George F. Kennan and the Making of American
Foreign Policy, 1947–1950

PRINCETON STUDIES IN

INTERNATIONAL HISTORY AND POLITICS

Series Editors
John Lewis Gaddis
Jack L. Snyder
Richard H. Ullman

History and Strategy by Marc Trachtenberg (1991)

George F. Kennan and the Making of American Foreign Policy,
1947–1950 by Wilson D. Miscamble, C.S.C. (1992)

George F. Kennan and the Making of American Foreign Policy, 1947–1950

Wilson D. Miscamble, C.S.C.

PRINCETON UNIVERSITY PRESS

PRINCETON, NEW JERSEY

Copyright © 1992 by Princeton University Press
Published by Princeton University Press, 41 William Street,
Princeton, New Jersey 08540
In the United Kingdom: Princeton University Press, Oxford

Library of Congress Cataloging-in-Publication Data

Miscamble, Wilson D., 1954-
George F. Kennan and the making of American foreign policy, 1947-1950 /
Wilson D. Miscamble.
p. cm. — (Princeton studies in international history and politics)
Includes bibliographical references and index.
ISBN 0-691-08620-6 (acid-free paper)
1. Kennan, George Frost, 1904-   . 2. United States—Foreign relations—1945-1953.
I. Title. II. Series.
E748.K374M57 1992   327.73—dc20   91-28336 CIP

This book has been composed in Linotron Times Roman

Princeton University Press books are printed on acid-free paper,
and meet the guidelines for permanence and durability of the
Committee on Production Guidelines for Book Longevity of the
Council on Library Resources

Printed in the United States of America

10 9 8 7 6 5 4 3 2

To Dad and Mum

Contents

List of Illustrations

Preface

In July 1947, the *New York Times Magazine* published a feature article by Brooks Atkinson, the *Times'* drama critic and former Moscow correspondent, entitled "America's Global Planner."[1] The subject of Atkinson's journalistic portrait was a foreign service officer, George F. Kennan, whom Secretary of State George C. Marshall had chosen to direct the newly established Policy Planning Staff in the Department of State. Kennan served as director of the Planning Staff through to December 31, 1949. Under him this group investigated a range of foreign policy problems staggering in their diversity and complexity. The core problem which confronted Kennan and dominated American foreign policy during his tenure, however, was how to respond to the antagonism and the apparent threat posed by the Soviet Union. Kennan's contribution in developing American foreign policy in response to the Russians is the subject of this study.

This work is not a biography, nor is it a survey of Kennan's ideas or a simple narrative of Kennan's activities devoid of context. Rather, its examination of Kennan's involvement in policy-making serves as a prism through which to view the wider spectrum of discussion and decision involved in devising the main lines of foreign policy during the crucial postwar period in American diplomacy. Kennan and his Planning Staff are suited uniquely for an investigation of this sort. Under his direction it lay close to the center of policy-making within the State Department which, with President Truman's approval, was the principal source of policy at this time.[2] The study then primarily casts light on what American policy was and on the process of its development. Assuredly, as a corollary, it identifies Kennan's role and ascertains his contribution. Does he deserve the appellation applied to him by Atkinson over four decades ago? If so, what does it mean?

Kennan's importance has long been recognized and his contribution has been the subject of much comment and controversy. In particular Kennan's role in formulating the so-called containment doctrine—he has been dubbed "the architect of containment," "the great theorist of containment," and "the founding father of containment,"—has provoked much discussion and de-

---

[1] Brooks Atkinson, "America's Global Planner," *New York Times Magazine*, July 13, 1947, pp. 9, 32–33.

[2] On the State Department's dominant role during the Truman presidency see I. M. Destler, Leslie H. Gelb, Anthony Lake, *Our Own Worst Enemy: The Unmaking of American Foreign Policy* (New York, 1984), pp. 168–71; and Barry Rubin, *Secrets of State: The State Department and the Struggle Over U.S. Foreign Policy* (New York, 1985), pp. 49–75.

bate.[3] Much of this unfortunately has been little more than a rehash of old arguments and a repetition of seeming verities. But the appearance of a number of recent studies specifically devoted to Kennan's thought has served to deepen further our understanding. Notable among these is the penetrating analysis of Kennan's views and ideas provided in John Lewis Gaddis's *Strategies of Containment*.[4] This outstanding work, which examines the whole of United States national security policy from World War II through the Nixon presidency, attempts to outline in a composite manner Kennan's geopolitical "code" as presented in the late 1940s. The works of David Mayers, Anders Stephanson, Walter L. Hixson, and Barton Gellman similarly are in their essence studies of Kennan's ideas and their development over time.[5] The emphasis here is quite different. This study moves beyond the analysis of ideas to their implementation and systematically appraises the extent to which Kennan's recommendations actually influenced policy. Kennan is viewed less as *theorist* and more as *policymaker*. The content of policy and the process of its formulation are the central focus.[6]

My approach has been to adopt what Barry Rubin has termed "a middle ground between two extremes: the dry diplomatic history that presents decisions as clear-cut and inevitable by omitting the clash and blend of motives, personalities, abilities, and even accidents that occur in the policy process, and the journalistic account focusing on gossip and personalities to the exclusion of fundamental issues and options."[7] Necessarily I have explored the nature of the relationships both among certain key policymakers—such as Kennan's with General Marshall and with Marshall's successor, Dean G. Acheson—and among influential groups within the State Department, such as the Division of European Affairs and the Policy Planning Staff. The story of American foreign policy in the late 1940s is partly one of bureaucratic battles

---

[3] For the direct quotations see Thomas M. Magstadt, "Understanding George Kennan," *Worldview* 27 (September 1984): 7; Norman Podhoretz, *The Present Danger* (New York, 1980), p. 17; William Taubman, *Stalin's American Policy: From Entente to Detente to Cold War* (New York, 1982), p. 166.

[4] John Lewis Gaddis, *Strategies of Containment: A Critical Appraisal of Postwar American National Security Policy* (New York, 1982).

[5] David Mayers, *George Kennan and the Dilemmas of US Foreign Policy* (New York, 1988); Anders Stephanson, *Kennan and the Art of Foreign Policy* (Cambridge, Mass., 1989); Walter L. Hixson, *George F. Kennan: Cold War Iconoclast* (New York, 1989): and Barton Gellman, *Contending With Kennan: Toward a Philosophy of American Power* (New York, 1984). One should also note the fine discussion of Kennan's thought in Michael Joseph Smith, *Realist Thought From Weber to Kissinger* (Baton Rouge, La., 1986).

[6] The fine collective biography by Walter Isaacson and Evan Thomas, *The Wise Men: Six Friends and the World They Made* (New York, 1986) is quite insightful on these questions but the huge scope of their subject perforce limits the depth of their investigation of the matters examined in this work.

[7] Rubin, *Secrets of State*, p. xi.

at the second echelon of the government. Tracing Kennan's actions provides an entree into these important disputes and their key participants.

I cannot claim to have captured in any full and objective fashion the world of the policymakers mentioned here with its inevitable compromises, ultimate objectives only dimly perceived, and constantly competing pressures that confused and obscured policy vision.[8] What I have aimed to do—with what success the reader must judge—is to avoid reading history backwards and imposing an artificial coherence on American foreign policy as it developed during 1947 to 1950. The historiography of the origins of the Cold War already is overly burdened with studies of this kind.[9] My hope is that this work, whatever its limitations, is one which grows "organically from the evidence" and which consequentially speaks with authenticity of the past.[10]

What might be termed interpretative extremism has been an occupational hazard for historians of postwar American diplomacy. But the concern for interpretation has generated more heat than light and has not always furthered the historian's first task of determining what actually happened. I have deliberately avoided grand interpretative assertions and have not sought to develop some neat interpretation which would permit my work to be easily categorized by writers of those perennial reviews of the Cold War literature. Nor have I aimed to make this work of history into one of historiography by endlessly questioning the existing literature. I have benefitted from this literature but have no desire to get bogged down in sterile debates between opposing schools within it.

As the foregoing hopefully makes quite clear my work is neither entrapped in some artificial methodological "sophistication" nor constrained by the need to conform to some overarching interpretation. It accepts the premise that individuals, such as Kennan, can and do make a difference in foreign policy formulation. Perhaps the focus in this study is overly concentrated on the United States and it is but another contribution to what the British scholar D. Cameron Watt has termed "American nationalist historiography" (although I should add I am not an American).[11] Yet an effort is made here to

---

[8] This relies on Lisle Rose's discussion of the gulf between "the writing of history and the effective making of it" in his "The Trenches and the Towers: Differing Perspectives on the Writing and Making of American Diplomatic History," *Pacific Historical Review* 55 (February 1986): 99.

[9] An example would be Daniel Yergin's *Shattered Peace: The Origins of the Cold War and the National Security State* (Boston, 1977), with its artificially constructed "Riga" and "Yalta" axioms.

[10] See Philip Gleason's "Methodological Confession of Faith," in his *Keeping the Faith: American Catholicism, Past and Present* (Notre Dame, Ind., 1987), pp. 216–25; direct quotation on p. 222.

[11] D. Cameron Watt, "Britain, the United States and the Opening of the Cold War," in Ritchie Ovendale, ed., *The Foreign Policy of the British Labour Governments, 1945–1951* (Leicester, 1984), p. 48.

take account of the influence upon American policy of and the constraints applied to it by other powers and their representatives. In some cases this was quite decisive.

This work is mainly one of a "splitter" as opposed to a "lumper" (to borrow J. H. Hexter's terminology which John Gaddis has made so familiar to American diplomatic historians).[12] My hope is that it will be of interest to "splitters" and "lumpers" alike. Despite the profuse literature on the origins of the Cold War—some might say because of it!—there is much yet to be understood about American foreign policy during the Truman administration. This work clarifies that American foreign policy from 1947 to 1950 was not simply a working out of a clearly delineated doctrine of containment. Although Truman and his advisers determined as early as 1946 that Soviet actions endangered American security and resolved to meet that danger, no explicit course of action was charted.[13] Only in a piecemeal and staggered manner did the Truman administration decide upon the major elements of the American response to the Soviet Union. Kennan operated close to the center of such decisionmaking and this study of his involvements clarifies how each policy element resulted from a complex of factors. This book reveals such factors and suggests that the much discussed containment doctrine did not dictate the policies determined from 1947 to 1950 but rather the policies gave form and meaning to the doctrine.

This study pays attention initially to the circumstances of the Planning Staff's establishment and to Kennan's selection as its director. It then scrutinizes the major elements of American foreign policy during the period from 1947 to 1950. Throughout this work the emphasis has been placed on revealing and comprehending how and why American foreign policy developed as it did. The goal is understanding, not judgment and condemnation.

[12] Gaddis, *Strategies of Containment*, pp. vii–viii.

[13] Deborah Welch Larson reveals well the fluidity in American policy during 1945–1946 in her *Origins of Containment: A Psychological Explanation* (Princeton, 1985).

Acknowledgments

IN THE COURSE of completing this study I have acquired debts to both people and institutions which I wish to acknowledge, although, of course, the responsibility for the study's contents belongs solely to me.

A number of people who participated in or observed the formulation of foreign policy described in this study were generous in permitting me to interview them. The full list is included in the bibliography but I must make special mention of four individuals. George F. Kennan took time from his busy schedule to speak with me and gave typically insightful and forthright responses to my questions. Mr. Kennan also took time to read many of the following chapters in draft form and carefully replied to specific questions arising from them. Kennan's assistance to me and my regard for him have not diminished the rigor with which I have sought to examine his role, as I trust the reader will agree. Kennan's friend and one-time Planning Staff colleague, John Paton Davies, met with me in his beautiful home in Asheville, North Carolina, and demonstrated there the powers of analysis which made him such a prescient commentator on Asian questions. Paul H. Nitze spoke with thoughtfulness and almost clinical care but with genuine regard for the man he succeeded as director of the Planning Staff, despite their profound differences over policy both then and subsequently. Kennan's largely unheralded but nonetheless effective bureaucratic rival, John D. Hickerson, described in detail and with relish his battles with the planning chief, especially over the North Atlantic treaty.

This manuscript had its origins in the doctoral dissertation which I completed at the University of Notre Dame under the wise and judicious direction of Vincent P. DeSantis, who has continued to be both a source of constructive criticism and ready encouragement during the substantial revision and enlargement of the dissertation for publication. Thomas Blantz, c.s.c., and Philip Gleason of the History Department and Alan Dowty of the Government Department of Notre Dame read the original dissertation and offered helpful suggestions. Tom Blantz has gone beyond the call of duty in his continued willingness to assist me with this project. He is a true friend. Richard H. Ullman of Princeton University read the entire manuscript and gave helpful comments on it. Chapter 2 on the Marshall Plan benefitted from the critical comments on an early draft of it generously offered by Robert H. Ferrell of Indiana University. Dr. Forrest C. Pogue, General Marshall's esteemed biographer, assisted me by sharing his knowledge of the reasons for the Planning Staff's establishment. Lawrence S. Kaplan of Kent State University gave comments on the manuscript, particularly the chapter on the North Atlantic Treaty, as did Sir

Michael Howard, now of Yale University. Robert Blum, David Anderson, William Stueck and Melvyn Leffler all gave comments on an earlier draft of chapter 7 on China. Thomas Schwartz and Hans-Jurgen Schroder did the same on an earlier draft of chapter 5 on the division of Germany. Joseph M. Siracusa introduced me to the study of American diplomatic history at the University of Queensland (now many years ago!) and he made his work on NSC 68 available to me. My colleagues Thomas Kselman and Donald Critchlow gave me key advice down the home stretch. Other historians who have assisted me in one way or another include Anna Kasten Nelson, the capable editor of the Policy Planning Staff papers written during Kennan's tenure as its director; Robin Winks; and Linda Killen. Jim King, c.s.c. and John Young, c.s.c. gave the manuscript discriminating "layman's" readings, while Steven Brady, Matt Cronin and Steve Ruemenapp assisted with its final preparation. Finally, I must express my deep gratitude to two "Gaddises"—firstly Gaddis Smith, Director of the Yale Center for International and Area Studies, who arranged for my fellowship year in the stimulating surrounds of Yale which made possible the completion of this study; and secondly, John Lewis Gaddis, Kennan's authorized biographer, who has given me real support on this project, commented on large parts of it in one form or another and urged me to publish it. In a way that is hard to explain John Gaddis's regular invitation to me to participate in the Baker Peace Studies conference which he organizes annually at Ohio University helped maintain my interest in completing this book when, in the midst of seminary studies, it was flagging somewhat. The trip to Athens, Ohio, invariably reignited the flame within me to "get back to Kennan."

In a less direct but no less indispensable way I am indebted to the historians of postwar American foreign policy whose work I have drawn from. The extensive bibliography lists these works. In a particular way I am indebted to the other Kennan scholars—John Lewis Gaddis, David Mayers, Anders Stephanson, Walter Hixson, Walter Isaacson and Evan Thomas—from whose work I have benefitted in varying degrees. Most of these scholars had access to my early work in dissertation form and I am glad to return the compliment here by making some use of their studies.

In a very basic way archivists and librarians have made my work possible and I must express appreciation to the staffs of the National Archives; the Harry S. Truman Library; the Library of Congress; the Seeley G. Mudd Manuscript and Firestone Libraries at Princeton; the MacArthur Archives in Norfolk, Virginia; the George C. Marshall Research Foundation in Lexington, Virginia; the Bentley Historical Library at the University of Michigan; the Butler Library at Columbia University; the Sterling and Mudd Libraries at Yale University; and the Theodore M. Hesburgh, c.s.c. Library at the University of Notre Dame. In particular I must thank Gerald Haines, a one-time staff member of the Diplomatic Branch of the National Archives, and Irwin Muehler, Warren Orvahl, Dennis Bilger, and Liz Safly of the Truman Library. Jean Holliday of the Seeley G. Mudd Manuscript Library at Princeton was most helpful in providing photographs. The *Washington Post* and *Life Magazine* generously granted me permission to publish photographs. Mr. Arthur Altschul gave me access to his father's papers at Columbia University and the estate of James V. Forrestal gave me permission to use materials from the Forrestal Papers at Princeton.

The editors of *Mid-America: An Historical Review* and *American Studies: New Essays from Australia and New Zealand* kindly have granted permission to use material previously published in article form. Frank Cass Ltd., the publishers of *Diplomacy and Statecraft*, did the same. Mrs. Catherine Box and Mrs. Ettie Oakman typed the manuscript at varying stages. Generous folk have provided me with fine accommodations on my research trips—Mrs. Heroldine Helm in Independence; Dick and Joanne Rentner in Virginia Beach— (Joanne, again let me apologize for not staying for the dinner party!); Jim and Sue Ragland and the Holy Cross Brothers Communities at Mackin and McNamara High Schools in Washington, D.C.; and John Young, c.s.c. in New Haven.

Institutional debts which I must note are to the History Department of the University of Notre Dame; to the Harry S. Truman Institute for National and International affairs for grants which funded my various research visits to the Truman Library; to the sponsors of the Notre Dame History Department's John Highbarger Award which helped finance my first research visit to Princeton; and to my religious community, the Congregation of Holy Cross who "carried" me for a year. I also must thank all the fine people at Princeton University Press who contributed to the preparation and production of this book. I am especially indebted to Malcolm DeBevoise, Christine Heslin Benincasa, and Bill Laznovsky for their assistance. It has been a pleasure to work with them.

George Kennan once pointed out "that the studying and writing of history is a relatively lonely occupation." I confess that occasionally I found it so but the interest and support of good friends sustained me and I am deeply grateful to them. I want to thank especially my *confreres* in the Congregation of Holy Cross led by Lucas Lamadrid, who wanted to see his name listed in these acknowledgments. Rector Thomas King, c.s.c., and all the men of Zahm Hall at Notre Dame, where I have the good fortune to live, offered real encouragement. Also I should mention that my students' inquiries about my book and their promises to purchase it prompted its completion. I look forward to autographing their copies! Lastly, I must thank my family who have supported me over a long period on this and all else I have undertaken. My parents and my sister and brother, Jenny and Phillip, have helped keep me honest and committed through their example and love. I'm not sure that my Mum will read all of this book to my Dad but I hope she will read the dedication which is but a token of my love and gratitude to Doug and Bobbie Miscamble of Brisbane, Australia.

Abbreviations Used in Text and Notes

AEC	Atomic Energy Commission
ARA	Office of American Republic Affairs, Department of State
BBC	British Broadcasting Commission
CEEC	Committee of European Economic Cooperation
CFM	Council of Foreign Ministers
CIA	Central Intelligence Agency
CIG	Central Intelligence Group
CINCFE	Commander of American Forces in the Far East
ECA	Economic Cooperation Administration
ERP	European Recovery Program
FEC	Far Eastern Commission
FRUS	Foreign Relations of the United States
GAC	General Advisory Committee (of AEC)
HSTL	Harry S. Truman Library
JCS	Joint Chiefs of Staff
JSSC	Joint Strategic Survey Committee
NA	National Archives
NCFE	National Committee for a Free Europe
NSC	National Security Council
OPC	Office of Policy Coordination
OSO	Office of Special Operations
OSS	Office of Strategic Services
PCI	Italian Communist Party
PPS	Policy Planning Staff
PSF	President's Secretary's File (Truman Papers)
SANACC	State-Army-Navy Coordinating Committee
SCAP	Supreme Commander for the Allied Powers (Japan)
SDPPSP	The State Department Policy Planning Staff Papers
SPG	Special Procedures Group (of CIA)
SWNCC	State-War-Navy Coordinating Committee
UNSCOP	United Nations Special Committee on Palestine
USA	United States Army
USAAF	United States Army Air Force
USN	United States Navy

Fig. 1. George F. Kennan as Director of the Policy Planning Staff, Department of State, 1947–1950. Reprinted with permission of George F. Kennan and the Seeley G. Mudd Manuscript Library, Princeton University.

George F. Kennan and the Making of American
Foreign Policy, 1947–1950

CHAPTER ONE

Director of the Policy Planning Staff

MARSHALL TAKES COMMAND AT STATE

On January 21, 1947, George Catlett Marshall, the organizer of victory as Army Chief of Staff during World War II and the personification of devotion to duty, replaced James F. Byrnes as secretary of state. A grim and menacing world situation faced him and his nation. The West European economies, plagued by severe shortages of food and coal during a brutal winter, appeared on the verge of collapse.[1] Such a collapse when joined to evident political weakness and psychological exhaustion seemed certain to redound to the benefit of local communists, particularly in France and Italy. Further, Great Britain's grave economic difficulties forced her to confront the painful reality that she was no longer a great power, to acknowledge her military weakness and to reduce her commitments throughout the world. Magnifying the threat to America's interests inherent in European economic and military weakness was the Soviet Union's seeming ambition and capacity to exploit it. By the time Marshall took his place in Harry S. Truman's cabinet the United States and the Soviet Union, the only nations to emerge from the war against Hitler's Germany as major powers, faced each other as suspicious adversaries. Their wartime cooperation, such as it was, largely ended with the defeat of the common foe. During the volatile and confusing period from the War's end to Marshall's appointment to head the State Department Soviet-American relations were characterized by a series of disputes—over Eastern Europe, Germany, Iran, economic issues and atomic energy.[2]

By the end of 1946 many American officials had concluded that the Soviet Union's antagonistic attitudes and actions endangered America's national security and they sought to meet the Soviet challenge.[3] As Soviet-American dif-

[1] West European difficulties resulted in large part from "the fearsome winter of 1946–47, which paralyzed transportation, impeded food and fuel deliveries and radicalized workers into politically explosive wage demands." Charles S. Maier argues that without this winter and its effect European economic recovery might have progressed without substantial American assistance. See Charles S. Maier, "The Two Postwar Eras and the Conditions for Stability in Twentieth-Century Western Europe," *The American Historical Review* 86 (April 1981): 343.

[2] Many of these issues are dealt with by James L. Gormley, *The Collapse of the Grand Alliance, 1945–1948* (Baton Rouge, 1987); and Hugh Thomas, *Armed Truce: The Beginnings of the Cold War, 1945–46* (London, 1987).

[3] On this see John Lewis Gaddis's essay "The Insecurities of Victory: The United States and the Perception of the Soviet Threat After World War II," in his *The Long Peace: Inquiries into the History of the Cold War* (New York, 1987), pp. 20–47.

ferences increasingly covered the diplomatic landscape the task of discerning Soviet intentions and of developing a suitable American response dominated the formulation of American foreign policy. But this process of developing a policy to check the perceived Soviet threat was still in its infancy when Marshall took office and it was by no means clear that the Truman administration possessed the capacity and the stamina to forge a coherent and sustainable policy. There was no clear course charted. No real direction had been set. Essentially Marshall inherited only a growing disposition to oppose Soviet ambitions and aggrandizement. He faced an enormous task, one at which a lesser person might have balked. But Truman had selected well. The president wanted a strong secretary of state and he got this in Marshall. With Truman's broad approval and full trust, the new secretary of state assumed responsibility to preside over the formulation of policy.

Marshall took control of a largely neglected and ineffective department where morale was exceedingly low.[4] During the Second World War Franklin Roosevelt substantially excluded the State Department from decision-making preferring to rely on his military advisers and a few personal advisers like Harry Hopkins. On succeeding to the presidency, Truman did not set out to by-pass the department and looked upon his secretary of state, James F. Byrnes, as his principal adviser on foreign policy. But Byrnes, like Roosevelt, generally ignored the department. His under secretary, Dean G. Acheson, later reflected that Byrnes "thought of the State Department as himself and Chip [Charles E.] Bohlen and Doc [H. Freeman] Matthews."[5]

The Department of State which Byrnes consigned to Marshall was beset with problems not only of morale but also of an administrative and organizational nature. After the war the department underwent a great expansion because it absorbed many of the functions and personnel of such wartime agencies as the Office of Strategic Services, the Office of War Information, and the Foreign Economic Administration.[6] Simultaneous with this bureaucratic burgeoning and partly as a consequence of it, confusion existed within the department over procedures and functional responsibilities involved in policy-making. The department writhed in confused channels of communication, lack of direction, and general impotence. Viewed as a whole it was a most unimpressive agency in formulating and developing policy. On the day Mar-

---

[4] Charles E. Bohlen, *Witness to History, 1929–1969* (New York, 1973), p. 258.

[5] Acheson quoted from transcript of conversation between Truman, Acheson, Hillman, Heller, and Noyes, Kansas City, Mo., February 16, 1955, Papers of Harry S. Truman: Post-Presidential File (hereafter "Truman Papers" with appropriate details), Harry S. Truman Library, Independence, Mo. (hereafter HSTL), Box 1. For discussion of Byrnes as secretary of state consult Robert L. Messer, *The End of the Alliance: James F. Byrnes, Roosevelt, Truman and the Origins of the Cold War* (Chapel Hill, 1982).

[6] Graham H. Stuart, *The Department of State: A History of Its Organization, Procedure and Personnel* (New York, 1949), pp. 427–32.

shall moved to the new State Department offices at Foggy Bottom, Truman's Chief of Staff, the taciturn Admiral William D. Leahy, wrote in his diary that "from long association with General Marshall on the Joint Chiefs of Staff, I am satisfied that he will accomplish a marked improvement in the efficiency of the Department of State."[7] Leahy proved prescient.

Marshall made full use of the State Department which he strengthened and trusted. During his tenure as secretary and that of his successor, Dean Acheson, the department would enjoy a "sort of Golden Age" in which it took the principal role in forming policy.[8] Clearly this owed much to the careful and constructive relationships that Marshall and Acheson maintained with Truman but the restoration of the State Department under Marshall also played a part. Marshall imposed a sense of order within the department and injected new life into its officers by giving them responsibility. Although there had been some apprehension within the department that the general would impose such rigid discipline and procedures that ideas would never make their way to the top, Marshall never used excessive or constricting means to establish orderly staff procedures and clear lines of authority.[9] He delegated Acheson, who stayed on as his under secretary for some months, to be his chief of staff and to run the department. Matters for his decision and his instruction would come through the under secretary.[10] Believing in staff work and deeply secure in himself, Marshall willingly placed responsibility for policy-making on subordinates from whom he invariably garnered loyalty and respect. The new secretary, in stark contrast to his predecessor, preferred to have problems largely resolved before they reached him.[11]

In addition to clarifying lines of command Marshall instituted some significant restructuring within the State Department whose "complete state of disorganization" shocked him.[12] At Acheson's urging he reversed Byrnes's decision to disperse intelligence and research work among the geographic divisions of the department and ordered it centered in one office.[13] More im-

[7] Diary entry, January 21, 1947, Diary of William D. Leahy, Papers of William D. Leahy, Manuscript Division, Library of Congress, Washington, D.C., Box 5.

[8] For a skeptical comment on "The Golden Days" see William N. Turpin, "Foreign Relations, Yes; Foreign Policy, No," *Foreign Policy* 8 (Fall 1972): 51–52.

[9] On the apprehension see Bohlen, *Witness to History*, p. 258.

[10] Acheson, *Present at the Creation*, p. 213.

[11] For details on Marshall's methods see Robert H. Ferrell, *George C. Marshall*, vol. 15 in *The American Secretaries of State and Their Diplomacy*, ed. Robert H. Ferrell (New York, 1966), p. 52. On Marshall see the magisterial biography by Forrest C. Pogue, *George C. Marshall*, 4 vols. (1963–87).

[12] Marshall revealed this in an interview with Forrest C. Pogue, November 20, 1956. See George C. Marshall Interviews and Reminiscences for Forrest C. Pogue: Transcripts and Notes, 1956–57, George C. Marshall Research Foundation, Lexington, Virginia, transcript p. 525. Marshall qualified his comment by saying "I don't know as you'd call it disorganization; you'd say lack of organization. They just didn't have any."

[13] Acheson, *Present at the Creation*, pp. 157–63, 214. On this also note Spruille Braden, *Dip-*

portant, Marshall established the Executive Secretariat when he consolidated a number of supposed coordinating units in the department into one organization. To head this unit he selected Carlisle H. Humelsine, a capable and trusted former aide who had organized a similar unit in the Pentagon during the war years. The secretariat welded the offices of the secretary and under secretary into one and ensured that no paper requiring action came to the secretary without having obtained all necessary clearances at lower levels. It then followed up on every decision made. The Secretariat under Humelsine was not directly concerned with the content of policy but was key to its considered formulation and effective implementation.[14]

And, of course, Marshall had the idea of forming a planning group in the State Department. He recalled that "I was horrified when I got into the State Department to find . . . that each subdivision was a separate industry—a compartment by itself—which is all of the nonsensical organization things I have ever heard of."[15] Marshall sought to establish a body which might assist him to develop policy coherently and, perhaps, exercise some oversight of the disparate divisions of the department to ensure they avoided working at cross purposes.[16] In his initial months in office and burdened with many pressing concerns he did little directly to create such a body although others in the department were cognizant of the crying need to "give strategic direction to policy."[17] Acheson, in particular, railed against "the sin of ad hocery" (sic) and emphasized the need for more coordination and planning.[18]

Appropriately perhaps, it was to Acheson that Marshall, in characteristic fashion, delegated the task of initiating the formation of the new planning group. To this end, during the first week of Marshall's secretaryship—January 24 to be precise—Dean Acheson called to his office George Frost Kennan, a foreign service officer then lecturing at the National War College. He informed Kennan, with whom he had become acquainted following the diplo-

---

lomats and Demagogues: The Memoirs of Spruille Braden (New Rochelle, N.Y., 1971), pp. 346–51; and Martin Weil, A Pretty Good Club: The Founding Fathers of the U.S. Foreign Service (New York, 1978), pp. 243–49.

[14] On the Executive Secretariat see Harvey H. Bundy and James Grafton Rogers, The Organization of the Government for the Conduct of Foreign Affairs (Washington, D.C., 1949), p. 78; and Smith Simpson, Anatomy of the State Department (Boston, 1967), p. 23.

[15] Marshall interview with Forrest Pogue, November 20, 1956, transcript p. 525.

[16] Kennan later explained that when Marshall took office only the under secretary and the Counselor were competent to advise the secretary over the entire range of foreign policy problems and "neither of these officials had both the time and the facilities to give careful and exhaustive study to long range problems of policy or problems of exceptional intricacy." Statement by George F. Kennan, May 26, 1960, in Organizing for National Security—Inquiry of the Subcommittee on National Policy Machinery, Senator Henry M. Jackson, Chairman, U.S. Senate, vol. 1 (Washington, D.C., 1966), p. 804.

[17] Harley Notter to Secretary of State (Byrnes), January 9, 1947, Papers of J. Anthony Panuch, HSTL, Box 9. Notter went on to argue for the creation of a "Policy Advisory Staff."

[18] Author's interview with James Reston, Washington, D.C., August 8, 1989.

mat's return from Moscow eight months earlier, that Marshall intended to establish a unit to plan and review policy within the State Department. Acheson could not elaborate specifically on its structure or functions because he was exploring unfamiliar terrain but he spoke of the need for "something in the nature of a Deputy Under Secretary."[19] He then approached Kennan on his willingness to accept such a position. Kennan's glands for power must have experienced a sudden explosion in activity at the prospect of his appetite for real influence in policy-making being satiated at long last. He indicated his readiness to take on a position where he "could really contribute to a successful American foreign policy" but pointed out his need to complete his tour of duty at the War College through the end of June.[20]

Kennan's War College obligations presented a complication and delayed his return to the State Department. Early in February Acheson spoke again with Kennan. He reported that after further consideration the policy coordination and review functions would be placed in the hands of the new secretariat but that Kennan was needed to head the planning unit. He accepted that Kennan could not give himself full-time to his State Department assignment until the conclusion of his work at the War College. But he obtained Kennan's agreement to assist part-time during the intervening period in the preliminary work of setting up a planning organization in the department.[21] He thereupon asked Kennan to submit an outline of the organization and personnel of a planning unit which he might clear with General Marshall.

The experience of the State Department itself contained little which could serve directly as a model. Planning had not been totally ignored, however, and the idea of a formal planning group was not entirely new. Early in January 1944, Secretary of State Cordell Hull created the Post-War Programs Committee and the State Department Policy Committee. Hull established these committees for a specific purpose—to consider problems arising out of World War II—and each committee consisted of departmental officers with other responsibilities. Hull's successor, Edward R. Stettinius, a master of style over substance, replaced these two committees with what he called the Secretary's Staff Committee made up of the assistant secretaries and other top officials

[19] Kennan's account of the origins of the Policy Planning Staff. A copy of this three-page, undated document—loaned to Dr. Forrest Pogue by George F. Kennan, February 1959—is found in Forrest Pogue Materials, George C. Marshall Library, Verifax 358.

[20] According to Kennan: "I said that it was my personal hope that after completion of this [War College] work I could retire to private life and perhaps accomplish something in the academic field, where I had been encouraged to think I might have something to offer. I was interested in remaining in Government work only if it were in a capacity where I could feel that I could do some good and really contribute to a successful foreign policy. From this standpoint, I could not decline to undertake the sort of position he had in mind." Kennan account, undated, Pogue Materials. Also see George F. Kennan, *Memoirs, 1925–1950* (Boston, 1967) (hereafter *Memoirs*, I), p. 213.

[21] Kennan account, undated, Pogue Materials.

and charged with a grandiose list of objectives, among them policy planning. This goal remained notably unfulfilled and the committee typically performed ineffectually in 1945 and 1946.[22] In reality the inheritance regarding planning from within the State Department consisted of a weak concern for the task and a number of either limited or pathetic attempts to manifest this concern. Perhaps there were some lessons on what to avoid but clearly Marshall's decision to establish a planning group did not derive from a desire to revive or revitalize any previous unit within the department. Kennan would have the opportunity in large measure to design and construct a new component in the structure of the State Department.

Marshall gave few detailed instructions to shape the structure and functions of his proposed planning body during the next three months, although he spoke of the need for it within the councils of the administration.[23] Certainly Kennan did not work to some detailed prescriptions provided by Marshall with only one exception. Marshall apparently did not want the Staff to be manned by "distinguished outsiders" who might restrict and pressure him. The Staff was to be drawn primarily from within the department.[24] Kennan sensed that Marshall wanted a unit "to fill, at least in part, the place of the Division of Plans and Operations to which he was accustomed in the War Department."[25] During World War II Marshall charged the Operations Division of the War Department with responsibility for the Army's part in strategic planning and direction of operations. In retrospect it seems unlikely that he conceived that the planning group in the State Department should perform a similar totality of functions as the Operations Division.[26] It is more likely that he viewed the Strategy and Policy group, a component of the Operations Division which focused on policy formulation rather than direction and implementation, as a more suitable model. But Marshall never identified what came to be called the Policy Planning Staff as modeled upon any particular group, despite his taking

[22] On these committees see "Background Annex" attached to Harley Notter to Sec. of State, January 9, 1947, Panuch Papers, HSTL, Box 9. James Reston referred to the antecedents of the Policy Planning Staff in "New Policy Staff Will Aid Marshall Frame His Plans," *New York Times*, April 25, 1947, p. 4. For further details on the work of the committees established by Hull see Harley A. Notter, *Postwar Foreign Policy Preparation, 1939–1945* (Washington, D.C., 1949).

[23] Marshall, in response to a proposal by Navy Secretary James V. Forrestal, told a Cabinet lunch meeting on March 4 that before the administration could approach the overall problem of Soviet-American relations from the standpoint of getting the help of business, "there would have to be a lot of work done by a planning staff." Diary entry, March 4, 1947, James V. Forrestal Diaries, Papers of James V. Forrestal, Seeley G. Mudd Manuscript Library, Princeton University, Princeton, N.J., p. 1510.

[24] Kennan, *Memoirs*, I, p. 327.

[25] Ibid., p. 313. Note that throughout the war this group was known as the Operations Division of the War Department General Staff. The "Plans" in the title was added after the war.

[26] For the institutional history of the Operations Division see Ray S. Cline, *Washington Command Post: The Operations Division* (Washington, D.C., 1951).

"great pride" in creating it. The general's central contribution came in his recognizing the need for a planning group and in his expectation, as Acheson remembered it, that the group would "look ahead, not into the distant future, but beyond the vision of the operating officers caught in the smoke and crisis of current battle and also . . . constantly reappraise what was being done."[27]

While General Marshall gave little detailed guidance most other departmental officials had no opportunity to offer any. The shape and functions of the planning group did not become subjects for formal discussion among the department's senior officers—the assistant secretaries and the directors of the regional offices. Acheson simply informed them of Marshall's intention at one of his under secretary's meetings.[28] This minor involvement of the operational divisions, both geographic and functional, deftly contributed to the lack of bureaucratic opposition to the Planning Staff. There was no situation and no forum for tactful opposition to the planning group's creation, although some officials—no doubt eager to defend the prerogatives of their bailiwicks—considered it unnecessary.[29] And, it was supported, after all, by the new secretary with his unparalleled stature and reputation. Also most officials did not perceive of this planning group as endangering the essence of their own divisions. The expectation was that it would complement rather than challenge the roles already played by their divisions. Reinforcing this feeling of acceptance by officers was the realization that the Planning Staff would be drawn largely from within the department. The planners would be fellow members of the "club" and known to them.[30] The Planning Staff would be a part of the department rather than being artificially imposed on it or placed in it. Kennan's selection as director symbolized this.

KENNAN'S SELECTION—THE "LOGICAL ONE"

Marshall's exact reasons for selecting Kennan cannot be determined definitively. As Marshall had spent all of 1946 preoccupied with his mission in China to reconcile the Kuomintang and Communist factions it seems unlikely

[27] Acheson, *Present at the Creation*, p. 214.

[28] Author's interview with Loy W. Henderson, Washington, D.C., June 26, 1978. (Henderson at this time was Director of the Office of Near Eastern and African Affairs.)

[29] Interview with Loy Henderson, June 26, 1978.

[30] The lack of opposition to the Planning Staff contrasts markedly with the fierce opposition to the earlier scheme to establish the Office of Research and Intelligence as a policy-making unit. See Weil, *A Pretty Good Club*, pp. 243–49. On the more favorable reception extended to the Policy Planning Staff see for example H. Freeman Matthews (Director of the Office of European Affairs) to George F. Kennan, May 13, 1947, Record Group 59—General Records of the Department of State (hereafter RG 59), Lot File 54D394, Records of the Office of European Affairs—1942–1947, National Archives, Washington, D.C. (hereafter NA), Box 17. Matthews told Kennan: "I have long felt that the Department has been deficient in over-all and long range planning. I feel that you and your associates will fill a long-standing need."

that he possessed sufficient familiarity with the records and qualifications of suitable candidates to make the choice himself. The historian Lloyd C. Gardner assumed so, arguing instead that Navy Secretary James V. Forrestal "sent" Kennan to Marshall to head the Policy Planning Staff to tutor Marshall in what the intense and ideological Forrestal considered his weak areas, "economic understanding and an awareness of the nature of communist philosophy."[31] Kennan himself suspected he received the appointment because of Forrestal's "influence."[32] Unquestionably, Forrestal took a particular interest in Kennan's career from early 1946 onwards and brought him before Marshall's attention but to suggest that Forrestal arranged Kennan's appointment exaggerates his importance and neglects the influence of both Walter Bedell Smith and Dean Acheson.[33]

"Beetle" Smith, an aide to Marshall at Fort Benning and in the office of Chief of Staff before serving as Dwight Eisenhower's deputy in the European campaign, now served as ambassador in the Soviet Union. He was a trusted friend whose judgement Marshall respected. On January 15 he wrote the secretary-designate congratulating him on his appointment and cautioning him on the difficult task ahead. He then offered some advice:

> You will, of course be briefed until you are full up to the ears, and I shall not add a word. But I will venture one suggestion. George Kennan, now senior state department instructor at the Army War College, and until recently my Minister-Counsellor here, knows more about the Soviet Union, I believe, than any other American. He speaks Russian better than the average Russian. And not only has he served here under four different ambassadors, but he has had about equally valuable service in Germany. I strongly recommend that you bring him with you [to the forthcoming conference in Moscow] as one of your staff. I know all of the Russian experts, here and in Washington, and they are all good, but Kennan is head and shoulders above the lot, and he is highly respected in Moscow because of his character and integrity.[34]

Such effusive praise from a tough-minded soldier assuredly had an impact on Marshall. In his reply to Smith he tersely informed him that "I am considering

---

[31] Lloyd C. Gardner, *Architects of Illusion: Men and Ideas in American Foreign Policy, 1941–1949* (Chicago, 1970), p. 283. Gardner supplied no direct evidence to support his contention and I have found none. For Forrestal on Marshall's weak areas see Forrestal to Paul G. Smith, March 10, 1947, Forrestal Papers, Box 76.

[32] Kennan, *Memoirs*, I, p. 354; and George F. Kennan to author, December 14, 1978. In the letter just cited Kennan also mentioned the possibility of the "military men with whom I was associated at the time in the War College" suggesting his name to Marshall but there is no evidence to support this.

[33] On Forrestal's bringing Kennan before Marshall see Forrestal to Kennan, February 17, 1947, Forrestal Papers, Box 24.

[34] Smith to Marshall, January 15, 1947, Papers of George C. Marshall, George C. Marshall Library, Box 137, Folder 26.

Kennan matter" but, indicative of Smith's influence, the secretary of state already had investigated the possibility of including Kennan as part of the delegation he would lead to the Moscow Council of Foreign Ministers meeting scheduled for March.[35]

Acheson never claimed that he suggested Kennan for this position but close associates of both men assumed this to be the case.[36] At a dinner party at his home early in March, 1947, Acheson confided that he had "induced him [Kennan] to come back into the Department of State to help in setting up planning and research."[37] What seems most likely is that Bedell Smith and perhaps Forrestal broached Kennan's name to Marshall and testified to his capabilities. In discussion with Acheson Marshall settled on Kennan as the person to head the planning unit he proposed. Acheson gave this decision enthusiastic endorsement and was delegated to recruit Kennan for the position. No other candidates were considered.[38] As Carlton Savage, a founding member of the Policy Planning Staff, later remarked: "Kennan was such a logical one for it."[39]

EDUCATION OF A DIPLOMAT

What had made Kennan the logical choice? He was born in Milwaukee in 1904, the only son of Kossuth Kent and Florence James Kennan. His mother died just two months after his birth and his relationship with his father, fifty-two at the time of Kennan's birth, was strained to say the least. His childhood was not happy and secure in the conventional sense. He has described himself as "a moody, self-centered, neurotic boy," who was shy and confided in no one. He remembered his father as "a man whom I must have hurt a thousand times in my boyhood, by inattention, by callousness, by that exaggerated shyness and fear of demonstrativeness which is a form of cowardice and a congenital weakness of the family."[40] With such searing if overly remorseful self-

[35] Telegram, Marshall to Smith, January 30, 1947, Marshall Papers, Box 133, Folder 21. At a meeting on February 4 Acheson told Kennan that because of his War College obligations "he had persuaded General Marshall, with some difficulty, not to include me on the list of those who were to go to Moscow." Kennan account, undated, Pogue Materials, Marshall Library, Verifax 358.

[36] Author's interview with John D. Hickerson, Washington, D.C., July 6, 1978; and author's interview with Carlton Savage, Washington, D.C., June 22, 1978.

[37] Journal entry March 9, 1947, in David E. Lilienthal, *The Journals of David E. Lilienthal*, vol. 2: *The Atomic Energy Years, 1945–1950* (New York, 1964), p. 158.

[38] In approaching Kennan, Acheson told him that he knew of "no one else in Washington who could do this job." Kennan account, undated, Pogue Materials, Marshall Library, Verifax 358. Acheson asked Loy Henderson around this time what he thought of Kennan as director of the proposed group. Henderson responded that "somebody like George would be excellent" which prompted Acheson's laconic observation that "there's nobody quite like George." Author's interview with Loy W. Henderson, June 26, 1978.

[39] Author's interview with Carlton Savage, June 22, 1978.

[40] George F. Kennan, *Sketches from a Life* (New York, 1989).

analysis it is little wonder that lonely, diffident, isolated, fumbling, awkward, introverted, self-pitying, aloof are but *some* of the adjectives used by others to describe the boy Kennan.[41] These should suffice to give a sense of his early experience, although this subject is gladly consigned to his biographer for further investigation.

Two episodes in Kennan's childhood bear more direct import on his future career. As an eight-year-old he made his first visit to Europe and stayed with his family in Germany for six months. There, his natural facility with languages was displayed for the first time and apparently he was "speaking German quite respectably by the time he left."[42] His gift with languages proved an important element in his subsequent career. Even more important, Kennan developed some identification and sense of connection with the cousin of his grandfather for whom he had been named. The elder George Kennan had explored Siberia and authored an account of the Czarist prison system that had won him much acclaim in Europe and North America and indeed among Russian liberals and dissidents.[43] On his only visit with his older relative and namesake Kennan's fascination with Russia had its origins.[44] The fascination was not fleeting.[45]

Kennan's personal travails continued through his adolescence and early adulthood. Dispatched to St. John's Military Academy at age thirteen, Kennan suffered there from loneliness.[46] Worse was to come. Spurred on by its "seductive depiction" in F. Scott Fitzgerald's *This Side of Paradise* Kennan applied and was accepted to Princeton University. There "he suffered greatly from and was appalled by the pervasive social snobbery, which effectively excluded him, and he spent an undistinguished four years as an undergraduate."[47] In his own words: "I left college as obscurely as I had entered it."[48] In his *Memoirs* Kennan recalled the young Princeton graduate he once was as "a dreamer, feeble of will, and something of a sissy in personal relations."[49] Two more recent observers have portrayed astutely the young Kennan's char-

[41] See the descriptions of Kennan's childhood and the observations regarding his character in Isaacson and Thomas, *The Wise Men*, pp. 72–75; Mayers, *George Kennan*, pp. 16–20; C. Ben Wright, "George F. Kennan, Scholar-Diplomat, 1926–1946," Ph.D. diss., University of Wisconsin, 1972, pp. 1–11.

[42] Isaacson and Thomas, *The Wise Men*, p. 73.

[43] See George Kennan, *Siberia and the Exile System*, 2 vols. (New York, 1891).

[44] This difficult visit is described marvelously in Isaacson and Thomas, *The Wise Men*, pp. 75–76.

[45] Kennan later movingly wrote: "I feel that I was in some strange way destined to carry forward as best I could the work of my distinguished and respected namesake." He had noted that "both of us devoted large portions of our adult life to Russia and her problems." Kennan, *Memoirs*, I, pp. 8–9.

[46] Issacson and Thomas, *The Wise Men*, p. 76.

[47] Mayers, *George Kennan*, p. 21.

[48] Kennan, *Memoirs*, I, p. 15.

[49] Ibid., p. 16.

acter as containing "a curious blend of arrogance and insecurity, haughtiness and self-pity, sensitivity and coldness, assertiveness and shyness."[50] With this curiously blended character Kennan set about to pursue a career. He carried from Princeton neither well-formed opinions regarding public affairs nor deep convictions regarding international relations, but despite this he decided to try for the newly formed Foreign Service and, to his surprise, he passed the qualifying examination.[51] A quarter century of service as a diplomat lay ahead.

Few diplomats rise initially in meteoric fashion and Kennan was not numbered among the chosen few. He had a long road to travel before he would exert real influence over policy. Beginning in the fall of 1926 he studied for seven months at the Foreign Service School in Washington and then set off to serve in the lowly post of vice-consul first in Geneva and then in Hamburg. Even in this early period he had a particular ambition. "I have strong hopes of learning enough Russian during the first part of my service to present the Department with a *fait accompli* when Russia is finally recognized," he wrote his father. "That would be more or less in the family tradition—to go to Russia."[52] Kennan settled reasonably adeptly into the role and persona of the diplomat. "In this new role as representative (however lowly) of a government rather than of just myself, the more painful personal idiosyncrasies and neuroses tended to leave me," he explained. "I welcomed the opportunity to assume a new personality behind which the old introverted one could retire."[53] Kennan's increasing comfort in the role of diplomat did not prevent an attempt on his part in 1928 to resign from the Foreign Service. Moved by personal concerns Kennan returned to Washington but a broken engagement removed the impetus for him to resign.[54] Instead his fortuitous presence in the city afforded him the opportunity to gain selection for a training program for language specialists. He would have three years of graduate study in Europe while remaining in the Foreign Service.

Kennan's decision to stay gave him a choice of languages—Chinese, Japanese, Arabic, or Russian. Of course he chose Russian immediately but this choice, made so early in Kennan's career, contributed directly to his selection as Director of the Policy Planning Staff. It is difficult to conceive of a Chinese, Japanese, or Arab specialist being appointed to this post in 1947. The China Lobby already had begun its devastating assault on the China hands. The Japan specialists remained in relative obscurity as General Douglas MacArthur and the military oversaw the occupation of Japan. The Arabists already were

[50] Issacson and Thomas, *The Wise Men*, p. 74.

[51] On this see Kennan, *Memoirs*, I, pp. 16–18; Isaacson and Thomas, *The Wise Men*, pp. 140–43.

[52] Kennan letter to his father quoted in Isaacson and Thomas, *The Wise Men*, p. 145.

[53] Kennan letter quoted in Isaacson and Thomas, *The Wise Men*, p. 145.

[54] Isaacson and Thomas discuss the aborted resignation and the initial reasons for it with characteristic deftness in *The Wise Men*, pp. 145–46.

involved in a losing argument within the administration over the Palestine question. But the selection of a Russian specialist made sense precisely because Soviet-American relations had come to dominate American foreign policy.

Kennan began to study Russian language, literature, history, and culture, while serving briefly as vice-consul in Tallinin in Estonia and as Third Secretary in Riga, Latvia. From 1929 through 1931 he pursued formal studies in the Seminary for Oriental Languages in the University of Berlin. Afterwards he returned as Third Secretary to the so-called Russian Section of the legation in Riga where the United States, in the absence of diplomatic relations with the government of the Soviet Union, kept a wary watch on the activities of Stalin and his associates.[55] Here, from 1931 to 1933, Kennan handled reportage on economic matters, and, as he later put it with understated precision "grew to mature interest in Russian affairs."[56] Much has been made of the hardline, avidly anti-Bolshevik thrust of the training which Kennan and his fellow Russian specialists received during this period and its supposed enduring impact on them.[57] Unquestionably the overseer of this program, Robert Kelley—who headed the Division of Eastern European Affairs, loved Czarist Russia and rabidly opposed American dealings with the Soviet Union—insisted on the trainees being solidly grounded in Russian history and culture at the expense of knowledge of Soviet ideology and practice.[58] Undoubtedly the antagonistic views towards the Soviet regime of Kelley and the Russian emigre teachers exerted some influence but they were not imposed on Kennan. He was simply not the type to accept the party line.

The first picture Kennan formed of the Soviet Union was not flattering but it was not in any striking manner inaccurate. Poring through the Soviet newspapers, journals, and magazines from his Riga outpost he was struck by Soviet propaganda—"at the unabashed use of obvious falsehood, at the hypocrisy,

[55] Natalie Grant, "The Russian Section, A Window on the Soviet Union," *Diplomatic History* 2 (Winter 1978): 107–15.

[56] Kennan, *Memoirs*, I, p. 68.

[57] Daniel Yergin makes the most with his "Riga Axioms" in *Shattered Peace*, pp. 17–41. See the helpful corrective in Daniel Harrington, "Kennan, Bohlen and the Riga Axioms," *Diplomatic History* 2 (Fall 1978): 423–37.

[58] For a detailed account of this program, which emphasizes its anti-Communist intent, see Frederic L. Propas, "Creating a Hard Line Toward Russia: The Training of State Department Soviet Experts, 1927–1937," *Diplomatic History* 7 (Summer 1984): 209–26. In his *Memoirs* Kennan recalled: "Once, at the outset of my study in Berlin, I wrote to Kelley, pointing out to him that the Berlin University, almost alone among the universities of the West at that time, had excellent courses and lecture series on strictly Soviet subjects: Soviet finances, Soviet political structure, etc. I asked whether he did not want me to take some of these. The answer was negative. The sense of what he said was: stick to your knitting; get the essentials of a good Russian cultural background; the rest can come later." Kennan, *Memoirs*, I, p. 33. For later comments of Robert F. Kelley see Foy D. Kohler and Mose L. Harvey, *The Soviet Union: Yesterday, Today and Tomorrow* (Miami, 1975), pp. 164–78.

and, above all, at the savage intolerance shown toward everything that is not Soviet."[59] But such views did not diminish his desire to visit the Soviet Union and to observe it more closely. The Eastern European Division refused his request to travel in the Soviet Union in 1932.[60] Kennan possessed little admiration for the Soviet system but he avoided entrapment in rigidly doctrinaire anti-Soviet views. He continued to oppose recognition of the Soviet regime up to 1933 because of its continued support for revolutionary activities but his views were not set in concrete by the Riga experience. And soon they were to be shaped by a different reality. Franklin D. Roosevelt had become president and he planned to establish diplomatic relations with the Soviet Union.

Moscow the First Time

In November 1933, Maxim Litvinov, the Soviet Commissar for Foreign Affairs, arrived in Washington and began negotiations with Roosevelt leading to the American recognition of and establishment of relations with the Soviet Union.[61] Kennan chanced to be in the city. During his studies in Berlin he had met and married an attractive, young Norwegian, Annelise Sorensen, a graceful and balanced woman who exercised something of a calming impact on her emotional and highly strung husband. Their first child, Grace, was born in Riga. Using the age and ill-health of his father and the older man's desire to see his new granddaughter Kennan wangled a leave. He headed for Washington, however, not Milwaukee. There, through the intervention of Loy W. Henderson and Charles E. Bohlen, two other Russian specialists who would be longtime colleagues, Kennan met the dashing William C. Bullitt whom Roosevelt had named as American ambassador to Moscow after successfully completing his talks with Litvinov. After some discussion, as the now familiar story goes, Bullitt asked, "Do you know Russian?" Kennan replied, "yes." Bullitt then asked, "I'm leaving on Monday for Moscow. Could you be ready in time to come along?" He could and he was.[62]

Kennan's response to Bullitt's request says something of the young diplomat's ambition and his burning desire to be involved in American relations with the Soviet Union at the outset.[63] Impressed by Bullitt's "enormous charm, confidence and vitality" Kennan traveled with his new superior across the Atlantic and Europe.[64] In a state of high excitement they reached the Soviet

[59] George F. Kennan, "Flashbacks," *New Yorker* 61 (February 25, 1985): 57.

[60] Propas, "Creating a Hard Line Toward Russia," p. 220.

[61] On the Roosevelt-Litvinov agreements see Robert Paul Browder, *The Origins of Soviet-American Diplomacy* (Princeton, 1953).

[62] The foregoing relies on Isaacson and Thomas, *The Wise Men*, pp. 150–57.

[63] One might note that Kennan's father died while he was accompanying Bullitt to Moscow in 1933.

[64] Kennan offers an insightful portrait of Bullitt in his "Introduction" to Orville H. Bullitt, ed.,

border on December 4 and Moscow on December 11. Heady days followed. Bullitt presented his credentials to President Mikhail Kalinin on December 13 and began a whirlwind series of meetings and banquets to launch the relationship on a strong footing and to make the necessary physical arrangements for the American mission.[65] Bullitt's hopes were high. He realized there had been little contact between the diplomatic corps and the Soviet government but he planned to change all that. He wrote home to Roosevelt that "the men at the head of the Soviet Government today are really intelligent, sophisticated, vigorous human beings and they cannot be persuaded to waste their time with the ordinary conventional diplomatist. On the other hand, they are extremely eager to have contact with anyone who has first-rate intelligence and dimensions as a human being. They were, for example, delighted by young Kennan."[66] Bullitt, after thus setting himself up for inevitable disillusionment with his grand expectations of being able to bridge the communication gap with the Soviets, returned to the United States to recruit the rest of his delegation. He delegated Kennan to continue the work of establishing the mission. In difficult, almost hectic, circumstances Kennan did what he could to prepare residential and work premises for the ambassador and his staff who returned in March of 1934.

On Bullitt's return Kennan was appointed as Third Secretary and, except for some time in Austria in 1935 because of ill health, he served in Moscow until the summer of 1937.[67] This period established Kennan as a serious political analyst of the Soviet Union and afforded him the opportunity to immerse himself in Russia and to deepen his loving yet tortuous relationship with this vast land.[68] He traveled whenever he could although he felt constrained by the restrictions placed upon him.[69] These restrictions bothered him. He wrote to his friend Charlie Thayer from his sick bed in Austria in May of 1935 that

---

For the President: Personal and Secret, Correspondence Between Franklin D. Roosevelt and William C. Bullitt (Boston, 1972), pp. v–xvi. (The direct quotation is from p. xv.)

[65] Bullitt's account of this trip written solely for Roosevelt is found in Bullitt, ed., *For the President*, pp. 61–73.

[66] Ibid., p. 65. The delight with Kennan presumably was aided by the fact that Kalinin and others had read the books on Siberia by the elder George Kennan. See Kennan, "Flashbacks," p. 57.

[67] For a description of the staffing and operation of the embassy by a colleague of Kennan's, who considered him the "outstanding individual of the embassy's staff," see Bohlen, *Witness to History*, pp. 16–18; Also see the thorough but dry memoir by Loy W. Henderson in Papers of Loy W. Henderson, Manuscript Division, Library of Congress, Box 19. This has now been published. See George W. Baer, ed., *A Question of Trust: The Origins of U.S.-Soviet Diplomatic Relations; The Memoirs of Loy W. Henderson* (Stanford, 1987).

[68] On Kennan's service in Moscow from 1933 to 1937 see Mayers, *George Kennan*, pp. 29–47; Isaacson and Thomas, *The Wise Men*, pp. 161–73; and Wright, "George F. Kennan, Scholar-Diplomat," pp. 56–106.

[69] For accounts of some of his trips to the countryside, "primarily to visit places where the writer, Anton Chekhov . . . had lived," see Kennan, *Sketches From A Life*, pp. 22–35.

"Moscow had me somewhat on the run. I was too fascinated by Russia to take the restrictions of a diplomatic status with equanimity, and was inclined to feel bitter about things."[70] But this time in Moscow was important for Kennan. He developed strong and lasting personal friendships with Charles Bohlen and Charlie Thayer which tempered some of his apparent aloofness and distance. And he developed, as one writer has put it, "an intellectual intimacy with some associates, notably Henderson and Bohlen, and with them began to refine and conceptualize various impressions of Soviet life."[71] Here in Moscow at close range, more so than in Riga, were formed Kennan's lasting views of the Soviets.

Kennan and Bohlen agreed that the Soviet leaders they observed could be understood only in the context of traditional Russian political practice. Ideology held limited significance. Stalin owed more and bore a closer resemblance to Ivan the Terrible than he did to Marx. David Mayers has pointed out correctly that Kennan appreciated that "in Stalin's Russia ethical barbarism had been wedded to the modern techniques of tyranny."[72] As translator for Bullitt's successor, Ambassador Joseph E. Davies, at the Great Purge trials, Kennan had this reality seared into his mind. Some, like the vapid Davies whom Kennan held in contempt, sought to disguise or to excuse the Stalinist brutalities in the interests of fostering improved relations with the Soviet Union.[73] Blessed with intellectual integrity and a mixture of courage, arrogance, and plain contrariness which forced him to make his opinion known, Kennan rejected this approach but his voice carried no weight at this point. Davies recommended he be transferred for "his health" and 1938 found him back in Washington assigned to the Russian desk in the State Department.[74]

PRAGUE TO LISBON

Kennan spent a desultory year on the Russian desk.[75] It was his first extended stay in the United States in over a decade and he evoked no enthusiasm for what he saw. He even drafted some chapters for a proposed book which advocated a form of authoritarian government for the United States. America's elite would run things freed from meddlesome politicians and powerful special interests and ethnic groups.[76] Such views also developed in part from his in-

[70] Kennan to Charles W. Thayer, May 22, 1935, Papers of Charles W. Thayer, HSTL, Box 3.

[71] Mayers, *George Kennan*, p. 33.

[72] Ibid., p. 35.

[73] Kennan realized that the Purge trials were only the tip of the Stalinist iceberg but he had no full sense of the extent of Stalin's tyranny which is revealed by Roy Medvedev in his *Let History Judge: The Origins and Consequences of Stalinism*, rev ed (New York, 1989).

[74] On Kennan's transfer see Wright, "George F. Kennan, Scholar-Diplomat," pp. 105–6.

[75] Kennan, *Memoirs*, I, pp. 85–86.

[76] For Kennan's recommendations see his "The Prerequisites: Notes on Problems of the United States in 1938," Kennan Papers, Box 25; and the analysis in Mayers, *George Kennan*, pp. 49–

creasing frustration with the ragged and unprofessional way in which American foreign policy was formulated and implemented. By now he held a firm
conviction that the application of his abilities would improve matters significantly. On occasion he tried to convey his views of the Soviet Union. Addressing an audience at the Foreign Service School, which he once had attended,
Kennan explained that "we will get nearer to the truth if we abandon for a
time the hackneyed question of how far Bolshevism has changed Russia and
turn our attention to the question of how far Russia has changed Bolshevism."
In making recommendations with respect to American policy he argued that
"the primary quality of this policy must be patience. We must neither expect
too much nor despair of getting anything at all."[77] But his lectures at this time
failed to attract policymakers of consequence. He gladly got out of Washington and returned to Europe. He arrived in Prague on September 29, 1938, the
day of the Munich Conference. Europe, once again, marched inexorably toward war.

Kennan's reputation in the Foreign Service slowly grew and his service in
Prague further enhanced it.[78] Kennan had strong views on the role of the foreign service officer and he strove to live up to his own standards. He had
developed a contempt for the effete, prissy, and overly social dimension of
much of what passed for diplomacy in Europe. As early as 1935 in a letter
trying to encourage Charlie Thayer to join the Foreign Service he outlined his
vision of "a corps of younger officers who will be scholars as well as gentle-
men, who will be able to wield the pen as skillfully as the tea-cup, and who,
with their combination of academic training and practical experience will
come to develop a point of view [regarding the Soviet Union] much stronger
and more effective than that of the Paris emigre crowd who made so much
fuss about themselves."[79] Kennan carried this general outlook to his diplomatic practice in German-occupied Prague. He reported extensively and took
pride in his own efforts, although few read what he wrote.[80] The sense of being
ignored gnawed deep into his sensitive personality but it did not dissuade him
from offering his views in long memorandums. More would follow and these
would be read but his hour had yet to come.

---

58. For a discussion of Kennan's thinking extending beyond this time period see Anders Stephanson, *Kennan and the Art of Foreign Policy*, pp. 215–29.

[77] Kennan lecture, "Russia," May 20, 1938, George F. Kennan Papers, Seeley G. Mudd
Manuscript Library, Princeton University, Princeton, N.J., Box 16.

[78] On Kennan's growing reputation note that George Messersmith, the American ambassador
in Vienna during Kennan's short service there following his recuperation from illness, wrote that
he was "one of the finest of our younger officers." See Jesse H. Stiller, *George S. Messersmith:
Diplomat of Democracy* (Chapel Hill, N.C., 1988), p. 75.

[79] Kennan to Thayer, May 22, 1935, Thayer Papers, Box 3. Kennan later formulated his recommendations for the Foreign Service at some length. This is discussed in Mayers, *George Kennan*, pp. 58–62.

[80] Kennan later published some of his reports from Prague. See George F. Kennan, *From
Prague After Munich: Diplomatic Papers, 1938–1940* (Princeton, 1968).

Upon the outbreak of war in Europe in September 1939, Kennan was trans- ⌐
ferred from Prague to the American embassy in Berlin where, now a First
Secretary, he served as administrative officer until the advent of Pearl Harbor
and the German declaration of war against the United States in December
1941. Kennan had no regard for the Nazis and he drafted a report in 1940
which argued that the only way to prevent German domination of Europe was
to destroy the Nazi regime.[81] He differentiated this regime from the German ⌐
people as a whole and he extended his sympathies to the internal opposition to
Hitler, especially its aristocratic elements. He exerted no special effort to assist the victims of Nazi terror but Walter Isaacson and Evan Thomas exaggerate in describing him as callous.[82] Kennan considered the ill-treatment of the
Jews to be ''a fantastically barbaric thing'' but he walked no extra mile in
aiding them.[83] David Mayers is more insightful when suggesting that Kennan
was ''chillingly passive and correctly bureaucratic when something bolder
was required,'' although this criticism could be extended far beyond American
diplomats in Berlin.[84] As for Kennan, he implemented the visa regulations
strictly in accord with the law and resented the threats made to him to engage
the assistance of Jewish groups in the United States and their congressional
supports.[85] Such activities ended with Hitler's decision to honor his alliance
with the Japanese after their December 7 attack on the U.S. Pacific Fleet. The
U.S. found itself formally at war with the Nazis and Kennan, together with
the remainder of the embassy staff, found himself taken into custody and interned for five months.[86]

Upon his release from internment Kennan served firstly during 1942–1943 ⌐
in Lisbon as Counselor and then charge d'affaires and next during 1943–1944
in London as Counselor to the European Advisory Commission (EAC). In each
case Kennan demonstrated his initiative and deepening sense that *he*, more so
than those formally charged with the responsibility, knew the correct course
for American diplomacy. In Portugal the issue of obtaining American military ⌐
rights to air and naval bases in the Azores saw him objecting to the instructions
of the American military establishment conveyed to him by the State Department cipher. Recalled to Washington, he managed, through the intervention
of Admiral Leahy and of Harry Hopkins, to gain entry to President Roosevelt
who resolved matters in Kennan's favor.[87] During his work as political adviser

[81] Kennan, *Memoirs*, I, pp. 116–19.

[82] They write: ''What was most distinctive, and disturbing, about Kennan's reporting from
Prague and Berlin in 1939 and 1940 was his callousness to the plight of those subjected to Nazi
terror.'' Isaacson and Thomas, *The Wise Men*, pp. 177–78.

[83] For Kennan's description see his Diary entry for October 21, 1941, in *Sketches From a Life*,
p. 75.

[84] Mayers, *George Kennan*, p. 78.

[85] Author's interview with George F. Kennan, Princeton, N.J., March 6, 1989.

[86] Kennan, *Memoirs*, I, pp. 135–39; and Charles Burdick, *An American Island in Hitler's
Reich: The Bad Nauheim Internment* (Menlo Park, Calif., 1987).

[87] Kennan provides a long but interesting account of this episode in his *Memoirs*, I, pp. 142–

to Ambassador John Winant on the EAC Kennan similarly intervened directly with the president to sort out the question of the boundaries for the Soviet Union's proposed occupation zone in Germany. Again Roosevelt accepted the diplomat's recommendations.[88] In the broad scheme of wartime decision making these are but minor episodes whose significance derives mainly from what they reveal about Kennan. Here stood a man, now turned forty and eager to play a larger role in foreign policy-making. He seized with alacrity what few opportunities passed his way but more generally he felt ignored and on the periphery—a position he did indeed occupy. Whatever personal insecurities may still have resided within him his convictions regarding his professional competence were not modest, especially when he compared himself to the incumbents of senior policy-making positions. Kennan at this time resembled a volcano rumbling within and building towards an explosion. The eruption would occur to most notice two years later in Moscow.

RUSSIA SEVEN YEARS LATER

W. Averell Harriman, the American ambassador in Moscow, needed to strengthen the political section of his embassy staff and to obtain a deputy head of his mission. After some false starts he succeeded in securing Kennan as Counselor of his embassy.[89] The early morning of July 1, 1944, found Kennan at the Russian airport in Tehran. He flew from there to Baku and thence to Stalingrad and on to Moscow. He confided to his diary that "on the entire four-and-a-half hour trip from Stalingrad to Moscow, across the black-earth district, I sat glued to the window, moved and fascinated to see before me again this great, fertile, mysterious country which I had spent so many years trying to understand."[90] It did not take long for him to share some of his understandings. Within several months of his return to the Soviet Union Kennan's intuitive judgments and his own firsthand observations combined to convince him that American policy was founded on a "dangerous misreading of the personality, the intentions, and the political situation of the Soviet leadership."[91] He took it upon himself to alert those charged with formulating American policy but his endeavors initially brought no recognition and little response.

His first major effort to sound the alarm and to distill the essence of what he

---

63. For some further documentation on the matter see *Foreign Relations of the United States* (hereafter *FRUS*), 1943, II, pp. 527–76.

[88] On this matter see Tony Sharp, *The Wartime Alliance and the Zonal Division of Germany* (Oxford, 1975), pp. 64–66; Bernard Bellush, *He Walked Alone: A Biography of John Gilbert Winant* (The Hague, 1968), pp. 198–201; and Kennan, *Memoirs*, I, pp. 164–87.

[89] W. Averell Harriman and Elie Abel, *Special Envoy to Churchill and Stalin, 1945–1946* (New York, 1975), p. 229.

[90] Diary entry, July 1, 1944, Kennan, *Sketches From A Life*, p. 84.

[91] Kennan, *Memoirs*, I, p. 225.

knew of Russia came in a long and complex essay entitled "Russia—Seven Years Later." This paper traced developments in the Soviet Union since his departure in 1937 and then went on to look at prospects for postwar Russia. He portrayed the Soviets as committed "to the concrete task of becoming the dominant power of Eastern and Central Europe."[92] C. Ben Wright has noted the "total disregard of Marxist-Leninist ideology" in the essay. "Having abandoned Communist dogma to occupy the throne of Ivan the Terrible and Peter the Great," Wright observed correctly of Kennan's argument, "Stalin is portrayed as a Russian nationalist pursuing the Tsar's program of territorial expansion."[93] Seven years might have passed but little had changed in Kennan's argument but it was no less apposite because of this. Only one thing appeared to be constant—his new ambassador, like the old, paid his views little attention. Kennan handed "Russia—Seven Years Later" to Harriman and heard no more of it. Harriman simply returned it to him without comment, although the ambassador did forward a sizable portion of it to Washington. One suspects that the self-consciously intellectual quality of the piece left the practical and hard-pressed Harriman—a man of action—distinctly unimpressed.

Harriman headed a wartime embassy and naturally devoted much of his long work days to questions of a military nature. To the extent he relied upon any advisers he turned substantially to his military staff led by General John R. Deane. Certainly he accorded Kennan no exalted place.[94] But as World War II entered its final year political issues among the Allied powers kept bursting forth and Kennan seized the opportunity to offer his views on them to Harriman. Most crucially, Poland's future was at stake and Kennan saw Soviet actions there as a litmus test that confirmed his broad analysis. On August 1, 1944, the Polish Home Army in Warsaw rose up against their Nazi oppressors wanting to liberate their capital before the arrival of the Red Army. The uprising was crushed as the Red Army waited on the other side of the Vistula and, more tellingly, as the Soviet Union denied Britain and the United States the right to use airbases in the Ukraine to supply the Polish fighters. In light of Soviet acquiescence in the suppression of the Warsaw uprising Kennan believed that "there should have been a full-fledged and realistic political showdown with the Soviet leaders: when they should have been confronted with the choice between changing their policy completely and agreeing to collaborate in the establishment of truly independent countries in Eastern Europe or forfeiting Western-Allied support and sponsorship for the remaining phases of their war effort."[95] Such a course was quite unacceptable to Roosevelt and

[92] "Russia Seven Years Later," September 1944, Annex in Kennan, *Memoirs*, 1, pp. 503–31; direct quotation from pp. 520–21.

[93] Wright, "George F. Kennan, Scholar-Diplomat," p. 266.

[94] On Harriman see Larry I. Bland, "W. Averell Harriman: The Liberal Cold Warrior," in Jules Davids, ed., *Perspectives in American Diplomacy* (New York, 1976), pp. 299–320.

[95] Kennan, *Memoirs*, 1, p. 211.

Churchill who were still intent not only on maintaining Soviet armies in the war against Germany but securing them subsequently for the war against Japan. This was the position which Harriman loyally represented but now he began to move to a firmer approach towards the Soviets, demanding a more quid pro quo relationship. Perhaps Kennan had exercised some influence on his toughening stance, although the impact of Stalin's actions on him seems more consequential.

Through late 1944 and into 1945 Kennan sustained a lonely campaign to convince policymakers to abandon the chimera of postwar collaboration with the Soviets and to adopt a sphere-of-influence approach to European issues which would limit the outward thrust of Soviet power.[96] Kennan proselytized Bohlen, now close to the center of American decision making as State Department liaison officer to the White House. Early in 1945 he wrote to his old friend recommending a program "to divide Europe frankly into spheres of influence." The Soviet domination of Eastern and Southeastern Europe would be acknowledged while the Western powers would move to establish a Western European federation capable of restricting Soviet influence and power.[97] Bohlen, in tune with the tenor of American domestic politics, dismissed Kennan's advice as naive, impractical and impossible to implement in a democracy—a criticism, incidentally, that was to be levelled regularly.[98] Kennan's views did not inform American strategy at the Yalta Conference. Roosevelt labored there to maintain cooperation with Stalin in order to ensure the Soviets' intervention in the Pacific War and their participation in the United Nations and to modify Soviet behavior in Eastern Europe.[99] Perhaps a naivete of sorts informed FDR's hopes for further cooperation with Stalin but it did not lead him to concede anything to Stalin which was not already within the grasp of the Soviet dictator—disgraceful and politically inspired Yalta "myths" to the contrary. Kennan never alleged that the Western democracies "gave very much away" at Yalta.[100] His objection focused on their continuing endeavors to collaborate with the Soviets and their unwillingness to appreciate that they were dealing "with a deadly and implacable adversary, whose hos-

[96] Kennan's advocacy of a sphere-of-influence approach and his "realpolitik prescription for the postwar world" is examined intelligently by Hugh De Santis, *The Diplomacy of Silence*, pp. 152–55 and pp. 166–67. As Arthur Schlesinger, Jr., pointed out in his "Origins of the Cold War," *Foreign Affairs* 46 (October 1967): 28–29, Kennan was not the only advocate of this approach. Henry L. Stimson and Henry A. Wallace also advocated this course.

[97] Kennan to Bohlen, January 26, 1945, Papers of Charles E. Bohlen, Library of Congress, Box 5.

[98] On Bohlen's response see his *Witness to History*, pp. 175–76; and T. Michael Ruddy, *The Cautious Diplomat: Charles E. Bohlen and the Soviet Union, 1929–1969* (Kent, 1986), pp. 32–33.

[99] On Yalta see John L. Snell, ed., *The Meaning of Yalta: Big Three Diplomacy and the New Balance of Power* (Baton Rouge, La., 1956).

[100] George F. Kennan, *American Diplomacy, 1900–1950* (Chicago, 1951), pp. 84–87.

tility was in no way diminished by the common war effort against Germany.''[101]

The Soviets set about over the next year confirming Kennan's analysis. Soviet security interests in Eastern Europe were interpreted by them to necessitate controlling the political lives of the countries they occupied. Through proxies and puppets supported by the Red Army's presence they gradually imposed their total domination over the region. In the interests of postwar cooperation the United States had been prepared to concede the Soviet Union a predominant influence in the region but slowly and in a disorganized manner it began to object to an enforced and total Soviet hegemony.[102] American policy under Roosevelt and, after April 12, 1945, under Truman meandered towards a firmer approach to the Russians.[103] The conference at Potsdam in July 1945, and the CFM meeting in Moscow in December 1945, were not arenas where this approach was adopted. Invited by Byrnes to attend some of the sessions at the Moscow gathering Kennan identified more with the firmer British position than that offered by the American Secretary of State. Kennan complained to his diary that Byrnes's ''weakness in dealing with the Russians is that his main purpose is to achieve some sort of an agreement, he doesn't much care what.''[104]

Kennan felt his exclusion from genuine participation in such meetings deeply but continued on with his work in Moscow. Harriman's failure to give him any serious briefing on the Yalta conference had provoked some resentment on his part toward the ambassador.[105] The China specialist, John Paton Davies, who arrived in Moscow early in 1945 to join the embassy staff and who developed a very close friendship with Kennan, remembers him suffering ''agonies of frustration'' during this time.[106] Kennan's inability to separate himself emotionally from professional matters and Harriman's neglect to give any public sign of appreciation for his Counselor's work contributed to this

[101] Kennan has a good discussion of Stalin in his ''An Historian of Potsdam and His Readers,'' *American Slavic and East European Review* 20 (April 1961): 292.

[102] Eduard Mark, ''American Policy Toward Eastern Europe and the Origins of the Cold War, 1941–1946: An Alternative Interpretation,'' *The Journal of American History* 68 (September 1981): 313–36; and Geir Lundestad, *The American Non-Policy toward Eastern Europe* (New York, 1975).

[103] On Truman's policy-making during his first year in office see Robert James Maddox, *From War To Cold War: The Education of Harry S. Truman* (Boulder, 1988); Fraser J. Harbutt, *The Iron Curtain: Churchill, America and the Origins of the Cold War* (New York, 1986); and Deborah Welch Larson, *Origins of Containment: A Psychological Explanation* (Princeton, N.J., 1985), pp. 127–301.

[104] Diary entry, December 19, 1945, in Kennan, *Memoirs*, I, p. 287. For a more sympathetic portrayal of Byrnes see Robert L. Messer, *The End of an Alliance: James F. Byrnes, Roosevelt, Truman, and the Origins of the Cold War* (Chapel Hill, N.C., 1982).

[105] Diary entry, March 23, 1945, C. L. Sulzberger, *A Long Row of Candles: Memoirs and Diaries, 1934–1954* (New York, 1969), p. 250.

[106] John Paton Davies, Jr., *Dragon By the Tail* (New York, 1972), p. 390.

agony.[107] But Kennan's frustration did not paralyze him. He continued to run the administrative side of the embassy, a not insignificant undertaking. He acted as charge d'affaires in Harriman's absence in which capacity he addressed the cheering throng of Russians in front of the American embassy on the day the Allied victory in Europe was announced.[108] He took a special interest in the work of the junior officers and would organize informal discussion sessions with them.[109] With Davies as informal tutor he began his education in Asian affairs and, as of old, he took whatever opportunities he could to travel. In June 1945, he journeyed as far as Novosibirsk in Siberia and Kuznetsk, near the Siberian-Chinese border. In September he accompanied a group of American congressmen from Moscow to Helsinki. On the latter trip Kennan briefly visited Leningrad. His own emotion and intensity at this time is well revealed by his diary entry from this trip where he confided that "I know that in this city, where I have never lived, there had nevertheless been deposited by some strange quirk of fate—a previous life, perhaps?—a portion of my own capacity to feel and to love, a portion—in other words—of my own life; and that this is something no American will ever understand and no Russian ever believe."[110] Russia constituted a veritable part of his being but somewhat typically this only deepened his sense of isolation.

By 1946, Kennan had had enough. Disillusioned and despondent he contemplated resigning from the foreign service and returning to the United States. He listed as his reasons his dissatisfaction with existing American policy, the feeling that his talents were not being fully utilized, a desire to establish "roots" in the United States for his young family, and his poor health.[111] Each of these factors weighed on his thinking but it seems clear that his frustrated ambition carried decisive force.[112] Kennan believed he had been on the periphery too long, ignored in favor of not simply less competent men but quite wrongheaded ones to boot. The time had come to get out or so he threatened.

---

[107] Author's interview with John Paton Davies, Asheville, North Carolina, August 12, 1986.

[108] Kennan, "Flashbacks," p. 60; and Sulzberger, *Long Row of Candles*, p. 49.

[109] Interview with William A. Crawford by C. Ben Wright, September 29, 1970, C. Ben Wright Kennan Biography Collection, Marshall Library, Box 8. (Crawford was Third Secretary of the Moscow Embassy in 1945.)

[110] On Kennan's travels see his *Sketches From A Life*, pp. 91–117. Direct quotation from p. 114.

[111] C. Ben Wright, "George F. Kennan, Scholar-Diplomat," pp. 377–78. See the communications of March 1946 concerning Kennan's possible resignation in George F. Kennan, Personnel File 123, State Department Records, NA.

[112] Kennan recalled that it was "entirely possible that I considered resigning from the Foreign Service in 1945 or early 1946. I was strongly out of accord with the policies of Tehran and Yalta, about which I had never been consulted. I felt keenly the fact that people such as Alger Hiss and Stettinius and Harry Hopkins, who knew nothing about Russia were at the President's side during all that time, whereas I was sidetracked in Moscow." Kennan to author, December 14, 1978.

THE LONG TELEGRAM AND KENNAN'S CAREER

Of course, Kennan's resignation never reached the State Department. The reason for this owed to developments instigated by a departmental request for an explanation of recent Soviet behavior manifested in particular by the so-called election speeches of Stalin and his associates in early February of 1946, and by the dispute over the Azerbaijan region of Iran.[113] The request found Kennan again acting as charge d'affaires, in the interim between Harriman's resignation and the arrival of Bedell Smith to replace him, and laid up in bed with cold, fever, sinus, and tooth trouble and yet another attack of the ulcers that bedeviled him. Despite his dolorous state Kennan recognized that this request was "it." His opinion was being sought out. After struggling since his return to Moscow to get a hearing for his views he decided to make the most of this opportunity. In his *Memoirs* he captures his sentiments: "They had asked for it. Now, by God, they would have it."[114] The volcano erupted and was noticed.

Kennan composed his response, the Long Telegram, lying in his sickbed. This imposed no great burden on him because he "felt his mind functioned better when his body was in a horizontal position."[115] With the embassy's military and naval attaches at his bedside he dictated an eight thousand word dispatch to his secretary Dorothy Hessman. Brigadier General Frank K. Roberts, the military attache, remembers making a couple of suggestions "as to items from the military point of view" but the work was overwhelmingly Kennan's.[116] Dated February 22, it was divided into five sections, "like an eighteenth-century Protestant sermon," as Kennan remarked with more telling insight than he may have intended. It traced the basic features, background, and prospects of Soviet foreign policy and their implications for American policy.[117]

Kennan's analysis held few surprises for the small number already familiar with his previous writings and advice. Examining the Soviet "outlook" he

[113] For the departmental request see Matthews to Kennan, February 13, 1946 (861.00/2-1346), State Department Records, NA, referred to in *FRUS* 1946, VI, p. 696 n. 44. Matthews had asked Elbridge Durbrow to draft a cable to "goose him [Kennan]" into giving his views. See Yergin, *Shattered Peace*, p. 167. On the issue of Iran and its effects on American policy toward the USSR see Bruce R. Kuniholm, *The Origins of the Cold War in the Near East: Great Power Conflict and Diplomacy in Iran, Turkey and Greece* (Princeton, 1980); and Gary R. Hess, "The Iranian Crisis of 1945–46 and the Cold War," *Political Science Quarterly* 89 (March 1974): 116–46.

[114] Kennan, *Memoirs*, I, p. 293.

[115] Dorothy Hessman (Kennan's secretary at the time) interview with C. Ben Wright, October 1, 1970, C. Ben Wright Kennan Biography Collection, Box 8, Folder 15. In this interview Hessman gives further details of the telegram's composition.

[116] For Roberts' recollections see his unpublished "Memoirs-Interlude, 1944–49" in Papers of Frank N. Roberts, HSTL, Box 3.

[117] Kennan, *Memoirs*, I, pp. 293–94.

discerned that the "party line is not based on any objective analysis of the situation beyond Russia's borders; that, it has, indeed, little to do with conditions outside of Russia; that, it arises mainly from basic inter-Russian necessities." For him the motivation for Soviet policy lay in the need of the Kremlin to justify its rule. Marxist dogma provided for the Kremlin inhabitants "the fig leaf of their moral and intellectual respectability"—a veritable cover for their tyranny—but at the bottom of the Kremlin's "neurotic view of world affairs" resided the "traditional and instinctive Russian sense of insecurity." Stalin needed an enemy to justify his rule. Coexistence was a charade. From such premises Kennan went on to predict that the Soviet Union would aim to increase in every way the "strength and prestige of the Soviet state" and, wherever considered timely and promising, to "advance the official limits of Soviet power." But Soviet power in the Kennan view was "neither schematic or adventuristic. It does not work by fixed plans. It does not take unnecessary risks. Impervious to the logic of reason, it is highly sensitive to the logic of force." Kennan asserted that Soviet power usually withdrew upon strong resistance and, he emphasized, "if the adversary has sufficient force and makes clear his readiness to use it, he rarely has to do so."[118] The implications for American policy were obvious.

The Long Telegram undoubtedly had an impact on the thinking of senior policymakers in Washington. "The timing of Mr. Kennan's communication . . . was strategic," Louis Halle claimed. "It came right at a moment when the Department . . . was floundering about, looking for new intellectual moorings. Now in this communication it was offered a new and realistic conception to which it might attach itself."[119] Now Halle overestimated both the intellectual void within the State Department and the degree to which the Long Telegram actually influenced policy but there can be no doubt that Kennan's cable exercised a catalytic effect upon departmental thinking especially as regards the possibility of the United States achieving any non-adversary relationship with the Soviet Union. Under Secretary Acheson considered that "his recommendations . . . were of no help; his historical analysis might or might not have been sound but his predictions and warnings could not have been better."[120] State Department Counselor, Benjamin V. Cohen, although noting that policy was already in transition, conceded that the Long Telegram "di-

[118] For the Long Telegram see Kennan to Secretary of State, February 22, 1946, *FRUS* 1946, VI, pp. 696–709. Direct quotations from pp. 699–701, 707. The literature on the Long Telegram is seemingly endless and can't be canvassed here. For a competent discussion see Mayers, *George Kennan*, pp. 97–102.

[119] Louis J. Halle, *The Cold War as History* (New York, 1967), p. 105. Kennan made a similar point in his *Memoirs*, I, p. 294. "It was," he wrote, "one of those moments when official Washington, whose states of receptivity, or the opposite, are determined by subjective emotional currents as intricately imbedded as those of the most complicated of Sigmund Freud's erstwhile patients, was ready to receive a given message."

[120] Acheson, *Present at the Creation*, p. 151.

rectly and indirectly . . . influenced Department thinking."[121] Harriman, now back in Washington, sent a copy of his former deputy's cable to Forrestal describing it as "well worth reading." Forrestal obviously agreed and, beginning his self-appointed role as Kennan's promoter, had the piece mimeographed and distributed to other members of Truman's cabinet and to higher officers throughout the armed services.[122]

Kennan's message helped construct the intellectual supports for the already developing disposition of firmness towards the Soviet Union. In this achievement Kennan's communication must be linked to the private and public efforts of the profoundly realistic Winston Churchill. The former British Prime Minister on a private visit to the United States in February 1946 lobbied Truman to challenge the Soviets in Eastern Europe and in his famous "Iron Curtain" speech at Westminster College in Fulton, Missouri, pointed bluntly to the reality of Soviet expansionism and called for Western action in response.[123] The combination of the Kennan and Churchill efforts moved the United States towards the "get tough" approach which was given occasional implementation during the remainder of 1946. It served also to erode the "policy legitimacy," as the political scientist Alexander George would term it, of notions of cooperation with the Soviet Union.[124] "From this time on," John Lewis Gaddis contends, "American policymakers regarded the Soviet Union not as an estranged ally, but as a potential enemy, whose vital interests could not be recognized without endangering those of the United States."[125] It is striking, however, to gauge how little a positive impact on policy this new perception of the Soviets actually exercised. A disposition to challenge and confront on particular incidents hardly constituted a coherent policy which could be explained to the American people. The Long Telegram in no sense put an end to the floundering in American policy formulation. After a detailed examination, Deborah Welch Larson astutely concluded that "at the end of a year of drift and indecision, of waffling between confrontation and collaboration, Truman still had no new policy, nor did he perceive any alternatives to the present

[121] Cohen quoted in Richard L. Walker and George Curry, *E. R. Stettinius and James F. Byrnes*, vol. 14 in *The American Secretaries of State and Their Diplomacy*, ed. Robert H. Ferrell (New York, 1964), p. 202.

[122] Harriman and Abel, *Special Envoy to Churchill and Stalin*, p. 548. On Forrestal's reactions see Walter Millis, ed., *The Forrestal Diaries* (New York, 1951), pp. 135–36.

[123] Churchill's private and public efforts are examined at length in Harbutt, *The Iron Curtain*, pp. 151–208. The more general role of the British in moving the U.S. to a firmer approach towards the Soviets is well examined in Terry H. Anderson, *The United States, Great Britain and the Cold War, 1944–1947* (Columbia, Mo., 1981).

[124] Alexander L. George, "Domestic Constraints on Regime Change in U.S. Foreign Policy: The Need for Policy Legitimacy," in Ole R. Holsti, Randolph M. Siverson, and Alexander L. George, eds., *Change in the International System* (Boulder, 1980), pp. 233–62.

[125] John Lewis Gaddis, *The United States and the Origins of the Cold War, 1941–1947* (New York, 1972), p. 284.

policies, except the unacceptable prospect of war."[126] Policy, as it turned out, could not be created by a document. It was much more complicated, a reality which historians wedded to the importance of a certain document sometimes neglect.

The Long Telegram exerted its most tangible impact on Kennan's career. With the receipt of the message in Washington Kennan's "official loneliness" came to an end. As a consequence of it, he later correctly recorded his "reputation was made," and his "voice now carried."[127] He had obtained the recognition as a Soviet expert which would be crucial in his selection by General Marshall to head the Policy Planning Staff. After a few months, during which he served as mentor to Ambassador Smith, Kennan was recalled to Washington.[128] At the instigation of James Forrestal, who had Kennan checked out by Naval Intelligence, Kennan received appointment in mid-April as Deputy for Foreign Affairs in the recently established National War College.[129] Kennan was happy about the appointment and so were his friends. John Davies after acknowledging that Kennan was ideal for this job went on to note that "it will represent enough of a change in routine for him to be able to regain his health."[130] Kennan knew the years in Moscow had been hard on him but he did not leave the Soviet capital intent on limiting his involvements. He wrote a friend that "some of the most dangerous tendencies in American thought about Russia [had] been checked, if not overcome." Now the task would be to "restrain the hot-heads and panic-mongers and keep policy on a firm and even keel."[131] He clearly expected that he would play some role in the future determination of American policy toward the Soviet Union.

BACK IN WASHINGTON—THE WAR COLLEGE AND THE TRUMAN DOCTRINE

Kennan began instruction at the National War College in September and until he moved back to the State Department in 1947 he lectured there to high-

---

[126] Larson, *Origins of Containment*, p. 301.

[127] Kennan, *Memoirs*, I, pp. 294–95.

[128] Walter Bedell Smith, *My Three Years in Moscow* (Philadelphia, 1949), pp. 47, 86.

[129] On the report of Naval Intelligence see the Memorandum from K. Tolley, Office of Chief of Naval Operations to Cpt. W. R. Smedberg, Aide to Secretary Forrestal, February 26, 1946, Papers of James V. Forrestal, Princeton, N.J., Box 24. Tolley reported that "Kennan is considered one of the most competent and intelligent observers in the Foreign Service; has had long experience in Russian affairs; is on his third Moscow tour; speaks Russian very well. He has long been an exponent of the realistic, wholly reciprocal approach to the Soviet problem. During Harriman's tenure of office as Ambassador, Kennan's attempts to formulate and recommend a firm policy were very definitely discouraged by Harriman, who derived considerable amusement from Kennan's earnestness in the matter."

[130] Davies comments in a letter from him to John F. Melby, May 8, 1946, Papers of John F. Melby, HSTL, Box 6.

[131] Kennan to Dr. Bruce Hopper (Pentagon, Washington), April 17, 1946, quoted in Wright, "George F. Kennan, Scholar-Diplomat," p. 378.

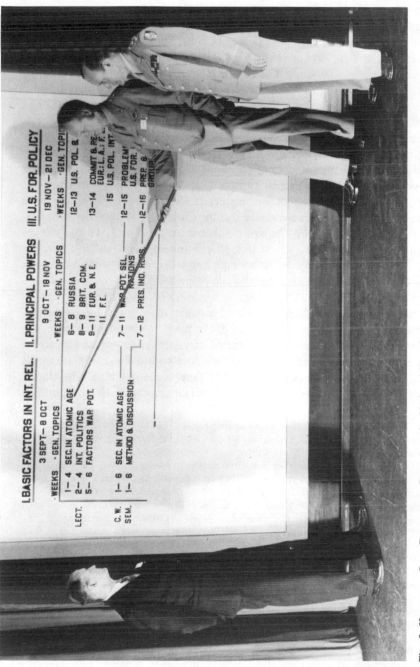

Fig. 2. Kennan as State Department Deputy at the National War College in 1946, along with General Ted Landon (with pointer), then Air Force Deputy at the College, and General Al Gruenther, then Executive Officer of the College. Note the course outline. Photo by Walter Sanders/*Life Magazine*/© *Time*, Inc., 1946. Reprinted with permission.

ranking military officers, Foreign Service officers, and an occasional cabinet member, particularly Forrestal. After returning from Moscow and prior to the beginning of term at the War College Kennan undertook an extensive speaking tour arranged by the Public Affairs section of the State Department and served as a consultant for one month to General Hoyt A. Vandenberg, the newly named Director of the Central Intelligence Group (CIG), the forerunner to the CIA.[132] His tenure at the War College witnessed him become a known figure in certain elite Washington circles. Dinner invitations in Georgetown and speaking engagements with weighty groups became a part of his experience.[133] Though not formally involved in the continuing process of defining Soviet intentions and designing a suitable American response, Kennan willingly gave advice on a number of occasions to those more deeply involved in this operation.[134] Indeed his anxiety to be more involved in policy-making was apparent and he readily announced his availability. "I am enjoying my work here immensely and I am convinced that the College is doing a highly important and constructive job," he wrote Acheson on October 8, 1946. "Meanwhile I am not bothering people in the Department anymore than I have to; but I am sure you and the Secretary both know that I am at your disposal at any time if there is anyway in which I can help."[135]

While he waited in the wings Kennan's lectures on geopolitics and strategy at the War College permitted him to hone his analysis of Soviet foreign policy, of the world situation in general, and of the needed American response. He appreciated well that the "war eliminated certain rival powers and created a vacuum into which some great power influence had to flow." This was the reality he discerned in eastern and central Europe and in China. The United States needed to address this new geopolitical circumstance. Kennan outlined

---

[132] For Kennan's extensive report of his tour see Kennan to Francis Russell, August 23, 1946, Acheson Papers, HSTL, Box 27. On his consultancy work see Philip S. Meilinger, *Hoyt S. Vandenberg: The Life of a General* (Bloomington, Ind., 1989), pp. 73–74.

[133] On the dinner parties note Diary entry, November 6, 1946, in Joseph P. Lash, ed., *From the Diaries of Felix Frankfurter* (New York, 1975), p. 292; and entry, March 9, 1947, in David E. Lilienthal, *The Journals of David E. Lilienthal*, vol. 2: *The Atomic Energy Years, 1949–1950* (New York, 1964), pp. 158–59. Kennan spoke to groups like the Yale Institute of International Studies and the National Defense Committee of the American Chamber of Commerce.

[134] In particular note his contribution to the so-called Clifford Memorandum. See Clark Clifford to Kennan, September 13, 1946; and Kennan to Clifford, September 16, 1946, Papers of George M. Elsey, HSTL, Box 63. This memorandum of September 24, 1946, entitled "American Relations with the Soviet Union" is in Elsey Papers, Box 63. On the writing and significance of the report see transcript of oral history interview with George M. Elsey, April 9, 1970, by Jerry N. Hess, HSTL, p. 266; and memorandum of conversation with Clark Clifford, June 2, 1966, by Herbert Feis, Papers of Herbert Feis, Manuscript Division, Library of Congress, Box 76. Clark Clifford tends to exaggerate the policy ramifications of his 1946 report in his recent memoir. See Clark Clifford with Richard Holbrooke, *Counsel to the President: A Memoir* (New York, 1991), pp. 123–29.

[135] Kennan to Acheson, October 8, 1946, Acheson Papers, HSTL, Box 27.

the "clash of outlooks between us and the Russians" but in doing so he did not infer that war between the two powers was inevitable—far from it. He argued that America could attain its ends by means short of war, by utilizing psychological, economic, political, and diplomatic over military measures.[136]

Early in 1947, Kennan outlined in summary form his analysis and recommendations regarding the problem of meeting the Kremlin in international affairs. Using the language that long would come to be associated with his name he argued that the "inherent expansive tendencies [of the Soviet Union] must be firmly contained at all times by counterpressure which makes it constantly evident that attempts to break through this containment would be detrimental to *Soviet* interests."[137] Here he introduced the word and developed the concept of containment. But notably his formulation of it—similarly to his recommendations in the Long Telegram—failed to highlight his preference for nonmilitary measures and, in fact, inferred the use of military force if need be to implement it.[138]

Kennan repeated this failure and inference in a paper titled "The Psychological Background of Soviet Foreign Policy," which he wrote at the specific request of James Forrestal in late January 1947.[139] Drafted in his northwest corner office of Theodore Roosevelt Hall at the War College, this essay—the most famous of all his writings—later was published as "The Sources of Soviet Conduct" in the July 1947 issue of *Foreign Affairs* under the authorship of "X."[140] The article publicly revealed the concept of containment which Kennan had attempted to propagate within the administration. "The main element of any United States policy toward the Soviet Union," Kennan initially

[136] See Kennan, "The Background of Current Russian Diplomatic Moves," December 10, 1946; Minutes of Organizational Meeting on Russia, June 12, 1946; Kennan, "Measures Short of War (Diplomatic)," September 16, 1946; all in Kennan Papers, Box 16.

[137] Kennan, "The Soviet Way of Thought and Its Effects on Foreign Policy," January 24, 1947, Kennan Papers, Box 16. (His emphasis.)

[138] For a view which argues that Kennan's formulation assumed the use of military containment see C. Ben Wright, "Mr. 'X' and Containment," *Slavic Review* 35 (March 1976): 1–31. The issue of what Kennan meant by containment and how it should be implemented has been the subject of much controversy. In addition to Wright's essay see John Lewis Gaddis, "Containment: A Reassessment," *Foreign Affairs* 55 (July 1977): 873–87; and Eduard Mark, "The Question of Containment: A Reply to John Lewis Gaddis," *Foreign Affairs* 56 (January 1978): 430–40.

[139] The initial impetus for this paper lay in Forrestal's request for Kennan to comment on a paper by E. F. Willett entitled "Dialectical Materialism and Russian Objectives," January 14, 1946, which may be found in Forrestal Papers, Box 17. For Forrestal's request to Kennan for him to write "on the same subject in your own way" relayed through John T. Connor see Connor to Kennan, October 31, 1946, Forrestal Papers, Box 70. For the paper, "The Psychological Background of Soviet Foreign Policy," January 31, 1947, see Forrestal Papers, Box 18.

[140] "X" [George F. Kennan], "The Sources of Soviet Conduct," *Foreign Affairs* 25 (July 1947): 566–82. For details on how the essay came to be published in *Foreign Affairs* see Kennan, *Memoirs*, I, p. 355.

informed Forrestal and subsequently the readers of the influential quarterly, "must be that of a long-term, patient but firm and vigilant containment of Russian expansive tendencies." He affirmed that "Soviet pressure against the free institutions of the Western world is something that can be contained by the adroit and vigilant application of counter force at a series of constantly shifting geographical and political points."[141]

With this article Kennan was accorded authorship of the containment doctrine and his notoriety established. But it must be made crystal clear that Kennan never obtained some equivalent of copyright over the notion of containment. He was neither a playwright who had prepared a script which now needed only to be acted out nor the single exegete consulted to clarify its implications. Containment as expressed in the "X" article represented no more than a broad approach. It was not a prescription for policy. It did not outline in any detail what exactly the United States should do. The temptation to characterize Kennan as a Moses-type figure descending to give the law of containment over to a disoriented group of American policymakers should be resisted. Others would play a role in defining and enfleshing containment and the doctrine would come to be understood only in light of these actions. And this process had begun before Mr. "X" became known to the readers of *Foreign Affairs*.

Well before "The Sources of Soviet Conduct" appeared in print, containment—as most people would come to understand it—received notable application first in Iran and then in Greece and Turkey. Kennan's own involvement in determining the policy on Greece and Turkey lends some substance to his claim that he desired to utilize primarily nonmilitary means to restrict Soviet expansionism. He played a tangential role in the early deliberations of late February concerning the American response to the British decision to withdraw their special support for Greece. He supported the view that the United States should fill the breech somewhat by extending economic assistance to Greece. Thereafter he had no further part in this matter until March 6 when he read a copy of the message drafted for President Truman to deliver to Congress. He then objected both to the tone of the message and its sweeping language but also to some of the specific actions it proposed, namely military aid to Greece and assistance to Turkey.[142] He offered a more subdued draft as an alternative but elicited no positive response.[143] Joseph Jones has noted the irony of Kennan, considered "the mastermind of the policy of containment,"

[141] "X," "The Sources of Soviet Conduct," pp. 575–76.

[142] A reasonable account of these deliberations leading up to the Truman Doctrine is provided by Joseph M. Jones, *The Fifteen Weeks* (New York, 1964). Jones apparently mistakes the time when Kennan first was called in on this matter. See the exchange of correspondence on this matter between Kennan and Loy Henderson and Henderson and Dean Acheson, March–April 1967, Papers of Loy W. Henderson, Manuscript Division, Library of Congress, Box 8.

[143] On Kennan's draft see Kuniholm, *The Origins of the Cold War in the Near East*, p. 418.

objecting to what, on the surface at least, appeared a manifestation of such a policy.[144] Kennan's objections came to nought and Truman delivered the message, the Truman Doctrine, on March 12.[145]

Interestingly, General Marshall shared some of Kennan's reservations over the language of Truman's message, believing that the speech contained "too much flamboyant anti-Communism." He expressed these reservations from Paris as he traveled to Moscow for the Council of Foreign Minister's meeting but the president, anxious to assure Senate approval of his proposal, rejected them.[146] Back at the War College Kennan questioned the universalist implications and tone of the president's message in a lecture in his Strategy, Policy and Planning Course.[147] He continued his work there even as he continued with his preparations to establish the planning group. Meanwhile Marshall struggled unsuccessfully to make progress in his negotiations in Moscow. The failure of the meeting was crucially important in forming his views of Soviet intentions and the requisite American response. This direct experience of dealing with the Soviets more so than reading any particular document, whether written by Kennan or another, motivated Marshall. "At the conclusion of the Moscow Conference," Marshall recalled, "it was my feeling that the Soviets were doing everything possible to achieve a complete breakdown in Europe." As he saw it, "the major problem was to counter this negative Soviet policy and to restore the European economy."[148]

Marshall perceived that the Soviet Union was not content to consolidate its East European empire but hoped to take advantage of the dislocation and desperation of Western Europe. On April 28 he arrived back in Washington. The very next day he called Kennan to his office and instructed him to return to the State Department immediately to establish the Policy Planning Staff. Referring to the deplorable state of Europe he directed Kennan and the Staff, which was still to be assembled, to address this problem and to make recommendations within two weeks. To Kennan's entreaty for more guidance he advised in distinctive fashion: "Avoid trivia."[149]

[144] Jones, The Fifteen Weeks, pp. 154–55.

[145] For Truman's message of March 12, 1947, see Public Papers of the Presidents of the United States: Harry S. Truman, 1947 (Washington, D.C., 1963), pp. 176–80. The significance of the Truman Doctrine and the reasons for it are discussed in Kuniholm, The Origins of the Cold War in the Near East, pp. 418–31.

[146] Bohlen, Witness to History, p. 261. On the apparent need for Truman to use flamboyant rhetoric to assure senatorial support and approval see Acheson, Present at the Creation, p. 219.

[147] Kennan, "National Security Problem," March 14, 1947, Kennan Papers, Box 17.

[148] Interviews with George C. Marshall, October 30, 1952, and February 18, 1953, by Harry B. Price, Papers of Harry B. Price, HSTL, Box 1. Also see Bohlen, Witness to History, p. 263; and John Foster Dulles to Arthur H. Vandenberg, March 29, 1947, and April 10, 1947, Papers of John Foster Dulles, Firestone Library, Princeton, N.J., Box 34.

[149] Kennan, Memoirs, I, pp. 325–26.

THE KENNAN CHARACTER

Some men might have balked at this demanding assignment, but not Kennan. Given the particular stage he had reached in his career, his personality and character, he welcomed it. Tall, lean, and balding, Kennan struck some acquaintances as "a rather academic-looking fellow."[150] His "quizzical blue eyes" struck more sensitive observers and gave some glimpse of the intensity and emotion that resided within the person who could appear cool and detached.[151] Kennan was a complex man. He was a sensitive and artistic man who loved music, liked to paint, and was widely read in American, English, German, and Russian literature—indeed, he had entertained the ambition of writing a life of Chekhov.[152] His moods and introspection bear some resemblance to those of Chekhov's characters. Those who got to know him at something beyond a superficial level found the contrasting elements or even contradictions in his personality most striking. Harrison Salisbury, who considered Kennan "my guide, my inspiration, my mentor on Russia," described him as "an optimist and a romantic" who "could also be, almost physically gloomy in a Spenglerian sense, and as realistic as a surgeon."[153] The British journalist Henry Brandon, who got to know Kennan in the late forties, pointed to his outer detachment and his inner passion and saw him as "a complex bundle of weary experience and precarious innocence."[154]

Whatever the contradictions, few disputed that Kennan possessed a brilliant mind capable of turning easily from one subject to the next.[155] His special expertise, of course, was the Soviet Union but he thought geopolitically and was unafraid, after appropriate study, to venture views on a quite varied range of subjects. His intellectual gifts and the integrity and fearlessness with which he applied them were to be the bedrock of Kennan's influence as Director of the Policy Planning Staff. Self-confident and independent in his judgments, he could argue them persuasively both orally and on paper. But his pride in his own intellectual ability and the passion he invested in the application of it held the seeds for much turmoil. Bohlen, his closest Foreign Service col-

---

[150] Lilienthal, *Journals of David E. Lilienthal*, 2, p. 158.

[151] Henry Brandon, *Special Relationships: A Foreign Correspondent's Memoirs From Roosevelt to Reagan* (New York, 1988), p. 36. Another person to comment on Kennan's eyes was the poet Stephen Spender who commented of him that "with his very bright blue eyes he looks like some tall, fair oriental philosopher who played football in his youth." Stephen Spender, *Journals, 1939–1983*, ed. John Goldsmith (London, 1985), pp. 168, 181.

[152] Brooks Atkinson, "America's Global Planner," p. 9.

[153] Harrison E. Salisbury, *A Journey For Our Times: A Memoir* (New York, 1983), p. 411.

[154] Brandon, *Special Relationships*, p. 36.

[155] Stanley Hoffman remarked that "seeing Kennan's mind is like looking at the mechanism of a fine watch." See Hoffman, "After the Creation, or the Watch and the Arrow," *International Journal* 28 (Spring 1973): 19. Also see Alfred Kazin, "Solitary Expert: The Case of George F. Kennan," *Atlantic Monthly* 221 (January 1968): 59–67.

league, recalled that matters became "personal" for Kennan—he couldn't "put his own feelings out of the way."[156] In this regard Kennan contrasted markedly with Bohlen himself, who was an operator, easy-going and well-liked even by those he disagreed with. Bohlen had none of the aloofness that Kennan sometimes affected nor did he take himself quite as seriously.[157] Kennan approached his new work in the State Department gravely and, one suspects, that he felt that fate had laid hands upon him and ordained him to formulate a proper American response to the Soviet challenge.

Kennan's complicated character did not prevent him from enjoying a very happy family life. Two more children were born after his return to Washington and his family proved a haven of security and contentment for him. His admirable desire to spend time with his wife and children removed him somewhat from the cocktails-before-dinner crowd. Kennan liked to pack up his family on weekends and retreat to the farm near Gettysburg in south-central Pennsylvania which he had purchased in 1942 and which was during these years the real family home and his place of legal residence.[158] Here he undertook rugged physical work and expended much sweat, which served as a respite from the demands of Washington and helped him counter the assorted illnesses that regularly assaulted his still delicate constitution.

Kennan's devotion to his family did not prevent him from extending his circle of friends and professional contacts in Washington. Bohlen he knew from his early days in the Foreign Service and many of his other State Department colleagues such as Loy Henderson also were well known to him. His time at the War College gave him the opportunity to meet a number of influential military figures such as Central Intelligence Group director Hoyt Vandenberg and Generals Al Gruenther and Ted Landon—his fellow deputy commandants. His service there gained him a respect from the military establishment which would pay handsome dividends in the years ahead when he worked in close cooperation with Pentagon representatives on committees of the National Security Council. But, it must be understood well, Kennan was not part of the circle of James Forrestal. He had no significant personal relationship with the nation's first Defense Secretary and very limited professional contact with Forrestal after his move to the State Department.[159] Kennan

[156] C. Ben Wright Interview with Charles E. Bohlen, September 29, 1970, C. Ben Wright Kennan Biography Collection, Box 8.

[157] On Kennan's "aloofness" note the recollection of Ralph Block who worked in the State Department's Public Affairs Office, 1947–50, and knew Kennan through John Paton Davies: "He always seemed to act as if he were [in] a religious novitiate of some kind. I had met him very briefly once through Davies, but he was very offhand with me. I was just one of those information people." Oral History Interview With Ralph Block by Jerry N. Hess, July 8, 1966, HSTL.

[158] Kennan, *Sketches from a Life*, pp. 158, 359–60.

[159] Author's interview with George F. Kennan, March 6, 1989. Kennan recalled that "he had no significant personal relationship with Forrestal" and could remember only two occasions when

appreciated well that Marshall was his principal audience and his avenue to influence over policy, although he did choose to develop his contacts with some weighty figures in the Washington press corps—Walter Lippmann, Joseph Alsop, and James Reston notable among them—whom he would engage in frank, off-the-record discussions.[160]

A group absent from Kennan's growing circle were politicians and their aides. He exhibited a certain disdain for Congress and a distaste for the task of prompting action from it. Bohlen recalled that Kennan had "trouble . . . in getting on, as it were, with the functioning of American democracy."[161] Kennan had spent nineteen of the first twenty years of active professional life outside the United States and these years had not deepened his appreciation for the American political system.[162] He had no prior direct experience of dealing with Congress and he resented the inevitable compromises that had to be made to placate it or to secure congressional support. He defined his job, with General Marshall's approval, as being to identify the national interest, in particular places and in general, and to place this before the secretary of state who thereupon might place it before the president. As Director of the Planning Staff he felt no special call to worry about domestic political realities and no obligation to write in light of what was politically possible. This task belonged rightly to the secretary and the president.[163] Such an approach, however, played into the hands of those who criticized Kennan for his lack of concern about domestic politics and opened him to the vastly overstated charge leveled—privately and much later—by fellow Soviet expert Llewellyn Thompson that he would "rather be right than pursue a politically feasible policy."[164]

Even with his developing circle of friends and contacts Kennan tended to be something of a loner, "more comfortable speaking from his own pulpit than joining a chorus" as Harrison Salisbury put it.[165] From the outset he expected to dominate the Planning Staff intellectually and, in fact, he soon had it formally confirmed that the responsibility for Staff decisions rested on him personally.[166] The Policy Planning Staff would be a very personal operation—

he met Forrestal in other than a professional way. Wright confirms this point in his "George F. Kennan, Scholar-Diplomat," pp. 416–17.

[160] Author's interview with James Reston, Washington, D.C., August 8, 1989. Reston described Kennan as "very voluble but very discreet."

[161] C. Ben Wright Interview with Charles E. Bohlen, September 29, 1970.

[162] Kennan mentions this and examines his "expatriate" experience in Sketches from a Life, pp. 362–63.

[163] Author's interview with George F. Kennan, March 6, 1989.

[164] Interview with Llewelyn E. Thompson by C. Ben Wright, October 2, 1970, C. Ben Wright Kennan Biography Collection, Box 8.

[165] Salisbury, A Journey for Our Times, p. 405. Llewellyn Thompson alleged that Kennan loved to be an "iconoclast" and to "buck the crowd." Wright interview with Thompson, October 2, 1970.

[166] Kennan to Carlton Savage, October 27, 1947, RG 59, Lot File 64 D563, Records of the

one member recalled it as "pretty much like Lincoln's Cabinet."[167] Staff members would act in support of Kennan—a small but talented supporting cast. Kennan certainly had no desire to head a large operation. He envisioned a small but influential group which wasted no effort on its own administration. His focus was policy and this was precisely what the Planning Staff directorship demanded.

FIRST STEPS

Even before his return to Washington Secretary of State Marshall sent messages back from Moscow calling for the establishment of the Policy Planning Staff and without delay.[168] Kennan, thereupon, allocated a few hours each day to the matter and set about dealing with such questions as staff, organization, and office space. On April 24, 1947, Acheson formerly announced at his regular under secretary's staff meeting Kennan's appointment as Director of the Staff and that of Carlton Savage, a former assistant to Cordell Hull who continued to work in the secretary of state's office after Hull's departure, as the Executive Secretary of the group. Although born in Salem, Oregon, Savage continued something of Hull's tradition as a courtly, Southern gentleman. He was dignified and hardworking and facilitated the operations of the Staff but played no substantial role in the policy domain.[169] On the same day that Acheson made his announcements, Kennan, obviously cognizant of the broad directive he would receive as a first assignment, wrote a memorandum calling for the assembling of documents on current economic trends in the United Kingdom, France, Italy, and the western zones of Germany and Austria. He wanted these to make an overall assessment of what these areas would need "(*a*) by way of relief, in order to keep human life going in case no programs of rehabilitation are undertaken beyond those already in existence, and (*b*) to

Policy Planning Staff, 1947–1953, NA (hereafter PPS Records), Box 33. Kennan informed Savage "as a matter of record" that "Mr. Lovett was definite in stating that the responsibility for Staff decisions rests on me personally, and that I cannot be expected to achieve unanimity within the Staff before I put forward an opinion."

[167] Oral History Interview with Isaac N. P. Stokes by Richard D. McKinzie, July 3, 1973, HSTL. Stokes explained: "George made all the decisions. I did set a precedent. I don't know if it was ever followed again, but I wrote a dissenting opinion once to a recommendation which I thought was clearly wrong."

[168] Joseph Jones makes this point in *The Fifteen Weeks*, p. 240. The point is confirmed by the exchange of correspondence between Marshall and Acheson on April 22, 1947, regarding the staffing of the planning unit. See Acheson to Marshall (control 5434), April 22, 1947, and Marshall to Acheson (control 7027), April 23, 1947, Records of PPS, Box 8.

[169] Author's interview with Carlton Savage, Washington, D.C., June 22, 1978; and Author's interview with John Paton Davies, August 12, 1986. Davies remembered Savage as always offering "the elemental American point of view."

effect complete rehabilitation of the economy and to render it self support-ing.''[170]

As the European and Economic Affairs divisions of the State Department gathered information for him on the European economic situation, Kennan continued his recruiting efforts. On April 29, the day of his conversation with Marshall, Kennan recommended to Acheson that only he, Savage, and John Paton Davies, Jr., be assigned permanently to the Staff at this time.[171] Carl Humelsine had arranged Savage's selection with Kennan's subsequent com-pliance.[172] Kennan undoubtedly chose Davies, his valued colleague in the Moscow embassy and a specialist in Far Eastern affairs. Kennan wanted more time to enlist permanent members and in this regard he attempted to persuade Norris Chipman, the Second Secretary of the American Embassy in Paris, and Dexter Perkins, Professor of American Diplomatic History at the University of Rochester to join the Staff.[173] But the needs of the moment did not permit only leisurely searches so Kennan asked Acheson for some provisional ap-pointments. Acheson quickly approved his request for Joseph E. Johnson, a broadminded and able former university professor who had served as director of the department's Division of International Security Affairs and who in-tended to return eventually to academic life. Kennan tried to get Edward S. Mason, Dean of the Graduate School of Public Administration at Harvard Uni-versity and the former head of the economic section of the Research and Anal-ysis Branch of the Office of Strategic Services, to serve as the economist on the Staff. But Mason, then in Moscow as an adviser to Marshall at the CFM meeting, preferred to return to his academic pursuits and turned down a direct request from the secretary.[174] As a backup Kennan asked for Paul H. Nitze whom he had met by chance on a train trip in 1944 and who subsequently had served in a number of different capacities in Foreign Economic Administration and on the U.S. Strategic Bombing Survey. Rather ironically in view of their later close association, Acheson blocked Nitze's appointment claiming he

[170] Kennan memorandum, April 24, 1947, *FRUS* 1947, III, p. 220 n. 2.

[171] Kennan to Acheson, April 29, 1947, PPS Records, Box 33. He asked also for the permanent appointment of George Butler when he completed his term as ambassador to the Dominican Re-public.

[172] Carlton Savage recalled that "Marshall's assistant Carl Humelsine came to me and wanted to know if I would become secretary of the Staff. I told him I hadn't applied for it but I was hoping I would be offered it. Then later on George Kennan came to see me and asked me if I'd take it. He didn't seem aware that Humelsine had already asked me." Savage had never met Kennan before this time. Author's interview with Carlton Savage, June 22, 1978.

[173] On Kennan's efforts see Kennan to Norris B. Chipman, March 18, 1947, Kennan Papers at Princeton, copied from Larry Bland Collection, Marshall Library; Kennan to Acheson, May 28, 1947 (re Perkins); Kennan to Marshall, June 13, 1947; Marshall to Perkins, June 25, 1947, PPS Records, Box 8.

[174] Oral History Interview with Edward S. Mason by Richard D. McKinzie, July 17, 1973, HSTL.

wasn't "a real economist" but "just a Wall-street operator."[175] As a result of Acheson's decision and Davies' inability to take up his appointment until late July, Kennan held the first formal meeting of the Policy Planning Staff on May 5, 1947, with the Staff comprising only himself, Savage, and Johnson.

Kennan had more success with obtaining a place for the Staff to work than he initially did in assembling it. When the person in the State Department who handled space allocation consulted with him the new Staff director chose close proximity and access to the secretary as the determinative priority. Kennan's office would be separated from Marshall's only by the Planning Staff conference room through which Kennan could gain entree to the secretary. This conference room, in which so much of the Staff's work was undertaken, was modest in size but Kennan thought this most appropriate. He recalled observing that "if we get too big to sit around this table we are done."[176] Kennan proved capable of resisting the endemic bureaucratic temptation to expand. The productivity, so to speak, of the Planning Staff suggests the wisdom of his action.

At the first meeting on May 5, the Staff carefully examined the departmental regulation formally establishing the group to obtain a clear understanding of the scope and nature of the work contemplated.[177] This regulation directed it to perform a number of vaguely stated functions—to formulate and develop a long-term program for the achievement of American foreign policy objectives; to anticipate problems; to undertake studies and prepare reports on broad politico-military problems; to evaluate the adequacy of current policy; and to coordinate planning activities within the department. Further, the regulation absolved the Staff from operational responsibility and in so doing denied it the right to issue directives to the operational divisions of the department or in turn to be subject to directives from the operational divisions. The Staff would report and be responsible to the under secretary and through him the secretary.[178] Such bureaucratic formulations disguised somewhat the close connection which Kennan hoped to establish between planning and operations. In

[175] Nitze remembered Kennan inviting him to join the Staff and then calling him up a day later to inform him that Acheson had vetoed the appointment. Author's interview with Paul H. Nitze, June 30, 1978, Arlington, Va. Also see Paul H. Nitze, *From Hiroshima to Glasnost: At the Center of Decision* (New York, 1989), p. 50; Strobe Talbott, *The Master of the Game: Paul Nitze and Nuclear Peace* (New York, 1988), pp. 41–46. Nitze had worked for the Wall Street firm of Dillon, Read and Company in the 1930s.

[176] Author's interview with George F. Kennan, March 6, 1989. For administrative details I also rely on author's interview with Carlton Savage, June 22, 1978. One should note that the Staff had adequate secretarial assistance. Kennan had as his personal secretary, Dorothy Hessman, who had served in this capacity since his days as Counselor in the Moscow embassy and would do so through Kennan's service as Director of Policy Planning.

[177] Minutes of Meeting, May 5, 1947, PPS Records, Box 32.

[178] The regulation is printed in U.S. Dept. of State, *Department of State Bulletin* (Washington, 1947), May 18, 1947, p. 1007.

trying to recruit Norris Chipman he had emphasized "that unless the work of this unit proves to be hard-hitting and realistic, and unless intensive and effective contact is established between planning and operations, then I think the experiment will be a short-lived one indeed and that none of us will be faced with the prospect of a dragging on for years in a series of sterile and dreary exercises in composition."[179] Kennan might have been proud of his prose style but he did not come to the Planning Staff to produce literature so much as to produce results.[180] This was not to be a detached, other-worldly group. In this Kennan would have Marshall's backing. Interviewed in 1956, the old General recalled that "I wanted that [the Policy Planning Staff] to handle the most important things we had."[181] The nature of his initial assignment to it confirms the validity of his recollection.

At its second meeting, three days later, the Staff moved on from the discussion of its directive and organizational matters to confront "the main problem in United States security today." They generally agreed that it was "to bring into acceptable relationship the economic distress abroad with the capacity and willingness of the United States to meet it effectively and speedily; that with Greece and Turkey taken care of and the Korean problem now being posed, the greatest and most crucial problem is in Western Europe; . . . that the problem is both political and economic, and not military (except insofar as maintenance of U.S. military effectiveness is concerned); that the approach to the political problem for the moment must be economic."[182] The connection between American security and the necessity of European economic recovery was clearly drawn and the political and economic nature of the problem, in the mind of Kennan and his colleagues, revealed quite bluntly. On May 14, Kennan wrote to Acheson that "the Policy Planning Staff has held two meetings devoted to an unavoidable study of its directives and to operational problems. Tomorrow it is to meet for the first time to sail into the substantial part of its work."[183] Kennan had completed his journey to the center of American foreign policy formulation.

[179] Kennan to Chipman, March 18, 1947, Kennan Papers, Larry Bland Collection.

[180] My formulation here borrows from the testimony of a later director of the PPS, Robert R. Bowie, who stated that "the purpose of a Policy Planning Staff is not merely to produce literature but to produce results." See "Planning in the Department," *Foreign Service Journal* 38 (March 1961): p. 22.

[181] George C. Marshall Interviews and Reminiscences for Forrest C. Pogue, November 20, 1956, Marshall Research Foundation, transcript p. 527.

[182] Minutes of Meeting, May 8, 1947, PPS Records, Box 32.

[183] Kennan to Acheson, May 14, 1947, PPS Records, Box 33.

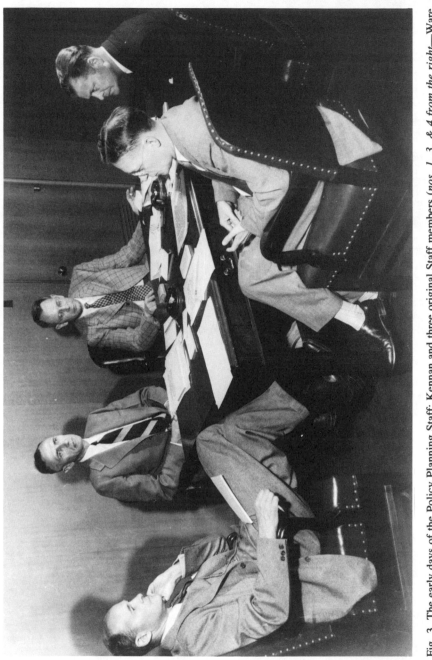

Fig. 3. The early days of the Policy Planning Staff: Kennan and three original Staff members (*nos. 1, 3, & 4 from the right*—Ware Adams, Joseph Johnson, and Carlton Savage) at a meeting in the Staff conference room, Summer 1947. Reprinted with permission of the *Washington Post*.

CHAPTER TWO

Launching the Marshall Plan

A CRISIS SITUATION?

Kennan's first major entry as director of the Policy Planning Staff into the arena of foreign policy formulation saw him contribute in an important manner to the development of what became known as the Marshall Plan. This Plan, known officially as the European Recovery Program (ERP), has long held an exalted place on the list of postwar American foreign policy achievements. The dramatic (and flattering) picture of a wholehearted and generous American effort reviving a dispirited and prostrate Europe was the staple of the early and somewhat hagiographic accounts of the Marshall Plan and lives on as evident in the celebratory comments of public figures at the time of its fortieth anniversary in 1987.[1] Whatever its impact on Europe, unquestionably the Marshall Plan marked a turning point in American diplomacy. It injected the United States into the midst of European affairs and marked a level of peacetime involvement there notably greater than in any preceding period. But recent scholarship has raised questions about the necessity of this American involvement, its origins, and its real purposes.[2] Illuminating Kennan's key participation in the making of the Marshall Plan affords the opportunity to address these questions and allows a richer appreciation for *how* the eventual policy emerged.

Alan S. Milward, an economic historian at the London School of Economics, has sought to slaughter a sacred cow of conventional interpretations of the Marshall Plan by disputing the very reality of the situation that supposedly called it forth. After amassing assorted statistical evidence he argued that Europe was not on the verge of economic collapse in the spring and summer of 1947. For him "the alleged economic crisis of the summer of 1947 in Western Europe did not exist, except as a shortage of foreign exchange caused by the

[1] For the early accounts see Harry B. Price, *The Marshall Plan and Its Meaning* (Ithaca, N.Y., 1955); and Joseph M. Jones, *The Fifteen Weeks* (New York, 1955). For the "celebratory comments" see, for example, Secretary George Schultz's address, "40th Anniversary of the Marshall Plan," May 26, 1987, Current Policy No. 964, Bureau of Public Affairs, Washington, D.C.

[2] See Alan Milward, *The Reconstruction of Western Europe, 1945–1951* (London, 1984); Michael J. Hogan, *The Marshall Plan: America, Britain and the Reconstruction of Western Europe, 1947–1952* (New York, 1987); Melvyn P. Leffler, "The United States and the Strategic Dimensions of the Marshall Plan," *Diplomatic History* 12 (Summer 1988): 277–306; Imanuel Wexler, *The Marshall Plan Revisited: The European Recovery Program in Economic Perspective* (Westport, Conn., 1983); and Charles P. Kindleberger, *The Marshall Plan Days* (Boston, 1987).

vigor of the European investment and production boom."[3] His argument, while noteworthy for its originality, goes completely against the grain of what everyone thought at the time.[4] Perhaps Theodore White, a reporter in Paris in 1947 and 1948, engaged in retrospective hyperbole in describing Europe as a bankrupt civilization—whose condition was "that of a beached whale that has somehow been stranded high beyond the normal tides and which, if not rescued, will die, stink and pollute everything around it."[5] But such views, even if more soberly expressed, were widely shared on both sides of the Atlantic. The influential Walter Lippmann publicly called attention to Europe's plight in March and April but officials within Truman's administration hardly needed to be briefed by him.[6] Secretary Marshall's sincerely held conclusions about Europe's dire prospects and the resultant opportunities they presented the Soviet Union were derived from his discussions in Moscow with Ernest Bevin and Georges Bidault and from reports from American representatives in Europe.[7]

Did the contemporary observers get it all wrong? Was there a real crisis or was it a deliberately manufactured one to serve other ends? Here Milward's own figures suggest a conclusion quite at variance with his own. The 1947 harvest was the worst in Europe in a century; the standard of living fell in 1947 in France, Belgium, and probably Italy; food consumption declined in Britain, France, Denmark, and Sweden in 1947; in Austria, Germany, and Italy caloric intake would not sustain health for long.[8] When both the impact of the winter of 1946–1947, which "paralyzed transportation, impeded food and fuel deliveries and radicalized workers into explosive wage demands," and the seeming strength of Communist forces in France and Italy with its implications for political upheaval are added to this then notions of a manufactured crisis ring rather hollow.[9] The food and fuel shortages and the dollar-shortage of the Europeans to finance their imports meant that "they faced production cutbacks and unemployment, malnutrition and hunger, monetary disorder and inflation,

---

[3] Milward, *Reconstruction of Western Europe*, pp. 1–17. Milward conveniently summarizes his argument in Alan S. Milward, "Was the Marshall Plan Necessary?" *Diplomatic History* 13 (Spring 1989): 237–38.

[4] This point is made by William Diebold, Jr., in his insightful "The Marshall Plan in Retrospect: A Review of Recent Scholarship," *Journal of International Affairs* 41 (Summer 1988): 430.

[5] Theodore H. White, *In Search of History: A Personal Adventure* (New York, 1978), p. 275.

[6] On Lippmann see Ronald Steel, *Walter Lippmann and the American Century* (Boston, 1980), pp. 440–41.

[7] Pogue, *George C. Marshall*, 4, p. 194.

[8] This point is made in Charles Kindleberger's essay "Did Dollars Save the World?" in his *Marshall Plan Days*, pp. 245–65. The argument draws especially from pp. 251–53 where Kindleberger summarizes material from Milward's first chapter.

[9] The impact of the winter is noted in Charles S. Maier, "The Two Postwar Eras and the Conditions for Stability in Twentieth-Century Western Europe," p. 343.

proliferating exchange controls and quotas.''[10] Milward could not quantify the political turmoil and the psychological exhaustion in Europe in early 1947, nor could he adequately assess an atmosphere that was charged, as Lawrence Kaplan argues, "with a fear of chaos or Communist control."[11] But these were precisely parts of the threatening reality that Kennan and his colleagues confronted. With four decades of hindsight one might argue with clinical detachment that Europe might have negotiated its own way out of the stormy economic and political waters in which it found itself in 1947. But American policymakers, operating in a situation of urgency and pressure, did not possess the luxury of testing this proposition. They preferred not to gamble with the well-being of Western Europe and with the security of the United States with which it was entwined.

DEPARTURE POINT

In undertaking the task of investigating Europe's problems and of developing proposals for the United States to assist European economic reconstruction Kennan did not start from scratch but built upon earlier efforts to address the issue. The seeds for what would become the Marshall Plan were sown not only within the Policy Planning Staff. Indeed, in pursuit of his effort "to cast the Marshall Plan in the context of America's twentieth-century search for a new economic order at home and abroad," the historian Michael Hogan traced the roots of the Marshall Plan to the "associative state" as it evolved in the post–World War I years, as it developed during the New Deal, and as it was amended during World War II.[12] The Marshall Plan involved no less than the projection of this American corporatism to Europe. This projection was most evident in the eventual administration of the Marshall Plan by the Economic Cooperation Administration (ECA) but also manifested itself in the ideas for an integration of the various European economies circulating at the expert level of the State Department early in 1947. Hogan's corporativist approach certainly provides a useful perspective from which to view the overall significance of the Marshall Plan but care must be taken in applying it too rigorously to the early development of this initiative. It conveys a sense of American policy emerging in a more consistent and premeditated way than was the case.[13] Certainly Kennan and his colleagues never possessed such clarity about the historical continuity of their actions nor a sense that they were working out of this corporativist approach.

[10] Leffler, "The Strategic Dimensions of the Marshall Plan," pp. 279–80.

[11] Lawrence S. Kaplan, "The Cold War and European Revisionism," *Diplomatic History* 11 (Spring 1987): 147.

[12] Hogan's argument is outlined in chapter 1 of his *The Marshall Plan*.

[13] William Diebold, Jr., makes this general point in "The Marshall Plan in Retrospect: A Review of Recent Scholarship," pp. 434–35.

As he scurried around to initiate his own efforts Kennan benefitted most from the solid policy deliberations of the ad hoc committee of the State-War-Navy Coordinating Committee (SWNCC) and from the unrelenting endeavors of Under Secretary Acheson to build a constituency for an aid program to Europe. At Acheson's request SWNCC established a committee in March 1947 to conduct studies of areas in the world requiring the aid of the United States.[14] Drawing largely upon the work of a dedicated group of third-level officials, the committee delivered an interim report on April 21 which by its own admission was tentative and based on limited information.[15] Nonetheless it contained key proposals that the Policy Planning Staff would develop.

The SWNCC committee emphasized economic interdependence among critical countries and stressed integration and coordination of economic programs of such countries in relation to American economic assistance. Thus it provided a guiding principle for much of the American effort to implement the Marshall Plan. The SWNCC committee report demanded that attention be given to "co-ordination of economic policy in occupied areas, particularly Germany and Japan, with general objectives in Europe and the Far East." Further, it argued that a program to increase European coal production should receive the highest priority.[16] Each of these aspects—coordination of economic programs, integration of Germany in overall European economic recovery, and a major boost in coal production—directly influenced Kennan and the Planning Staff and were appropriated by it. The SWNCC discussions made a significant additional contribution by mobilizing the State Department, especially its economic sections.

Dean Acheson demonstrated his concern for European rehabilitation not only by his establishment of the SWNCC committee. He declined to rest upon this action and worked throughout April and May to stimulate public discussion and consideration of the issue. His concern manifested itself most clearly in his speech to the Delta Council in Cleveland, Mississippi, on May 8. Here Acheson described the world's and especially Europe's desperate economic plight and outlined the implications of this for American policy. Convinced of the efficacy of extending American assistance he suggested that it be concentrated in "areas where it will be most effective in building world political and

---

[14] Acheson to Robert P. Patterson, March 5, 1947, *FRUS* 1947, III, pp. 197–98; and memorandum by State Department member of SWNCC (Hilldring), March 17, 1947, *FRUS* 1947, III, pp. 198–99. For further description of the context in which Marshall Plan policy-making was initiated see Scott Jackson, "Prologue to the Marshall Plan: The Origins of the American Commitment for a European Recovery Program," *The Journal of American History* 65 (March 1979): 1043–68.

[15] Report of the Special *Ad Hoc* Committee of the State-War-Navy Coordinating Committee, April 21, 1947, *FRUS* 1947, III, pp. 204–19. On the writing of this report see Ben T. Moore to Clair Wilcox, July 28, 1947, *FRUS* 1947, III, p. 240.

[16] Report of the Special *Ad Hoc* Committee of the SWNCC, April 21, 1947, *FRUS* 1947, III, pp. 204–19.

economic stability."[17] He always kept the link between political ends and economic means to the fore in his analyses. Acheson's speech in Cleveland, Mississippi, devised no plan but vividly portrayed the situation and indicated the need for some action. This speech was not targeted primarily at the Mississippi farmers who heard him deliver it. He wanted instead to get attention among congressional and opinion leaders. James Reston of the *New York Times,* whom he briefed in advance regarding his speech, served compliantly as Acheson's "transmission belt" and gave his ideas wide distribution.[18] Acheson's efforts resemble those of one who tills the soil to ensure that the seeds once planted will grow.

Kennan, of course, brought with him his own ideas regarding assistance to Europe. He had considered the matter during the early months of 1947 and revealed his thoughts in a number of lectures in early May. On May 6 he spoke at the National War College and argued that any scheme for economic rehabilitation must provide for the maximum of economic collaboration and exchange among the European nations. While suggesting utilization of the machinery of the European Economic Commission to develop such collaboration, he pointed to the vulnerability of this United Nations-sponsored group to Russian interference. He emphasized rehabilitation as opposed to relief and cautioned that aid to Europe would not imply universal commitments. When referring to Europe, he explained, that "a fairly comprehensive and pretty far-reaching program has to be drawn up, or else we might as well let go of that area right now."[19] Three days later in an address at the Naval Academy he noted that when the United States simply poured "dollars and relief supplies into a foreign area," they tended to "sink away like water in the sand." Such aid was a mere "palliative rather than a cure for the economic distress to which it is a response." Kennan called for an aid program designed to "bring about rehabilitation and not only relief."[20]

Kennan shared his evolving views on European recovery with Walter Lippmann, the doyen of the Washington press corps. Forrestal had advised Lippmann to see Kennan and during several lunches in early May these two men, strikingly similar in both their capacity to theorize and their desire to influence policy, shared ideas thus initiating a remarkable intellectual relationship. Lippmann recalled talking to Kennan at length and having "a very good understanding" with him. Kennan outlined for the distinguished columnist many of the ideas later embodied in the ERP concept and Lippmann offered certain

[17] Dean G. Acheson, "The Requirements of Reconstruction," May 8, 1947, *Department of State Bulletin,* May 18, 1947, pp. 991–94.

[18] Author's interview with James Reston, August 8, 1989.

[19] George F. Kennan, "Problems of U.S. Foreign Policy After Moscow," May 6, 1947, Kennan Papers, Box 17.

[20] George F. Kennan, "Current Problems of Soviet-American Relations," May 9, 1947, Kennan Papers, Box 17.

ones in return.[21] Most notably he suggested that the European countries should get together and forge a recovery program to present to the United States.[22] This would facilitate European economic and political cooperation. Kennan eventually afforded this proposal a central place in the Staff's recommendation to Marshall, although it ultimately foundered on the reef of the European inability to act in concert. Kennan and Lippmann also agreed that an American aid program could not appear as "either an American ploy to dominate Europe or a blatant anti-Soviet maneuver."[23] European initiative would address the former concern while an offer for the Soviets to participate in the aid program would dampen any criticism based on the latter.

INITIAL EFFORTS

By the time Kennan and his fledgling Staff began serious discussions, the recognition that Europe needed economic assistance was widespread and ideas as to how to aid the Europeans were numerous. A crying need existed for some order and coherence to be given to the many ideas, for some method to meet the acknowledged needs of the Europeans. Here is where Kennan and the Policy Planning Staff came into their own. At their second meeting on May 8, Kennan, Savage, and Johnson had settled upon a rough procedure to confront the issues they faced. They divided the question of the economic rehabilitation of Europe into short-term and long-term problems and agreed that, although time didn't permit them to develop fully a program for the long-term problem, "some sort of immediate action is necessary for psychological reasons."[24] This division and the recommendation for immediate action survived the two additional weeks of debate and argument within the Staff prior to the presentation of its report on May 23.

Kennan obtained three additional members for his Staff after the May 8 meeting, each of whom plunged into the pressured environment of its work on aiding Europe. Kennan had no formal training in economics and had sought to compensate for this deficiency by recruiting first Edward Mason and then Paul Nitze for the Staff. Denied the services of these men he attracted Jacques Reinstein, a young economist who recently had helped negotiate the peace treaty with Italy. He also garnered the services of Ware Adams, an experienced foreign service officer with particular knowledge of Germany and Austria. Finally Kennan drew into the work of the Planning Staff Colonel Charles H. Bonesteel of the War Department's Plans and Operations Division, an able

[21] Oral History Interview with Walter Lippmann, April 8, 1950, Butler Library, Columbia University, New York, transcript pp. 258–59; and Kennan to Walter Lippmann (draft letter—unsent), April 6, 1948, Kennan Papers, Box 17.

[22] Ronald Steel, *Walter Lippmann and the American Century*, pp. 440–42.

[23] Ibid., p. 441.

[24] Minutes of Meeting, May 8, 1947, PPS Records, Box 32.

soldier temporarily assigned to the State Department.[25] The Planning Staff accorded Bonesteel tacit as opposed to formal membership because of a concern to avoid having a "military member" on the group but Bonesteel participated vigorously in the Staff's work.[26] He had attended the Moscow Conference with Marshall and had a firm grasp on the nature of the European problems and a commitment to framing an integrated response to it. He would later serve as the State Department's coordinator of European Recovery Program activities. Incidentally, Kennan also tried to obtain the services of Professor Emile Despres, a Williams College economist, but quickly retracted his offer when it appeared that this appointment might be politically controversial. He refused to have his attention diverted by a personnel dispute from the primary task of framing policy recommendations.[27]

As director of the Policy Planning Staff Kennan asked his colleagues to express their thoughts freely and to subject all ideas to critical analysis. Such an approach ensured some intense debates. In the work of the Staff Kennan's evolving thoughts provided the locus for discussion. The other Staff members sought to modify and refine them. For Kennan it was not a painless experience. His associates were, he recalled, "sufficiently stout in argument to put me personally over the bumps, to drive whole series of cliches and oversimplifications out of my head, to spare me no complications, and to force me into an intellectual agony more intensive than anything I had ever previously experienced," which for Kennan was saying something.[28] It is hard to recapture the intensity and pressure under which the Staff worked in these initial days but it was such that one night Kennan in order "to recover [his] composure, left the room and walked, weeping, around the entire building."[29] The sense that they were involved in a policy initiative of crucial importance pervaded their meetings and the consultations they held with other department officials, especially those with State Department economic experts like Harold Van B. Cleveland, Ben T. Moore and Charles Kindleberger.[30]

After lengthy meetings on May 15, Kennan again sought to clarify what the

[25] On the further staffing see Kennan, Memoirs, I, p. 328; author's interview with Carlton Savage, June 22, 1978; and the plaintive letter from Ware Adams to Ambassador Laurence A. Steinhardt, August 26, 1947, Papers of Laurence A. Steinhardt, Manuscript Division, Library of Congress, Washington, D.C., Box 54.

[26] The reservation about a "military member" relies upon author's interview with Carlton Savage, June 22, 1978.

[27] This matter is discussed more fully in Mayers, George Kennan, pp. 128–29.

[28] Kennan, Memoirs, I, p. 328.

[29] Ibid.

[30] Cleveland was Assistant Chief, Division of Investment and Economic Development; Moore was the Assistant Chief of the Division of Commercial Policy; and Kindleberger was the Chief of the Division of German and Austrian Economic Affairs. On their specific contribution and that of the economic sections consult Jones, The Fifteen Weeks, pp. 242–43.

Staff's responsibility involved.[31] He acknowledged the work of the SWNCC committee and concluded that this group should bear the burden of detailed planning for European recovery. The Staff aimed only to submit "a set of principles" to frame a master plan for American assistance to Western Europe. But in light of the need for immediate action for psychological reasons he advocated a program aimed at boosting European coal production.[32] Kennan took these views to a discussion with Under Secretary Acheson on May 19 and obtained Acheson's approval to present them formally.[33] In what would become the familiar approach on the Staff Kennan decided to draft the report himself. This he did over the next two days and by May 22 it was ready to be discussed in a day-long session with his Staff colleagues and with Bohlen, George C. McGhee, special assistant to the Under Secretary of State for Economic Affairs, and H. Freeman Matthews, Director of the Office of European Affairs.[34] Upon their advice Kennan made minor alterations in his draft memorandum, titled "Policy with Respect to American Aid to Western Europe." The following day he sent it to Acheson as the first document of the Policy Planning Staff.[35]

STRATEGY FOR A PLAN

The May 23 report (PPS/1) argued that the American effort in aiding Europe should be directed not to the combatting of communism as such but to the restoration of the economic health and vigor of European society. The target should be the economic maladjustment which made Europe susceptible to Communist exploitation. The short-term problem was to decide upon immediate action to halt the economic disintegration in Europe. Here the Staff recommended the "production of coal in the Rhine Valley and its movement to places of consumption in Europe." The report emphasized this measure, which implied using some German economic rehabilitation to facilitate overall European economic recovery, and promised more details on it in the near future.[36]

Although stressing the "enormous complexity and difficulty" of the long-term problem, the Planning Staff report offered an "overall approach" to its solution. The pivotal element of this approach placed the burden of developing an aid program on the Europeans. In words that Marshall would borrow for

[31] Minutes of Meeting, May 15, 1947, PPS Records, Box 32.

[32] Memorandum by the Director of the Policy Planning Staff, May 16, 1947, *FRUS* 1947, III, pp. 220–23.

[33] Minutes of Meeting, May 19, 1947, Records of PPS, Box 32.

[34] Ibid., May 22, 1947.

[35] "Policy with Respect to American Aid to Western Europe," enclosed with Kennan to Acheson, May 23, 1947, *FRUS* 1947, III, pp. 223–30.

[36] Ibid. On the relationship of the Staff's short- and long-term recommendations to Germany see John Gimbel, *The Origins of the Marshall Plan* (Stanford, 1976), pp. 199–201.

his famous speech Kennan's report advised that "the formal initiative must come from Europe; the program must be evolved in Europe; and the Europeans must bear the basic responsibility for it." The American role should consist of "friendly aid in the drafting of a European program and of later support of such a program, by financial and other means, at European request." Notably, Kennan specified that the aid program should be a joint one and not simply a series of individual requests and that it should aim to bring Europe to a self-supporting basis. In regard to the need for a comprehensive program the report mentioned the possible use of the European Economic Commission in formulating this program but pointed to the danger of Russian interference in this forum.[37]

Kennan's report was obviously not a plan for American assistance in European economic recovery. Essentially it proposed only a strategy to provide such a plan and this principally involved the Europeans themselves. What Kennan and his Staff colleagues had done effectively was to begin the complex task of transforming disparate ideas and policy recommendations into practice. The importance of this contribution must be acknowledged. As Marshall himself recalled, "Kennan's memorandum was probably the nearest thing to the basis for the ERP proposals particularly in regard to the important . . . 'how to do it.' "[38] Similarly, Kennan's initial contribution should not be exaggerated. There was still a great distance to travel before arrival at the final destination of an implemented recovery program.

Kennan's proposals received an indirect but substantial boost from the somewhat complementary efforts at this time of the Under Secretary of State for Economic Affairs, Will Clayton. Clayton, a wealthy Texas cotton broker before coming to Washington, had returned to Washington from the International Trade and Employment Conference in Geneva on May 19 in order to seek Truman's veto of a wool tariff bill which threatened his negotiations there. While in Washington and spurred on by departmental deliberations on this matter and by his firsthand observations in Europe, he addressed what he described as the European crisis. In a memorandum of May 27 he reemphasized the point made by Acheson, Kennan, and others that "without further prompt and substantial aid from the United States, economic, social and political disintegration will overwhelm Europe." Claiming that "the facts are well known" Clayton went on to estimate European aid requirements as $6–7 billion dollars annually over three years. Although Clayton—perhaps influenced by Kennan's recommendation—mentioned that American aid should be

---

[37] "Policy with Respect to American Aid to Western Europe," *FRUS* 1947, III, pp. 223–30. The connection between extending aid in terms of joint European requirements and American ideas of European integration is examined in Armin Rappaport, "The United States and European Integration: The First Phase," *Diplomatic History* 5 (Spring 1981): 122–26.

[38] Interview with George C. Marshall by Harry B. Price, February 18, 1953, Harry B. Price Papers, HSTL, Box 1.

based on a European plan he seemed more concerned with ensuring a prominent American role in the plan's development and implementation. As he put
it starkly, "the United States must run this show."[39] As subsequent events
revealed Clayton's remarks contained some prescience but his memorandum's
role was limited. It certainly was not the basis for the Marshall Plan as Clayton
and some historians were to claim.[40] Clayton, like Acheson, weighed in
heavily with a clear portrayal of the need for action.

Clayton's more important contribution in the early stages of the development of the Marshall Plan occurred at a meeting on May 28 which Marshall
called with the senior officers of the department to discuss the Planning Staff's
recommendations. Here Clayton graphically described Europe's economic
woes and powerfully advocated the need for American action. According to
Acheson Marshall agreed that it would be folly "to sit back and do nothing."
Clayton injected an even greater sense of urgency into the American deliberations and prompted Marshall to push ahead more quickly with his plans for a
policy initiative. This meeting however used the Staff's May 23 report as the
basis for its substantive discussions. Against reservations regarding the European capacity to frame an effective program Kennan forcefully restated the
need for European "responsibility and parentage" of a reconstruction plan.[41]
Anxious to avoid the opprobrium of dividing Europe Kennan advised Marshall
to "play it straight" in terms of leaving the door open to Soviet and eastern
European participation in any aid plan. Such an offer to the Russians would
test their good faith. Such advice was somewhat disingenuous as both Kennan
and his fellow Soviet expert Bohlen saw it as unlikely that Stalin would respond positively. To do so on the terms of European economic cooperation
which the Americans might expect would threaten Soviet control of their east
European sphere.[42] Marshall listened and kept his own counsel.

[39] "The European Crisis," memorandum by Will Clayton, May 27, 1947, *FRUS* 1947, III, pp.
230–32. For a discussion of Clayton's differences with the Kennan approach on European initiative see Charles P. Kindleberger, "Origins of the Marshall Plan," July 22, 1948, *FRUS* 1947,
III, p. 244.

[40] Clayton wrote of his May 27 memorandum in 1950 that "this was the basis of Secretary
Marshall's speech at Harvard . . . and was the basis of the Marshall Plan." Clayton to Ellen St.
John Garwood, January 7, 1950, Papers of Will Clayton, HSTL, Box 60. Not surprisingly, among
those who echo Clayton's assertion are his daughter Ellen Garwood in *Will Clayton: A Short
Biography* (Austin, 1958); and the editor of his papers, Frederick J. Dobney, in his "Introduc-
tion" to *Selected Papers of Will Clayton* (Baltimore, 1971), p. 14.

[41] Summary of discussion by Ward P. Allen, May 28, 1947, *FRUS* 1947, III, pp. 234–36. The
power of Clayton's oral presentation and Marshall's response is noted in Acheson, *Present at the
Creation*, pp. 231–32.

[42] Bohlen recalled that "Kennan and I . . . did not feel that the Soviet Union would accept
American verification of the use of goods and funds. Furthermore, we did not think the Soviet
Union would be able to maintain its control over Eastern Europe if those countries were able to
participate in the cooperative venture." Bohlen, *Witness to History*, pp. 264–65.

MARSHALL'S SPEECH

Marshall's actions are rather curious at this time. Despite the evident seriousness with which he viewed the situation in Europe the secretary of state hardly personified force and decisiveness in moving to address it. Only on May 28 did he inform President James B. Conant of Harvard University that he would come there a week later to receive an honorary degree. He told Conant that he would not make a formal address but would offer a few remarks and perhaps "a little more" to the gathered alumni, graduating class, and friends. Marshall's biographer commented aptly that "the 'little more' was to have global reverberations."[43] Marshall's almost cautious movement towards his Harvard speech and the little advance significance which he accorded it might owe something to his concern about "the emotional anti-Russian attitude in the country" which he had revealed in an off-the-record session with a few influential reporters soon after his return from Moscow. Marshall had emphasized to these reporters "the necessity to talk and write about Europe in terms of economics instead of ideologies."[44] In this sense he and Kennan were on the same wavelength and this suggested that the Staff's recommendations would receive his approval.

While Marshall moved towards his speech in a restrained manner his under secretary, Acheson, worked deliberately to ensure that the speech would strike a responsive chord with the British. As early as May 22 he lunched with John Balfour, the head of the Chancery at the British Embassy, and with Gerald Barry, the editor of the London *News Chronicle*, and briefed them that American thinking on aid to Western Europe was now being done "in continental rather than in national terms." Balfour eventually got off a dispatch to the Foreign Office reporting his conversation and included with it a copy of James Reston's article in the *New York Times* of May 27, entitled tellingly "US Studies Shift of Help to Europe as Unit in Crisis."[45] Interestingly, Kennan had also been in conversation with Balfour, with whom he had served in the Lisbon diplomatic corps during World War II. The American official, informally, shared with the British diplomat his thoughts as the American position evolved, remarks which Balfour recalled "took the form of post-prandial musings without method."[46] Acheson was not content with his contact

[43] Pogue, *George C. Marshall*, 4, p. 209.

[44] See notes by Arthur Krock on briefing by General Marshall, undated, Papers of Arthur Krock, Seeley G. Mudd Manuscript Library, Princeton University, Princeton, N.J., Box 1 (Book 1, p. 192).

[45] Balfour to Neville Butler in the Foreign Office, May 29, 1947, quoted in Henry Pelling, *Britain and the Marshall Plan* (Houndmills, Basingstoke, 1988), p. 8.

[46] On Kennan's conversations with John Balfour see Pogue, *George C. Marshall*, 4, pp. 215–16. Also see John Balfour, *Not Too Correct An Aureole: The Recollections of a Diplomat* (Salisbury, Wiltshire, 1983), pp. 89, 116–18.

through Balfour. On June 2 he saw Leonard Miall of the BBC, Malcolm Muggeridge of the *Daily Telegraph*, and Rene McColl of the *Daily Express*. According to Acheson he primed them to take note of Marshall's Harvard address.[47] And Miall, in particular, played a key role in conveying the message of Marshall's speech across the Atlantic.

Neither Kennan nor the Staff as a whole participated in the actual preparation of General Marshall's Harvard speech. The duty of drafting this address fell to Bohlen who made full use of the Planning Staff's May 23 report and Will Clayton's memorandum. Acheson and Clayton saw Bohlen's draft and made suggestions. Presumably Marshall received broad approval from Truman for the speech but the president rarely entered into the substantive deliberations on this initiative. The secretary of state made his own revisions, indeed some while traveling north to Boston. From the steps of Memorial Church in Harvard Yard on June 5 Marshall read his speech without any show of drama or flair.[48] Fortunately for the secretary of state at this time style had not completely overwhelmed substance and Marshall's audience beyond Harvard Yard examined the content of what he said there.

Marshall began by describing the economic plight of Europe, and here his debt to Clayton was obvious. But the positive proposals in his speech drew upon the recommendations of Kennan and his Staff even though the ideas behind them did not all originate with them. Marshall affirmed that any American aid policy would be "directed not against any country or doctrine but against hunger, poverty, desperation and chaos." He declared that assistance should not be extended on a piecemeal basis. There was a need for a comprehensive and cooperative effort by the Europeans which would provide for "a cure rather than a mere palliative." He insisted that the initiative for a joint European recovery program must come from Europe. The role of the United States, he asserted, "should consist of friendly aid in the drafting of a European program and of later support of such a program so far as it may be practical for us to do so."[49]

To acknowledge that Kennan's report made the principal contribution to Marshall's June 5 speech does not imply that claims for his and the Planning Staff's paternity of the Marshall Plan should be conceded.[50] As the historian John Gimbel has noted, no plan was presented at Harvard.[51] Marshall was well

[47] On Acheson's efforts see Pogue, *George C. Marshall*, 4, pp. 216–17. Note that Miall maintained that Acheson did not make specific mention of Marshall's speech.

[48] For details of Marshall's speech see Bohlen, *Witness to History*, pp. 263–64; Jones, *The Fifteen Weeks*, pp. 254–55; Pogue, *George C. Marshall*, 4, p. 214; and Charles L. Mee, Jr., *The Marshall Plan* (New York, 1984), pp. 100–103.

[49] Remarks of secretary of state, June 5, 1947, *Department of State Bulletin*, June 15, 1947, pp. 1159–60.

[50] Hadley Arkes is one of a number of scholars who make this claim. See his *Bureaucracy, The Marshall Plan and the National Interest* (Princeton, 1972), pp. 51–52.

[51] Gimbel, *Origins of the Marshall Plan*, p. 15.

aware of this and wrote his ambassador in Paris soon after that "the scope and nature of the program is not yet foreseeable."[52] What Marshall did at Harvard, in essence, was to make public the strategy for a plan which Kennan had formulated for him. Having been persuaded that the Europeans should have the principal task of formulating a recovery program he issued a call for them to do so. While his speech "marked the beginning not the end of the process which produced the European Recovery Program," its significance should not be diminished. As Ernest Bevin's biographer, Alan Bullock, has observed, the American policymakers—Marshall, Acheson, Clayton, Kennan, and in the background Truman—"were clear that it was a new departure in American foreign policy" and one which "would require exceptional efforts on their part to get Congress and the nation to accept."[53] The Marshall speech, however, gained its real significance because of the responses it provoked.

EUROPEAN RESPONSE AND AMERICAN FOLLOW-UP

Marshall's Harvard speech galvanized British Foreign Secretary Bevin and his French counterpart, Georges Bidault, into action designed to develop an economic recovery program. After hearing Leonard Miall's report of Marshall's speech over the BBC Bevin, at his most robust and forceful, seized the initiative.[54] As Bullock accurately described, "he threw all his energy into conjuring up a European response of sufficient weight and urgency to give substance to Marshall's offer of American support."[55] Bevin and Bidault began discussions in Paris on June 17, to which they then invited Soviet participation. Marshall had made it clear at a press conference on June 13 that in referring to Europe he included the Soviet Union so Bevin, despite reservations, had little choice but to extend this invitation. To the surprise of some, the Soviets announced their willingness to participate in discussions at foreign minister level and these were scheduled for Paris in late June.

In the days preceding the meeting of the three foreign ministers the Americans sought to give guidance to the European response. The British were the crucial contact point and vehicle for the Americans in ensuring that the pro-

[52] Marshall to Jefferson Caffery, June 12, 1947, *FRUS* 1947, III, pp. 249–51. Note also that Will Clayton in discussions with British officials in London on June 25 said that "he did not want to give the impression that he had laid out any well thought-out plan or scheme." Memorandum of conversation, June 25, 1947, III, pp. 283–84.

[53] Bullock, *Ernest Bevin: Foreign Secretary*, p. 403.

[54] Bevin's actions can be traced in detail in Bullock, *Ernest Bevin: Foreign Secretary*, but see also, on British actions, Pelling, *Britain and the Marshall Plan*, pp. 11–15; Lord Strang, *Home and Abroad* (London, 1956), p. 289; and Peter G. Boyle, "The British Foreign Office and American Foreign Policy, 1947–48," *Journal of American Studies* 16 (December 1982): 385–88.

[55] Bullock, *Ernest Bevin: Foreign Secretary*, p. 404. Bullock also noted that "it is arguable that Bevin's action in the next few days was his most decisive personal contribution as Foreign Secretary to the history of his times."

ʳgram developed along acceptable lines. Will Clayton and the new American ambassador in London, Lewis Douglas, helped clarify for Bevin the role the United States expected Britain to play. They rejected Bevin's request for some form of senior status for Britain, a virtual partnership which would place Britain in a special financial relationship with the United States. Clayton conveyed the American view that Britain must be treated "as part of Europe" because "special assistance to the U.K. partner would violate the principle that no piecemeal approach to the European problem would be undertaken."[56] The British resented the implied diminution of their role but their dependence on the Americans for economic support left them few options.[57]

While refusing the British a broker's role to the other European countries the Americans still relied on them most in building the structure of the Marshall Plan. Back in Washington Kennan and Bohlen called by the British embassy on June 24 and conveyed to Lord Inverchapel, the ambassador, and John Balfour the terms for Soviet participation in the plan. Kennan aimed to make it clear to the British so that they in turn could do the same for the Russians that the Soviet Union and the east European countries could participate only if they were prepared to engage in the economic cooperation Marshall had called for. In particular the Soviets would need "to permit their satellites to enter fully into economic relations with their Western neighbors." If the Russians rejected this approach, said Kennan, "the Americans wanted the Europeans to understand that America would like, then, to go with a plan for Western Europe alone."[58] Kennan in effect told the British to make demands on the Soviets which likely would force them out of the evolving recovery program.

Bevin needed little encouragement from the Americans to take a firm position with the Soviets when they began their meetings on June 27. With Bidault's support he stressed European economic cooperation and called for a study of the contribution which European countries could themselves make to each other's recovery. Molotov predictably rejected this approach. He complained that a comprehensive reconstruction program would meddle in the internal affairs of sovereign nations. Bidault and Bevin held firm against Molotov's complaints voiced in an increasingly threatening tone.[59] The result was predictable. Bevin reported to Jefferson Caffery that "this conference will break up tomorrow. I am glad that the cards have been laid on the table and that the responsibility will be laid at Moscow's door. They have been trying

---

[56] Memorandum of Clayton's meeting with British Cabinet members, June 24, 1947, *FRUS 1947*, III, pp. 268–73.

[57] Bullock points to the "conflict between poverty and pride" for the British who "were financially dependent on the Americans for their economic survival, yet wanted to be treated as an equal partner in dispensing aid to the Europeans." *Ernest Bevin: Foreign Secretary*, p. 415.

[58] This relies on Mee, *The Marshall Plan*, pp. 124–26. (Mee drew from Inverchapel's report of this meeting—FO 371/62401-9936).

[59] Georges Bidault, *Resistance* (New York, 1967), pp. 150–51.

to sabotage it in the conference room from the very beginning."[60] On July 2 Molotov withdrew from the conference and returned to Moscow the next day. Undaunted, Bevin and Bidault immediately invited twenty-two European countries to send representatives to Paris to formulate a recovery plan. Although the Soviet Union forced the eastern European nations to decline, the representatives of sixteen nations convened in Paris on July 12, intent on responding to the challenge Marshall had extended on June 5—to draft a program of European recovery.

The Soviet departure prompted a collective sigh of relief in Washington. Kennan had never thought it likely that the Soviets would pay the price of participation in an integrated European economy. They were neither prepared to open up their economy to outside influence nor willing to reduce their control over their east European satellites. Kennan recalled that "we put Russia over the barrel. Either it must decline or else enter into an arrangement that would mean an ending of the Iron Curtain. When the full horror of [their] alternatives dawned on them they left suddenly in the middle of the night."[61] The Russian departure allowed the United States to reaffirm the purpose of the aid program as originally conceived. Europe was to be strengthened economically and politically to counter the perceived Soviet threat. The strategy of European economic integration ironically had served effectively to further the strategy of political containment.[62]

PROBLEMS: SHORT-TERM AND LONG-TERM

While the dramatic events occurred in Paris Kennan and his colleagues doggedly continued their work in relative anonymity in Washington. Completion of their May 23 report had meant no reduction in the intensity of their activities. The Planning Staff simply drew breath and plunged forward to examine what it earlier had labeled the short-term and long-term problems. Upon the submission of the May 23 report the Staff turned immediately to consider the European coal situation in close consultation with a group of State Department economic officials headed by C. Tyler Wood, deputy to the Assistant Secretary for Economic Affairs, and Charles Kindleberger.[63] On May 29 it discussed papers on the European coal shortage and on German coal production prepared in the economic offices and it debated a proposal from Clayton that the United States take over Ruhr coal production. All this was a prelude to drawing up its own recommendations which were compiled in draft form on

---

[60] Caffery to secretary of state, July 1, 1947, *FRUS* 1947, III, pp. 301–3.

[61] Harry B. Price Interview with George F. Kennan, February 19, 1953, Harry B. Price Papers, HSTL, Box 1.

[62] Hogan argued in a related but somewhat different manner that "the strategy of integration, as much as the strategy of containment, . . . shaped American policy, [and] wrecked the chances for Soviet (and Eastern European) cooperation." Hogan, *The Marshall Plan*, p. 53.

[63] Minutes of Meetings, May 23, and 26, 1947, PPS Records, Box 32.

June 1. After some revision it took form as the second paper of the Planning Staff entitled plainly, "Increase of European Coal Production." Kennan gave it to Acheson on June 2.[64]

The Staff's study of the European coal situation, not surprisingly, concluded that the deficient production of coal in Britain and in the Ruhr-Aachen fields of Germany constituted a decisive bottleneck in European economic rehabilitation. It suggested a number of measures to overcome the deficiency and emphasized the necessity of obtaining British cooperation. To the latter end it recommended discussions with the British government as an essential first step and arrangements were soon made to hold such a meeting.[65] The War Department quickly sought the view of General Lucius Clay, the American Military Governor in Germany, on the German part of the Staff's recommendations. The Planning Staff had suggested a capital loan to the coal industry secured by exports and had proposed to supply additional machinery. Clay disputed the recommendations from Kennan's group, a practice he would repeat. The self-styled American proconsul argued that removal of uncertainty regarding mine ownership and responsibility constituted the main problem in German coal production.[66] Clay triumphed on this matter. Future discussions centered on issues of ownership and administration, particularly the British desire to nationalize the Ruhr coal fields.[67] The Staff had offered its recommendations on coal production in response to what it saw as the "short-term problem" but its contribution to American action on the coal issue was limited to affirming the intimate relationship between an increase in German production and Europe-wide economic recovery and to prompting discussions between Britain and the United States on German coal production.

The historian John Gimbel emphasizes the importance of the Planning Staff's memorandum on the European situation in an effort to prove his thesis that "the Marshall Plan originated as a crash program to dovetail German economic recovery with a general European recovery program in order to

[64] Minutes of Meetings, May 29, 1947 & June 2, 1947, PPS Records, Box 32. A copy of PPS/2—"Increase of European Coal Production," June 2, 1947, is in PPS Studies-1947, PPS Records, Box 3. The paper is included in Anna Kasten Nelson, ed., *The State Department Policy Planning Staff Papers 1947* (New York, 1983), pp. 12–19. (Hereafter citations for PPS papers not published in the *Foreign Relations* series will be referenced to Nelson's valuable published collection [*SDPPSP* and year] as well as to the archival source.)

[65] As a result of preliminary discussions in June arrangements were made to discuss at the official level technical problems connected with increased coal production in the Ruhr and neighboring mining areas in Germany. These conversations began in Washington on August 12. See "Report on the Anglo-American Talks on Ruhr Coal Production," September 10, 1947, *FRUS* 1947, II, pp. 959–62.

[66] Clay's reactions as reported by his political adviser, Robert Murphy, are in Murphy to Secretary of State, June 17, 1947, *FRUS* 1947, II, pp. 924–25. Also note Gimbel's discussion in *Origins of the Marshall Plan*, p. 209.

[67] On future discussions see memorandum by Kenyon C. Bolton, September 22, 1947, *FRUS* 1947, II, pp. 962–66. For Gimbel's analysis of this question see *Origins of the Marshall Plan*, pp. 207–19.

make German economic recovery politically acceptable in Europe and in the United States."[68] The coal memorandum of June 2 seen in context does not support his thesis. The recommendations in this memorandum aimed to solve what the Staff called the short-term problem and thus to halt *European* economic disintegration. They did not derive from any desire to pacify the army over occupation policy in Germany nor out of a desire to rehabilitate the western zones of Germany as an end in itself.[69] The Staff's reasoning was directly opposite to that presented by Gimbel. Its major concern lay with Europe and it supported increasing German coal production and boosting German economic recovery only as vehicles to reach the main goal.[70]

The larger focus of Kennan's Planning Staff was made manifest by its actions through the rest of June and July. After completing the coal memorandum Kennan directed Staff study of a range of questions related to European recovery. At the request of Under Secretary-designate Robert Lovett, who had been prompted by the Republican Chairman of the Senate Foreign Relations Committee Arthur H. Vandenberg, the planning group examined the effect of foreign aid on the United States domestic economy and natural resources.[71] Kennan appreciated that the subject required much further study and deftly framed a recommendation for this on June 19 which Lovett accepted and conveyed to Truman.[72] Just three days later the president announced the formation of three committees to give further guidance to American efforts to assist Europe. The first, headed by Secretary of the Interior Julius Krug, would examine the state of American national resources while the second, under Edwin G. Nourse, the Chairman of the Council of Economic Advisers, would look at the impact on the national economy of aid to other countries. The final committee, an explicitly nonpartisan one, would "determine the facts with respect to the character and quantities of United States resources available for economic assistance to foreign countries."[73] Truman tapped his Secretary of

[68] For Gimbel's thesis and for his emphasis on the Staff's coal memorandum see *Origins of the Marshall Plan*, pp. 4, 203.

[69] Gimbel infers this in ibid., pp. 248–49.

[70] Kennan recalled that the Planning Staff "regarded German recovery as an essential part of any general European recovery. But," he explained, "our interest in European recovery did not start from, or proceed from, any interest in German recovery for its own sake. Not that we were against it—we just had broader interests." Kennan to author, February 22, 1979. Also note that John J. McCloy, W. Averell Harriman, and Paul H. Nitze denied that "the Marshall Plan had been designed specifically to solve the German situation." See Charles W. Sydnor, Jr., "Some Architects of U.S. Occupation Policy Respond: Summary of a Roundtable," in *U.S. Occupation in Europe After World War II*, ed. Hans Schmitt (Lawrence, Kans., 1978), pp. 136–37.

[71] On Vandenberg's role see Arthur H. Vandenberg, Jr., *The Private Papers of Senator Vandenberg* (Boston, 1952), pp. 375–77.

[72] For Kennan's recommendation see PPS/3, "Studies Relating to the Impact of Aid to Foreign Countries on U.S. Domestic Economy and Natural Resources," June 19, 1947, PPS Studies-1947, PPS Records, Box 3; and Nelson, ed., *SDPPSP 1947*, pp. 20–25.

[73] For Truman's statement announcing the creation of the three committees see *FRUS* 1947, III, pp. 264–66.

Commerce and Kennan's former chief in Moscow, Averell Harriman, to head this body which eventually included experts and representatives of business, labor, agriculture, and the universities. This last committee, which was labeled for its chairman, played an important role in the selling of the Marshall Plan to Congress and the American people. All three committees owed their existence primarily to Vandenberg's suggestion and influence but the Staff's role in their foundation illustrated the crucial place it had obtained in relation to the secretary and under secretary of state. Kennan's Policy Planning Staff had become the key group which sifted through the various ideas and suggestions and transformed some into recommendations for action. The early work on the Marshall Plan allowed Kennan to avoid any compartmentalization of planning away from crucial day-to-day decision-making. Kennan quickly had secured his place in the midst of this process and retained it through Marshall's tenure at State.

The Planning Staff devoted special consideration to economic circumstances in Italy, Britain, France, and Germany during July as it worked on a follow-up paper to its May 23 report. On July 23 Kennan presented Lovett, the Wall Street banker and former Assistant Secretary of War whom Marshall had appointed as Acheson's successor, with a long paper (PPS/4) entitled "Certain Aspects of the European Recovery Program from the US Standpoint."[74] This piece, which had been discussed widely within the State Department, grew out of and expanded upon the Staff's initial report. It dealt with the "long-term problem" as defined in the earlier memorandum. Despite its detail it did not constitute a blueprint for aiding Europe. In notes he prepared for Marshall on July 21 Kennan told his chief that "we have no plan," and that the "Europeans must be made to take responsibility" for designing one.[75] Kennan still relied on the European capability to forge a coherent aid program. What he aimed to do in his report was to clarify American purposes and strategy.

Kennan emphasized two major sources of American interest in European recovery. The first related to the economic interest of the United States in Europe stemming from the latter's role as a market and as a supplier of products and services to the U.S. Here, Kennan elucidated that the aid to Europe contributed to the economic interest of the United States, an argument important for the "selling" of the aid program domestically. The second and more important related to America's security interest in preserving "a continuation in Europe of a considerable number of free states subservient to no great power."[76] This objective from the outset had provided the central motivation for American assistance to Europe. This aid was largely a defensive measure

[74] PPS/4, "Certain Aspects of the European Recovery Program from the U.S. Standpoint," July 23, 1947, PPS Studies-1947, PPS Records, Box 3; and Nelson, ed., *SDPPSP 1947*, pp. 26–68.

[75] "GFK Notes for Secy Marshall," July 21, 1947, *FRUS* 1947, III, pp. 335–37.

[76] See section 1 of "Certain Aspects of the European Recovery Program from the U.S. Standpoint," PPS Records, Box 3.

aimed at preventing economic disintegration which the Soviet Union through local Communist parties might exploit. Other goals—such as economic revival in the western zones of Germany and integration of the European economies—were efficacious only because they served this primary objective.[77]

After outlining the American interest Kennan turned in this report to examine the central requirements for securing it. He stressed the revival of industrial and agricultural production and the need to target key areas such as the European transportation network. He maintained his preference for European initiative and reemphasized the necessity of a joint program among the Europeans. The report gave special consideration to Britain and Germany. Britain's balance of payments problem was considered sympathetically but the Staff held that Britain must be incorporated in the overall recovery program. Germany's importance to European recovery was restated and the need for action on this issue confirmed despite "the feelings of the French Government with respect to questions of military and economic security." To conclude his analysis Kennan turned to the implications of an American aid program to Europe on foreign policy in general. He rejected the notion that the European aid program might receive some larger application. He differentiated Europe, where the problem was one of "releasing the capacity for self-help already present," from non-European areas where for the most part the need was not for "the release of existing energies but the creation of new ones."[78] In this matter Kennan's ideas aligned with Senator Vandenberg who opposed any attempt to "WPA the earth" but supported the "Marshall idea" of helping "those who help themselves and who are prepared to demonstrate that they are making practical plans to this end."[79]

The Europeans bore responsibility for the making of such practical plans. The sixteen nations which convened in Paris on July 12 promptly constituted themselves as the Committee of European Economic Cooperation (CEEC) under British chairmanship. Sir Oliver Franks, a tall, florid Oxford philosopher and a leading wartime civil servant, chaired the working sessions after Bevin's departure. Four technical committees were established to consider food and agriculture, coal and steel, power, and transportation. The participants selected an Executive Committee comprised of Britain, France, Italy, Norway, and the Netherlands. After making these organizational arrangements the work of the conference slowed as individual nations began to pursue their own economic objectives, such as the British reluctance to alter their foreign trade arrangements and the French refusal to give ground either on German eco-

---

[77] Leffler seemingly accords revival of the western German zones equal status as an American objective in his "The United States and the Strategic Dimensions of the Marshall Plan," pp. 277–78.

[78] "Certain Aspects of the European Recovery Program from the U.S. Standpoint," PPS Records, Box 3.

[79] Arthur H. Vandenberg to Alton T. Roberts, August 12, 1947, Papers of Arthur H. Vandenberg, Bentley Historical Library, The University of Michigan, Ann Arbor, Michigan, Box 2.

nomic recovery or on their insistence that the Monnet Plan for industrial mod-
ernization be incorporated in the program. The American officials located in
Paris to support and advise the European delegates—Will Clayton, Lew
Douglas, Clay's political adviser Robert Murphy, and Jefferson Caffery—
grew increasingly perturbed at the European failure to act in concert and to
develop a coherent plan. Early in August these four men met to evaluate the
progress of Marshall's proposal. Paul Nitze, at the time Deputy Director of
the Office of International Trade Policy, traveled from Washington to bring
the most recent thinking within the administration to the group. He used the
Planning Staff's July 23 memorandum to guide the group's discussion. Clayton and the three ambassadors expressed discontent with the Paris negotiations.[80] They recommended that the time had come to extend the "friendly
aid" in drafting the recovery program which Marshall had promised at Harvard.[81]

Similar sentiments emerged in Washington. Concern had developed that the
Marshall plan lacked direction. Ben T. Moore captured this well when he confided to a friend that "the 'Marshall plan' has been compared to a flying sau-
cer—nobody knows what it looks like, how big it is, in what direction it is
moving, or whether it really exists."[82] The energetic new head of the Office
of European Affairs, John D. Hickerson, joined in suggesting that the Europeans should be provided with more detailed advice.[83] Lovett, acting as secretary in Marshall's absence at the Inter-American Conference on Peace and
Security in Brazil, felt pulled in opposite directions. He recognized the cogency of the advice of the American officials in Paris but was reluctant to
weaken a key plank in the Marshall proposal—that the initiative must come
from Europe. Lovett, nonetheless, perceived that the Europeans preferred to
draw up a "shopping list" and had neglected to stress "the elements of self-
help and mutual aid."[84] To add to the pressures upon him the Planning Staff
right at this very time issued a reminder to Lovett of the absolutely urgent need
in Europe for American assistance. In a paper, appropriately titled "The Time
Factor in a European Recovery Program," the Planning Staff sounded the
alarm that "if a program of U.S. aid is not acted upon by the Congress before
the end of the year, there is little likelihood that such a program, as now conceived, could be successful." Intent on addressing the urgency problem the
Staff unavoidably dealt with the question of American involvement in forming
the European program. In a clear retreat from the earlier position on European
initiative the Staff reasoned that "if time-consuming delays are to be avoided

[80] Memorandum by Wesley C. Haraldson on "Paris Discussions on the Marshall Plan, August
4 to August 6, 1947," August 8, 1947, FRUS 1947, III, pp. 345–50. Paul H. Nitze, From Hiroshima to Glasnost: At the Center of Decision (New York, 1989), pp. 54–55.

[81] Caffery to Secretary of State, August 6, 1947, FRUS 1947, pp. 343–44.

[82] Moore to Wilcox, July 28, 1947, FRUS 1947, III, pp. 239–41.

[83] Hickerson memorandum, August 11, 1947, FRUS 1947, III, pp. 351–55.

[84] Lovett to Clayton and Caffery, August 14, 1947, FRUS 1947, III, pp. 356–60.

after the completing of the Paris Conference and if the United States is to influence the general character of the program developed at Paris, our influence must be brought to bear now."[85]

KENNAN TO PARIS

The efforts of Clayton and his colleagues in Paris brought little results. The Europeans "still refused to transcend national sovereignties, permit the CEEC to examine country requirements critically, or adjust national production and investment programs to the needs of Europe as a whole."[86] By the third week of August with the reports of the technical committees filtering in Franks and the Executive of the CEEC offered some tentative estimates of the total aid required of the United States. The Oxford don mentioned the astronomical figure of $28.2 billion over four years.[87] Clayton immediately told him that such a figure was "out of the question."[88] Caffery reported home that the European program was little more than "an assembly job of country estimates" which failed to address the structural economic problems besetting the continent.[89] Back in Washington Lovett appreciated the situation with crystal clarity. He cabled Marshall in Brazil that "the present grand total of the shopping list approach is unreasonable." Furthermore, he pointed out not only the huge total request foreshadowed by the Europeans but also that "these huge sums will not accomplish the rehabilitation over a four-year period, still leaving a deficit at the end of that time."[90] The under secretary proceeded to recommend some action to confront this unfortunate situation.

Lovett recommended to Marshall that the United States be prepared to allow the Paris conference to be extended for two weeks to develop a more satisfactory and acceptable plan. More immediately he suggested that Kennan and Bonesteel be dispatched to Paris to represent the American position more effectively. Lovett colored matters in diplomatic niceties by suggesting to Marshall that Clayton and Caffery "have been out of touch with headquarters for some months and may not be wholly familiar with the work that has been done here."[91] In reality he lacked confidence in their ability.[92] He turned to Kennan and to Bonesteel, now his assistant on European recovery matters, to fill the

---

[85] PPS/6, "The Time Factor in a European Recovery Program," August 14, 1947, PPS Studies-1947, PPS Records, Box 3; and Nelson, ed., SDPPSP 1947, pp. 71–75.

[86] Hogan, The Marshall Plan, p. 72.

[87] Pelling, Britain and the Marshall Plan, pp. 17–18.

[88] Troutman to Secretary of State, August 25, 1947, FRUS 1947, III, pp. 377–79.

[89] Caffery to Lovett, August 26, 1947, FRUS 1947, III, pp. 380–83.

[90] Lovett to Marshall, August 24, 1947, FRUS 1947, III, pp. 372–75.

[91] Ibid.

[92] Charles L. Mee, Jr., is both insightful and entertaining on this whole episode in his The Marshall Plan, pp. 180–85.

breech. Marshall responded: "I concur completely in your views and action proposed."[93]

Kennan's journey to Paris marked a new stage in his role as Director of the Policy Planning Staff. Not only would he be involved integrally in the day-to-day formulation of policy in Washington but he would be called on directly to participate in its implementation overseas. He traveled to Paris as an increasingly noted and publicly discussed figure. *U.S. News and World Report* on August 8 had deemed him and Bohlen "People of the Week."[94] The publication in the July issue of *Foreign Affairs* of the article "The Sources of Soviet Conduct" by "X"—soon identified as Kennan—sparked enormous discussion and won him unsought notoriety. Some of this he carried to Paris where he and Bonesteel arrived on August 28. One historian rightly has noted that "of all the Americans in Paris, the Europeans had no trouble sensing at once that George Kennan was the significant one in the crowd."[95]

Kennan and Bonesteel met first with Clayton, Caffery, and Douglas. They used as a basis for discussion a department policy statement on aiding Europe which listed the fundamental objectives and essential elements of a program desirous of obtaining American approval. Here the Americans agreed on a position which they then conveyed to the CEEC Executive Committee in a frank exchange.[96] The Europeans revealed aspects of their preliminary plan, which now included an estimate of $29.2 billion of required outside aid and gave no indication that Europe would be self-supporting at the end of the specified four-year period. In response, with Kennan in the lead, the Americans stated their reservations and criticisms and outlined what were for them "essentials" of a viable plan. The Europeans heard that the Americans were "not attempting to dictate to the Conference" but merely stating their "view of essentials for winning approval of the American people." Kennan also tried to convey his message of the necessity for more realism and genuine cooperation in European planning in private discussions and at various social occasions he attended but his combined efforts had little impact.[97] "The conferees," as Hogan has summarized, "remained as reluctant as ever to take measures that meant transcending national sovereignties or reducing living standards."[98] Their intransigence gouged a deep impression on Kennan and he returned quickly to Washington to formulate recommendations to respond to it.

[93] Marshall to Lovett, August 25, 1947, *FRUS* 1947, III, p. 375.

[94] *U.S. News and World Report*, August 8, 1947, pp. 50–51.

[95] Mee, *The Marshall Plan*, p. 187.

[96] For the departmental policy statement see Lovett to Clayton and Caffery, August 26, 1947, *FRUS* 1947, III, pp. 383–89. For a record of the various deliberations see Clayton for Secretary and Lovett, August 31, 1947, *FRUS* 1947, III, pp. 391–96.

[97] Mee, *The Marshall Plan*, p. 191.

[98] Hogan, *The Marshall Plan*, p. 75. Also see Bullock, *Ernest Bevin: Foreign Secretary*, pp. 457–58.

The planning chief slammed the inability of the European diplomats to engage in realistic, honest discussions in which aid requests and economic projections received critical analysis. He informed Marshall, now returned from South America, that the Paris conference revealed "all the weakness, the escapism, the paralysis of a region caught by war in the midst of serious problems of longer-term adjustment, and sadly torn by hardship, confusion and outside pressure." Not surprising in light of this evaluation he warned that the United States "must not look to the people in Paris to accomplish the impossible. . . . No bold or original approach to Europe's problems will be forthcoming." The Europeans were incapable of meeting the essential conditions which he and Clayton had sought to outline. They remained trapped by their "strong emphasis on national sovereignty."[99] What could be done?

Kennan offered Marshall a procedure to deal with the inauspicious circumstances in Paris. He advised that the Americans accept the Paris Conference report only as a basis for subsequent discussion during which they should try to reduce the size of the European requests. After this stage the European proposals should receive final consideration within the executive branch of the government in which it should be decided unilaterally what to present to the Congress. Kennan explained rather bluntly but honestly that "this would mean that we would listen to all that the Europeans had to say, but in the end we would not *ask* them, we would just *tell* them what they would get." This represented quite a transformation from the earlier stance of relying upon the Europeans to develop the aid program. In the eyes of American policymakers the Europeans had failed to formulate an acceptable plan. Kennan sought to overcome the impasse. He soothed whatever concerns he might have had about imposing a plan on the Europeans by observing that "this was what some of the more far-sighted Europeans hope we will do." Such a course would involve time-consuming and complex deliberations but this conflicted with Europe's urgent need for assistance. To meet this troublesome situation Kennan recommended an interim aid program to "buy . . . time in which to deal deliberately and carefully with the long-term program."[100] Marshall and Lovett found the Kennan procedure persuasive. In broad terms they proceeded to implement it.

THE BURDEN OF BEING MR. "X"

Immediately upon Kennan's return from Paris, Walter Lippmann greeted him with a series of no less than fourteen columns devoted to contesting the thesis and implications of Kennan's "X" article, "The Sources of Soviet Con-

[99] Kennan, "Situation with Respect to European Recovery Program," September 4, 1947, *FRUS* 1947, III, pp. 397–405.
[100] Ibid.

duct."[101] Even before his departure for Paris, the "X" article had served to bring much public note to Kennan. *Reader's Digest* and *Life* reprinted long excerpts from it and newspapers discussed it, thereby ensuring an audience far beyond the foreign policy elite who read *Foreign Affairs*. Lippmann's serious and lengthy retort, however, succeeded in vesting upon the "X" article virtually the status of official doctrine. Ironically, the renowned columnist's slanted interpretation helped establish in the public mind the very strategy of containment which he aimed to contest.

Lippmann determined to cast the arguments of the "X" article in the starkest terms, a task facilitated by the loose construction and ambiguous language of the piece which permitted a variety of interpretations.[102] He paid no attention to qualifications Kennan had made. He accused Kennan of overemphasizing the role of ideology in Soviet foreign policy at the expense of traditional Russian security motives but largely ignored Kennan's point that Soviet leaders had "found in Marxist theory a highly convenient rationalization for their own instinctive desires." He directly linked Kennan's article to the Truman Doctrine and then to the notion of global and military containment of the Soviet Union. He did this despite knowing full well that Kennan had objected to the global implications of the Truman Doctrine and that his work on the European aid program testified to his preference for political and economic measures over military containment. Lippmann needed a severe portrayal of containment to allow for his memorable criticism that it was a "strategic monstrosity" because it conceded to the Kremlin the "strategical initiative" and because the United States could not expect to muster "unalterable counterforce" at all the points where the Soviets might encroach. Lippmann presciently predicted that, because of the limits of American power, containment (as he defined it) could "be implemented only by recruiting, subsidizing and supporting a heterogeneous array of satellites, clients, dependents and puppets." Instead of attempting to stretch American military resources to every corner of the globe Lippmann advocated a political settlement in Europe designed to allay Russian fears—the reunification and demilitarization of Germany with a withdrawal of American and Soviet forces from Europe, both West and East.[103]

Lippmann's critique annoyed Kennan who felt with some justification that

[101] Lippmann's columns appeared in his "Today and Tomorrow" syndicated column in the *New York Herald Tribune* on Sept. 2, 4, 6, 9, 11, 13, 16, 18, 20, 23, 25, 27, 30, and Oct. 2, 1947. They may be found in the Robert O. Anthony Collection of Walter Lippmann, Sterling Library, Yale University, Box 39. They later were compiled and published as Walter Lippmann, *The Cold War* (New York, 1947).

[102] Kennan provides an excellent discussion of the ambiguities of the 'X' article in his *Memoirs*, I, pp. 360–61.

[103] Lippmann, *The Cold War*; and Kennan, "The Source of Soviet Conduct." See also the discussion in Steel, *Walter Lippmann and the American Century*, pp. 443–45; and Anders Stephanson, *Kennan and the Art of Foreign Policy*, pp. 100–102.

it misrepresented his position, as astute commentators recognized at the time.[104] Confined to a hospital bed in April 1948 he wrote a lengthy response to Lippmann in which, after noting their earlier discussions on a European recovery scheme, he noted that "I am a little non-plussed to find myself sternly rebuked as the author of the 'Truman Doctrine' and confronted with the Marshall Plan as an example of constructive statesmanship from which I might derive a useful lesson and improve my way."[105] Kennan resented his identification by Lippmann with military containment universally applied when the columnist knew quite well that Kennan pursued a different approach. Although Kennan failed to send his letter, he later responded to Lippmann directly when he trapped him and his wife in a parlor car on the train to New York and held forth for the whole trip. No doubt it was a revenge of sorts. Kennan's regard for and intellectual friendship with Lippmann survived the whole episode over the "X" article and they subsequently consulted on other matters. Kennan suspected that Lippmann's pointed criticism of his article owed something to Lippmann's resentment at the attention which the article brought *Foreign Affairs* and its editor, Hamilton Fish Armstrong. Lippmann's wife formerly had been married to Armstrong and upon their separation, prior to her marriage to Lippmann, a bitter Armstrong effectively banned Lippmann from the pages of *Foreign Affairs*. Whatever the truth of this matter, it assisted Kennan to understand Lippmann's critique.[106]

The Kennan-Lippmann debate over containment has been the focus of much scholarly attention but its relevance for this study resides in its impact on Kennan and on the policy he contributed to developing. Here Lippmann's famous critique possessed only little importance. Lippmann might have implanted in Kennan's mind ideas for a new approach on Germany but these would not reach fruition for almost a year. But on other substantive policy matters Lippmann's response to the "X" article exercised little influence on Kennan. The director of the Policy Planning Staff still saw the United States as involved in "a long-range fencing match" with the Soviets in which the weapons were "political, rather than military, means."[107] This was the approach that guided

---

[104] See, for example, Frank Altschul's piece, "The Cold War," *New York Herald Tribune*, September 16, 1947, in which Altschul observed that "Mr. Lippmann ascribes to the word 'counter-force,' as used by Mr. X, the narrow meaning of military power; and he construes a policy of containment as a program of fitful and adventurous military intervention in the most unlikely places. The result is a complete distortion of the ideas so cogently presented by Mr. X. For in his view military power, on which Mr. Lippmann places so much emphasis is but one element in a policy of containment. Diplomatic skill, economic resources, moral leadership — these, too, must play their part in the struggle. There is no reason to believe that Mr. X intends to overlook any of them."

[105] Kennan to Lippmann, April 6, 1948 (unsent), Kennan Papers, Box 17.

[106] Author's interview with George F. Kennan, March 6, 1989.

[107] Kennan had offered this view of the Soviet-American relationship in a speech on "Soviet-American Relations Today," May 12, 1947, Kennan Papers, Box 17.

his specific recommendations throughout the development of the European recovery program.

The attention which Lippmann and other commentators afforded the "X" article caused Kennan some professional concerns. General Marshall had established a principle that "planners don't talk." Kennan recalled that "the last thing he had expected was to see the name of the head of his new Planning Staff bandied about in the press as the author of a programmatical article—or an article hailed as programmatical—on the greatest of our problems of foreign policy."[108] The secretary of state called in his planning chief and bluntly asked for an explanation. Presumably quivering a little, Kennan noted the origins of the piece and also that it had been duly cleared for publication by the appropriate official committee. The latter satisfied Marshall and he never raised the matter with Kennan again, but his demeanor during the conversation conveyed effectively that this was not an episode to be repeated. Thoughts of writing a public response to Lippmann or a follow-up essay to clarify misunderstandings vanished. Kennan let "The Sources of Soviet Conduct" take on a life of its own, feeling, as he later put it, "like one who has inadvertently loosened a large boulder from the top of a cliff and now helplessly witnesses its path of destruction in the valley below."[109]

Kennan's relationship with Marshall easily survived the episode of the "X" article publicity because Marshall had developed an appreciation for his planning chief from the solid work he had performed on the European aid proposal. He extended neither familiarity nor favoritism to Kennan whom he continued to address by his last name. Strict professionalism characterized their relationship, as it did with all Marshall's dealings with subordinates. But Marshall's regard for Kennan manifested itself in his willingness to assign important tasks to him and in his readiness to adopt his recommendations. Marshall possessed the security to choose able subordinates and to rely upon them, and Kennan had emerged by September of 1947 in the front rank of such officials. The assertion—by Dean Rusk's biographer—that "Marshall ignored Kennan as much as possible" has no grounding in evidence.[110] It is, in a word, false. Not one to dispense praise liberally, Marshall wrote Kennan in light of his work during 1947 that "I just want you to know in a rather formal manner how much I appreciate the splendid work you have been doing here in the Department. Your calm and analytical approach to our problems is most comforting and your judgement is a source of great confidence to me."[111] Such

[108] Kennan, *Memoirs*, I, p. 357.

[109] Ibid., p. 356.

[110] Thomas J. Schoenbaum, *Waging Peace and War: Dean Rusk in the Truman, Kennedy and Johnson Years* (New York, 1988), p. 137.

[111] Marshall to Kennan, January 6, 1948, George C. Marshall Papers, Box 133. In a letter written after his final retirement from government service Marshall told Kennan: "I admired and

appreciation was pure balm for Kennan and only increased his regard for Marshall which already had reached a high level. He knew he worked with a "great man" and admired "his unshakeable integrity, . . . his ironclad sense of duty; [and] his imperturbability . . . in the face of harassments, pressures and criticisms."[112] He left no stone unturned in his efforts to serve the secretary and in a subtle exercise in bureaucratic imperialism claimed a share in the speechwriting assignment for the secretary.[113]

Kennan held Marshall's new deputy, Under Secretary Robert Lovett, in somewhat less esteem. Kennan did not know Lovett before his arrival in the State Department and never moved within his social circle. While he respected Lovett he saw him essentially, and one might add accurately, as an "operator" who brought few ideas or concepts on foreign policy to his position.[114] Lovett expended a good deal of his energy on domestic political matters, especially relations with the Congress, which Kennan gladly gave a wide berth.[115] This difference in emphasis helped ensure that Kennan worked quite well with Lovett, whom Kennan thought treated him with some wariness. Kennan sought primarily to formulate policy while Lovett aimed to obtain congressional backing for it and to implement it effectively. This dichotomy should not be drawn too tightly because there was some overlap in the work of both men, but it provides some sense of their respective contributions as is evident in their continuing work on the Marshall Plan.

Kennan's being Mr. "X" did not notably affect his relations with other officials in the State Department. No aura surrounded him. His public reputation did not secure his views from criticism. His contribution depended as always on the quality and persuasiveness of his recommendations. Of course his wide-ranging responsibilities as Planning Staff Director, which placed no issue outside his concern, gave him a special role in the department. He dealt with officials from every division of the State Department and his liberal cooperation with the division of Economic Affairs on the aid program to Europe demonstrated his willingness and facility for this. Needless to say Kennan

---

respected your judgement, and you were of great help to me during what I consider a very difficult period." Marshall to Kennan, February 17, 1953, George C. Marshall Papers, Box 231.

[112] Kennan, *Memoirs*, I, p. 345; and author's interview with George F. Kennan, March 6, 1989. On the day before he left the State Department in August 1950, Kennan wrote General Marshall that "I look back on my association with you here as the greatest of the privileges I have known in the quarter century of government work." Kennan to Marshall, August 24, 1950, Documents loaned to Dr. Forrest Pogue by George F. Kennan, Marshall Library, Verifax 358.

[113] A speechwriter, Joseph Jones, complained to his boss Francis Russell in the Public Affairs Division that "I believe he [Kennan] considers that it is his function now to write the secretary's speeches." Jones to Russell, June 30, 1947, Jones Papers, HSTL, Box 2.

[114] Author's interview with Kennan, March 6, 1989.

[115] Paul Nitze refers to Lovett's emphasis on dealing with Congress and notes that "I considered his abilities to be more in the direction of tactical skill than profound analysis," in his *From Hiroshima to Glasnost*, p. 51.

eventually found himself involved in disagreements with other elements in the department—the most notable being with John D. Hickerson and the Office of European Affairs as we shall see—but such conflict owed nothing to the publication of the "X" article. Only Dean Rusk, who as Special Assistant for Political Affairs handled matters concerning the United Nations, appeared to dislike and resent Kennan for his public notoreity, although even in this relationship the difference developed as much out of their substantive disagreement over the emphasis which the United States should place on the United Nations.[116]

Within the Planning Staff Kennan's dominance had been established before publication of his famous article and this simply continued. By September Joseph Johnson had departed for the groves of academe but John Paton Davies had arrived back from Moscow and taken up his position, and George Butler had returned from his ambassador's post to assume his responsibilities as deputy director of the Staff. These two men added valuable experience and capacity for independent judgment to the Staff. Even with their arrival Kennan still operated under tremendous pressure. In a lecture at the National War College on September 18 he recalled that the previous year he had complained about "the despotism of the military tyrants like General Gruenther" who had expected him to produce lectures on short notice. He went on to observe that "when I look back now from my present duties on that period, it seems that I was about as strapped for time as one of those fellows you see fishing in the Potomac off the docks."[117] Invitations poured in for Kennan/Mr. "X" to speak but for the most part, with Lovett's express approval, he turned them down. As Director of the Planning Staff he had other things to do.

ONWARDS TO A RECOVERY PROGRAM

With Kennan's recommendations as their guide Marshall and Lovett authorized American officials to contact the Europeans and to convince them that the CEEC report should be labeled "provisional" and subject to revision to take account of American principles. The Americans also obtained an agreement to postpone the formal meeting of ministers by a week to allow for their further efforts to reduce the combined European request. Through direct representa-

---

[116] Schoenbaum, *Waging Peace and War*, pp. 137–38.

[117] Kennan, "Formulation of Policy in the USSR," September 18, 1947, Kennan Papers, Box 17. As early as June, Kennan complained about the time pressures in his job. He told an audience at the National War College: "Now the essence of the task of planning is that you are supposed to keep yourself free of trivialities and concentrate on pure thought. The theory is that all you really need for the job is a good quiet stump and something to whittle. If everyone had this same conception of a planner's role, that too would make things easier; but the number of people who lay claim to your attention and your time surpasses belief. And the worst part of it is that you can never explain to your bosses the nature of your distractions and get any sympathy from them. They say it is all your own fault." Kennan, "Planning of Foreign Policy," June 18, 1947, Kennan Papers, Box 17.

tions in the various European capitals and through the endeavors of Clayton and his associates in Paris the Americans persuaded the Europeans to lessen their aid requirements.[118] The revised text of the CEEC report, now asking for $22 billion, was ready for the European foreign ministers to sign in Paris on September 22. After the ceremony at the Quai d'Orsay the report made its way to the Americans for consideration. The task of fashioning an acceptable program to present to Congress now passed to the State Department's Advisory Steering Committee. Kennan necessarily could not serve on this group which subjected European data on production, financial, and trade policy to detailed and searching examination. Although he headed one of the auxiliary groups to the Advisory Steering Committee—the objectives subcommittee—charged with reviewing the broad aspects of the program as it developed, his regular involvement in Marshall Plan questions declined from this point. Once the Europeans presented their report officials like Lewis Douglas, Nitze, and Bonesteel supervised by Lovett assumed the lion's share of responsibility for developing and implementing the Marshall Plan.[119]

Kennan's influence lingered. His concern that interim aid be extended to Europe while the larger program took shape guided policymakers. Secretary Marshall and President Truman informed a conference of congressional leaders in late September that "unless funds are made available by the first of the year the governments of France and Italy will fall to the Communists and a long-term program of rehabilitation of Europe will be impossible of accomplishment."[120] With Marshall again absent at a United Nations meeting in New York Lovett framed recommendations for Truman to address the crisis situation.[121] Truman acted upon them and called Congress into session on November 17 when he addressed a joint sitting of both houses proposing over half a billion dollars in short-term aid. On December 15 the legislation was approved and $522 million was soon on its way to Italy, France, and Austria.

After complicated consideration of the CEEC request the administration slashed this figure to $17 billion. This was what the Europeans were told they would get. On December 19, Truman submitted to Congress a message on "A Program for U.S. Aid to European Recovery." He proposed aid for the first fifteen months—from April 1, 1948 to June 30, 1949—of $6.8 billion, together with a further $10.2 billion in the three succeeding years. An Economic Cooperation Administration would be formed to administer the aid, headed by an officer appointed by the president but subject to confirmation by the Senate. There also would be a Special Representative to liaise with the continuing

---

[118] On the representations see Lovett's memorandum, September 7, 1947, *FRUS* 1947, III, pp. 412–15. On the activities of Clayton and his subordinates in Paris see the various exchanges in *FRUS* 1947, III, pp. 421–35.

[119] Nitze, *From Hiroshima to Glasnost*, pp. 56–66.

[120] Diary of Admiral William D. Leahy, September 29, 1947, Leahy Papers, Box 5.

[121] Lovett to Truman, October 13, 1947, *FRUS* 1947, III, pp. 478–81. Pogue discusses these matters in greater detail in *George C. Marshall*, 4, pp. 234–36.

organization in Europe.[122] Thus the European Recovery Program set off to run the gauntlet of congressional scrutiny. Here Marshall and Lovett played masterful roles. The secretary skillfully used his stature and nonpolitical reputation to forge a bipartisan coalition to support the program now identified with his name. His deputy worked long hours placating congressional concerns, massaging congressional egos, and adjusting to or deflecting congressional amendments. Lovett's intimate and well-manicured relationship with Senator Vandenberg paid handsome dividends. After inevitably placing his own stamp on the bill by limiting the initial appropriation to $5.3 billion over a twelve-month period, Vandenberg garnered unanimous support for the Economic Cooperation Act from his Foreign Relations Committee.[123] Spurred on by the Communist coup in Czechoslovakia and the continuing crisis atmosphere abroad, the full Senate approved the measure 69 votes to 17.[124] The House passed its version of the legislation on March 31, by 329 votes to 74. A House-Senate conference soon reached a compromise on the two versions of the bill. After both the House and the Senate voted in favor of the amended measure Truman signed it into law on April 3, 1948. After almost a year of intense and complicated deliberations and discussions the Marshall Plan had become a reality.

Truman's signature brought the Economic Cooperation Administration (ECA), charged with the administration of American aid to Western Europe, into existence. Truman selected Paul G. Hoffman, president of the Studebaker Corporation and a prominent Republican internationalist, as its chief administrator.[125] Hoffman, in turn, persuaded Averell Harriman to give up his Cabinet position to take the second ranking job in the ECA—the post of special representative in Europe. Together Hoffman and Harriman oversaw the implementation of the European Recovery Program, extending economic assistance while promoting the integration of the European economies and the adoption of American labor and management practices designed to boost productivity.

[122] President's Message to Congress, December 19, 1947, *US Department of State Bulletin* 17 (1947), pp. 1233–43.

[123] On Vandenberg's important role see David R. Kepley, *The Collapse of the Middle Way: Senate Republicans and the Bipartisan Foreign Policy, 1948–1952* (New York, 1988), pp. 12–13.

[124] On the crisis atmosphere see Leffler, "Strategic Dimensions of the Marshall Plan," pp. 287–89

[125] Alan R. Raucher, *Paul G. Hoffman: Architect of Foreign Aid* (Lexington, Ký., 1985), pp. 64–79. Kennan had some reservations about the administration of ERP by Hoffman and the ECA. In February of 1948 he wrote : "The most significant feature of the emerging recovery program is that it is to be conducted by this Government as a technical business operation and not as a political matter. We must face realistically the fact that this will reduce drastically the program's potential political effect and open up the road to a considerable degree of confusion, contradiction and ineffectiveness in this Government's policies toward Europe." See Kennan, "Review of Current Trends: U.S. Foreign Policy" (PPS/23) February 24, 1948, PPS/Records, Box 3; and Nelson, ed., *SDPPSP 1948*, pp. 103–34.

As Michael Hogan has revealed in great detail the European governments dexterously deflected much American direction and exercised "a considerable degree of autonomy within the framework of the ERP."[126] The Marshall Plan did not "remake Europe in an American mode" but in response to American efforts and pressures the West Europeans developed their own solutions.[127] The extent of the Marshall Plan's contribution to the European economic revival which occurred in the late 1940s—a subject that attracts considerable scholarly attention—lies outside the province of this study.[128] But by April 1948, when the first installments of ERP assistance reached Europe, Kennan already judged the Marshall Plan a stunning success.

KENNAN AND THE POLITICAL IMPACT OF THE MARSHALL PLAN

Kennan had played a crucial role in the early development of the Marshall Plan. He was most responsible for the initial American strategy of encouraging the Europeans, acting jointly, to formulate a recovery program. He provided decisive guidance on how to deal with the Soviets and through his lobbying influenced the British position on this matter. After his visit to Paris in late August 1947, the planning chief recommended a modified two-stage approach—firstly, interim aid and, secondly, American formulation of a long-term plan after receiving the European proposal—which Marshall implemented. Kennan deserves an honored place on the team of midwives which delivered the Marshall Plan. He and his Planning Staff were justifiably proud of their achievement. Kennan appreciated that his work on the Marshall Plan had secured his position as a key policy adviser to Marshall. More important, however, Kennan saw the Marshall Plan contributing impressively to the political and strategic objectives of the United States in its contest with the Soviet Union.

For Kennan the Marshall Plan was the decisive first step in establishing a political balance of power in Europe. In an analysis of the world situation written in October of 1947 Kennan explained that "I would not hesitate to say that the first and primary element of 'containment,' as used in that ["X"] article, would be the encouragement and development of other forces resistant

---

[126] Hogan, *The Marshall Plan*, p. 444.

[127] Ibid., p. 445; and Milward, *The Reconstruction of Western Europe*, p. 502.

[128] The debate centers on how essential Marshall Plan aid was to European recovery. Alan Milward, of course, argues that "the postwar European world would have looked much the same without it." See his "Was the Marshall Plan Necessary?" p. 252. Hogan insists that without the Marshall Plan there would have been "a serious crisis in production that would have come with the collapse of critical dollar imports." Hogan, *The Marshall Plan*, p. 431. Charles Maier argues that "U.S. aid served, in a sense, like the lubricant in an engine—not the fuel—allowing a machine to run that would otherwise buckle and bind." Maier, "The Two Postwar Eras and the Conditions for Stability in Twentieth-Century Western Europe," pp. 341–43. Also see Richard Mayne, *The Recovery of Europe: From Devastation to Unity* (London, 1970), pp. 117–21.

to communism.'' The problem in the immediate post-hostilities period, he went on to note, ''rested in the fact that with the power of Germany, Italy, and Japan destroyed and with England and China desperately weakened, Russia was surrounded only by power vacuums.'' Initially, some of these could only be filled by direct American action, such as in Greece, but for him this was undesirable. ''It should be a cardinal point of our policy,'' he continued, ''to see to it that other elements of independent power are developed on the Eurasian land mass as rapidly as possible, in order to take off our shoulders some of the burden of 'bipolarity.' '' Herein lay the ''chief beauty of the Marshall Plan'' because ''it had outstandingly this effect.''[129] Kennan offered these views before any economic assistance actually reached Europe. Gathering the Europeans together and engaging them upon the task of planning for their own economic rejuvenation served a signal purpose. The Marshall Plan project threw the Communist forces in Western Europe on the defensive and gave new confidence to non-Communists. Kennan later recalled that ''the psychological success at the outset was so amazing that we felt that the psychological effect was four-fifths accomplished before the first supplies arrived.''[130]

When he concluded his substantive work on the Marshall Plan in late 1947 Kennan still discerned the Soviet Union as poised to take advantage of the power vacuum left in Europe by Germany's defeat. The Soviet program of expansion, utilizing primarily political rather than military means, continued to have as its immediate end the seizure of power in Italy, France, Greece, and Czechoslovakia. As such it presented a serious potential threat to the security of the United States because the resources of Western Europe when combined to those of Russia could produce overwhelming power. To safeguard America from this threat Kennan recommended the restoration of ''something of the balance of power'' to enable the Europeans to assume for themselves part of the burden of halting Soviet advances. The Marshall Plan contributed centrally to this end and stood firmly in the tradition of enlightened national self-interest. Kennan, however, opposed American military guarantees to Europe or the stationing of American forces there as unwise and ineffective in combating the Soviet threat.[131] His stance did not meet universal agreement within the Truman administration when the issue of some form of Atlantic Security pact was thrust to the fore late in 1947 at the instigation of Ernest Bevin. At this time Kennan had turned his primary attention from the Marshall Plan to the perilous situation in the eastern Mediterranean.

[129] Kennan to Lyon, October 13, 1947, PPS Records, Box 33.
[130] Kennan interview with Harry P. Price, February 2, 1953.
[131] Kennan's views are revealed in ''Resume of World Situation,'' November 6, 1947 (PPS/13), *FRUS* 1947, I, pp. 770–77; Kennan, ''Relations with Russia,'' speech to the Governors, Federal Reserve System, December 1, 1947; and Kennan, ''Preparedness as Part of Foreign Relations,'' talk to Armed Services Committee, January 8, 1948, Kennan Papers, Box 17.

CHAPTER THREE

Mediterranean Crises: Greece, Italy, and Palestine

AT THE VORTEX

Early in 1949 Kennan journeyed up to New York to address a "small private dinner" of eighty or so members of the Council on Foreign Relations gathered at The Harold Pratt House. There he lamented to the assembled members—worthies in New York's legal, business, and academic circles—that, while the Planning Staff had been formed to consider matters of long-range foreign policy, from the outset it had been constantly diverted "into consideration of immediate and pressing questions of current policy."[1] Kennan's observation held telling force especially for the Staff's activities during the period covering the last months of 1947 through April of 1948. As Kennan and his Staff brought the main part of their work on the Marshall Plan to a close a host of other urgent problems descended upon them like a hailstorm. A mere listing of just some of Kennan's concerns during this period serves to suggest their diversity and complexity—policy in Germany, especially with regard to the western zones; the nature and extent of American assistance for an increasingly unsteady Chiang Kai-shek in China; the pressing need for modifications in occupation policy in Japan; a response to the Bevin proposals for a western military union; a suitable approach to Eastern Europe over which the Soviets—as demonstrated by the Czech coup—intently tightened their grip. Any one of these issues provided sufficient difficulties to test the mettle of a policymaker but Kennan, aided by his small band of colleagues, participated in the debate on every one of them as we shall see in subsequent chapters. But this was by no means the limit of his activities during this turbulent period.

During the winter of 1947–1948 the United States confronted foreboding situations in both Greece and Italy where fears were raised of Communist seizures of power. To add more explosive potential to the Mediterranean cauldron, by late 1947 it had become apparent that the Jews and Arabs in Palestine could not frame a lasting and acceptable settlement. The question of the future disposition of Palestine emerged as yet another major and troublesome issue in American diplomacy. A "politically astute" person might have avoided involvement on this matter in light of its domestic political significance but Kennan rather courageously made no effort to back away from it. Plunging

---

[1] For the details of this dinner, including the guest list, and for a summary of Kennan's remarks see Archives of the Council on Foreign Relations, New York, Record of Meetings, 1949.

ahead, where perhaps angels might have feared to tread, the Planning Staff contributed notably to the policy debate on the American response to events in Italy, Greece, and Palestine, although with considerably different results.

Kennan's involvement on such a wide range of foreign policy issues owed much to the key place he was assigned in the bureaucratic apparatus established upon the passage of the National Security Act in July of 1947. This landmark legislation established an independent air force and mechanisms to coordinate the efforts of the national defense establishment, namely a Secretary of Defense and a committee of the service chiefs, the Joint Chiefs of Staff (JCS). It also transformed the Central Intelligence Group (CIG) into an independent department, renamed the Central Intelligence Agency (CIA). Finally, it created the National Security Council (NSC) under the chairmanship of the president with the secretaries of state and defense as its key members, to coordinate policy formulation. Truman decided against regular attendance at the NSC meetings and designated the secretary of state to chair it in his absence. He preferred to wait upon the considered recommendation of the NSC and to make his decisions regarding policy upon its receipt.[2] The president, in fact, trod rather lightly in the domain of foreign policy formulation, with some notable exceptions—Palestine being first among them.

The substantive work of the NSC took place elsewhere than in the White House. Truman appointed a former St. Louis banker and wartime naval intelligence officer, Admiral Sidney Souers, as the first executive secretary of the NSC. But Souers possessed no ambition to play the policy formulation role craved by some future presidential advisers on national security. Demonstrating both good sense and real skill he limited his role to coordination and left the actual policy-making to others.[3] Naturally the Cabinet-level officials had the final authority regarding what moved forward to the president. However, they were like officers on the bridge. They depended on the engine room to provide them with the wherewithal to move forward and the true engine room

---

[2] See Anna Kasten Nelson, "President Truman and the Evolution of the National Security Council," *Journal of American History* 72 (September 1985): 360–78. One should note that only after amendment of the National Security Act in 1949 was provision made for a statutory chairman of the JCS or for a Department of Defense. The full membership of the NSC consisted of the President; the Secretaries of State, Defense, the Army, the Navy, and the Air Force; and the Chairman of the National Security Resources Board. On the establishment and operation of the NSC also see Alfred D. Sander, "Truman and the National Security Council: 1945–1947," *Journal of American History* 59 (September 1972): pp. 369–88; Stanely L. Falk, "The National Security Council Under Truman, Eisenhower, and Kennedy," *Political Science Quarterly* 79 (September 1964): 403–34; and James S. Lay, Jr., and Robert H. Johnson, "Organizational History of the National Security Council," in U.S. Senate, Committee on Government Operations, *Organizing for National Security*, vol. 2 (Washington, D.C., 1961), pp. 417–31.

[3] He proved himself "the quiet manager, the facilitator, the perfect coordinator of an interdepartmental council." See Nelson, "President Truman and the Evolution of the National Security Council," pp. 365–66.

of the NSC in the late 1940s was a body known as the Consultants on which each NSC member placed one representative. Marshall appointed Kennan as the State Department Consultant and over the next eighteen months he worked in close contact with the other Consultants to frame the basic statements of national security policy accepted and implemented by the Truman administration. Kennan's participation on the NSC Consultants placed him at the vortex of policy formulation and provided him with contacts and influence well beyond the State Department.

In his work on the Consultants Kennan joined three military representatives—Lieutenant General Albert C. Wedemeyer, Deputy Chief of Staff, Plans and Operations, of the Army Department; Vice Admiral Forrest Sherman, Deputy Chief of Naval Operations; Lieutenant General Lauris Norstad, Deputy Chief of Staff, Operations, Department of the Air Force—and another civilian, Daniel C. Fahey of the National Security Resources Board. Three other officials participated as observers in activities of the Consultants—Rear Admiral Roscoe H. Hillenkoetter, Director of the CIA; Major General Alfred M. Gruenther, a former colleague of Kennan's at the National War College, from the Joint Staff of the JCS; and John H. Ohly, Special Assistant to the nation's first Secretary of Defense, James Forrestal.[4] With Souers supervising the administrative details, the Consultants worked together with notable effectiveness. In pointed contrast to those who develop reputations for bureaucratic expertise by their ability to frustrate or scuttle proposals from other departments, the initial Consultants cooperated well and saw themselves engaged upon a common endeavor. Kennan considered his relations with his Armed Service opposites to be "excellent" and opined that "the national defense authorities appear to be pleased with the arrangement and to feel that they now have, for the first time, an adequate point of contact with the [State] Department on general policy matters below the Under Secretary and Secretary level."[5]

Kennan emerged quickly as the key member of the Consultant group. His influence stemmed primarily from the fact that the State Department undertook to develop most initial drafts for consideration by the NSC Consultants. Not surprisingly, Kennan turned the Policy Planning Staff into the essential agency in the department to serve the needs of the NSC. One student of the National Security Council has noted that "as the NSC began to function, many Policy Planning Staff papers became blueprints for NSC documents."[6] A vir-

---

[4] The Consultants are listed in the NSC's report, "Policies of the Government of the United States of America Relating to the National Security," vol. 1, 1947–48, in Truman Papers, PSF, Box 195. Note that each consultant could appoint a deputy. Kennan assigned his Planning Staff deputy, George Butler, to fill this position.

[5] See PPS/15, "Report on Activities of Policy Planning Staff—May to November, 1947," November 13, 1947, PPS Records, Box 3; and Nelson, ed., *SDPPSP 1947*, p. 144.

[6] Anna Kasten Nelson, "Introduction," in *SDPPSP 1947*, p. xix. Nelson has commented that

tual symbiotic relationship developed between the Planning Staff and the NSC with Kennan as the connecting link. The NSC relied on the State Department planners for much of its staff work while the Policy Planning Staff obtained elevated recognition and responsibilities through its integral involvement in the National Security Council policy process. This new recognition, of course, was limited to the rarefied circles of Washington policymakers.[7]

In light of the Staff's increased responsibilities Kennan instituted some new procedures. He recognized that he would not be able to take personal responsibility for every paper and hence accepted a system whereby a Staff member would be assigned responsibility for preparing a draft. This draft would then come to the whole Staff and, where appropriate, representatives of the operational Offices of the State Department, the Service Departments, and outside consultants.[8] Kennan, however, remained the central figure on the Staff and reveled in this role. In an appraisal of the usefulness of the Planning Staff which he wrote for Lovett and Marshall in mid-November 1947, Kennan exuded satisfaction with its operations and with the contribution which he and his fellow planners had been able to make. He reaffirmed his desire to avoid "bigness" and restated his intention "to keep the organization small and flexible, and to prevent its becoming water-logged with internal administrative problems."[9] Kennan held to this objective even as the demands on the Planning Staff multiplied ominously in the winter of 1947–1948. The Staff consisted of fewer than ten members right through until the latter part of 1949.

CRITICAL SITUATIONS

In October 1947, the newly reorganized CIA produced a report examining the current situation in the Mediterranean and the Near East which captured well the challenges the United States confronted there. The intelligence analysts immediately outlined the strategic importance of the region asserting that "access to the oil of the Persian Gulf area and the denial of control of the Medi-

---

"although the defense establishment initiated as many studies as the State Department did, the latter—specifically the PPS—organized and wrote the papers and thus had a critical impact on the NSC during the Truman administration." Nelson, "President Truman and the National Security Council," p. 370.

[7] Sidney Souers certainly appreciated the contribution of Kennan and the PPS. On his resignation as executive secretary of the NSC he wrote thanking Kennan and commented to him that "the record of the Council's activities reflects the influence of your contributions more clearly than anything I might say. Not so apparent to anyone who has not been part of the team is the effective and broad staff coordination that you helped establish through the NSC Consultants and Staff, and the relationships of these two groups with the Policy Planning Staff and similar planning groups in the other departments and agencies." See Souers to Kennan, February 1, 1950, Papers of Sidney W. Souers, HSTL, Box 1.

[8] The new procedures are recorded in PPS Minutes, September 29, 1947, PPS Records, Box 32.

[9] See PPS/15, "Report on Activities of Policy Planning Staff—May to November, 1947," November 13, 1947, PPS Records, Box 3; and Nelson, ed., SDPPSP 1947, p. 140.

terranean to a major, hostile, expansionist power are deemed to be essential to the security of the U.S." They identified the major threat to U.S. interests and security as lying in Soviet penetration into the Mediterranean and Near East, either directly, through satellites, or through local Communist action. The CIA report then proceeded to list the "critical situations in order of importance," placing Italy first, then Greece, and then the Arab states.[10] Italy's economic crisis was of such dimensions that the CIA analysts argued that it demanded prompt and effective aid to prevent an economic collapse which could lead to a Communist accession to power. In Greece the Communist challenge had advanced further, despite the promulgation of the Truman Doctrine and the limited economic and military assistance program which Congress approved. There the CIA accused the Soviet Union, acting indirectly through its satellites, of being engaged in a forcible attempt to seize part of the country. In bureaucratic parlance, which served to disguise the urgency of the situation, the report suggested that "unless an early pacification and economic and political rehabilitation of the country are achieved, the situation, already at an advanced state of deterioration, may well pass beyond the possibility of effective remedy." The CIA also raised the specter of the Soviet threat in regard to the Arab states. Having concluded that Arab determination to resist partition of Palestine was such that any attempt to enforce that solution would lead to armed conflict, the report observed that this would present an opportunity for the extension of Soviet influence. But Palestine needed to be understood in terms beyond Soviet interference. The CIA warned that U.S. support for partition of Palestine might lead the Arab states to take their own steps to undermine American economic and strategic interests.[11] The perceived Soviet challenge in this region combined with British weakness had prompted the actions associated with the Truman Doctrine early in 1947, but that was only an opening salvo in the American response. In the year after Truman's historic speech the United States struggled to maintain its security interests in the Mediterranean.

Italy in the years immediately after World War II reeled from economic and political disorder.[12] Deterioration in Italian political and economic conditions was a recurring theme in the reporting from Rome of the American ambassador, James Clement Dunn.[13] The coalition government led by the Christian Democrat Alcide De Gasperi produced only political paralysis and further eco-

[10] CIA, "The Current Situation in the Mediterranean and the Near East," October 17, 1947, Truman Papers, PSF, Box 254. The CIA also listed Iran as a critical situation and then gave the following ranking for "Less Urgent Situations in Order of Importance"—Turkey, Egypt, French North Africa, Libya, Spain.

[11] Ibid.

[12] John Lamberton Harper gives details in *America and the Reconstruction of Italy, 1945–1948* (Cambridge, 1986). In addition to Harper's study on U.S.-Italian relations see also James Edward Miller, *The United States and Italy, 1940–1950: The Politics and Diplomacy of Stabilization* (Chapel Hill, 1986).

[13] See, for example, Dunn to Secretary of State, May 3, 1947, *FRUS* 1947, III, pp. 889–91.

nomic distress. In June of 1947, De Gasperi, in a daring political move, dismissed the Communists and the left-wing Socialists led by Pietro Nenni from his government. He eventually formed a government of Christian Democrats in collaboration with a number of minor parties—Liberals, Republicans, and, somewhat later, the more moderate Socialist faction led by Guiseppe Saragat. De Gasperi's action polarized the Italian polity and drew forth a fierce response from the parties of the Left which "reacted with a growing campaign of violence that seemed to presage a civil war."[14] Although the Communists (PCI) under Palmiro Togliatti probably retained some capacity for action independent of the Kremlin, the Americans viewed Communist strength in Italy as Soviet strength. A Communist electoral victory or seizure of power would serve to bring Italy into the Soviet orbit with disastrous consequences for American interests in Western Europe.

Kennan and the Planning Staff were deeply aware of Italy's travails as a result of their Marshall Plan deliberations. Precisely because of the "gravity and urgency" of the situation Kennan had pushed successfully for interim economic assistance to tide Italy over until the arrival of assistance under the general Recovery Program.[15] By the fall of 1947, however, anxiety developed in the Truman administration that such economic assistance would not suffice to stabilize the Italian political situation and allow De Gasperi to defeat the Communist political challenge. Furthermore, American policymakers gave increasing credence to the possibility of the Communists launching a violent assault against the De Gasperi government. In light of such American fears Under Secretary Robert Lovett requested the Policy Planning Staff in mid-September to make recommendations "for use in the event that the Communists should take over Northern Italy."[16] Kennan undertook to draw up these recommendations himself.

Lovett had made a similar request of the Planning Staff with respect to Greece a month beforehand. Revealing a bent for contingency planning, the under secretary asked Kennan and his colleagues for recommendations in case the Communists should grab power in Greece.[17] In August 1947 such a Communist victory could not be ruled out. Soon after the British replaced the Germans in Greece in October of 1944 they suppressed, after vicious fighting, a Communist-led revolt by the left-wing National Liberation Front (the EAM) and its military arm, the National People's Liberation Army (ELAS). Two years later, after elections in March of 1946 installed a conservative, royalist gov-

[14] James E. Miller, "Taking Off the Gloves: The United States and the Italian Elections of 1948," *Diplomatic History* 7 (Winter 1983): 36.

[15] For an example of the Planning Staff's concern for Italy see PPS Minutes, June 12, 1947, PPS Records, Box 32.

[16] Kennan refers to Lovett's request in PPS Minutes, September 18, 1947, PPS Records, Box 32.

[17] Kennan reported Lovett's request to his colleagues in PPS Minutes, August 14, 1947, PPS Records, Box 32.

ernment dominated by Constantine Tsaldaris's reactionary Populist Party and in response to rightist repression, a new Communist insurgency developed. By the end of 1946 a full-scale and bloody civil war engulfed the country. But the British refused to bear the price of sustaining the Greek government any longer and through Truman's Greek-Turkish Aid Program of March 1947 the United States accepted this responsibility which it understood in terms of containing Soviet influence in Greece.[18]

After careful investigation the historian Lawrence S. Wittner concluded that "despite the American emphasis on Soviet responsibility for the civil war in Greece, no solid evidence emerged to indicate that the rebellion there was motivated (or even appreciably assisted) by Stalin's foreign policy."[19] Although admitting that the Soviet satellites—Yugoslavia, Bulgaria, and Albania—extended support to the Communist insurrection, Wittner determined that the United States had been "blinded by Cold War dogma" and had rejected opportunities for negotiation and compromise which might have ended the terrible bloodshed of the civil war.[20] His analysis, however, tends to isolate Greece from its international context and to ignore its vital location. By mid-1947, as the Greek civil war raged on, American policymakers worried little about the exact relationship between the Kremlin and the Greek Communists. Their concern was to prevent the cession of what they genuinely considered a highly strategic part of the world's surface to forces they judged antagonistic to the United States.[21] This concern certainly guided the endeavors of the Policy Planning Staff.

Around the same time that the British limited their commitment to Greece, thereby forcing the American hand there, they also announced their failure to

[18] For further detail on the situation in Greece and on American policy there see Bruce R. Kuniholm, *The Origins of the Cold War in the Near East: Great Power Conflict and Diplomacy in Iran, Turkey, and Greece* (Princeton, 1980); Lawrence S. Wittner, *American Intervention in Greece, 1943–1949* (New York, 1982); John O. Iatrides, ed., *Greece in the 1940s: A Nation in Crisis* (Hanover, N.H., 1981); Howard Jones, *"A New Kind of War": America's Global Strategy and the Truman Doctrine in Greece* (New York, 1989); and David Reynolds, "The Origins of the Cold War: The European Dimension, 1944–1951," *Historical Journal* 28 (June 1985): 479–515.

[19] Wittner, *American Intervention in Greece*, p. 255.

[20] Ibid., p. 254.

[21] PPS draft paper, "U.S. Policy in the Event of a Communist Victory on the Greek Mainland," attached to PPS Minutes, August 22, 1947, PPS Records, Box 32. The CIA defined Greece's "strategic importance" in this manner: "Greece is the last Balkan state resisting Soviet domination. Should the USSR obtain control of Greece directly or through satellites, the USSR would: (a) complete its domination of the Balkans; (b) be able to extend and consolidate the position in the Aegean which control of Macedonia and Thrace would give the Soviet Union; (c) secure Salonika, historical southern terminus of the land route from the Danubian basin; and (d) gain a strategic position in the Eastern Mediterranean, thereby outflanking Turkey and the Dardanelles, threatening the Suez, and endangering the polities of the Near East." CIA, "The Current Situation in Greece" (ORE 51), October 20, 1947, Truman Papers, PSF, Box 254.

forge a settlement between Arabs and Jews which would permit them to terminate smoothly their League of Nations mandate in Palestine taken up at the end of World War I. Consequently, on February 25, 1947, the British simply turned the entire problem over to the United Nations which formed a special committee to consider it. This situation inevitably drew the United States into a deeper involvement on this most complex and emotional issue, the true resolution of which still remains beyond the abilities of the principal antagonists.[22] The next year found the United States government "divided, frustrated and confused in its policy."[23] President Truman failed to establish a definite and clear approach for the United States and subsequently different elements within his administration began a long battle to determine the American position. Truman oscillated between them while exhibiting considerable irritation with the various principals in the dispute over Palestine.[24]

The debate over policy on Palestine pitted the State Department against certain influential members of Truman's White House staff, most notably presidential counselor Clark Clifford, whose views on the Middle East were distilled through a coarse filter of concern to secure American-Jewish support for Truman's reelection bid in 1948.[25] Within the State Department responsibility on this issue rested with the Office of Near Eastern and African Affairs, headed by Loy W. Henderson, and the Office of Special Political Affairs, headed by Dean Rusk.[26] Henderson, a courageous and determined man and a

[22] The literature on American policy on the partition of Palestine and the creation of Israel is extensive. Important works include: Kenneth Ray Bain, *The March to Zion: United States Policy and the Founding of Israel* (College Station, Texas, 1979); Michael J. Cohen, *Palestine and the Great Powers, 1945–1948* (Princeton, N.J., 1982); Zvi Ganin, *Truman, American Jewry, and Israel, 1945–1948* (New York, 1979); John Snetsinger, *Truman, the Jewish Vote and the Creation of Israel* (Stanford, 1974); Evan M. Wilson, *Decision on Palestine: How the U.S. Came to Recognize Israel* (Stanford, 1979); Wm. Roger Louis and Robert W. Stookey, eds., *The End of the Palestinian Mandate* (Austin, 1986); the relevant sections of Peter Grose, *Israel in the Mind of America* (New York, 1983); Steven L. Spiegel, *The Other Arab-Israeli Conflict: Making America's Middle East Policy, from Truman to Reagan* (Chicago, 1985); and Robert J. Donovan, *Conflict and Crisis: The Presidency of Harry S. Truman, 1945–1948* (New York, 1977).

[23] Peter Grose, "The President versus the Diplomats," in Louis and Stookey, eds., *The End of the Palestinian Mandate*, p. 44.

[24] For an example of Truman's irritation see his handwritten comment on a memorandum to Admiral William Leahy where he observed that "Greeks and Jews suffer from an inferiority complex as well as a persecution complex. I've tried to help both and so far they've only given me a pain in the neck." Memorandum on "The Greek Situation," July 18, 1947, Joint Chiefs of Staff (Leahy) Files, Modern Military Records, NA, File 123, Box 19.

[25] For a discussion of Clifford's early linkage of the Palestine question and Truman's reelection bid see Richard S. Kirkendall, "Election of 1948," in Arthur M. Schlesinger, Jr., *History of American Presidential Elections, 1789–1968*, vol. 8 (New York, 1985), pp. 3110–11.

[26] For details on the State Department and the making of policy on Palestine, especially the NEA and Loy Henderson, see Evan Wilson, *Decision on Palestine*, pp. 5–11; George McGhee, *Envoy to the Middle World: Adventures in Diplomacy* (New York, 1983), pp. xviii–xix; Oral History Interview with Loy W. Henderson by Richard D. McKinzie, June 14 & July 5, 1973,

fervent anti-Communist, believed that the Zionist goal of establishing a Jewish state in Palestine would be detrimental to the interests of the United States. His State Department colleagues sided with him on this, and not, one must add, out of any demonstrable anti-Semitism despite the damaging charges leveled against the State Department's "Arabists."[27] In contrast, the able and well-placed Clifford, out of a mixture of humanitarian and domestic political motives, held a distinctly pro-Zionist position.[28]

The United Nations Special Committee on Palestine (UNSCOP) issued its report at the end of August recommending that the British mandate be terminated and that Palestine be partitioned into a Jewish state and an Arab state, although within some form of economic union. The Jews supported partition as a step in the direction of a sovereign state while the Arabs opposed it. Truman eventually announced his support of partition despite the reservations of the State Department that American forces might be required to enforce it and that it would promote an alignment between the Arab states and the Soviet Union. On November 29, 1947, after a vigorous lobbying effort by pro-Zionist Americans, the General Assembly approved the partition proposal by thirty-three votes to thirteen with ten abstaining.[29] As Zvi Ganin has noted this vote "was a watershed in Jewish history, for it gave explicit recognition to the Jewish claim of sovereignty in Palestine."[30]

The General Assembly's November 29 vote for partition hardly resolved matters. With the Arabs' violent rejection of the proposal, questions quickly arose as to how it could be implemented. The British made it quite clear that they would not execute the plan and decided instead to accelerate their withdrawal from Palestine. The Mandate would end May 15, 1948 (6 p.m., May 14, Washington time.) To prescient observers it appeared likely that the partition plan could not be implemented without the intervention of forces from member nations of the UN. The issue of whether the United States should be involved in some enforcement of the partition plan quickly confronted policymakers and it attracted the attention of Kennan and his Staff. Just a few days before the UN vote, on November 24, Secretary of the Army Kenneth Royall

HSTL; Oral History Interview with Edwin M. Wright by Richard D. McKinzie, July 26, 1974; Oral History Interview with Fraser Wilkins by Richard D. McKinzie, June 20, 1975, HSTL.

[27] Evan Wilson's *Decision on Palestine* is persuasive on this point.

[28] For Clifford's own account see his "Factors Influencing President Truman's Decision to Support Partition and Recognize the State of Israel," in Clark M. Clifford, Eugene V. Rostow, and Barbara W. Tuchman, *The Palestine Question in American History* (New York, 1978), pp. 24–45. Clifford affords his involvement on the Palestine question pride of place in his recent memoir. See his introductory chapter, "Showdown in the Oval Office," in Clifford with Holbrooke, *Counsel to the President*, pp. 3–25.

[29] Robert Donovan gives some details of this in *Conflict and Crisis*, pp. 329–31. Donovan also persuasively suggests that Truman himself was not aloof from the American lobbying. Also note Wilson, *Decision on Palestine*, pp. 125–28; and Bain's conclusion in *The March to Zion*, p. 182.

[30] Ganin, *Truman, American Jewry, and Israel, 1945–1948*, p. 146.

had placed Palestine on the NSC agenda. Kennan and his fellow NSC Consultants met on December 12, after the UN vote, and they agreed that the State Department should prepare the initial draft of an NSC report on the United States' position on the Palestine problem.[31] Despite the extent and range of other pressing concerns Kennan undertook to wrestle with this most thorny issue.

ASSISTING THE ITALIAN GOVERNMENT

Lovett's charge to the Planning Staff to draw up contingency plans in the event that the Communists should take over Northern Italy drew an immediate response from Kennan. By September 22 he had produced a working draft which he subjected to the scrutiny of the other Staff members. In light of the military implications of the paper he also consulted with Generals Gruenther and Norstad and Admiral Sherman among others.[32] Although some disagreement existed on the Staff regarding whether the Italians should be expected to request the suspension of withdrawals of American forces, Kennan proceeded to finalize and distribute the paper.[33] He made it clear that "the ultimate aim of the Italian Communist Party" was "the complete subjugation of Italy to Soviet control," but raised considerable doubts about the short-term possibility of an armed Communist insurrection. He interpreted the increased Communist pressure through propaganda, popular demonstrations, and strikes as primarily an effort to force their "renewed participation in the Italian government by parliamentary means." A Communist resort to force was less likely, at least pending the final withdrawal of Allied forces from Italy scheduled for December 5 (and required under the peace treaty by December 15). Nonetheless, Kennan refused to rule out the possibility and consequently offered a plan for American action in the event of the Communist seizure of Northern Italy. Because he held that Soviet control of the Italian peninsula would jeopardize U.S. interests in Europe and the Mediterranean, Kennan argued that "the National Interest would require that the greatest possible support be given the Italian government in its effort to maintain itself and eventually to regain the territory seized by the Communists."[34] All this was sufficient for Lovett. After discussions with Forrestal he referred the Italian situation to the National Security Council for its formal consideration, and it became the very first issue on the NSC agenda.[35] In an explicit demonstration of the connection between

[31] For details of Royall's intervention and the Consultants decision see the editorial note, *FRUS* 1947, V, p. 1283.

[32] Minutes of Meeting, September 22, 1947, PPS Records, Box 32.

[33] PPS/9, Memorandum by the PPS, September 24, 1989, *FRUS* 1947, III, pp. 976–81.

[34] Ibid.

[35] See Nelson, "President Truman and the Evolution of the National Security Council," p. 360.

the Policy Planning Staff and the NSC, Kennan's paper became the point of departure for NSC consideration.[36]

Kennan played an important role in framing the context for the NSC deliberations. He agreed that the stability of the De Gasperi government depended fundamentally on its ability to obtain adequate economic support from the United States, and he helped formulate the proposal for interim aid for France and Italy which worked its way through to congressional approval in mid-December. But the planning chief's cautionary diagnosis of the Italian situation and the general European situation conveyed the view that additional political and military assistance might be necessary to enable De Gasperi to withstand the Communist challenge. On November 6, Kennan submitted to Secretary Marshall an assessment of the world situation which forecast that Moscow, in response to the Marshall Plan initiative, would tighten its grip on Eastern Europe and "clamp down completely on Czechoslovakia." He raised the likelihood that the Kremlin might order the Communist parties in France and Italy "to resort to virtual civil war in those countries as soon as our right to have troops in Italy expires." The Soviets aimed, argued Kennan, "to bring chaos in Europe and dissuade us from proceeding with the aid program."[37] Marshall accepted Kennan's analysis and shared it with the president and Cabinet the following week.[38] Influenced by such assessments, what one scholar has referred to as "the vision of a class war in Western Europe" took hold in Washington throughout November and December.[39] Kennan helped create this "vision" and, of course, he contributed to American planning to deal with it.

On November 14 the National Security Council met to formulate the position of the United States with respect to Italy. The NSC simply appropriated the analysis sections from Kennan's earlier paper (PPS/9) and moved on to recommend strengthened measures to assist De Gasperi. Economic assistance headed the list but NSC members also recommended further assistance to the Italian armed forces to strengthen their capability to counter threats to Italian internal security and territorial integrity.[40] While the NSC determined that the United States should not use force directly in an internal Italian conflict, it indicated that it would utilize selected naval and air bases in Italy if the Communists made an outright grab for power. And it decided that if the Communists seized control of parts of Italy before December 15, the U.S. should

[36] Kennan reported to his colleagues on October 7 that "the Policy Planning Staff's papers on Italy and Greece were being considered by the National Security Council and that future Staff papers with a military aspect would presumably follow the same course." Minutes of PPS, October 7, 1947, PPS Records, Box 32.

[37] PPS/13 "Resume of World Situation," November 6, 1947, *FRUS* 1947, I, pp. 770–77.

[38] See note 1, *FRUS* 1947, I, pp. 770–71.

[39] Miller, *The United States and Italy*, p. 238. Miller points out that "the crisis atmosphere existed initially only in Washington and was then transferred to Italy." See p. 234.

[40] NSC 1/1, "The Position of the United States with Respect to Italy," November 14, 1947, *FRUS* 1948, III, pp. 724–26.

suspend the withdrawal of its troops specified under the Italian peace treaty.[41] For fear of embarassing De Gasperi's government the NSC held off on plans to run training flights from Germany into Italy designed to make the Italian airfields operational for fighter aircraft.[42] The president quickly gave his approval for these measures and directed that they be implemented.[43]

Such measures had no immediate impact in Italy where the Communists launched a major campaign of political agitation, strikes, and violence against the government which lent credibility to the alarming predictions of a full-scale civil war.[44] In response to the threatening situation De Gasperi asked on November 28 that the United States delay the final withdrawal of its occupation troops from December 5 until December 15. President Truman soon agreed. The suspension of the troop withdrawal prompted another intervention by Kennan. Although not responsible for Italy in any operational sense he maintained a close involvement on policymaking because of Italy's crucial importance. On December 1 he wrote Lovett of his "hunch" that, in light of the suspended troop withdrawal, the president should issue a strong statement bluntly warning that the United States would not permit minority factions to overthrow the Italian democracy. The Planning Staff director described his recommendation as "a bold step" but argued "the time has come when we must either fish or cut bait. If this step is taken, I doubt that civil war will materialize in Italy."[45] Moved also by De Gasperi's request for a similar statement, which Dunn relayed, Lovett accepted Kennan's idea and a strong statement was drawn up.[46] Secretary of State Marshall, in London for the CFM meeting, objected to the severity of the draft and prompted its modification prior to its release by the White House on December 14.[47] Even as modified,

[41] Ibid., pp. 725–26.

[42] Secretary of the Air Force Symington had requested such flights but Lovett had expressed the State Department's reservations. See Minutes of the 2d Meeting of the NSC, November 14, 1947, Truman Papers, PSF, Box 203; and Record of Actions by NSC, November 14, Truman Papers, PSF, Box 191.

[43] Truman's memo to the Executive Secretary of the NSC attached to NSC 1/1, Truman Papers, PSF, Box 203.

[44] See the analysis of the Italian situation by Samuel Reber, Acting Director, Office of European Affairs, November 28, 1947, FRUS 1948, III, pp. 727–29. John Lamberton Harper in his *America and the Reconstruction of Italy*, p. 148, has referred to the American fear of the PCI as "obsessive." Based on the Communist activities in the last quarter of 1947 this assessment is open to dispute.

[45] Kennan to Lovett, December 1, 1947, PPS Records, Box 33. Kennan further noted of his proposal: "In any case, this would enable us to test the character of public and congressional opinion in this country and to know how far we could go if trouble does start."

[46] For De Gasperi's request see Dunn to Secretary of State, December 5, 1947, FRUS 1948, III, pp. 736–37. The State Department's initial draft is included in Lovett to Marshall (in London), December 11, 1947, FRUS 1948, III, p. 746. This statement warned that "this country did not fight a war in Italy to see the Italian people again subjected to the totalitarian rule of a foreign inspired minority."

[47] For Marshall's reservations see Marshall to Lovett, December 12, 1947, FRUS 1948, III, pp. 748–49. Truman's eventual statement is included in note 2 of this entry.

James Edward Miller accurately has described it as a "clear warning to the PCI that force would be met with force" and as a sign that the United States now "would openly confront the PCI."[48]

Kennan's initiatives had helped move the United States to a much more interventionist stance with regard to Italy. In cooperation with Lovett, Ambassador Dunn and both his NSC Consultant colleagues, and the State Department's operational officers, Kennan carried the United States from a position where it relied largely on the promise of economic assistance to support Italy to one where it more readily utilized political and military pressures to defeat the perceived Communist threat. This set the stage for even more vigorous intervention—overt and covert—on the part of the United States in the early months of 1948 as Italy prepared for its national elections.

COMBAT FORCES TO GREECE?

Kennan and his Staff viewed Greece in like manner to Italy as yet another theater in the dangerous conflict with the Soviet Union. The Staff first gave sustained attention to Greece in mid-August 1947 upon Lovett's question of what the United States should do if the Communists took over there, a question which itself reflected the deteriorating Greek situation. The Staff considered the issue through the latter half of August and consulted with Loy Henderson, Director of the Office of Near Eastern and African Affairs (NEA), and officers of his division.[49] On August 22 the Staff discussed a draft paper which outlined actions to be undertaken if and when the U.S. government decided that it could not prevent the Communist domination of the Greek mainland. The Staff did not hold failure in Greece as inevitable but it made recommendations for that eventuality including training of non-Communist guerrillas, ending the Greek aid program, continuing recognition of the non-Communist Greek government which might be relocated in Crete, and projecting American military strength in the area.[50] The Planning Staff paper eventually was referred to the National Security Council for consideration but attention within the Truman administration concentrated on preventing the situation which would necessitate such measures.[51] Kennan and his Staff colleagues redirected their attention to how the United States should aid the Greek government in resisting the Communist forces.

From October 16 to November 7 Kennan participated in conversations between diplomatic and military representatives of Great Britain and the United States reviewing strategic and political problems in the Eastern Mediterranean

[48] Miller, *The United States and Italy*, p. 241.

[49] See PPS Minutes, August 14, 18, and 20, 1947, PPS Records, Box 32.

[50] PPS paper, "U.S. Policy in the Event of a Communist Victory on the Greek Mainland," August 22, 1947, PPS Records, Box 32.

[51] For reference to the referral of the Greek paper to the NSC see PPS Minutes, October 7, 1947, PPS Records, Box 32.

and the Middle East. Here the United States affirmed its commitment to the security of the region and its corollary of maintaining both the territorial integrity and political independence of Italy, Greece, Turkey, and Iran.[52] It pledged to make full use of its political, economic and, if necessary, military power in carrying out this policy. While the U.S. delegates clarified that their nation would exhaust political and economic means before resorting to the actual use of force, by the end of these conversations the question of the use of American combat forces in Greece emerged as the key issue for consideration of the Truman administration. The reason was quite obvious. Even with the political, economic, and military assistance of the Greek-Turkish Aid Program, the Tsaldaris government—notable mainly for its incompetence and right-wing rigidity—made no headway against the Communist guerrillas. The Greek army, even with the assistance of the British Military Mission, proved remarkably ineffective owing to disgraceful weaknesses in its leadership and command structure.[53] The situation demanded additional measures.

The United States Army displayed no enthusiasm for dispatching combat troops to Greece, recognizing that such a move would spread forces even more thinly around the world and perhaps require a partial national mobilization.[54] Dwight Eisenhower, the Army Chief of Staff, recommended instead the furnishing of operational advice to the Greek armed forces to supplement the existing program of military assistance. In the plan accepted by the National Security Council and approved by the president, the United States would form an Advisory and Planning Group of around ninety officers in order to provide high staff advice to the Greek forces. The American officers would not engage in combat.[55] The issue of combat troops would not go away, however. At a meeting of the National Security Council on December 17, Admiral Souers admitted he was at a loss as to the extent of the measures the Council was willing to take in Greece. Lovett, acting-secretary during Marshall's absence at the London CFM, pointed to the inconsistency of the American withdrawal of troops from Italy at the exact same time that it was considering placing troops in Greece, which he added was "one of the worst possible areas in which to fight."[56] He gained a deferral on any decision on this matter pending

[52] For a statement of the "basic conclusions" reached in these talks—known as "The Pentagon Talks of 1947"—see PPS/14, "Eastern Mediterranean and Middle East," November 11, 1947, in Nelson, ed., *SDPPSP 1947*, pp. 137–38. For the memberships of the respective delegations see *FRUS* 1947, V, pp. 582–83.

[53] For further details on these points see Jones, *"A New Kind of War,"* pp. 96–97.

[54] See the recollections of General Omar Bradley in Omar N. Bradley and Clay Blair, *A General's Life* (New York, 1983), pp. 474–75.

[55] Marshall refers to Eisenhower's proposal in forwarding it to Truman as a recommendation of the NSC. See Memorandum for the President, "Extension of operational advice to the Greek Armed Forces," November 3, 1947, Truman Papers, PSF, Box 193. Truman approved the memorandum the following day.

[56] See Minutes of 4th NSC Meeting, December 17, 1947, Truman Papers, PSF, Box 203.

the return for consultations of Major General Walter G. Livesay, who oversaw the existing logistical military assistance program in Greece.

On the day after Christmas when Livesay met in Washington with senior State Department officials the issue of committing U.S. combat troops moved to the center of discussion. At this meeting, after hearing Livesay's report, the Army's Assistant Chief of Staff for Plans, Major General A.V. Arnold, now called for a decision to be made to send American troops to Greece if the Greeks failed to clear up the guerrilla situation. Loy Henderson strongly supported this position and Lovett agreed that perhaps a decision should be made even though he recognized the administration had no existing authority to send combat troops. Kennan acted as a brake on his fellow officials, warning that the U.S. should give careful consideration to sending combat troops, even as part of a UN force. In a cautionary tone he observed that "we might find ourselves in a difficult position from which it would be hard to withdraw and equally hard to keep other nations from withdrawing the contingents they contributed."[57] This meeting broke up without attempting to reach final decisions but it had flushed out the two principals in the State Department debate over committing troops—Loy Henderson and George Kennan. As Howard Jones has commented, they "became the focal points of the ongoing controversy."[58]

Henderson presented his views forcefully and without complicating qualifications. For him Greece was "the test tube which the peoples of the whole world are watching in order to ascertain whether the determination of the Western Powers to resist aggression equals that of international communism to acquire new territory and new bases."[59] He wanted the United States to furnish Greece with the funds, materials, and the U.S. troops necessary to eliminate the guerrilla bands and to end what he saw as Communist aggression. For him the success of American foreign policy generally demanded that a firm stand be taken there.[60] In contrast, Henderson's former subordinate in Riga had misgivings about taking so firm a stand in Greece. His views struck a military observer as not as clear-cut as Henderson's but they grew out of his questions and concerns about sending combat troops. Kennan admitted that it was a "simple matter" to determine when to send the troops in but, in a telling observation—and one that incidentally might well have been raised in other contexts in postwar American diplomacy—he noted that it wasn't "clear as to when and how we would get them out." Furthermore, the role such troops might play remained ill-defined. Were they to participate in an occupation or

---

[57] See Memorandum of Conversation, December 26, 1947, *FRUS* 1947, V, pp. 466–69.

[58] Jones, *"A New Kind of War,"* p. 120.

[59] Memorandum by Henderson, December 22, 1947, *FRUS* 1947, V, pp. 458–61.

[60] Henderson's position is well summarized in Memo for Wedemeyer from T.W.P.[?]: "State Department Views Reference Greek Problem," December 29, 1947, Plans and Operations Division Decimal File, 091. Greece Sec. II–III, U.S. Department of Army Records, Xerox 3521, Marshall Library.

military government, he asked? Finally Kennan questioned how such a policy in Greece related to America's overall stance in the Middle East and Mediterranean and he specifically queried how it related to the Palestine issue.[61]

With the lines thus drawn, Henderson and Kennan engaged in an intense, although politely waged, battle to determine the ultimate American policy. Henderson's position made the initial running and was reflected in an NSC document (NSC 5) of January 6, which declared that "the United States should be prepared to send armed forces to Greece or elsewhere in the Mediterranean, in a manner which would not contravene the spirit of the Charter of the United Nations, if it should become clear that the use of such forces is needed to prevent Greece from falling a victim to direct or indirect aggression and that Greece would thereby be afforded a reasonable chance of survival."[62] The NEA director wrote a strong memorandum to Marshall on January 9 emphasizing the need for American decision to commit combat troops.[63] But then what Lawrence Wittner referred to as "a bureaucratic counterattack" challenged the Henderson line.[64] Kennan and the Planning Staff led it. After expressing "fullest sympathy" for Henderson's insistence on a strong policy, the Staff questioned "whether the dispatch of U.S. armed forces would necessarily be the most efficacious means of achieving the final objective and whether an advance decision to send troops, if things get worse in Greece, would be a sound and suitable way to express . . . [the American] determination" to prevent Greece from falling victim to direct or indirect aggression. Kennan indicated that he agreed with Henderson on what needed to be done but expressed his doubts that regular U.S. forces were "the proper tool" to do it. In a skillful maneuver he did not rule them out completely but argued that there was not "an adequate basis" to decide on an issue of this gravity. The Planning Staff noted the weaknesses in command of the existing U.S. military assistance group in Greece and argued the need for a fully qualified individual to make balanced and comprehensive recommendations before any decision was made.[65]

Kennan understood well that his principal audience was Secretary Marshall and that this man, who placed such stock in military planning, would question any precipitous and vague committal of military forces. And so Marshall did. On January 13, 1948, Lovett informed a meeting of the National Security Council that Marshall felt the present NSC document had to be "re-worked."

[61] Kennan's position summarized in Memo for Wedemeyer from T.W.P. [?], December 29, 1947.

[62] NSC 5, "The Position of the United States with Respect To Greece," January 6, 1948, *FRUS 1948*, IV, pp. 2–7.

[63] Henderson to Secretary of State, January 9, 1948, *FRUS 1948*, IV, pp. 9–14.

[64] Wittner, *American Intervention in Greece*, p. 238. Wittner's discussion of this bureaucratic battle is well done and has guided my own analysis here.

[65] PPS/18, "United States Policy with Respect To Greece," January 10, 1948, Nelson, ed., *SDPPSP 1948*, pp. 27–33.

Reflecting the influence of Kennan's advice, Lovett reported Marshall's view that the document "dealt in too abstract terms with the dispatch of troops; and that it contained no adequate appraisal of the likely consequences of the action envisaged." For Marshall, there would need to be a clear definition of what combat forces sought to do and what forces would be required to do it before serious consideration could be given to dispatching them.[66] Given Marshall's prestige it is hardly surprising that the other NSC members accepted his view. They directed that the NSC Staff rework NSC 5 in light of the Policy Planning Staff's report and the discussion at their meeting.[67] Kennan's counterattack had met with success and his position now held the field.

The bureaucratic battle was by no means over, however. Henderson was nothing if not relentless and when a second draft of the NSC document (NSC 5/1) on Greece appeared on February 2, which reflected the views of Kennan and the Planning Staff, he criticized its failure to "decide now that, with the consent of the Greek Government, [the United States] will send troops to Greece if necessary to prevent Greece from falling under Soviet domination."[68] But the tide was running against the NEA director. The military evinced no enthusiasm for intervention in Greece and the Joint Chiefs of Staff continued to make it clear that such action probably would necessitate a partial mobilization.[69] American officials also feared getting bogged down in Greece when dangerous situations also existed in Italy and Palestine. At a meeting on February 12 the NSC, with Marshall in attendance, approved a paper on Greece which called for "strengthening the present U.S. Assistance program to Greece, using all feasible means short of the application of U.S. military power."[70] Truman approved the paper the next day and directed that it be implemented.[71] With this presidential decision the prospect of sending combat troops to Greece declined markedly, although characteristically Henderson refused to end his advocacy of this step.[72]

[66] Marshall's views as reported by Lovett are recorded in Kennan Memorandum, Meeting of the National Security Council, January 13, 1948, *FRUS* 1948, IV, p. 27. Also see Minutes of the 5th Meeting of the NSC, January 13, 1948, Truman Papers, PSF, Box 203.

[67] For the NSC's decision see NSC's Record of Actions No. 22, January 13, *FRUS* 1948, IV, p. 28. This can also be found in Truman Papers, PSF, Box 191.

[68] Henderson's views of February 10, 1948, are included in editorial note, *FRUS* 1948, IV, pp. 39–41.

[69] Defense Secretary Forrestal reported this at the NSC meeting, February 12, 1948, Minutes of 6th Meeting of NSC, Truman Papers, PSF, Box 203.

[70] NSC 5/2, "The Position of the United States with Respect to Greece," February 12, 1948, *FRUS* 1948, IV, pp. 46–51. For the discussion at this meeting see Minutes of the 6th Meeting of the NSC, February 12, 1948, Truman Papers, PSF, Box 203.

[71] For Truman's approval see his signature dated February 13, 1948, on Souers memorandum attached to NSC 5/2, February 12, 1948, Truman Papers, PSF, Box 203.

[72] On Henderson's continued support for the use of force see Wittner, *American Intervention in Greece*, pp. 238–39. The final blow to committal of combat troops came on April 1, 1948, when the Joint Chiefs of Staff concluded that the dispatch of American troops to Greece would

Following the debate over committing combat troops Kennan's involvement on the Greek issue lessened.[73] But he gave full support to the variety of measures which the United States executed in 1948 to sustain the Greek government, including the sizable financial support which enabled the Greeks to increase greatly their security forces. He welcomed the appointment, at Marshall's suggestion, of Major General James A. Van Fleet to command the American advisory group in Greece and approved this capable soldier's effort to instill in the Greeks "the will to win."[74] At no point did Kennan favor any compromise with the Communist forces. In May 1948 he told Marshall that "the problem in Greece is merely one of cessation of aggression and does not call for discussion or negotiation of any kind."[75] Final victory did not come easily, but bitter and costly fighting in 1948 paved the way for the final crushing of the insurrection in 1949. The objective that Henderson and Kennan shared equally had been achieved. Greece had been denied to the Soviet sphere.[76]

The suppression of the Greek insurgency resulted, as John Iatrides has demonstrated well, from a combination of political, military, domestic, and foreign factors. The Tito-Stalin split and the subsequent abandonment of the insurgents by the Yugoslavs hurt the Greek Communists severely. But ultimately the American support for the Greek government enabled it to emerge victorious. Without this assistance, "the insurgents might have continued to harass the government almost indefinitely."[77] Such crucial assistance to the Greeks did not result specifically from the recommendations of George Kennan and the Policy Planning Staff. They were merely a part of the broad consensus which favored assistance to the Greek government in order to stem the perceived Soviet tide. From the time of the Truman Doctrine onwards American officials unwaveringly agreed that the United States should exercise its power to preserve a non-Communist government in Greece. The question

---

be "militarily unsound." JCS memorandum quoted in John O. Iatrides, ed., *Greece in the 1940s*, p. 215. Also see NSC 5/3, May 23, 1948, and the reference to NSC 5/4, June 4, 1948, both in *FRUS* 1948, IV, pp. 93–95, 101.

[73] While it lessened, it did not end. The Planning Staff considered questions related to Greece in April and May of 1948. See Minutes of Meetings, April 30, May 20 and 24, 1948, PPS Records, Box 32. Toward the year's end Gordon Merriam of the Planning Staff completed a "Report on U.S. Aid to Greece" evaluating the effectiveness of U.S. efforts. See PPS 44, November 24, 1948, *FRUS* 1948, IV, pp. 195–203.

[74] On Van Fleet's appointment and Marshall's instruction to him to instill in the Greeks the "will to win" see Pogue, *George C. Marshall: Statesman*, p. 398.

[75] Kennan to Marshall, May 12, 1948, PPS Records, Box 33.

[76] The consequences of the American actions in Greece are beyond the purview of this study. Not surprisingly opinions vary considerably. Wittner argues that "by adopting a counterrevolutionary orientation, the U.S. government facilitated the dominance in Greece of conservative, reactionary, even fascist elements." See Wittner, "American Policy in Greece," in Iatrides, ed., *Greece in the 1940s*, p. 237. William Hardy McNeill adopted a more positive view of American assistance in his *Greece: American Aid in Action, 1947–1956* (New York, 1957).

[77] Iatrides, ed., *Greece in the 1940s*, pp. 216–19.

the policymakers faced was how to obtain this goal. Here Kennan played an important part in determining the nature and scope of the American assistance. When a snowballing sentiment to commit American armed forces developed he placed the effective obstacles in its path. With Marshall's support and the general reluctance of the military to extend its overseas commitments, Kennan blocked this proposal. The significance of this step is difficult to gauge, but one only needs to imagine the implications of a scenario in which American troops fought and died in Greece in 1948 to appreciate that it was of real consequence.

In his "X" article Kennan had called for "the adroit and vigilant application of counterforce at a series of constantly shifting geographic and political points."[78] Greece represented an interesting test case for Kennan and his recommendations there suggest conclusively that his preference in implementing containment was for political and economic measures over direct American military involvement. The Planning Staff Director believed that "the use of U.S. regular armed forces to oppose the efforts of indigenous Communist elements within foreign countries must generally be considered as a risky and profitless undertaking, apt to do more harm than good."[79] Kennan, however, was quite prepared to utilize the threat of application of U.S. military power in the hope that this might cause the Russians to restrain local Communist forces.[80] And, as we shall see, in what he perceived as desperate circumstances, he even recommended U.S. military action. But Greece was not the place. Nor was Palestine, an issue on which Kennan found himself allied to the redoubtable Henderson.

KENNAN AND THE RETREAT FROM PARTITION

In "The Resume of World Situation," which Kennan prepared for Marshall's use in early November 1947, he predicted that the Middle East was in for "a rocky time." The Palestine situation had been "badly fouled up" and violent conflict seemed likely. Such circumstances would present "favorable opportunities for the Russians to fish in muddy waters" which Kennan asserted "they would exploit to the limit."[81] Kennan's sense that the Middle East held such dangerous potential prompted him to arrange for the appointment to the Planning Staff of a Near-East specialist. He selected Henry Serano Villard, apparently on the recommendation of Loy Henderson who described Villard as possessing "a lot of courage in his quiet way."[82] In communicating with

[78] "X" [Kennan], "The Sources of Soviet Conduct," p. 576.

[79] See PPS/23, "Review of Current Trends in U.S. Foreign Policy," February 24, 1948, *FRUS 1948*, I, p. 519.

[80] Ibid.

[81] PPS/13, "Resume of World Situation," November 6, 1947, *FRUS 1947*, I, p. 775.

[82] Oral History interview with Carlton Savage, June 22, 1978. Savage did some of the intermediary work on this appointment and Henderson's description of Villard was made to him.

Henderson Kennan had noted "the highly crucial nature of the things which are happening in the area handled by your office," and expressed the need to have someone on the Staff "who is familiar with your problems and your thoughts and who has your personal confidence."[83] Villard, who served as Henderson's deputy in NEA during 1946–1947, certainly possessed these qualifications. By the time the Policy Planning Staff came to give detailed consideration to the Palestine question after the UN partition vote, he was established as the member who gave Kennan most assistance in this area.

The Policy Planning Staff began work on its paper for the NSC on the Palestine question in early December and worked intensively on the subject over the next two weeks. Villard advised Kennan that "Arab passions and feelings of nationalism which have been aroused by the UN [partition] decision will seriously damage U.S. prestige in the area." The harmful consequences for the U.S. would serve Soviet policy. Furthermore Villard, after referring to the Soviet opportunity to introduce Communists and fellow travelers amidst the expected increase in immigration to Jewish Palestine, raised the rather fantastic specter of "a Communist dominated Jewish state in Palestine within the next year or two."[84] On December 9 Colonel William Eddy, who recently had returned from a visit to Saudi Arabia, Syria, Lebanon, and Palestine, briefed the Staff. He reported to Kennan and his colleagues of the deep Arab bitterness against the United States and attributed this to the Arab sense that U.S. support of partition came "as a blow from a friend." Eddy suggestively commented that if the United States henceforth pursued a strictly neutral policy in the Arab-Jewish dispute, then, after some years, it might regain its favored position in the Arab world.[85] He inferred that the United States should avoid any involvement with the implementation of partition which the Arabs planned to oppose. Eddy's views added support to those of his superiors in the defense establishment including the Joint Chiefs of Staff, who as early as October made clear their opinion that involvement in the Palestine controversy was disadvantageous to American national security.[86] Kennan and his Staff appreciated this position and also were cognizant of the CIA analyses claiming that partition would require military enforcement.[87]

By December 17 Kennan completed a draft paper which outlined two alter-

[83] Kennan to Henderson, August 27, 1947, PPS Records, Box 33.

[84] Villard to Kennan, "Comment on Paper on Soviet Policy," December 5, 1947, PPS Records, Box 23.

[85] For Eddy's comments see Minutes of Meeting, December 9, 1947, PPS Records, Box 32. For a more extensive report of Eddy's views see "The Future of US-Arab Relations," December 10, 1947, which CIA Director Hillenkoetter passed to Admiral Leahy (who noted that the president read it), in Truman Papers, Naval Aide Files, Box 13.

[86] For reference to the JCS decision see Leahy diary, October 10, 1947, Papers of William D. Leahy, Library of Congress, Box 5.

[87] CIA, "The Consequence of the Partition of Palestine" (ORE 55) November 28, 1947, Truman Papers, PSF, Box 254.

native recommendations, both of which represented a substantial retreat from partition. The first proposed referring the Palestine problem back to a special session of the UN General Assembly at which the U.S. might either offer a " 'middle of the road' " solution or suggest a UN trusteeship for Palestine. The second simply proposed that in light of the impossibility of implementing the Palestinian partition, no steps should be taken to that end. The United States would oppose sending UN troops to enforce partition and would maintain its own arms embargo on Palestine.[88] In either case Kennan sought to distance the United States from the UN partition scheme upon which the Jewish hopes for a sovereign state rested. Kennan subjected his draft paper to the critique of his Staff colleagues and also consulted with Loy Henderson and Dean Rusk. Rusk refrained from endorsing the Staff paper while Henderson—"the arch-enemy of Zionism"—welcomed the Staff's conclusions which reflected his own views on partition.[89]

On January 20, 1948, Kennan shared his views on Palestine with a wider audience within the administration, especially Marshall and Lovett. The paper (PPS/19), written while Kennan juggled his involvements on the Greek and other issues, focused on Palestine in light of the security interests of the United States. Kennan and his colleagues revealed no sympathy for the Jewish aspirations for a national homeland and gave no indication that either the Holocaust or the dislocation and suffering of Jewish refugee survivors of that dastardly crime weighed in their calculations. At issue for them was the national interest of the United States—control of the eastern Mediterranean and the Suez Canal; securing the supply of oil from the Middle East, the increased amount of which was crucial to the success of the Marshall Plan in Europe; the maintenance of stability in and good relations with the Arab states, deemed crucial in limiting Soviet influence in the region. The Staff document reviewed the situation in the Middle East paying special attention to the Arab determination to resist partition and to the antagonism which the Arabs would bear for the United States if it attempted to enforce it. The Soviet Union's capacity to exploit the situation created by the partition proposal also received substantial attention. In an alarming portrayal, the Staff concluded of any attempt to enforce partition that "so numerous would be the ramifications of mounting Arab ill will, of opening the door to Soviet political or military penetration, and of generally chaotic conditions in Palestine and neighboring countries that the whole structure of peace and security in the Near East and Mediterranean

[88] A draft of this paper (501.BB Palestine/12-1747) is in the State Department files. This draws from the section of it published in *FRUS* 1947, V, pp. 1313–14.

[89] For the further Staff consideration of the paper on Palestine see Minutes of Meetings, December 18 and 19, 1947, and January 5, 12, and 19, 1948, PPS Records, Box 32. The Staff met with Henderson and Rusk on December 19. For the description of Henderson see Bain, *The March to Zion*, p. 185.

would be directly and indirectly affected with results impossible to predict at this stage in detail but certainly injurious to U.S. interests."[90]

Having contested the workability of partition and surveyed its deleterious strategic consequences for the United States, the Staff moved to its recommendations for American policy. Most fundamentally it opposed any further initiative to implement or to aid partition. This departure point led on to further steps—opposition to the dispatch of armed forces, American or otherwise, to Palestine to implement partition; and the maintenance of the arms embargo. Kennan and his colleagues advised that the United States should distance itself from the problem and "divest" itself of "the imputation of international leadership in the search" for its solution. Kennan expected that future events would make clear that partition was not viable at which point he suggested the United States might then recommend that the matter be returned to the UN General Assembly where other options such as a federal state or a trusteeship might be explored.[91] Through his policy recommendations Kennan aimed to ensure that the United States refrained from getting involved in a Palestinian quagmire in some futile attempt to implement partition. He sought to cement American security interests, as he saw them, by distancing the U.S. from endeavors to create a Jewish state in Palestine. Kennan held membership in what Robert Donovan has referred to as the "school within the Department of State and the Pentagon" which held that "war in the Middle East and loss of Arab friendship would be too high a price to pay for a Jewish state."[92]

The reaction to Kennan's paper varied considerably. Marshall avoided direct comment and he and Lovett continued publicly to support the General Assembly recommendation on partition. Lovett on receiving the Staff paper indicated to Kennan that it was not of real use. Kennan recalls that Lovett commented that he had hoped the Planning Staff would come up with "something different." The politically attuned under secretary hoped, in fact, that the Staff might chart a way out of the international and domestic political conundrum in which the Truman administration found itself.[93] But Kennan's stance closely resembled Henderson's which Truman's political advisers found so troubling as they faced the prospect of a tough election contest in 1948. Nonetheless, the Planning Staff's recommendations instigated a new

[90] pps/19, Report by the pps on "Position of the United States with Respect to Palestine," January 19, 1948, *FRUS* 1948, V, pp. 546–54.

[91] Ibid., pp. 553–54. Remarkably, Kennan and the Planning Staff framed their recommendations as beneficial to Jews throughout the world, including the United States. pps/19 argued that "in the U.S., the position of Jews would be gravely undermined as it becomes evident to the public that in supporting a Jewish state in Palestine we were in fact supporting the extreme objectives of political Zionism, to the detriment of overall U.S. security interests."

[92] Donovan, *Conflict and Crisis*, p. 371.

[93] Author's interview with Kennan, March 6, 1989.

debate within the administration on partition and moved the State Department to weaken its support for it.

Dean Rusk, now director of the newly created Office of United Nations Affairs (UNA), raised objections to the Staff paper on Palestine alleging that it lacked the completeness to serve as a basis for the major change in policy that it recommended. After severely criticizing British behavior in Palestine, Rusk questioned the Planning Staff's criticisms of the viability of the partition plan. Always enamored of utilizing the United Nations, Rusk considered that the verdict remained to be delivered on this point. In such a situation he considered it wise for the State Department to take steps to support the General Assembly resolution.[94] Rusk neither wanted nor thought it possible that the U.S. could distance itself from the Palestine situation as Kennan advocated. Lovett respected Rusk's views on this matter and assigned them sufficient weight that he delayed approving the circulation of Kennan's report to NSC members because of the future Secretary of State's objections.[95]

Rusk's position and Lovett's decision predictably prompted an immediate response from Kennan. He sent Lovett on January 29 a detailed point-by-point commentary and critique of Rusk's memorandum, but aware of the inverse relationship between length of document and careful consideration by some readers he encapsulated his points in a brief cover letter. Kennan accused Rusk of seeking only temporary relief and of doing so at the expense of American relations with the British and the Arabs and "at the cost of further involvement in commitments leading toward international enforcement of the [UN] Palestine decision." The Planning Staff director advised that the respite obtained by continuing to support partition would be brief and he raised the possibility that such continued U.S. support would lead to a point where the United States held "major military and economic responsibility for the indefinite maintenance by armed force of a *status quo* in Palestine fiercely resented by the bulk of the Arab world." Kennan then argued that the American public would not approve such action which led him conveniently back to his position against further U.S. involvement on the issue while extricating itself from existing commitments. For Kennan it was a "clear-cut issue of policy" and the sooner a decision was taken the better.[96] This constituted a forceful and effective retort to Rusk and with Henderson also weighing in against the UNA director momentum gathered in the State Department to move formally away from

[94] Memorandum by Rusk to Lovett, January 26, 1948, *FRUS* 1948, V, part 2, pp. 556–61. On Rusk's position see Schoenbaum, *Waging Peace and War*, pp. 166–69.

[95] For reference to PPS/19 being held up by Rusk's objections to it see Minutes of Meeting, January 28, 1948, PPS Records, Box 32.

[96] Memorandum of Kennan to Lovett (PPS 19/1), January 29, 1948, with attached Annex A, "Personal Comments by Mr. Kennan on Mr. Rusk's Memorandum of January 26, 1948," January 29, 1948, *FRUS* 1948, V, part 2, pp. 573–81.

support for the partition plan.[97] This sentiment met with the approval of Defense Secretary Forrestal, the Joint Chiefs of Staff, and the analysts in the CIA, all of whom held deep reservations concerning the partition plan.[98]

Marshall and Lovett moved cautiously, however. They refused permission for the Staff's paper to go forward for NSC consideration in its existing form.[99] Upon Lovett's request the Planning Staff reworked it to outline a range of alternatives which the United States might pursue along with an estimate of their consequences. This was ready by February 11 and Marshall approved its distribution to the NSC for consideration but made clear that its status was that of a working paper and that it did not represent the State Department's position.[100] In a clear demonstration of the sensitivity of the issue and of his own caution, when Marshall outlined the courses of action reviewed in the revised Staff paper at a meeting of the National Security Council on February 12 he made very clear that none of them had his approval as yet.[101] The revised PPS document placed three possible choices before Marshall and his NSC colleagues: (a) full support for partition, including the use of armed force; (b) a passive approach, with no further steps to aid or implement partition; and (c) a reversal of support for partition, while seeking through the UN to formulate a new solution such as a federal state with Jewish and Arab areas or some form of international trusteeship.[102] The Staff's analysis favored the third option. Disastrous strategic consequences ruled out the first. The passivity option was judged to be domestically unacceptable and, furthermore, it would consign the Middle East to chaos and "undermine any possible future intervention on legal or moral grounds in Greece or Italy." While the final option would provoke the Zionists, it would attract Arab support, assist the U.S. to regain is strategic position, and thereby serve the national interest and strengthen American national security.[103]

[97] For Henderson response to Rusk, February 6, 1948, *FRUS* 1948, V, part 2, pp. 600–603. The NEA director told Rusk that "The Palestine Partition Plan is manifestly unworkable. I think that with each passing day our task will be rendered more difficult and that by mid April general chaos will reign in Palestine." For a further exposition of Henderson's views, as he recalled them for William Quandt some two decades later, see Henderson to Quandt, April 11, 1969, Henderson Papers, Library of Congress, Box 11.

[98] For Forrestal's views and those of the JCS, as expressed by Gen. Gruenther, Forrestal's diary, January 24, 1948, Forrestal Papers, quoted in *FRUS* 1948, V, p. 633. On Forrestal's opposition to Zionism see also Grose, *Israel in the Mind of America*, pp. 260–61. For an example of the CIA's analysis see "Possible Developments in Palestine" (ORE 7-48), February 28, 1948, Truman Papers, PSF, Box 255.

[99] For Kennan's report on their refusal see Minutes of Meeting, February 9, 1948, PPS Records, Box 32.

[100] See Butler to Lovett, February 11, 1948, and the attached PPS/21, "The Problem of Palestine," February 11, 1948, *FRUS* 1948, V, part 2, pp. 619–25.

[101] Forrestal diary entry, February 12, 1948, in Millis, ed., *The Forrestal Diaries*, pp. 371–72.

[102] PPS/21, "The Problem of Palestine," p. 622.

[103] Ibid., pp. 624–25.

The real decision on U.S. policy apparently rested with Marshall. Uneasy ¬ with the domestic political considerations influencing the president, especially the pressures exerted by the American Jewish community, on February 19 the secretary of state met with him and received an assurance that "whatever course we considered the right one we could disregard all political factors."[104] Marshall then told Truman that a statement was being prepared for the U.S. Ambassador to the United Nations, Warren Austin, to make in the Security Council. The preparation and content of this statement marked the secretary of state's decision to move towards the third option favored by the Policy Planning Staff. With Lovett now taking personal responsibility for policy formulation on this matter in order to prevent leaks which would ignite a fierce Jewish reaction, a draft statement was prepared for Austin's delivery. This statement repeated American support for partition but held that the UN had no responsibility to enforce it. The Austin statement was a preliminary step away from partition. In the memorandum to Truman, which accompanied the draft of Austin's statement, the State Department conveyed its expectation that upon the UN Security Council's recognition of the collapse of partition the U.S. would request the UN General Assembly to reconsider the whole matter. Some form of trusteeship would be necessary.[105] Truman endorsed Austin's speech and in doing so, as Bain has noted, "he authorized a major change in U.S. policy which constituted a subtle but decisive step away from the partition resolution."[106]

At this point it seemed evident that Kennan and the Policy Planning Staff had played an influential role in modifying American policy in the Middle East. This modification took on an even firmer character in the ensuing weeks. ↲ After Austin's speech at the UN on February 24 only the Soviet Union and the Ukraine demonstrated any enthusiasm for partition. Marshall and Lovett decided to take the additional steps already foreshadowed to Truman. Marshall informed the president on March 5 that, upon recognizing its inability to proceed with partition, the Security Council should refer the Palestine problem back to the General Assembly. The State Department recommended that the U.S. now announce its support for the establishment of a trusteeship over Palestine. On March 8, Truman approved the new policy and Marshall thereupon instructed Austin to announce it at the United Nations which the ambassador did on March 19.[107]

The Austin announcement sparked an enormous outcry. Just the day before Austin spoke, Truman, after yielding to the request of his old friend and former business partner Eddie Jacobsen, met with Chaim Weizmann and assured

[104] Memorandum from Marshall to Lovett, February 19, 1948, *FRUS* 1948, V, p. 633.

[105] State Department to President Truman, February 21, 1948, *FRUS* 1948, V, pp. 637–40.

[106] Bain, *The March to Zion*, p. 188.

[107] These events are described in greater detail and with appropriate documentation in Bain, *The March to Zion*, pp. 189–90.

the Jewish leader there would be no change in American support for partition.[108] Charges of State Department perfidy and presidential pusillanimity and confusion were liberally aired. Truman affected bewilderment at the policy reversal.[109] He supposedly told Clark Clifford that Marshall and Lovett "have made me out a liar and a double-crosser," a presidential accusation that kindly might be labeled as unfair.[110] The president, upset at the domestic and international criticism leveled at him, quickly backed away from support for the trusteeship scheme and this proposal foundered unceremoniously. At a press conference on March 25, at which he faced a barrage of questions, Truman emphasized his continued support for partition while casting the trusteeship proposal as merely a transitory measure offered in an effort to avert violence. State Department plans to reverse American support for the UN partition plan, which Kennan had played such an important role in framing and promoting, withered quickly.

Following the trusteeship debacle Truman essentially let events take their own course. The State Department now focused its efforts mainly on obtaining a cease-fire in Palestine where Jewish-Arab clashes escalated. In the White House an increasingly assured Clifford, intent on strengthening Truman's appeal to Jewish voters in the upcoming presidential campaign, worked to get the arms embargo lifted so as to facilitate greater support for the Israelis.[111] And the White House counselor effectively laid the groundwork for early recognition of the state which Jewish leaders reaffirmed their determination to establish in the Promised Land as soon as the British mandate ended. In these circumstances Kennan played no further role. Indeed, Marshall himself largely backed away from dealing with Palestine matters, although he opposed the immediate recognition of Israel. In the end the secretary left it to the more

[108] Donovan, *Conflict and Crisis*, pp. 373–75, has good description of Jacobsen's efforts to persuade Truman to see Weizmann. These ended with Truman telling his old friend: "You win, you bald-headed son of a bitch. I will see him." For Jacobsen's own account of his activities see his letter of Dr. Josef Cohn which covers events from February 20 to June 1, 1948, in Chaim Weizmann Archives, Rehovoth, Israel, held in Truman Library, Box 1.

[109] Truman told his Staff meeting on March 20 "that he never knew anything about the intention to take this action yesterday and learned of it only this morning." One staff member in attendance confided to his diary that the president "seemed shocked and depressed. He has repeatedly in the past asserted the determination of the United States to stick by its decision and to support the United Nations." Diary entry, March 20, 1948, Papers of Eben Ayers, HSTL, Box 16.

[110] Clark Clifford, "Factors Influencing President Truman's Decision to Support Partition and Recognize the State of Israel," p. 36. Clifford outlined here the qualifications Truman made prior to giving his approval to the Trusteeship proposal. See pp. 35–36. Lovett's defense of the State Department is included in Humelsine to Marshall, March 22, 1948, *FRUS* 1948, V, part 2, pp. 749–50. Fair-minded accounts of the whole episode are provided by Herbert Feis in *The Birth of Israel: The Tousled Diplomatic Bed* (New York, 1969), pp. 51–59; and Donovan, *Conflict and Crisis*, pp. 372–79.

[111] Clifford, "Memorandum on Conference on Palestine," March 24, 1948, Truman Papers, PSF, Box 184. On Clifford's political efforts see Donovan, *Conflict and Crisis*, p. 380.

phlegmatic Lovett, a consummate negotiator, to work with Clifford on the statement granting diplomatic recognition to Israel which the White House released on May 14, 1948, some sixteen minutes after that state had come into existence.[112] Israel's army thereupon proceeded to implement partition and to secure the existence of the state they subsequently have defended and expanded.

The creation of the Israeli state drew the Policy Planning Staff back to the issue. On May 17, Kennan and the Staff members decided to examine the implications of the situation in light of the termination of the British mandate.[113] Kennan, who refused to disguise his anger and shock at the course of U.S. policy, wrote Marshall on May 21 conveying the Staff's deep apprehensions at the continuing direction of this policy. He warned that the course the United States now pursued could lead it to assume "major responsibility for the maintenance and security of a Jewish state in Palestine" and could bring the U.S. "into a conflict with the British over the Palestine issue." In rather hyperbolic terms he warned that such actions not only would threaten American national interests in the Middle East and Mediterranean but also "disrupt the unity of the western world and . . . undermine our entire policy toward the Soviet Union." Additionally the "disintegration of the United Nations" was a possibility.[114] Marshall and Lovett held a less extreme assessment of the consequences of American support for Israel but they agreed that the Staff might prepare a paper for the NSC on the subject.[115] The State Department planners expended substantial effort on this project through June of 1948, but eventually their total irrelevance to policy determination on this issue dawned upon them.[116] In July Kennan ended their endeavors to frame a long-term policy for Palestine.[117]

Kennan's efforts to derail American support for the partition of Palestine met with some initial success. He proved instrumental in convincing Marshall and Lovett to move away from partition and to support a trusteeship arrange-

[112] Clifford notes Lovett's role in Clifford et al., *The Palestine Question in American History*, p. 41. On the decision-making involved in the recognition of Israel see Cohen, *Palestine and the Great Powers*, pp. 379–90.

[113] See Minutes of Meetings, May 6, 14, and 17, 1948, PPS Records, Box 32.

[114] Kennan to Marshall, May 21, 1948, *FRUS* 1948, V, part 2, pp. 1020–21.

[115] For Lovett's view to which Marshall indicated his assent see Lovett to Marshall, May 21, 1948, *FRUS* 1948, V, part 2, pp. 1021–22. George Butler announced the PPS intention to prepare a paper on Palestine and sought Marshall's approval in Butler to Marshall and Lovett, June 3, 1948, PPS Records, Box 31.

[116] On the work of the PPS see Minutes of Meetings, June 2, 7, and 11, 1948, PPS Records, Box 32.

[117] Gordon Merriam, who replaced Villard as Middle East expert on the Staff in April, reported to his Staff colleagues on July 12 that Kennan had "said that short-term developments now occurring so rapidly left no basis on which to attempt at this time to develop a long-term policy paper on Palestine." Minutes of Meeting, July 12, 1948, PPS Records, Box 32. Merriam did in fact continue to work on a paper on U.S. policy towards Israel but it was never presented.

ment. But on this issue persuading Marshall did not suffice to guarantee the adoption of Planning Staff recommendations as the policy of the Truman administration. The White House rather than the State Department played the determining role. Ultimately, President Truman, under the weight of domestic political pressures, refused to go along with his diplomats' advice and Kennan's work came to naught. Truman's decision owed more to humanitarian and political considerations than to the dispassionate appraisal of American strategic interests upon which Kennan founded his recommendations. Questions of morality and justice did not really enter into Kennan's calculations. Jewish aspirations for statehood and the tragic experiences of persecution that impelled them left him unmoved. He demonstrated neither particular concern for Holocaust victims nor, for that matter, displaced Palestinians.[118] His actions found their roots in a concern to avoid costly American military commitments in Palestine and to block Soviet penetration of the Middle East. From our present vantage point, we might conclude that Kennan overstated the negative strategic consequences of Israel's establishment; but, this said, it must be appreciated that his views were sincerely held and honorably offered. Imputations of anti-Semitism on his part as a motivating force are grossly unfair, indeed scurrilous.[119] His recommendations on Palestine/Israel reveal a detachment, indeed coldness, to painful and tragic human realities but this attitude emerged from his geopolitical approach to the world. Notably the very same concern that principally motivated his actions in Italy and Greece also operated in Palestine. That concern—to block the expansion of the Soviet sphere—prompted a renewed and uncharacteristic intervention on his part in Italy around the time his real influence on the Palestine question came to an end.

KENNAN'S PANIC

Having helped develop the policy of vigorous support for the Italian government in the latter part of 1947, Kennan's day-to-day involvement on this issue declined somewhat in the early months of 1948 as he focused on other issues and as the Office of European Affairs under John Hickerson maintained firm control of policy. Of course, the planning chief continued to consider the preservation of non-Communist control of Italy as vital and he watched with approval as the United States beefed up its aid to the De Gasperi government.[120] Even with the increased assistance, anxiety for Italy did not appreciably diminish and by February Washington moved Italy back to the forefront of its

[118] Bain makes this criticism of the State Department in general. See *March to Zion*, p. 200.

[119] Kennan referred to such imputations in interview with author, March 6, 1989.

[120] For details on the supply of U.S. equipment to the Italian armed forces see the report, "Provision of U.S. Equipment to the Italian Armed Forces," January 16, 1948, *FRUS* 1948, III, pp. 757–62.

security concerns. On February 10, 1948, the NSC staff issued an update of the policy paper on Italy (NSC 1/1) which confronted policymakers with two alarming prospects—the first had the PCI securing control of the Italian government following victory in the elections scheduled for April, while the second had the Communists mounting an armed insurrection following their defeat in these elections. Either the ballot box or the barrel of a gun would serve as instruments to establish the Communists in Rome. The new document reaffirmed that the United States would make full use of its political, economic and, if necessary, military power to prevent Italy falling under Soviet domination.[121] It presaged an open campaign to blunt the PCI challenge.[122]

Into this already tense situation the events in Prague in late February came as a lightning bolt. Although Kennan had predicted a Communist coup in Czechoslovakia, Klement Gottwald's toppling of President Eduard Benes on February 25 and the subsequent assassination of the respected non-Communist foreign minister Jan Masaryk shocked the West. The actions of the Czech Communists were viewed as establishing a precedent that might be followed in cases like Italy.[123] In response, the Truman administration, agitated further by a "war alert" issued by General Clay on March 5, stepped up its efforts to defeat the PCI. On March 8 the National Security Council met again and it authorized (in NSC 1/3) secret operations by the CIA in Italy, including covert funding of the Christian Democrats and Saragat's Socialists, and covert arms shipments.[124] Additional overt actions followed—support for further interim aid to Italy, assurances that efforts would be made to keep the disputed port city of Trieste in Italian hands, threats to cut off all assistance to Italy if the Communists were elected, and a major propaganda campaign.[125]

Kennan played no significant role in designing these actions although his concern for Italy ran deep. As the Italian situation entered the climatic month prior to the election he found himself away from Washington on a trip to consult with General Douglas MacArthur in Japan. George Butler ran the Plan-

[121] NSC 1/2, "The Position of the United States with Respect to Italy," February 10, 1948, FRUS 1948, III, pp. 765–69. Miller provides more discussion in The United States and Italy, p. 246. On the likelihood of the Communists resorting to civil war if they lost see also CIA, "The Current Situation In Italy," February 16, 1948, Truman Papers, PSF, Box 255.

[122] Miller gives details in his "Taking Off the Gloves: The United States and the Italian Elections of 1948," pp. 45–47.

[123] Leffler makes this point in "The United States and the Strategic Dimensions of the Marshall Plan," p. 288.

[124] NSC 1/3, "Position of the United States with Respect to Italy in the Light of the Possibility of Communist Participation in the Government by Legal Means," March 8, 1948, FRUS 1948, III, pp. 775–79. On the efforts of the CIA see William R. Corson, The Armies of Ignorance: The Rise of the American Intelligence Empire (New York, 1977), pp. 298–301; Tom Braden, "The Birth of the CIA," American Heritage (February 1977), p. 13; and Robin W. Winks, Cloak and Gown: Scholars in the Secret War, 1939–1961 (New York, 1987), pp. 382–87, which focuses on the role of the CIA's man in Italy, James Jesus Angleton.

[125] Miller, "Taking Off the Gloves," pp. 47–50.

ning Staff in Kennan's absence but he made every effort to keep his absent chief informed of Italian events. Other Planning Staff members, most regularly Villard, stood in for Kennan at the staff level discussions of the NSC which laid the groundwork for NSC 1/3.[126] Like Kennan they considered Italy vital to western security and their sense of the urgency of the situation deepened following a briefing on March 1 for them by Arnold Wolfers, professor of international relations at Yale. Wolfers, who had just returned from a trip to Italy during which he interviewed all the principal actors, told the Staff that the Italian election was crucial for all of Europe. "If Italy goes Red," the distinguished academic held, "Communism cannot be stopped in Europe."[127] The likelihood that Italy would go "Red" appeared to increase as March progressed. On March 10 Ambassador Dunn cabled Marshall of "deepening anxiety and pessimism on the part of the non-Communist elements." He mentioned reports of "hedging" by the normally anti-Communist middle and upper classes, including the flight of capital and preparations to emigrate.[128] These communications of impending PCI victory struck a raw nerve on the Policy Planning Staff director lodged on the other side of the globe.

On March 15 Kennan, now in Manila on his way home, decided to try to influence policy by long distance. He communicated to Marshall and Lovett that, while the Russians were "basically over-extended in eastern Europe," this had prompted their apparent urgent determination to "break [the] unity of western Europe and disturb the ERP pattern." The Soviets, in his view, needed to do this in order to maintain their grip on eastern and central Europe, "because resulting material contrast, added to the incurable desire of all eastern and central European peoples to be considered part of western civilization" would bode ill for long-term Russian control. The upshot was that a dangerous, new element existed. Italy held the key position. If the Communists won the election there, America's whole position in the Mediterranean, and also in western Europe, would probably be undermined. Kennan feared that the PCI would secure victory through intimidation and in these circumstances he argued against elections being held. From this analysis Kennan moved directly to his policy recommendations which, to put it mildly, were not framed to appeal to the faint-hearted. He suggested that the Italian government should "outlaw [the] Communist Party and take strong action against it before [the] elections." This would provoke the Communists to civil war which would give the U.S. grounds to reoccupy Foggia fields and other military facilities.

[126] For indications that the Planning Staff was considering the draft of NSC 1/3 see Minutes of Meetings, March 3, 4, 5, and 6, 1948, PPS Records, Box 32.

[127] For Wolfers' briefing the PPS see Minutes of Meeting, March 1, 1948, PPS Records, Box 32. For a fuller statement of the Yale professor's views see Memorandum by Major-General S. E. Anderson, March 2, 1948, in Records of Office of Western European Affairs Relating to Italy, RG 59—Records of Department of State, Box 4.

[128] Dunn to Marshall, March 10, 1948, *FRUS* 1948, III, pp. 845–46.

The result would be "much violence and probably a military division of Italy; but," Kennan concluded, "we are getting close to the deadline and I think it might well be preferable to a bloodless election victory, unopposed by ourselves, which would give the Communists the entire peninsula at one coup and send waves of panic to all surrounding areas."[129]

Kennan's extraordinary recommendations went nowhere. Although Butler loyally reported to Staff members that he would take up Kennan's suggestions with Assistant Secretary Norman Armour, Hickerson dealt them an immediate and fatal blow.[130] The Office of European Affairs director made three points. Firstly, he agreed with Kennan that outlawing the Communist party would cause civil war. Next, he noted that the "non-Communist parties have a good chance of winning election without any such drastic steps," which allowed him to conclude, "therefore action recommended by GFK seems unwise. Instead, U.S. Gov[ernmen]t should do everything it properly can to strengthen non-Communist forces and parties."[131] Hickerson's way prevailed and with De Gasperi skillfully turning the April 18 election into a choice between "western democracy versus eastern totalitarianism"—a virtual "referendum on communism"—the Christian Democrats and their non-Communist allies emerged victorious, cementing themselves in power and bonding Italy firmly to the West. Talk of a Communist insurrection subsided.[132]

Kennan's suggestion to outlaw the PCI has received much more attention from historians than it deserves in terms of its actual impact on policy. It has been scrutinized by exegetes of Kennan's writings to shed light on what he meant by "counterforce" in the "X" article and how he intended to utilize military power in implementing containment.[133] However, one should appreciate that his Manila cable hardly constituted considered policy advice. It did not represent a new emphasis on military containment at the expense of the political and economic containment that he had long espoused. Kennan's recommendations, hastily conceived and poorly considered and so potentially calamitous in their consequences, must be put down to a panic of sorts on his part.[134] His fear of seeing Italy shift to the Soviet sphere and the dire consequence of this shift on the rest of Western Europe incited his advice. Ironically Hickerson, who would be Kennan's major bureaucratic opponent in the debate over the North Atlantic Treaty and who favored more explicitly military forms

[129] Kennan to Marshall, March 15, 1948, FRUS 1948, III, pp. 848–49.

[130] For Butler's commitment to take up Kennan's suggestions see Minutes of Meeting, March 15, 1948, PPS Records, Box 32.

[131] Hickerson's comment in FRUS 1948, III, p. 849.

[132] The first quotation is from Dunn to Marshall, March 10, 1948, FRUS 1948, III, p. 845; the second is from Miller, The United States and Italy, p. 248.

[133] Stephanson provides an interesting discussion in Kennan and the Art of Foreign Policy, pp. 97–100.

[134] William Taubman in Stalin's American Policy, p. 169, suggests that Kennan "nearly panicked."

of containment, deflected him on the Italian issue and ensured the application of the political and economic measures that Kennan himself preferred.

FATHER OF COVERT ACTION?

The Christian Democratic victory in Italy soothed some of Kennan's anxieties concerning the Soviet threat to the Mediterranean. It also provoked further consideration on his part of the most appropriate measures to turn back the Soviet challenge. The covert activities of the CIA impressed him and in May 1948, he recommended the creation of a permanent organization capable of undertaking the kind of missions that the CIA had performed in Italy on a rather ad hoc basis. His recommendation and his consequent involvement placed Kennan in the midst of the development of covert activities by the United States. His involvement in this area clarifies beyond question that his role was not that of a theorist detached from the making of foreign policy but that of central player in the national security apparatus.

Kennan early on demonstrated a concern with intelligence questions. In 1945 he had recommended large-scale, special intelligence efforts aimed at the Soviet Union.[135] In June of 1946 he labored briefly for General Hoyt Vandenberg and CIG. At this point he didn't suggest covert operations but calls for such activities were heard, especially from the influential Harvard historian William Langer. In July 1946, Langer, the respected wartime head of the Research division of the Office of Strategic Services, argued "the case for funding 'covert activities' at a national intelligence authority meeting."[136] The first U.S. clandestine operations probably were initiated toward the end of 1946 but these apparently were of a minor nature and not part of a coherent program.[137] The passage of the National Security Act in 1947 transformed the CIG into the CIA and made it responsible to the National Security Council. Under its first director, Rear Admiral Roscoe Hillenkoetter, the agency initially concentrated on collection of intelligence, both overt and covert, and on the production of national current intelligence and national estimates.[138] Hillenkoetter

---

[135] Kennan to Secretary of State, September 30, 1945, *FRUS* 1945, V, p. 885.

[136] See Trevor Barnes, "The Secret Cold War: The C.I.A. and American Foreign Policy in Europe, 1946–1956. Part I," *The Historical Journal* (June 1981), p. 405. Anne Karalekas, "History of the Central Intelligence Agency," Senate Select Committee to Study Governmental Operations with Respect to Intelligence Activities (Church Committee), *Final Report*, Book IV (Washington, D.C., 1976), p. 26, notes that in 1946 Secretary of War Robert Patterson also suggested covert action.

[137] This is the conclusion of Trevor Barnes, a careful researcher, in "The Secret Cold War," p. 405.

[138] The literature on the CIA is huge. On its foundation see Braden, "The Birth of the CIA," pp. 4–13; Karalekas, "History of the Central Intelligence Agency," pp. 1–41; Ray S. Cline, *Secrets, Spies and Scholars: Blueprint of the Essential CIA* (Washington, D.C., 1976), pp. 81–106. Also of value are two recently declassified internal histories completed as part of a CIA history series:

displayed no desire to take on the operational functions necessary to wage the covert "psychological warfare" against the Soviet Union that a chorus of policymakers led by Forrestal demanded by the end of 1947. The CIA director, in fact, almost avoided the additional responsibility. The Defense Department wanted to assign all propaganda—including covert psychological warfare—to the State Department. Marshall objected, however, and argued vehemently against State's responsibility for covert action fearing that exposure of such activities would embarrass the department and discredit U.S. foreign policy.[139] Truman sided with his Secretary of State and on December 14 the National Security Council adopted a directive (NSC 4/A) which charged the CIA with covert psychological operations. On December 22, Hillenkoetter established the Special Procedures Group (SPG) in the CIA's existing Office of Special Operations (OSO) to execute this responsibility.[140] Over the next few months the SPG initiated some "limited and amateur" actions aimed at Central and Eastern Europe—unattributed publications, radio broadcasts, and the like.[141]

The SPG action in Italy constituted a qualitatively different action than these covert media activities and, characteristically, Hillenkoetter tried to avoid it. When Forrestal came and asked him if the agency would take up the cudgels and help defeat the PCI by interfering directly in the election campaign, the CIA chief sought advice from his general counsel, Lawrence Houston, who doubted the new organization had that legislative authority.[142] But under pressure from the defense establishment and with the president's approval, Hillenkoetter decided the CIA could undertake such covert actions when ordered to do so by the National Security Council. When such instructions came from the NSC, the Italian operation sprang into being and with such pleasing results to all involved in it—results so pleasing, that as one writer has observed, it prompted "a surge of American enthusiasm for covert operations as the weapon of choice in the back-alley struggles of the Cold War."[143] Kennan

Arthur B. Darling, *The Central Intelligence Agency: An Instrument of Government to 1950* (Washington, D.C., 1953), lodged in Modern Military Records, NA, Washington, D.C.; and Ludwell Lee Montague, *General Walter Bedell Smith As Director of Central Intelligence, October 1950–February 1953* (Washington, D.C., 1971) in Modern Military Records, NA. Darling's history is very sympathetic to Hillenkoetter. Montague spends the first part of his study challenging Darling's interpretation. John Lewis Gaddis in "Intelligence, Espionage, and Cold War Origins," *Diplomatic History* (Spring 1989), pp. 191–212, provides an excellent overview of the effectiveness of U.S. and Soviet intelligence operations.

[139] This relies on Karalekas, "History of the Central Intelligence Agency," pp. 27–28.

[140] Karalekas, "History of the Central Intelligence Agency," p. 28; Darling, *The Central Intelligence Agency: An Instrument of Government to 1950*, chap. 7, pp. 32–39.

[141] Karalekas, "History of the Central Intelligence Agency," p. 29.

[142] On this see Braden, "The Birth of the CIA," p. 13; and Corson, *The Armies of Ignorance*, pp. 294–99.

[143] Thomas Powers, *The Man Who Kept the Secrets: Richard Helms and the CIA* (New York, 1979), p. 31.

channeled this enthusiasm into support for his recommendation that the U.S. develop a permanent covert political action capability.

Kennan's recommendation took shape in the latter days of April. On May 3 he, his Staff colleagues, and a number of senior department officials, among them Bohlen and Henderson, discussed a memorandum he had completed on April 30 examining the "inauguration of organized political warfare."[144] After obtaining the general approval of the group Kennan took it forward to the NSC consultants for discussion. He proposed that the State Department, but more specifically the Policy Planning Staff, oversee "a 'directorate' for overt and covert political warfare." While the State Department would guide the new group, the latter, along with its concealed funds and personnel, would not be associated with it in a formal way.[145] After some modification by the consultants, Kennan's proposal went to the NSC which on June 18 endorsed it as NSC 10/2, "a directive authorizing a dramatic increase in the range of covert operations directed against the Soviet Union, including political warfare, economic warfare, and paramilitary activities."[146]

NSC 10/2 established the Office of Special Projects, soon renamed the Office of Policy Coordination (OPC), to undertake the increased array of covert actions which it envisaged.[147] Although technically located within the CIA, the CIA director possessed little control over OPC which operated independently from the rest of the agency. In a reflection of Kennan's influence, the NSC directive gave the secretary of state authority to name the OPC director who would receive policy guidance from designated representatives of the secretaries of state and defense, known as the 10/2 panel. OPC "was to be an instrument of policy, not an instigator."[148] Eager to exercise a determining role over the policies implemented by OPC, Kennan proposed himself as the State De-

---

[144] Minutes of Meeting, May 3, 1948, PPS Records, Box 32. The Staff had earlier discussed covert activities in a meeting focused on the establishment of "Freedom Committees." In a meeting with other State Department officials on April 9 at which Kennan was absent, "many serious questions were raised as to the practicability and advisability of undertaking the covert activities envisaged in this paper, and it was generally agreed that further study should be given to this subject." Minutes of Meeting, April 9, 1948, PPS Records, Box 32.

[145] All this relies on Karalekas, "History of the Central Intelligence Agency," p. 29; and Darling, *The Central Intelligence Agency: An Instrument of Government to 1950*, chap. 7, pp. 40–46.

[146] Karalekas, "History of the Central Intelligence Agency," p. 29. Barnes, "The Secret Cold War," pp. 413–14, is also helpful in comprehending the formulation of NSC 10/2. He notes the role of Allen Dulles.

[147] NSC 10/2, "National Security Council Directive on Office of Special Projects," June 18, 1948, may be found in Thomas H. Etzold and John Lewis Gaddis, eds., *Containment: Documents on American Foreign Policy and Strategy, 1945–1950* (New York, 1978), pp. 126–27. For a thoughtful discussion of the system established by NSC 10/2 see Corson, *Armies of Ignorance*, pp. 303–5.

[148] Cline, *Secrets, Spies and Scholars*, p. 103.

partment representative. Marshall, in yet another indication of regard for his planning chief, appointed him forthwith. Kennan thereby extended his tentacles further through the national security system and secured for himself a part in planning the covert action program that the United States implemented in 1948–1949.

In view of the later excesses of the CIA Kennan came to regret his involvement in the development of the agency's covert capability and assessed it as "the greatest mistake I ever made," but in 1948 such remorse lay well into the future.[149] Once the National Security Council approved NSC 10/2 Kennan actively participated in its implementation and ensured that his prerogatives as State Department representative were guaranteed. In discussions with Hillenkoetter and Souers in August 1948, Kennan stated that he would need "to have specific knowledge of the objectives of every operation and also the procedures and methods employed in all cases where those procedures and methods involved political decisions."[150] Kennan claimed the responsibility to decide which individual projects were politically desirable. The political warfare activity would be conducted as an instrument of U.S. foreign policy and Kennan hoped to man the controls.

In September Marshall appointed Frank Wisner, then serving as Deputy Assistant Secretary of State for Occupied Areas, to direct OPC. Wisner, a Mississippian and a graduate of the University of Virginia law school, had served during the war in OSS in Istanbul, as station chief in Rumania, and finally as Allen Dulles's wartime deputy.[151] He relished his new position and quickly established OPC as an operating concern moved by his visceral opposition to the Soviets and the absence of any of Hillenkoetter's caution about covert actions. Kennan welcomed the appointment of Wisner whom he knew well and, in marked contrast to most of his other bureaucratic colleagues, met socially at the Bohlens or at Joseph Alsop's. In the early days of OPC their relationship was a close one, although Kennan later would criticize Wisner's proclivity to pursue unsound schemes.[152]

Kennan's new responsibilities in the intelligence domain meant some change in the operation of the Policy Planning Staff. The Staff remained Ken-

---

[149] Kennan interview with author, March 6, 1989. See also his testimony before the Church Committee, October 28, 1975, quoted in Karalekas, "History of the Central Intelligence Agency," p. 31. For Kennan's own account of the development of covert capabilities, which tends to downplay his own role, see Memoirs, II, pp. 202–3.

[150] Kennan quoted in Karalekas, "History of the Central Intelligence Agency," p. 30. For an account which is critical of the leading role which Kennan seized see Darling, The Central Intelligence Agency: An Instrument of Government to 1950, chap. 7, pp. 61–66.

[151] On Wisner see Sig Mickelson, America's Other Voice: The Story of Radio Free Europe and Radio Liberty (New York, 1983), pp. 14–15; Winks, Cloak and Gown, p. 54; and Powers, The Man Who Kept the Secrets, pp. 91–97, which examines the tragic end of his career.

[152] Kennan interview with author, March 6, 1989.

nan's support unit and so inevitably it also became caught up to some extent in the intelligence oversight work. John Davies eventually would play a role in advising on intelligence operations, especially in the Far East.[153] To obtain full-time assistance in the intelligence area Kennan brought Robert P. Joyce, a Foreign Service officer and good friend of his, to the Staff at the end of 1948.[154] Joyce, a Yale graduate who had served as an oss agent in Yugoslavia and then as the political officer at Allied Supreme Headquarters for the Mediterranean Theater, acted as Kennan's deputy in liaison work with opc.[155] He also gave Kennan special advice on intelligence operations in the East European area. Prior to the Korean War this region received the most attention from opc and, as we shall see, Kennan contributed to a number of covert operations, some of which recently have attracted bitter criticism.[156]

Kennan was not pulled reluctantly into the shadowy world of secret operations. His embarrassment about the later behavior of the Central Intelligence Agency has led him to minimize the role he expected opc to play. In testimony before the Church Committee on the Intelligence Activities of the United States Kennan recalled that he and his associates who conceived opc "thought that this would be a facility which could be used when and if an occasion arose when it might be needed. There might be years when we wouldn't have to do anything like this."[157] But Kennan approached covert actions with enthusiasm in 1948 and does not appear to have made apparent any sentiment on his part that covert operations would be limited in scope. Nor did he display any reservations concerning the extralegal character of much of what opc would undertake. The end of stemming the Soviet tide justified these new means. And not only did he play the central role in conceiving opc but he ensured that he would be involved in supervising its activities. He entered fulsomely into the pursuance of political warfare against the Soviet Union and developed a taste for intelligence work that lingered long after he departed from the Policy Planning Staff, although in fairness to Kennan his later involvements were mainly

[153] On some of the cia's Asian actions see William M. Leary and William Stueck, "The Chennault Plan to Save China: U.S. Containment in Asia and the Origins of the cia's Aerial Empire, 1949–1950," *Diplomatic History* (Fall 1984), pp. 354–57.

[154] Joyce attended his first Staff meeting in December 1948, see pps Records, Box 32. The Kennans and the Joyces were friends socially. Mrs. Kennan confided to Joseph Alsop that it was "a great addition to Washington to have them back." She also mentioned that the Joyces spent Christmas (of 1948) with them at the farm. See Annelise Kennan to Joseph Alsop, Alsop Papers, Box 4.

[155] On Joyce see Winks, *Cloak and Gown*, pp. 220, 355, 396; and Interview with James McCargar, Washington D.C., February 28, 1990.

[156] See for example Christopher Simpson's *Blowback: America's Recruitment of Nazis and Its Effects on the Cold War* (New York, 1988). The actions of Kennan and Joyce in this area are dealt with in chapter 6 on "Titoism, Eastern Europe and Political Warfare."

[157] Kennan testimony, October 28, 1975, quoted in Karalekas, "History of the Central Intelligence Agency," p. 31.

in the area of intelligence analysis.[158] He turned down an offer from Allen Dulles in 1953 to join the CIA.[159]

"No Fruits Have Dropped"

To comprehend the evolution of American foreign policy in the early years of the Cold War an appreciation of the uncertainty and anxiety that gripped policymakers is essential. The pressures and fears they worked under should not be dismissed simply as exaggerated by those who benefit from decades of hindsight. Rather, they should be acknowledged for the authenticity with which they were held and, indeed, for their legitimacy. The Communist challenges in Greece and Italy should not be lightly dismissed even though their direct connection to the Kremlin might have been limited. The mood of the period may be gauged by the title of article by Joseph and Stewart Alsop in the *Saturday Evening Post*, "If Russia Grabs Europe," which asked "what will we do if the Kremlin controls the Continent?"[160] Policymakers like Kennan labored feverishly to ensure that this question remained theoretical. By mid-year of 1948 Kennan, for one, believed that they largely had succeeded in their efforts. In the letter he wrote but never sent to Walter Lippmann, Kennan asked the columnist to compare the situation in April 1948 with that of a year earlier. In 1947 Kennan observed that "it was almost impossible to see how Europe could be saved." As of 1948 he argued, with Greece and Italy no doubt in mind, that while "Europe is admittedly not over the hump . . . no fruits have dropped." Western Europe could pursue its recovery in a climate of "new hope."[161]

Kennan contributed notably to this favorable circumstance for the United States. Tracing his involvement affords the opportunity to view the development of American policy. In the cases of Greece, Italy, and (at least, for the State Department) Palestine, a fundamental concern to prevent the expansion of the Soviet sphere or Soviet influence provided the raison d'être for action. But, it is crucial to understand, this gave policymakers only a disposition, a

---

[158] The Office of National Estimates of the CIA had an outside panel of consultants to evaluate draft estimates. In 1950 Kennan began his service on this group—known as the "Princeton Consultants" because they met at the Princeton Gun Club—which also included Hamilton Fish Armstrong and Vannevar Bush. See Karalekas "History of the Central Intelligence Agency," p. 19; In 1956 Wisner contacted Kennan for advice on how to utilize the Khrushchev speech to the Twentieth Party Congress which the CIA had obtained. See, Winks, *Cloak and Gown*, p. 413. Kennan also involved himself vigorously in the work of the CIA-funded Congress for Cultural Freedom during the fifties. See Peter Coleman, *The Liberal Conspiracy: The Congress for Cultural Freedom and the Struggle for the Mind of Postwar Europe* (New York, 1989).

[159] Kennan, *Memoirs*, II, p. 176–77.

[160] Joseph and Stewart Alsop, "If Russia Grabs Europe," *The Saturday Evening Post*, December 20, 1947, p. 15.

[161] Kennan to Lippmann, draft letter, April 6, 1948, Kennan Papers, Box 17.

way of looking at issues. It did not provide guidance on what exactly to do. Actual policies emerged from the bureaucratic process in which Kennan participated so vigorously. He mixed it up well with his colleagues, disagreeing with Henderson on dispatching combat troops to Greece, with Rusk over the implementation of partition in Palestine, and, to a lesser extent, with Hickerson on the outlawing of the Communist party in Italy. Looking at these three episodes gives the lie to notions that the United States possessed a coherent strategy by this point. In the Palestine instance, other factors overwhelmed strategic concerns. Greece and Italy possessed similarities but policy for each was determined somewhat independently. Grasping the individual character of each episode of policy-making is essential in discerning how the Truman administration gave meaning to the notion of containment. There were no tested methods for implementing containment. The instruments were seized on in a rather haphazard manner as the adoption of political warfare and covert operations illustrates. By mid-1948 momentum had built to respond to the perceived Soviet threat in a more explicitly military manner. As always, Kennan found himself in the midst of the debate.

CHAPTER FOUR

The North Atlantic Treaty

BEVIN'S INITIATIVE

The North Atlantic Treaty holds a position of unquestioned importance in the history of postwar American diplomacy. Signed in Washington, D.C., on April 4, 1949, by the representatives of twelve European and North American countries, this Treaty—and the organization, NATO, formed to give substance to its guarantees—proved a cornerstone of American foreign policy. The United States agreement to the Treaty formally marked a new epoch in the nation's foreign policy, for not since 1800, when it disengaged itself from its French alliance, had the American government been bound in peacetime by a treaty of alliance. The North Atlantic Treaty provided the crucial foundation for transatlantic security and stands among the principal accomplishments of the Truman administration.[1] Tracing the evolution of the Treaty and identifying its architects affords a clearer view of the process of making foreign policy and, of course, it clarifies Kennan's role in this process.

The initial stimulus for the North Atlantic Treaty came not from the Truman administration nor even from an American, but from British Foreign Secretary Ernest Bevin. Tough and realistic, the former trade union leader held few illusions about the Soviet Union. Like other leaders of the British Labour Party he refused to forget the Nazi-Soviet pact.[2] He recognized quickly the danger of Soviet expansionism, and upon the failure of initial efforts aimed at accommodating the Soviets, he swung the Labour Party behind a firm approach, despite the carping criticism of some Labour left-wingers led by Richard

---

[1] On the origins of the North Atlantic Treaty see Lawrence S. Kaplan, *The United States and NATO: The Formative Years* (Lexington, Ky., 1984); Timothy P. Ireland, *Creating the Entangling Alliance: The Origins of the North Atlantic Treaty Organization* (Westport, Conn., 1981); Alan K. Henrikson, "The Creation of the North Atlantic Alliance, 1948–1952," *Naval War College Review* 32 (May–June 1980): 4–39, and Parley W. Newman, Jr., "The Origins of the North Atlantic Treaty: A Study in Organization and Politics," Ph.D. diss., Columbia University, 1977. See also the accounts of three participants—a Canadian, an Englishman, and an American, respectively—in the Treaty's formulation: Escott Reid, *Time of Fear and Hope: The Making of the North Atlantic Treaty, 1947–1949* (Toronto, 1977); Sir Nicholas Henderson, *The Birth of NATO* (London, 1982); and Theodore C. Achilles, "U.S. Role in Negotiations that Led to Atlantic Alliance," parts 1 & 2, *NATO Review* 27 (August & October 1979): 11–14, 16–19.

[2] Donald Cameron Watt makes the point that "the hostility and suspicion shown by the British Labour leadership towards the Soviet Union had been a consistent element in their thinking on international matters since the Nazi-Soviet pact." See his *Succeeding John Bull: America in Britain's Place, 1900–1975* (Cambridge, 1984), p. 120.

H. S. Crossman and Michael Foot.[3] Bevin knew instinctively that the Soviet Union under Stalin constituted an inveterate enemy to the democratic socialist parties of Europe. When in late September of 1947 the Soviets and eight other European Communist parties, including the French and Italian, established the Cominform—an organization devised by Moscow to control more tightly local Communist parties—and embarked on a course of political warfare, Bevin felt confirmed in his views.[4] Perhaps he did not foresee in all its tragic detail—the arrests, persecutions, purges, liquidations—the movement to one-party totalitarian regimes wherever the Red Army held sway, but he grasped the central reality and acted to prevent the further imposition of Communist dictatorships beyond the line Churchill had described graphically as the Iron Curtain.[5]

By late 1947 Bevin, his outlook now dominated by an acute perception of the Soviet threat, considered it essential to construct some form of defensive system in Western Europe.[6] Upon the collapse of the London Council of Foreign Ministers in December 1947 Bevin broached this broad subject to Secretary of State Marshall. He vaguely proposed "not a formal alliance, but an understanding backed by power, money and resolute action," which would serve to guarantee West European security and would prevent the Soviets from filling the power void in Europe.[7] Bevin's deliberately vague proposal initiated the series of discussions and negotiations leading to the signing of the North Atlantic treaty and the eventual formation of NATO.

---

[3] Bevin's endeavors to line up the Labour Party behind his firm approach and his conflict with the so-called "Keep Left" group is discussed in Wayne Knight, "Labourite Britain: America's 'Sure Friend'? The Anglo-Soviet Treaty Issue, 1947," *Diplomatic History* 7 (Fall 1983): 267–82.

[4] On the establishment of the Cominform and its initial declaration see Taubman, *Stalin's American Policy*, pp. 172, 176–78.

[5] Bevin's concern must have been deepened by the vicious Communist assaults on the nontotalitarian left—kindred spirits to him ideologically—in Eastern Europe. For a contemporary account that outlines the frightful fate of the democratic socialists of Eastern Europe (Poland, Hungary, Czechoslovakia) see Denis Healey, ed., *The Curtain Falls: The Story of the Socialists of Eastern Europe* (London, 1951).

[6] Lord Gladwyn, *The Memoirs of Lord Gladwyn* (London, 1972), pp. 208–9. Bevin, as Escott Reid notes, was influenced in his thinking by Gladwyn Jebb. Reid, *Time of Fear and Hope*, p. 68. Bevin's thinking at this time can be traced in more detail in Bullock's biography but also see Ritchie Ovendale, *The English-Speaking Alliance: Britain, the United States, the Dominions and the Cold War, 1945–1951* (London, 1985), pp. 66–68; Richard A. Best, Jr., *"Co-operation with Like-Minded Peoples": British Influences on American Security Policy, 1945–1949* (Westport, Conn., 1986), pp. 150–54; and Ray Merrick, "The Russia Committee of the British Foreign Office and the Cold War, 1946–47," *Journal of Contemporary History* 20 (July 1985): 453–68. Attention to Bevin's role in such works has been part of the "tidal wave of publications [which] has appeared on Britain and the Cold War" over the last decade. For an insightful discussion of this literature see Bert Zeeman, "Britain and the Cold War: An Alternative Approach. The Treaty of Dunkirk Example," *European History Quarterly* 16 (July 1986): 341–67.

[7] British memorandum of conversation, undated, *FRUS* 1947, II, pp. 815–16. Also note the Oral History Interview with John D. Hickerson by Richard D. McKinzie, November 10, 1972; January 26 and June 5, 1973, HSTL, transcript pp. 52–54.

Having mentioned his ideas in general terms to Marshall, Bevin moved next to give them more concrete form and to obtain the endorsement of his Cabinet colleagues for them. In early January 1948 he laid before the Cabinet a memorandum entitled "The First Aim of British Foreign Policy," which clearly conveyed his views and deserves to be quoted at length. The Labour Foreign Secretary argued that

> it must be recognized that the Soviet Government has formed a solid political and economic block behind a line running from the Baltic along the Oder, through Trieste to the Black Sea. There is no prospect in the immediate future that we shall be able to re-establish and maintain normal relations with European countries behind that line . . .
>
> In the situation in which we have been placed by Russian policy halfmeasures are useless. If we are to preserve peace and our own safety at the same time, we can only do so by the mobilization of such a moral and material force as will create confidence and energy on the one side and inspire respect and caution on the other. The alternative is to acquiesce in continued Russian infiltration and helplessly to witness the piecemeal collapse of one Western bastion after another.

Bevin admitted that "we shall be hard put to it to stem the further encroachment of the Soviet tide" but went on:

> It is not enough to reinforce physical barriers which still guard our western civilization. We must organize and consolidate the ethical and spiritual forces inherent in this western civilization of which we are the chief protagonists. This in my view can only be done by creating some form of union in Western Europe, whether of a formal or informal character, backed by the Americas and the Dominions.[8]

After gaining Cabinet approval for his proposal on January 8, Bevin—who emerges as a principal architect *and* builder of the Western response to the Soviet Union—resumed his efforts to engage the United States in his plans.[9]

The Policy Planning Staff's involvement in the origins of the North Atlantic Treaty differed from its initial contribution to the Marshall Plan because this treaty originated in a European (Bevin's) proposal and because the Europeans, especially the British, helped to define the subject and to shape the character and content of most of the discussions. Moreover, the continuous exchanges and actual negotiations which took place with the Europeans in conjunction with and as part of the American process of policy determination meant that the issue, whatever its long-term implications, was one not only of planning but also of operations. As a consequence Kennan and the Staff received no exclusive charge from Marshall to develop American policy on this issue.

---

[8] "The First Aim of British Policy," January 4, 1948, C.P. (48) 6, CAB 129/23, quoted in Best, *"Co-operation with Like-Minded Peoples,"* pp. 151–52.

[9] On Cabinet approval see Best, *"Co-operation With Like-Minded Peoples,"* p. 154.

From the outset other groups within the State Department, most notably the Office of European Affairs headed by John Hickerson, helped shape the American response.

Marshall tellingly turned to both Kennan and Hickerson for their views of Bevin's proposals which were conveyed by the British Ambassador in Washington, Lord Inverchapel, on January 13. In a covering letter Inverchapel reported that Bevin continued his efforts to create a "Western Union" and intended to propose that Britain and France jointly offer bilateral treaties to Belgium, Holland, and Luxembourg along the lines of the Treaty of Dunkirk of March 1947, in which Britain and France had agreed to come to each other's defense in the case of renewed German aggression. Such treaties seemingly would be aimed at Germany but in reality their main target would be the Soviet Union. This move comprised the initial step in Bevin's larger plan to construct a "Western democratic system," with the backing of the Americas and the Dominions, which would include not only the five treaty nations but also Scandinavia, Italy, Greece, perhaps Portugal, and, when circumstances permitted, Spain and Germany. Bevin, in seeking "assurance of salvation" from the "Communist peril" strove for the "consolidation of Western Europe." He did not, either in this proposal to Marshall or in his famous speech to Parliament on January 22, suggest a formal alliance—especially in the form of a multilateral defense pact—nor did he request direct American participation. He proposed a more vague "understanding" to be backed by "power, money and resolution." But his aim was clear—to halt Soviet infiltration and "the piecemeal collapse of one Western bastion after another."[10]

KENNAN VERSUS HICKERSON

John D. (Jack) Hickerson sympathized with Bevin's objectives from the very first. An energetic and outgoing Texan, the head of the Division of European Affairs had been present at the London CFM with Marshall and, at the secre-

---

[10] British Ambassador to the Secretary of State, January 13, 1948 (enclosing "Summary of a Memorandum Representing Mr. Bevin's Views on the Formation of a Western Union), *FRUS* 1948, III, pp. 3–6. For Bevin's speech to Parliament on January 22, 1948, see *Parliamentary Debates*—House of Commons, 5th Series, vol. 446 (London, 1948), pp. 386–411. Some historians have interpreted the North Atlantic Treaty as primarily a means to soothe French security concerns regarding Germany but this was not Bevin's central concern. The significance of Bevin's actions should not be underestimated. Richard Best has argued insightfully that "Bevin's grand design for the free world as anticipated in his cabinet memoranda and in his speech to the House of Commons represents a major turning point in postwar history." As Best points out: "in the historiography of the period it has been given little attention, while buckets of ink have been expended on explications of the Truman Doctrine and Churchill's speech at Fulton. Yet Bevin's policy, as first publicly set forth in January 1948, was perhaps much more significant." This was because "the creation of the Western European Union by the Treaty of Brussels of March 1948 was a direct result of Bevin's initiative; Brussels was NATO in embryo." See Best, *"Co-operation with Like-Minded Peoples,"* p. 156.

tary's instruction, had scouted out further details on Bevin's proposal. He was soon convinced of the need for some form of collective defense arrangement and he diligently and skillfully proceeded to work to secure it.[11] Hickerson had joined the Foreign Service in the 1920s but in 1931 he transferred to the civil service and thereafter remained in Washington serving mainly in the Division of West European affairs. During the war he bore responsibility for British Commonwealth Affairs where his commitment to strong Anglo-American relations never wavered.[12] Such attitudes predisposed him to be receptive to the Bevin initiative. In fact his deputy, Theodore C. Achilles, recalled that Hickerson, well lubricated with "fishhouse punch," told him on New Year's eve 1947 at the Metropolitan Club, "I don't care whether entangling alliances have been considered worse than original sin since George Washington's time. We've got to negotiate a military alliance with Western Europe in peacetime and we've got to do it quickly."[13]

With some advance notice of Bevin's thinking Hickerson wasted no time in responding to Marshall's request for comments on the proposals Inverchapel conveyed on January 13. Just six days later he reported to Marshall that Bevin's objective was "magnificent." But he described the first step—the extension of the Dunkirk Treaty—as "highly dubious." Hickerson had expended much thought on this question and deftly proposed as an alternative a regional collective security pact modeled on the Treaty of Rio de Janeiro. He contended quite openly that American adherence would be required for such a pact to become effective.[14] He thereupon took an important step beyond Bevin in laying the conceptual foundation for the North Atlantic Treaty.

One day after Hickerson, Kennan replied to Marshall. Although in some doubt as to what the British had in mind, he welcomed the idea of a Western Union which would contribute to restoring the balance of power in Europe and he recommended that Marshall extend American sympathy to the undertaking. Like Hickerson Kennan criticized Bevin's proposal of treaties with the Benelux nations modeled on the Treaty of Dunkirk. But whereas Hickerson argued that it was the wrong approach to obtain the desired goal of a military alliance, Kennan opposed it because he objected to the actual goal itself. "Military union," he claimed, "should not be the starting point. It should flow from the political, economic and spiritual union—not vice versa." Kennan welcomed

[11] Author's interview with John D. Hickerson, Office of the Atlantic Council of the United States, Washington, D.C., July 8, 1978; and Oral History Interview with Theodore Achilles, HSTL, pp. 7–15.

[12] For details on Hickerson see Weil, *A Pretty Good Club*, p. 84; and Best, *"Co-operation With Like-Minded Peoples,"* p. 119.

[13] Achilles Oral History, HSTL. Despite arduous research I have not succeeded in determining the exact ingredients of fishhouse punch. I should like to thank Rev. Arthur S. Harvey, C.S.C., for his assistance on this matter.

[14] Hickerson to Secretary of State, January 19, 1948, *FRUS* 1948, III, pp. 6–7.

only this latter form of union reflecting his view that the Soviet threat in Europe was primarily political not military, that the principal danger resided in "stooge political elements" within West European countries not from direct ⌐military invasion, a view he proffered frequently to Marshall. Similar to his advice on the Marshall Plan, Kennan recommended that "the initiative must come from Europe" and that the Europeans should not "bother their heads" in the initial stage about the American relationship to the proposed Union.[15] His recommendation to Marshall grew out of the same broad strategic advice advocating the restoration of a balance of power in Europe which undergirded his support for the Marshall Plan.[16]

The replies from Hickerson and Kennan alerted the observant that on this matter the two men would be adversaries. Subsequently, Hickerson with notable singlemindedness molded the Office of European Affairs into an institutional bastion of support for a security pact in which the Americans would participate.[17] He self-consciously saw himself as leading the fight within the U.S. government for American membership in a collective defense arrangement. He possessed neither Kennan's broader view nor his close access to the secretary of state but he compensated by his finesse and stamina as a bureaucratic infighter. He constantly worked to build support for his position. In sharp contrast, Kennan tended to rely on the admittedly not inconsiderable force of his personality and on the persuasion of his own argument to win his case. He actually neglected to seek additional support for his position, a practice evident even in his relations with his Planning Staff colleagues. Kennan

[15] Kennan to Secretary of State, January 20, 1948, *FRUS* 1948, III, pp. 7–8. For Kennan's advice to Marshall on the nature of the Soviet threat see his Memoranda to the Secretary of State, January 6, 1948, and February 3, 1948, PPS Records, Box 33. In the January 6 memorandum Kennan stated bluntly his belief that it would be "a mistake for us to press for the creation of *major* military strength in the Western European area as a whole." His reasons were: "(a) It would strain the economic resources of the countries and divert them from other and more important tasks. (b) It could not be done without restoring Germany's armed strength. This was plainly undesirable. (c) It would mean mistaking the nature of the problem." On this last point Kennan reiterated his view that "the Soviet effort in Europe is a *political* one, not a *military* one." Kennan shared similar views with other audiences. On January 8, 1948, he told the Senate Armed Services Committee at a gathering in Secretary Royall's office that the Russian program "is a political program in which they do not expect to use military force on an international scale. It would be neither wise nor effective for us to attempt, except possibility in very exceptionable circumstances, to use our armed forces to combat these activities at this stage of the game. In many respects they are not susceptible to being combatted by armed force; and any failure on our part to recognize this fact might cause more harm than good." See "Preparedness As Part of Foreign Relations," January 8, 1948, Kennan Papers, Box 17. See also Kennan to Frank Altschul, February 2, 1948, Altschul Papers, File 113 a.

[16] PPS/13, "Resume of World Situation," November 6, 1947, *FRUS* 1947, I, p. 771. Kennan argued here that "our best answer . . . is to strengthen in every way local forces of resistance, and persuade others to bear a greater part of the burden of opposing communism. The present 'bipolarity' will, in the long run, be beyond our resources."

[17] See the oral history interviews with Hickerson and Achilles, HSTL.

extended his advice to Marshall on Bevin's proposal not on behalf of the staff but for himself. He failed to consult his staff colleagues formally on this issue and, as we have seen, it devoted most of its efforts during January of 1948 to the troubling question of Palestine.

In his *Memoirs* Kennan stated that he could not recall having anything to do with the American reply to Bevin's January 13 proposal. He suspected that the tenor of the reply was influenced by the views of John Foster Dulles, whom Marshall had taken on as an advisor in the interests of bipartisanship.[18] A close reading of the reply Marshall sent to Bevin through Inverchapel suggests Kennan is wrong on both counts for the secretary of state's response displayed the influence not of Dulles but of Kennan himself. Borrowing heavily from the language of Kennan's memorandum, Marshall welcomed European initiative on this issue and referred favorably to the proposed strengthening of material and spiritual links between the West European nations but he notably neglected to mention specifically military links and assumed that the whole question would be the subject of further study. Although not explicitly arguing against a military pact he gave it no endorsement and gave absolutely no intimation that the Americans would participate actively in such an endeavor.[19]

Marshall's cautious response proved sufficiently encouraging for the British and led them on to new attempts to involve the Americans more directly.[20] In the following days Inverchapel met with the ubiquitous Hickerson who extended encouragement and advice.[21] Hickerson always conducted himself with the utmost propriety and yet, in retrospect, it is apparent that the British government appropriately might have paid part of his salary so helpful was he to its interests. Coached by Hickerson Inverchapel next met with Under Secretary Lovett and relayed to him a suggestion from Bevin for a defense agreement between Britain and the United States to reinforce the proposed political and defense organization of Western Europe. He requested informal, secret discussions of this matter with the American government. The British now had revealed their true intention to seek some form of military alliance involving the United States as a guarantor of West European security. Immediately sensitive to the domestic political implications of such a proposal, Lovett drew back. He declined to agree even to the holding of informal conversations,

---

[18] Kennan, *Memoirs*, I, p. 398.

[19] Secretary of State to British Ambassador, January 20, 1948, *FRUS* 1948, III, pp. 8–9. Truman claimed that Marshall consulted with him and that he authorized this message. See Harry S. Truman, *Memoirs*, vol. 2: *Years of Trial and Hope* (Garden City, N.Y., 1956), p. 243.

[20] In tracing British policy one should appreciate the general point made by Donald Cameron Watt that from London's perspective the main feature of the immediate postwar years was "a desperate and frustrating effort to prevent the ebbing away of American interest, involvement and commitment to Europe." D. C. Watt, "Britain and the Cold War in the Far East," in Yonosuke Nagai and Akira Iriye, eds., *The Origins of the Cold War in Asia* (New York, 1977), p. 89.

[21] Memorandum of conversation by Hickerson, January 21, 1948, *FRUS* 1948, III, pp. 9–12.

stating that this question would require careful consideration by the National Security Council, the president, and the Congress.[22]

Lovett's reluctance temporarily deterred Bevin but the British statesman already had his hands full with the Anglo-French proposals to the Benelux countries. The policymakers in these three countries led by the capable Belgian Prime Minister Paul-Henri Spaak rejected Bevin's Dunkirk Treaty approach of separate bilateral defense treaties. Instead, they successfully counter-proposed a regional arrangement established under Articles 51 and 52 of the United Nations and modeled on the Rio Treaty. Following a series of exchanges among the five nations in February and actual negotiations in early March a multilateral economic, cultural, and defense treaty—the Treaty of Brussels—was signed on March 17, thereby creating the Western Union.[23]

As these weighty events took place on the eastern side of the Atlantic, the Americans continued to grapple with the issue. Marshall and Lovett maintained their cautious response to further European solicitations and simply advised that the initiative must come from Europe and that the United States could not become involved directly.[24] On February 24, in an overall examination of American foreign policy problems, Kennan supported their cautious stand. He advised that encouragement be given to the European Union and saw that it might have beneficial effects in terms of the economic integration that the Marshall Plan advocated. But he recommended further study before reaching any position on American links to this Union.[25] Two days later he departed on his trip to Japan assuming, as he later recalled, "that the whole matter would remain open until my return."[26] It did not.

THE PLANNING STAFF MINUS KENNAN

Events in Europe, particularly the Communist coup in Czechoslovakia compounded by General Clay's warning on March 5 that "war may come with dramatic suddenness," reshaped the context in which decisions were made and convinced American policymakers of the inadequacy of the wait and see approach pursued to this point.[27] Truman's concern about Soviet expansion

[22] Memorandum of conversation by Lovett, January 27, 1948, *FRUS* 1948, III, pp. 12–14; and Inverchapel to Lovett, January 27, 1948, *FRUS* 1948, III, pp. 14–16.

[23] Lord Gladwyn, *Memoirs*, pp. 212–13. On the contribution of the United States, particularly of Americans outside the executive branch, to the conclusion of the Treaty, see Lawrence S. Kaplan, "Towards the Brussels Pact," *Prologue* 12 (Summer 1980): 73–86.

[24] See memorandum of conversation by Hickerson, February 7, 1948, *FRUS* 1948, III, pp. 21–23.

[25] PPS/23 "Review of Current Trends in U.S. Foreign Policy," *FRUS* 1948, I, pp. 510–11.

[26] Kennan, *Memoirs*, I, p. 399.

[27] On Clay's warning see Clay to General Stephen G. Chamberlin, March 5, 1948, in Jean Edward Smith, ed., *The Papers of General Lucius D. Clay: Germany 1945–1949*, 2 vols. (Bloo-

deepened. At a briefing from Marshall on March 5 he scribbled a note to himself: "Will Russia move first? Who pulls the trigger? Then where do we go?"[28] In a forceful speech to Congress on March 17 the president called for the restoration of Selective Service to bolster the American military.[29] Meanwhile, and not surprisingly, Hickerson's discreetly incessant campaign within the State Department to gain American adherence to a treaty with the Europeans took on new force and directness. On March 8 in a memorandum to Marshall he called for the president and the National Security Council to consider "the possibility of U.S. participation in a North Atlantic-Mediterranean regional defense arrangement based on Articles 51 and 52 of the U.N. Charter and including initially Great Britain, France, Benelux and Italy," and he suggested consultations with representatives of these nations.[30] His well-planned efforts now produced results. With Truman's approval, Marshall wrote Inverchapel on March 12 requesting him to inform Bevin that the Americans were "prepared to proceed at once to joint discussions on the establishment of an Atlantic security system."[31]

The troubling events in Europe and the negotiations in Brussels also attracted attention from the Policy Planning Staff, now operating without its director. In a briefing to the Staff on March 1 Yale's Arnold Wolfers had stressed that Bevin's Western Union proposal would lack meaning if the proposed organization did not possess the military backing of the United States.[32] His remarks stimulated Staff members' interest and prompted action on their part. On March 3 they agreed to seek Lovett's approval for a Staff study of the problem of Western Union.[33] This gained, on March 8, George Butler, presiding over the group in Kennan's absence, assigned a new Staff member, Bernard Gufler, to get information on which to develop a paper from Hicker-

---

mington, Ind., 1974), II, pp. 568–69. For further details of the events in Europe see Henrikson, "The Creation of the North Atlantic Alliance," pp. 10–13.

[28] Truman's handwritten comments are attached to a Memorandum by Marshall of March 5, 1948. Here Truman outlined his principal requests of the Congress—"Pass E.R.P.—Universal [Military] Training & restore draft—Implement defense program." Then he gave a staccato history of postwar U.S.-Soviet relations—"Tehran, Yalta, Potsdam, Moscow, Paris, London, Rumania, Bulgaria, Hungary, Austria—Assets etc., Czechoslovakia, Finland, Turkey and Greece, Marshall, Plan, China, Korea"—before asking: "Shall we state the case to the Congress—name names and call the tune(?) Will Russia move first? Who pulls the trigger? Then where do we go?" Truman's handwritten note, March 5, 1948, Truman Papers, PSF, Box 154.

[29] Truman's speech of March 17, 1948, in Public Papers of the Presidents: Harry S. Truman, 1948 (Washington, D.C., 1964), pp. 182–86. For background on this speech and Truman's dinner speech of the same day to the Society of the Friendly Sons of St. Patrick in New York, in which he castigated Henry A. Wallace, see George Elsey memorandum to Clark M. Clifford, Elsey Papers, HSTL, Box 21.

[30] Memorandum by Hickerson, March 8, 1948, FRUS 1948, III, pp. 40–42.

[31] Secretary of State to Inverchapel, March 12, 1948, FRUS 1948, III, p. 48.

[32] Minutes of Meeting, March 1, 1948, PPS Records, Box 32.

[33] Ibid., March 3, 1948.

son's key assistant, Theodore Achilles.[34] Gufler had served in the State Department's Special War Problems division during World War II but then had
left it for a two-year stint as a stockbroker. He only recently had rejoined the
department and soon would be dispatched to the staff of Clay's Political Adviser in Berlin. On temporary duty with the Planning Staff he brought neither
special expertise nor strong views to this matter but simply served, as requested, as an information gatherer. A week after initiating its work on this
question the Staff met and discussed the Western Union issue. Achilles joined
them, and apparently with his prompting the Staff agreed that, because of the
urgency of the situation, this question should be given priority. The Staff's
willingness to seek information and counsel from Achilles suggests that it either did not fully appreciate or chose to ignore the fact that Kennan's view
differed fundamentally from that of Hickerson and Achilles. The Staff's discussion over the following two days revealed that its members viewed the
issue quite differently from their absent chief. It is not surprising that Kennan
remembers being "drawn up short, upon my return to the Department in April
1948, to realize how little I had succeeded in conveying to him [Butler] and
to the others my own view of what was and what was not needed in Europe at
that time."[35]

In framing its views on the American relationship to the Western Union, the
Planning Staff under Butler consulted widely. In a meeting on March 16, also
attended by Hickerson and Achilles among others, the Staff agreed that the
United States should not seek to join the Brussels Pact but should give it military backing. Furthermore, in the long run the United States should look forward to some pact of mutual assistance between itself and the Western European countries.[36] The discussion continued the next day at a Staff meeting
which brought together most of the senior officials of the department with an
interest in this matter—Norman Armour, the Assistant Secretary of State for
Political Affairs; Charles Bohlen, the Counselor; Hickerson, Achilles, and
Llewellyn E. Thompson from the Office of European Affairs; Loy Henderson
and Joseph C. Satterthwaite from the Office of Near Eastern and African Affairs; and Durward V. Sandifer from the Office of United Nations Affairs.
There was some disagreement over the Staff suggestion that the United States
propose a U.S.–Western Union mutual defense agreement within the framework of the United Nations Charter. In this proposed accord the contracting
parties would consider an armed attack against any one of them an attack upon
all of them and each would assist in countering the attack.[37] Presumably it was

[34] Ibid., March 8, 1948.
[35] George F. Kennan to author, April 23, 1979.
[36] Minutes of Meeting, March 16, 1948, PPS Records, Box 32.
[37] Ibid., March 17, 1948. A copy of the Planning Staff draft paper of March 17, 1948, on "The
Position of the United States with Respect to Western Union and Related Problems," is attached
to the minutes of that day.

Bohlen who disagreed with the suggestion, for when it was discussed further on March 19 by a similar group minus the Counselor a draft paper was readily agreed upon and prepared for Secretary Marshall.[38]

Butler submitted the Planning Staff report (PPS/27) concerning "Western Union and Related Problems" on March 23. Reflecting Hickerson's influence it advised against American participation in the Western Union but argued both for the "initiation of political and military conversations with members of the Western Union and other selected non-Communist states" and for "a mutual defense agreement under the Charter of the United Nations."[39] PPS/27 outlined the provisions such a treaty should contain including that an attack on one party would be considered an attack on all and would draw a response from all, that each party should determine for itself whether an attack within the meaning of the agreement had occurred, and that upon the determination of an attack all the parties should consult immediately to coordinate their efforts. These provisions, of course, resemble many of those found in the North Atlantic Treaty signed a year later and suggest the importance of the Planning Staff contribution. In similar manner to its work on the European Recovery Program, the Staff's role consisted in organizing and arbitrating among a number of ideas and suggestions to develop a coherent recommendation on the subject. In this case, however, none of the major ideas in the Staff's paper had its origins with the planners; but once adopted and shaped by them, the proposals gained added weight. The Staff report served as the basis for a formal American policy favoring a North Atlantic Treaty.[40] One day after receiving it, but without taking a position on it, Marshall sent it to Admiral Souers, NSC executive secretary, as a working paper for consideration by the NSC staff with a view to its possible approval by Council members.[41] The Planning Staff proposal, which in reality was a vehicle for Hickerson's ideas, thus entered the policy-making process beyond the State Department.

[38] Minutes of Meeting, March 19, 1948, PPS Records, Box 32. For Butler's discussion paper for this meeting which outlined the various proposals for support of Western Union, see *FRUS* 1948, III, pp. 58–59. Bohlen's disagreement is inferred because he opposed a defense treaty favoring instead "a unilateral United States declaration accompanied by the provision of military equipment by the United States." Reid, *A Time of Fear and Hope*, p. 106.

[39] PPS/27, "Western Union and Related Problems," March 23, 1948, *FRUS* 1948, III, pp. 61–64. Note that after submitting this paper the Planning Staff met separately with Dean Acheson and Leo Pasvolsky and requested their views on the subject. Both supported the Staff's ideas but warned that there should be congressional participation in the development of policy. Minutes of meetings, March 25, 1948 (144th and 145th meetings), PPS Records, Box 32.

[40] Two careful scholars, Cees Wiebes and Bert Zeeman, argue that "this report laid down future American policy." See Cees Wiebes and Bert Zeeman, "The Pentagon Negotiations, March 1948: The Launching of the North Atlantic Treaty," *International Affairs* 59 (Summer 1983): 351–63.

[41] Marshall's letter to Souers is not to be found in State Department files. For details of its contents see the reference to it in George H. Butler to Lovett, April 6, 1948, covering letter to PPS/27/1, PPS Records, Box 3.

TALKS WITH THE BRITISH AND THE CANADIANS

Just as the Planning Staff completed its paper on Western Union the joint discussions Marshall had agreed to hold with the British began in Washington. The Staff paper effectively served as a brief for the American delegation. By mutual consent the British and the Americans invited Canada to participate in these talks in order to involve directly another likely participant in a security pact and to obtain the invariably level-headed and helpful contribution of its diplomats.[42] The Americans declined, however, to involve the French at this point. They were deemed a security risk—ironic in light of Soviet spy Donald Maclean's membership in the British delegation—and also threatened to complicate and divert the discussions by introducing their deep-seated security fears concerning the Germans.[43] The delegates from the three countries met under great secrecy in the Pentagon where Major General Alfred Gruenther, director of the joint staff of the JCS, served as rapporteur. The composition of the delegations shifted slightly during the course of six meetings held from March 22 through April 1, but the primary participants were the American ambassador in London Lewis Douglas, Hickerson, Butler, and Achilles for the United States; Lord Inverchapel and Gladwyn Jebb from the Foreign Office for the British; and for the Canadians, Under-Secretary of State for External Affairs Lester Pearson and their ambassador in Washington, Hume Wrong.

Although the talks took place within the Pentagon complex where security and secrecy could be better maintained, civilian and military defense officials played but a minor role in formulating and representing the American position on this matter which laid the central foundation of Western defense for decades. The military were actively engaged in copious planning efforts of one sort or another but much of it simply was not influential in developing American foreign policy and defense commitments.[44] During much of 1948 the

---

[42] The Canadian involvement in and perspective on the formation of NATO is well covered in Reid's *Time of Fear and Hope*. See also James Eayrs, *In Defence of Canada: Growing Up Allied* (Toronto, 1980). The Canadian contribution came particularly in Article 2 of the eventual treaty—the idea that it should not be just a military alliance but should have a political, economic, social, and even spiritual character. This point is made by John Holmes in Peter Stursberg, ed., *Lester Pearson and the American Dilemma* (Toronto, 1980), pp. 63–64. Henrikson evaluates the Canadian contribution in "The Creation of the North Atlantic Alliance," pp. 17–18.

[43] Wiebes and Zeeman, "The Pentagon Negotiations, March 1948," p. 356.

[44] Melvyn P. Leffler outlines a great deal of this military planning in his "The American Conception of National Security and the Beginnings of the Cold War, 1945–48," *American Historical Review* 89 (April 1984): 346–81. John Lewis Gaddis correctly questions what impact this planning had on actual policy in his comment on Leffler's article in *American Historical Review* 89 (April 1984): 382–83. On the limits of the military's planning see the comment from Alexander L. George and Richard Smoke that "it is not a great exaggeration to say that for about five years after the end of the war, the United States and the West lacked any systematic strategy or theory

American military turned in upon itself in the so-called unification battle where the Army, Navy, and Air Force fought each other over allocations of functions, missions, and money.[45] An increasingly pressured Forrestal merely struggled to control the intense rivalries and jealousy among the services.[46] He brought little to the discussions which gave birth to the North Atlantic Treaty. Gruenther had Forrestal's confidence and undoubtedly kept the Secretary of Defense informed but that was largely it.[47] Nor did the Joint Chiefs of Staff offer substantive advice, although their reservations about American overcommitment were known.

At the initial meeting on March 22 the delegations considered three possibilities: (1) linking the United States and Canada to the Brussels Pact, (2) a new Atlantic alliance, and (3) a vague worldwide treaty based on Article 51 of the UN Charter.[48] With Hickerson guiding the American contribution the first and third proposals soon were dropped and attention concentrated on the second, an effort to create a Western Mutual Defense Pact.[49] Thereafter the delegates set about resolving some of the most difficult issues inherent in such an arrangement. They addressed the nature and obligations of the mutual assistance pledge (the crucial article 5 of the eventual treaty), examined the responsibilities of member states in situations of indirect aggression, and discussed questions regarding territorial scope and membership.[50] The Americans naturally drew from the Planning Staff document which, after all, reflected the ideas of delegates Hickerson, Achilles, and Butler. The British and Canadians dealt carefully with the Americans, appreciating well that the whole proposal depended on U.S. participation. By April 1 the parties agreed upon a joint paper recommending a collective defense treaty for the North Atlantic area. While some disagreements remained, this document outlined the essential elements of the western security pact.[51]

---

linking military planning to foreign policy objectives." See George and Smoke, *Deterrence in American Foreign Policy: Theory and Practice* (New York, 1974), p. 21.

[45] On this see Steven L. Rearden, *History of the Office of the Secretary of Defense: The Formative Years, 1947–1950* (Washington, D.C., 1984), pp. 29–43, 385–405.

[46] For a contemporary portrait of Forrestal see Hanson W. Baldwin, "Big Boss of the Pentagon," *New York Times Magazine*, August 29, 1948, pp. 9, 38–39.

[47] On the close working relationship between Forrestal and Gruenther see Oral History Interview with John H. Ohly by Richard D. McKinzie and Theodore A. Wilson, November 30, 1971, HSTL, transcript p. 29.

[48] On these proposals see Wiebes and Zeeman, "The Pentagon Negotiations, March 1948," pp. 353–54.

[49] For the minutes of these meetings see *FRUS* 1948, III, pp. 59–61, 64–67, 69–71. On these conversations see also Lord Gladwyn, *Memoirs*, pp. 214–16; and Lester B. Pearson, *Mike: The Memoirs of the Right Honourable Lester B. Pearson, 1948–1957* (New York, 1973), pp. 43–44.

[50] For discussion on each of these issues see Wiebes and Zeeman, "The Pentagon Negotiations, March 1948," pp. 357–61.

[51] The paper is included in the Minutes of the Sixth Meeting of the United States-United Kingdom-Canada Security Conversations, April 1, 1948, *FRUS* 1948, III, pp. 71–75.

All the delegates understood that the result of their collaboration bound only working-level officials. But the British and the Canadians knew that the support of their governments was guaranteed. Such assurance was not the possession of the American delegates. The British sensed how problematic American participation in a mutual defense treaty still was.[52] Hickerson and his colleagues knew this only too well, but with calm resolution they formulated a strategy of action designed to secure their nation's commitment to the proposed alliance. Firstly, Marshall's and Lovett's approval was necessary, and then Butler would have to introduce a revised paper to the NSC and through it obtain the support of Secretary of Defense Forrestal. After National Security Council approval, both the president's endorsement and the concurrence of congressional leaders, especially Senator Vandenberg, would be needed. Only then could the United States pursue the formal steps to the treaty, invitations to and discussions with other nations, also outlined in the paper. The American delegates immediately began to execute their strategy and to overcome the formidable hurdles before them.[53]

Lovett was the first point of contact. In Marshall's absence at the Inter-American Conference in Bogota in early April, he was acting secretary with full authority to make decisions on the matter of the North Atlantic Treaty. Lovett had no particular substantive contribution to make but he predictably worried over how the alliance proposal would be received domestically, especially by the eightieth Congress with which he had expended such effort in obtaining the passage of the ERP legislation.[54] During the morning of April 6 he met with Hickerson, Loy Henderson, Dean Rusk, Achilles, and Butler. There he indicated a more positive stance towards the joint proposal. Consequently discussion focused on a revision of PPS/27 of March 23 in light of the U.S.-U.K.-Canada working paper of April 1. The new document refined the initial Planning Staff text emphasizing the precedent of the Rio Treaty and delineating the area to be covered by the proposed agreement. Butler returned the revised version to the acting secretary that afternoon.[55]

[52] Inverchapel mentioned on March 31 that "there were signs that Hickerson had been encountering resistance to his idea of a Pact during soundings of his colleagues in State Department." And, Bevin on April 6 wrote to Prime Minister Attlee that "the chances of eventual agreement by the U.S. Government on proposals for a Treaty are now reckoned as little better than fifty-fifty." Both quoted from Wiebes and Zeeman, "The Pentagon Negotiations, March 1948," pp. 361–62.

[53] The sequence of steps is outlined in the minutes of the final meeting in FRUS 1948, pp. 71–75.

[54] The British were quite unsure of Lovett's commitment to an Atlantic Pact. Inverchapel reported to London on March 31, 1948, that "even Lovett himself is not altogether convinced of the necessity for a treaty." Quoted in Wiebes and Zeeman, "The Pentagon Negotiations, March 1948," p. 362.

[55] Butler to Lovett, April 6, 1948; and PPS/27/1, "The Position of the United States with Re-

Lovett then began what he did best—negotiating support for a policy or proposal formulated by others. On April 7 he met with Truman and gave him a copy of the revised paper (PPS/27/1) carefully explaining that neither he nor Marshall had taken a position on it. This marked the first time that the White House had been consulted seriously about the proposed treaty, an indication of the central role of the State Department under Truman and also of the president's limited role in policy formulation. Lovett returned to see Truman the next day and asked for permission to begin approaches to certain key congressional figures to lay the foundations for senatorial ratification of a possible treaty. Truman gave him the "green light."[56] Lovett then authorized the submission of PPS/27/1 to the National Security Council as a replacement of the earlier staff version.[57] Admiral Souers distributed it as NSC 9 entitled "The Position of the U.S. with Respect to Support for Western Union and Other Related Free Countries."[58] Much had happened during the time Kennan was away from the department!

THE VANDENBERG RESOLUTION AND KENNAN'S BELATED OPPOSITION

Upon receiving Truman's approval to open discussions with congressional figures Lovett moved quickly to build bipartisan support for a North Atlantic Treaty. This meant that once again he took on the role of emissary to Arthur Vandenberg, the Republican Chairman of the Senate Foreign Relations Committee. Vandenberg led the internationalist wing of the Republicans but he and John Foster Dulles, who advised him, were not prepared to give the Truman administration any ready endorsement for its plans. Lovett advised Clark Clifford at the White House on April 12 of his troubles clearing the proposal on Capitol Hill and of Vandenberg's desire "to think about it at great length."[59] Lovett then performed the elaborate ritual of courting Vandenberg and inevitably agreed to the Senator's placing his own stamp on the process.[60] This

---

spect to Western Union and Related Problems," PPS Records, Box 3; and Nelson, ed., *SDPPSP 1948*, pp. 165–70.

[56] See George M. Elsey's "Western Union Chronology" April 13, 1948, which gives summary details of Lovett's April 7 and 8 meetings with Truman, in Elsey Papers, HSTL, Box 66.

[57] See *FRUS* 1948, III, p. 78 n. 1.

[58] For NSC 9 see National Security Council Documents in Modern Military Records, Modern Military Branch, NA, Box 2.

[59] Elsey's "Western Union Chronology," April 13, 1948, Elsey Papers, Box 66.

[60] On Lovett's discussions with Vandenberg held on April 11, 18, and 27, 1948, see Lovett's memoranda in *FRUS* 1948, III, pp. 82–84, 92–96, 104–8. General Marshall and John Foster Dulles also participated in the final meeting. See also Vandenberg, Jr., ed., *The Private Papers of Senator Vandenberg*, pp. 404–9; John Foster Dulles, *War or Peace* (New York, 1950), pp. 95–96; Dulles's memorandum on the April 27 meeting with Lovett in Dulles Papers, Box 37; and Vandenberg to Dulles, May 10, 1948, Vandenberg Papers, Box 3. The White House Staff felt that Lovett failed to keep them sufficiently informed of his activities. On April 30 George Elsey, Clifford's principal assistant, recorded in his journal: "I have been needling Clifford to find out

came with the so-called Vandenberg Resolution (S. Res. 239) which the Senate passed on June 11, 1948.

Through the Vandenberg Resolution the Senate voiced the opinion that the United States should among other measures associate itself ''by constitutional process, with such regional and other collective arrangements as are based on continuous and effective self-help and mutual aid, and as affect its national security.'' It further declared that the United States should make clear ''its determination to exercise the right of individual or collective self-defense under Article 51 of the United Nations Charter should any armed attack occur affecting its national security.''[61] The importance of the Vandenberg Resolution does not lie in any contribution or clarification it made to the final version of the North Atlantic Treaty whose main outlines were sketched already in PPS/27/1. Its true significance resides in the public endorsement it gave to American participation in collective defense arrangements thereby convincing the administration of congressional support for the implementation of such a policy.[62]

The need to get Vandenberg and the Senate Republicans on side had slowed the progress towards a treaty. This gave Kennan the opportunity to resume his opposition to the idea of an alliance when he returned to the State Department in late April, following his trip to Japan and a bout of illness. During Lovett's discussions with Vandenberg the Planning Staff remained very active on this issue, assisting the under secretary with the assorted revisions to PPS/27/1 designed to gain the rather bombastic senator's support.[63] Ironically, even Kennan was drawn into this work upon his immediate resumption of duties with the Staff. In late April and May he played something of a dual role. He participated in the difficult, technical task of drafting and redrafting papers on a proposed defense treaty for submission to the NSC while at the very same time he questioned the whole concept of a defense treaty.[64] Although unhappy over the paper the Staff had submitted during his absence, he didn't want to disown

---

what State Dept. is up to, as I am curious and anxious to get into it, and mistrustful of where State will leave Truman in this deal.'' Elsey journal, April 30, 1948, Elsey Papers, HSTL, Box 33. Also see Elsey memorandum of May 5, 1948, on Western Union in Elsey Papers, HSTL, Box 66. Elsey's complaint is another indication of Truman's limited role in the formulation of the American stance on the North Atlantic Treaty.

[61] For the text of the resolution (S. Res. 239) and for the final vote upon it see U.S. Congress, *Congressional Record* 80th Congress, 2d session, vol. 94, part 6 (Washington, D.C., 1948), pp. 7791, 7846.

[62] For details of Vandenberg's contribution—somewhat overestimated—and the significance of the Vandenberg Resolution see Daryl J. Hudson, ''Vandenberg Reconsidered: Senate Resolution 239 and American Foreign Policy,'' *Diplomatic History* 1 (Winter 1977): 46–63.

[63] See minutes of meetings, April 12 and 15, 1948, PPS Records, Box 32.

[64] See Kennan to Souers, April 23, 1948, *FRUS* 1948, III, pp. 100–103; and Kennan to Lovett, May 7, 1948, *FRUS* 1948, III, pp. 116–19.

it completely and this ambivalence influenced the form of his opposition expressed on April 29 to Marshall and Lovett.

Kennan believed that the proposed alliance was unnecessary. Speaking not only for himself but also for Bohlen, who substantially shared his views, the chief planner argued that what worried the Europeans was not whether the Americans would be on their side in the event of a Russian attack but that there was no "agreed concept" to guide American and European actions should such an attack occur. Kennan's view of the Czech coup as a defensive move by the Soviets designed to consolidate their sphere led him to consider an outright military attack unlikely but for the purpose of his analysis he addressed this danger. He argued that the West Europeans required from the United States "not so much a public political and military alliance but rather realistic staff talks to see what can be done about their defense."[65] In these circumstances he advised against a congressional resolution at that time. Rather than directly attacking the whole proposal head-on Kennan attempted a diversionary action and offered an alternative to draw the American effort away from the idea of a political-military alliance for which he saw neither need nor value. He and Bohlen offered the "dumbbell" option of informal guarantees from North America to Europe backed by such military advice as might be helpful to allow the Europeans to cooperate effectively in organizing their own defense. This constituted a much less concrete and permanent American commitment than the formal alliance approach. As in his earlier comments upon Bevin's initial proposal Kennan aimed to keep the Europeans focused primarily on building their own political and economic strength. He considered his alternative would furnish sufficient reassurance to the Europeans and disputed the position, best represented by Bevin and Hickerson, that an alliance was necessary to provide the sense of military strength and security which would afford political stability and economic development in Europe.

One of Kennan's difficulties in persuading Marshall and Lovett lay in the fact that the British—to this point the only European country consulted—gave no indication of any enthusiasm for Kennan's proposed course of action. Instead, Kennan's intervention caused them a good deal of concern. The Foreign Office feared Kennan's influence with Marshall and by the end of April the British worried that "the Kennan-Bohlen line was gaining ascendancy" as there were indications of weakened State Department support for the security pact. One British scholar has described the British concern that "what had been thought to be a settled policy, at least as far as the State Department was concerned, now appeared open for debate. Everything gained at the Pentagon

---

[65] Memorandum by Kennan to Marshall and Lovett, April 29, 1948, *FRUS* 1948, III, pp. 108–9. Also see Kennan, *Memoirs*, I, p. 409. On Kennan's and Bohlen's opposition see Reid, *Time of Fear and Hope*, pp. 106–8.

talks now seemed lost.''[66] The chance of American retreat from support of a mutual defense treaty appeared on the near horizon and to prevent it the British vigorously stressed their own support for a North Atlantic pact.

The British stance proved a difficult obstacle for Kennan but it was not the only one. By the time he could bring his ideas to bear Lovett had completed the bulk of his conversations with Vandenberg. Marshall himself had joined them for a meeting on April 27, where firm understandings had been reached regarding American participation in a mutual defense pact. Marshall on his return from Bogota largely accepted much of what Lovett had accomplished on the matter almost as a fait accompli. His deep bond with his deputy ensured that Kennan's counsel came too late to convince either man to alter course. The agreements with Vandenberg tended to lock American policy in place and Kennan's departmental superiors rejected his advice to delay or modify the treaty.[67] Too much had been agreed upon already—with Vandenberg, with the British and Canadians—for Kennan to block the momentum towards a formal alliance. Similarly, the continued reservations of the Joint Chiefs of Staff were ineffective.[68]

Although committed to American participation in a mutual defense treaty Marshall moved cautiously on the matter. He refused to take hasty action and waited for the National Security Council and the president to indicate their support and for the Vandenberg resolution to pass the Senate before taking further steps.[69] On June 14 the British ambassador, now Sir Oliver Franks, called on the secretary of state to inquire when the broader discussions with other likely treaty participants might begin. Marshall told Franks that in view of the Senate's vote he now was prepared to act. Kennan attended this meeting and expressed the view, which Marshall supported, that the proposed conversations should be "entirely exploratory."[70] Marshall stated this explicitly when on June 23 the British, French, Canadian, Belgian (also acting for Luxembourg), and Netherlands Embassies were advised of the American willingness to begin top secret exploratory talks pursuant to the Vandenberg Resolu-

[66] Martin H. Folly, "Breaking the Vicious Circle: Britain, the United States and the Genesis of the North Atlantic Treaty," *Diplomatic History* 12 (Winter 1988): 73.

[67] For an attempt on Kennan's part to modify the treaty see Kennan to Marshall and Lovett, May 7, 1947, PPS Records, Box 33. Here he sought to have paragraph 5 of the Vandenberg Resolution removed. This paragraph requested "maximum efforts to obtain agreements to provide the United Nations with armed forces as provided by the [UN] Charter."

[68] On the reservations of the JCS see Wiebes and Zeeman, "The Pentagon Negotiations, March 1948," pp. 362–63.

[69] NSC approval was assured after its meeting on May 20 but formal approval of NSC 9/3 came from the NSC on July 1, 1948. President Truman approved it and directed that it be implemented the next day. See *FRUS 1948*, III, pp. 140–41. Also see the discussion in Truman, *Years of Trial and Hope*, pp. 245–46.

[70] Memorandum of conversation, June 14, 1948, *FRUS* 1948, III, pp. 136–37.

tion.[71] Unbeknownst to the French and the Benelux and despite the Kennan/ Marshall qualification most of the exploration had already been completed.

THE WASHINGTON EXPLORATORY TALKS

Lovett opened the exploratory talks on July 5 in Washington, D.C., where they continued throughout the summer of 1948 under the added tension brought on by the Soviet blockade of Berlin imposed on June 24. Several formal meetings, each chaired by Lovett, were held—five during the first three days and the last two in early September during the final days of this series of discussions. The bulk of the real work during these conversations occurred within the so-called International Working Group which held fifteen meetings between July 12 and September 9.[72] At the formal meetings Lovett exercised no firm leadership, leaving it to Oliver Franks and Lester Pearson to push the negotiations further. In the working group it was a different story. Here the Americans took the lead. The regular American participants were Hickerson, Achilles, Samuel Reber, and W. J. Galloway from the Office of European Affairs, while Kennan and Bohlen attended occasionally. Hickerson directed proceedings. A British participant recalled that "perched forward on the edge of his chair, [Hickerson] would dispose of difficulties, drastically, like a man swatting flies, and when confronted with new suggestions he would welcome them eagerly in the manner of an auctioneer receiving bids."[73] Hickerson related well to the Europeans and worked closely with the British and the Canadians and usually could carry the day. Some of his toughest moments came from his fellow American, George Kennan.

After recognizing that some kind of North Atlantic security pact would be created Kennan acquiesced and accepted this in order to retain some influence on policy formation.[74] During the discussions of the International Working Group he labored to limit the scope and nature of the proposed pact prompting

[71] See Secretary of State to Embassy in France, June 23, 1948, *FRUS* 1948, III, p. 139. It is possible that Marshall's decision to remain "exploratory" resulted mainly from the advice of John Foster Dulles who did not wish the United States to enter into any firm commitments until after the presidential elections of that year. Dulles, *War or Peace*, p. 97.

[72] For the minutes of the seven formal meetings of the Washington Exploratory Talks on Security, July 6–September 10, 1948, and the minutes or editorial summaries of the fifteen meetings of the International Working Group, July 12–September 9, 1948, see *FRUS* 1948, III, pp. 148– 250 (inter alia). For an excellent account of these discussions see Henderson, *The Birth of NATO*, pp. 35–64.

[73] Henderson, *The Birth of NATO*, pp. 59. Sir Nicholas Henderson also commented that "without Hickerson's unflinching faith in the Pact it is doubtful whether the Working Party could have made the progress it did in the summer and whether any scheme would have been worked out in time for early consideration in the New Year."

[74] Escott Reid suggests that by the end of August "Kennan had been converted to support of the treaty" and he portrays the Canadians as influential in his conversion. Reid, *Time of Fear and Hope*, p. 108–12. Reid exaggerates, however, for Kennan was never a convert.

disagreements with and evoking opposition from Hickerson.[75] Kennan argued for a pact limited to the seven countries represented at these meetings and aimed to exclude the Scandinavians and especially Italy.[76] Hickerson favored the broader pact and in the end he carried both his superiors and his working group colleagues with him on the matter. The joint paper produced during these talks reflected Hickerson's views over those of Kennan. The Europeans, like Hickerson, preferred the deeper American commitment. Neither Kennan nor Bohlen could sway them.[77]

The joint paper that emerged from the Washington talks deemed the security of Western Europe to be "immediately threatened" by the Soviet Union and that of North America as "seriously affected." It asked how Western Europe and North America could join together for mutual aid against the common danger to achieve their security. Not surprisingly, the proposed solution was United States and Canadian association with the West Europeans in a North Atlantic security arrangement. Little attention was devoted to practical measures to enflesh the guarantees of the proposed treaty. As Ernest May has remarked, "When the Atlantic alliance was conceived, its parents did not think much about how it might grow up. They were concerned mostly with a healthy birth." The emphasis was placed on obtaining the potential American commitment to Western Europe's defense through the proposed treaty. In discussing the territorial scope for this treaty no strict limits were set as Kennan had wanted. Even Italy was viewed as a potential full member along with nations who more obviously belonged in a North Atlantic security pact. The paper went on to discuss the nature of such a pact and, reflecting Hickerson's influence, emphasized the precedent of the Rio Treaty and the importance of the agreement conforming to the framework outlined in the Vandenberg Resolution.[78]

Upon acceptance of the paper Lovett asked the delegates to transmit it to their governments for comment as a preliminary stage to further progress to-

[75] For the Kennan-Hickerson disagreements see Kennan to Lovett, August 31, 1948, *FRUS* 1948, III, p. 255. For the attached Annex A and Annex B referred to in Kennan's letter see PPS Records, Box 33. Also note memorandum of the thirteenth meeting of the International Working Group, September 2, 1948, *FRUS* 1948, III, pp. 226–28.

[76] On Kennan's continuing opposition to Italian inclusion in the North Atlantic Treaty see E. Timothy Smith, "The Fear of Subversion: The United States and the Inclusion of Italy in the North Atlantic Treaty," *Diplomatic History* 7 (Spring 1983): 139–55.

[77] The European delegates regarded both Kennan and Bohlen favorably even though disagreeing with them. Nicholas Henderson observed that "it is a measure of their extraordinary skill and of the enormous appeal of their personalities that, although Bohlen and Kennan had so frequently to strike so negative a note, they never aroused the least personal resentment on the part of the representatives of the other powers." *The Birth of NATO*, p. 60.

[78] Memorandum by the Participants in the Washington Security Talks, July 6–September 9, submitted to their respective governments for study and consent, September 9, 1948, *FRUS* 1948, III, pp. 237–48.

ward the treaty. In reality further progress depended upon one government only, that of the United States. But, in terms of policy-making, the American government began to mark time while awaiting the result of the 1948 presidential election and the expected change of administration. When Truman surprisingly retained office after his feisty campaign against Thomas Dewey the administration immediately proceeded ahead with the negotiations for a North Atlantic Security Pact.

KENNAN'S FINAL OPPOSITION AND THE CONCLUSION OF THE NORTH ATLANTIC TREATY

With the prospect of further negotiations in the near future Kennan submitted a paper to Marshall and Lovett on November 24, 1948, in an endeavor to clarify certain points in the American position. Kennan later suspected that he submitted it "more for the record . . . than for any other reason," but since he wrote in a very persuasive form it might be judged that he still hoped to influence policy.[79] Although submitted in the name of the Planning Staff, the document contained his personal views. Earlier he had discussed it with his Staff colleagues but did not subject it to rigorous collective analysis.[80] It represented his final major attempt to sway policy. He did it again not by launching a frontal assault on the idea of a security pact—that was now a given—but by seeking to reduce both its significance and to limit its territorial scope.

Kennan warned that a formal security arrangement was not the answer to the Soviet attempt to dominate Europe. It would not "appreciably modify the nature or danger of Soviet policies," which he again described primarily in political rather than military terms. Kennan conceded that a security pact was advantageous only as it operated to "stiffen the self-confidence of the Western-Europeans" in the political war against the Soviet Union. It was disadvantageous, indeed dangerous, because its preoccupation with military affairs worked "to the detriment of economic recovery and of the necessity for seeking a peaceful solution to Europe's difficulties." For Kennan the proper course of action lay in achieving economic recovery and political stability in Europe rather than in the construction of a military alliance. He consistently had expressed these views from the time Bevin first raised the issue almost a year before. As for the territorial scope of the proposed treaty Kennan argued that it should be restricted to the North Atlantic area narrowly defined. He warned of unfavorable consequences if the treaty ranged farther afield. To include Italy would only lead to a "series of demands from states still farther afield that they be similarly treated." A move beyond the North Atlantic area would mean that there was "no logical stopping point in the development of a system

[79] For Kennan's later suspicions see *Memoirs*, I, p. 409.
[80] Minutes of meeting, November 22, 1948, PPS Records, Box 32.

of anti-Russian alliances until that system had circled the globe.''[81] Kennan aimed to avoid such a globalized containment.

The planning chief's fervent opposition to an enlarged Atlantic alliance reflected even deeper concerns which he now voiced. A larger alliance incorporating most of the countries involved in the ERP program "would amount to a final militarization of the present dividing-line through Europe." This not only would damage the chances for German and Austrian settlements but also would lock the Eastern European satellites under permanent Soviet domination. Kennan admitted that "it may not be possible for us to prevent a progressive congealment of the present line of division" but he approvingly restated the goal of present American policy as being to secure the eventual peaceful "withdrawal of both the United States and the U.S.S.R. from the heart of Europe." By this point he had expended much energy on a proposal for a German reunification settlement which involved the Red Army's withdrawal from Europe's center. He desperately wanted to pursue it and naturally advised against actions "which tend to fix, and make unchangeable by peaceful means, the present line of east-west division.''[82]

Marshall apparently sympathized with some of Kennan's points but the secretary planned to resign and he refrained from involving himself. He left matters to Lovett and the under secretary showed no interest in accommodating Kennan's suggestions. Lovett implicitly rejected Kennan's analysis by presenting the North Atlantic Security Pact not as detrimental to European economic recovery but "as an essential supplement to the Marshall Plan.''[83] And Lovett it was who oversaw the Washington talks—adjourned in September—which reopened on December 10, 1948.

During the course of these December conversations the delegates initiated, with the approval of their governments, the actual drafting of a treaty. To assist in this task an International Working Group again was established. Kennan chaired it and headed the American delegation to it, an indication of the important position he retained in the department.[84] Kennan aided in thrashing out the very language of a pact, as he later noted, with which he found himself in substantial disagreement.[85] Those who have not worked in government

---

[81] Memorandum by Kennan, November 24, 1948, enclosing PPS/43, "Considerations Affecting the Conclusion of a North Atlantic Security Pact," *FRUS* 1948, III, pp. 283–89.

[82] Ibid.

[83] For Kennan's note regarding Marshall's comments see *FRUS* 1948, III, p. 284 n. 2. For Lovett's comments see Acting Secretary of State to U.S. Special Representative in Europe (Harriman), December 3, 1948, *FRUS* 1948, III, p. 303.

[84] Of course, Hickerson was also part of the American delegation and argued, with some success, that "the treaty should be written in such simple language that 'even a milkman in Omaha can understand it.' " Achilles, "U.S. Role in Negotiations that Led to Atlantic Alliance," part I, p. 14.

[85] For Kennan's appointment and work on the "International Working Group" see *FRUS* 1948, III, p. 315 n. 1; and Kennan, *Memoirs*, I, p. 413.

might find this circumstance overly replete with irony. They should note Kennan's salutary observation that "not every official in a government apparatus may expect to have his own views prevail (mine certainly did not); yet unless he is prepared to abandon his job and his usefulness then and there, he often has to try to make himself useful within the framework of a policy of which he personally disapproves."[86] It is some testimony to Kennan's commitment to the work of the State Department and to the reliance of that body on him that he played this role in concluding the North Atlantic Treaty.

From this point the movement to the passage of the treaty had an inexorable momentum. On December 24 the International Working Group presented to the so-called Ambassadors Committee chaired by Lovett a draft treaty which it approved the same day for submission to the various governments.[87] This served as the basis for further negotiations from January to April of 1949, conducted under the direction of the new secretary of state, Dean Acheson.[88] During this period the Planning Staff again unsuccessfully tried to keep Italy out of the Treaty and it gave some advice on establishing an organization to lend substance to the guarantees of the Treaty but its impact on policy-making on these subjects was minimal.[89] By this time Kennan had turned his full attention to the related question of Germany's future. On April 4, 1949, the North Atlantic Treaty was signed. After being overwhelmingly approved by the Senate it took effect on August 24, 1949.[90] In its first year of existence little flesh and sinew, in terms of actual defense cooperation and an organizational structure, were added to the skeletal outline of the treaty. Neither the executive branch nor the Congress evoked enthusiasm to commit sizable num-

[86] Kennan's "Reply" to C. Ben Wright's "Mr. 'X' and Containment," *Slavic Review* 35 (March 1976): 35–36.

[87] Report of the International Working Group to the Ambassadors Committee, December 24, 1948, *FRUS* 1948, III, pp. 333–43.

[88] Minutes of the 11th to 18th meetings of the Washington Exploratory Talks on Security, January 14–March 15, 1948, *FRUS* 1949, IV, pp. 27–224 (inter alia). For Acheson's account see *Present at the Creation*, pp. 276–84. For an analysis of the major issues during the 1949 negotiations see Henrikson, "The Creation of the North Atlantic Alliance," pp. 17–25.

[89] On opposition to Italy's inclusion in the Pact see memorandum by George H. Butler, March 2, 1949, PPS Records, Box 33. See also on the question of Italy's admission, Smith, "The Fear of Subversion: The United States and the Inclusion of Italy in the North Atlantic Treaty," pp. 150–55. One should note that as late as February 28, 1949, President Truman and the influential Senators Tom Connally, Walter George, and Arthur Vandenberg all leaned against initial Italian membership in the Treaty. The pressure from the Europeans, especially the French, led to the Italian admission. On the position of the president and the senators see Acheson's memoranda of February 28, 1949, in Dean Acheson Papers, HSTL, Box 64. The Italians campaigned to be included and this made it more difficult to exclude them. See Miller, *The United States and Italy, 1940–1950*, pp. 268–71. On the question of organization see Butler's memorandum to Achilles, March 24, 1949, in Records of Charles E. Bohlen, Subject File, Box 8.

[90] On Senate approval see Vandenberg, Jr., *The Private Papers of Senator Vandenberg*, pp. 498–500; Tom Connally, *My Name Is Tom Connally* (New York, 1954), pp. 332–33; and James T. Patterson, *Mr. Republican: A Biography of Robert A. Taft* (Boston, 1972), pp. 435–39.

bers of troops or to expend large amounts of money to substantiate the guarantees of the North Atlantic Treaty. In reality "it took the Korean War and the
related security crisis in Europe to transform NATO from a loose mutual defense pact into a permanent military alliance, with U.S. troop commitments
and a formal command structure under U.S. leadership."[91]

THE TREATY'S PARENTAGE AND PURPOSE

Success, it is said, has many fathers and this proved literally true for the North
Atlantic Treaty. George Kennan rightly has never claimed any paternity
rights. His continued reservations about the alliance treaty prompted one associate to remark that "he probably disliked NATO because he had neglected
to invent it."[92] He later described the Treaty as "the first of the major undertakings of American policy in General Marshall's time with relation to which
I failed to exert any effective influence."[93] In deciding to participate in a regional military alliance in the North Atlantic, American policymakers rejected
Kennan's views on how to respond to the Soviet threat in Europe. Although
he initially opposed the whole notion of a security pact, Kennan eventually
accepted some form of treaty as inevitable and then worked to limit its nature
and geographical scope. He was unsuccessful because in the end most American and European policymakers, shaken by the Czech coup and the Berlin
Blockade, disagreed with the Kennan line that a military alliance was not only
unnecessary but also counterproductive in thwarting the Soviet threat. The
Europeans, in particular, saw that the assurance provided by the Alliance
would bolster their efforts to resist Soviet pressure. A number of other factors
contributed to Kennan's defeat in the battle over the North Atlantic Treaty—
his absence from the department and hence the policy debate during the crucial
weeks of March and April of 1948; his unwillingness or inability to carry the
members of his Planning Staff with him on this issue and to build the Staff
into an institutional opponent of a military alliance; Marshall's substantial
devolution of authority on this issue to Lovett, thereby denying to Kennan a

---

[91] David Reynolds, "The Origins of the Cold War: The European Dimension, 1944–1951,"
Historical Journal 28 (June 1985): 510. For details of the development of the organizational
structure and military forces of NATO see Lawrence S. Kaplan, *A Community of Interests: NATO
and the Military Assistance Program, 1948–1951* (Washington, D.C., 1980); Kaplan, "The Korean War and U.S. Foreign Relations: The Case of NATO," in Francis H. Heller, ed., *The Korean
War: A Twenty-Five Year Perspective* (Lawrence, Kans., 1977), pp. 44–53; Ernest R. May, "The
American Commitment to Germany, 1949–55," *Diplomatic History* 13 (Fall 1989): 431–60; Walter LaFeber, "NATO and the Korean War: A Context," *Diplomatic History* 13 (Fall 1989): 461–
77; and Ted Galen Carpenter, "United States' NATO Policy at the Crossroads: The 'Great Debate'
of 1950–1951," *The International History Review* 8 (August 1986): 388–415.

[92] Jacob Bean, *Multiple Exposure: An American Ambassador's Unique Perspective on East-
West Issues* (New York, 1978), p. 37.

[93] Kennan, *Memoirs*, I, p. 397.

prime source of his power—his access to and influence on Marshall; and finally the bureaucratic infighting skill of the proponents of the Treaty, especially Hickerson and the Office of European Affairs.

Hickerson and the Office of European Affairs made the crucial contribution in ensuring American involvement in the North Atlantic security pact. From the time of Bevin's initial proposal Hickerson forcefully sought a regional security pact modeled on the Rio Treaty. He was a primary participant in all the discussions which brought the treaty to fruition and his Office did much of the staff work on the issue. Working effectively in conjunction with European proponents of the treaty, Hickerson and the Office of European Affairs provided crucial intellectual and bureaucratic support for the North Atlantic pact. Theodore Achilles did not indulge in hyperbole and unwarranted praise of his former chief when he described Hickerson as more responsible than any other person "for the nature, content and form of the Treaty and for its acceptance by the Senate."[94] Hickerson is one of the true fathers of containment as that concept came to be understood and implemented in Europe, much more so than Kennan. Recognition of his large role as "the main architect of NATO" is, however, largely limited to the band of scholars who study this matter in detail and to the group of NATO boosters gathered in The Atlantic Council of the United States.[95] But failure to appreciate Hickerson's importance clouds an understanding of how American foreign policy was made.

In a limited way Kennan did make a minor contribution to the North Atlantic Treaty's successful conclusion through his work in April and May drafting papers on a proposed defense treaty and that in the International Working Group during December 1948. But the work of his colleagues on the Planning Staff, especially during his absence in Japan, warrants greater recognition. The Staff's paper of March 23, 1948, recommended American adherence to a mutual defense treaty and outlined many of its eventual major provisions. Lovett used this paper as the basis for his discussions with Vandenberg and it also served as the groundwork for the NSC document which ultimately received the approval of the National Security Council and the president. The Staff acted less as the originator than as the organizer of and arbitrator among ideas. This was a useful function and it was supplemented by the assistance lent to Lovett by Staff members, and in George Butler's case, by actual participation in negotiations with other nations.

Now all of this is not to suggest that American policy simply flowed upwards. Responsibility for policy cannot be attributed solely to these second-

[94] Oral History Interview with Theodore Achilles, HSTL, transcript p. 36.

[95] Gier Lundestad described Hickerson as "the key person and in many ways the main architect of NATO" in his "Empire By Invitation? The United States and Western Europe, 1945–1952," *SHAFR Newsletter* 15 (September 1984): 8. Achilles played an important role in The Atlantic Council of the United States in the 1970s so it's hardly surprising that Hickerson's role was appreciated there.

level officials. Truman, Marshall, and, to a greater extent, Lovett, modified, approved, and implemented the policy recommendations of their State Department subordinates and share responsibility for policy with them. But the role of the president and his senior officials was not central to the actual content of policy. Their role focused more on the execution of policy rather than its formulation. In this process Lovett took the lead especially in dealing with the Europeans and lining up congressional support. Truman's role was quite limited and his performance on this issue tends to confirm that he simply delegated a good deal of responsibility in the domain of foreign affairs except in moments of genuine crisis.[96]

Additionally, the evolution of American support for a North Atlantic treaty can only be understood in the context of the events taking place in Europe— the breakdown of any semblance of four-power cooperation at the London CFM, the Czech coup, the March war scare, the fears concerning Italy, and the Soviet blockade of Berlin. These developments gave impetus to the efforts of the Europeans to engage the Americans in a formal alliance guaranteeing their security and they ensured strong senatorial support for such an alliance by seemingly confirming the need for it. Ultimately the pressures from the Europeans, especially the British in the early months, must be counted as crucial in bringing NATO into existence. This was not an American initiative but an American response to European requests and Gier Lundestad captures well the situation which resulted from the American commitment as an "empire by invitation."[97] In acknowledging the European contribution particular note must be paid to the importance of that stout-hearted English socialist, Ernest Bevin. It was he who initiated serious discussions about a western security system involving the United States and, taking their lead from him, British officials played a sustaining part in all the discussions even though they skillfully consigned leadership on the matter to the United States from mid-1948 on. Bevin's signature of the North Atlantic Treaty was the single most satisfying act of his term of office as Foreign Secretary.[98] He is, like Hickerson, a legitimate father of containment.

Some historians have portrayed NATO in terms of an attempt to allay French security concerns regarding a resurgent Germany.[99] Unquestionably the reassurance which the Treaty provided the French comprised a beneficial side-

---

[96] Moments of crisis would include the initial period surrounding the imposition of the Berlin Blockade and the early days of the North Korean invasion of South Korea. For a contemporary discussion of Truman's delegation of authority in foreign affairs see John Fischer, "Mr. Truman's Politburo," *Harper's Magazine* 202 (June 1951): 29–36.

[97] Lundestad, "Empire By Invitation?" p. 1.

[98] Lord Strang, *Home and Abroad* (London, 1956), p. 289.

[99] Ireland in *Creating the Entangling Alliance* has argued this case most persuasively. An important distinction needs to be made here. After the actual negotiation of the North Atlantic treaty the French did exercise considerable influence over American actions (e.g., the tangible presence of U.S. troops in Europe) in order to address their concerns regarding Germany.

effect but the evidence that this was a primary motivation of NATO's founders is tenuous at best, with perhaps the exception of the French themselves. At the root of the actions of Bevin and Hickerson and the others responsible for the North Atlantic Treaty was concern at the threat posed by the Soviet Union. A more persuasive, although also unconvincing, view of NATO's origins is that it resulted from a misreading, indeed an exaggeration or oversimplification, of the Soviet threat.[100] Kennan held to a version of this view. In a long analysis of "The Soviet Union and the Atlantic Pact" written during his ambassadorship in Moscow in 1952 he explained:

> Large numbers of people, both in Western Europe and the United States, were incapable of understanding the Russian technique of penetration and "partial war" or of thinking in terms of this technique. They were capable of thinking about international developments only in the old-fashioned terms of full-fledged war or full-fledged peace. It was inconceivable to them that there could be real and serious threats to the independence of their countries that did not come to them in the form of foreign armies marching across frontiers; and it was natural that in undertaking to combat what they conceived to be a foreign threat they should have turned to the old-fashioned and familiar expedient of military alliance. They had understood that there was a threat; but they had not understood the nature of that threat, and were hardly capable of doing so.[101]

But here Kennan caricatured the positions of the Treaty proponents. Bevin, Hickerson, and company did not expect the Red Army to come barreling to the Atlantic at any moment, although they never completely ruled it out. Like Kennan they saw the Soviet threat not simply in explicitly military terms. For them, the danger for Western Europe lay in the power of intimidation the Soviets possessed over those whom their military threat cast a shadow and in their opportunism to strike if a seizure of power was possible.[102] The real purpose of NATO lay in its facilitation of political stability and economic development. Political and economic containment welded with military containment in an inexorable mix.[103] And, it must be admitted that the alliance, even

---

[100] Lawrence Kaplan leans in this direction in his *The United States and NATO: The Formative Years*.

[101] Kennan's "The Soviet Union and the Atlantic Pact," September 8, 1952, in Kennan, *Memoirs*, II, pp. 333–34.

[102] Hickerson had put this position to Marshall and Lovett in his March 8, 1948, memorandum. To quote it at length: "The problem at present is less one of defense against overt foreign aggression tha[n] against internal fifth-column aggression supported by the threat of external force, on the Czech model. An essential element in combatting it is to convince non-Communist elements that friendly external force comparable to the threatening source is available. Absence of any sign of friendly external force was undoubtedly a major factor in the limp Czech collapse. Willingness to fight for liberty is closely related to the strength of the help available." Hickerson to the Secretary, March 8, 1948, *FRUS* 1948, III, pp. 40–42.

[103] For the State Department's linking of the Atlantic Pact to ERP and to European Integration

as it has adapted itself to changed circumstances and new members, essentially delivered what its founders envisioned. It locked the United States to the defense of Western Europe and behind American protection Europe enjoyed a remarkable period of political stability and economic growth.

Kennan lamented the militarization of containment that NATO initiated and the rigidity it brought to the European situation. He had hoped to see a more politically unified and economically integrated Western Europe develop which would dilute the bipolar quality of the international environment. Although such a strategy might have been viable, it was not to be. But forty years hence this European entity is emerging, albeit slowly, while the Soviet Union has relinquished its political domination of Eastern Europe. NATO's purpose seems likely to change. Expectations have been expressed already that it might serve as a constructive instrument in reshaping the European future. Those who plot its future course and design the new architecture for Europe might judge the concerns of its founders rather archaic but they will do well to appreciate why this alliance came about as they seek to use it to extend the political freedom and economic growth long enjoyed by its present members.

---

see *FRUS* 1949, IV, pp. 240–41. Note that military containment would await NSC 68 and the Korean War, however, before its full expression.

CHAPTER FIVE

The Division of Germany

THE GERMAN PROBLEM

The disagreement between the western powers and the Soviet Union over Germany stood at the heart of the Cold War conflict. Germany, or more accurately the power vacuum brought about by the defeat of central Europe's great power, constituted the fundamental problem of any postwar European settlement. The issue was resolved eventually—at least for four decades—by the creation of two German states. Such a development was not envisaged at the end of World War II. At the Potsdam Conference held outside the ruins of Berlin in July 1945, Stalin, Truman, and Clement Attlee decided against dismembering Germany. Instead they determined that it should be occupied for as long a period as would be necessary to create a vaguely defined new democratic governmental structure and to ideologically reorient—to denazify—the German people. While this was being done Germany was to be administered as one political and economic entity by a single governing body, the Allied Control Council, sitting in Berlin. The unanimous policy decisions of the Council composed of the representatives of the occupying powers—Britain, the Soviet Union, the United States, and eventually France—were to be implemented in each of the four German zones by the respective occupying authority. No permanent division of the country was planned. Yet by the end of 1949 Germany had been partitioned. Two quite distinct states emerged—the Federal Republic of Germany, a democracy tied to the West, and the German Democratic Republic, a Soviet satellite. This rupture of the German nation solidified the split of Europe as a whole.

In reality, by breaking Germany up into separate geographic occupation zones in 1945 the victorious Allied powers immediately divided their vanquished foe. In the absence of any agreement on specific programs to give meaning to the generalities agreed to at Potsdam the Allied Control Council proved ineffective in governing Germany as a single entity. As a consequence of their failure each occupying power applied its own ideas in its own zone. The temporary administrative division of Germany began to harden into a permanent political separation in the summer of 1946 when the Americans and the British merged their zones into an economic union, known as Bizonia. The Russians promptly denounced the arrangement as a harbinger of permanent division. This economic merger did not signify the abandonment by the Americans of the goal of German unification which they unsuccessfully sought at the Foreign Ministers' conferences at Moscow in March and in London during November and December of 1947. The failure of the London CFM to agree on a four-power German settlement, however, did induce a major redirection in policy. Impelled by a desire to reduce their own occupation costs and to develop the western portion of Germany as a contributor to West European economic recovery, the United States and Great Britain conferred with a reluctant, cautious France and the Benelux countries on the major elements of the German problem. After difficult negotiations held intermittently in London from January to June of 1948 an agreement was reached which proposed the creation of a West German government and state.[1]

The Soviet Union vehemently opposed both the discussions in London and the policies, the so-called London Program, formulated there. To prevent this Program's implementation, especially its initial step providing for the introduction of a separate currency for West Germany, and in order to force the Western powers back to the negotiating table to reach an all-German settlement satisfactory to themselves, the Soviets instituted a blockade of the Western sectors of Berlin, which lay wholly within their zone of occupation.[2] As is well known the Americans and the British eventually responded imaginatively to this total restriction on surface traffic into Berlin with an airlift of supplies to the besieged city which they maintained until the Soviets lifted the blockade in May of 1949.[3] The almost legendary success of the airlift should not obscure the fact that, despite the protracted series of restrictions and disagreements in the previous months, the imposition of the full blockade on June 24 surprised most American policymakers who reacted with a marked lack of

[1] This brief survey of postwar developments in Germany and of the German policies of the Allied powers draws upon John Gimbel, *The American Occupation of Germany: Politics and the Military, 1945–1949* (Stanford, 1968), pp. 245–57; John H. Backer, *The Decision to Divide Germany: American Foreign Policy in Transition* (Durham, N.C., 1978); Bruce Kuklick, *American Policy and the Division of Germany: The Clash with Russia over Reparations* (Ithaca, N.Y., 1972); R. Harrison Wagner, "The Decision to Divide Germany and the Origins of the Cold War," *International Studies Quarterly* 24, no. 2 (June 1980): 155–90; Earl F. Ziemke, "The Formulation and Initial Implementation of U.S. Occupation Policy in Germany," in Hans A. Schmitt, ed., *U.S. Occupation in Europe after World War II* (Lawrence, Kans., 1978), pp. 27–44. For accounts by American policymakers within Germany see Lucius D. Clay, *Decision in Germany* (New York, 1950), pp. 346–57, 394–96; and Robert D. Murphy, *Diplomat Among Warriors* (New York, 1964), pp. 310–15.

[2] On Soviet motives note Adam Ulam, *The Rivals: America and Russia Since World War II* (New York, 1971), p. 148, who argued that the Soviet Union's principal objective was not to force the West out of Berlin but rather "a resolution of the German problem as a whole." The CIA considered the Soviet purpose was "to force the resumption of Four-Power negotiations about Germany under conditions largely favorable to the USSR," in order "to delay the implementation of a program for Western Germany." CIA, Review of World Situation, August 19, 1948, Truman Papers, PSF, Box 204.

[3] For further details on the blockade, the airlift, and the impact of each in Berlin see W. Phillips Davison, *The Berlin Blockade: A Study in Cold War Politics* (Princeton, 1958); and Frank Howley, *Berlin Command* (New York, 1950), pp. 192–206.

decisiveness.[4] Even General Lucius Clay, the forceful and tough-minded American Military Governor in Germany, who initiated the airlift, lacked faith in its effectiveness to overcome the blockade. He told the editor of *Neue Zeitung*, after announcing the beginning of the airlift, that "I wouldn't give you that [snap of fingers] for our chances."[5] It was viewed as a mere palliative rather than a solution. In a situation of dramatically heightened international tension the blockade thrust the German problem to the forefront of American concerns. Not surprisingly it attracted Kennan's attention.

DEVELOPMENT OF A PROPOSAL

From the initiation of the Soviet blockade it was apparent that the Western powers might find it necessary to agree to another four-power meeting on Germany in order to regain road and rail access to Berlin. In July 1948, when the capacity of the airlift to sustain Berlin over a long period was still doubted, Kennan and the Planning Staff undertook to study whether such a meeting should be held and, if so, what should be proposed to the Soviets at it. Kennan's involvement on this question resulted in a wide-ranging proposal as significant in its implications as anything he put forward as director of the Policy Planning Staff. Ultimately his proposal met with rejection, a painful and punishing blow which eventually would lead him to question his own continued participation in the policy-making process.

Kennan possessed a grasp of German culture and language similar to his command of Russian.[6] From his childhood visit, through his service as vice-consul in Hamburg, his graduate studies in Berlin, and his service in the German capital on the eve of World War II he keenly observed German thought and life. His experience and knowledge gave him a confident assurance in the consideration of German issues. His views on Germany as the war in Europe came to an end were dictated, however, by an urgent desire to limit Soviet expansion. Such views had prompted his support for the sphere of influence approach which he had conveyed to Bohlen on the eve of the Yalta conference and led him to advocate explicitly the division of Germany. He disparaged the Potsdam arrangements and declared in classic Kennan prose that

[4] On American decision-making see Avi Shlaim, *The United States and the Berlin Blockade, 1948–1949: A Study in Crisis Decision-making* (Berkeley, 1983); and Wilson D. Miscamble, "Harry S. Truman, The Berlin Blockade and the 1948 Election," *Presidential Studies Quarterly* 8 (Summer 1980): 306–16.

[5] Clay quoted in Eugene Davidson, *The Death and Life of Germany: An Account of American Occupation* (New York, 1961), pp. 202–3.

[6] James W. Riddleberger, himself a German expert, recalled of Kennan that "his German is just about as close to perfect as any Anglo-Saxon I've heard who didn't learn it as a first language when he was young." Oral History Interview with James W. Riddleberger by Richard D. McKinzie and Theodore A. Wilson, HSTL, June 24, 1971.

the idea of a Germany run jointly with the Russians is a chimera. The idea of both the Russians and ourselves withdrawing politely at a given date and a healthy, peaceful, stable, and friendly Germany arising out of the resulting vacuum is also a chimera. We have no choice but to lead our section of Germany—the section of which we and the British have accepted responsibility—to a form of independence so prosperous, so secure, so superior, that the East cannot threaten it. This is a tremendous task for Americans. But it is an unavoidable one; and along these lines, not along the lines of fumbling unworkable schemes of joint military government, must lie our thinking.[7]

Kennan's open support for dismemberment was sustained throughout 1946 at the same time that the redoubtable General Clay exerted every effort to work jointly with the Soviets and to obtain successful four-power cooperation.[8] On March 6, 1946, Kennan warned bluntly that the Soviets aimed to establish a Communist Germany and that the continued pursuit by the United States of a unified Germany played into their hands. Against the specter of a Communist-dominated Germany Kennan recommended the development of the Western zones "on [a] relatively independent basis with constructive programs looking toward integration of these zones into general economic patterns of western Europe."[9] He brought such views back to Washington and to his directorship of the Planning Staff.

Kennan continued his advocacy for a division of Germany through 1947. Late in the year, before the London CFM Conference, Kennan advised Marshall to "insist on keeping Western Germany free of communistic control." He explained that if the Soviets attempted to get them out of West Germany under arrangements leaving it defenseless against Communist penetration then the Americans would have no choice but to disagree, "to proceed to make the best of a divided Germany" and to "bring the western part of Germany into some acceptable relationship to the other western European countries."[10] The thrust of his advice, which ironically resembled the policy finally pursued by

[7] Kennan, *Memoirs*, I, p. 258. For a discussion of Kennan's views on Germany during World War II see David Mayers, "Nazi Germany and the Future of Europe: George Kennan's Views, 1939–1945," *International History Review* 3, no. 4 (November 1986): 550–72.

[8] On Clay's efforts see Wolfgang Krieger, "Was General Clay a Revisionist? Strategic Aspects of the United States Occupation of Germany," *Journal of Contemporary History* 18, no. 2 (April 1983): 165–84; and Jean Edward Smith, "General Clay and the Russians: A Continuation of the Wartime Alliance in Germany, 1945–1948," *Virginia Quarterly Review* 64, no. 1 (Winter 1988): 20–36.

[9] Kennan to Secretary of State, *FRUS* 1946, V, pp. 518–19.

[10] PPS/13, "Resume of World Situation," November 6, 1947, *FRUS* 1947, I, pp. 770–71, 774. Note that Kennan viewed Germany as being of central strategic importance. In September 1947, he expounded that "the vital issue of world politics, particularly in the relations between this country and Russia, is the German settlement." Kennan, "World Political Situation," Speech to Business Advisory Council, Department of Commerce, September 24, 1947, Kennan Papers, Box 17.

the United States against Kennan's later counsel, was for the economic rehabilitation of the Western zones of Germany and their integration into Western
Europe. He also implied the establishment of a West German state. The Planning Staff subjected this latter issue to preliminary analysis in November
1947, and called in Yale's Arnold Wolfers and Professor Calvin B. Hoover of
Duke University to aid in the deliberations.[11] The planners intended their own
deliberations and the consultations with Wolfers and Hoover to serve as the
basis for a policy paper on Germany. But for a number of reasons, among
them Kennan's foray to Japan, his subsequent hospitalization with a severe
case of ulcers, and the Staff's preoccupation during his absence with the question of a North Atlantic security pact, it never produced this paper. During the
first half of 1948 the Staff failed to make any formal recommendations as to
the appropriate course of political action in Germany.[12] But the Soviet blockade had a riveting impact and drew Kennan back to this issue. This time his
recommendations differed markedly from the views he had offered on Germany through the end of 1947. Kennan was in the process of undergoing a
conversion on this issue which transformed him into the foremost proponent
of German unification within the Truman administration.

At a meeting on July 15, 1948, Kennan and the other Staff members discussed the Berlin situation with Charles Bohlen, who urged them to produce
a paper. Kennan assessed that the initiation of negotiations in Moscow between Western representatives and Stalin presaged an early meeting of the
CFM. With this in mind and with Lovett's immediate concurrence the Planning
Staff agreed on August 2 to urgently prepare proposals on Germany for such
a meeting.[13] Between this point and August 12, Kennan led his colleagues in
an examination of the complex problem. In most of their discussions they were
joined by the State Department officers primarily responsible for operational
policy in Germany including Charles E. Saltzman, the Assistant Secretary of
State for Occupied Areas; Jacob D. Beam and Howard Trivers from the Division of Central European Affairs; and Paul Nitze from Economic Affairs.
Kennan also had General Albert C. Wedemeyer designate two talented officers
from his Plans and Operations Division of the Army Department—Lieutenant
Colonels J. W. Coutts and E. S. Hartshorne—to participate in the discussions

[11] A question list prepared for the discussion with the outside consultants had two main head-
ings: "1. Do we still want a united Germany?" and "2. How about a partition imposed by failure
to reach agreement at London?" This list is attached to Minutes of Meeting, November 10, 1947,
PPS Records, Box 32. For the Planning Staff meetings with Wolfers and Hoover see Minutes of
Meeting, November 12 & 14, 1947, PPS Records, Box 32.

[12] Although the Staff put the German question on the back burner as their other concerns
mounted, in May they did discuss the specific matter of developing improved channels of communication between the State Department and the Office of the Military Governor in Germany to
ensure a more effective implementation of U.S. policy. See Minutes of Meetings, May 17, 1948
(183d meeting) and attachment, PPS Records, Box 32.

[13] Minutes of Meetings, July 15, 1948; August 2, 1948 (237th meeting), PPS Records, Box 32.

to provide military opinion on the alternative proposals put forward.[14] Kennan dominated the discussions and the product of the Staff labors reflected his ideas.

The Planning Staff paper of August 12 (PPS/37) on "Policy Questions Concerning a Possible German Settlement" described a choice between firstly a "sweeping settlement of the German problem," involving withdrawal of occupation forces from the major portion of Germany, termination of the military government, and establishment of a German government with real power and independence, and secondly a continuation of a divided Germany with the vigorous implementation of the London Program.[15] The heart of the paper comprised an analysis of the advantages and disadvantages of the first alternative. On the positive side Kennan discerned most crucially that it "would avoid congealment of Europe along the present lines." Furthermore, it would solve the Berlin crisis, permit the Americans to take advantage of the favorable political situation existing in Germany, ensure the withdrawal of Soviet forces to the east, and greatly reduce the size and cost of the American military establishment in Germany. On the negative side, Kennan perceived that a general settlement would be a great risk complicating both the European Recovery Program and the Western Union discussions. Additionally, it would mean "the re-establishment of Germany as the only great state in central Europe," and involve the abandonment of the London Program, then in the early stages of implementation. Although he confessed that the alternatives posed a real dilemma, Kennan doubted there would be "a future time when disengagement [from] Germany will be any easier for us than it is today," and so he argued that the United States should seek the broad settlement of the German question. Only if this attempt failed should the Western Allies proceed with the London Program.

Kennan's strikingly new position was incited by the Berlin crisis but resulted from a cluster of interrelated factors.[16] His reservations about the militarization of containment, which had prompted his objections to a western military alliance, and his recognition that the Marshall Plan's success augured well for the establishment of a political balance of power in Europe provided the context for his thinking. His realization that German public opinion leaned strongly in favor of the West negated his earlier fears of Communist penetration and control there and of the possibility that German power could be joined to that of the Soviet Union. Optimistically, he began to envisage a retraction of Soviet military and political power and the return to a more normal and, he

[14] Minutes of Meetings, August 2–12, 1948, PPS Records, Box 32.

[15] PPS/37, "Policy Questions Concerning a Possible German Settlement," August 12, 1948, *FRUS* 1948, II, pp. 1287–97.

[16] Anders Stephanson provides an insightful account of Kennan's conversion from partition to reunification in his *Kennan and the Art of Foreign Policy*, pp. 130–45. Also see David Mayers, *George Kennan and the Dilemmas of US Foreign Policy*, pp. 145–47.

thought, stable European system. There seems little doubt that the imperious views of Walter Lippmann directly influenced his thinking in this regard. Lippmann's response to the "X" article had argued that the withdrawal of the armies of occupation was a prerequisite for a "tolerable peace" in Europe. Washington's premier journalistic sage went further and advocated a demilitarized and neutralized Germany as the essential condition for troop withdrawals and the restoration of a balance of power.[17] As we have seen, the Lippmann critique of the "X" article weighed heavily on Kennan. He considered it carefully during his recuperation in the hospital in April of 1948 and it seems likely he had discussions with Lippmann on German issues after he returned to his desk in the State Department. Early in July 1948 Lippmann wrote to Ambassador Lewis Douglas of his own concern regarding America's German policy. He then criticized the War Department's influence over this policy and apprised Douglas with the assurance of one who possesses firsthand information that "the planning people in the State Department are also very unhappy about the development and in private say that they have no real voice in the shaping of policy."[18] PPS/37 represented Kennan's effort to inject his voice into the formulation of American policy on Germany.

INITIAL REACTIONS AND FURTHER CONSIDERATION

Upon its submission to Secretary Marshall, the Planning Staff memorandum proposing a general settlement in Germany was circulated for comment within the department. The first response to it received by Kennan came from his principal antagonist on the North Atlantic Treaty, the unrelenting and seemingly ubiquitous John Hickerson. The chief of the European Affairs division warned bluntly that "the dangers of the proposed approach outweigh its advantages and that it would not be in the interests of the United States to make this proposal." Conditioned by the same caution that had dictated his position on the military alliance, Hickerson explained that "it would be highly dangerous to agree to unite Germany along the lines you propose until Western Europe is stronger, both economically and militarily."[19] Lovett's reaction typically was more ambivalent. Not wanting to play a decisive personal role in the determination of policy he simply wrote on the cover of Kennan's memoran-

---

[17] See Walter Lippmann, "The Cold War: VIII," September 18, 1947, and "The Cold War: XI," September 25, 1947, Robert O. Anthony Collection of Walter Lippmann, Yale, Box 39.

[18] Lippmann to Lewis Douglas, July 9, 1948, in John Morton Blum, ed., *Public Philosopher: Selected Letters of Walter Lippmann* (New York, 1985), p. 515.

[19] Hickerson to Kennan, August 31, 1948, *FRUS* 1948, II, p. 1287 n. 1. PPS 37 also drew adverse comments from others in the Office of European Affairs including Jacob Beam and Theodore Achilles. Kennan sent these written reactions on to Marshall and Lovett, described them as "worthy of careful attention" but expressed his disagreement with them. Kennan to Secretary and Lovett, September 8, 1948, PPS Records, Box 15.

dum: "This needs much more discussion with the Secretary."[20] As for Marshall, he responded more favorably although tentatively. He gave Kennan the green light to continue study of an all-German settlement but recommended that the Planning Staff should seek the advice of a group of outside consultants. Kennan recalled that PPS/37 evoked from his superiors only a troubled and thoughtful silence, although he admitted that "we were encouraged—or permitted, at least—to continue our exploration" of an all-German proposal.[21] But this recollection, a characteristic self-portrait of Kennan as a voice crying in the wilderness, does Marshall an injustice. The secretary retained an open mind on this question and definitely encouraged his planning chief to pursue his investigation of it.

The Planning Staff quickly assembled a distinguished group of outside consultants to aid its consideration of policy toward Germany. The prominence and foreign policy expertise of the consultants attested to the serious purpose of the deliberations. Foremost among the consultants was Dean Acheson, the former under secretary of state who would be named Marshall's successor in just four months. Joining the future secretary were Hamilton Fish Armstrong, the editor of *Foreign Affairs*; Sarah Gibson Blanding, the president of Vassar College; William R. Castle, like Acheson a former under secretary of state; John L. Collyer, the president of the B. F. Goodrich Company; James B. Conant, the president of Harvard University; Brooks Emeny, the president of the Foreign Policy Association; Marion B. Folsom, the treasurer of Eastman Kodak company; John M. Hancock, a partner in the Wall Street firm of Lehman Brothers; Joseph M. Proskauer, a senior member of the law firm of Proskauer, Rose, Goetz and Mendelsohn; Charles P. Taft, the president of the Federal Council of Churches of Christ in America; and Edmund Walsh, S.J., the well-known Jesuit priest who was a regent of the School of Foreign Service at Georgetown University. Marshall accorded a high status to these representatives of the interlocking legal, business, academic, and religious circles which constituted the American foreign policy establishment, and he made sure to attend their opening session with the Planning Staff. He asked the consultants to give their views on what U.S. policy should be on the German problem if a CFM meeting were to be held soon. In a manner that indicated he did not consider a policy of German division as predetermined he revealed that he sought a better approach to this problem, if possible. He assured the group that "we are seeking for an understanding [with the Soviets] in good faith."[22]

The special consultative group met with the Planning Staff during Septem-

[20] Lovett's comment, which is written on the copy of this paper in the PPS files, is referred to in *FRUS* 1948, II, p. 1288 n. 1.

[21] Kennan, *Memoirs*, I, p. 422.

[22] For Marshall's comments see Minutes of Meeting, September 15, 1948, PPS Records, Box 32.

ber 15 and 16.[23] The consultants generally agreed that the ultimate objective in Germany should be the removal of the de facto division. They supported the withdrawal of occupying forces, the termination of military government, and the establishment of a German government with wide powers—a program which closely resembled the policy alternative favored by Kennan in PPS/37. The consultants further recommended that discussions be held with the Soviets to consider the implementation of this program, although they cautioned that the United States should do this in cooperation with Britain and France. This support for Kennan's preferred course was diminished, however, by serious questioning on the consultants' part of Soviet willingness to accept such a program on terms agreeable to the Americans. In light of their reservation on this score they advised that the Western allies should proceed vigorously with their existing arrangements for West Germany. Despite these doubts about the likely Soviet acceptance of a four-power settlement, Kennan gleaned sufficient encouragement from the consultants' approval of the value of such a scheme to inform Marshall that he would continue work on the question and, in light of the consultants' suggestions, draw up a detailed program for him.[24]

PROGRAM A

Before dealing with Kennan's formulation of the detailed program it is essential in order to appreciate the context and climate for its reception to delineate briefly developments within Germany. The work of establishing a separate West German state had begun on July 1, 1948, when the occupation authorities had called the minister-presidents of the eleven West German Lander (states) to Frankfurt and empowered them to summon a constitutional assembly by September 1 to draft a democratic constitution. The delegates of the German Parliamentary Council began to meet in Bonn on September 1, but only after overcoming serious reservations about abandoning the Soviet zone of Germany and also, it must be added, after being subjected to some Western persuasion and pressure.[25] The delegates proceeded to draw up a Basic Law (their surrogate for a constitution) for what would become the Federal Republic during the very same time as the Planning Staff developed its proposal. The

[23] The verbatim transcript of the final session (and other related documents) of the Special Consultative Group on German Policy, collated on September 23, 1948, are found in PPS Records, Box 15. Also see Minutes of Meetings, September 15 and 16, 1948 (277th & 278th meetings), PPS Records, Box 32. The PPS Report, "Position To Be Taken by the U.S. at a CFM Meeting," November 15, 1948, FRUS 1948, II, pp. 1320–24, noted that "of the group of outside consultants called in to examine this program on September 15–16, all but two (Mr. Armstrong and Father Walsh) appeared to favor a course of action along the lines of Program A."

[24] Kennan to Marshall, September 17, 1948, PPS Records, Box 33.

[25] These developments are discussed in detail in Gimbel, *The American Occupation of Germany* but see in particular his "Summary of Events Leading to the West German Government," pp. 253–57.

efforts of the German delegates, however, served to attract and further congeal support among policymakers such as General Lucius Clay for a settlement involving the division of Germany.[26] Clay, who felt he had given cooperation with the Soviets in Germany his best effort, now developed a deep and vocal commitment to the plans for West Germany.[27] The British and the French likewise firmed in their support for German partition—a position toward which they had always leaned.[28]

These political developments in West Germany created suspicion regarding the development of an all-German settlement which would negate the work expended in implementing the London Program. Compounding this sentiment were persistent doubts over the efficacy and value of negotiations with the Soviet Union. Such doubts were only increased by the failure of the talks to end the Berlin blockade which the Western representatives in Moscow conducted with Stalin and Molotov.[29] Furthermore, the surprising success of the airlift—both in supplying Berlin and as a symbol of Western commitment to freedom against Soviet oppression—removed the urgency and much of the pressure from the Americans, British, and French even to agree to negotiate with the Soviets over either Berlin or Germany as a whole.[30]

Despite these developments querying the feasibility of a four-power settlement in Germany, Kennan vigorously pursued his study of this question. His own commitment to German unity on both an intellectual and an emotional level deepened significantly. After a brief diversion to investigate the more narrow issue of Berlin and the airlift, the Staff labored throughout October over the broader German problem.[31] Kennan continued to exercise a dominant

[26] This point in fact has been made by Kennan in *Memoirs*, I, p. 443.

[27] For an indication of Clay's views see his letter to James F. Byrnes, September 18, 1948, in Jean Edward Smith, ed., *The Papers of Lucius D. Clay: Germany 1945–1949*, vol. 2 (Bloomington, Ind., 1974), pp. 858–60. Clay wrote: "I am convinced that a strong western German government reoriented toward western Europe would do much to restore the political and economic balances in Europe in our favor." Charles Bohlen warned on August 4, 1948, that the suspension of the London Program "would certainly be violently opposed by General Clay and Ambassador Murphy." Bohlen to Secretary Marshall, August 4, 1948, Records of Charles E. Bohlen, Box 5.

[28] For a discussion of the British position see Josef Foschepoth, "British Interest in the Division of Germany after the Second World War," *Journal of Contemporary History* 21, no. 3 (July 1986): 391–411. For an exploration of Bevin's "instinctive anti-Germanism" and his fears of a revived Rapallo-type treaty see Kenneth O. Morgan, *Labour in Power, 1945–1951* (Oxford, 1984), pp. 255–57. The severe French attitude on Germany is well known. For an effort by Walter Lippmann to persuade Jean Monnet of the value of an all-German settlement see Lippmann to Monnet, September 30, 1948, in Blum, ed., *Public Philosopher*, p. 524.

[29] On the failure of these negotiations see Bedell Smith, *My Three Years in Moscow*, pp. 237–53.

[30] Despite the airlift's achievement the Americans did seek further negotiations with the Russians for a Berlin settlement. For details of this and Kennan's support for the measure see Philip C. Jessup, "The Berlin Blockade and the Use of the United Nations," *Foreign Affairs* 50 (October 1971): 163–73.

[31] On the Staff's discussion of the Berlin issue see Minutes of Meeting, September 27 and 28, 1948, PPS Records, Box 32.

influence over his colleagues. He established the main lines of thought and his colleagues assisted in fleshing them out. In this task Kennan received the most substantial assistance from Ware Adams, a competent foreign service officer with experience in Germany and Austria, who shared Kennan's preference for a unified Germany and who had rejoined the Planning Staff in June 1948 after an earlier temporary appointment at the time of the Marshall Plan formulation.[32] Kennan, Adams and the other Staff members also brought representatives of relevant State Department divisions and from the Plans and Operations Division of the Army Department into their discussions.[33]

The focus for the discussions was a derivation of Kennan's earlier reunification proposal providing for the withdrawal of all occupation garrisons to the perimeter of a German state. Not all members of the enlarged working group agreed on the desirability and the feasibility of such a settlement. But according to Ware Adams' minutes there existed a "general agreement that it should be framed and put forward in a sincere intention to secure its adoption."[34] By late October a document outlining detailed prescriptions for policy had been completed. After intensive analysis and final redrafting by Kennan, the Planning Staff paper (PPS/37/1), known as Program or Plan A, was submitted to Marshall on November 12, 1948.[35]

In submitting Program A to Marshall Kennan alerted him to the larger group which had devised it and he took pains to explain that this group had not sought to answer the question as to whether the United States should actually present a positive proposal of its nature at that specific time. He accurately conveyed the group's view that this should be Marshall's decision.[36] But in a separate paper the planning chief aimed to persuade the secretary of state to implement Program A provided that the United States could obtain "advance assurance of a wide enough degree of British and French acquiescence to maintain basic three-power unity." He reasoned that putting his German Program forward would seize the initiative for the Americans, offset charges that they did not want a settlement with Russia and, by evincing a readiness to negotiate, keep the international situation flexible so as to mitigate "the congealment of the present division of Germany and Europe." Realistically, Kennan admitted that Program A was unlikely to be accepted at that juncture but he argued persuasively that its offer might "help keep open the door for an

[32] Oral History Interview with Ware Adams by C. Ben Wright, September 30, 1970, Wright Papers, Box 8.
[33] For details of these discussions see Minutes of Meetings, September 20 to November 1, 1948, PPS Records, Box 32.
[34] Minutes of Meeting, October 14, 1948, PPS Records, Box 32.
[35] PPS 37/1, "A Program for Germany" (Program A), November 12, 1948, FRUS 1948, II, pp. 1325–38. For the text in full see PPS Records, Box 15. Also note Kennan, Memoirs, I, pp. 423–26.
[36] Kennan to Marshall, November 12, 1948, FRUS 1948, II, pp. 1324–25.

eventual peaceful withdrawal of the Russians from central Europe.''[37] It could provide the basis for negotiations. Finally, there was no alternative to it other than accepting the division of Germany.

Program A can still be read with interest and profit. It stands among the most creative attempts to resolve the German problem. Kennan and his planning colleagues proposed a new control machinery for Germany followed by the election and establishment of a provisional government for the whole country. Simultaneously military government through Germany would be terminated. The forces of all four occupying powers would be withdrawn to specified perimeter garrison areas. These major components of the program and the measures to implement them were outlined in impressive detail. There could be no disputing that this constituted a thoughtful assault on the troublesome German issue. And, it contained within it the basis for a genuine negotiating position to place before the Russians. Program A was not naive in its approach to the Soviet Union. It was predicated on the assumption that anti-Communist forces would win a working majority in any election and on a belief in the ability of the Germans to maintain a government capable of resisting Communist political pressures. If these factors were not considered likely, then the whole program would be abandoned. In such circumstances the Americans would be forced to press ahead with the London Program for the West German zones.[38]

Kennan immediately arranged for the distribution of the Program A proposal.[39] He appreciated the need to generate support for it among other figures concerned with German policy. But the initial reaction was adverse. Robert Murphy, General Clay's political adviser and the senior State Department official in Germany, found it ''a very worthwhile document and as blueprints go it should be valuable.'' But Murphy, a tough-minded and skilled diplomat who had represented the United States in Vichy France and in the complicated politics of North Africa during World War II, criticized the proposal in letters to Jacob Beam of the Central European Division and to General Marshall's special assistant, Marshall S. Carter. He continued to emphasize using ''Western Germany to the greatest extent possible as our political and military bridgehead.''[40] Murphy also relayed General Clay's grave reservations about the troop withdrawal component of Program A. Clay now believed that the pres-

[37] See PPS Report, "Position To Be Taken by the U.S. at a CFM Meeting," November 15, 1948, *FRUS* 1948, II, pp. 1320–24.

[38] PPS 37/1, "A Program for Germany" (Program A), November 12, 1948, *FRUS* 1948, II, pp. 1325–38.

[39] Kennan sent copies of Program A to Marshall S. Carter in Paris where he was attending the United Nations meeting with General Marshall in order that Carter could distribute them to Clay, Murphy, and others. See Kennan to Carter, November 12, 1948, PPS Records, Box 33.

[40] For the initial Murphy quotation see his letter to Jacob Beam, December 7, 1948, *FRUS* 1948, II, p. 1320 n. 1. For the second quotation see Murphy to Marshall S. Carter, January 14, 1949, PPS Records, Box 15.

ence of the American army was all that kept Europe stable and that to withdraw it would be to "practically turn the show over to Russia and the Communists without a struggle." He dismissed the periphery theory of stationing
garrison forces in ports and on the rim of Germany as "totally impractical."[41]
Clay had a reputation for being sure that his judgment was correct after he
reached it and for insisting upon it with fiery determination but Kennan was
unintimidated by the military governor's repute.[42] With powerful logic he replied to Murphy and presumably through him to Clay that "if our troops remain, Russia's troops remain. If Russia's troops remain, zonal boundaries
remain. If zonal boundaries remain, there can be no serious talk of a solution
of the German problem as a whole."[43]

Clay and Murphy had committed such effort to implement the London Program that it is not surprising that they exhibited reluctance in pursuing any
alternative, but Kennan hoped for a more favorable reception from other policymakers less closely identified with the West German arrangements. Again
he was disappointed. Charles Bohlen had notified him before Program A was
submitted formally of his doubts concerning a policy which meant, in effect,
"an attempt to unify Germany by giving the Germans themselves an opportunity to try it." Bohlen also predicted that Kennan's plan to withdraw troops
would have a most unfavorable impact on the French given their "neurosis on
security."[44] The working group had not been convinced by his misgivings and
Kennan had hoped that his old friend would feel differently upon seeing the
final document. He did not because ultimately he thought it impossible to persuade the Russians to withdraw from East Germany. Even more vigorous opposition came predictably from Hickerson, although he directed it not at Program A itself but at the recommendation for its implementation. In stark
contrast to Kennan's approach he advised that the United States "not take the

---

[41] General Clay's views, which were completely at odds with Program A, were expressed to
Secretary Forrestal. See Millis, ed., *The Forrestal Diaries*, pp. 506–7.

[42] On Clay's reputation see Oral History Interview with Robert Lovett by Jean Smith, May 4,
1971, Eisenhower Administration Project, Columbia University, New York.

[43] Kennan to Murphy, December 24, 1948, PPS Records, Box 33. Kennan further explained to
Murphy: "Yet if we were again to appear in the CFM, we would have to have *some* suggestion for
such a solution. We could not just sit silent and let the Russian propagandists work out on us as
on a punching bag. Better—it seemed to us—to make clear the terms on which we *could* envisage
a withdrawal of forces, than to allow ourselves to appear as those who oppose any movement
toward solution in the German problem."

[44] For Bohlen's doubts see his letter to Kennan, October 25, 1948, Records of Charles E.
Bohlen, Box 5. Bohlen reported to Kennan from Paris that "The French neurosis on security is
even stronger than I had anticipated before coming here and the one faint element of confidence
which they cling to is the fact that American troops, however strong in number, stand between
them and the Red Army. If you add to that the strong fears to be generated with the prospect of
returning power to Germans at the present juncture, I am sure that the general line of approach
suggested in your letter would have a most unfavorable reaction in France and probably in Holland
and Belgium as well."

initiative in presenting Program A since to do so would risk breaking the united western front and might prejudice the plans we are successfully pursuing in the greater part of Germany.'' He dismissed Program A as ''an 'ideal' Program'' and supported the continuation of the existing policies in the larger part of Germany under Western control.[45] Hickerson garnered the support of the Office of the Assistant Secretary for Occupied Areas in opposing the Staff proposal's implementation. Only the Office of the Assistant Secretary of Economic Affairs, through Paul Nitze, concurred with the Staff.[46]

The criticisms and objections to Program A blocked its further progress. Lovett ordered Kennan to reconsider his recommendation in light of the critical comments made of it.[47] General Marshall, who had encouraged Kennan in developing this proposal designed to prevent the permanent division of Germany, made no decision concerning it and apparently did not comment upon it. Marshall was tied up away from Washington at the meeting of the United Nations General Assembly in Paris during the period of Program A's presentation.[48] Kennan lost his direct access to the secretary of state which undoubtedly contributed to Marshall's failure to comment on the all-German proposal. In all likelihood, however, Marshall's failure to express his opinion and to act upon it resulted mainly from his imminent departure from office and his unwillingness to constrain those who would replace him. Whatever the reason the unresolved debate on German policy, which the failure to accept or reject Program A exemplified, was part of the legacy he consigned to his successor, Dean Gooderham Acheson.

ACHESON RETURNS TO STATE

President Truman chose an experienced and capable international lawyer to replace General Marshall. Acheson readily agreed to leave his practice at the prestigious law firm of Covington and Burling to take the reins at State. He had left the firm before in 1941 and had served subsequently as Assistant Secretary of State for Economic Affairs (1941–1944) and for Congressional Relations (1944–1945) before taking on the under secretaryship of state under both James F. Byrnes and George Marshall.[49] Such service gave him personal

[45] Hickerson to Office of Secretary of State, November 23, 1948, PPS Records, Box 27.

[46] For Economic Affairs concurrence see Paul H. Nitze to Office of Secretary of State, November 26, 1948, PPS Records, Box 27. Nitze recalled working with Kennan on this question and of being of ''the same mind'' on it. He also remembers that Chip Bohlen ''thought Kennan and I were nuts on the German question.'' Author's interview with Paul H. Nitze, Arlington, Va., June 30, 1978. For reference to the non-concurrence of the Office of the Assistant Secretary for Occupied Areas see *FRUS* 1948, II, p. 1320 n. 1.

[47] Lovett memorandum, December 1, 1948, *FRUS* 1948, II, p. 1320 n. 1.

[48] On Marshall's activities during this period see Pogue, *George C. Marshall: Statesman*, pp. 404–12.

[49] For Acheson's own account of his service see *Present at the Creation*, pp. 169–328.

familiarity with many of the major issues of postwar American diplomacy. Along with this knowledge Acheson brought to his new position high intelligence and a notable capacity for hard work. And, crucially, he came with a close relationship with Truman which flourished during his tenure in office and was the bedrock of his strength as secretary of state. He served the president loyally for four years and Truman reciprocated with unswerving support for Acheson, who managed to accumulate more than his fair share of enemies over that time. Dean Rusk even speculated that Truman selected the new secretary for the loyalty and friendship he had demonstrated during the 1948 election campaign when Acheson the private citizen at times had waited in lonely vigil to meet the president on his return to Union Station from his whistle-stop tours.[50]

Acheson cut an impressive figure. Tall and handsome with his brushed-up mustache, impeccable clothing, and erect, almost military, bearing, he seemed to define the requirements of "what a Yale man is supposed to look like."[51] His appearance gave ample hints of his privileged background—son of the Episcopal bishop of Connecticut, Groton, Yale, Harvard Law School, and a clerkship with Justice Louis Brandeis. His background and education decisively influenced his career. He possessed a peculiarly American form of noblesse oblige along with others of his generation because, as his British friend Noel Annan recalled, "they had been taught at school and college to serve their country first and care for their reputation and fortune second."[52]

Acheson appears to have had neither doubts that he should assume the position nor concerns about his abilities to fill it. His self-assurance and seeming arrogance annoyed some. He possessed not only a sharp mind but a sharp tongue with which he voiced frank evaluations of people and ideas. His friend Archibald MacLeish noted that Acheson "did not shrink at making enemies and had almost no tolerance for what he felt was inferior intellect or stupid questioning."[53] Acheson's acerbic edge separated him from Marshall and Lovett who had exercised such great tact in dealing with others and in garnering support for their endeavors. Comparing Acheson and Marshall, Paul Nitze noted that the former "was a more intelligent and brilliant man, but often he could not resist humiliating people whose support he could have used."[54]

Acheson found no need to exaggerate his already formidable intelligence

[50] See Rusk's reflections recorded in Schoenbaum, *Waging Peace and War*, p. 192.

[51] This is David McCullough's observation given in a speech at "Dean Acheson, A Remembrance," Washington, D.C., April 6, 1989. I am grateful to Mr. McCullough for supplying me with a copy of his remarks.

[52] Noel Annan, "Dean Acheson," *The Yale Review* 77, no. 4 (October 1988): 477. This article has influenced my portrayal of Acheson. On this point see also Walter Isaacson and Evan Thomas, *The Wise Men*, the elegant collective biography which examines the contribution of the Acheson generation.

[53] MacLeish quoted in Barry Rubin, *Secrets of State*, p. 64.

[54] Nitze, *From Hiroshima to Glasnost*, p. 67.

with any pretense at intellectual hauteur. Justice Brandeis "taught him to be both a pragmatist and an empiricist" and it was a lasting lesson. In his approach to making foreign policy Acheson "was very much a practical man, one who eschewed visionary schemes." He approached problems simply, had little time for theory and was "influenced by solid evidence and concrete situations."[55] Acheson actually liked to participate in discussions at the early stages of policy formation.[56] He was not the type to wait for a policy recommendation to come to him. He brought energetic leadership to the State Department and a respect for and a willingness to utilize its personnel.

Acheson's strong character and notable talents did not mean, however, that he arrived at the State Department in January 1949 with his mind made up on the crucial issues of American diplomacy. His confidence resided in his belief that he could develop appropriate policies and did not rest on any delusion about himself as an oracle. Acheson came prepared to confront challenging foreign-policy issues and to work hard on their resolution. In doing so he wanted to hear the arguments, to debate the strengths and weaknesses of various positions and to forge the best course for the United States. In this undertaking he knew he needed the support of others.

With Marshall's retirement Lovett considered his duty done and returned back to Brown Brothers, Harriman on Wall Street in an effort to improve his physical and financial well-being. To replace him Acheson chose, at Truman's suggestion, James E. Webb who had served well as Director of the Bureau of the Budget. With studied understatement Acheson recalled that "Webb knew more about administration than about foreign policy."[57] Indeed, close observers assumed that Webb had been appointed to oversee the reorganization of the State Department along the lines suggested by the so-called Hoover Commission (of which Acheson had been vice-chairman), including its recommendation that the permanent State Department establishment in Washington be amalgamated with the Foreign Service.[58] Webb's brief was not so specific, although he did tend to focus on administrative arrangements. Acheson accepted Webb not because he expected any significant contribution on policy from him—and none was forthcoming—but because he appreciated that Truman felt comfortable with Webb and this would cement presidential confidence in the State Department.[59] To fill the lacunae in policy-making Acheson appointed Dean Rusk to a new position as deputy under secretary for substan-

[55] The above draws on the insightful analysis of Isaacson and Thomas in *The Wise Men*, pp. 126, 323–24, 362.

[56] Barry Rubin makes this point in *Secrets of State*, p. 65.

[57] Acheson, *Present at the Creation*, p. 332.

[58] For speculation by Walter Lippmann that Webb had been brought in to reorganize the State Department see Lippmann to Jean Monnet, January 10, 1949, in Blum, ed., *Public Philosopher*, pp. 525–26.

[59] Acheson, *Present at the Creation*, p. 332.

tive matters and he largely took on the task of coordinating the work of the geographic and functional divisions.[60] Also Acheson appointed his friend Philip Jessup, a professor of international law at Columbia, to be ambassador-at-large. But as Jessup's wife observed, "Such a position would also entail a share in the framing of foreign policy. *This* is the part that 'sold' the idea to Phil."[61] Jessup expected to work closely with Acheson and the Policy Planning Staff under Kennan.

The new under secretary's appointment did not bode well for Kennan. Webb was warned early on by an associate, Alvin Roseman, that the Foreign Service and the Foreign Service Officers who headed up the geographic offices were disturbed by his appointment because as Budget director he had questioned the "whole concept of the Foreign Service as a separate 'elite corps.' "[62] Perhaps tension over this matter underlay the strained relations that developed between Webb and senior Foreign Service officers including Kennan. Whatever the case, in the transition from Lovett to Webb the planning director lost out. Lovett had not always agreed with Kennan but he had accepted and facilitated his access to Marshall. Webb, in the supposed interests of good administration eventually would limit Kennan's direct dealings with Acheson. Three decades after they served together in the State Department Webb's dislike for Kennan (and Bohlen) remained unrestrained.[63] His presence in the State Department made Kennan's more difficult. But problems with Webb were far from Kennan's mind when Acheson returned to State because the Policy Planning Staff director assumed that he would be working directly with the secretary.

Kennan had a more personal and social relationship with Acheson than he did with General Marshall. Marshall had totally ignored the Washington social scene. He never went to dinner at Walter Lippmann's or Joe Alsop's. Acheson did and, in fact, played some role in introducing Kennan to this circuit, although Kennan was a more reticent participant. While not close friends Kennan and Acheson had maintained a good personal relationship since Kennan returned to Washington to take up his position at the War College.[64] Kennan

[60] On Rusk's position see Schoenbaum, *Waging Peace and War*, pp. 193–94.

[61] Lois K. Jessup, "At Large with My Ambassador; Notes from the Diplomatic Sidelines," edited family letters, February 1, 1949, Papers of Philip Jessup, Library of Congress, Washington, D.C., Container B1.

[62] Alvin Roseman to Webb, January 12, 1949, James E. Webb Papers, HSTL, Box 23.

[63] In 1980 Webb jibed that Kennan "who had never lived in a democracy" would "come in and say, 'You and the President have to go up there and make Congress do the following.' " As for Bohlen, he repeated an Achesonian quip to the effect that "I can't run foreign policy out of Chip Bohlen's restaurant." He sarcastically referred to their desire to be "the great towering experts" on whom "Truman, Acheson and everybody else depended." Joint Oral History Interview by Hugh Heclo and Anna Nelson on "The Truman White House" with Charles Murphy, Richard Neustadt, David Stowe, and James Webb, February 20, 1980, HSTL.

[64] Author's interview with Kennan, March 6, 1989.

greeted Acheson's appointment with approval and lost no time in briefing him on what he thought needed to be done both in terms of policy and "the tools of the trade," the means to implement it.[65] Acheson in turn came to his new position with a high opinion of Kennan based especially on a recollection of his fine work at the time of the Marshall Plan formulation. He clearly intended to work closely with him and to signify this he soon appointed Kennan the department's Counselor, a post vacated by Bohlen and usually regarded as that of a top policy adviser to the secretary. Kennan retained his directorship of the Policy Planning Staff. Perhaps he might have preferred the deputy under secretary's post which went to Rusk, where he would have possessed line responsibility for coordinating the geographic and functional divisions, but his continued directorship of the Staff certainly augured well for his playing a significant role in the formulation of foreign policy under Acheson's leadership.[66] But Kennan began his service under Acheson in a somewhat strained and anxious mood. He told Acheson that he was troubled by "the pressures of an insistent, prodding world reality which is already breathing down our necks" and warned that "I am really not interested in carrying on in government service unless I can feel that we have at least a sporting chance of coping with our problem."[67] The German question comprised a central element of that problem.

ACHESON AND THE FORMULATION OF GERMAN POLICY

The new secretary of state did not assume his office with fixed views on German policy. His willingness early in 1949 to seek advice on the subject from the banker and foreign policy commentator, James P. Warburg—who warned insistently against the creation of a separate West German state—indicated something of his open mind.[68] Although not committed to any policy line,

[65] See Kennan to Acheson, January 3, 1949, PPS Records, Box 33. This letter supposedly was written before Kennan knew of Acheson's appointment but it reads suspiciously otherwise.

[66] My speculation that Kennan might have preferred Rusk's position results from Kennan's emphasis in his letter to Acheson of January 3, 1949, of the need for a "permanent under-secretary" of the department. Kennan to Acheson, January 3, 1949, PPS Records, Box 33.

[67] Ibid. Kennan told Acheson: "I'd rather be at Yale, or where-you-will,—any place where I could sound-off and talk freely to people,—than in the confines of a department in which you can neither do anything about it nor tell people what you think ought to be done."

[68] James P. Warburg, *The Long Road Home: The Autobiography of a Maverick* (New York, 1964), pp. 255–58. According to Warburg: "Throughout 1949, until the point of no return was passed, I did my utmost to persuade Acheson not to create a separate West German state." Acheson had an association and close friendship with Warburg going back to the 1930s. See their quite extensive correspondence in Papers of Dean G. Acheson, Sterling Memorial Library, Yale University, New Haven, Conn., Box 33. On Warburg also see William C. Berman, "James Paul Warburg: An Establishment Maverick Challenges Truman's Policy Toward Germany," in Thomas G. Paterson, ed., *Cold War Critics: Alternatives to American Foreign Policy in the Truman Years* (Chicago, 1971), pp. 54–75.

Acheson possessed some familiarity with German issues. As Byrnes's under secretary of state he had some hand in the German policy implemented during 1946 and had contributed to a proposal aimed at forestalling the definitive division of Germany.[69] More recently, he had participated as a consultant in the Planning Staff's deliberations on an all-German settlement and given a general endorsement to its proposal. Also he brought to the State Department an awareness of the importance of the German problem derived from Kennan's private endeavors to orient him.[70] And he could not have missed Walter Lippmann's fiercely critical comments concerning the London Program which he voiced in his column on the eve of Acheson's arrival at State.[71] Along with the final negotiation of the North Atlantic Treaty, the American attempt to resolve this problem dominated Acheson's first six months in office.

On January 24, just three days after taking his oath of office, Acheson secured President Truman's agreement to the State Department's preparation of a paper on German policy to be sent through the NSC to the president for his approval. Acheson illustrated the regard he had for Kennan and pointed to the role he expected him to play by directing the Policy Planning Staff to devise this paper.[72] Simultaneous with Acheson's initiation of the study of German policy within the State Department the Army secretary, Kenneth C. Royall, sought to establish an inter-departmental group to consider German problems.[73] When he raised his idea with other Cabinet members on January 26,

[69] Acheson's involvement on the German question during 1946 is discussed in W. W. Rostow, *The Division of Europe after World War II: 1946* (Austin, 1981).

[70] In his long letter of January 3 Kennan stressed the proper handling of the German problem as indispensable to a successful foreign policy. Kennan to Acheson, January 3, 1949, PPS Records, Box 33.

[71] See especially Lippmann's "The Dark Prospect in Germany," December 30, 1948, a "Today and Tomorrow" column included in the Robert O. Anthony Collection of Walter Lippmann, Box 39.

[72] Acheson's memorandum of conversation with the president, January 24, 1949, PPS Records, Box 15. See also Savage to Kennan, January 24, 1949, PPS Records, Box 15, in which Savage reported Acheson's instructions; and Minutes of Meeting, January 26, 1949, PPS Records, Box 32.

[73] Perturbed both by the risk inherent in the Berlin situation and by the prolongation of military and political tensions in Europe, Royall had concluded that the United States should "take the initiative in suggesting a specific long-range plan designed to meet these troublesome situations." Surprisingly, given his position, the Army Secretary called for "a major move which would solve our Berlin difficulties by including them in a new *modus vivendi* for Germany as a whole." See Royall to Secretary of Defense, January 19, 1949, *FRUS* 1949, III, pp. 82–84. Royall, aware of the existence of Program A which he referred to as "Mr. Kennan's Plan," proposed a substitute plan as a basis for further discussion. Acheson received a copy of Royall's memorandum on January 26 and requested Kennan's opinion of it. The planning chief sympathized with Royall's basic objective but described many of his specific suggestions as unrealistic in view of the work done by his planning group in the fall of 1948. Kennan took this opportunity to forward a copy of Program A to Acheson. See Kennan to Secretary of State, January 27, 1949, RG 59, General

Acheson insisted the proper procedure was to act through the NSC, and to have Royall's proposed group designated as an NSC working subcommittee and to assign it the task of restating American policy toward Germany. Acheson secured Truman's approval of this procedure the following day and on January 28 the NSC established a working subcommittee composed of the secretaries of state, defense, army, and the head of the Economic Cooperation Administration. In addition, the NSC organized a steering group of representatives of these officials—on which Acheson notably placed Kennan who acted as its chairman—and charged it with drawing up a statement of American policy towards Germany.[74] This arrangement linked the state and NSC investigations of German policy. It might have been expected that the intra-departmental study initiated by Acheson on January 24 would serve as the first stage of the NSC investigation and that through this framework decisions regarding the course to pursue in Germany would be reached expeditiously. The expectation was not fulfilled.

Kennan talked with Lippmann as he began his deliberations. Lippmann—who described himself as "one in whom *l'esprit de l'escalier* is strongest the morning after"—wrote to Kennan after such a discussion and counseled that the State Department should only assume responsibility for the German occupation when "an unequivocal set of principles" had been accepted. Foremost among these principles was "that the German problem is soluble only (as per your [Kennan's] memorandum) within the framework of a European (not a West European) system." Like Kennan, Lippmann did not want to recognize the permanence of the Iron Curtain. He wanted the liquidation of military government and the withdrawal of occupation troops as "a real and present objective, not a remote and theoretical one."[75] Lippmann's support encouraged Kennan in the validity of the approach enshrined in Program A but the journalist's endorsement, however satisfying in an intellectual sense, did not assist him in pushing his case within the administration.

In fact he found it hard to focus attention on broad policy questions. When the Policy Planning Staff approached the German question its discussions were soon diverted to the particular matter of the administration of the German occupation.[76] Kennan realized that the continued surfacing of day-to-day operational problems seriously interfered with the formulation of broad policy

Records of the Department of State, Decimal File 1945-1949, NA, Washington, D.C. (hereafter Decimal File), 740.00119 Control (Germany)/1-2549.

[74] For details see Acheson's "Germany" memorandum, January 26, 1949, Decimal File, 740.00119 Control (Germany)/1-2649. See also his memorandum on "Meeting with the President," January 27, 1949, Decimal File, 740.00110 Control (Germany)/1-2749. For the deliberations of the NSC see Acheson's proposal in Truman Papers: Records of NSC, HSTL, Box 10.

[75] Lippmann to Kennan, February 1, 1949, Papers of Walter Lippmann, Sterling Memorial Library, Yale University, Box 81.

[76] Minutes of Meetings, February 2, 3, 4, and 7, 1949, PPS Records, Box 32.

and he complained of this to Acheson early in February.[77] Acheson's response was delay. Despite his expressed desire to settle upon long-term German policy, he moved cautiously and did not hurry to facilitate its determination by providing for a structured debate on it in which presumably Program A might have been accepted or rejected. By the end of February Kennan had managed to gain the NSC Steering group's acceptance of a report identifying major areas for decision on Germany but no final conclusions had been reached on these.[78] In this stagnant context he decided to visit Germany to gather firsthand information to assay his own thoughts on policy and to evaluate the London Program policies now, he thought, assuming a dangerous permanence.

Before his departure for Germany Kennan offered an assessment of the German situation in an obvious attempt to provoke discussion of general German policy. He argued that the only solution to the German problem lay in terms of Europe. He criticized the arrangements for a West German state on the grounds that it would become "the spokesman of a resentful and defiant nationalism" capable of negotiating with the Russians to regain the eastern German provinces. In lieu of establishing a formal West German government, he suggested forming a provisional West German administration possessing wide powers but leaving sovereignty in the hands of the occupying nations.[79] Kennan intended this demarche to reduce the solemnity and significance of a division of Germany under the terms of the London Program and thereby to provide some basis for further negotiation with the Russians along the lines of Program A. He sought to preserve the possibility of his larger objective—"the retraction of Soviet power from Eastern Europe."[80]

When the State Department officers concerned with operations in Germany—(Jacob Beam, John Hickerson, Henry Byroade, and Robert Murphy)—examined Kennan's proposal, they argued in chorus that it was too late for the United States to change its position regarding the establishment of a West German government owing to commitments made within Germany and with Britain and France. Kennan deferred to their position when he met with Acheson to discuss his proposal and elicited a surprising reaction. The secretary regretted Kennan's deferral and told him he had been "almost persuaded by the cogency of . . . [his] argument." He then admitted his ignorance as to how the United States had decided to establish a West German government and, in a manner suggesting that he was not partial to this development, wondered aloud if it had not been "the brainchild of General Clay" rather than a

---

[77] For Kennan's complaint see his report to Acheson, February 8, 1949, Decimal File, 740.00119 Control (Germany)/2-849.

[78] "Report by the Steering Group to the NSC Sub-Committee on the German Questions," February 14, 1949, Decimal File, 740.00119 Control (Germany)/2-1449.

[79] See Kennan's untitled paper, March 8, 1949, PPS Records, Box 15, which is also in FRUS 1949, III, pp. 96–102.

[80] For Kennan's objective see Minutes of Meeting, March 1, 1949, PPS Records, Box 32.

governmental decision. Then, mentioning Kennan's forthcoming trip to Germany, Acheson resolved to put off decision on German policy until his planning director's return. Acheson did not interfere with the implementation of the program to establish a West German government but he concluded by asking Kennan to "bring back up-to-date information and his personal appraisal of the present situation to form the basis for long-range policy."[81]

Thomas Schwartz aptly has described Acheson's approach on the German issue as a "two-track policy" and surely this is evident here.[82] In a related sense it is accurate to conclude that as of early March 1949 the secretary of state had not yet decided upon the course to pursue on the German problem. Indeed, Acheson had specifically obtained Truman's approval not to be rushed into assuming State Department responsibility for the German occupation "until we had arranged our ideas about policy."[83] To comprehend the development of America's German policy in 1949 this openness of Acheson's part must be appreciated. Both of Acheson's capable biographers have failed to illuminate this point. The suggestion that "Acheson gave lip service to the idea of German unification, but . . . did not consider it a practical possibility," describes the secretary's attitude after the Paris meeting of the Council of Foreign Ministers in May but not before it.[84] One must at this point also correct the view, most persuasively offered by Kennan himself (although admittedly referring not just to this issue), that Acheson valued him as "an intellectual gadfly on the hides of slower colleagues" but did not take him fully seriously when it came to the final, responsible decisions of policy.[85] On the German question Acheson valued Kennan's counsel and planned to consider his advice in the final determination of policy.[86]

[81] Minutes of Meeting, March 9, 1949, pps Records, Box 32. For Kennan's meeting with Acheson see Memorandum of Conversation by Murphy, March 9, 1949, *FRUS* 1949, III, pp. 102–5.

[82] Thomas Alan Schwartz, "From Occupation to Alliance: John J. McCloy and the Allied High Commission in the Federal Republic of Germany, 1949–1952," Ph.D. diss., Harvard University, 1985, p. 70.

[83] Acheson's memorandum of conversation with the president, February 28, 1949, Acheson Papers, HSTL, Box 64.

[84] Gaddis Smith, *Dean Acheson*, vol. 16, in *The American Secretaries of State and Their Diplomacy*, ed. Robert H. Ferrell (New York, 1972), pp. 79–81. Smith's argument, concurred in by David S. McLellan, that Acheson's policy "was to press for the maximum development of German power as a counterpoise to the Soviet Union" may characterize his eventual German policy but it does not identify his policy—or rather *lack* of policy—in his first months in office. See David S. McLellan, *Dean Acheson: The State Department Years* (New York, 1976), p. 147.

[85] Kennan, *Memoirs*, I, p. 427. On this point one must avoid the temptation to let one's interpretation be colored by Acheson's later searing judgment that Kennan had never "grasped the realities of power" if one is to explain accurately how America finally settled its German policy. For Acheson's later views see *New York Times*, January 12, 1958; and Dean G. Acheson, "The Illusion of Disengagement," *Foreign Affairs* 36 (April 1958): 371–82.

[86] The night before Kennan left from Washington he accompanied Acheson to his home for a long discussion. Acheson also gave Kennan permission to speak not only with officials in Ger-

OPERATIONAL NECESSITIES AND LONG-TERM POLICY

Kennan left Washington on March 10 and spent the next two weeks meeting with American occupation officials, including General Clay, elected and appointed German officials, and a number of unofficial German contacts. He visited West Berlin, Frankfurt, and Hamburg, conversing, observing, and thinking. The experience did nothing to diminish either his personal distaste for the American military occupation authorities or his opposition to the London Program. He later admitted to feeling simply oppressed "with the enormity of the responsibility we had incurred and of our inadequacy to it."[87] Kennan did succeed in raising doubts and pessimism in Clay's mind over the commitment of the United States government to the establishment of a West German government.[88] With an irony that neither man fully appreciated they substantially had reversed their positions from those they had advocated in 1945–1946. What remained consistent was the contempt each held for the opposite view. But, aside from unsettling Clay, Kennan's visit failed to produce any major insights capable of influencing decisively the debate over long-term policy. And, in his absence from Washington, decisions were made with important implications for such policy.

During Kennan's time in Germany developments of considerable impor-[1] tance had occurred on two fronts. Acheson agreed to hold discussions on Germany with the British and French Foreign Ministers coincident to their visits to the United States in early April to sign the North Atlantic Pact.[89] The prospect of these discussions required the United States to reach some conclusive negotiating position on German issues. And, Professor Philip C. Jessup, serving as Acheson's ambassador-at-large, had begun secret negotiations with Jacob Malik, the Soviet representative to the United Nations, portending a lifting

---

many but also with Ambassadors Douglas (London), Caffery (Paris), and Harriman (ECA), and with the Belgian Prime Minister Paul-Henri Spaak on the German question. Clearly Kennan took this mission seriously. For his meeting with Acheson see the entry in Acheson's appointment book, March 9, 1949, Acheson Papers, HSTL, Box 45. For the permission see memorandum of conversation, Secretary's Daily Meeting, March 10, 1949, RG 59, Records of the Department of State—Office of Executive Secretariat, NA, Box 1.

[87] Kennan, *Memoirs*, I, p. 439. For further details on Kennan's visit see Kennan, *Sketches from a Life* (New York, 1989), pp. 119–26; and Notes and miscellaneous Papers Relating to George Kennan's Visit to Germany, March 10–21, 1949, Kennan Papers, Box 23.

[88] For reference to Kennan's conversation with Clay see Acting Political Adviser for Germany (Riddleberger) to Secretary of State, March 26, 1949, *FRUS* 1949, III, p. 231. Riddleberger wrote: "In talking to me this morning, I had the strong impression that Clay's pessimism over the establishment of a West German Government was intensified by his conversation with Kennan from which Clay deduced a lack of determination on the part of the U.S. to push ahead vigorously with the establishment of the West German Government."

[89] Memorandum of Conversation, Secretary's Daily Meeting, March 16, 1949, Executive Secretariat Records, Box 1.

of the blockade of Berlin and the convening of the CFM.[90] The meeting of the CFM surely would introduce the question of some form of four-power agreement on Germany. Confronted with these developments and revealing again his desire for Kennan's advice, Acheson ordered the Planning Staff director to come home for discussions on both the Jessup-Malik exchange and the broad German question prior to the arrival of Ernest Bevin and Robert Schuman.

Acheson had expected to consider long-term policy upon Kennan's return but requirements on the operational level in preparation for the talks with his British and French opposites now took precedence. Because differences over the implementation procedure and operational terms of the London Program—especially the drafting of a new Occupation Statute—would be major topics of these talks, Acheson was forced to devote attention to them. By agreeing to discuss Germany with the British and the French Acheson quite undeliberately hampered the possibility of a serious examination of long-range policy. The demands for present tactics prevented an effort to chart a new strategy for the future. Kennan's report to Acheson on March 29—proposing that the United States end the military occupation, ease restrictions with Germany, and seek arrangements for four-power control—was submerged under the more immediate task of preparing for the meeting with Bevin and Schuman.[91] On March 31, the day of his first conversation with Bevin, Acheson submitted for Truman's approval a paper—influenced greatly by Robert Murphy who had returned to the department to work on German affairs—outlining the American responses to issues likely to be raised in these talks. The paper, which gained presidential assent, did not disavow the ultimate goal of a united Germany but it ran counter to the policy line Kennan offered. It identified the American objective as aimed at integrating as large a part of the German people as practicable into the West European structure. Further, it recommended that the London Program for a West German government "not be postponed or suspended for the purpose of negotiating as to the lifting of the Berlin blockade or the establishment of a four zone German government."[92] It represented the views of those who were fearful of any compromise on Germany.

The meetings of the three Western foreign ministers served to augment the already substantial pressure to cement the division of Germany or, perhaps more accurately stated, to terminate any further attempts at German reunification. When he met with Bevin and Schuman, who had effected a notable moderation in France's German policy, Acheson found that they desired *West-*

---

[90] On the Jessup-Malik talks see Philip C. Jessup, "Park Avenue Diplomacy—Ending the Berlin Blockade," *Political Science Quarterly* 87 (September 1972): 377–400.

[91] On Kennan's report see editorial note in *FRUS* 1949, III, pp. 137–38; and Memorandum of Conversation, Secretary's Daily Meeting, March 29, 1949, Executive Secretariat Records, Box 1.

[92] Secretary of State to the President, March 30, 1949, *FRUS* 1949, III, pp. 140–55.

ern Germany integrated into *Western* Europe.[93] In this situation the foreign ministers reached what Acheson later described as "almost prodigies of agreement" on Germany during their week of discussions.[94] By April 8 they reached accord on principles to govern the exercise of powers by their governments following the establishment of the German Federal Republic. They transformed this understanding on principles into practical terms by approving a new and much simplified occupation statute and trizonal fusion agreement. The foreign ministers also determined that with the establishment of a provisional German government in the Western zones the military governors should be replaced by civilian authority—a tripartite Allied High Commission with headquarters in Bonn—to exercise all but explicit military functions.[95] In essence these agreements, along with the Basic Law (constitution) the West Germans were themselves completing, provided the framework and the implementation for a West German state.[96]

Having arrived at these accords only after protracted discussion it was perhaps natural for Britain and France to look upon them virtually as ends in themselves and as resolving affirmatively the question of whether to divide Germany—although they could not publicly admit the latter. But for the Americans the matter of the division of Germany had not been resolved finally. Acheson admitted as much when he told Joseph Bech, the foreign minister of Luxembourg that "as a result of Mr. Kennan's trip to Germany we had been trying to think of something that could be done in order to solve the German problem."[97] The issue surfaced again immediately after the conclusion of Acheson's talk with Bevin and Schuman as a result of Jessup's continuing conversations with Jacob Malik. Jessup reported to Acheson on April 11 that the Soviets would lift the blockade and participate in a CFM meeting on condition that a West German government not be established before or during such a meeting. While refusing to acquiesce so as to avoid the appearance of duress and to display his bargaining strength, Acheson forced the Russians to concede the point and on May 4 unconditional agreement was reached for the lifting of the blockade on May 12. This was a prelude to convening a Council

[93] Michael Hogan discusses these matters in his *The Marshall Plan*, pp. 198–99. Note that Schuman used his influence against a narrowly nationalistic French policy toward Germany. He leaned increasingly to the idea of a West European union including Germany. See Robert W. Keyserlingh, *Fathers of Europe: Patriots of Peace* (Montreal, 1972), pp. 104–6. On French policy see the chapter "France and the German Problem, 1945–1949," in F. Roy Willis, *The French in Germany, 1945–1949* (Stanford, 1962), pp. 45–66.

[94] Acheson, *Present at the Creation*, p. 272. For the British (Bevin's) perspective on these discussions see Alan Bullock's *Ernest Bevin*, pp. 665–69.

[95] For the "Agreements on Germany" see *FRUS* 1949, III, pp. 177–83.

[96] For Konrad Adenauer's account of developments within West Germany see his *Memoirs, 1945–53*, trans. by Beate Ruhm von Oppen (Chicago, 1965), pp. 131–40.

[97] Memorandum of Conversation with Joseph Bech, April 1, 1949, Acheson Papers, Box 64.

of Foreign Ministers meeting in Paris on May 23 to consider questions concerning Germany in general and Berlin in particular.[98]

PHILIP JESSUP REVIVES PROGRAM A

The likelihood of a CFM meeting, however, brought to the fore the question of whether the United States should seek an all-German settlement. Acheson decided to appoint Jessup, who had not been deeply involved previously, to collate opinion on the matter so as to facilitate a decision. In response to Jessup's solicitation of views Ware Adams of the Planning Staff forwarded on April 15 Kennan's recommendation that the basic principles and detailed implementation of Program A be considered.[99] Jessup found Kennan's view persuasive. "Isn't it true," he pointedly asked Adams, "that everything we can learn from historical experience indicates that the permanent or long-continuing suppression of a nation like Germany is impossible?" He then observed that "if I am correct on this, shouldn't we keep in mind in framing a long-range policy the eventuality of a restored Germany?"[100] With Jessup's sponsorship the Staff proposal seriously reentered the policy-making cauldron at a meeting which Acheson held with Webb, Bohlen, Kennan, Murphy, Rusk, and Jessup on April 18. Two distinct views emerged. The first, presumably pushed by Murphy, aimed to maintain the split in Germany because West Germany was a more manageable unit for integration into Western Europe. The second view, undoubtedly presented by Kennan, sought to end the division of Germany on condition that the division of Europe was terminated as well. This depended on the withdrawal of the Red Army to the east. In a written report to Acheson on this meeting—the very holding of which is evidence that the secretary of state was still deliberating over German policy—Jessup advised that the "formulation of United States policy in anticipation of a meeting of the Council of Foreign Ministers should seek to provide an optimum program." Significantly, he suggested that Program A could serve as the basis of this program.[101]

Kennan had found an ally in Jessup, whom Acheson respected highly and considered a personal friend.[102] But the secretary himself needed to be con-

[98] Memorandum of Conversation, Secretary's Daily Meeting, April 11, 1949, Executive Secretariat Records, Box 1.

[99] Jessup's solicitation is referred to in Ware Adams to Jessup, April 15, 1949, *FRUS* 1949, III, pp. 856–58. For Kennan's recommendation see his "Position of the United States at any Meeting of the Council of Foreign Ministers on Germany that May Occur," pp. 858–59.

[100] Jessup to Adams, March 19, 1949, PPS Records, Box 15.

[101] Jessup to Acheson, "Formulation of Policy for a Meeting of the Council of Foreign Ministers," April 19, 1949, *FRUS* 1949, III, pp. 859–62.

[102] Acheson and Jessup had a friendship extending back to the 1930s. See their correspondence in the Papers of Philip C. Jessup, Containers A1, B1, B3. Kennan commented on the closeness of the Acheson-Jessup relationship in interview with author, March 6, 1989.

vinced if Program A was to be adopted as American policy. Acheson, quite uncharacteristically, seemed unsure of himself. On April 21 he admitted to being "all confused about the German business."[103] His thinking is difficult to discern largely because he continued to pursue something of a dual approach on the matter. On April 28 he publicly stated that the recent tripartite agreements on West Germany did not mean the abandonment of hope for a solution applicable to all of Germany but rather meant that the American, British, and French were not prepared to wait indefinitely for a four-power agreement before acting in the Western zones. Further, he advised that his government would not agree to a general solution for Germany which did not provide basic safeguards and benefits of the existing West German arrangements and that until such a solution was achieved the United States would "continue to lend vigorous support to the development of the Western Germany program."[104] Some observers, like Assistant Secretary of the Army Tracy Voorhees, assumed Acheson's speech meant proceeding without question along the steps toward West German government and considered Acheson's references to German unification as mere lip service.[105] As Voorhees soon discovered, however, Acheson's words about an all-German settlement had real content. He was still open to a genuine attempt to reunify Germany.[106]

Acheson permitted discussion to continue within the State Department on Program A and, notably, on May 4 Under Secretary Webb forwarded the nucleus of it to Secretary of Defense Louis Johnson for the consideration of the Defense Establishment, particularly the Joint Chiefs of Staff.[107] Although Robert Murphy informed Voorhees that Acheson had not approved the paper, its transmittal had a most unsettling impact on the Army Department. There

[103] Memorandum of Conversation, Secretary's Daily Meeting, April 21, 1949, Executive Secretariat Records, Box 1.

[104] Dean G. Acheson, "Current Situation in Germany," Address before the American Society of Newspaper Publishers, April 18, 1949, *Department of State Bulletin* 20 (May 8, 1949): 585–88.

[105] For Voorhees assumption see Teleconference TT-2185 between Voorhees, Door, and Clay, May 5, 1949, Smith, ed., *Clay Papers*, II, p. 1140.

[106] Acheson's position is revealed somewhat by his remarks to the British ambassador, Sir Oliver Franks, on May 2, 1949. According to Acheson: "I told Sir Oliver that these present negotiations might lead to little more than a lifting of the blockade. In a Council of Foreign Ministers we may have little real chance for agreement but we would have a serious propaganda problem with which to deal. This propaganda would primarily concern German opinion. We must therefore be bold in our approach in order to deal adequately with propaganda aspects but in doing so make proposals which we think would in fact be the basis for a reasonable settlement. By undue timidity we might be pushed back to the defensive and seriously damage our propaganda position." Acheson's memorandum, May 2, 1949, PPS Records, Box 15.

[107] Webb to Johnson, May 4, 1949, referred to in Johnson to Acheson, May 14, 1949, *FRUS* 1949, III, p. 875. For Johnson's request to the JCS see his Memorandum, "Military Considerations in the Conclusion of Any Agreement with Respect to Germany," May 5, 1949, Truman Papers, PSF, Box 178.

the proposals for Germany which it outlined were taken very seriously indeed. Voorhees raced the text to Clay and asked for immediate comment. The American proconsul in Germany responded first with specific criticisms but soon launched into a general and emotional attack describing the broad approach of the paper as "suicidal to our objectives." Claiming it was unnecessary and alleging that "we hold all the cards," Clay argued that "the Soviets will accept occupation statute and Bonn republic." He viewed the elements of Program A, especially the troop withdrawals, as a major threat not only to the West German political arrangements but to the whole security of Europe, declaring that they were a prescription for turning Germany over to the Soviets.[108]

Clay's assessment of Program A as unrealistic and dangerous confirmed him in his view that "Kennan is all theory" and no doubt his blood boiled at having to defend his German stance against a mere theoretician.[109] But the intense Clay was never afraid to fight and the next day, having calmed down a little, he repeated his objections in a more moderate tone yet in a manner acknowledging the seriousness with which he viewed this proposal for a renewed attempt to reunify Germany. He explained that "with great effort and considerable financial sacrifice by our own people, we have established in Germany the base from which West Germany with its 45 million people look to the West and eagerly desires to be included in the association of western European nations." For him this was too substantial an achievement to give up or even to risk. Resorting to the analogy of war, he concluded that "we have won the battle but under the State Department proposal are writing an armistice as if we lost the battle."[110]

Clay's opinion carried weight but it was insufficient to kill discussions of Program A in the daily sessions Acheson held with his advisers—Jessup, Murphy, Rusk, Kennan, Bohlen, Hickerson, and Beam—to prepare for the forthcoming CFM meeting. On May 10 Acheson outlined the problem as he saw it and dispatched a copy of this synopsis to Bevin and Schuman. Working from a major premise which placed concern with the future of Europe above Germany as a problem by itself, he noted the progress achieved in integrating the part of Germany which the West controlled into a free and democratic Europe and he stated that this would not be jeopardized by seeking a unified Germany as in itself good. But Acheson, unlike Clay, considered German unification as a potentially viable alternative to the division of Germany. "Just as the unification of Germany is not an end in itself," he explained, "so the division of

[108] Teleconference TT-2185 between Voorhess, Door, and Clay, May 5, 1949, Smith, ed., *Clay Papers*, II, pp. 1139–51.

[109] John D. Backer, *Winds of History: The German Years of Lucius DuBignon Clay* (New York, 1983), pp. 277–78.

[110] Clay to Voorhees, May 6, 1949, Smith ed., *Clay Papers*, II, pp. 1151–55. See also Clay's later comments in his *Decision in Germany* (New York, 1950), pp. 438–39.

Germany is not an end in itself." He went on to mention "a possible regrouping of troops" as deserving of the "most careful study" and as "essential to any further unification of Germany and of Germany with the West." He also referred to the conditions under which a four-power plan should operate, a clear indication of his willingness to countenance an all-German settlement.[111]

In addition to forwarding this outline of his thinking to the British and French foreign ministers, Acheson gained Truman's approval of it and he authorized Jessup and Bohlen to mention that Program A had received consideration with the American government during preparatory discussions they were to hold with British and French officials prior to the CFM meeting.[112] His friend Warburg pointedly encouraged Acheson assuring him that "so far as Germany is concerned, I realize that the real problems lie ahead, but at least we are now going to face them instead of running away from them."[113] All this suggests that Acheson was prepared to investigate the practicality of an all-German settlement and the possibility of its acceptance by the other Western powers. For him the test for German unification was whether it could be achieved under conditions which helped the security and stability of Europe. David McLellan is incorrect when he asserts that Acheson "could not take Kennan's proposal (Program A) seriously [because] it would sow doubts in European minds and deal a setback to American strategy for a revivified Europe."[114]

BRITISH/FRENCH OBJECTIONS AND THE PARIS CFM MEETING

The likely consequences of Acheson (or Jessup and Bohlen) pressing on the British and French the need for a proposal providing for a quadripartite German settlement is a moot point for a combination of factors intervened to crush the chances of the serious discussion of Program A. Important among these factors was the blunt advice of the Joint Chiefs of Staff Chairman, General Omar Bradley, that the effect of Program A's proposed troop withdrawals into the German port areas would be to back the British and the Americans into indefensible positions while the Russian forces would not be moved far enough east to remove their threat to West Germany and all of Western Europe. Bradley's military assessment was endorsed by Secretary of Defense Johnson and presented as the position of the whole National Military Establishment.[115] With the troop withdrawal component of Program A portrayed as

---

[111] Secretary of State to Embassy in the United Kingdom, May 11, 1949, enclosing "An Approach to the CFM," *FRUS* 1949, III, pp. 872–74.

[112] For Truman's approval see Acheson's memorandum, May 12, 1949, Acheson Papers, HSTL, Box 64. For the authorization to Jessup and Bohlen see Kennan, *Memoirs*, I, p. 444.

[113] Warburg to Acheson, May 5, 1949, Acheson Papers (Yale), Box 33.

[114] McLellan, *Dean Acheson*, p. 159.

[115] Bradley's formal objection is contained within Johnson to Acheson, May 14, 1949, *FRUS*

a threat to European security it is not surprising that, as Acheson offhandedly and rather disingenuously remarked in his memoirs, "interest in this approach waned."[116]

The major provocation and impetus for Acheson to distance himself from Program A was provided by the reverberations in Europe following the publication on May 12 of a story by James Reston, carried on page one of the *New York Times*, reporting in detail Program A's proposal for troop withdrawals.[117] Kennan later described this as a "spectacular *coup de grace*" for Program A, designed to frighten the British and the French before Jessup and Bohlen could explain it to them.[118] If this was the goal of Reston's source—presumably either from the Pentagon or a Kennan opponent from State—then he achieved it successfully because as Bohlen recalled Reston's article "raised a good deal of hell in Europe."[119] The British and French understandably reacted instantly against the proposal. Deep British fear of the Soviet Union and their reluctance at even negotiating with the Russians guaranteed that they would take what seemed the more secure course—that of establishing a western German state tied to the West.[120] An American official precisely captured the British attitude as "more concerned with preventing Soviet incursions into the West than in maneuvering the Soviets out of the East."[121] They were afraid to countenance any proposal which might reduce the American political and military presence in Western Europe. The French agreed, both for this reason and also because of their own peculiar security rationale which saw the integration of the western part of Germany into Western Europe as a brake on a resurgent Germany and a safeguard against renewed German aggression. In short, the French feared a unified Germany.[122]

Jessup moved immediately to quell the furor and to prevent a damaging rupture among the Western allies on the eve of their meeting with the Soviets.

1949, III, pp. 875–76. Note however that in conversation with Acheson and his advisers Bradley had offered an alternative troop redeployment proposal. He suggested that U.S. and U.K. troops "occupy restricted areas along the Rhine, rather than at the ports of Bremen and Hamburg." Memorandum of conversation (10 a.m. meeting), May 12, 1949, PPS Records, Box 15.

[116] Acheson, *Present at the Creation*, pp. 291–92.

[117] James Reston, "U.S. Plan Weighed: Big 3 Would Withdraw to Ports in the North Under Proposal," *New York Times*, May 12, 1949, p. 1.

[118] Kennan, *Memoirs*, I, p. 444.

[119] Bohlen, *Witness to History*, pp. 285–86. As to Reston's source—like a good reporter he could not recall who had leaked these details to him! Author's interview with James B. Reston, Washington, D.C., August 8, 1989.

[120] On Bevin's concerns see Bullock, *Ernest Bevin*, p. 693. Bullock admits that Bevin "was far more concerned to prevent [the London Program] being undermined than he was to explore the possibilities of re-unifying Germany." For Bevin's negative reaction to a "possible regrouping of troops in Germany," see Bevin to Secretary of State, May 13, 1949, *FRUS* 1949, III, pp. 874–75.

[121] Memorandum by Charles W. Yost to Jessup, May 21, 1949, *FRUS* 1949, III, pp. 890–92.

[122] For a discussion of the French see ibid.

He assured Schuman on the very morning of his arrival in Paris that Reston's story bore no substance. The next day he repeated assurances to suspicious British and French officials that the United States did not favor either the withdrawal of its forces or any disposition of them which would weaken American influence in Europe.[123] Jessup was struck by the vehemence of the British and French views. He wrote Kennan from Paris that "one thing which has stood out in my mind in our conversations with the French and the British is that they are not yet ready to think in the broad European terms which have been behind your planning. Had we come here with 'Program A' (even if unhampered by the really serious effects of the Reston article), I do not think we could have secured tripartite agreement on it."[124]

Thus Program A was not presented to the Europeans. The British and the French were unwilling to run the risks involved in submitting a serious unification proposal to the Russians. Combined with Bradley's military advice their unwillingness compelled Acheson to retreat from initiating legitimate discussions on an all-German settlement.[125] Meeting with the National Security Council on May 18, two days before his own departure for Paris, he cautiously stated his intention to probe the Soviet attitude and outlined the difficulties involved in extending democratic government in Germany. He noted the military establishment's objection to the regrouping and reduction of occupation forces and then outlined the basic position he would take to Paris—namely, "that we should continue to go ahead with the Western German government, and that any unification of Germany as a whole should grow out of that."[126] He concluded that this was the less painful course than trying to unite Germany first.

Acheson was not persuaded by a final attempt by Kennan, made on the very day of his departure, to convince him of the efficacy of an approach to Germany based on Program A. Nor would he accept Kennan's advice that "the

[123] For Jessup's comments see his report in Bruce to Secretary of State, May 14, 1949, *FRUS* 1949, III, p. 878.

[124] Jessup to Kennan, May 24, 1949, PPS Records, Box 15.

[125] Kennan agrees as to "the decisive importance of the French and British views" and maintains that "they made a deep impression on Mr. Acheson: first, I think, because while he did not know much about Europe, he assumed that they did; secondly, because they largely coincided with those of our own military establishment, and thirdly, because they had the support of the Western European Division in the Department of State." Letter, Kennan to author, August 10, 1979.

[126] Acheson explained that "he felt that if we were to stop Western German development now and attempt to get unification we would lose the momentum already acquired and greatly discourage the Germans. He felt there would be fewer and less painful difficulties by going ahead with the Western German government than by attempting to unite Germany first." See Memorandum for the President (containing summary of discussion at the 40th meeting of the National Security Council), May 18, 1949, Truman Papers, PSF, Box 220. It seems Acheson first had reached this conclusion only after a second long meeting with his advisers on May 12, 1949. See Memorandum of Meeting, May 12 (2 p.m.), 1949, PPS Records, Box 15.

British and French . . . be asked to bear the main burden of presentation and defense of the western position (on Germany) in the CFM'' and that the United States indicate that ''it had deferred extensively to their views in these matters.'' The depth of Kennan's feelings on the issue emerged in his bitter complaint to Acheson about spending ''eight weeks last fall working out what we felt would be a logical program for advance towards the unification of Germany [when] piece by piece, in our deliberations here and in the concessions we have made to French and British feelings in Paris, the essentials of this program have been discarded and the logic broken up.''[127] Acheson, of course, rejected Kennan's advice on deferring to the British and French so as to deny the Soviets any opportunity to gain a wedge to splinter Western unity. To ensure such unity the American secretary of state twice met with his British and French counterparts before the beginning of the CFM conference in Paris's *Palais Rose*.[128] Here he fully acquiesced in and adopted as his own the negative outlook towards German unification of Bevin and Schuman, to whom he related well. Acheson's view, which then translated into *the* American position on Germany, was more a product of the Western resolution of policy prior to the Paris meeting than the source of that resolution. The revisionist historians Joyce and Gabriel Kolko exhibit a curious national egoism in mistakenly describing the proposal put to the Russians as ''America's terms on Germany.''[129] The western proposal eventually put to the Russians was a genuine tripartite proposal, which in fact—as Kennan recognized—owed as much to Britain and France as to the United States. The British and the French acted as a brake on, indeed a fatal barrier to, any American initiative.

In the CFM meeting Foreign Minister Andrei Vyshinsky presented the Soviet position on Germany and demonstrated, as Acheson correctly recalled, ''that the Russians had nothing to propose for Germany as a whole and sought only to recover the power to block progress in West Germany.''[130] The Soviet failure to make a forthright proposal for German reunification convinced Acheson of the futility of seeking a four-power settlement and suggests that even a serious western proposal, like Program A, would have garnered little response from the Russians.[131] They shared with the French a powerful fear of a unified,

[127] Kennan to Acheson, May 20, 1949, *FRUS* 1949, III, pp. 888–90.

[128] On these meetings see Acheson to President and Acting Secretary of State, May 22, 1949, *FRUS* 1949, III, pp. 892–94. Note that even though he accepted the British/French view on troop withdrawals, Acheson talked about this as necessary in the future.

[129] Joyce and Gabriel Kolko, *The Limits of Power: The World and United States Foreign Policy, 1945–1954* (New York, 1972), p. 501.

[130] See Proposal of the Soviet Delegation to the Council of Foreign Ministers, May 25, 1949, *FRUS* 1949, III, pp. 1040–41; and Acheson, *Present at the Creation*, p. 297.

[131] It is hard to imagine Stalin's Soviet Union acquiescing in a settlement that would have implied a Germany linked integrally to the West in economic and political terms even if neutralized in a military sense. Kennan himself later acknowledged this in a dispatch from the Moscow embassy in 1952. He observed that ''whether they [Soviets] could have been brought actually to

resurgent Germany.[132] The experience of this meeting permanently colored Acheson's views of Soviet intentions and set him firmly along the path to his later strategy of "negotiation from strength."[133] With Bevin acting as spokesman the Western side rejected Vishinsky's arguments and counterproposed the establishment of a federal government for all of Germany by extending the Bonn constitution—the Basic Law for the Federal Republic of Germany—to the whole country thereby making it one economic and political unit.[134] As Kennan later commented, and as the Western Ministers actually realized at the time, this proposal "envisaged acceptance *in toto* by the Soviet government of arrangements worked out exclusively on the Western side without their participation, and thus implied something like an unconditional capitulation of their position in Germany."[135] Predictably Vishinsky rejected the proposal charging that it meant the dismemberment not the unification of Germany.[136] This deadlock at the Paris CFM conference—the last East-West meeting at Foreign Minister level for nearly five years—sounded the death knell for efforts to reunify Germany. That nation's division was now formalized.

The Paris CFM meeting had not interfered with the process of establishing the West German state. On May 8 the Western military governors had approved the Basic Law presented by the German Parliamentary Council and after ratification by all the Lander (states) except Bavaria this document was promulgated on May 23. The West German political forces immediately moved to give concrete expression to this constitutional document. Elections throughout West Germany were held on August 14. The new Bundestag convened on September 7 and voted Theodor Heuss and Konrad Adenauer as

accept a withdrawal of forces from Germany on the basis of a continued demilitarization of that country and genuine freedom for German political life is difficult to say—the probabilities were against it." See Kennan's Dispatch 116, "The Soviet Union and the Atlantic Pact," September 8, 1952, in George F. Kennan, *Memoirs, 1950–1963* (Boston, 1972), p. 340.

[132] According to Paul Nitze Acheson authorized Bohlen "informally to sound out the Soviets on whether they would entertain a proposal similar to Plan A." Bohlen did so with General V. I. Chuikov, the Soviet Military Governor for the Eastern Zone who volunteered: "The Germans hate us. It is necessary that we keep our forces in Germany." Nitze, *From Hiroshima to Glasnost*, pp. 71–72. Bohlen tried to be "a voice of moderation" at the Paris CFM without success. See Daniel F. Harrington, "Kennan, Bohlen and the Riga Axioms," *Diplomatic History* 2, no. 4 (Fall 1978): 433–34.

[133] On this see Coral Bell, *Negotiations from Strength: A Study in the Politics of Power* (London, 1962), pp. 23–40. Acheson admitted exactly this in a letter to Hans J. Morgenthau written in January 1957, when he observed that "my own firsthand attempt to work out something in regard to Germany in May, 1949, added me to the list of those whose experience convinced them that so long as it appeared in Russian eyes that there were soft spots, those soft spots would be probed." Acheson to Morgenthau, January 16, 1957, in David C. McLellan and David C. Acheson, eds., *Among Friends: Personal Letters of Dean Acheson* (New York, 1980), pp. 121–22.

[134] Proposal of the United States, United Kingdom, and French Delegations to the Council of Foreign Ministers, May 28, 1949, *FRUS* 1949, III, pp. 929–31.

[135] Kennan, *Memoirs*, I, p. 446.

[136] Vishinsky's rejection as reported to Truman in *FRUS* 1949, III, pp. 929–31.

president and chancellor, respectively, of the new state. Adenauer's cabinet was sworn in on September 20 fulfilling the final prerequisite for the entrance into force of the new Occupation Statute. The next day the three civilian high commissioners received Adenauer and the members of his government, accepted formal notification of their taking office and declared the new Occupation Statute as legally in force. This date marked the end of military government in West Germany and ushered in a period of gradual advance toward full sovereignty under the mild reign of the civilian High Commission, during which time the institutions and political forces of the Federal Republic operated increasingly without restraint except in the areas of foreign affairs and defense.[137] Thus sovereignty flowed back to Germany—but to a Germany that would remain divided for well over a generation.

ACHESON, KENNAN, AND THE DIVISION OF GERMANY

In the long view the division of Germany was the consequence of Hitlerism, of a lost war, and of fundamental mistrust and disunity among the victorious occupying powers. Germany remained divided because none of the occupying powers would accept the risks of unification. Resolution of this issue in this way, and more precisely the American acceptance of this resolution, represented rejection of the advice offered by George Kennan in Program A. In understanding America's German policy it is important to appreciate that this rejection took place not when Acheson became secretary of state but just prior to the Paris CFM meeting in May of 1949. It took place then because American military advice portrayed the troop withdrawal component of Program A as dangerous to West German and European security and, more so, because of the influence on Acheson of British and French opposition to attempts at German reunification. Additionally, the momentum of existing occupation arrangements and the forceful bureaucratic support from some of their American formulators—such as Clay, Murphy, and Hickerson—tended to constrain an alteration in America's German policy. These conclusions reveal that American policy on the German problem from mid-1948 to May of 1949 should not be characterized simply as a premeditated effort calculated to divide Germany. Marshall's willingness to have Kennan develop a reunification proposal and the attention paid to it by Acheson prove otherwise. Both secretaries of state allowed a dual approach on German policy—in broad terms, the continued implementation of the London Program on the one hand while seriously exploring at different points the possibility of an all-German settlement. Neither

---

[137] For a brilliant account of John J. McCloy's tenure as American High Commissioner of Germany see Thomas Alan Schwartz, *America's Germany: John J. McCloy and the Federal Republic of Germany* (Cambridge, Mass., 1991). See also John Ford Golay, *The Founding of the Federal Republic of Germany* (Chicago, 1958); and Peter Merkl, *The Origins of the West German Republic* (New York, 1963).

man appreciated fully that the continued pursuit of the former wrecked whatever possibility there may have been to obtain the latter. Nor should American policy be presented as resulting from a desire to utilize the western zones of Germany in the strategy of containing the Soviet Union. As late as mid-1949 West Germany's part in the containment policy was not defined clearly. The major concern for American policymakers rested with the passive security risk of all of Germany—especially the industries of the Ruhr—falling under Soviet influence or domination.[138] Acheson's decisions at this point were not influenced by any notions of developing West Germany as an active military resource against the Soviet Union. That would come later.

This examination of German policy evokes some comments on the positions of Acheson and Kennan and on their relationship. Although the division of Germany and Europe later became the subject of an intense dispute between the two statesmen—which climaxed following Kennan's BBC Reith lectures in December 1957, advocating the withdrawal of military forces from the center of Europe—this should not cloud an assessment of their stands as of the first part of 1949.[139] The temptation to portray Acheson from his first day in office as pressing "for the maximum development of German power as a counterpoise to the Soviet Union," should be avoided.[140] In contrast to this characterization, Acheson in the period before the Paris CFM displayed openness and even indecision. He presided over a labored debate over German policy rather than the bold implementation of a policy already molded by him. Kennan staunchly advocated one side of that debate. Whatever may have occurred later, during early 1949 Acheson solicited Kennan's advice, considered it seriously, and actually explored the possibility of its implementation.

Acheson believed he had reasoned his way to the best course among the alternatives offered. It represented an exercise of his intellect. But for Kennan not only his intellect but his emotions had been engaged deeply on this issue. Kennan felt bitter and disillusioned when Acheson chose the alternate course to the one he had fashioned and offered. He expressed his frustration to the British journalist Henry Brandon—for whom he would stretch out on his office couch and spill his mind rather in the manner of a psychiatrist's patient—arguing that the United States "had done 'almost irreparable damage' with its policies in Germany."[141] Kennan's anger resulted from his clear appreciation of the historic dimension of the events concerning the division of Germany.

---

[138] For an excellent analysis of Germany's part—or lack thereof—in the containment strategy see Wolfgang Krieger, "Was General Clay a Revisionist?" pp. 165–84.

[139] For Kennan's revised lectures see his *Russia, The Atom and the West* (New York, 1958). For an indication of the dispute, the intensity of which was mainly engendered by Acheson, see "Acheson Rebuffs Kennan on Withdrawal of Troops," *New York Times*, January 12, 1958, pp. 1, 24–25.

[140] Smith, *Dean Acheson*, p. 79.

[141] Brandon, *Special Relationships*, p. 43.

The die was cast. The creation of the western military alliance through the North Atlantic Treaty and the formation of a West German state meant the congealment of the division of Europe and the foregoing of any realistic chance to extract the Soviets from Eastern Europe. Kennan struggled to prevent this and failed. For a proud man the pain of this defeat struck deep. While he continued his work on European issues after this point and committed a major effort to the issue of European integration he increasingly found himself marching to the beat of a different drummer than Acheson and most of his colleagues.[142]

Kennan also sensed a subtle but important change in his own role in the department. He judged it as a relative diminution of his importance despite the fact that his additional appointment as Counselor of the State Department was announced right at this time. He continued to participate in the policy-making councils but other influential individuals had emerged in this domain. Under General Marshall Kennan welcomed the chance to consult widely and then to bring forth a coherent recommendation for the secretary. His was a central role. Now, under Acheson, he found himself but one among a number of competing voices and his voice no longer carried so well. Marshall seemingly had treated all his subordinates with professional detachment. Acheson clearly related more closely to some of his aides such as Jessup and the State Department's Legal Adviser, Adrian "Butch" Fisher, than to others.[143] Kennan began again to fear being excluded from the inner circle of policy-making. The memory of the long years when he had been virtually ignored increased his anxiety at the prospect. His sensitivity exaggerated the implications of his altered role in the department. Nonetheless, Acheson's decision on German policy marked a fundamental defeat for Kennan. From this point forward he developed a greater willingness to assume the role of in-house dissenter, although this became more evident later in the year with his work on European integration and the development of the hydrogen bomb.

One comes in the end to the question of the correctness of the decision to agree implicitly to the division of Germany. The historian can ask but cannot answer it definitively for it is related integrally to the reality of a Soviet threat to West Germany and Western Europe. As Kennan later pointed out, because he did not believe this a reality he "was concerned not so much to provide protection against the possibility of such a [military] attack . . . as to facilitate the retirement of Soviet forces" closer to traditional Russian boundaries.[144] His proposal for German reunification sought this goal and also to end a national division which Kennan viewed as inherently unstable and, because of German revanchism, potentially explosive. Ultimately Acheson came down

---

[142] For a good summary of the work on European integration see Mayers, *George Kennan and the Dilemmas of US Foreign Policy*, pp. 149–52.

[143] Author's interview with George F. Kennan, March 6, 1989.

[144] Kennan, *Memoirs*, I, p. 464.

against Kennan on this issue, and influenced by Bevin and Schuman, he joined these European statesmen in accepting the German division thus setting a course, according to a later insightful critic of Kennan, "less dangerous than any other arrangement," because this partition avoided the restoration of fluidity and of risk to the European situation.[145] Certainly Kennan underestimated both the stability that subsequently prevailed in Europe and the facility with which the West Germans would build a liberal democracy and sustain it for a period more than double that of Germany's first republic and triple that of Hitler's "Thousand Year Reich." And yet the basic issue of a divided Germany, which Kennan confronted, remained unresolved and refused to disappear.[146] Four decades later it suddenly rose again to challenge the capacities of policymakers with its vast implications for the future of Europe and the international structure forged in the late 1940s.

[145] This was the criticism of Raymond Aron as reported by Kennan in his *Memoirs*, II, p. 253. See also Raymond Aron, *Memoires* (Paris, 1983), pp. 278–83.

[146] For Kennan's thinking on this as of early 1989, just prior to the disintegration of the Communist regimes of Eastern Europe, see George F. Kennan, *The German Problem: A Personal View* (Washington, D.C., 1989).

CHAPTER SIX

Titoism, Eastern Europe, and Political Warfare

Consolidation of Soviet Control

The might of the Red Army brought Soviet power into the very heart of Europe as World War II came to an end. Stalin capitalized on his military strength and proceeded over the next three years to consolidate his control over East Central Europe—Poland, Hungary, Czechoslovakia, Rumania, Bulgaria, Yugoslavia, and Albania. In 1946 and increasingly in 1947 the Soviets severely curtailed the influence of the West in the region and moved to eliminate all political opposition.[1] The scene bore a depressing and tragic familiarity in countries like Rumania, Hungary, and Poland—opposition political leaders forced to flee, imprisoned, or killed; independent political parties suppressed; genuine elections and any vestiges of real democracy eliminated. In Yugoslavia, where Soviet control was less direct, the Communist leader Josip Broz Tito proved himself an eager disciple of Stalin and vigorously pursued the creation of a one-party police state. With the Czech coup in February of 1948 the Communists essentially had full control of every government. The ''iron curtain'' truly descended as the Soviet client states were denied any autonomy. In July of 1947 the Soviet Union had forbidden them to participate in the Marshall Plan and this action reflected the pattern of Soviet domination. In September the foundation of the Cominform (Communist Information Bureau) provided the structures that bound the satellites to Moscow.[2]

In the face of such Soviet actions the United States found its own policy options for Eastern Europe increasingly limited. Despite the ritual protestations against spheres of influence, American policymakers had been prepared to concede to the Soviet Union predominant influence in this region so long as the Soviets ''allowed a large measure of domestic political autonomy.''[3]

---

[1] For fine accounts of this tragic process see the essays in Thomas T. Hammond, ed., *Witnesses to the Origins of the Cold War* (Seattle, 1982); and Denis Healey, ed., *The Curtain Falls: The Story of the Socialists of Eastern Europe* (London, 1951).

[2] For background on Stalin's ambitions in Eastern Europe see Vojtech Mastney, *Russia's Road to the Cold War: Diplomacy, Warfare, and the Politics of Communism, 1941–45* (New York, 1979).

[3] See Eduard Mark, ''American Policy toward Eastern Europe and the Origins of the Cold War, 1941–1946: An Alternative Interpretation,'' *Journal of American History* 68 (September 1981): 318. Also see Mark's ''Charles E. Bohlen and the Acceptable Limits of Soviet Hegemony in Eastern Europe: A Memorandum of 18 October, 1945,'' *Diplomatic History* 3 (Spring 1979): 201–13; and Geir Lundestad, *The American Non-Policy Towards Eastern Europe, 1943–1947: Universalism in an Area not of Essential Interest to the United States* (New York, 1975).

James F. Byrnes worked to secure an "open Soviet sphere" as opposed to an "exclusive sphere" but without any success.[4] Even limited political autonomy apparently troubled Stalin who obviously felt no necessity to placate American sensibilities on this issue. Eventually his refusal and the blatant imposition of Communist regimes provoked a response. Because such measures as political representations and linking trade credits to political reform proved quite ineffective, the American response involved mainly verbal protestations at the Soviet actions and, as we have seen, a major endeavor to secure Western Europe and the Mediterranean from further Soviet expansion.[5]

George Kennan was not numbered among those well-meaning souls shocked by the totality and brutality of Soviet control in Eastern Europe. From the time of his return to Moscow in 1944 he had argued for a frank recognition of spheres of influence in Europe and for a clear disassociation of the United States from Soviet actions. Appreciating well that the United States had little influence over events within the Soviet domain he argued that it should avoid bearing any political and moral responsibility for them.[6] When the ailing Harry Hopkins came to Moscow as Truman's envoy in May 1945 to fashion with Stalin a compromise political settlement for Poland, Kennan told him frankly that "we should accept no share of the responsibility for what the Russians proposed to do in Poland." "Then you think it's just sin," Hopkins rejoined, "and we should be agin it." "That's just about right," Kennan responded.[7] At base it was a question of power realities. The United States lacked the wherewithal to influence effectively developments in the region behind the advance lines of the Red Army. Back in Washington at the War College Kennan held firmly to his view. At the end of a Kennan lecture a listener asked why something couldn't be done to challenge the Soviet Union's grasp of Eastern Europe. "The fact of the matter is," he replied, "that we do not have power in Eastern Europe really to do anything but talk. You see what I mean. It seems to me this issue is rather a theoretical one. There is no action we can take there except to state our case."[8]

Once esconced as Director of the Policy Planning Staff, however, Kennan expanded his imagination with regard to policy options for Eastern Europe. It was at his suggestion that Marshall Plan aid was offered to the Soviet Union and its East European satellites. The terms of such aid meant that the East Europeans would need to integrate their economies with those of the West thereby reducing the extent of Soviet hegemony. Kennan's objective was two edged: to place responsibility for the division of Europe firmly on the Soviets

---

[4] Mark, "American Policy toward Eastern Europe," p. 329.

[5] On American measures see Robert Garson, "The Role of Eastern Europe in America's Containment Policy, 1945–1948," *The Journal of America Studies* 13 (April 1979): 84–87.

[6] See Kennan, *Memoirs*, I, p. 235.

[7] Ibid., p. 212.

[8] Quoted in Daniel Yergin, *Shattered Peace*, p. 255.

if they and their satellites refused to accept the proposed conditions; or, if they accepted, to force the abandonment of "the exclusive [Soviet] orientation of their economies."[9] Furthermore, Kennan hoped that the expected Soviet rejection "would strain Moscow's relations with its satellites."[10] His hopes came to naught as the Soviets moved to cement further their domination of Eastern Europe in the latter half of 1947. In Rumania the National Peasant Party was suppressed while in Hungary Prime Minister Ferenc Nagy was forced to resign and the Small Farmers Party was emasculated.

Kennan viewed these political events in the Balkans with dismay. He even recommended to Lovett that the United States withhold its ratification of the peace treaties reached with Rumania, Bulgaria, and Hungary as a mark of its displeasure. He argued that the Balkan treaties "as they stand hold no benefits for this country and contain numerous clauses which we know full well will never be implemented and give us no real protection against the insolent noncompliance of the treaties with which we will certainly be faced."[11] Kennan also turned the attention of the Planning Staff to the issue of trade with the Soviet Union and Eastern Europe. He assigned the economist Jacques Reinstein to prepare a paper on the subject.[12] But the Staff's investigation was overtaken by competing recommendations on this issue offered by the Commerce Department and by an ad hoc Eastern European Economic Working Party drawn mainly from the Economic divisions of the State Department. Lovett asked the Staff to arbitrate between the different means of regulating the rather small levels of trade with the Soviet bloc.[13] The Staff's response (PPS/17) of November 26, 1947, meandered through a survey of the factors involved and contributed little, although it supported restrictions on exports to the Soviet Union and Eastern Europe.[14] Ultimately it was the proposal pushed by Secretary of Commerce Averell Harriman which gained approval from the National Security Council and adoption as U.S. policy. This provided for "the immediate termination, for an indefinite period, of shipments from the United States to the USSR and its satellites of all commodities which are critically short in the United States or which would contribute to the Soviet military

---

[9] Kennan, *Memoirs*, I, p. 341.

[10] John Lewis Gaddis makes this point in his essay "The Strategy of Containment," in Thomas H. Etzold and John Lewis Gaddis, *Containment: Documents on American Policy and Strategy, 1945–1950* (New York, 1978), p. 32.

[11] Kennan to Lovett, July 30, 1947, PPS Records, Box 33.

[12] Minutes of PPS Meetings, September 29, 1947; October 7, 1947; November 3, 1947.

[13] For the Staff consideration of these proposals which involved them in discussions with officials from both the Economic divisions of State and the Commerce Department see Minutes of Meetings, November 18, 1947; November 24, 1947; and November 25, 1947, PPS Records, Box 32.

[14] PPS/17, "United States Exports to the U.S.S.R. and the Satellite States," November 26, 1947, *FRUS* 1948, IV, pp. 489–98.

potential.''[15] Through this selective embargo the U.S. aimed not to force positive, incremental political changes in Eastern Europe but to inflict economic damage on Moscow and its satellites. American policymakers now accepted the painful reality that Stalin's hold on Eastern Europe was unyielding. Change could come "only through slow atrophy or some kind of revolution."[16] Kennan shared and had helped shape this view.

In the "Resume of World Situation" which he wrote for General Marshall in early November 1947 and which the secretary of state shared with President Truman and the full Cabinet on November 7, Kennan observed that the halt in the Soviet political advance in Western Europe "necessitated a consolidation of Communist power throughout Eastern Europe."[17] With some prescience he predicted that the Soviets would find it necessary "to clamp down completely in Czechoslovakia." Permitting even the appearances of freedom in Czechoslovakia risked its becoming "a means of entry of really democratic forces into Eastern Europe in general."[18] Kennan predicted that the Russians could maintain their power behind the Luebeck-Trieste line for some time by the exercise of "sheer police methods" but he thought the task would become increasingly difficult for them. Over the long haul he considered it "unlikely that approximately one hundred million Russians will succeed in holding down permanently, in addition to their own minorities, some ninety millions of Europeans with a higher cultural level and with long experience in resistance to foreign rule."[19] Kennan, however, did not foresee the crumbling of Russian rule in Eastern Europe on the near horizon and he offered no suggestions to further such a development. With Kennan's premises widely accepted within the Truman administration, policymakers assumed, as Robert Garson has argued, that it would be "internal contradictions and strain [which] would eventually erode the Russian grip."[20] Senior policymakers accepted that their opportunities to contest Soviet control in Eastern Europe were minimal and focused on the other pressing issues demanding their attention. Kennan himself juggled more issues than a circus performer during the late months of 1947 and the early months of 1948—aid to Greece, aid to China, Palestine, occupation policy for Japan—and found little time to devote to Eastern Europe. But midlevel offi-

[15] Report by the NSC, "Control of Exports to the USSR and Eastern Europe," December 17, 1947, FRUS 1948, IV, pp. 511–12.
[16] Robert Garson makes this point in his fine article, "Role of Eastern Europe in America's Containment Policy, 1945–1948," p. 86.
[17] PPS/13, "Resume of World Situation," November 6, 1947, FRUS 1947, I, pp. 770–77.
[18] Ibid., p. 773.
[19] Ibid., p. 774. Kennan thought enough about the eventual likelihood of dissolution of Soviet power in Eastern Europe to warn that it would be a dangerous time for world stability because "the Kremlin may then feel itself seriously threatened internally and may resort to desperate measures."
[20] Robert A. Garson, "American Foreign Policy and the Limits of Power: Eastern Europe, 1946–50," Journal of Contemporary History 21 (July 1986): 353.

cials maintained their concern for developments in the Soviet bloc. Foremost among these was Kennan's friend and fellow Staff member, John Paton Davies.

UTILIZATION OF REFUGEES FROM THE SOVIET WORLD

John Davies thought it important to make use of refugees from the Soviet world. In a paper (PPS/22) which obtained the endorsement of his colleagues on February 5, 1948, Davies pointed to the presence of hundreds of thousands of refugees from the Soviet bloc in Europe and Asia. He then noted the failure of the United States to make any systematic attempt to draw on the intelligence information in the possession of these individuals, despite the fact that the USSR and the satellite states were becoming "terra incognita." The lack of information and knowledge regarding what he termed "Eurasia" distressed Davies because he saw that it left the U.S. "ill-equipped to engage in the political and psychological conflict with the Soviet world, now forced upon us." In light of this analysis he argued that the United States needed "to utilize refugee resources available in free Europe and free Asia to fill the gaps in our current official intelligence, in public information, and in our politico-psychological operations."[21]

Davies possessed creativity and imagination and naturally he had recommendations to offer as to how these refugee assets should be exploited. He suggested that the Departments of State, Army, Navy, and Air Force and the CIA promptly should undertake a screening program of refugees.[22] Through this program qualified social scientists, physical scientists, and specialists in broadcasting and translating for propaganda purposes would be brought to the United States. To obtain the most benefit from the social scientists he proposed that "an institute for basic social science research on the Soviet world" be established in Washington staffed by refugee scholars working in collaboration with American specialists.[23] Somewhat disingenuously, because he thought such scholars would assist the fledgling intelligence community, Davies wanted the Institute to pursue its research openly and to maintain contacts with the American academic community. To this end he recommended that it be financed by private rather than government funds and he indicated that "certain prominent American citizens" already were investigating possibilities in this regard. General William Donovan, the wartime head of the Office

[21] PPS/22, "Utilization of Refugees from the Soviet Union in U.S. National Interest," February 5, 1948, Nelson, ed., *SDPPSP 1948*, pp. 88–90.
[22] Davies gave the specific responsibility to the State-Army-Navy Coordinating Committee (SANACC)—see PPS/22 "Utilization of Refugees from the Soviet Union," pp. 90–92.
[23] See Annex A to PPS/22, "Institute," February 5, 1948, Nelson, ed., *SDPPSP 1948*, pp. 93–95.

of Strategic Services, apparently had agreed to lend assistance on this venture.[24]

George Butler, acting-Director of the Staff in Kennan's absence, forwarded Davies' proposal to Lovett on February 19 and the under secretary of state forwarded it to the NSC Secretariat. There Admiral Souers determined that no need existed to send this paper through to the National Security Council and he returned it to be acted upon by the SANACC. Davies revised his proposal placing more emphasis on encouraging defections from the Soviet bloc and adding a recommendation that SANACC, along with a representative of the Department of Justice, also be charged with "submitting recommendations regarding the possible utilization of refugee political leaders in U.S. national interests."[25] Lovett approved the revised document and transmitted it to SANACC and the CIA for implementation but even before Lovett's action, State Department officials had outlined the general ideas for the institute to East European emigre leaders.[26]

Davies energetically pursued his project, although the full extent of his activities remains elusive. He already had specific individuals in mind whom he wished to bring to the United States and he immediately undertook to arrange this. His contact on the ground in occupied Germany was a protege of William Bullitt, Carmel Offie, who went on to become a special assistant to Frank Wisner at OPC but who at this time served on the staff of Robert Murphy, General Clay's political adviser.[27] On March 8, before Lovett formally had given the green light for his project, Davies contacted Offie about Nikolai N. Poppe, whom he described as "an outstanding authority on Mongolian and Turki areas."[28] According to Davies, Poppe, whose potential value as an intelligence source had been noted by U.S. Army Intelligence in 1947, languished in a Displaced Persons camp in the British zone of Germany and was on the verge of suicide.[29] Davies asked Offie to "keep him alive" and mentioned plans being made to make use of Poppe. Offie had some difficulty tracking Poppe down but Davies persisted in his efforts to obtain his services explaining that the "importance of Poppe lies in fact that we are most mea-

[24] Reference to Donovan's involvement is found in a telegram from Davies to the ambassador in Greece, Henry F. Grady, October 12, 1948, Decimal File, 800.43 Eurasian Institute/10-1248.

[25] PPS 22/1, March 4, 1948, Nelson, ed., *SDPPSP 1948*, pp. 97–102.

[26] See, for example, the Memorandum of Conversation by the Acting Chief of the Division of Eastern European Affairs (Francis B. Stevens), March 8, 1948, *FRUS* 1948, IV, pp. 404–6.

[27] For basic information on Carmel Offie I rely on my interview with Mr. James McCargar, Washington, D.C., February 28, 1990.

[28] Telegram, For Offie from Davies, March 8, 1948, Decimal File, 800.4016 DP/3-848.

[29] On Military Intelligence's awareness of Poppe's value see the memo by Col. Peter P. Rodes, "Personnel of Possible Intelligence Interest," May 22, 1947, printed in full in Christopher Simpson, *Blowback: America's Recruitment of Nazis and Its Effects on the Cold War* (New York, 1988), p. 120.

gerly informed of Mongolia and Central Asia.''[30] Only after some searching, dealings with the British, and complicated travel arrangements involving his being given a false name (Joseph Alexandris) was Poppe brought to the United States in May 1949.[31] On arrival in the United States by U.S. Military Transport plane Poppe moved to Washington and worked for some time in OPC before eventually taking up a position of professor of Far Eastern Languages at the University of Washington. According to Poppe's own account during his Washington sojourn he wrote reports concerning "the sciences in the Soviet Union, the organization of universities and research institutes, and the internal political conditions, particularly the purges in universities and research institutes."[32]

In his book *Blowback: America's Recruitment of Nazis and Its Effects on the Cold War*, Christopher Simpson, an investigative reporter, used Poppe as an example to help substantiate his case that Kennan and Davies were principals in a clandestine American program to bring former Nazis and German government officials to the United States.[33] Poppe, a one-time member of the Soviet Academy of Sciences, crossed to the German side in August 1942 when they occupied the city of Mikoyan Shakhar in the Caucasus where he was teaching. He collaborated in minor ways with them in establishing a quisling government in the Karachai minority region of the USSR. In 1943 he moved west with the retreating Germans out of fear and in order to leave the Soviet Union. He accepted a position at the Wannsee Institute in Berlin where he joined other collaborators in preparing intelligence reports on developments in the Soviet Union for the benefit of Hitler's regime. Poppe denied any involvement, either direct or indirect, in war crimes.[34] But even if Poppe's denials met the strictest veracity tests he was still burdened with the problem of what the ethicists term "dirty hands"—his collaboration with and service of the Nazi government. There need be no attempt made to disguise this. This accepted, what can be said of Davies' shadowy efforts to recruit him? Simpson has no doubt that it was quite wrong and morally culpable. Writing with the disposition of a hanging judge he lambasts Davies and Kennan (for this and other episodes), heaping scorn on them for their willingness to associate with

---

[30] Telegram, For Offie from Davies, March 18, 1948, Decimal File, 893.00 Mongolia/3-1848.

[31] On all of this see the cable traffic, Decimal File, 861.00/10-2248; 861.00/10-2948; 861.00/11-248; 861.00/11-848; 861.00/11-1548; 861.00/11-1648; 861.00/11-1648; 861.00/12-2248; 861.00/12-2248. The final travel arrangements involving the false name were handled by Davies' colleague Robert Joyce. See Personal for Riddleberger from Kennan (Joyce), May 4, 1949, Decimal File, 800.4016 DP/5-449.

[32] Nicholas Poppe, *Reminiscences*, ed. Henry G. Schwartz (Bellingham, Wash., 1983), pp. 199–200.

[33] Simpson, *Blowback*, pp. 118–21.

[34] For his own account see Poppe, *Reminiscences*, pp. 153–84. Simpson presents Poppe in a much less favorable light and suggests that he was at a minimum associated with war crimes. See *Blowback*, p. 119.

those who were less than pure. His accusatory tone rings shrilly and ignores the complex context and the tense atmosphere in which Davies (in this instance) operated. With the Czech coup, Stalinist domination throughout Eastern Europe, General Clay's war warning of March 1948, and the Soviet blockade of Berlin providing something of the context for his actions, Davies focused on developing the intelligence resources of the United States on the Soviet Union. In the messy and pressured reality of policy-making at that time he accorded this objective priority and in doing so he sought to utilize individuals whose past activities were ambiguous or clouded.

Of course Davies' efforts to utilize refugee expertise were not concentrated solely on Poppe. He participated in the interdepartmental discussions with representatives from the Armed Forces, the CIA, and the Department of Justice to establish a screening process for refugees. And by the end of May he informed Offie in Frankfurt that "progress on establishment of institute now appears running ahead of screening development."[35] To facilitate progress in the latter area Davies traveled to Europe in June 1948 where he had various discussions to develop a list of candidates for his proposed institute. In Paris he reviewed a preliminary list of candidates drawn up by Sergei Melgunov, a Russian historian and leader of an anti-Soviet group in Paris.[36] He enlisted Melgunov to visit the American zone in Germany to interview candidates.[37] Although he kept Kennan informed of his activities, Davies clearly emerged as the point man on this project. Information with regard to individuals believed to be in possession of valuable intelligence on the Soviet Union and satellites was channeled to him.[38] He relished his responsibilities in this area and involved himself deeply in the State Department's cooperation with Frank Wisner's OPC. It was through this organization that his efforts were increasingly channeled. After a seemingly favorable initial response, his Eurasian Research Institute foundered on the rock of lack of finances. By October 1948 Davies was writing to his father-in-law, Henry F. Grady, the American ambassador in Greece, asking him to give General Donovan names of persons on the West Coast "whom he might approach for financial support [of] Institute."[39] Such support did not materialize and Davies' proposed Eurasian Research Institute was never established.[40] But Davies' work with regard to it had moved the

[35] Telegram, From Offie for Davies, May 27, 1948, Decimal File, 800.43 Eurasian Institute/5-2748.
[36] Reference to this is found in Telegram, From Chipman for Offie, June 14, 1948, Decimal File, 800.43 Eurasian Institute/6-1448.
[37] On Melgunov's plans see Telegram, From Chipman for Offie, June 23, 1948, Decimal File, 800.43 Eurasian Institute/6-2548.
[38] See Telegram, John Wiley (Tehran) to Davies, July 27, 1948, Decimal File, 800.43 Eurasian Institute/7-2748.
[39] Telegram, For Ambassador from Davies, October 12, 1948, Decimal File, 800.43 Eurasian Institute/10-1248.
[40] Simpson states that many of the Eurasian Institute's "recruits were eventually integrated into

Policy Planning Staff into an important new area—intelligence operations, especially those involving refugees from the Soviet bloc. It was one that secured a major involvement from Kennan, Davies, and Robert Joyce (after he joined the Staff) through their liaison work with opc in the latter half of 1948 and through 1949. To understand fully the operations of the Policy Planning Staff during Kennan's tenure as Director this dimension of its activities must be appreciated.

COUNTERING THE SOVIET THREAT I

The Soviet success in consolidating power in Eastern Europe prompted responses beyond those of John Davies. The secretariat staff of the National Security Council leapt into the fray in March 1948 in an effort to appraise the nature of the Soviet threat and to chart a course to respond to it. Its initiative sparked deliberations on this subject which continued through the summer of ⌐1948 and which necessarily involved Kennan and the Planning Staff. In late February in a long review of trends in U.S. foreign policy Kennan had predicted to Marshall that if the line could be held in Western Europe and the Mediterranean and Soviet penetration consequently limited to the Iron Curtain then "the Russians will be prepared, for the first time since the surrender, to do business seriously with us about Germany and about Europe in general."[41] Kennan's optimism led him to make some suggestions for the day when the Russians might agree "to talk realistically." In particular he recommended that secret preparatory discussions be conducted with them by someone whose ⌐qualifications rather noticeably matched his own. How else can one interpret his suggestion that "those discussions can be successfully conducted only by someone who: (a) has absolutely no personal axe to grind in these discussions, even along the lines of getting public credit for their success, and is prepared to observe strictest silence about the whole proceeding; and (b) is thoroughly acquainted not only with the background of our policies but with Soviet philosophy and strategy and with the dialectics used by Soviet statesmen in such discussions." The clinching evidence that Kennan strove to outline a job description for himself came with his final suggestion that "it would be highly desirable that this person be able to conduct conversations in the Russian language. In my opinion, this is important with Stalin."[42] Beyond pushing his personal barrow, Kennan recommended that the United States wait for the Soviets to realize that they weren't going to expand any further and, upon their

the Munich-based (and cia-financed) Institute for the Study of the USSR during the early 1950s." *Blowback*, p. 115.

[41] pps/23, "Review of Current Trends, U.S. Foreign Policy," February 24, 1948, Nelson, ed., *SDPPSP 1948*, p. 118.

[42] pps/23, "Review of Current Trends," pp. 119–21.

doing so, to begin serious negotiations on the issues dividing them. This was a rather sanguine view and one not universally shared.

The NSC staff offered a more alarmist analysis. In a paper sent to the Planning Staff for its consideration on March 18 the NSC staff held that "the ultimate objective of Soviet-directed world communism is the domination of the world. To this end, Soviet-directed world communism employs against its victims in opportunistic coordination the complementary instruments of Soviet aggressive pressure from without and military revolutionary subversion from within."[43] The report counted down the countries that already had fallen to the Soviets and listed Italy, Greece, Finland, and Korea as among the others now immediately threatened. In what might have been taken as a criticism of Kennan's approach the NSC report argued that "a defensive policy cannot be considered an effectual means of checking the momentum of communist expansion and inducing the Kremlin to relinquish its aggressive designs." Such an approach allowed the Soviets to retain what they already had. The NSC staff called instead for a "counter-offensive policy" although they were rather vague about what this meant. They called for a strengthening of the American military establishment and endorsed the implementation of the European Recovery Program and the Western Union proposal but, aside from a suggestion that underground resistance movements be encouraged in countries behind the Iron Curtain, they had little new to offer.[44]

In Kennan's absence in Japan the Planning Staff considered the NSC report and circulated it within the State Department. There, the directors of the regional divisions criticized it as "too general to be useful."[45] Under some pressure from the military consultants to the NSC who strongly desired the adoption of a paper like this, Butler consulted with Kennan, now back from Japan and recovering his health in Walter Reed hospital. The chief planner sympathized with the directors of the regional divisions and asked that the paper on Soviet-Directed World Communism be kept off the NSC agenda until he and General Marshall had studied it.[46] It was at this point that Kennan and Bohlen, encouraged by the passage of ERP and the favorable outcome of the Italian elections, reintroduced to Marshall the possibility of some approach to the Russians designed to lay the groundwork for serious discussions. Marshall took up the suggestion in late April, although he did not call on Kennan to undertake this

[43] Minutes of Meeting, March 18, 1948, PPS Records, Box 32. Attached to these minutes is a copy of the NSC report, "The Position of the United States with Respect to Soviet-Directed World Communism."

[44] NSC Report, "The Position of the United States with Respect to Soviet-Directed World Communism."

[45] George Butler reported this criticism to his Staff colleagues in Minutes of Meeting, April 6, 1948, PPS Records, Box 32.

[46] Ibid.

delicate mission. He entrusted the responsibility to his ambassador in Moscow, Walter Bedell Smith.[47]

Smith duly made his secret approach to Vyacheslav Molotov on May 4. He rehearsed for the Soviet Foreign Minister the problems in U.S.-Soviet relations since the conclusion of the war with Germany and restated American policy. Then, in a manner reflecting Kennan's influence, Ambassador Smith revealed that his government did "not despair by any means of a turn of events which will permit us to find the road to a decent and reasonable relationship between our two countries." He assured Molotov that "the door is always wide open for full discussion and the composing of our differences."[48] Molotov responded to Smith on May 9 in a formal note which concentrated on defending Soviet international behavior but which also announced a Soviet willingness to better relations with the U.S. and so to proceed "towards a discussion and settlement of the difference existing between us."[49] But the Soviets blatantly torpedoed the possibility of any such discussion on May 11 when Molotov publicly announced that the Soviets would join the Americans in talks. The U.S. government considered the Molotov announcement an exercise in Soviet propaganda and psychological warfare designed in the words of Elbridge Durbrow, Smith's deputy in Moscow, to "undercut USA leadership [of] western countries by sowing elements [of] distrust among our friends not consulted in advance."[50] Predictably, the West Europeans were perturbed by the American action.[51] Marshall, however, vigorously and successfully fought the brushfires of their discontent and soothed their anxieties that the U.S. might undertake bilateral negotiations with the Soviets without prior consultation with its Western friends.[52]

The Smith-Molotov exchange had exploded in the face of the Truman administration and it served to sour many American policymakers on the possibility of serious negotiations with the Soviets. Bedell Smith set the tone by describing the "Soviet maneuver" as evidence "that [the] Kremlin has not [the] slightest idea of any compromise solution at this time."[53] Even the Plan-

---

[47] For the initial instructions to Smith see Lovett to Smith, April 24, 1948, *FRUS 1948*, IV, pp. 834–35; and Marshall to Smith, April 29, 1948, *FRUS 1948*, IV, pp. 840–41. Also see Kennan, *Memoirs*, I, pp. 346–47.

[48] Smith's statement included in Smith to Marshall, May 4, 1948, *FRUS 1948*, IV, pp. 847–50.

[49] Molotov's statement in Smith to Marshall, May 10, 1948, *FRUS 1948*, IV, pp. 854–57.

[50] For Durbrow's discussion of Molotov's statement see Durbrow to Marshall, May 11, 1948, *FRUS 1948*, IV, pp. 858–59.

[51] See, for example, Memorandum of Conversation by Marshall of his discussion with British Ambassador, Lord Inverchapel, May 11, 1948, *FRUS 1948*, IV, pp. 860–61.

[52] Marshall to Douglas (for Bevin), May 11, 1948, *FRUS 1948*, IV, pp. 861–62. Also see General Marshall's public statement, May 12, 1948, *Department of State Bulletin* 18, no. 464 (May 23, 1948): 683–85.

[53] Caffery (for Smith) to Marshall, May 12, 1948, *FRUS 1948*, IV, p. 863. Also see Smith's discussion of the whole episode in his *My Three Years in Moscow*, pp. 157–67.

ning Staff, with Kennan in the chair, was forced to admit that "the action of the Russians in publishing the communication indicates that they have no desire seriously to enter into discussions on points at issue."[54] Of course, Kennan did not give up on the possibility of negotiation with the Soviets, as we have seen on the German question, but the perception of a deliberate and bloody-minded Soviet sabotage of Smith's initiative revealed to all the difficulty of this process and strengthened the hand of those who saw negotiations as pointless.

The failure of Smith's effort only served to highlight the need for a clearer formulation of American policy toward the Soviet Union. Once back at his desk at the Planning Staff after recovering his health Kennan placed the NSC paper on Soviet-Directed World Communism aside and began to draw up his own on this broad subject. On June 7 he reported to the Staff that he had completed a draft of a paper on "Objectives of U.S. Policy toward USSR."[55] This paper consisted of a more sophisticated analysis of the Soviet threat and a more full discussion of American policy to meet it. Before Kennan could begin to navigate it through to approval by the National Security Council a striking event occurred which required him to undertake some revision. The unity of the Soviet bloc was sundered.

TITOISM AND THE AMERICAN RESPONSE

The split between Stalin and Tito completely surprised Kennan, as it did most everyone else in the West. The Planning Staff director shared the conventional view that Tito and the Yugoslavs acted at the beck and call of the Kremlin. Indeed, Kennan had characterized the Yugoslav leader in late 1946 as "a bird dog which has been so well trained that it has been taught to heel and no longer needs to go on the leash."[56] Tito's aggressiveness towards and willingness to confront the West in the years following World War II over issues like Trieste and support for the Communist guerrillas in Greece confused Washington into considering him little more than an extension and tool of Soviet power, the most loyal satellite of all.[57] No one picked up on the 1947 observations of the American chargé d'affaires in Belgrade, John M. Cabot, that the Yugoslavs might "not always blindly follow Russian instructions."[58] Even the early

---

[54] Minutes of Meeting, May 12, 1948, PPS Records, Box 32.

[55] Ibid., June 7, 1948.

[56] Address, October 22, 1946, Kennan Papers, Box 16, quoted in Stephanson, *Kennan and the Art of Foreign Policy*, p. 89.

[57] Robert M. Blum has analyzed the American failure to foresee Tito's clash with Stalin in "Surprised by Tito: The Anatomy of an Intelligence Failure," *Diplomatic History* 12 (Winter 1988): 39–57. On the Trieste matter see Roberto G. Rabel, *Between East and West: Trieste, the United States and the Cold War, 1941–1954* (Durham, 1988).

[58] Cabot to Marshall, June 7, 1947, *FRUS* 1947, IV, pp. 806–7. See also John M. Cabot, *First*

warning signals of the split detected by the Embassy in Belgrade and conveyed to the State Department on June 18, 1948, prompted no response beyond a telling silence.[59] But the Cominform's expulsion of the Yugoslav Communist party in an angry denunciation issued at its meeting in Bucharest on June 28 ended doubts of the break between Stalin and his supposed ally Tito. The Yugoslav leader's heresy ultimately lay in his obtaining and his largely maintaining power independent of Moscow, and the rift between the two Communist systems ran deep.[60] Presumably Stalin thought Tito's government would collapse but it did not.[61] Instead it gave birth to a distinct political course—Titoism—thereby presenting a new and unexpected challenge to policymakers in the West.

Kennan played the central role in forging the American response to Tito's break with Stalin. In what can only be termed a virtuoso performance he prepared within two days the basic document which in its essentials "guided American policy into 1949."[62] Kennan possessed only a general background on Yugoslavia. He and the Staff had recommended in late 1947 that the United States maintain its tough negotiating stance in refusing to release Yugoslav gold reserves in the United States until the Yugoslavs settled assorted American claims against them.[63] But aside from this issue Kennan devoted little time to Yugoslav matters prior to June 28. Then the situation changed dramatically and Kennan urgently prepared a paper, at Under Secretary Lovett's request, in order to furnish guidance for American diplomatic officials in light of the Cominform's denunciation of the Yugoslav Communist Party. He discussed it

---

Line of Defense: Forty Years' Experiences of a Career Diplomat (Washington, D.C., 1979), p. 34.

[59] For the embassy's warning see Reams to Marshall, June 18, 1948, *FRUS* 1948, IV, p. 1073. For the recollections of a participant in the production of this cable and comments on the lack of response from the State Department see Charles G. Stefan, "The Emergence of the Soviet-Yugoslav Break: A Personal View from the Belgrade Embassy," *Diplomatic History* 6 (Fall 1982): 387–404.

[60] For details on the Soviet-Yugoslav break see Robert Bass and Elizabeth Marbury, eds., *The Soviet-Yugoslav Controversy, 1948–58: A Documentary Record* (New York, 1959); Adam B. Ulam, *Titoism and the Cominform* (Cambridge, 1952); Hamilton Fish Armstrong, *Tito and Goliath* (New York, 1951); and Vladimir Dedijer, *The Battle Stalin Lost: Memoirs of Yugoslavia, 1948–1953* (New York, 1970).

[61] Adam Ulam argues that "megalomania persuaded Stalin that Tito and his miserable partisans would be cast at his feet in chains by their frightened associates. 'I shall shake my little finger and there will be no Tito,' he is alleged to have said, and though this may not be a literal quotation, that is how he felt." Ulam, *The Rivals: America and Russia Since World War II* (New York, 1971), p. 140.

[62] This accurate assessment of the importance of Kennan's work belongs to Lorraine M. Lees. See her fine article, "The American Decision to Assist Tito, 1948–1949," *Diplomatic History* 2 (Fall 1978): 410.

[63] PPS/16, "Unlocking of Yugoslav Gold," November 17, 1947, Nelson, ed., *The State Department Policy Planning Staff Papers 1947*, pp. 147–51.

with the other Staff members on the morning of June 30 and later that day Lovett gave it his approval.[64]

Kennan appreciated that Tito's defiance of the Kremlin created "an entirely new problem of foreign policy for this Government."[65] Mentioning the possibility of further disintegration of the Soviet satellite area he observed that the American attitude toward the Yugoslavs would set an important precedent and might influence whether other satellites followed Tito's lead. He called for extreme circumspection in handling this issue. Kennan noted that Yugoslavia remained a Communist state with an ideology hostile to the West. He deemed it an "undignified error" to accept that Tito was now a "friend" because he had fallen out with Stalin—(and in fact it took Tito some time to wean himself from his militant anti-Western sentiments). This said, and without ruling out some patching up of the rift, Kennan zeroed in on the significance of Tito's break with Stalin: "A new factor of fundamental and profound significance has been introduced into the world communist movement by the demonstration that the Kremlin can be successfully defied by one of its own minions. By this act, the aura of mystical omnipotence and infallibility which has surrounded the Kremlin power has been broken. The possibility of defection from Moscow, which has heretofore been unthinkable for foreign communist leaders, will from now on be present in one form or another in the mind of every one of them." But caution was required in dealing with Tito and Kennan warned against two extremes. Firstly, any Western moves to fawn on Tito would be exploited by Moscow and would only undermine his position. Yet, if the West coldly rejected Tito and repulsed any advances he might make, Moscow would use this to prove that Communist states had no choice but to stay within the fold—"that desertion only places them at the mercy of the wolves of capitalism." The correct approach lay in a cautious middle way. Thus, Yugoslavia's emerging independence would be welcomed without disguising American distaste for the unsavory character of its internal regime. But this regime would not stand in the way of "a normal development of economic relations" provided Yugoslavia adopted a cooperative attitude in its international dealings. The initiative lay with Tito's regime. If it "should demonstrate a wish to establish better relations with the west," Kennan advocated, "this Government would not stand in the way of such a development." The United States should not rush, however, to any precipitous action.

Marshall approved Kennan's proposals on July 1 and arranged for them to be sent to Clark Clifford to bring to the president's attention.[66] On July 6 the

[64] Minutes of Meeting, June 30, 1948, PPS Records, Box 32.

[65] PPS/35, "The Attitude of This Government Toward Events in Yugoslavia," June 30, 1948, *FRUS* 1948, IV, pp. 1079–81. All subsequent quotations in this paragraph are drawn from this document.

[66] See Marshall's handwritten note on the cover of his copy of PPS/35 lodged in PPS Records, Box 33.

Kennan document, now designated NSC 18, was circulated to the National Security Council for information but no formal meeting was held to approve it because Marshall already had set about implementing its recommendations, buoyed by the fact that Bevin and the British supported a similar, cautious course.[67] Using Kennan's paper as his guide he rejected advice from a number of quarters including the embassy in Belgrade that the United States adopt a more active policy in support of Tito.[68] He turned down a two-stage proposal from Under Secretary of the Army William Draper under which a secret approach would be made to ascertain if Tito desired to discuss improved relations, a favorable response to which would be followed by a visit to Belgrade by Draper and Averell Harriman.[69] The secretary of state explained to Army Secretary Kenneth Royall that "the situation is too fluid at present" to undertake the Draper proposal.[70] Continued observation and assessment of the situation was necessary. The president and the Cabinet, preoccupied with the concurrent crisis brought on by the blockade of Berlin, agreed.[71]

The Yugoslav policy which Kennan formulated and the Truman administration adopted required patience. As Robert Lee Wolff portrayed it, "The United States must quietly hold open for Tito a door through which he might pass when he should choose to do so."[72] The United States managed this operation with finesse and skill. Within three weeks of the Yugoslav excommunication from the Cominform agreement was reached on a settlement involving the frozen Yugoslav assets (mainly gold) in the U.S.[73] The Yugoslavs also began to look to the West for trade but Marshall moved carefully on this, informing the Belgrade embassy that "any steps we may be prepared to take to assist Tito will require most careful appraisal in light [of] all prevailing circumstances."[74] The Americans waited for the Yugoslavs to demonstrate a

[67] For Bevin's position see Douglas to Secretary of State, June 30, 1948, *FRUS* 1948, IV, p. 1078. For Marshall's reference to Bevin's position see Marshall to Royall, July 7, 1948, *FRUS* 1948, IV, p. 1087.

[68] Lees discusses the recommendations for a more active policy and Marshall's rejections in "The American Decision to Assist Tito," p. 411.

[69] For Draper's proposal see Draper to Royall, July 6, 1948, *FRUS* 1948, IV, pp. 1085–87. For Draper's recollection of the circumstances of his suggestion see Memo of Conversation between General William H. Draper and Mark L. Chadwin, July 5, 1967, Harriman Papers, Box 867.

[70] Marshall to Royall, July 7, 1948, *FRUS* 1948, VI, p. 1087. Marshall referred to the cautionary stance adopted by the British to support his decision. For discussion of British policy see Beatrice Heuser, *Western 'Containment' Policies in the Cold War: The Yugoslav Case, 1948–53* (London, 1989), pp. 43–80.

[71] Reference to the president's and Cabinet's agreement is found in Marshall's memorandum to Lovett, July 9, 1948, *FRUS* 1948, IV, p. 1087 n. 4.

[72] Robert Lee Wolff, *The Balkans in Our Time*, rev. ed. (Cambridge, Mass., 1974), p. 410.

[73] On this settlement see Editorial Note, *FRUS* 1948, IV, p. 1093; and the discussion on this matter in David L. Larson, *United States Foreign Policy Toward Yugoslavia, 1943–1963* (Washington, D.C., 1979), pp. 185–86.

[74] Marshall to Embassy in Yugoslavia, July 28, 1948, *FRUS* 1948, IV, p. 1099.

more independent foreign policy from the Soviets, something they markedly failed to do at the Danubian Conference in Belgrade in July, which convened to negotiate new navigational arrangements for the Danube. There the Yugoslavs marched in lockstep with the Soviets to the detriment of the position of the United States. Despite this, restraint characterized the American position. [75]

Having charted the main lines of the American approach Kennan turned to other pressing matters, especially the formulation of Program A for Germany, during the fall of 1948. He kept his eye on Yugoslav policy but saw little need for modifications. At a meeting of the National Security Council on September 30 Kennan, in reply to an inquiry from Secretary of Defense Forrestal, indicated that he could see no need for any change in policy because "our 'hands off' policy had been so successful." [76] As the year came to an end, however, Kennan recognized that some redirection in policy might be necessary. In November 1948 he readily agreed to a suggested addition from John Hickerson of the Office of European Affairs to his June 30 policy statement providing that the United States would consider carefully any proposals by the Yugoslavs for improved trade relations. On this issue, Kennan and Hickerson found themselves in agreement. They accepted the department's decision to deny approval for the export of oil-drilling equipment to Yugoslavia but supported Under Secretary Lovett's decision to expedite trade items for which export license applications had been made. [77] External events prompted a further sentiment that the United States might need to adopt a more sympathetic approach to Yugoslavia's economic needs. The propaganda warfare launched by Moscow against the "Fascist Tito clique" and the massing of Soviet ground forces on the Yugoslav frontier largely ended doubts that the Yugoslav rift with Stalin was for real. More seriously, Moscow launched economic warfare against Yugoslavia, systematically isolating her from the Cominform bloc on which she had been dependent for substantial quantities of raw materials and some manufactured goods. This economic quarantine forced Tito to reorient his economy more towards the West. In December 1948 he signed a trade agreement with Great Britain and indicated his willingness to exchange strategic raw materials for increased trade with the West. In such circumstances American officials concluded that they needed to more actively assist Tito to stave off Soviet pressures. Kennan played a decisive role in this new stage of America's Yugoslav policy.

The American embassy staff in Belgrade led by Ambassador Cavendish Cannon and his deputy R. Borden Reams had campaigned for a more forth-

[75] For further discussion of it see Lees, "American Decision to Assist Tito," pp. 111–13.

[76] National Security Council meetings, memorandum for the president, October 1, 1948, Truman Papers, PSF, Box 220.

[77] Memorandum, Hickerson to Kennan, November 26, 1948, *FRUS* 1948, IV, pp. 1117–18. For Kennan's response see *FRUS* 1948, IV, p. 1118 n. 4.

coming United States policy toward Tito from the outset but without success. Kennan's more cautious approach prevailed. But when the Planning chief alerted his superiors to the need for alterations in this approach they were adopted quickly. His second major policy proposal, distributed formally on February 10, 1949, exercised the same decisive impact on policy as the first and charted the way for U.S. relations with Tito through the remainder of 1949 and beyond. Robert Joyce, who had served in Belgrade before World War II, with the OSS in the Balkans during the War and in Trieste afterward, assisted Kennan in its preparation and gathered support for its conclusions from officials from the regional divisions such as John Campbell who was the Yugoslav desk officer in the Southeast European Affairs office of the Division of European Affairs.[78] In PPS/49, "Economic Relations between the United States and Yugoslavia," Kennan offered a series of recommendations aimed at relaxing "U.S. export license controls in favor of Yugoslavia in order to strengthen Tito's resistance to the Kremlin."[79] While noting that Tito's attitude toward the West had "softened only slightly," Kennan affirmed the profound character of the rift between the Yugoslav leader and Stalin. He argued that American interests demanded that Tito's position should not be made more difficult by American actions, because the only alternative to Tito was "a Cominformist regime completely subservient to Moscow." Aside from this negative alternative Tito brought positive advantages. "It is in the obvious interests of the United States," Kennan explained, "that 'Titoism' continue to exist as an erosive and disintegrating force operating within the Kremlin's power sphere." Kennan did not disguise the reality that Tito ran a police state but he asserted vigorously—almost to the point of rhetorical overkill—that "much as we may dislike him, Tito is presently performing brilliantly in our interests in leading successfully and effectively the attack from within the Communist family on Soviet imperialism. Tito in being is perhaps our most precious asset in the struggle to contain and weaken Russian expansion. He must be allowed to prove on his own Communist terms that an Eastern European country can secede from Moscow control and still succeed." After such an assessment of Tito's value Kennan not surprisingly proceeded to recommend a relaxation of the trade and credit restrictions on Yugoslavia. He called for this without demanding that Tito be forced to pay a public price in specific political concessions, although he suggested that the American ambassador in Belgrade remind the Yugoslavs quietly but firmly that U.S. interests were damaged by certain Yugoslav actions, especially by their support for the Communist guerrillas in Greece. Such subtle pressure would suffice while the United States

[78] Oral History Interview with John C. Campbell by Richard D. McKinzie, June 24, 1974, HSTL, transcript pages 138–39.

[79] PPS/49, "Economic Relations between the United States and Yugoslavia," February 10, 1949, Nelson, ed., *The State Department Policy Planning Staff Papers 1949*, pp. 14–24. Subsequent quotations in this paragraph are drawn from this document.

pursued its primary objective, "to keep Tito strong enough to continue his resistance to the Cominform."

Kennan's proposal was quickly adopted as national policy. After a full discussion of his document at a meeting chaired by Under Secretary of State James Webb on February 14 a slightly modified version was dispatched to the National Security Council.[80] The Council accepted the recommendations for a policy of relaxation over export controls to Yugoslavia and sent the report to the president. Truman wasted no time and approved it the following day.[81] In a gradual manner the new policy was implemented. Direct trade between the two countries increased during 1949. In August 1949 the U.S.—over the objections of Secretary of Defense Louis Johnson—agreed to the export of a steel finishing mill to Yugoslavia, despite its being deemed a "war potential" item.[82] The following month the Export-Import Bank, an American institution, extended a $20 million loan to the Yugoslavs. By the end of the year permission had been granted for the Yugoslavs to purchase such war potential items as civil aircraft and equipment and aviation gasoline. Washington also concluded a civil aviation agreement with Belgrade and encouraged expanded Yugoslav trade arrangements with West European countries.[83] All had been done in an effort to help secure Tito in power which, of course, as 1949 ended he still held to firmly despite the Soviet pressures against him. The policy's success manifested itself also in Tito's political actions. He closed his frontier with Greece sealing the fate of the Greek Communists and Yugoslav diplomatic representatives became somewhat more vocal in their criticism of the Soviet Union. Such independence led the United States to support the successful Yugoslav bid for a seat on the United Nations Security Council in October 1949.

The policy Kennan recommended laid the groundwork for the sound U.S.-Yugoslav relationship. It was constructed cautiously and carefully and always with a clear recognition of the significance of Tito's break with Stalin. Kennan held that in its implications it was "as important for Communism as Martin

[80] For the discussion and modified document see Minutes of the Under Secretary's meeting, February 14, 1949, *FRUS* 1949, V, pp. 863–68.

[81] For NSC and Truman's approval see Editorial Note, *FRUS* 1949, V, p. 868. For the report see NSC 18/1, "Economic Relations between the United States and Yugoslavia," February 15, 1949, Truman Papers, PSF, Box 205. (Upon approval by the NSC and Truman it was designated NSC 18/2.)

[82] Lees provides a full account of the struggle between State and Defense over the steel mill in "American Decision to Assist Tito," pp. 416–18.

[83] Wolff, *The Balkans in Our Time*, pp. 411–12. For further details also see Larson, *United States Policy Toward Yugoslavia*, pp. 204–13. The Planning Staff had helped formulate a tough general civil aviation policy toward the USSR and its satellites demanding reciprocal transit and commercial landing rights. See NSC 15/1, "U.S. Civil Aviation Policy Toward the USSR and Its Satellites," July 12, 1948, *FRUS* 1948, IV, pp. 451–56. This was a slight modification of PPS/32 of June 11, 1948.

Luther's proclamation was for the Roman Catholic Church."[84] His measured approach largely guided the United States policy which effectively and skillfully assisted Tito.[85] The policy received further development after Kennan had left the State Department when the Truman administration decided to extend direct assistance, including military advice and aid, to Tito's regime.[86] But such steps were based on the solid foundations Kennan had done so much to lay. In formulating this policy Kennan had no need to engage in the bureaucratic battles that beset him on other issues. The State Department's policy-making on this issue was quick and decisive, perhaps a reflection of the clarity with which Kennan set forth America's strategic and political interests in Yugoslav independence and Titoism. Most likely a similar policy would have been formulated even had Kennan not been in the department such was the weight of U.S. interests.[87] But, this said, there is still need to acknowledge Kennan's crucial role—something done so far by only a few specialist historians.[88] During the Kennedy administration Kennan served as American ambassador to Yugoslavia, a Yugoslavia still fiercely independent of Soviet domination. Presumably and justifiably he took some pride in his own role in

[84] See Kennan's talk at the Council on Foreign Relations, "Long Term Questions of U.S. Foreign Policy," February 16, 1949, Archives of the Council on Foreign Relations (New York), Records of Meetings.

[85] The final contribution of the Policy Planning Staff under Kennan's directorship to the formulation of policy on Yugoslavia came with PPS/60, "Yugoslav-Moscow Controversy as Related to U.S. Foreign Policy Objectives," September 12, 1949, *FRUS* 1949, V, pp. 947–54. This document advocated the extension of military assistance to Yugoslavia in the event of its being attacked by the Soviet Union or the Soviet satellites—which the Staff did not deem likely. On the formulation of the paper see Minutes of Meeting, September 9, 1949, PPS Records, Box 32. This paper was subjected to some criticism at an Under Secretary's meeting, much to Kennan's displeasure, and returned to the Staff for reworking. Joyce took on the responsibility for this and was guided by a "formula" which held that "at such time as it becomes clear that such action is necessary to strengthen Tito's hand with his own people we will inform him that he can expect aid from the U.S. in the event of an attack by the U.S.S.R. or the Satellites." See Minutes of Meeting, September 26, 1949, PPS Records, Box 32. For the criticism see Record of the Under Secretary's Meeting, September 16, 1949, *FRUS* 1949, V, pp. 959–61. For Kennan's displeasure see his *Memoirs*, I, pp. 465–66.

[86] On the nature of this assistance and the factors that prompted it (including the devastating drought that struck Yugoslavia in 1950) see Henry W. Brands, Jr., "Redefining the Cold War: American Policy toward Yugoslavia, 1948–60," *Diplomatic History* 11 (Winter 1987): 41–53; and Robert M. Hathaway, "Truman, Tito and the Politics of Hunger," in William F. Levantrosser, ed., *Harry S. Truman: The Man From Independence* (New York, 1986), pp. 129–49; and John C. Campbell, *Tito's Separate Road: America and Yugoslavia in World Politics* (New York, 1967), pp. 22–29.

[87] As John C. Campbell has commented: "The reasons of self-interest for the United States and the entire West, however, were so clear that any other course would have been a triumph of ideological fervor over good sense." John C. Campbell, *Tito's Separate Road*, p. 19.

[88] Lorraine Lees is a worthy representative of this group. Kennan himself makes little of his contribution in this area in his Memoirs.

fashioning the American policy which had contributed to such independence.[89]

COUNTERING THE SOVIET THREAT II

Once he had provided urgent counsel on Yugoslav policy Kennan turned his attention back to the comprehensive survey of U.S. policy toward the Soviet Union which he had undertaken in order to improve on the overly broad study offered by the NSC secretariat staff. Furthermore, Defense Secretary Forrestal emphasized the crucial need to clarify basic national objectives in order to formulate a sound military program thereby adding to the demand for such a study.[90] Now Kennan had to incorporate the reality that the international Communist movement was no longer monolithic into his analysis and to frame his recommendations for U.S. strategy in light of the Tito-Stalin split. He labored throughout July and revised his paper (PPS/38) titled "United States Objectives with Respect to Russia."[91] He submitted it to Lovett on August 18, 1948.

Kennan introduced his long paper by noting that the Soviet Union constituted the outstanding problem for U.S. foreign policy but that up to that point there had been "no clear formulation of basic U.S. objectives with respect to Russia."[92] He rectified that situation arguing that the United States had but two fundamental objectives with regard to the Soviet Union—firstly, to reduce Moscow's power and influence to a point where it not longer constituted "a threat to the peace and stability of international society"; and, secondly, to bring about a basic change in the "theory and practice" of Soviet international relations. After detailed explication of each objective he posed the questions of how each might be pursued. Notably with regard to the first objective and referring to the East European satellite area he called for U.S. policy "to place the greatest possible strain on the structure of relationships by which Soviet domination of this area is maintained." This might be done through the use of economic power—here he gave the offer of Marshall Plan funds to the Soviet

[89] Kennan described his tour of service in Yugoslavia as "one of the richest, most pleasant, and most rewarding of the personal experiences of a Foreign Service life." Kennan, *Memoirs*, II, p. 269.

[90] Memorandum by Forrestal to NSC, July 10, 1948; and Forrestal to Truman, July 10, 1948, *FRUS* 1948, I, pp. 589–92.

[91] Kennan wrote to his friend Frank Altschul while working on this paper: "We do our best to analyse the Russian moves on the chess board but we are working under handicaps, making our plans in a glass cage and seeking the innumerable clearances required by the normal processes of three democratic governments, yet opposed by a group of people who can take their decisions with great secrecy and rapidity." Here he clearly had decision-making with regard to the Berlin blockade in mind but it indicates his mood as he worked on PPS/38. See Kennan to Altschul, July 20, 1948, Altschul Papers, File 113a.

[92] PPS/38, "United States Objectives with Respect to Russia," August 18, 1948, Nelson, ed., *SDPPSP 1948*, pp. 372–411. Subsequent quotations in this paragraph draw from this document.

bloc and the strains it presumably put on relations within it as an example. Propaganda, or as Kennan politely put it "informational activity," represented another weapon in the U.S. arsenal. Encouraging and facilitating the satellite governments to extricate themselves from Soviet control took on added feasibility in light of the Yugoslav episode. Kennan implied other rifts might occur because "the Kremlin leaders are so inconsiderate, so relentless, so overbearing and so cynical in the discipline they impose on their followers that few can stand their authority for very long." And of course, there was his bedrock point which he had made myriad times—that of "building up the hope and vigor of western Europe to a point where it comes to exercise maximum attraction to the peoples of the east." As well as outlining such aims and methods to achieve the U.S. objective Kennan clarified that the U.S. should NOT aim "to place the fundamental emphasis of our policy on preparation for an armed conflict, to the exclusion of the development of possibilities for achieving our objectives without war." Measures short of war attracted his support. As David Mayers has noted Kennan held to the conviction that "non-military strategies could be used to weaken Soviet hegemony in Eastern Europe."[93]

As for the second objective—bringing about some real change in the Soviet theory and practice of international relations—Kennan resorted to a similar argument that he had put forward in his "X" article, "The Sources of Soviet Conduct." He described the West as unable to alter the basic political psychology of the men in the Kremlin but argued that these Soviet leaders were "prepared to recognize *situations*, if not arguments." The task was to create situations which would convey to the Soviets the disadvantages to them of emphasizing conflict in their dealings with the West.[94] This obviously is what Kennan's notion of containment was meant to bring about and he did not expect it in the short-term.[95] His efforts to strengthen Western Europe and to block Soviet expansionist moves were aimed to create such situations.

Kennan's paper contained much more, including his rather esoteric discourse of what aims the United States should pursue in any war with Russia which contained long discussions of whether the United States would preserve the existing Soviet state (minus the Baltic nations) or partition it; what role the United States would play in determining who would rule a Russia freed from Communist rule and so forth. Perhaps some in the policy-making community read these parts carefully but there is little evidence of it. Nonetheless, the Kennan paper was conveyed to the National Security Council where it was

---

[93] Mayers, *George Kennan and the Dilemmas of Foreign Policy*, p. 157.

[94] PPS/38, "United States Objectives with Respect to Russia," pp. 372–411.

[95] John Lewis Gaddis provides an insightful analysis of this in his "The Strategy of Containment," in Thomas H. Etzold and John Lewis Gaddis, eds., *Containment: Documents on American Policy and Strategy, 1945–1950* (New York, 1978), pp. 33–34.

designated NSC 20/1.[96] After some consideration and some slight reworking the National Security Council adopted it—now designated NSC 20/4—as policy on November 23, 1948, and President Truman approved it the next day.[97] NSC 20/4 provided the basis for subsequent analysis of American policy towards the USSR but its immediate impact on policy implementation was relatively minor. Actual policy continued to emerge in a rather ad hoc manner. The exercise had not been a waste for Kennan, however. He and his Staff, especially John Davies and Robert Joyce, began to focus much attention on the first objective of NSC 20/1—the retraction of Soviet power. It involved them in the murky domain of political warfare.

POLITICAL WARFARE

Kennan's and the Staff's involvement in what we may broadly term political warfare was well established by the time he completed his paper examining U.S. objectives toward the Soviet Union. As we have seen (chapter 3), prompted by the seeming success of covert operations in the Italian election campaign, Kennan played the leading role in conceiving the Office of Policy Coordination and in ensuring that he as Director of Policy Planning would be involved in supervising its activities. Intent on utilizing political warfare as an instrument of U.S. foreign policy he successfully had claimed the responsibility to decide which projects were politically desirable. Also, through Davies' activities the Planning Staff already was well involved in the effort to recruit refugees to contribute to various aspects of the political/psychological contest with the Soviets. The launching of OPC brought the Planning Staff's involvement in this area to a qualitatively new stage. The Policy Planning Staff and the Office of Policy Coordination were related integrally in the first years of the latter's existence. While it was lodged within the CIA for administrative reasons the Director of Central Intelligence exercised no authority over Wisner's OPC. It was responsible to the State Department and essentially Kennan exercised this responsibility, although given the pressure of other demands he could not devote his major effort to this. John Paton Davies and Robert Joyce were Kennan's liaison officers to OPC and filled some of the breach. They maintained frequent contact with the officials of OPC, visiting its offices regularly and calling OPC officials to the State Department, and they were the source of some of the initiatives undertaken by the new organization.[98]

The Office of Policy Coordination formally came into operation on September 1, 1948. Wisner held his first meeting with his then small staff on Septem-

[96] The full text of NSC 20/1 is available in Etzold and Gaddis, eds., *Containment*, pp. 173ff.

[97] For NSC 20/4 see *FRUS* 1948, I, pp. 662–69.

[98] On the contacts between the Planning Staff and OPC I rely on interviews with two of the early appointees to OPC. Interview with Franklin Lindsay, Washington, D.C., February 27, 1990; and Interview with James McCargar, Washington, D.C., February 28, 1990.

ber 8. Apparently there had been some expectation that the new body would be given a grace period to get well established but various pressures upon Wisner made this impossible.[99] Wisner faced the demands from policymakers like Kennan to contribute quickly to the struggle against the Soviets. By September 17 he framed a plan for expansion and devised an organizational chart dividing the functional activities of the Office into major groupings: psychological warfare by press, radio, and other devices; political warfare; economic warfare; preventive direct action such as support of guerrillas, sabotage, and related subversive practices; front organizations and war plans.[100] An air of tension wafted through the new organization created in part by Wisner's own intense and activist temperament and by a sense of fear generated by the Soviet threat. One senior officer recalls "running around like mad" and of undertaking actions in light of what was perceived as a most dangerous international situation.[101] In this category must surely go the endeavors to organize "stay behind" organizations which would harass Soviet occupation forces if the Red Army swept into Western Europe.[102]

The Planning Staff contribution to the work of OPC focused more on efforts to dislodge the Soviets from what they already occupied. An important preliminary step to any such action was obtaining good but increasingly inaccessible intelligence on what exactly was going on in the Soviet bloc.[103] Davies had this in mind in trying to tap into refugee expertise for his Eurasian Institute. He continued his efforts to obtain the services of such individuals but the Staff also saw the benefit of obtaining German expertise in this area. Along with Carmel Offie of Wisner's staff Davies took the initiative to bring to the United States Gustav Hilger, the Minister Counselor of the German Embassy in Moscow at the outbreak of World War II.[104] During the war Hilger worked for Foreign Minister Joachim von Ribbentrop providing advice primarily on So-

[99] On the expectation see interview with Franklin Lindsay, February 27, 1990.

[100] This relies directly on Darling, *The Central Intelligence Agency: An Instrument of Government to 1950*, chap. 7, p. 67.

[101] Interview with Franklin Lindsay, February 27, 1990.

[102] Ibid. Anne Karalekas notes that "until 1950 OPC's paramilitary activities (also referred to as preventive direct action) were limited to plans and preparations for stay-behind nets in the event of future war. Requested by the Joint Chiefs of Staff, these projected OPC operations focused, once again, on Western Europe and were designed to support NATO forces against Soviet attack." Karalekas, "History of the Central Intelligence Agency," p. 36.

[103] In commenting that it was not until 1949 that the CIA placed its own secret agents in Russia, the Agency's Harry Rositzke recalled that "it was our almost total ignorance of what was going on in the 'denied area' behind the Iron Curtain that helped create the false image of a superpowerful Soviet Union." Rositzke, *The CIA's Secret Operations: Espionage, Counterespionage and Covert Action* (New York, 1977), p. 15.

[104] Telegram for Murphy from Kennan (J. Davies), September 20, 1948, Decimal File, 862.00/9-2048. For the exchanges regarding the method of bringing Hilger into the country see Decimal File, 862.00/9-2148; 862.00/9-2548; 862.00/9-2748; 862.00/9-2848; 862.00/9-3048; 862.00/10-448. James McCargar recalled Offie's role in interview with McCargar, February 28, 1990.

viet affairs.[105] At the war's end he surrendered to U.S. forces and apparently was brought to the United States for debriefing and, according to Simpson, "for secret employment as a high-level analyst of captured German records on the USSR."[106] Eventually he was returned to Germany where he maintained contact with the Americans. In the fall of 1948 Davies thought it would be advantageous to utilize Hilger's unquestioned expertise on the Soviet Union and he and his family were brought to Washington where the former German diplomat worked within OPC analyzing Soviet strategy.[107] Here Kennan had some dealings with him, the impact of which appears minor. It is important to note in light of the charges leveled at Kennan of operating a program to bring ex-Nazis into the United States, that the Planning Staff director played only a minor role in Hilger's importation—(presumably Davies kept him informed in a general way).[108] Also one must note that Hilger, whom Davies certainly did not consider sympathetic to the Nazis, already served as an intelligence operative for the United States. Davies' effort aimed to attain maximum benefit from him. He considered this in a similar vein to the concurrent efforts being made to employ German scientists such as the rocket expert Wernher von Braun. Each action was fraught with moral ambiguity and raises difficult questions of means and ends which a historian legitimately might leave to the reader prepared to wrestle with their ethical implications. This historian would suggest, however, that a moral category utilized in the just war tradition—namely proportionality—might be helpful in any such ethical evaluation. Proportionality maintains that the evil involved in a particular action must not be greater than the harm which would result if the action were not performed. In light of this consideration and in view of both the abysmal ignorance of developments in the Soviet Union and the context of confrontation in U.S.-Soviet relations, one should avoid any hasty or kneejerk condemnation of the actions of Kennan and Davies.

Just as OPC, through Davies and Offie, made use of Gustav Hilger, so it

[105] Simpson in *Blowback*, pp. 112–14 provides more details including some tangential connections between Hilger and the murder of Jews. While I find many of Simpson's conclusions questionable his doggedness as a researcher cannot be denied.

[106] Simpson, *Blowback*, p. 114.

[107] James McCargar remembers seeing Hilger hard at work in an office at OPC and assumed he was working on Soviet issues. Interview with McCargar, February 28, 1990. Nikolai Poppe also met Hilger in Washington in 1949 and claimed that "he had been brought to the United States in order to help with plans for a future German government." He asserted that "the existence of the Adenauer government was to a large extent the result of Hilger's activities." *Reminiscences*, p. 200. There is little evidence to support Poppe's recollection.

[108] The charges are, of course, those of Simpson in *Blowback*. Note that Kennan wrote to Simpson: "I do not recall seeing him [Gustav Hilger], or having any contact with him, in the period between the end of the war and his arrival in this country. I do not recall having had anything to do with, or any responsibility for, bringing him to this country; nor do I recall knowing, at the time, by what arrangements he was brought here." Simpson, *Blowback*, p. 116. He stands by these statements. Author's interview with Kennan, March 6, 1989.

readily cooperated with another German, one who brought much more than his own personal expertise on the Soviet Union. General Reinhard Gehlen had served as head of military intelligence for *Fremde Heere Ost* (Foreign Armies East) of the German Wehrmacht where he built up a strong espionage network. Upon Hitler's defeat he microfilmed his extensive files and hid the films. He eventually negotiated a deal of sorts with the American military whereby he "offered the Americans access to his microfilms and use of the agents in place left behind as the Russian armies had overrun eastern Europe" in return for his continuing role in supervising his intelligence network.[109] Gehlen in fact signed a written contract with the U.S. War Department in May 1949 and his intelligence system aimed its efforts on the Soviet bloc. While Gehlen's formal agreement linked him to the War Department his field activities linked him closely to OPC where Carmel Offie served as a key liaison.[110] Kennan and his colleagues undoubtedly approved of the cooperation with Gehlen's outfit, which grew more extensively at Wisner's initiative after 1949. Gehlen, who went on to serve as director of the West German Federal Intelligence Service in 1955, maintained a tight control over his organization which most observers assume contained some former Nazis.[111] No one from the Planning Staff or OPC raised questions. They thought instead of how to utilize this valuable asset.

The main thrust of OPC's activities up to the Korean War centered on various Central and Eastern European refugee operations. A full and accurate account of OPC's early operations—an account that would require the opening of the records of the CIA—remains to be written. Yet some sense of its activities, which Kennan in broad terms approved, can be garnered. Recruitment among the refugees from the Soviet bloc—Ukrainians, Poles, Byelorussians, Balts, and anti-Stalinist Russians—continued, including groups who out of their hatred for Stalinist terror and tyranny had associated with the Nazis. Efforts were made, some in conjunction with Gehlen, to organize guerrilla training for refugee groups and plans made to mount operations behind the Iron Curtain.[112] Those who suggest that these efforts amounted to a revival or replication of the Nazi-sponsored Vlasov Army perpetrate an exaggeration.[113] With hind-

[109] On Gehlen's background see Robin Winks, *Cloak and Gown*, p. 454. For more details see Heinz Hohne and Hermann Zolling, *Network: The Truth about General Gehlen and His Spy Ring* (London, 1972).

[110] On Offie's role see interview with James McCargar, February 28, 1990.

[111] See the comment of Gregory F. Treverton, *Covert Action: The Limits of Intervention in the Postwar World* (New York, 1987), p. 39.

[112] For some details see John Prados, *Presidents' Secret Wars: CIA and Pentagon Covert Operations Since World War II* (New York, 1986), pp. 36–44, 52–60.

[113] Predictably this group includes Simpson, *Blowback*, pp. 8, 88, 100–103. See also John Loftus, *The Belarus Secret* (New York, 1982). Loftus charges Wisner of working with Gehlen to build a paramilitary force from the Byelorussian SS. He refers to them as Wisner's "Nazi proteges" (p. 81) and makes a feeble attempt to link Kennan to this operation. Andrey Andreyevich

sight it is obvious that most of these covert exercises, which usually were thoroughly penetrated by Soviet agents, possessed a sad, almost pathetic quality as in the case of the Albanian episode which we shall examine. In the end OPC proved effective in Eastern Europe only in propaganda and in intelligence gathering.[114] Interestingly, Kennan made his most direct contribution in these areas.

RADIO FREE EUROPE/RADIO LIBERTY

Kennan instigated and helped nurture two of the most significant political/ psychological operations undertaken by the United States in the era of the Cold War. These were Radio Free Europe, which beamed propaganda toward the Eastern bloc exclusive of the USSR and East Germany, and Radio Liberation from Bolshevism which broadcast to the Russians and is better known as Radio Liberty. These radio efforts complemented the State Department's openly funded Voice of America in an endeavor to spread the American point of view behind the Iron Curtain. Despite the impact of Soviet jamming they succeeded over the years in piercing to some extent the totalitarian blanket of control over information and opinion which the Soviet Union imposed within its domain and in providing details of dissident activity in support of human rights there.

In conventional accounts of the origins of Radio Free Europe the story is simply told. Kennan and a number of colleagues were troubled by the numbers of exiles and refugees who were paying visits to the State Department seeking support, although they had no official role. Kennan came to the conclusion "that the proper place for help and comfort lay not in the official chambers of the United States government but in the hearts of the American people."[115] Early in 1949, with Acheson's approval, he approached Joseph Grew—former ambassador to Japan, former under secretary of state, and an elder in the American foreign policy establishment—and asked him to establish a private group to deal with the refugees, to extend some sustenance to them, and to utilize their talents. Grew and his old friend and former State Department colleague, DeWitt Clinton Poole, thereupon organized a committee of prominent individuals and on June 1, 1949, the Free Europe Committee (the name was

---

Vlasov, a general in the Red Army, was captured by the Germans in 1942. He decided to assist the German war effort in an attempt to bring down communism and organized troops among those who had surrendered to the Germans. Vlasov surrendered to the Americans in May 1945 and was returned to the Soviets who ultimately executed him. For details see Nicholas Bethell, *The Last Secret: Forcible Repatriation to Russia, 1944–7* (London, 1975), pp. 68–72; and Catherine Andreyev, *Vlasov and the Russian Liberation Movement, 1941–1945: Soviet Reality and Emigre Theories* (Cambridge, 1987).

[114] Treverton, *Covert Action*, p. 40.

[115] This account of RFE's origins is drawn from Robert T. Holt, *Radio Free Europe* (Minneapolis, 1958), pp. 9–16. The rest of the paragraph relies on his account.

soon changed to the National Committee for a Free Europe—NCFE) was incorporated. In July 1949, a Radio Committee chaired by a New York banker and Kennan friend Frank Altschul was established by NCFE and charged with putting the voices of the exiles on the air addressed to their own peoples in their own languages. By 1950 Radio Free Europe broadcast tapes prepared in New York from transmitters in West Germany.[116]

This conventional account ignored the continuing and essential role of the United States government in the operation of Radio Free Europe and Radio Liberty. After Kennan saw Grew and persuaded him to become involved in forming the Free Europe Committee he didn't simply fade back into the bureaucratic woodwork. Along with Wisner he played an instrumental role in fostering the growth of this venture. Davies' experience with the Eurasian Institute had taught Kennan the valuable lesson that such undertakings as these could not be sustained by private fundraising. Although the National Committee for a Free Europe (NCFE) launched a well-publicized fund-raising campaign—"Crusade for Freedom"—donations from nongovernmental sources covered a miniscule share of its costs.[117] The bulk of its funding came initially and secretly from OPC and after that body's full incorporation into the CIA from the agency itself. The money was channeled to NCFE and thus to the radio organizations through such august private institutions as the Rockefeller Foundation and the Ford Foundation's Russian Research Committee. Without such funding the organization would never have made it off the ground. Kennan's contribution extended beyond this crucial arrangement of the financial backing for the organization. Through his discussions with Grew he helped arrange for the appointment of the other major figures involved in the infancy of the NCFE—Allen Dulles (whose law firm of Sullivan and Cromwell handled legal matters for the new body) and Frank Altschul. Both Dulles and Altschul were Kennan's personal friends and men with whom he could deal privately and frankly.[118] Dulles chaired the executive committee of NCFE and Altschul headed the radio operations. With men such as these in control Kennan's influence was exercised informally and in a manner which left no paper trail. They agreed with him that NCFE was not a philanthropic organization aimed

[116] Holt, *Radio Free Europe*, p. 14.

[117] On the funding of Radio Free Europe/Radio Liberty see Cord Meyer, *Facing Reality: From World Federalism to the CIA* (New York, 1980), pp. 110–12; and Sig Mickelson, *America's Other Voice: The Story of Radio Free Europe and Radio Liberty* (New York, 1983), pp. 20–22. As Mickelson notes: "The new corporation almost immediately began to spend money in substantial amounts. It expanded its headquarters space in the Empire State Building several times in a few months, requested communications consultants to prepare technical recommendations, and started to employ staff." And, all of this "without any visible means of financial support and within only weeks of the day when Kennan had gone to see Grew" (p. 20).

[118] Kennan refers to his friendship and his cooperation with Dulles on intelligence matters in *Memoirs*, I, p. 202. On his friendship with Altschul see their correspondence in Altschul Papers, Columbia University.

at caring for exiles and refugees. It was an institution to work in conjunction with American foreign policy and to engage vigorously in the political/psychological campaign against the Soviet Union.[119] Kennan watched with approval as, under the guidance of his friends and with the continuing financial support from OPC, Radio Free Europe and Radio Liberty developed and as NCFE assisted in the development of a dizzying array of national exile organizations intent on contesting Soviet domination of their various homelands. This was the kind of political warfare he favored.

EAST EUROPEAN POLICY

In addition to initiating and supporting various elements of the political warfare program against the Soviets, the Policy Planning Staff during 1949 played an important part in formalizing the policy they were in the process of implementing. In June Robert Joyce produced a paper which sought to provide guidelines for handling defectors. He wanted the State Department to coordinate the process in important cases so as to derive from defectors "the maximum advantage in the fields of intelligence information and psychological exploitation."[120] He and Davies already devoted significant attention to this work.[121] More substantial was the Staff's effort to formulate a general policy toward Eastern Europe. This they completed over the summer and on August 25 PPS/59, "United States Policy Toward the Soviet Satellite States in Eastern Europe" was submitted for approval.[122] The Staff aimed to improve and intensify American efforts to reduce and eliminate "dominant Soviet influence in the satellite states of Albania, Bulgaria, Czechoslovakia, Hungary, Poland and Rumania."

This attempt to codify a general East European policy had its origins in discussions which the Staff held in March 1949 with American ambassadors and ministers to the East European nations and the Soviet Union. Kennan outlined the goal of forcing the retraction of Soviet power and explained that "we should be able to determine what are the weak spots on which to hammer

[119] Mickelson, *America's Other Voice*, pp. 20–22. Interview with James McCargar, February 28, 1990 was helpful for background here.

[120] PPS/54, "Policy Relating to Defection and Defectors from Soviet Power," June 29, 1949, Nelson, ed., *The State Department Policy Planning Staff Papers 1949*, pp. 75–81. For evidence of Joyce's authorship see Minutes of Meeting, June 10, 1949, PPS Records, Box 32.

[121] A classic case is Davies' and Joyce's consideration of the case of ex-Brigadier General Valentin Gonzales (whose *nom de guerre* was "el campesino"), who had served with the Spanish Republican Army, escaped to the Soviet Union, and then fled to Iran late in 1948. See the corre spondence concerning him in Decimal File, 800.43 Eurasian Institute/12-2848; 800.43 Eurasian Institute/12-2948; 800.43 Eurasian Institute/3-2849; 800.43 Eurasian Institute/5-1849; and 861.00/1-849.

[122] PPS/59, "United States Policy Toward the Soviet Satellite States in Eastern Europe," August 25, 1949, Nelson, ed., *The State Department Policy Planning Staff Papers 1949*, pp. 124–38.

relentlessly and also to determine whether we want in the first instance some form of Titoism.''[123] Much of the debate over this policy focused on this latter point. Ambassador Bedell Smith, recently returned from the Soviet Union, argued that the Russians feared Titoism more than anything else. He advocated that it be fostered and explained that ''the United States does not fear communism if it is not controlled by Moscow and not committed to aggression.''[124] The Planning Staff members shared this more subtle view and John Davies eventually developed a draft which placed emphasis on fostering Titoism. There arose some objection that this too readily accepted Communist regimes, which still denied basic freedoms to their citizens. John C. Campbell, then the Assistant Chief of the Division of Southern European Affairs, remembered ''rather extensive and sometimes bitter arguments'' over the point.[125] In the end Davies gave a little ground on the point without foregoing his emphasis on Titoism. The Staff document urged that the United States should, ''as the only practical expedient,'' seek to achieve the reduction of Soviet power by ''fostering Communist heresy among the satellite states, encouraging the emergence of non-Stalinist regimes as temporary administrations, even though they be Communist in nature.'' It clarified , however, that the United States would aim in the long term to replace these with ''non-totalitarian governments desirous of participating with good faith in the free world community.''[126] The real enemy in the short term, however, was Soviet power and expansionism not communism per se. Kennan, Davies, and their colleagues favored the emergence of nationalist Communist leaderships in the Eastern European countries. This very prospect apparently troubled Stalin sufficiently that purges of supposed ''national Communist'' leaders like Gomulka in Poland, Rajk in Hungary, and Clementis in Czechoslovakia were carried out during 1948–1950.[127] The Staff failed to appreciate in 1949 the ferocious

[123] Minutes of Meeting, March 1, 1949, pps Records, Box 32. In attendance at this meeting were Minister Selden Chapin (Hungary), Minister Donald R. Heath (Bulgaria), Minister Arthur Schoenfeld (Romania), and former ambassador to the Soviet Union Walter Bedell Smith, as well as representatives from the European Division of the State Department.

[124] Minutes of Meeting, March 1, 1949, pps Records, Box 32. Further discussion on this issue continued in March and April. See Minutes of Meetings, March 2 and 29, 1949; April 1 and 20, 1949, pps Records, Box 32. Also see Memorandum by Robert P. Joyce, April 1, 1949, FRUS 1949, V, pp. 10–13, which gives a more detailed account of the discussions at the April 1 pps meeting. Among the conclusions recorded by Joyce were that ''we should encourage a healthy nationalism within the satellite countries as an antidote to the iron controls exercised by Moscow. Titoism within the Soviet orbit should be encouraged and fostered wherever possible and by all means of propaganda.''

[125] Oral History Interview with John C. Campbell, June 24, 1974, hstl, transcript pp. 156–59. Davies' draft was discussed with officials from the geographic bureaus at a meeting on June 2. See Minutes of Meeting, June 2, 1949, pps Records, Box 32.

[126] pps/59, ''United States Policy Towards the Soviet Satellite States in Eastern Europe,'' p. 137.

[127] For details see Thomas W. Wolfe, Soviet Power and Europe, 1945–1970 (Baltimore, 1970), pp. 22–23.

extent to which the Soviets would go to maintain their hold over the satellite nations. Its suggestion that rifts in the Communist world might grow "to the point where there would be two opposing blocs in the Communist world—a Stalinist group and a nonconformist faction, either loosely allied or federated under Tito's leadership" proved overly optimistic. (The Sino-Soviet split did create something of this sort.)

The Planning Staff paper was eventually submitted to the National Security Council and after due consideration and slight modification approved by the president in December 1949.[128] Truman accepted as a practical immediate expedient that the United States policy preferred "schismatic Communist regimes" and thus would seek "to foster a heretical drifting-away process on the part of the satellite states."[129] Neither the president, the Policy Planning Staff, nor any other agency of the United States government expected that this would occur quickly. They accepted the assessment of the CIA that the "separation of any Cominform Satellite from the Soviet orbit is unlikely under current conditions." As the CIA argued the circumstances that had enabled Tito to challenge Stalin in Yugoslavia did not prevail elsewhere in Eastern Europe.[130] The question then was how to implement this policy, how to take the offensive in the contest with the Soviets. Here there was little new on offer. The policy accepted in December formalized what already was occurring— trade and credit restrictions, propaganda, support for emigre organizations, and covert operations. Such tactics were not expected to occasion immediate change in Eastern Europe. There was a becoming modesty concerning the expectations of the policy and a realization that much depended on developments within the East European countries themselves. But this policy was simply not one of passive acceptance of the Stalinist regimes. In retrospect it possessed more feasibility and intellectual integrity than its successor in the Eisenhower administration which publicly promised liberation without knowing how to deliver on it.[131]

COVERT ACTION—THE ALBANIAN EPISODE

Kennan's personal contribution to the projects sponsored by OPC concentrated in the realms of propaganda and formation of emigre organizations through the NCFE. But the Planning Staff also maintained a weighty involvement in OPC's covert paramilitary operations undertaken to weaken Soviet dominance

[128] On the NSC approval see NSC Action No. 264, December 8, 1949, Truman Papers, PSF, Box 191. Truman approved it on December 13, 1949.
[129] See NSC 58/2, "United States Policy Toward the Soviet Satellite States of Eastern Europe," December 8, 1949, FRUS 1949, V, pp. 42–54.
[130] CIA Intelligence Memorandum No. 248, "Satellite Relations with the USSR and the West," November 7, 1949, National Security Council Records, HSTL, Box 2.
[131] My thinking here is influenced by Bennett Kovrig, The Myth of Liberation: East-Central Europe in U.S. Diplomacy and Politics since 1941 (Baltimore, 1973), p. 90.

in Eastern Europe. The most significant such undertaking went beyond the general policy goal of seeking to stimulate further Titoism and actually aimed to dislodge the Communist regime headed by Enver Hoxha in Albania. Kennan's subordinate, Robert Joyce, played a role in planning this operation and maintained an oversight role during its implementation. Joyce, with his experience with OSS in the Balkans during World War II, possessed a bent for operations. He was in the words of Franklin Lindsay of OPC "a doer not an ivory tower thinker."[132]

The initiative for an attempt to bring down Hoxha, who still was aligned with Stalin at this time, originated with the British. After the Tito-Stalin split they found the temptation impossible to resist. Albania—"the smallest and weakest link in the Soviet bloc"—found itself locked in between Yugoslavia and Greece and cut off from direct land contact with the Soviets. Intelligence reports suggested that it was "a poverty-stricken land torn by discontent and internal strife" now deprived of the support which the Yugoslavs had provided. It appeared susceptible to a subversion operation which would infiltrate guerrilla fighters into Albania and have them exploit the known opposition to Hoxha's Stalinist control. A more general uprising, a veritable counterrevolution, might be the result.[133] Stalin's control of the Balkans would be weakened further.

The British Secret Intelligence Service (SIS/MI6) decided to proceed with this operation early in 1949 but they desired to involve the Americans. In March 1949 SIS's William Hayter traveled to Washington for discussions on Anglo-American intelligence cooperation in a number of areas. A part of these discussions was devoted to planning for the Albanian operation. Wisner and Joyce led the American delegation in these talks. The two allies quickly agreed on procedures on Albania.[134] Wisner demonstrated particular enthusiasm hoping that the "Albanian operation would be 'a clinical experiment' in rolling back Communism in Eastern Europe."[135] The British, who had assets in the region, took the lead on the operational side while the Americans accepted primary responsibility to assist in the creation of an Albanian exile committee which might serve various propaganda functions and form the nucleus for an alternative regime.[136] The British provided a base on Malta and the training and equipment for recruits drawn from Albanian exiles—referred to as "pixies"— who had escaped to Italy and Greece when Hoxha's Communists came

---

[132] Interview with Franklin Lindsay, February 27, 1990.

[133] On British decision-making on Albania consult Nicholas Bethell, *The Great Betrayal: The Untold Story of Kim Philby's Biggest Coup* (London, 1984), pp. 33–37. For a good summary see Winks, *Cloak and Gown*, p. 396.

[134] Bethell, *The Great Betrayal*, p. 39.

[135] Winks, *Cloak and Gown*, p. 397.

[136] Interviews with Franklin Lindsay, February 27, 1990; and James McCargar, February 28, 1990.

to power. The Americans through the Committee for a Free Europe helped establish the Albanian National Committee and eventually installed Hassan Dosti as its leader after the suspicious death of Midhat Frasheri in October 1949.[137] Broad control of the operation was exercised by a Special Policy Committee seated in Washington and consisting of Joyce from the State Department, Franklin Lindsay from OPC, Earl Jellicoe of the British Embassy, and Kim Philby—the British traitor—then the representative of SIS in Washington.[138] Joyce certainly kept a close eye on this operation although OPC handled the day-to-day responsibilities for the American side.[139]

The fine details of this unusual operation which extended from 1949 to 1952 need not detain us here. Suffice it to say that the initial British-sponsored efforts landed a few small parties on the Albanian coast but they accomplished nothing having been thwarted by highly alert Albanian security forces.[140] The Americans thereupon took a larger responsibility on the operational side and during 1951 parachuted a number of Albanians into their homeland on covert missions. This effort proved equally unsuccessful—indeed, one careful student has remarked of it that "seldom has an intelligence operation proceeded so resolutely from one disaster to the next."[141] The reason seems clear. Presumably Philby, in service to his true master, briefed his Soviet contact on the Anglo-American plans at least in general outline.[142] Suitably warned, Hoxha's counterintelligence service and his security forces easily quashed the attempt to overthrow him and in the process demonstrated just how difficult it was to unsettle a police state with an underground movement. In such police states it proved difficult to transform the passive opposition and resistance of the populace into open rebellion.[143] Active opposition simply seemed futile.

[137] Bethell provides the fullest account of all of this. I rely also on my interview with James McCargar.

[138] Interview with Franklin Lindsay, February 27, 1990. Also see Kim Philby's *My Silent War* (London, 1968), p. 143. Philby refers to the work of the Special Policy Committee and describes Joyce as "a convivial soul with experience of Balkan affairs."

[139] For indications of Joyce's close involvement on this issue see various cables and memorandums in Decimal File, 875.00/4-2749; 875.00/5-649; 875.00/5-1249.

[140] Bethell, *The Great Betrayal*, pp. 90–91.

[141] The quotation is from Robin Winks in *Cloak and Gown*, p. 399. Winks provides a good summary of the American directed part of this operation. See pp. 397–400. Also see Prados, *Presidents' Secret Wars*, pp. 45–52.

[142] This is certainly the argument of Bethell in *The Great Betrayal*, pp. 198–99. One should note, however, Frank Lindsay's argument that Philby was too valuable an asset to have risked on this matter. Lindsay argues that Hoxha's security forces had penetrated the Albanian exile groups and as a result the Anglo-American operations leaked badly. Interview with Lindsay, February 27, 1990.

[143] As John Gaddis has observed: "From all that we know, Anglo-American efforts to conduct covert operations inside the Soviet Union and Eastern Europe in the early postwar years were thoroughly unsuccessful." In making this judgment Gaddis refers to Anglo-American efforts in

KENNAN AND THE AMERICAN INTELLIGENCE COMMUNITY

Joyce's participation in the attempt to bring down the Albanian government illustrated the extent of involvement of the Planning Staff under Kennan's direction in the intelligence operations area. Joyce had substantial leeway in his actions but he operated as Kennan's representative and as such the representative for the State Department as a whole. Undoubtedly he kept Kennan informed of his activities. His participation highlights the crucial relationship that the Staff under Kennan's leadership maintained with OPC. It formed the bridge between the State Department and intelligence operations. But, as the activities of Kennan, Davies, and Joyce make clear, the Staff did not limit its role to approving projects conceived by others. They entered into the fray and helped develop the wide array of activities pursued by the Office of Policy Coordination. Ironically and sadly, Davies' very inventiveness in planning political warfare projects was to be used against him in a most disgraceful way during the McCarthyite witch-hunt through the State Department.[144]

While Kennan played an important part in instigating America's covert political warfare campaign it soon took on dimensions that he could not have foreseen. He had encouraged the development of OPC with Europe—East and West—in mind. But events in Asia overtook his more modest and measured plans. With the outbreak of the Korean War, OPC under Wisner's driven leadership pursued paramilitary missions in Asia. As Anne Karalekas pointed out in the history written for the Senate Select Committee investigating U.S. intelligence activities (the Church Committee), "OPC's participation in the [Korean] war effort contributed to its transformation from an organization that was to provide the capability for a limited number of ad hoc operations to an organization that conducted continuing, ongoing activities on a massive scale. In concept, manpower, budget, and scope of activities, OPC simply skyrocketed."[145] The comparative figures for 1949 and 1952 tell the story. In 1949 OPC spent $4.7 million; in 1952, $82 million. In 1949 OPC had 302 employees and 7 field stations; by 1952 it had 2,812 plus 3,142 overseas contract personnel and maintained 47 stations.[146]

Kennan had resigned as director of the Policy Planning Staff by the time this great expansion took place. His departure and the arrival of General Walter Bedell Smith as the new director of Central Intelligence in 1950 also meant an alteration in the chain of command for OPC. The formidable Smith's first substantive move on taking up his position at the CIA was to establish his con-

Poland, the Baltic states, and the Ukraine, as well as Albania. See John Lewis Gaddis, "Intelligence, Espionage and Cold War Origins," *Diplomatic History* 13 (Spring 1989): 199.

[144] On this see Kennan, *Memoirs*, II, pp. 202–7.

[145] Karalekas, "History of the Central Intelligence Agency," p. 31.

[146] Karalekas provides these figures in ibid., pp. 31–32.

trol over the Office of Policy Coordination.[147] In October he simply asserted his authority over OPC and given his prestige—he had been Eisenhower's wartime chief of staff and a former ambassador to the Soviet Union—State and Defense readily accepted the new arrangement which ended the State Department's direct role in guiding OPC. The change resulted from three factors, as Ludwell Lee Montague pointed out in his official history of Smith's tenure as DCI: ''(1) Kennan, who was determined to control covert warfare, and Hillenkoetter, who was deemed inadequate for that role, were both gone. (2) Smith had reached his own understanding with the Secretaries of State and Defense. (3) All concerned were happy to accept General Smith's forthright assumption of command of covert action operations.''[148] Thereafter, Smith incorporated OPC into the mainstream of the agency's activities and eventually integrated it with the Office of Special Operations (OSO), the CIA's clandestine intelligence collection branch.[149] Smith's actions in asserting his control over covert operations only serve to magnify the extraordinary role played by Kennan in determining the initial nature of American involvement in this area—an area, which in the 1950s and 1960s would prove to be a vehicle for American actions which ran quite contrary to its democratic traditions.[150] In light of what the CIA became it is perhaps understandable that Kennan disassociates himself from it and deems his involvement in the creation of its covert capability his worst mistake. But mea culpas from him appear unnecessary. The specific sins of the sons should not be visited on the fathers.

In the end the efforts of Kennan and the Planning Staff to foster Titoism in Eastern Europe and to force the retraction of Soviet power there produced little. Only the political earthquake in that region during the winter of 1989–1990—fostered by the indefatigable Solidarity movement in Poland and ultimately permitted by Mikhail S. Gorbachev—ended Soviet domination of the region, at least on the political, economic, social, and cultural planes. In pursuing their efforts during 1948 and 1949 Kennan and his colleagues had expected no miraculous results. Realistically they struggled to stimulate and to exploit fissures to weaken Stalin's power. It was an approach they examined not only in Eastern Europe but also in the Far East—in China.

[147] Montague, *General Walter Bedell Smith as Director of Central Intelligence*, II, pp. 52–57.
[148] Ibid., pp. 57–58.
[149] For a brief account of these developments see Gregory F. Treverton, *Covert Action: The Limits of Intervention in the Postwar World* (New York, 1987), pp. 40–42.
[150] On the larger point see Rhodri Jeffreys-Jones, *The CIA and American Democracy* (New Haven, 1989).

CHAPTER SEVEN

The Limits of America's China Policy

THE KENNAN-DAVIES PARTNERSHIP

From the nineteenth century when Yankee traders ventured forth in search of their share of the fabled China market and devoted missionaries embarked to convert to Christianity its vast millions China exercised a peculiar hold on the American imagination. John Hay's Open Door Notes of 1899–1900 designed primarily to establish the concept of equal trade opportunity for all nations in China and thereby to secure access for American goods and capital came to be portrayed as an admirable American defense of Chinese territorial integrity. Through the decades of the twentieth century the United States readily cast itself in the role of special friend of China, a virtual benefactor.[1] The United States welcomed the establishment of the Chinese republic in 1911 upon the overthrow of the Manchu dynasty and extended some support to its founder, Sun Yat-sen, and his successor, Chiang Kai-shek.* Prodigious challenges soon confronted Chiang in his efforts to secure control of the turbulent country buffeted by social and economic turmoil. In the 1920s a civil war broke out pitting Chiang's Nationalists against the Communist forces led by Mao Tse-tung. A decade later, after failing in his efforts to crush Mao, Chiang faced a militarily more formidable foe when the Japanese launched their attack upon China in 1937. In the subsequent years prior to Pearl Harbor and more so afterwards the United States encouraged China in its opposition to Japan, although it never accorded the China Theater a high priority in its strategic planning. Franklin Roosevelt, perhaps in an effort to compensate for the limited tangible support he extended, granted China major power status symbolized by his meeting with the Chinese leader at Cairo in 1943 and by China's inclusion as a permanent member of the security council of the fledgling United Nations in 1945.[2]

The accoutrements of big power status failed to mask the reality of Chiang's internal weakness. His Kuomintang (KMT) government's most notable characteristics lay in the fields of intrigue, mismanagement, and corruption. Upon

---

* This chapter uses the traditional Wade-Giles system of romanizing Chinese characters as it was in use during the events described.

[1] My thinking here benefits from the ideas of David L. Anderson. See Anderson's *Imperialism and Idealism: American Diplomats in China, 1861–1898* (Bloomington, Ind., 1985).

[2] For further details see Michael Schaller, *The United States and China in the Twentieth Century* (New York, 1979).

the defeat of the Japanese the long-simmering conflict between the Nationalists and the Chinese Communist Party (CCP) threatened to explode again. While extending some assistance to Chiang's government, the Truman administration tried to avert a full-scale civil war. At Truman's request, General Marshall traveled to China in December 1945, to mediate the conflict. But the General's extensive efforts throughout 1946 to forge a coalition government ended in complete failure.[3] When he returned to the United States to become secretary of state in 1947 the need for an incisive reappraisal of America's China policy accompanied him. As the policy debate developed during 1947 it focused on the question of how extensive should be the American involvement in China in support of Chiang Kai-shek against the Communists.[4] George Kennan played a crucial role in formulating the State Department's ultimately successful case against the American military's desire for a deep American commitment on the Nationalist side and he continued to advise on America's policy toward China until 1950. That Kennan, a Soviet specialist with limited background in the Far East, contributed so significantly to policy in this area resulted from his strong partnership with John Paton Davies, Jr.

The early careers of George Kennan and John Davies possess a parallel quality. After joining the Foreign Service both became area specialists of sorts. Kennan, of course, focused on the Soviet Union. Davies, the son of American missionary parents who had been born in the western Chinese province of Szechwan and who attended Yenching University in Peking for some time before graduating from Columbia University, specialized in Chinese affairs. During the 1930s he served initially in the American consulate in Kunming, then in the American consulate in Mukden, Manchuria, and finally in the embassy in Hankow, where Chiang established a temporary seat of government after the Japanese attack. Like Kennan, Davies early on demonstrated a penchant for analysis and a deep commitment to understanding the character and culture of the country on which he concentrated his considerable abilities.[5]

[3] On the Marshall mission see John Robinson Beal, *Marshall in China* (Garden City, N.Y., 1970); and Steven I. Levine, "A New Look at American Mediation in the Chinese Civil War: The Marshall Mission and Manchuria," *Diplomatic History* 3 (Fall 1979): 349–75. For Marshall's own recollections of his mission, written at Truman's request in May 1954, see his "Memorandum on China," May 18, 1954, Truman Papers, PSF, Box 174.

[4] There are a number of excellent studies of Sino-American relations prior to the Korean War. See William Whitney Stueck, Jr., *The Road to Confrontation: American Policy Toward China and Korea, 1947–1950* (Chapel Hill, 1981); Russell D. Buhite, *Soviet-American Relations in Asia, 1945–1954* (Norman, Okla., 1982); Robert M. Blum, *Drawing the Line: The Origins of the American Containment Policy in East Asia* (New York, 1982); Nancy Bernkopf Tucker, *Patterns in the Dust: Chinese-American Relations and the Recognition Controversy, 1949–1950* (New York, 1983); Warren I. Cohen, "Acheson, His Advisers and China, 1949–1950," in Dorothy Borg and Waldo Heinrichs, eds., *Uncertain Years: Chinese American Relations, 1947–1950* (New York, 1980), pp. 13–52; and Edwin W. Martin, *Divided Counsel: The Anglo-American Response to Communist Victory in China* (Lexington, Ky., 1986).

[5] For biographical details on John Davies see his own *Dragon by the Tail: American, British,*

Both men became important members of the respective small groups of specialists who focused on Russia and China and the evolving political experiments in each country. Kennan and his colleagues like Bohlen, Llewellyn Thompson, and Elbridge Durbrow formed a comparable group to the "China hands" among whom John Carter Vincent, John Stewart Service, O. Edmund Clubb, and Davies figured prominently.[6]

America's entry into World War II found Davies working in the Division of Far Eastern Affairs but eager to escape his Washington desk and to experience something of the war. To this end he arranged to be attached to the staff of General Joseph ("Vinegar Joe") Stilwell, the commanding general of U.S. Forces in the China-Burma-India Theater and Chiang's chief of staff. Although formally designated a second secretary of the American embassy, now located in Chungking, Davies worked directly for Stilwell and enjoyed great freedom in doing so. From early 1942 until the end of 1944 Davies engaged in penetrating analysis of the Chinese maelstrom. He early recognized that a major impact of the Japanese invasion would be an upsurge in the civil war between Chiang's forces and those of Mao. He bluntly pointed to the corruption of the KMT, to its lack of a popular base, and to the unlikely possibilities of its agreeing to any genuine political or social reforms. He warned that the United States should avoid both an unalterable commitment to Chiang and entanglement in the civil war on his side. Rather, the U.S. should accommodate itself to the forces of Chinese nationalism. To this end Davies engaged in dialogue with the CCP and traveled to the Communist stronghold in Yenan to meet with Mao and his lieutenants like Chou En-lai.[7] He favored direct military cooperation between the United States and the Chinese Communists in an effort to further the war effort against Japan and to reduce the dependency of the CCP on the Soviet Union. While he enjoyed the patronage and protection of Stilwell Davies offered his insightful analyses with immunity, although some KMT politicians intrigued against him. A major source of such intrigue was T.V. Soong, Chiang's brother-in-law and foreign minister, who unsuccessfully schemed to replace Davies with his own confidante, Captain Joseph

Japanese and Russian Encounters with China and One Another (New York, 1972); and his more recent "The China Hands in Practice: The Personal Experience," in Paul Gordon Lauren, ed., *The China Hands' Legacy: Ethics and Diplomacy* (Boulder, 1987), pp. 37–57. Also see David Halberstam, *The Best and the Brightest* (New York, 1972), pp. 111–13, 379–92.

[6] On Davies and his fellow China specialists see E. J. Kahn, Jr., *The China Hands: America's Foreign Service Officers and What Befell Them* (New York, 1975).

[7] Davies' wartime views are outlined well and at some length in Michael Schaller, *The U.S. Crusade in China, 1938–1945* (New York, 1979), pp. 44–45, 116–18, 139–43, 199–204. For recollections of his work with Davies in the China-Burma-India Theater and at Yenan see John K. Emmerson, *The Japanese Thread: A Life in the Foreign Service* (New York, 1978), pp. 152–53, 206–9. And for a revealing account of Davies' activities at Yenan see Theodore H. White, *In Search of History: A Personal Adventure* (New York, 1978), pp. 180–206.

Alsop.[8] But with Stilwell's recall in October 1944, Davies' vulnerability increased markedly. His critical views of the KMT and his promotion of cooperation with the CCP eventually brought him into conflict with the newly appointed and rather unstable American ambassador, Patrick J. Hurley.[9] Hurley, a bumptious innocent abroad, grandly assigned himself to reconcile the conflict between the KMT and CCP but when the political negotiations between the two sides broke down in December 1944 he needed a scapegoat. He absurdly charged Davies with persuading the CCP to break off negotiations with Chiang's regime and ordered him from China. The State Department quickly dispatched Davies to the American embassy in Moscow, a post he previously had requested both to escape the "rancid" atmosphere prevailing in Chungking and because it would provide an excellent vantage point to observe the Soviet influence on the Chinese Communists.[10] In Moscow Davies renewed his acquaintance with George Kennan, now the Embassy counselor and Ambassador Harriman's deputy.

Davies first met Kennan in 1937 on a brief visit to Moscow as he made his way home for leave via the Trans-Siberian railroad. Kennan invited him to lunch and subjected him to a vivid account of the "eerie proceedings" taking place at the show trials Stalin inflicted upon those he planned to eliminate.[11] They did not maintain personal contact in the ensuing years but quickly resumed their conversation when Davies came to the Moscow embassy in 1945. There they forged a deep professional and personal friendship. It was a time of professional difficulty for both men. Davies had been purged from his post in China and Hurley went on to attack him recklessly and publicly before the Senate Foreign Relations Committee in 1945. Kennan suffered from a quite different problem. He felt ignored and frustrated. Perhaps these professional difficulties served to link them more closely because during this time each man developed a deep respect not only for the other's knowledge and abilities but also for his character. The lasting bond between them—which assured Kennan's strenuous and eloquent defense of Davies during his McCarthyist ordeal—dated from their service in Moscow.[12] So too did Kennan's education in East Asian affairs.

Kennan readily acknowledged Davies' tutelage and later attributed to him credit for "whatever insight I was able to muster in those years into the nature

[8] Alsop, of course, emerged at the war's end as a prominent Washington columnist and Kennan acquaintance. For details see Davies, "The China Hands in Practice: The Personal Experience," pp. 44–47.

[9] For a more sympathetic portrayal of Hurley see Russell D. Buhite, *Patrick J. Hurley and American Foreign Policy* (Ithaca, N.Y., 1973).

[10] For Davies' description of the atmosphere in Chungking and his request made to Charles Bohlen see author's interview with John Paton Davies, Jr., Ashville, N.C., August 12, 1986.

[11] Davies, *Dragon by the Tail*, p. 184.

[12] On Davies' ordeal and Kennan's involvement see Kahn, *The China Hands*, pp. 244–85; Kennan, *Memoirs*, II, pp. 200–215; White, *In Search of History*, pp. 383–87.

⌐of Soviet policies toward the Far East.''[13] Prior to his contact with Davies, Kennan had no abiding interest in the Far East. But he possessed what Davies remembers as a "listening mind," and he gained from the China expert some appreciation of the situation in China and of the relative strengths of the KMT and the CCP. Also Kennan was prepared to consider the possibility that not every Communist movement was run directly out of Moscow when Davies advanced his thesis regarding the "semi-independence" of the CCP. Long before Tito's rift with Moscow laid bare the reality that international communism was not centrally controlled from the Kremlin, Davies sensed the potential for independence among the Chinese Communists. He perceived a division within the Chinese Communist oligarchy between the ideological dogmatists allied to the Soviet Union and a more pragmatic group including Chou En-lai, Chu teh, and Mao Tse-tung himself. The pragmatism of this group was founded on their having a separate geographic area to govern, their own apparatus for party control such as secret police and propaganda machinery, and the extent of their own military achievement and capability. Davies believed that this pragmatist group would be more nationalistic in behavior than its ideological counterpart. He placed such views before Kennan during 1945 and, while Kennan did not endorse them, at least in Davies' recollection he did not reject them.[14]

Davies and Kennan began their cooperation on matters concerning China during this time. A visit from Ambassador Hurley to Moscow in April 1945 occasioned the most notable instance of their joint endeavors. En route from Washington back to his post in Chungking, Davies' nemesis went to Moscow to ascertain Soviet intentions regarding China. After discussions with Stalin Hurley naively reported that the Soviet leader endorsed American policy which accorded Generalissimo Chiang Kai-shek the leadership role in any postwar coalition government.[15] Kennan and Davies disagreed with this favorable assessment of the Soviet stance and drew attention to Stalin's inability to speak for the CCP. With Davies' assistance Kennan wrote a report to the State Department warning that the Soviet leader could not be relied upon to support America's position on China.[16] Advised by Davies, Kennan maintained this suspicious position regarding Soviet intentions in China until he left Moscow but their combined efforts had no discernible impact in Washington.[17] Such impact on China matters would await Kennan's appointment to the Policy Planning Staff.

[13] Kennan, *Memoirs*, I, p. 239.

[14] The above relies on interview with John Davies, August 12, 1986.

[15] Hurley to Truman, April 17, 1945, in U.S. Department of State, *United States Relations with China* (hereafter *China White Paper*) (Washington, D.C., 1949), pp. 94–96. Also see Buhite, *Patrick J. Hurley and American Foreign Policy*, pp. 188–238.

[16] Kennan to Secretary of State, April 23, 1945, *FRUS* 1945, VII, p. 343.

[17] For another example of the Kennan-Davies effort to warn about Soviet intentions in China,

In the interim period during his service at the National War College Kennan confronted the related questions of the strategic importance of China and the desirability of the United States becoming deeply involved there. In geopolitical terms Kennan perceived China as essentially a power vacuum similar in some respects to central Europe.[18] This common diagnosis did not draw from Kennan a common remedy. In May of 1947 just as he prepared to take up his Planning Staff position he distinguished between "the danger of Communism in highly strategic areas such as Greece or Austria, where a Communist victory might have very, very serious results for us and our allies, and a Communist victory in other places where it is not apt to have those results—China, for example." Central Europe was of vital importance but China was a more peripheral concern. Kennan also contested the argument that the stratagem applied in Greece and Turkey was applicable to or practical in China. "If I thought for a moment that the precedent of Greece and Turkey obliged us to try to do the same thing in China," he told an audience at the War College, "I would throw up my hands and say we had better have a whole new approach to the affairs of the world. I don't think it is possible in China. China could take all of the national budget we could direct to it for the next twenty-five years and the problems would be worse at the end of that time than they are today."[19]

Kennan's unwillingness to involve the United States in an effort in China similar to what he recommended for it in Europe was hardened by a belief that there was a "good chance that you let the Russians alone in China they will come a cropper on that problem just as everybody else has for hundreds of years."[20] Kennan told a University of Virginia audience in February 1947 that if the Chinese Communists "ever expand to a point where they could command the majority of the resources of China and where they would represent a major military force in their own right, the men in the Kremlin would suddenly discover that this fluid, subtle oriental movement which they thought they held in the palm of their hand had quietly oozed away between their fingers."[21] Such views clearly reflected the influence of John Davies on Kennan. Kennan's strategic assessments of China—his according Europe a higher priority than Asia and also his assigning Japan priority over China—were his own but his evaluations of both the risks involved in intervention there and the

---

which also notes the nationalistic coloration of the CCP see Kennan to Secretary of State, January 10, 1946, *FRUS* 1946, IX, pp. 116–19.

[18] See Kennan's speech, Minutes of Organizations meeting on Russia, June 12, 1946, Kennan Papers, Box 17.

[19] The foregoing quotations are from Kennan, "Problems of U.S. Foreign Policy After Moscow," May 6, 1947, Kennan Papers, Box 17.

[20] Ibid.

[21] Kennan, "Russian-American Relations," February 20, 1947, Kennan Papers, Box 16.

possibility of the Chinese Communists establishing their independence from the Kremlin found their roots in Davies' advice.

On April 29, 1947, the very day Marshall asked him to head the Planning Staff Kennan requested of Under Secretary Acheson that only he, Carlton Savage, the executive secretary, and John Paton Davies, Jr., be assigned permanently to the new group at that point.[22] Savage was recommended to him but Kennan chose Davies himself. The China specialist was Kennan's first choice to join him on the Policy Planning Staff and this despite the fact that Patrick Hurley already had denounced Davies before the Senate Foreign Relations Committee.[23] Kennan remained untroubled that Davies might be a politically risky appointment. He thought only of gaining Davies' knowledge and ability for his planning team. This choice brought Davies back from the Moscow embassy and placed him in a position where in tandem with Kennan he could contribute directly to the policy-making process on China. The years ahead provided plenty of scope for their partnership.

IN SEARCH OF A POLICY

Kennan and Davies came to a State Department floundering in its efforts to develop a coherent China policy. The complete failure of Marshall's mediation efforts had indicated the need for a reappraisal of America's China policy from the beginning of 1947 and the new secretary of state soon requested suggestions for constructive steps which might be taken on this question.[24] The marked deterioration in the military position of the Nationalists in the second quarter of 1947 added further fuel to the fire of demands for a new policy for China. The Joint Chiefs of Staff strode onto the scene in June 1947 and proposed a policy of extensive support for Chiang Kai-shek. The Joint Chiefs judged that "the military security of the United States will be threatened if there is any further spread of Soviet influence and power in the Far East." Consequently, they argued that the United States needed to maintain the Nationalist government. To do this they advocated the provision of "sufficient assistance to that Government to eliminate all Communist armed opposition."[25] John Carter Vincent, the Director of the Office of Far Eastern Affairs in the State Department, opposed the Joint Chiefs' proposals. He advised Marshall against becoming caught in the web of China's civil conflict

---

[22] Kennan to Acheson, April 29, 1947, PPS Records, Box 33.

[23] On Hurley's denunciation in December 1945, see Davies, *Dragon by the Tail*, p. 420.

[24] For a reference to Marshall's request see Forrestal to Marshall, February 27, 1947, Forrestal Papers, Box 75.

[25] Memorandum by the Joint Chiefs of Staff to State-War-Navy Coordinating Committee, June 9, 1947, *FRUS* 1947, VII, pp. 842–45.

and he contested the JCS view of the importance of China to the national security of the United States.[26]

Marshall declined to make a clear decision for or against the JCS proposal. Instead he offered President Truman a means to postpone resolving the fundamental difference of opinion within the administration. At the secretary of state's suggestion Truman decided to send a mission to China led by General Albert C. Wedemeyer to make an objective survey of the situation there as a basis for future policy.[27] Wedemeyer, who earlier had replaced Stilwell as U.S. Commander of the China Theater and chief of staff to Chiang, then served as deputy Army chief of staff for plans. No doubt Marshall also hoped that Wedemeyer might be able to use his influence with Chiang to persuade the Chinese leader to undertake those political, military, and economic reforms deemed necessary to give his government a solid base from which to defeat the Communists.

The results of the Wedemeyer mission proved disappointing for Marshall. Wedemeyer submitted his report to the president on September 19, 1947. He recommended not only far-reaching economic and political reforms within the country but also large-scale economic and military aid for China.[28] Notably, Wedemeyer refused to make the latter dependent on the former as the State Department member of his mission, Philip Sprouse, recommended.[29] As Chiang displayed no intention to pursue the suggested course of reform, Wedemeyer's refusal meant that he largely adopted the approach of the Joint Chiefs of Staff. He wanted to boost Chiang's fortunes with a strong commitment of American support. His proposals failed to convince Marshall. The secretary of state persuaded Truman that the report should not be released to the public and authorized its analysis within the State Department where various elements of Wedemeyer's overall proposal were considered and then rejected.[30] The problem for Marshall lodged in the fact that while rejecting Wedemeyer's approach he had no cohesive policy alternative to offer to the

[26] Memorandum by the Director of the Office of Far Eastern Affairs to Secretary of State, June 20, 1947, *FRUS* 1947, VII, p. 849.

[27] On Marshall's decision to send Wedemeyer to China and Truman's directive to him see the documents in *FRUS* 1947, VII, pp. 635–41. See also Marshall's "Memorandum on China," May 18, 1954, Truman Papers, PSF, Box 174; and William Whitney Stueck, *The Wedemeyer Mission: American Politics and Foreign Policy during the Cold War* (Athens, Ga., 1984), pp. 7–13.

[28] The text of Wedemeyer's report may be found in *China White Paper*, pp. 764–74. On his activities in China and for an analysis of his report see Stueck, *The Wedemeyer Mission*, esp. p. 77. For Wedemeyer's own account see Albert C. Wedemeyer, *Wedemeyer Reports* (New York, 1958), pp. 382–97.

[29] Sprouse discusses his proposal and his inability to persuade Wedemeyer to adopt it in Oral History Interview with Philip D. Sprouse by James R. Fuchs, February 11, 1974, HSTL, transcript pp. 69–71. See also Sprouse to Wedemeyer, August 23, 1947, *FRUS* 1947, VII, pp. 752–53. Sprouse's proposal is discussed and contrasted with Wedemeyer's in Stueck, *Wedemeyer Mission*, pp. 77–79.

[30] Stueck, *Wedemeyer Mission*, pp. 86–93.

president and to convey to Congress and the public. He knew what he didn't want to do but found it much more difficult to conclude what he should do.

It was in this situation of continuing flux and uncertainty that Kennan injected himself into the debate over China policy. He did it simply by walking through the door that separated his office from that of the secretary of state and introducing the subject to Marshall. In the manner of a lawyer leading a witness, Kennan, who must have known of Marshall's quandary over policy, explained that the Planning Staff had not undertaken to present recommendations on China because of the appreciation of Staff members of Marshall's own familiarity with the subject. "To my surprise," Kennan later explained— hopefully with tongue-in-cheek—to Walton Butterworth who had replaced John Carter Vincent, "he [Marshall] replied that he would like to know our views anyway, just out of curiosity, because he felt that he had been so close to the problem that he was not sure that he could see it in perspective and would like to have a more detached view."[31] Little wonder that Marshall succumbed to Kennan's temptation to request the Staff's views on China. Precisely at this time he confronted urgent appeals from the Nationalists for more assistance and faced insistent pro-Nationalist congressional pressure.[32] His need to construct a viable policy to address the Chinese situation was pressing. After his conversation with the secretary Kennan assembled the Staff that same day, informed them of Marshall's request, and asked Davies to take the initiative in the matter.[33]

Kennan's decisive intervention at this point must be appreciated if the formulation of America's policy toward China is to be understood accurately. The fact that Marshall in late October involved Kennan and his Staff, who had not previously been involved in consideration of the Wedemeyer report, indicates that the secretary was still searching for a policy to adopt and to present to Truman. Kennan, aided as always by Davies, came to Marshall's rescue. He framed his eventual policy recommendation on China within the overall strategic advice he placed before Marshall—that is, there were but five industrial regions of the world with the capacity to develop major military strength. China was not one of them. Japan was. In the Kennan schema, Japan *not* China was the country in the Far East most vital to American security. With this departure point and well aware of America's limited means and its need to differentiate among its interests, Kennan reported to Marshall in early November that "while a collapse of the National Government would be deplorable, it probably would not be a catastrophe for American interests in China." He frankly expressed doubts that any foreign intervention in China, including

---

[31] Kennan to Butterworth, October 29, 1947, PPS Records, Box 33. In this memorandum Kennan asked Butterworth if he had any objection to the Staff forwarding its views.

[32] For details see Ernest R. May, *The Truman Administration and China, 1945–1949* (Philadelphia, 1975), pp. 28–29.

[33] Minutes of meeting, October 21, 1947, PPS Records, Box 32.

that by the United States, could produce beneficial results and counseled against any direct American intervention in support of Chiang. American assistance could not prevent his collapse. But Kennan noted the existence of a "highly vocal body of opinion in this country advocating U.S. aid to the National Government." He observed that "for practical reasons" this opinion could not be ignored and so argued "that the United States should extend the minimum aid necessary to satisfy American public opinion, and, if possible, to prevent any sudden and total collapse of the Chinese Government."[34] In a nutshell his policy was simply to extend enough aid to placate the pro-Nationalist domestic clamor.

Marshall accepted Kennan's recommendation that some aid would need to be extended to China primarily for domestic political reasons. He had a program drawn up which was quite modest in comparison to the aid then being committed to Europe and which carried the bonus of helping secure congressional support for the European Recovery Program. On February 18, 1948, Truman sent a request to the Congress asking for an appropriation of $570 million in nonmilitary assistance for a fifteen-month period. Marshall's defense of this limited economic aid program clearly reflected Kennan's thinking and virtually borrowed his phrasing. Diminishing China's strategic importance, the secretary told the Senate Foreign Relations Committee that it didn't "possess the raw material and industrial resources which would enable it to become a first-class military power within the foreseeable future." He proceeded to inform the committee that "we cannot afford, economically or militarily, to take over the continued failures of the present Chinese Government to the dissipation of our strength in more vital regions." Marshall explained the limited extension of aid only on the grounds that "it would be against U.S. interests to demonstrate a complete lack of confidence in the Chinese Government and to add to its difficulties by abruptly rejecting its request for assistance."[35] After reducing the duration of the program to twelve months and rearranging the amount appropriated to $436 million, Congress passed the China Aid Act on April 2, 1948.[36]

[34] Kennan to Marshall, November 4, 1947, PPS Records, Box 13.

[35] For Marshall's statement see *China White Paper*, pp. 380–84. Kennan and Butterworth had played important roles in preparing the statement and in ensuring that it was Marshall rather than a subordinate who presented it to Congress. See Butterworth's memorandum, January 24, 1948, *FRUS* 1948, VIII, pp. 459–61; and Kennan's memorandum to Marshall and Lovett, January 26, 1948, PPS Records, Box 33. Also note Kennan's comments on the draft of Marshall's statement where he argued: "I hold no brief for the language use here, but I think we must be prepared to meet and challenge the assertion that our national security would be virtually undermined by a disintegration of the National Government in China. In my thinking, this is the crux of the whole problem, and I see no way of hitting it except by the head-on assertion that the communists will probably not take over all of China and could not make a dangerous military power out of China if they did." Kennan to Marshall Carter, February 10, 1948, PPS Records, Box 13.

[36] For further details see May, *The Truman Administration and China*, pp. 30–31.

The passage of this act temporarily concluded the policy-making process on China within the State Department. It demonstrated the department's dominance over the military in fashioning America's China policy. Indeed, Marshall had presented his limited aid proposal as a fait accompli to Defense Secretary Forrestal and the national military establishment. Despite reservations they were forced to accept this measure although they were unpersuaded by the logic that undergirded it.[37] Ultimately the China Aid Act failed to end the drifting quality which had characterized America's policy toward China throughout 1947 because the course adopted made neither a full commitment to Chiang nor a complete break with him. With hindsight the policy's flaws are evident for all to see because the limited assistance it provided further antagonized the Communists without measurably aiding the Nationalists. It placed the United States in the precarious position of extending aid to a regime which it fully expected to collapse in the not too distant future. Angus Ward, the U.S. Consul General in Mukden, aptly captured the position when he reported to his colleague John Cabot on his return to China from home leave in February 1948 that "the Department has written off China as lost, is merely trying to prolong the agony by aid measures and avoid the blame for the collapse when it comes."[38] Nonetheless, given the American domestic political situation and especially the need to guarantee congressional support for the ERP this was probably the most realistic policy that could have been developed.[39]

Kennan's importance in devising the new policy of limited assistance, which Marshall recommended, Truman accepted, and for which Congress provided, must be acknowledged. His specific recommendation of limited assistance without deep American commitment was hardly original but he best articulated this position and firmed the consensus on the matter within the State Department, where he and Davies cooperated well with the Division of Far Eastern Affairs led by Butterworth. Kennan's intervention stiffened Marshall's resolve to reject the Wedemeyer/military approach and it served to confirm further the secretary's willingness to rely upon his planning chief. This recommendation reflected Davies' view that Chiang's prospects were dim and the cost of saving him astronomical. The distinctive Kennan contribution lay in enunciating the view that China was relatively unimportant to America's

[37] For the thinking of Forrestal and the JCS see Rearden, *The Formative Years*, pp. 215–17.

[38] See Cabot's diary entry of February 8, 1948, in Cabot, *First Line of Defense*, p. 39.

[39] While admitting that "the China Aid Bill was designed partially to soothe pro-Nationalist American public opinion and to speed the legislative process on European aid," John H. Feaver argues that "the demands of domestic politics would not have presented a major obstacle had the Truman administration really wanted to sever all ties with the Nationalist government in 1947 or early 1948." This assessment of the political situation may or may not be correct. What is relevant, however, and what Feaver ignores is that the Truman administration policymakers believed that congressional and public support for the Nationalist regime was of such significance that it had to be accommodated. See John H. Feaver, "The China Aid Bill of 1948: Limited Assistance as a Cold War Strategy," *Diplomatic History* 5 (Spring 1981): 107–20.

security and that it should be placed low on the list of American priorities. This advice provided a key rationale for refraining from direct involvement in the Chinese civil war and proved an extremely efficacious counter to the views of the American military. Kennan had provided Marshall with arguments to sustain the course favored by his own instincts and which the secretary's ambivalence on any major intervention in China throughout 1947 suggested. Through his access to and influence upon Marshall Kennan established himself as a principal formulator of America's China policy in late 1947 and early 1948.

Kennan possessed a firm conviction regarding the validity of the approach he advocated. When Joseph Alsop, now campaigning openly in Washington on behalf of Chiang and the KMT, wrote to Kennan complaining that "the real explanation of our present China policy lies in the search for reasons why nothing should be done," the chief planner remained quite unmoved.[40] In fact in notes he scribbled on China, possibly as a preliminary to drafting a response to Alsop, he mused that "perhaps the main reason America has done nothing about the course of developments in China is that no-one has been able to suggest any[thing] very practical or effective which Am[erica] might do." With Alsop presumably in mind he reflected that "to some, that may seem a depressing reason; but," no doubt with himself and the other policymakers in mind, he continued, "to those who must bear responsibility for action it is a valid one."[41]

In making his recommendations to Marshall, Kennan did not raise the possibility of the Chinese Communists acting independently of Moscow. Although he was aware from Davies of some potential for such action and had himself raised this possibility with Lovett as early as June 1947, at this point he did not perceive any basis to found policy upon.[42] The crucial factors for him were firstly the enormity and the danger involved in seeking to rescue Chiang, and secondly the reality that China could not threaten the security of the United States. These two factors were to remain of central importance in Kennan's approach to China but the startling events in Yugoslavia in mid-1948 raised indirectly the question of the relationship between the CCP and the Soviet Union, and its implications for American policy in China.

THE DIFFICULTY OF DETACHING FROM CHIANG

The Yugoslav example was perceived conspicuously as related to China. Suggestions as to the possibility of some form of Chinese Titoism were many once

[40] Alsop to Kennan, February 18, 1948, Papers of Joseph and Stewart Alsop, Box 3.

[41] Notes on "China," February 1948, in Kennan Papers, Box 23.

[42] See Kennan to Lovett, June 23, 1947, PPS Records, Box 13. Here Kennan argued that "in case the Communists were to succeed in taking over the greater part of the country, I doubt that they would retain the ideological fibre of their movement or the present degree of dependence on Moscow."

the Yugoslavs had demonstrated that a Communist regime could break with Moscow. The parallel between Tito and his regime and Mao and the CCP seemed a "natural one" as Nancy Bernkopf Tucker has observed.[43] In August 1948, the U.S. ambassador in China, John Leighton Stuart, observed that "the Chinese Communists in recent months have been guilty of precisely those sins for which Tito is being attacked."[44] But attention did not focus on means to exploit this potential independent tendency of the CCP. Rather, the State Department got caught up blocking renewed attempts to bolster Chiang's faltering regime.

By September of 1948 the course of China's civil war had proved disastrous for the Kuomintang. The best of Chiang's troops were destroyed in Manchuria and as demoralization set in Nationalist soldiers increasingly deserted to the Communist side. Mao's forces now controlled Manchuria and most of China north of the Yangtze River.[45] The continual stream of reports of Nationalist reverses ensured that even by midyear, when the China Aid Act provisions barely had begun to be implemented, the Army Department initiated new discussions on China policy within the National Security Council apparatus. In these discussions Kennan's Planning Staff emerged as an able defender of the position reached during the policy reappraisal culminating in the China Aid Act. When the Army Department and the Joint Chiefs of Staff called in late July for additional aid to be supplied to the Nationalist Chinese, Kennan vigorously opposed them.[46] The Joint Chiefs based their argument on the need to "buy time" in China but Kennan, as Thomas Etzold has remarked, "thought the price too high."[47] Kennan joined by his Staff colleagues forcefully put this case during the latter half of 1948 and gave their considered views in a Staff paper (PPS/39) on "U.S. Policy Toward China," on September 7, 1948.[48]

PPS/39 had been in preparation since the beginning of 1948. In February and March the Staff undertook a preliminary survey of the problem and called in outside specialists on China, including Professors John K. Fairbank of Harvard and David N. Rowe of Yale, and former American ambassador to China, Nelson T. Johnson, for an exhaustive examination of the issues involved.[49]

---

[43] See Tucker's discussion in *Patterns in the Dust*, pp. 29–30.

[44] Stuart to Secretary of State, August 4, 1948, *FRUS* 1948, VII, p. 399.

[45] For a fine account of the disintegration of Nationalist China see A. Doak Barnett, *China on the Eve of Communist Takeover* (New York, 1963).

[46] For the Army Department's view see NSC 22, "Possible Courses of Action for the U.S. with Respect to the Critical Situation in China," July 26, 1948, *FRUS* 1948, VIII, pp. 118–22; and for the Joint Chiefs' comments see NSC 22/1, August 6, 1948, *FRUS* 1948, VIII, pp. 131–35.

[47] Thomas H. Etzold, "The Far East in American Strategy, 1948–1951," in Etzold, ed., *Aspects of Sino-American Relations Since 1784* (New York, 1978), p. 114.

[48] PPS/39, "To Review and Define United States Policy Toward China," September 7, 1948, *FRUS* 1948, VIII, pp. 146–55.

[49] For the meetings with the China specialists see Minutes of Meetings, February 10, 1948 (Fairbank); February 11, 1948 (Rowe); March 2, 1948 (Johnson), PPS Records, Box 32.

The policy planners made little progress on the paper because their differences with the military on the question of aid foreshadowed a split on the overall China problem. According to deputy-director George Butler the Staff decided "to wait on the persuasive influence of events in China to demonstrate the validity of this [State] Department's analysis." By the end of July, spurred by the Army Department's demarche, the Staff considered "the time now about ripe for this Department to submit a position paper on China to the NSC."[50] In preparing the paper the Staff made use of the assistance of a number of the department's China specialists including Philip Sprouse and Edmund Clubb, who was visiting Washington on leave from his position as the American Consul-General in Peking. The Staff's paper also bore the concurrence of Walton Butterworth as head of the Far Eastern Division of the department.

In response to the Army Department's proposal the Policy Planning Staff advanced a more pessimistic but more realistic evaluation regarding Nationalist prospects for retaining power. Principally authored by Davies, the Staff's paper claimed that the "Kuomintang and the National Government have so declined in strength that they may be assumed to be on the verge of losing their long struggle with the Chinese Communists." Only all-out American aid, including direct American military intervention, could reverse the course of the civil war. But the Staff firmly opposed such action which they recognized would be of "huge, indefinite and hazardous proportions." After ruling out American intervention the Staff worked from the long-held Davies premise that "China's destiny is largely in its own hands." It recommended that the United States "not become irrevocably committed to any course of action or any one faction in China"—a clear warning against too deep an attachment to Chiang.[51]

In advocating this pragmatic course, the Staff examined at some length the prospect of Titoism in China, a subject which Davies had examined consistently since his days in China during the war.[52] The Staff paper speculated as to the Kremlin's concern to control the CCP and observed that "Moscow faces a considerable task in seeking to bring the Chinese Communists under its complete control, if for no other reason than that Mao Tse-tung has been entrenched in power for nearly ten times the length of time that Tito has." Nationalism was integral to the success of the Chinese Communists and when the fighting stopped this would become apparent. The likelihood of tensions between the Chinese Communist leadership and their brethren in the Kremlin was almost gleefully reported as was the corollary that "the possibilities which such a situation would present us, provided we have regained freedom of ac-

---

[50] Memorandum by George Butler, July 27, 1948, *FRUS* 1948, VIII, pp. 122–24.

[51] PPS/39, "To Review and Define United States Policy Toward China," pp. 146–55.

[52] For examples of Davies' continuing reflection on this matter before the actual Tito-Stalin break see his letter to Melby, Schutheis, and Ludden, March 1, 1948, Papers of John F. Melby, HSTL, Box 3. Also note Melby reply to Davies, July 13, 1948, Melby Papers, Box 6.

tion, need scarcely be spelled out."[53] Davies, Kennan, and their Staff colleagues assumed that somewhere in the near future division would develop in relations with the CCP and the Soviet Union. In such a situation they expected that the United States would be able to exploit this rupture to its advantage. This, however, was a possibility for the future. No recommendations were made to establish serious links with the CCP or to initiate contacts which might foster the Titoist prospect among Mao and his comrades.

The principal task at hand for the United States in the view of Davies and Kennan was to detach itself from the Nationalists and to regain freedom of action in China. The situation in China appeared so fluid and such a maze that they made no attempt to chart a detailed course of action. Pragmatism was the key. To counter alternative recommendations the Staff persuasively insisted that military strength could not be effectively applied in China "except at prohibitive cost."[54] This Staff paper forcefully checked the Army Department's July proposal for deeper American involvement in support of the Nationalists. It presented a convincing plea that the United States accommodate itself to the passage of the "mandate of heaven" to Mao, if circumstances placed this mantle upon him.

Kennan sent this paper forward to Marshall and Lovett for their approval, suggesting it be laid before the NSC Staff as a working paper reflecting the views of the State Department. Marshall made some minor suggestions but expressed agreement with the paper's conclusions and Lovett authorized its submission to the NSC.[55] The State Department accepted the Planning Staff's analysis and broadly instructed Ambassador Stuart in accord with it. The ambassador was told firmly that "underlying our recent relations with China has been fundamental consideration that U.S. must not become directly involved in Chinese civil war and U.S. must not assume responsibility for underwriting CHIGOVT militarily and economically."[56] But the Defense Department remained unconvinced. In the NSC the Defense Department representatives indicated dissatisfaction with the definition of existing United States policy with respect to China.[57] Kennan found especially troubling the "widespread feeling, which Secretary Forrestal appears to hold, that we 'have no policy' with relation to what is now happening in China and something should be done

[53] PPS/39, "To Review and Define United States Policy Toward China," pp. 148, 153–54.

[54] Ibid., pp. 154–55. See also author's interview with John Davies, August 12, 1986.

[55] For Marshall's comments see his memorandum to Kennan, September 18, 1948, PPS Records, Box 13. For Lovett's authorization see Kennan's memorandum to Lovett, October 4, 1948 (on which approval is indicated), PPS Records, Box 13.

[56] Lovett to Stuart, October 26, 1948, *FRUS* 1948, VII, pp. 512–17. Further indicating the influence of the Staff paper Lovett also explained to Stuart that "this Govt. plainly must preserve maximum freedom of action."

[57] Kennan refers to the dissatisfaction with U.S.-China policy in a lengthy letter to Admiral Sidney W. Souers of the NSC, November 22, 1948, PPS Records, Box 33.

about it.''[58] He appreciated well that this allegation of an absence of policy in reality attacked the existing policy of avoiding deep involvement in China and aimed to push the United States toward greater support of the Nationalists.

Continuing disagreement over the extent of American commitment to Chiang dominated the policy debate within the Truman administration during the next few decisive months. Far from getting into a position in which it might maneuver to exploit Chinese Communist indications of independence from Moscow, the American government bogged down in reducing its commitment to Chiang and failed to explain its China policy in straightforward terms to the American people. Kennan tried to break the logjam in both areas. He sought without success to persuade Marshall to defend his China policy in public. On November 26 he referred to ''the confusion and bewilderment in the public mind regarding our China policy'' and counseled the secretary that ''it is now less important to cover up the inadequacies of the Chinese Government than it is to regain the understanding confidence of the American public, without which we cannot effectively implement China policy.'' As early as August, Kennan had objected to American restraint in the face of Chiang Kai-shek's complaints about the lack of U.S. aid which, as he realized correctly, placed the Truman administration ''in a defensive position,'' as Chiang brazenly blamed the U.S. for what were his own mistakes. By late November, Kennan wanted to remove any need for the administration to be defensive and suggested that efforts be made—a presidential statement and the preparation of materials by the State Department—to correct ''misapprehensions in the mind of the American public regarding our relations with China.''[59] He wanted the American public to understand that, despite U.S. assistance, the Nationalists were on the verge of defeat and that culpability for their situation lay squarely with themselves.

Kennan also confronted the Forrestal view head-on, stating bluntly to all NSC members that it was ''unrealistic and indefensible . . . to assume that we could decisively affect the course of events in China without taking upon ourselves the major responsibility.'' As the Nationalists' continued resistance to the Chinese Communists could not be guaranteed, the logical next step would be the American assumption of the burden of fighting Mao if a CCP victory was to be prevented. This he opposed vociferously. He concluded by offering to give careful study to any suggestions ''for a blanket policy which would hold out promise of producing results beneficial from the standpoint of this country '' and by noting that the State Department had no such suggestions

[58] Kennan memorandum to Marshall and Lovett, November 24, 1948, *FRUS* 1948, VIII, pp. 211–12.

[59] PPS/45, ''U.S. Policy Toward China in the Light of the Current Situation,'' November 26, 1948, *FRUS* 1948, VIII, pp. 214–15. For Kennan's objections in August see his Memorandum to General Marshall Carter, August 23, 1948, PPS Records, Box 13.

itself and was "skeptical of the feasibility of any such ideas."[60] He challenged the critics of existing American policy—among them the Defense Secretary— to put up a viable alternative or to shut up. Kennan's challenge attracted no immediate takers but his efforts failed to move the administration toward a more detached position on China.

In the end Truman simply lacked the will to cut the links with Chiang. He agreed that it was important for the American people to know the facts about China, including the complete military and economic failure of the KMT but the president refused to do anything about it. He demurred when Marshall placed Kennan's suggestion of a presidential statement, which would defend U.S. policy while pointing to Chiang's ineptitude, before him at a Cabinet meeting on November 26. As Marshall later recounted, Truman felt such action "would place us in the position of having administered the final blow to the Government of the Generalissimo."[61] Kennan's suggestion eventually was adopted six months later when criticism of the administration's China policy had become even more emotional and fierce and when the public was less susceptible to a reasoned analysis of the situation in China and to a defense of the American policy there. Rather ironically it was Kennan—usually disparaged for his lack of concern with domestic political matters—who recognized the immediate need to cut the ground from the fuming critics, the so-called China lobby. Other supposedly politically attuned figures, including the president, procrastinated and condemned the administration to the defensive on this issue throughout 1949 and beyond when it would be tagged with "losing" China.

Unwilling to reveal Chiang's myriad failures to the American public the president also declined to end completely his support for the Chinese leader, even though Marshall and his subordinates were resigned by the end of 1948 to an eventual Communist victory in China, a view confirmed by the assessments of the military and the CIA.[62] On December 30, 1948, Lovett cabled

[60] See Kennan to Souers, November 22, 1948, PPS Records, Box 33. Kennan forwarded a slightly different version of this letter (a summary paragraph was added) to Marshall as a Staff paper. See PPS/39/1, "U.S. Policy Toward China," November 23, 1948, *FRUS* 1948, VIII, pp. 208–11.

[61] Marshall to Lovett (with copy to Kennan), November 26, 1948, PPS Records, Box 13. According to Forrestal, Marshall himself argued against the Kennan proposal to go to the American public "to explain the inadequacies of the Chiang Kai-shek government." Marshall told the cabinet "that this would administer the final *coup de grace* to Chiang's government." Millis, ed., *The Forrestal Diaries*, pp. 533–34.

[62] See the message from Major General David Barr, head of the Army Advisory Group in China, December 18, 1948, in R.G. 218, U.S. Joint Chiefs of Staff Records, Central Decimal File, 1948–1950, Modern Military Branch, NA, Box 106. Barr observed that "only a policy of unlimited United States aid, including the immediate employment of United States Armed Forces to block the southern advance of the communists, which I emphatically do not recommend, would enable the Nationalist Government to maintain a foothold in Southern China against a determined communist advance." The CIA noted on December 10, 1948, that "the rapid disintegration of the

Ambassador Stuart that the United States still recognized and continued to extend aid to the Chinese Government in accordance with the China Aid Act.[63] Such was the vapid China policy which Marshall turned over to Dean Acheson.

ACHESON AND "A MORE REALISTIC POLICY"

Acheson received a baptism of fire for on the very day he assumed his office Chiang, at least in name, resigned his and turned over leadership of the Nationalist Government of Li Tsung-jen. "I arrived," Acheson later wrote of Chiang, "just in time to have him collapse on me."[64] Acheson possessed little direct experience of Chinese affairs and readily accepted the existing State Department view that Western Europe held the highest priority. He devoted his main energies early in 1949 to the German issue and the final negotiations of the North Atlantic Treaty but unavoidably confronted the question of providing additional aid to the remnants of the Kuomintang. He immediately agreed with his advisers led by Kennan and Walton Butterworth, whom he made Assistant Secretary of State for Far Eastern Affairs, that it was useless to aid the Nationalists further. Briefed on the Titoist possibilities in China, in February Acheson advanced through the NSC and then obtained Truman's approval for a policy "to exploit through political and economic means any rifts between the Chinese Communists and the USSR and between the Stalinist and other elements in China both within and outside the Communist structure."[65] In March he frankly told the Senate Foreign Relations Committee: "We have got to the point where in fact there is nothing more constructive that is coming out of this [Nationalist] government." Opposing the provision of more aid to the Nationalists he advocated "a wait, look, see policy" toward China.[66] Obviously Acheson accepted more readily than his predecessor the thrust of the Planning Staff's recommendation to Marshall in PPS/39 that the United States should pursue a pragmatic approach in China and keep its options open. In early April, when Bevin arrived for the signing of the North Atlantic Treaty, the American Secretary of State explained to his British counterpart that the U.S. had decided against any further support for the National regime beyond

---

Nationalist Army indicates that organized resistance to the military forces of the Chinese Communist Party will probably cease within a few months." CIA, "Chinese Communist Capabilities for Control of All China" (Report ORE 77-48), December 10, 1948, Truman Papers, PSF, BOX 256.

[63] Lovett to Stuart, December 30, 1948, FRUS 1948, VII, p. 704.

[64] Acheson, Present at the Creation, p. 257.

[65] NSC 34/2, "U.S. Policy Toward China," February 28, 1949, FRUS 1949, IX, pp. 491–95. For Truman's approval see Memorandum by the Acting Executive Secretary of the NSC, March 3, 1949, FRUS 1949, IX, p. 499.

[66] U.S. Congress, Senate, Committee on Foreign Relations, Economic Assistance to China and Korea, 1949–1950 (Washington, D.C., 1974), pp. 30–41.

the China Aid Act due to expire in June and that it would henceforth "pursue a more realistic policy respecting China."[67]

As Acheson brought the Truman administration to a position where it planned to wait upon and observe the course of events in China, attention continued to be given to the question of Chinese Titoism. From Shanghai U.S. Consul-General John Cabot advised that the United States should be receptive to initiatives from the CCP.[68] In Washington Davies maintained a close watch for signs of CCP independence from Moscow. In late January he wrote Kennan that "a strong odor of bad fish is emanating from Sino-Soviet relations."[69] In February he gave off-the-record briefings on the Titoist possibility in China to C. L. Sulzberger of the *New York Times* on which Sulzberger based a series of articles on the subject.[70] Davies clearly expected the realization of his long-held view that the Chinese Communists would act without direction from the Kremlin.[71] While noting the potential for Titoism in China no sustained consideration was given to how it might be fomented. The American approach bore some similarity to that applied in Yugoslavia. The emphasis, as with Tito, centered upon waiting and letting the CCP indicate by its actions a desire for improved relations with the United States. Those officials like Cabot, who wanted to pursue the Titoist option more aggressively, were not at the senior levels of policy-making. The dominant position early in 1949 was one of waiting for "the dust to settle."[72] The possibility for Sino-Soviet differences to develop was well appreciated but the method for exploiting them was delayed for future consideration.

During the first half of 1949 Kennan's involvement on the China question diminished somewhat. In part this was due to his preoccupation with the German problem but it also resulted from the fact that the Planning Staff had no role in managing the details of the bilateral relationship. Nevertheless, the Planning Staff's influence was still quite pervasive. Its analysis of the situation within China and of China's relative strategic importance permeated the State Department and its recommendations were unchallenged within the depart-

[67] Memorandum of Acheson-Bevin conversation, April 4, 1949, *FRUS* 1949, VII, pp. 1138–41.

[68] Cabot's efforts are discussed in Tucker, *Patterns in the Dust*, p. 31. Also see Cabot, *First Line of Defense*, pp. 56–67.

[69] Davies to Kennan, January 25, 1949, PPS Records, Box 13.

[70] See the articles by C. L. Sulzberger in the *New York Times*, February 11, 15, 18, and 21, 1949, *FRUS* 1949. For Davies as the briefer see Cyrus L. Sulzberger, *A Long Row of Candles: Memoirs and Diaries, 1934–1954* (New York, 1969), pp. 384–87.

[71] Kennan continued to find Davies' analysis persuasive. He told a meeting at the Council on Foreign Relations on February 16, 1949, that "there is now some evidence . . . to indicate that both the Chinese Communists and the Soviets are apprehensive about each other." See Kennan, "Long-Term Questions of U.S. Foreign Policy," Archives of the Council of Foreign Relations, Record of Meetings, 1949.

[72] Acheson, *Present at the Creation*, p. 306.

ment. While Acheson was advised principally by Butterworth the content of this advice was essentially that which the Staff had presented to Marshall late in 1948. Unlike the questions of the North Atlantic Treaty and German policy, the China issue did not find Kennan at odds with the relevant operational division. Kennan and Davies of the Planning Staff and Butterworth and his colleagues from the Office of Far Eastern Affairs shared the same view and supported each other in holding to it against pressure from outside the administration. Davies shared personal friendship and easy familiarity with the China specialists while many of the latter, such as Philip Sprouse, held Kennan in esteem.[73] Kennan and Butterworth, Princeton classmates who held each other in high regard, engaged in none of the bureaucratic battling that occurred between the Planning Staff director and John Hickerson of the Office of European Affairs.[74] Kennan and Davies found no need to intervene on overall China policy when they agreed with Butterworth's actions. They did seek, however, to influence the American approach on specific questions, among them the defense of the China policy in the domestic political arena, the American stance on Formosa, and the question of dealing with the Chinese Communists.

The domestic criticism of the administration's policy toward China increased under Acheson's secretaryship as the Nationalist regime writhed through its death throes. The new secretary showed little disposition to bear ill-founded criticism in silence and in sharp contrast to his respected predecessor he proved willing to counter the charges of the China lobby. In mid-May he informed Truman of the preparation of a White Paper recording United States policy toward China and documenting Kuomintang incompetence and corruption. He got presidential approval to publish its findings regardless of the damage it might do to Chiang, who remained in real control of the Nationalists.[75] This White Paper originated in John Davies' suggestion, in which Kennan concurred, to John F. Melby that a full-length account of American policy be prepared.[76] Melby assisted by Philip Sprouse and others compiled

[73] Sprouse remembered Kennan as a "tremendously impressive man, intellectually superior and fearless." Oral History Interview with Philip D. Sprouse, February 11, 1974, HSTL.

[74] Of his relationship with Butterworth, Kennan recalled that "Butterworth and I were classmates in college and had been associated in our respective positions in the American Legation in Lisbon during the war. We remained good friends down to his death." Kennan to author, February 2, 1981. Note also that he found Butterworth to be "much more the 'operator' than the man of conception." Marshall Green, who worked for Butterworth at the time, remembered that "Butterworth and Kennan had great respect for each other." Author's interview with Ambassador Marshall Green, Department of State, Washington, D.C., July 6, 1978. On Kennan's work with Butterworth in Lisbon see Kennan, Memoirs, 1, pp. 145–47.

[75] Acheson to Truman, May 12, 1949, FRUS 1949, IX, pp. 1365–67; and Clark M. Clifford to Acheson, May 17, 1949, FRUS 1949, IX, p. 1367.

[76] For details of the White Paper and its compilation see Davies interview with author, August

the White Paper under the general direction of Butterworth.[77] As they did so
Kennan advised Acheson that "the Executive should aggressively assume the
offensive" on the China issue. He urged the earliest possible publication of
the White Paper as the first step in such an offensive and suggested further
measures including a major speech by the president. This should have as its
theme that "the Executive resisted irresponsible, sentimental and partisan
pressures in this country for an adventurous China policy which would have
played straight into the hands of the Kremlin and have committed this country
to a deep involvement and incalculable squandering of its prestige, manpower
and treasure." Kennan seemed emotionally caught up in proclaiming that the
administration's China policy was "a triumph of good sense over a proposed
gamble with our deepest national interests and security."[78] This strong recommendation to publish the White Paper reinforced Acheson's own resolve
and convinced him to override the reservations of Secretary of Defense Louis
Johnson and the Joint Chiefs of Staff to the document's publication.[79]

Kennan's eagerness to take the battlefield against the China lobby tended to
cloud his judgment about the international implications of American actions.
Neither he nor Davies raised any objection to Acheson's letter transmitting the
White Paper to Truman which not only savaged Chiang's Nationalists for their
ineptitude but also charged that "the Communist leaders have foresworn their
Chinese heritage and have publicly announced their subservience to a foreign
power, Russia."[80] Such accusations contributed nothing to keeping open the
possibility of accommodation between the U.S. and the Chinese Communists—indeed, quite the opposite. Mao reacted furiously against them and the
White Paper served to heighten the barrier to normal relations.[81]

12, 1986; Kahn, *The China Hands*, pp. 203–4; Philip Sprouse to Walton Butterworth, July 25,
1971, Papers of Walton W. Butterworth, Marshall Library, Lexington, Va., Box 1.

[77] Marshall Green remembered Butterworth's involvement and said of him: "His heart and soul
were in that White Paper." Author's interview with Marshall Green, July 6, 1978.

[78] Kennan to Acheson, June 28, 1949 (attached is a handwritten note "Communicated orally,
GFK"), PPS Records, Box 13. Kennan's emotional involvement can be sensed from the correspondence sent to him concerning the China issue by Joseph Alsop. See Alsop's letters of June 6 and
September 21, 1949, Alsop Papers, Boxes 4 and 5, respectively. In the latter letter Alsop talked
of being "deeply wounded" by Kennan in an argument on the subject.

[79] For reference to the doubts of Louis Johnson and the JCS see Acheson's memorandum of
conversation with the president, July 25, 1949, RG 59, Executive Secretariat Records, Box 3.
Acheson may not have needed Kennan's advice to proceed with the publications of the White
Paper given his own determination in this regard. See Cohen, "Acheson, His Advisers and China,
1949–1950," p. 25.

[80] Letter of Transmittal, Acheson to Truman, July 30, 1949, *China White Paper*, p. xvi.

[81] On the Chinese reaction see Steven M. Goldstein, "Chinese Communist Policy Toward the
United States: Opportunities and Constraints, 1944–1950," in Borg and Heinrichs, eds. *Uncertain Years*, p. 264; and Robert P. Newman, "The Self-Inflicted Wound: The China White Paper
of 1949," *Prologue* 14 (Fall 1982): 153–55. Note that Newman also argues that the White Paper

The decisive importance which Kennan gave to the need to respond to domestic critics when framing his recommendations on China emerged also in his advocacy of a series of actions "designed to demonstrate a positive and affirmative policy in the Far East." He explained to Acheson that "these acts will, of course, speak louder than any words and will serve to take the eye of both the public and Congress off the record of the past."[82] Influenced by Davies, he saw the question of what to do about Formosa as just the opportunity to demonstrate such a positive and affirmative approach.[83] On July 6, 1949, he proposed that the United States use unilateral force to assert its authority over Formosa. He gave no particular consideration to the impact such a move would have on the Communists in China. Quite simply he deemed the island strategically important and wanted to prevent its falling to the Communists and to deny it to the Kuomintang, envisioning instead a regime independent of the mainland. He realized that his proposed action would be unlikely to gain the approval of Acheson or the NSC but in a rhetorical flourish he argued, that if it were executed "with sufficient resolution, speed, ruthlessness and self-assurance, the way Theodore Roosevelt might have done it, it would not only be successful but would have an electrifying effect in this country and throughout the Far East."[84] Acheson rejected Kennan's proposal—which in

also proved deleterious in the domestic political context. For discussion of the congressional response to the White Paper see Kepley, *The Collapse of the Middle Way*, pp. 45–47.

[82] Kennan to Acheson, June 28, 1949, PPS Records, Box 13.

[83] Kennan's suggestion on Formosa must be understood in the context of the discussions then taking place within the administration on the Formosa question. The State Department had decided on January 14 that the United States should undertake "diplomatic and economic" measures to keep Formosa out of Communist hands. Doubting that these would suffice, Davies developed the suggestion that the U.S. should foster a Taiwanese independence movement so that if future direct American military intervention to prevent the island falling to the Communists was required it could be disguised as support for Taiwanese self-determination rather than as a selfish American effort to secure only its own strategic interests. Acheson received the suggestions for an independent Formosa with caution and sent Livingston Merchant of the Far Eastern Division to investigate the possibility. Merchant questioned the viability of an independent Taiwan and advised that the U.S. abandon its efforts to deny the island to the Communists. It was at this point that Kennan injected himself into the debate with his proposal for unilateral American action. For the January 14 decision see Memorandum from Lovett to Truman, January 14, 1949, *FRUS* 1949, IX, pp. 265–67. For Davies' suggestions see Davies note, January 14, 1949, PPS Records, Box 13. His ideas were reflected in NSC 37/2, February 3, 1949, *FRUS* 1949, IX, pp. 281–82. For Merchant's report see Merchant to Secretary of State, May 4, 1949, *FRUS* 1949, IX, pp. 324–26. Also see Oral History Interview with Livingston Merchant by Richard D. McKinzie, Washington D.C., May 27, 1975, HSTL, transcript pp. 31–33. The decision-making on Formosa is described more fully in Cohen, "Acheson, His Advisers and China, 1949–1950," pp. 25–32; and Russell D. Buhite, " 'Major Interests': American Policy Toward China, Taiwan and Korea, 1945–1950," *Pacific Historical Review* 47 (August 1978). 432–40.

[84] Memorandum by Kennan, July 6, 1949 (enclosing PPS/53, "United States Policy Toward Formosa and the Pescadores," June 23, 1949), *FRUS* 1949, IX, pp. 356–64. The Staff's paper, PPS/53, was drafted originally by Davies and then revised by Kennan after Staff discussion. See Minutes of Meetings, June 15, 17, 22, and 27, 1949, PPS Records, Box 32.

retrospect seems singularly inappropriate and rather incongruous given his views on limiting U.S. involvement in China—ironically upon advice from the Joint Chiefs of Staff.[85] The secretary of state used similar criteria in deciding to avoid entanglement in Formosa as Kennan had developed and used to limit American involvement on the Chinese mainland. Despite further attempts by Philip Jessup and Dean Rusk to persuade him to change his mind on the matter Acheson held firm and accepted that the Communists would conquer Formosa eventually.[86] Because the president agreed with him, Acheson's view prevailed.[87]

No Paper Tiger—The Failure to Foster Chinese Titoism

The question of how to pursue relations with the Chinese Communists occupied the State Department through 1949 and into 1950. Both Kennan and Davies participated fully in the discussions. The Planning Staff's paper (PPS/39) of September 1948, recommending that the United States pursue a pragmatic approach intimated that it would look favorably upon reaching terms with the ultimate victors in the Chinese conflict, especially since Mao was viewed as a possible Asian Tito. Yet, despite the desire of policymakers like Kennan and Davies and most everyone else in the State Department to see the Soviet Union and the Chinese Communists at odds, the tactic of encouraging Titoism in China was never implemented seriously. The Truman administration did adopt in early March a quite liberal trade policy designed to encourage the Chinese to distance themselves from the Soviet Union.[88] But this carrot was neither offered temptingly nor supplemented meaningfully. The administration failed

[85] Acheson did give the Kennan proposal some consideration but when the Joint Chiefs advised that the strategic importance of Formosa did not justify overt military action "so long as the present disparity between our military strength and our global obligations exists," he decided against it. For his initial consideration see Summary of Secretary's Daily Meeting, July 29, 1949, Executive Secretariat Records, Box 1. For the advice of the Joint Chiefs see Joint Chiefs of Staff to Secretary of Defense, August 17, 1949, *FRUS* 1949, IX, p. 377.

[86] Warren Cohen discusses the efforts of Rusk and Jessup in "Acheson, His Advisers and China, 1949–1950," pp. 28–29.

[87] For Truman's agreement note that he told Under Secretary Webb on October 31, 1949, that "the Communists could take Formosa almost on their own timetable," and he instructed Webb to arrange for American citizens to get off the island. Webb's minute of meeting with the president, October 31, 1949, Executive Secretariat Records, Box 3. For the formal acceptance of this position by the National Security Council see NSC 48/2, "The Position of the United States with Respect to Asia," December 30, 1949, NSC Records, Box 3.

[88] On trade policy see NSC 41, "U.S. Policy Regarding Trade with China," March 3, 1949, *FRUS* 1949, IX, pp. 826–34. The rationale for this policy, in Michael Schaller's words, was that "it might serve as a carrot encouraging acceptable political behavior by China." See his discussion in *The American Occupation of Japan: The Origins of the Cold War in Asia* (New York, 1985), pp. 190–91. Also see David Allan Mayers, *Cracking the Monolith: U.S. Policy Against the Sino-Soviet Alliance, 1949–1955* (Baton Rouge, 1986), p. 40.

to turn off completely the life-support sytem of American aid to the National-ists that helped sustain Chiang and which so antagonized his foes.[89] And, the administration refused to act upon what *may* have been Communist overtures to American diplomats in China—the invitation extended by Chou's aid, Huang Hua, for Ambassador John Leighton Stuart to visit Peking;[90] and the possible demarche by Chou En-lai for improved relations extended through the Australian journalist Michael Keon.[91] These possible overtures have fu-eled a lively debate among historians over "missed opportunities" or a "lost chance" in China, although recent evidence suggests that Mao held little in-terest in reaching out to the Americans.[92] In any case, these perceived over-tures were insufficient for the United States. The Americans waited for more significant demonstrations of CCP independence from Moscow but these were not forthcoming. In American eyes Mao moved in quite the opposite direction especially when on June 30, 1949, in an address commemorating the 28th anniversary of the founding of the Communist Party in China, he declared his policy of "leaning to one side"—that of the Soviet Union.

Davies especially took offense at Mao's hostility to the United States and his apparent subservience to the Soviet Union. He read Mao's speech as sig-nifying that Chou En-lai and the supposed pragmatists had lost out to Liu Shao-chi and the pro-Soviet hardliners.[93] His actions in response suggest the fury of an angry parent. The Chinese were refusing to behave as he wished.

[89] As late as early 1950 some aid was still getting through to Chiang and the U.S. government placed no restrictions on Chiang's procurement of military supplies from commercial firms with his own funds.

[90] On the Chinese overture see Yu-ming Shaw, "John Leighton Stuart and U.S.-Chinese Com-munist Rapprochement in 1949: Was There Another 'Lost Chance in China'?" *The China Quar-terly*, no. 89 (March 1982): 74–96. See also Stueck, *The Road to Confrontation*, pp. 122–25; Martin, *Divided Counsel*, pp. 27–39, 43–48; and for Cabot's diary entries of July 1 and 2 which strongly favored Stuart's visit to Peking see *First Line of Defense*, p. 68.

[91] For the initial report of Chou's supposed demarche through Keon see Clubb to Secretary of State, June 1, 1949, *FRUS* 1949, VIII, pp. 357–60.

[92] For a good summary of the debate over whether there was "an opportunity for early rap-prochement between the United States and the Chinese Communists," see Warren I. Cohen, "The United States and China Since 1945," in Cohen, ed., *New Frontiers in American-East Asian Relations* (New York, 1983), pp. 141–43. Also see Zhigong Ho, " 'Lost Chance' or 'Inevitable Hostility?' Two Contending Interpretations of the Late 1940s Chinese American Relations," *SHAFR Newsletter* 20 (September 1989): 67–78. For a strong case challenging the significance of these "overtures" see Steven Goldstein, "Chinese Communist Policy Toward the United States: Opportunities and Constraints, 1944–1950," in Borg and Heinrich, eds., *Uncertain Years*, pp. 270–78. On the recent evidence—namely conversations with Chinese officials—see Warren Co-hen's conclusion that "Chinese officials who participated in the diplomacy of the late 1940s put little stock in the idea, so popular among American scholars, of a 'lost chance' to establish good relations between the United States and the People's Republic in 1949." Warren I. Cohen, "Con-versations with Chinese Friends: Zhou Enlai's Associates Reflect on Chinese American Relations in the 1940s and the Korean War," *Diplomatic History* 11 (Summer 1987): 284.

[93] Interview with Davies, August 12, 1986.

He favored Stuart's visit to Peking primarily because it would allow the American ambassador to give the Communists a "curtain lecture" on the treatment of American officials in China.[94] He set about to devise forms of pressure to exert on the Chinese "to compel them to respect the United States and moderate their behavior." In mid-August he persuaded Kennan and Jessup to join him in formulating a program of "frank hostility to the Chinese Communists" to demonstrate American strength. Later that month he set out some specific punitive measures including the use of air power to disabuse the Chinese of the notion that the United States was "a paper tiger," although even he had misgivings about the severity of the measures he suggested.[95] Acheson refused to countenance any such direct military actions in a notable demonstration of good judgment. But he did not object when Kennan, as the State Department representative on the OPC oversight committee, gave an implicit endorsement for OPC to provide financial support for General Claire Chennault's Civil Air Transport (CAT) so that the airline might "facilitate CIA secret operations" in China, including the transport of supplies to remnant forces still battling the Communists.[96]

It is helpful for an understanding of Kennan's position and American policy-making on China to come to grips with Davies' thinking. He illustrates well the problem that Americans faced in pursuing the Titoist option in China. Clearly he appreciated the nascent tensions that existed between the CCP and the Soviet Union. He fully expected that the U.S. would have the opportunity to exploit such tensions which derived from Chinese nationalism and independence. But neither Davies nor any other significant policymaker offered a considered program to foster a Sino-Soviet split. No concerted effort was made from the American side to regularize contacts with the Chinese Communists. Like Davies, the United States adopted essentially a reactive posture to the ⌜possibility of Chinese Titoism. Beyond the trade liberalization no positive measures were taken to encourage the Chinese to adopt a more independent stance. Rather, the U.S. waited to judge Chinese actions. This was the situation that prevailed through June of 1949. As in Yugoslavia, favorable actions would elicit a positive American response. Truman accepted this approach and directed American diplomats on June 16 "to be most careful not to indicate

[94] Davies to Kennan, June 30, 1949, *FRUS* 1949, VIII, pp. 768–69.

[95] The program devised by Kennan, Davies, and Jessup is referred to by Cohen in "Acheson, His Advisers and China, 1949–1950," pp. 39–40. For Davies' own proposal see his memorandum to Kennan, August 24, 1949, PPS Records, Box 13. As to Davies' doubts, he attached a handwritten note: "George, I hope this won't seem too extreme. I have misgivings myself."

[96] For details on this interesting episode see William M. Leary, *Perilous Missions: Civil Air Transport and CIA Covert Operations in Asia* (University, Ala., 1984), pp. 67–83; quotation from p. 82. On this see also John Prados, *Presidents' Secret Wars: CIA and Pentagon Covert Operations Since World War II* (New York, 1986), pp. 62–67.

any softening toward the Communists but to insist on judging their intentions by their actions."[97]

The refusal of the CCP to act in the independent manner which Davies and Kennan had foreshadowed for it in 1947 and 1948 deeply offended the policy planners. Their extraordinarily swift move from eager anticipation of Sino-Soviet division in early 1949 to the belligerent stance they adopted toward the CCP by midyear is rooted partly in that offense. Their somewhat condescending attitude toward China and the CCP also contributed. Davies, who also persuaded Kennan, curiously expected the Chinese to reach out for American support. The audacity of the CCP in rejecting the possibility of future American "benevolence" and in attacking the U.S. angered both men. They failed to comprehend the depth and basis of resentment toward the U.S. which resided in the CCP—a resentment rooted in Marxist ideology and bitterness at the extent of American support for Chiang—and they reacted against Chinese hostility.[98] In June 1949 Kennan described the Chinese Communists as a " 'grievously misguided and confused people' who should be given nothing until they abandoned 'the Iron Curtain psychology' and 'their attitude of arrogancy (sic) contempt toward the West.' "[99] Davies' recommendation of measures to pressure and harass the Chinese developed from similar sentiments.

This clash of CCP actions with the expectations of Davies and Kennan transformed two of the most likely candidates to push the Titoist option into advocates of harsh measures toward the CCP.[100] And it left the Truman administration without any significant policymaker who adopted a restrained view of the Chinese actions and indicated a willingness to take initiatives toward the CCP. In fact, Acheson had the role of point man on this matter forced upon him but there were limits to his efforts. Neither he nor any other senior policymaker advocated dismissing Mao's comments as partly rhetorical. No one cautioned as to the weight that should be applied to them in light of Mao's own domestic political needs or his obligation to placate Moscow. No one counseled that the

[97] Memorandum by Webb of Conversation with the President, June 16, 1949, FRUS 1949, VIII, p. 388. Also relevant here is Webb to Clubb, June 14, 1949, FRUS 1949, VIII, pp. 384–85.

[98] On this point see David Mayers, Cracking the Monolith, p. 61. Chinese leaders recently interviewed by Warren Cohen perceived the United States "as relentlessly hostile toward China beginning with Hurley's ascendancy in early 1945." They claimed to be unaware of any efforts at rapprochement by the American side. Cohen, "Conversations with Chinese Friends," pp. 286–87.

[99] Kennan, "An Estimate of the International Situation," June 13, 1949, quoted in David McLean, "American Nationalism, the China Myth, and the Truman Doctrine: The Question of Accommodation with Peking, 1949–1950," Diplomatic History 10 (Winter 1986): 41–42.

[100] Kennan's sentiments as of late August can be gauged from his remarks in a conversation with John Cabot, back in the Department from Shanghai. As recorded in Cabot's diary: "He [Kennan] held forth rather emphatically re Chinese policy. George apparently wants something of a showdown with the Chinese commies." Cabot, First Line of Defense, p. 74.

United States could ride out the storm of anti-Western actions of the Chinese, now at the pinnacle of their revolutionary triumph, and await the arrival of the calmer seas of national self-interest.[101] Davies, who given his earlier views on the independent strain in the CCP, was the natural one to adopt such a stance and to bring Kennan along with him, went in a vastly different direction. In fact, David McLean insightfully has noted the absence from the American policy debate of ''any sustained advocacy of normalization of relations with Chinese communism such as that which occurred in the upper echelons of the British government during 1949.'' McLean argued that the State Department ''believed that there was in fact very little that the United States could do to encourage a Sino-Soviet split.''[102] This misses the real approach and stance of the Americans. Most U.S. policymakers, even among the group who readily anticipated a Peking-Moscow split, thought there was little the United States *should* do to further this split. It was up to the Chinese to adopt an independent position in relation to the Soviet Union just as Tito had done. The U.S. would move thereupon to exploit the fissure by indicating receptivity to Chinese initiatives. The litmus test was Chinese actions.

THE QUESTION OF RECOGNITION

Mao's proclamation of a Chinese People's Republic (PRC) on October 1, 1949, confronted the Americans with the issue of formal recognition. Truman indicated on October 3 that he felt ''we should be in no hurry whatever to recognize this regime.''[103] That same day the administration laid down the American prerequisites for recognition. The P.R.C. had to be in control of the government, govern with the assent of the Chinese people, and fulfill its responsibilities under international law.[104] To aid in the determination of a policy on the matter Acheson convened a conference of a number of China specialists from October 6 to 8. The majority view of the conference was ''that a stabilization of relationships through quick recognition would be desirable from the standpoint of commercial considerations, the ideological effect on the Chinese people and to put the political orientation of the Communist leadership to-

[101] This was essentially the British approach. See Martin, *Divided Counsel*, pp. 63–72.

[102] McLean, ''American Nationalism, the China Myth and the Truman Doctrine,'' pp. 33, 35. In making his case McLean refers especially to the testimony of Philip Jessup before the Senate Foreign Relations Committee. When asked about the likelihood of Chinese Titoism, Jessup admitted it as a possibility but commented that ''we do not think it safe to bank on it.'' Jessup testimony of October 12, 1949, in U.S. Congress, Senate, Committee on Foreign Relations, *Review of the World Situation* (Historical Series), 81st Cong. (Washington, D.C., 1974), p. 99.

[103] Webb's memorandum of his meeting with Truman, October 3, 1949, Executive Secretariat Records, Box 3.

[104] See the report of the public presentation of policy in *New York Times*, October 4, 1949, p. 1.

wards the Soviet Union under strain."[105] Acheson agreed with this view. Counseled by his Consultants on China policy—Raymond Fosdick, the former president of the Rockefeller Foundation, and Everett Case, the president of Colgate University—the secretary of state placed two alternative objectives before the president in mid-November. The first aimed "to oppose the Communist regime, harass it, needle it and if an opportunity appeared to overthrow it." The second, which Acheson indicated the Consultants and China specialists favored, proposed to attempt to detach the Communist regime "from subservience to Moscow and over a period of time encourage those vigorous influences which might modify it." This second alternative, he reassured Truman, "did not mean a policy of appeasement any more that it had in the case of Tito."[106]

Acheson leaned toward recognition but, as David Allan Mayers argues, the secretary of state "believed that for formal, full Sino-American relations to be palatable to his compatriots a show of good faith by China was required."[107] In the last quarter of 1949 the United States waited for China to demonstrate its good intentions—waited for it to pass the litmus test to improved relations. The Chinese hardly rushed to oblige. Having just won a long struggle against a foe supported by and identified with the United States they possessed no inclination to design their actions to accommodate American sensibilities. On October 24 Chinese Communist officials arrested Angus Ward, the American Consul-General in Mukden, Manchuria, and charged him with spying. This arrest placed a colossal roadblock before any early move toward recognition. Truman reacted furiously against Ward's incarceration and even spoke of mounting a naval blockade on coal traffic into Shanghai in retaliation so that "the Communists would understand that we meant business."[108] The State Department diverted him from this measure by questioning the significance of

[105] See Francis H. Russell to Kennan, October 13, 1949, enclosing "Summary of Some of the Views Expressed at Consultative Meeting on Problems of U.S. Policy in China," PPS Records, Box 13. For the full Record of Roundtable Discussion by twenty-five Far Eastern Experts with the Department of State on "American Policy Toward China," October 6, 7, and 8, 1949, see Truman Papers, PSF, Box 174. The participants included Professors John K. Fairbank, Edward O. Reischauer, Bernard Brodie, and Owen Lattimore along with public figures such as Harold Stassen and John D. Rockefeller III. General Marshall also participated. Kennan was part of the State Department contingent and briefed the Conference on the subject of "China in the world picture."

[106] Acheson's memorandum of conversation with Truman, November 17, 1949, Executive Secretariat Records, Box 3.

[107] Mayers, *Cracking the Monolith*, p. 55.

[108] Webb memorandum of meeting with the president, November 14, 1949, RG 59, Records of the Office of Chinese Affairs, 1945–50, NA, Box 14. Under Secretary Webb asked Truman, "Would he actually use force to stop the coal traffic if they refused to obey orders from our Naval Forces?" to which the president replied that "if we meant to go into this matter we should be prepared to sink any vessels which refused to heed our warning."

the coal shipments into Shanghai but the proposal suggests Truman's attitude at the time.[109]

Ward's arrest prompted Kennan to make his last attempt as Planning Staff director to influence his nation's China policy. Now he departed markedly from the policy of hostility and coercion which he had joined Davies in recommending in August. He separated from Davies and advocated immediate recognition and movement toward normalization of relations. Kennan judged the imprisonment of Consul-General Ward as Soviet-inspired and designed both to retaliate for the American arrest of officials of the Soviet AMTORG Trading Corporation in New York and to embitter further relations between the U.S. and the P.R.C. Kennan resisted being manipulated by the Soviets in this way and moved to obstruct it. Addressing his comments to Acheson, Webb, Jessup, Rusk, and Butterworth, the planning chief argued that "the greatest single external threat to the complete Stalinization of China is that the U.S. should establish normal relations with the Chinese Communists and once more bring its influence to bear in that country, even if on a more restricted basis." Kennan now saw that the American interest lay in bringing about a rapid normalization of relations with Peking, which he claimed the Chinese would welcome. "If the Chinese Communist leaders did not entertain this view," he explained, "they would not have formally advised our Consul-General in Peking that they were open to recognition," which Chou En-lai had done on October 1, 1949. Kennan, with an air of resignation, then criticized the false and emotional basis of the opposition to recognition observing that "if recognition had all the moral tones and implications of friendship which is being imputed to it in connection with the Chinese Communists, we could not possibly now be maintaining official relations with Tito, not to mention the Soviet and Satellite Governments." Except for the Ward case there was no real reason not to recognize Mao's government. After this analysis Kennan then recommended the immediate solution of the Ward case which he thought could be done through a deal involving the release of the AMTORG officials. The way would then be opened for normalization of relations with Peking.[110] But Kennan's views on China policy in late 1949 attracted much less attention than those offered in late 1947 and his adroit proposal went unheeded.

Truman and Acheson saw no need to act expeditiously. They appreciated

[109] See Butterworth to Acheson, November 17, 1949, Records of the Office of Chinese Affairs, Box 14.

[110] For details of the AMTORG case, which involved the arrest of five Soviets for failing to comply with the provisions of the Foreign Agents Registration Act, see the correspondence and memoranda in *FRUS* 1949, V, pp. 762–65. For Kennan's comments see Kennan to Rusk, November 17, 1949, and the attached paper "Mr. Ward, the Russians and Recognition," PPS Records, Box 33. The importance of the AMTORG case for the Russians can be measured by the fact that when Soviet foreign minister Vyshinsky called on Acheson on November 7, 1949, this was the only matter of substance which he raised. See Memorandum of Conversation, November 7, 1949, Papers of Dean Acheson, HSTL, Box 64.

that Britain—motivated by Bevin's thought "that there was no point not recognizing something that was there"—was on the verge of according recognition to the Peking regime but they preferred to hold back.[111] On December 20
the secretary reminded the president that their policy was to make no decision
regarding recognition of the Chinese Communist regime "until the matter had
developed further."[112] The National Security Council strengthened this position on December 30 when it agreed to avoid recognizing the Chinese Communist regime until it was in the American interest to do so.[113] But the Chinese
refused to behave in a manner, as Edmund Clubb later commented, "that
would permit the United States gracefully to extend recognition."[114] They
would not live up to what Acheson termed their "international obligations"
which meant protecting American property interests and the rights of American diplomats and diplomatic property. After he left office Acheson explained
to Hans Morgenthau that "it seemed to us at the time that it was premature to
go to recognition in the absence of some assurance (and none was forthcoming) from the Chinese that they would honor their international engagements,
including decent treatment for our nationals in their power."[115] But, as the
historian Lisle Rose has pointed out, for the Chinese to have met these American defined "international obligations" would have meant their surrendering
"at the very moment of triumph that revolutionary, anti-Western fervor which
had brought them victory in the first place."[116] This they refused to do.

In a move which compounded the anger over the earlier imprisonment of
Angus Ward, the Chinese in January 1950 seized the buildings which the
Americans had converted into the offices of the Consulate-General in Peking,
despite warnings that this would provoke the withdrawal of all official American personnel from China.[117] Mao's lengthy discussions with Stalin in Moscow in January 1950, leading to the conclusion of the Sino-Soviet Mutual

[111] Bevin's thought remembered by Lord Franks in Oral History Interview with David Mc-
Lellan, Oxford, June 27, 1964, HSTL, transcript pp. 8–9. Britain extended recognition on January
6, 1950. On this issue see R. Ovendale, "Britain, the United States and the Recognition of Communist China," *The Historical Journal* 26 (March 1983): 139–58. The U.S. had tried to discourage quick British movement toward recognition. See the details in the sections on the Far
East in the State Department's "Weekly Review," October 12 and November 9, 1949, Truman
Papers, Confidential File, Box 55.

[112] Acheson's memorandum of conversation, December 20, 1949, Executive Secretariat Records, Box 3.

[113] NSC 48/2, "The Position of the United States with Respect to Asia," NSC Documents, Modern Military Records, NA, Box 3.

[114] O. Edmund Clubb, *The Witness and I* (New York, 1974), p. 23.

[115] Acheson to Morgenthau, January 16, 1957, in McLellan and Acheson, eds., *Among
Friends: Personal Letters of Dean Acheson*, pp. 121–22.

[116] Lisle A. Rose, *Roots of Tragedy: The United States and the Struggle for Asia, 1945–1953*
(Westport, Conn., 1976), p. 209.

[117] Details of this seizure are provided by Clubb, who was the Consul-General at the time, in
The Witness and I, pp. 82–85.

Assistance Treaty on February 14, further hardened American sentiment against recognition and ended prospects for any reconciliation in the short term. Such Chinese actions, Michael Schaller has argued persuasively, caused even most of the "moderates" on China policy, who hoped for a Sino-Soviet split and leaned towards recognition of the Peking regime, to lose "nearly all faith in rapprochement with the Chinese Communists by the spring of 1950."[118] Schaller included in the "moderate" category Acheson, Kennan, Davies, Edmund Clubb, Philip Sprouse, Philip Jessup, and Walton Butterworth. Schaller is correct in his basic point, although his assessment of Kennan ignored the Planning Staff's director's willingness to grant immediate recognition to the Communist Chinese government.

INEVITABLE HOSTILITY?

With the Korean War and the ensuing direct confrontation between American and Chinese troops, Sino-American relations passed into a period of bitter hostility. Although neither side sought the Korean conflict, it served to enlarge and set in concrete the antagonisms which existed before its outbreak. Not only did the Korean War destroy any possibility of normal relations but it also provoked policy reversals on the part of the United States regarding the defense of Formosa and the further extension of military aid to Chiang Kai-shek, who had reasserted his formal leadership of the Nationalist government now lodged on that island.[119] These reversals poisoned U.S.-Sino relations. The Korean War brought to an end the American effort over the previous three years to disengage from the Nationalist Chinese and to hold open the possibility of relations with the victorious Chinese Communists.[120]

[118] Michael Schaller, "Consul-General O. Edmund Clubb, John P. Davies, and the 'Inevitability' of Conflict between the United States and China, 1949–1950: A Comment and New Documentation," *Diplomatic History* 9 (Spring 1985): 150.

[119] In a statement on January 5, Truman declared that the United States would stay out of the Chinese civil war, had no interest in Formosa and, while extending limited economic support would give no military aid to the Nationalists. In his famous speech to the National Press Club on January 12, 1950, Acheson publicly outlined his "defensive perimeter" concept which included Japan, the Ryukyus, and the Philippines but notably excluded Formosa and any part of the mainland such as Korea. Truman's statement, January 5, 1950, *Department of State Bulletin* 22 (January 16, 1950): 79–91; Acheson's speech on "Crisis in Asia—An Examination of U.S. Policy," January 12, 1950, *Department of State Bulletin* 22 (January 23, 1950): 111–18. With the outbreak of the Korean War Truman reversed these policy statements and interposed the U.S. 7th Fleet in the Taiwan Strait, effectively preventing any Communist invasion of Formosa.

[120] Robert Blum has made a similar point: "When North Korea invaded the South, administration officials who had championed the tattered Titoist policy for the previous eighteen months kicked it over in an evening, without much apparent regret and with full public support." See his *Drawing the Line*, p. 215. On the impact of the Korean War on American policy see also Tucker, *Patterns in the Dust*, pp. 195–207; and Robert Jervis, "The Impact of the Korean War on the Cold War," *Journal of Conflict Resolution* 24 (December 1980): 563–92.

Kennan and Davies had been instrumental in formulating this policy with both its strengths and undoubted weaknesses. In the policy reconsideration leading to the China Aid Act, Kennan, advised by Davies, took a leading part in developing the State Department's position of limited assistance without deep involvement. By describing China as relatively unimportant to America's security Kennan provided the crucial rationale for avoiding direct American involvement in the Chinese civil war. During 1948 Kennan, again aided by Davies, effectively defended these positions against attempts by the national military establishment to involve the U.S. more deeply in China on the side of the Nationalists. The positions provided the policy foundations from which Acheson during 1949 sought to complete American disengagement. Thus, they also provided the crucial basis for what Richard Lowenthal has called "the greatness of President Truman" in dealing with the Communist threat which "consisted in the fact that the same man who stopped Stalin's European offensive—by the Truman Doctrine, the Marshall Plan, the Berlin airlift and the creation of NATO—also had the insight to cut American losses in China, because he understood that the absence of a cohesive force opposed to Communism in that country could not be replaced by American military intervention from outside."[121] They had helped prevent a potentially disastrous intervention against communism on the Asian mainland. Unavoidably one contrasts this approach with the costly decision of the policymakers of the Kennedy and Johnson administrations who, when confronted with the "chronic weakness that afflicted South Vietnam," chose to take over the burden of the fighting.[122]

A number of factors account for Kennan's influence at this stage of the formulation of America's China policy. The persuasiveness of his analyses and policy recommendations, which honestly confronted realities in China, were fundamental. General Marshall's high regard for him gave such policy recommendations an added weight. Kennan's geopolitical perspective furthered his effectiveness and influence on policy. He spoke on China not as a specialist or "China hand" but as a strategist concerned with responding to the perceived Soviet threat throughout the world. His recommendations on China were not formed in a vacuum. Precisely because of this Kennan emerged as a most effective opponent of the military's desire for deepening American involvement in China. Additionally, Kennan and Davies cooperated well with the Far Eastern Division of the State Department headed by John Carter Vincent and Walton Butterworth. They reinforced each other on the basic elements of China policy and consequently the State Department presented a rather consistent and unified position in the councils of the Truman

[121] Richard Lowenthal, "The Shattered Balance: Estimating the Dangers of War and Peace," *Encounter* 55 (November 1980): 9.

[122] On this point see George C. Herring, " 'Peoples Quite Apart': Americans, South Vietnamese, and the War in Vietnam," *Diplomatic History* 14 (Winter 1990): 22–23.

administration enhancing its ability to resist the requests of the Kuomintang, to negate the advice of the military, and to withstand the increasing pressure of domestic opposition.

Kennan and Davies worked closely and well together. On the China issue Davies served Kennan as a tutor of sorts. Kennan revealed a fine capacity to learn and gained from Davies during 1947 a fuller appreciation of the grievous weaknesses of Chiang's regime and of the improbability of its success in any prolonged conflict with the Chinese Communists. This appreciation figured centrally in the recommendations he framed for Marshall in November 1947 which influenced the policy he defended throughout 1948. Davies' insistence on "scolding" the Chinese Communists "for subservience to the Russians as a means of provoking them to behave more like nationalists" also affected Kennan, especially in mid-1949.[123] This led him to join Davies and Jessup in proposing a program of "frank hostility" to compel the Chinese Communists to respect the United States.

Kennan and Davies helped alert American policymakers to the possibility of conflict in relations between the Kremlin and the CCP and to the related prospect of a rapprochement of sorts with the CCP. But this was as far as they went. Having framed guidelines for relations with the Tito regime in Yugoslavia, they applied the same approach—although not in a forced or conscious manner—to dealing with the Chinese Communists. This approach might be described as empirical in that American policy was determined in response to and conditioned upon the concrete actions of the Chinese.[124] Kennan and Davies should not be attributed sole authorship for the empirical approach. This view that the actual Chinese behavior was all important pervaded the administration from Truman and Acheson downwards. Yet certainly both policy planners contributed to the widespread acceptance of this approach. And, of perhaps equal importance, Kennan and Davies failed to formulate and to offer within the councils of the Truman administration a more positive program to drive a wedge between the Soviets and the Chinese. The distinction is crucial and bears repetition. While Kennan and Davies raised the possibility of Titoism in China they did not advocate measures, aside from Davies' tough scolding approach, to encourage and induce this. In November 1954 John Davies wrote to General Daniel Noce, the inspector general of the Army and the chairman of the board to determine Davies' loyalty, and addressed the question of whether he was the chief advocate of the "separability of the Chinese Communists from Moscow." Davies denied being "the leading proponent in the Department of State." He noted that "I knew no proponents of such a dogma. I did believe, however, that certain factors suggested such a possibil-

[123] Cohen, "Acheson, His Advisers and China, 1949–1950," p. 21.
[124] Deborah Welch Larson's *Origins of Containment*, p. 252, has been suggestive for me here.

ity and that the question should be examined.''[125] Davies, facing accusations
of Communist sympathies and worse, surprisingly underplayed his tough approach to the Chinese Communists but his recollection accurately highlights
the limited efforts of the Truman administration to foster Chinese Titoism.
John Lewis Gaddis's suggestion that by December 1949 the Truman administration ascribed to "a well thought-out strategy of using Titoism to roll back
Soviet influence in the Communist world" conveys an exaggerated impression
of the American pursuit of Titoism in Asia.[126] It implies a coherence in America's policy toward China which it never possessed.

The empirical approach specified that the Truman administration would respond to Chinese actions. Whether a more positive policy regarding rapprochement with the Chinese would have produced a more favorable response
is much debated.[127] Certainly the Chinese—both past and present—give little
indication of being swayed by conciliatory offerings and gestures.[128] There
appears to have been little appreciation of the subtleties of the American position on the part of the Chinese. Ignorance and deep suspicion characterized
their attitudes.[129] In recent interviews the associates of Chou En-lai confirmed
as much and also recalled that "China was committed to the Soviet side" and
intent on demonstrating to Stalin "that China was *not* a 'Tito-like' state."[130]
The likely receptivity of the CCP to any American overtures must be questioned.[131] Certainly this appears the case in the short term and beyond that we
are in the realm of those sad words, what might have been.[132] In the end, what

[125] Davies letter to Noce, November 2, 1954, quoted in Davies, "The China Hands in Practice:
The Personal Experience," pp. 52–53. Also note Davies' comment in letter to author, January
14, 1987, that "in 1949 and early 1950 the opportunities for the United States Government to
foster Titoism in China were slight."

[126] Gaddis, *Strategies of Containment*, p. 70.

[127] For a useful survey of the principal participants in this debate see Robert J. McMahon, "The
New Cold War in Asia: Toward a New Synthesis?" *Diplomatic History* 12 (Summer 1988): 312–
15.

[128] Steven Goldstein holds vigorously that a more positive American policy would *not* have
prompted a favorable Chinese response. He argues that "there was no 'lost chance' [in China] for
the simple reason that neither side was in a position to take a chance." See his "Chinese Communist Policy Toward the United States," p. 278.

[129] The CIA provided information to Truman from a classified source in November 1949, that
"Communist Party leaders appear to be completely ignorant about American economic, political
and social facts; they believe the United States is a poverty-stricken nation of slave laborers exploited by Wall Street billionaires who wish to exploit China through Chiang. These leaders have
no access to contrary information and thus believe that it is impossible to develop good relations
with the United States now." Hillenkoetter memorandum, November 21, 1949, Truman Papers,
PSF, Box 250.

[130] Warren Cohen, "Conversations with Chinese Friends," p. 287.

[131] This is done well in Edwin Martin's *Divided Counsel* which also notes that the British,
despite their efforts to get along with the Chinese, got little by way of a positive response.

[132] Edward Friedman in his fine review of Martin's book skates toward this area of thin ice
when he asks: "What would have happened had the United States not kept backing the armed

cannot be debated is that a policy involving U.S. overtures to the Chinese was never implemented. The deliberations and actions of Kennan and Davies through most of 1949 help explain why it was not.

Kennan resigned as Director of the Policy Planning Staff at the end of 1949. He had separated himself from the line of his friend John Davies of scolding the Chinese. He now argued for recognition of the Peking government. Furthermore, during the early days of the Korean War, immediately prior to his departure from the State Department, Kennan opposed any attempt to move beyond the *status quo ante* on the Korean Peninsula. In addition, he advocated the admission of the People's Republic of China to the United Nations.[133] His recommendations hit a brick wall. The empirical approach, which he had done his part to construct, prevailed in the Truman administration. Especially after the Chinese intervention in the Korean War Truman vociferously opposed any political normalization with Peking. He fumed to Justice William O. Douglas, who advocated such a course, that "as long as I am president, if I can prevent it, that cutthroat organization will never be recognized by us as the Government of China and I am sorry that a Justice of the Supreme Court has been willing to champion the interest of a bunch of murderers by a public statement."[134] Over twenty years, and, one must add, much empirical evidence of differences between Peking and Moscow were to pass before the Nixon/Kissinger initiatives began the normalization in Sino-American relations.[135]

---

loser in China's civil war, stopped at the 38th parallel and not fought China in Korea, not had China condemned in the United Nations as an aggressor, not led a stiff international boycott against Beijing?" Edward Friedman, "Was Chinese-American Hostility Inevitable?" *Reviews in American History* 15 (September 1987): 504.

[133] Kennan, *Memoirs*, I, pp. 486–97. Stueck refers to Kennan as "the only high-ranking State Department official to urge diplomatic flexibility." He discusses Kennan's efforts in *The Road to Confrontation*, pp. 200–205.

[134] See Truman to Douglas, September 13, 1951, and Douglas's persuasive response of September 25, 1951, Truman Papers, PSF, Box 118.

[135] While prospects for normalizing relations with the P.R.C. did come to end with the Korean War, official efforts to promote a Sino-Soviet split did not. Indeed, it seems John Foster Dulles worked to this end. See John Lewis Gaddis, "Dividing Adversaries: The United States and International Communism, 1945–1958," in his *The Long Peace*, pp. 147–94. See also David Mayers, *Cracking the Monolith* in this regard. One should note also that John Paton Davies, who was fired by John Foster Dulles in November 1954, for having "demonstrated a lack of judgement, discretion and reliability," also had to wait until after the election of Richard Nixon to have his name finally cleared. See Kahn, *The China Hands*, pp. 258–61, 283–85.

CHAPTER EIGHT

Japan and Southeast Asia

MacArthur and the Japanese Occupation

In determining its China policy the Truman administration confronted the basic decision of whether or not to involve the United States to the extent that it would influence fundamentally the course of events within China. In Japan the situation varied markedly. Here such American involvement was accepted as a given. The central issue was not whether but rather in what direction the United States should seek to influence events in Japan. What changes should the United States seek to impose on the Japanese polity and society? What international role should Japan be permitted? These were questions that attracted George Kennan's attention from 1947 onwards and led to one of his most decisive interventions in the formation of his nation's foreign policy, an intervention so consequential in its implications that it alone richly warrants his inclusion among the important policymakers of the postwar era.

In mid-August of 1945 the long and destructive Pacific war came to an end as the unprecedented and indiscriminate explosive power of the atomic bombings of Hiroshima and Nagasaki forced the Japanese leaders to concede defeat.[1] General Douglas MacArthur received Japan's formal surrender aboard the battleship *Missouri* on September 2, 1945, and then moved to his Tokyo headquarters as Supreme Commander for the Allied Powers (SCAP) to direct the Allied occupation. "Never in history," MacArthur, in characteristically grandiloquent style, later alleged, "had a nation and its people been more completely crushed than were the Japanese at the end of the war."[2] While the Carthaginians might have objected to this sweeping judgment there was the sense of truth about it. When the American troops moved to occupy Japan they discovered much of the country in ruins. One historian has described it as "a ravaged land, whose urban dwellers lived amidst rubble, . . . shorn of the resources of empire and normal trade, inundated by some six-million pathetic civilian repatriates and returned servicemen, plagued by food shortages of staggering complexity and gutted by runaway inflation."[3] The Japanese

---

[1] On the ferocity of the Pacific War see John W. Dower, *War Without Mercy: Race and Power in the Pacific War* (New York, 1986).

[2] Douglas MacArthur, *Reminiscences* (New York, 1964), p. 281.

[3] J. W. Dower, *Empire and Aftermath: Yoshida Shigeru and the Japanese Experience, 1878–1954* (Cambridge, Mass., 1979), p. 293.

waited in shock and fear to see what MacArthur, who came quickly to personify the Allied occupation, would inflict upon them.

In contrast to Nazi Germany where the whole infrastructure of government collapsed and was replaced by occupation regimes in the various zones, in Japan the occupying authority chose to work through existing institutions. Far from punishing Emperor Hirohito, General MacArthur, after redefining the imperial prerogatives and attributes, permitted him to remain as Japanese head of state and sought to use him to implement the occupation. Furthermore, the existing governmental system continued with a scap superstructure placed over it. Japan avoided partition, operating instead as one administrative unit run by a government obliged to comply with scap directives. In determining the direction of the occupation MacArthur possessed the guidance of a presidential statement of August 29, 1945, entitled "United States Initial Post-Surrender Policy for Japan."[4] This outlined the broad goals of demilitarization and democratization. In his efforts to achieve them MacArthur enjoyed substantial autonomy. He regarded officialdom in Washington with suspicion and such was his prestige that few in the American capital sought to challenge or influence him. The representatives of the other Allied powers, among them Britain, China, and the Soviet Union, were sequestered on an ineffective Allied Council where they talked harmlessly and had little impact on occupation policy. Courtney Whitney, a key scap courtesan, argued in a grandiloquent manner similar to that of his master that "no proconsul, no conqueror, no generalissimo ever had more power over his subjects than MacArthur had over the people of Japan. His authority was supreme."[5] Despite the exaggeration here, MacArthur did exercise enormous power and he began to use it to effect major changes in Japan.

From his headquarters in the Dai Ichi insurance company's building opposite the emperor's palace scap demonstrated, in the words of another of his key aides, that "though the Emperor continued to reign, it was MacArthur who ruled."[6] The goal of demilitarization was vigorously pursued. The Japanese armed forces, numbering perhaps six million, were disarmed and demobilized. Those lodged overseas were repatriated to the home islands. Trials for war criminals were instituted. Parallel to these measures MacArthur launched a major program of democratization to transform Japan from a feudal society to a capitalist and, he hoped, Christian democracy. Discussion of the wide range of political and social reforms is beyond the scope of this study but one need only note such measures as the new Japanese constitution especially with its article on the renunciation of war, the emperor's renunciation of divinity, the change in the locus of sovereignty from the person of the emperor to the

---

[4] For the presidential statement see *Department of State Bulletin* 13 (September 23, 1945): 423–27.

[5] Courtney Whitney, *MacArthur: His Rendezvous With History* (New York, 1956), p. 229.

[6] Charles A. Willoughby, *MacArthur, 1941–1951* (New York, 1954), p. 305.

people, the extension of suffrage to women, the restoration of civil liberties, the revisions of the legal codes, the disestablishment of Shinto as a state religion, the liberalization of the educational system and curriculum, the encouragement of formation of trade unions, and the abolition of feudal land tenure to gain some appreciation of the changes wrought upon Japan.[7]

MacArthur approached his task of national rebuilding with an essentially paternalistic attitude towards the Japanese. He decided that they responded to "the *mystique* of the unseen ruler" so he barricaded himself behind what one occupation official called "the bamboo screen."[8] He met with few Japanese beyond the emperor and the various Prime Ministers. His remoteness applied also to officers of SCAP. Only a few occupation officials gained regular access to his Olympian heights, among them Brigadier General Whitney, who headed the Government Section; Major General William F. Marquat, who lead the Economic and Scientific Section; and Major General Willoughby, MacArthur's G-2 responsible for Intelligence. His isolation extended in a way even to his own country. He last had visited the United States in 1937 and declined invitations to return home to accept the gratitude and congratulations of his nation and to meet with President Truman. He deemed his own presence in Japan to be too crucial.

Destiny appeared to have prepared MacArthur to play the part of remote ruler.[9] He possessed a commanding presence, a suitably American imperial manner, and a surfeit of self confidence. His success as a general and military strategist during the Pacific War gave him a heroic aura which he utilized to the full. He spoke always with great certainty and in a way that left many listeners in awe and convinced of his genius. But MacArthur suffered from a seemingly unquenchable ambition and need to prove himself. From this developed his vanity, his suspicion of those who might obstruct or restrict him, and his barely disguised contempt for higher military and civilian authority. Such was MacArthur's ambition and contempt for those presently in authority in the United States that he deeply desired to be nominated for and elected to the presidency in 1948. And, as the historian Howard Schonberger has re-

[7] The literature in English on the occupation and on American policy-making during it is large and growing. Among the more important studies are: Michael Schaller, *The American Occupation of Japan: The Origins of the Cold War in Asia* (New York, 1985); Howard B. Schonberger, *Aftermath of War: Americans and the Remaking of Japan, 1945–1952* (Kent, Ohio, 1989); Theodore Cohen, *Remaking Japan: The American Occupation as New Deal*, ed. Herbert Passin (New York, 1987); Meirion and Susie Harries, *Sheathing the Sword: The Demilitarization of Japan* (New York, 1987); and Robert E. Ward and Sakamoto Yoshikazu, *Democratizing Japan: The Allied Occupation* (Honolulu, 1987).

[8] Cohen, *Remaking Japan*, p. 67.

[9] For biographical details on MacArthur at this time see D. Clayton James, *The Years of MacArthur*, vol. 3, *Triumph and Disaster, 1945–1964* (Boston, 1985); Michael Schaller, *Douglas MacArthur: The Far Eastern General* (New York, 1989); and William Manchester's popular and overly laudatory *American Caesar: Douglas MacArthur, 1880–1964* (Boston, 1978).

vealed, MacArthur's "every word and action in Japan was taken with an eye to supplementing his war-hero status in the United States with a reputation as a peacemaker and competent administrator over a civilian government," so as to further his presidential ambition.[10]

A Peace Treaty in 1947?

While the twin goals of demilitarization and democratization were pursued, economic conditions in Japan continued to deteriorate. But these troublesome economic circumstances proved an inadequate barrier when MacArthur decided the time was ripe to move towards a peace settlement with Japan. Cognizant of his own domestic political necessities the general wanted to wrap up the occupation in time for him to return triumphantly in advance of the 1948 elections. With this apparently as a principal factor in mind he surprised Washington in March of 1947 by announcing that the main work of the occupation had been completed and that the reforms he initiated had taken root. With Japan disarmed and on its way to becoming a political democracy MacArthur declared that the U.S. should withdraw its troops and negotiate a treaty with the former enemy. MacArthur sought to decouple the occupation from economic recovery in Japan arguing that the latter would occur after the occupation's end when other nations resumed normal trading patterns with the Japanese.[11]

MacArthur's comments provoked deliberations within the State Department during mid-1947 over the nature of a peace treaty. Rather than resulting in an agreed draft treaty for presentation to America's allies in the Pacific War—gathered formally on the Far Eastern Commission (FEC)—these discussions prompted a full reconsideration of occupation policy in Japan. Kennan played an instrumental role in instigating this reconsideration and figured prominently in shaping the revisions in policy which resulted from it. His efforts to derail a specific treaty proposal drew him into the determination of broad policy toward Japan.

In July of 1947 State Department officials met with representatives of the other member countries of the FEC in an endeavor to arrange a conference for preliminary discussions on a peace treaty for Japan. On August 6 the Japan specialist Hugh Borton, then serving as Chief of the Division of Northeast Asian Affairs and working under the impression that it was the State Department's "desire to call a peace conference for Japan as soon as possible," distributed copies of a draft peace treaty to senior officers of the State, Navy, and War Departments in an attempt to secure agreement to a document for

---

[10] Schonberger, *Aftermath of War*, p. 6 for quotation and pp. 40–81.

[11] This relies on Schaller, *Douglas MacArthur*, pp. 142–43; and Schonberger, *Aftermath of War*, p. 71.

submission to a conference of the FEC countries.[12] Borton's draft treaty "reflected the general idea that all precautions must be taken against a Japanese military renaissance" and included provisions for long-term Allied control and supervision of Japan's military potential, industrial capacity, and raw material stockpiles.[13]

On receiving his copy Kennan assigned John Paton Davies to look over it "informally."[14] The China specialist also served as Kennan's key aide on Japan and indeed on Asian matters in general. It did not take him long to respond to the draft treaty which disturbed him greatly. Four days later he reported to Kennan that the treaty in no way contributed to what he took to be the central American objective of creating a stable Japan integrated into the Pacific economy and friendly to the United States. On the contrary, it seemed preoccupied with restrictive measures overseen by international supervision which would provide the Soviet Union with a dangerous entree into the direction of Japanese affairs. In fact Davies, newly returned from Moscow and with his experience there fresh in his mind, went so far as to describe the Borton draft treaty as providing opportunities for the Russians to encourage "sovietized totalitarianism." Not surprisingly he recommended further discussions to harmonize the treaty with fundamental American objectives in Japan.[15] This counsel immediately persuaded Kennan and he sent Davies' recommendation directly to Under Secretary Lovett. He accompanied it with his own observation that the United States should formulate its objectives with regard to Japan—which he tellingly remarked had not been done "with any degree of concreteness"—before drafting a peace treaty.[16] Here Kennan skillfully shifted the emphasis from specific consideration of the Borton draft treaty to a larger investigation of American policy toward Japan. He also tempted the under secretary to involve the Planning Staff directly on this matter and with good effect.

Lovett quickly agreed that the draft treaty was "wholly inadequate in present form" and dispatched it back to the Division of Northeast Asian Affairs. He also formally requested that the Policy Planning Staff give its views on a peace treaty with Japan, thereby involving it directly in departmental deliberations on policy toward Japan. Having largely completed its work on the European Recovery Program and despite the arguments of officers from the Northeast Asian Affairs division that "no long delays be allowed to occur in connection with the peace-making process," the Staff decided to investigate

[12] Memorandum from Borton to Bohlen and others, August 6, 1947, *FRUS* 1947, VI, pp. 478–79.
[13] Frederick S. Dunn, *Peacemaking and the Settlement with Japan* (Princeton, N.J., 1963), pp. 58–59.
[14] Minutes of meeting, August 7, 1947, PPS Records, Box 32.
[15] Davies to Kennan, August 11, 1947, *FRUS* 1947, VI, pp. 485–86.
[16] Kennan to Lovett, August 12, 1947, *FRUS* 1947, VI, pp. 486–87.

the question at length.[17] In so doing Kennan and his colleagues seized the initiative on this matter within the State Department away from the formally responsible officers like Borton, James K. Penfield, and Max Bishop. They also maneuvered themselves into a position to lead a challenge to the direction MacArthur had imposed on the occupation. The initial outcome of these efforts was the gradual decline in prospects for an early peace treaty. MacArthur's call for a peace treaty in 1947 had been effectively sidetracked.

QUESTIONING OCCUPATION POLICY

In mid-August the planning group began consultations on Japanese matters. Of necessity they met with the Japan specialists from the Office of Far Eastern Affairs, among them Penfield, Borton, and Bishop, but these meetings failed to alleviate the Staff's substantive reservations about the approach reflected in Borton's draft treaty. To gain the military's perspective the Staff consulted with representatives of the Navy and War Departments lead by Rear Admiral E. T. Woolridge, Assistant Chief of Naval Operations, and Brigadier General Cortlandt Schuyler of the Army's Plans and Operations Division.[18] These meetings laid some preliminary foundations for a coalition of the State and Defense departments against SCAP. Additionally, the Staff called upon the expertise of some of the old Japan hands—Joseph C. Grew, the former ambassador to Tokyo and under secretary of state; Joseph Ballantine, a former head of the Far Eastern Division; and Eugene Dooman, formerly counselor in the American embassy in Tokyo.[19] All three men were certified members of the "Japan lobby" which from early 1947 pushed for the economic rehabilitation of Japan.[20] All three disagreed emphatically with the punitive concepts of Borton's draft peace treaty. And all three, respected elders for Kennan and his associates, influenced the more restrained views developing in the Planning Staff on a peace treaty with Japan. With Davies in the lead, and in Kennan's occasional absence also in the chair, the Staff wrestled with the complex issues involved. Here Kennan and the Staff's wider geopolitical perspective came to the fore. They did not narrowly focus on Japan but looked at that country in light of the new international situation brought on by Soviet enmity. From this

[17] For this argument see James K. Penfield to Kennan, August 14, 1947 (which includes a note on "Urgency of a Peace Settlement with Japan," by Max W. Bishop of the Northeast Asian Affairs division), Department of State Records, Decimal File, 740.011 P.W. (Peace)/8-1447.
[18] Minutes of Meetings, August 18, 25, 26, and 29, 1947; and September 2, 1947, PPS Records, Box 32.
[19] Minutes of Meetings, September 9, 1947 (Grew); September 10, 1947 (Ballantine); September 11, 1947 (Dooman), PPS Records, Box 32.
[20] See Howard Schonberger, "The Japan Lobby in American Diplomacy, 1947–1952," *Pacific Historical Review* 46 (August 1977): 335–36.

vantage point grew their belief that Japan must be politically and economically strengthened and linked in with America's own strategic objectives.[21]

Kennan presented the results of the Staff's study of the problems connected with the Japanese peace treaty to Secretary Marshall on October 14, 1947. This study (PPS/10) notably conveyed the need for Japan to be politically and economically stable before the signing of a peace treaty so that it might be capable of preventing Communist penetration and disruption.[22] As in Europe the specter of internal collapse and chaos which might be exploited by Communists most perturbed Kennan. After discussing the mechanics of negotiating a peace treaty, the Staff paper turned its attention to the contribution of existing occupation policy to developing political and economic stability in Japan. Unwilling to reach definite conclusions in light of the limited facts available to it, the Planning Staff deftly placed MacArthur's occupation under review by posing the fundamental issue as to "whether the directions under which SCAP is now operating are such as to make the maximum contribution to Japan's eventual ability to meet the strain of renewed economic independence." The Staff reported that it had heard directly opposite opinions on this question. The negative view held that the "present purge and decartelization policies" ran counter to the requirements of future political stability and economic vigor in Japan. SCAP categorically rejected this view.[23] In order to resolve this basic difference the Staff paper advised further discussions with SCAP. In his covering letter, Kennan recommended that a high official of the department concerned with policy matters be sent to review all essential points with MacArthur.[24] Of course, he suggested no names but one would not be deemed overly suspicious to infer that Kennan herein announced his own availability for the mission.

This preliminary paper from the Planning Staff quickly altered the whole framework of the State Department's approach to Japan. Apprised by the Staff of the dangers of any early relinquishment of control over Japan, attention within the department shifted away from the provisions of a peace treaty to the question of current occupation policy. Having previously sidetracked the peace treaty proposal the Staff now derailed it. In doing so they received indirect support from the failure of American efforts, due to Soviet and Chinese opposition, to arrange for a conference to discuss a peace treaty.[25] With the

[21] Minutes of meeting, August 25, 1947, PPS Records, Box 32.

[22] PPS/10, "Results of Planning Staff Study of Questions Involved in the Japanese Peace Settlement," October 14, 1947, FRUS 1947, VI, pp. 537–43.

[23] MacArthur's views are evident in the exchange between the War Department and the Supreme Commander. See Civil Affairs Division of War Dept. to MacArthur (No. 86537), September 22, 1947, in Admiral Leahy Files, JCS Files, Modern Military Records, NA, Box 7.

[24] Kennan to Marshall and Lovett, October 14, 1947, FRUS 1947, VI, pp. 536–37.

[25] On this see Butterworth's memorandum to Marshall on "Japanese Peace Treaty Discussions," September 22, 1947, State Department Records, Decimal File, 740.0011 P.W. (Peace)/9-2247.

advisability of a peace treaty questioned from within and the logistics of arranging for one proving burdensome, the United States simply ceased its efforts to make progress on this issue. Attention focused instead on the determination and implementation of occupation policy within Japan. The important, indeed seminal, character of PPS/10 is revealed in the way it redefined the American objectives in Japan and as a corollary the criteria for assessing occupation policy. Matters related to demilitarization and democratization were largely ignored. Concern focused on Japan's political and economic stability, and the occupation was to be judged on whether or not it served this end. Howard Schonberger correctly described the Planning Staff paper as the "document that became the basis for the National Security Council's NSC 13 series that governed Japan policy in 1948 and 1949."[26]

Secretary Marshall approved the Staff's study and accepted Kennan's recommendation that an official go to Japan for discussions with MacArthur.[27] The question of whom to send then arose. Aware of MacArthur's capacity to dominate his visitors, Lovett believed the proposal "only as sound as the man we send" and suggested the newly installed Director of the Office of Far Eastern Affairs Walton Butterworth, "since the only other two officers I would be happy about (Kennan and Bohlen) are not available."[28] Butterworth from virtually the moment of his appointment had agreed with the Kennan-Davies approach on Japan and, as on China matters, he cooperated well with the Planning Staff. But Marshall apparently balked at dispatching him to Tokyo. In yet another indication of his high regard for Kennan he wanted his planning chief to undertake this mission. Perhaps Marshall wanted to match Kennan's confidence in his own judgments and his substantial capacity for sweeping geopolitical assessments against those of MacArthur. After some deliberation it was decided that Kennan should visit Japan as soon as this could be arranged to study the whole problem on the spot and to formulate recommendations for American policy.[29]

Because of other demands cascading upon him—Italy, Greece, Palestine, China—Kennan delayed his departure for Japan until late in February of 1948. During the interim from the presentation of PPS/10 until his departure his views hardened on the inappropriateness of MacArthur's occupation policies. The strategic point of departure for Kennan lay in his belief, which of course he also had put to Marshall in relation to China policy, that Japan was the country in the Far East vital to American security because of its military-industrial potential.[30] Influenced by the astute Davies, Kennan minimized the possibility

[26] Schonberger, *Aftermath of War*, p. 72.

[27] For advice as to Marshall's approval see the note from Carlisle Humelsine to Kennan, October 29, 1947, State Department Records, Decimal File, 740.0011 P.W. (Peace)/10-2947.

[28] Lovett's handwritten comments are on Kennan's memorandum transmitting PPS/10, October 14, 1947, PPS Records, Box 33.

[29] Kennan, *Memoirs*, I, p. 377.

[30] See the section on the Far East in PPS/23, "Review of Current Trends: U.S. Foreign Policy,"

of a direct Soviet military threat to Japan but foresaw a real danger of Communist-inspired internal upheaval. The more closely he examined MacArthur's occupation policies the more inappropriate he found them to prevent such an upheaval because, as he judged them, they failed to foster political and economic stability.

Kennan revealed his views on October 31 when lunching with Navy Secretary Forrestal and Army Secretary Royall. According to Forrestal, Kennan said it had become clear "that the socialization of Japan had proceeded to such a point that if a treaty of peace were written and the country turned back to the Japanese it would not be possible, under the present economic machinery, for the country to support itself." He went so far as to raise the possibility of economic disaster and "near anarchy," which he explained was "precisely what the Communists would want."[31] Kennan severely condemned the program of breaking up the Zaibatsu (the large Japanese corporations) then being implemented by MacArthur in an effort to break up the enormous concentrations of wealth and hence to further Japanese democratic reform. Kennan preached to the converted in addressing Forrestal and Royall. As he later reported to Lovett, both men "voiced considerable concern over the situation of the Japanese economy."[32] They shared his concern at the direction of the occupation. Like them, Kennan evinced no real concern for developments in Japan on their own terms. He appeared not only quite uninterested in and unperturbed by the fact that the Zaibatsu had proved willing partners of the Japanese militarists but also unconcerned that their preservation would limit the genuine openness of the Japanese economy. He possessed no reforming zeal or inclination. His motivation rested solidly in his strategic concerns that Japan be prevented from succumbing to Soviet influence.[33]

Kennan placed his reservations about occupation policy directly before Marshall early in November in his general report on the world situation. In what had now become his familiar argument he alleged that the occupation policies had been "effective in disarming Japan and destroying the old patterns of militarism; but they have not produced, nor are they designed to produce, the political and economic stability which Japanese society will require

February 24, 1948, *FRUS* 1948, 1 (part 2), pp. 523–26. Also note Kennan, *Memoirs*, I, pp. 374–75.

[31] Diary entry October 31, 1947, in Millis, ed., *The Forrestal Diaries*, p. 316.

[32] Kennan to Lovett, October 31, 1947, PPS Records, Box 33.

[33] An indication of Kennan's strategic vision and focus is provided in his speech, "Problems of Far Eastern Policy" which he gave to the Council of Secretary of the Navy Sullivan on January 14, 1948. Here he outlined "two major objectives in Japan for the sake of our own security and to prevent Japan from falling into Russia's hands." These were: "(1) a stable, internally strong Japanese government and (2) a sufficient degree of disarmament to prevent the Japanese from threatening us." Kennan noted "that we have probably overdone the disarmament and not favored stability at all." See Kennan Papers, Box 17.

if it is to withstand communist pressures after we have gone."[34] He advised the secretary of state to correct this deficiency until which time Japan could not be safely released from the occupation regime. A thorough reexamination of policies was required. In December Kennan went further in his criticism alleging that the Russians "must consider that the general trend of developments in Japan during the occupational period has heretofore been favorable to their ultimate aims." Displaying no need to investigate matters on the spot in order to reach conclusions, Kennan referred to the policies of democratization, decartelization, and demilitarization, and argued forcefully that they eliminated "from influence in Japanese society elements which the Communists, for selfish political reasons, would wish to see eliminated." He remarked again on the "dubious prospects for future economic stability in Japan," and especially set the sights of his criticism on the "break-up of the Zaibatsu holdings."[35]

Kennan did not develop his views within a vacuum. They sprouted and grew within a milieu of questioning and criticism of American policy in Japan both within and outside the administration. Much of the questioning centered upon the program for Zaibatsu dissolution approved by the Far Eastern Commission and outlined in the document FEC-230.[36] But this specific criticism reflected a wider dissatisfaction with the reform measures which supposedly hampered economic recovery. During 1947 this dissatisfaction was increasingly expressed publicly.

Outside the administration Harry F. Kern, the foreign affairs editor of *Newsweek*, organized a small but influential lobby group which he developed into the American Council on Japan. Through it he launched a sustained campaign against the purge of businessmen and the Zaibatsu dissolution program generally.[37] Throughout 1947 he used the pages of *Newsweek* to assail the economic policies of the occupation. In the summer of 1947 he wrote a cover story criticizing the Zaibatsu dissolution and other occupation economic programs.[38] It is likely that Davies read this story and it may have influenced his initial critical assessment of Borton's restrictive and punitive draft peace treaty. In the December 1, 1947 issue of *Newsweek* Kern published portions of a report by an American lawyer, James Lee Kauffman, attacking in a powerful broadside the whole range of the occupation's economic reform measures and specifically assaulting FEC-230.[39] Kauffman, who had practiced law

---

[34] PPS/13, "Resume of World Situation," November 6, 1947, *FRUS* 1947, I, p. 775.

[35] Kennan to Butterworth, December 16, 1947, PPS Records, Box 23.

[36] The complete text of FEC-230 is included in Eleanor M. Hadley, *Antitrust in Japan* (Princeton, N.J., 1970), pp. 495–514.

[37] Kern's activities and their impact on policy formation are discussed comprehensively in Howard Schonberger, "The Japan Lobby in American Diplomacy, 1947–1952," pp. 327–59.

[38] *Newsweek*, June 23, 1947, pp. 36–42.

[39] See "A Lawyer's Report on Japan Attacks Plan to Run Occupation . . . Far to the Left of Anything Now Tolerated in America," *Newsweek*, December 1, 1947, pp. 36–38.

in Tokyo prior to the war where he represented important American interests like General Electric, Westinghouse, and Ford, was retained by American business interests—principally the Ford subsidiary Libby-Owens-Ford (a leading glass manufacturer) which had sizable Japanese investments—to critique SCAP's economic policies.[40] Prior to its partial release in *Newsweek*, Kauffmann's full report circulated among powerful Washington policymakers with devastating effect.[41] John Biggers, the president of Libby-Owens-Ford Glass company, discussed it and dispatched a copy to Commerce Secretary Averell Harriman.[42] Forrestal and Royall apparently possessed familiarity with its contents. And an important new figure on the scene, who emerged quickly as a key participant in Washington's discussions concerning the occupation, Under Secretary of the Army William Draper knew the details of the report and found them very persuasive.

Kauffman's report stimulated and confirmed the emerging consensus of dissatisfaction with the economic policies being pursued by MacArthur in Japan.[43] The need for a new policy to provide for Japan's economic rehabilitation was recognized widely. Draper, a former vice-president at Wall Street's Dillon, Read & Co., worried particularly that Japan's economic collapse would mean a further drain on the financial resources of the United States. Further, he saw that the SCAP economic policies complicated the possibility of obtaining appropriations from Congress which might aid Japan to move to a self-supporting state.[44] His more explicit economic concerns dovetailed neatly with Kennan's strategic concerns. The two men quickly formed an effective partnership. The challenge confronting the Washington policymakers, however, lay in how to translate their concerns into alterations in MacArthur's policies. The Secretary of the Army took it upon himself to voice his concerns publicly in a speech in San Francisco on January 6, 1948, although he avoided any direct criticism of MacArthur. Both the State and Army Departments, Royall observed, "realize that for political stability to continue and for free government to succeed in the future there must be a sound and self-supporting economy."[45] Royall's speech was noted in Japan, at least by the Japanese. Yoshida Shigeru, the future Prime Minister, later described it as "the first

[40] On Kauffman see Cohen, *Remaking Japan*, pp. 366–67; and Meirion and Susie Harries, *Sheathing the Sword*, pp. 207–8.

[41] A copy of the full report dated September 6, 1947, may be found in Harriman Papers, Box 246.

[42] Biggers to Harriman, October 2, 1947, Harriman Papers, Box 246.

[43] The impact of the Kauffman report is discussed in Schonberger, "Japan Lobby in American Diplomacy," pp. 331–36. For an indication of dissatisfaction see the comments of Royall, Forrestal, and Lovett, at the NSC meeting of December 17, 1947. See Minutes of 4th meeting of NSC, Truman Papers, PSF, Box 203.

[44] On Draper and his concerns see Schonberger, *Aftermath of War*, pp. 161–70.

[45] Royall as quoted in Hadley, *Antitrust in Japan*, p. 138.

public indication of a new emphasis'' in policy aimed at providing Japan with ''a healthy and autonomous economy.''[46] But SCAP remained unmoved.

Despite Royall's speech and the attack on the FEC-230 program during January by Republican Senator William F. Knowland of California, an unintimidated MacArthur vigorously proceeded with the plan to break up companies considered to be excessive concentrations of economic power.[47] MacArthur's defiant actions prompted discussions in Washington among the key second-level officials from State and Army who, in effect, had taken over the preparation of the administration's policy on this major issue. Kennan and Draper were joined by Butterworth and General Schuyler. Kennan reported on these discussions to Lovett on February 24. After noting that all four agreed, he advised the under secretary to instruct the American representative on the FEC to withdraw FEC-230 on the ground that circumstances had so changed since its submission ''that it no longer represents the current views of the American Government.''[48] Kennan argued that the withdrawal of FEC-230 would mean that ''the decks will be cleared for a basic re-examination of our policy with regard to [the] Japanese economy'' which should follow the visits to Japan which he and an Army department delegation led by Draper were about to make. His suggestion was rather disingenuous given that this basic reexamination of policy had been underway from the time of the preparation of PPS/10. When Kennan set out for Japan he could hardly play the part of a neutral observer intent on weighing the merits of the positions of both MacArthur and the occupation critics. The Planning Staff director numbered himself among those critics and with Draper acted as the key organizer of them. He already knew in which direction he wanted the occupation to go. His trip was not an exercise in gathering information. It was a part of a larger process to alter SCAP's policies.

A VISIT TO MACARTHUR

Kennan departed from Seattle on February 28 accompanied by Brigadier General Schuyler and Marshall Green, a young officer from the Division of Northeast Asian Affairs and a future Assistant Secretary of State for East Asian and Pacific Affairs, who served as Kennan's ''amanuensis.''[49] Green recalled that on this his first journey to the Orient Kennan read (more likely reread) the

[46] Yoshida Shigeru, *The Yoshida Memoirs: The Story of Japan in Crisis* (London, 1961), p. 40.

[47] Hadley, *Antitrust in Japan*, pp. 139–44; Cohen, *Remaking Japan*, pp. 168–69.

[48] Kennan to Lovett, February 24, 1948, PPS Records, Box 33.

[49] Green applied this description to himself. See author's interview with Amb. Marshall Green, July 6, 1978. Others in Kennan's small party included Colonel Harry O. Paxson and Lt. Col. Malcolm Gilchrist of the Army Department's Plans and Operations Division, and Miss Dorothy Hessman, Kennan's secretary.

Fig. 4. Kennan in Japan: The Policy Planning Staff Director pictured here during a conference with Japanese Prefecture officials in the office of Major General Joseph Swing (*left*), Commander, I Corps, Kyoto, Japan, March 8, 1948. Reprinted with permission of George F. Kennan and the Seeley G. Mudd Manuscript Library, Princeton University.

works of his namesake and distant relative on Siberia and that in an intellectual sense he arrived in Japan "from Vladivostock."[50] However this may be, Kennan appreciated keenly the delicacy of his mission and later remarked that it "was like nothing more than that of an envoy charged with opening up communications and arranging the establishment of diplomatic relations with a hostile and suspicious foreign government."[51] Although he was the most important State Department official to visit Japan since the beginning of the occupation—(and would remain so until John Foster Dulles's trip in June 1950 to launch discussions on a peace treaty)—Kennan told Butterworth that he "wished to avoid giving the impression of this being a high-powered mission."[52] Probably to ensure that his modest objectives circulated through the Washington rumor mills he wrote to Joseph Alsop that he did not expect to learn much "from such a flying visit." Nonetheless, as he told his journalist friend, "I may get a clearer view of some of the American personalities now involved" and he hoped to vindicate his "theory that just the smell of places . . . [would] help to plant an association and an interest and to turn abstraction into reality."[53]

The key American personality for Kennan to reach was Douglas MacArthur. Secretary Marshall, rather like a coach giving instructions, had cautioned Kennan to let MacArthur do the talking in the initial stages of their discussions and only after the Far Eastern General had said all he had to say should the planning chief bring forward the considerations of Washington.[54] The first part of Marshall's advice proved easier to carry out than the second. Kennan's party arrived in Tokyo after the long flight across the Pacific to be met with "a good deal of suspicion."[55] MacArthur immediately summoned Kennan for what Michael Schaller has referred to as a "ritual humiliation" and subjected him to a long monologue over lunch.[56] Caesar's occupation of Gaul was cited as the only comparable successful military occupation to MacArthur's own. The general waxed at length on his mission to bring Japan "both democracy and Christianity" and opined with assurance that the Japanese "were thirsty for guidance and inspiration." A weary Kennan remembered sitting "motionless in my humble corner."[57] After dismissing him, MacArthur shunted him off to receive a number of bland briefings from the staff of SCAP. The general

[50] Interview with Amb. Marshall Green, July 6, 1978.

[51] Kennan, *Memoirs*, I, p. 382.

[52] Kennan to Butterworth, February 10, 1948, PPS Records, Box 33.

[53] Kennan to Alsop, February 23, 1948, Papers of Joseph and Stewart Alsop, Box 3.

[54] Memorandum of conversation between Marshall and Kennan, February 19, 1948, PPS Records, Box 33.

[55] Author's interview with Amb. Marshall Green, June 6, 1978.

[56] Schaller, *Douglas MacArthur: The Far Eastern General*, p. 150.

[57] For Kennan's recollection of MacArthur's remarks and his reaction see his *Memoirs*, I, p. 384. See also Kennan's memorandum, "General MacArthur's Remarks at lunch," March 1, 1948, *FRUS* 1948, VI, pp. 697–99.

supposedly had greeted the news of Kennan's visit with ''a grim and cryptic: 'I'll have him briefed until it comes out his ears,' '' and his actions confirm this.[58]

Such treatment might have dampened the ardor of lesser men but Kennan, with Marshall's sage advice no doubt ringing in his ears, was not easily put off. Disguising his distaste for MacArthur, on March 2 Kennan politely wrote on the stationery of the Imperial Hotel thanking him for the briefings and ''the local hospitality'' but reminding him of his official mission, ''which,'' he explained, ''is to inquire—and to carry back to Gen. Marshall—your view of the broad framework of concepts which ought to underlie the decisions we shall soon have to take concerning our future course in Japan, and to give you any information that may be useful to you on the pattern of our over-all foreign policy problems, as we see them in Washington.''[59] Kennan's deferential tone might have gained him a second audience with MacArthur but it was at this point that Marshall Green's ''tactful effectiveness in liaison with the intermediate levels of SCAP'' came into play and provided the vehicle for Kennan to stimulate MacArthur's interest in him and to ensure his renewed access to the general.[60] Green had served in the Tokyo embassy before the war as private secretary to Ambassador Joseph Grew and he knew personally a number of the officials in SCAP who also had served in Tokyo in the prewar period. Green arranged through his former colleague Stanton Babcock—the prewar military attaché in Tokyo, now on MacArthur's staff—for Kennan to give a briefing on the Soviet Union to MacArthur's principal lieutenants, the senior officers of SCAP. Kennan delivered a ''brilliant presentation'' which traced the rise of Soviet power and influence ''right out of the mists of time when they were living in the forests of the steppes up to modern times.''[61] He revealed that MacArthur was not the only person capable of sweeping historical generalizations and geopolitical assessments and his SCAP audience was duly impressed.

Kennan's speech brought MacArthur's intelligence chief (''G-2''), General Charles Willoughby, to his hotel room one night eager to speak about the dangers of communism.[62] A long-time MacArthur aide—he had escaped with him from Corregidor—Willoughby was known without affection as ''Charles the Terrible.'' Born in Germany he favored reactionary politicians and military

[58] Kennan, *Memoirs*, I, p. 383.

[59] Kennan to MacArthur, March 2, 1948, MacArthur Archives, Norfolk, Virginia, R.G. 5, Box 32.

[60] The description of Green is from Kennan, *Memoirs*, I, p. 383.

[61] Interview with Amb. Marshall Green, June 6, 1978.

[62] Interview with Kennan, March 6, 1989. Kennan in his *Memoirs*, I, p. 385, suggests that General Willoughby saw him before his talk and organized it. I find Marshall Green's explanation for Kennan's presentation more persuasive and suggest that Willoughby visited Kennan after hearing his talk.

authoritarians and advised Kennan as to the virtues of General Francisco Franco in Spain. He hated Communists and applied that political label recklessly to various New Deal–type political activists involved in the occupation.[63] Indicative of the Byzantine rivalries of SCAP, he had long been suspicious of those officials clustered especially in General Courtney Whitney's Government Section who had pushed much of the reform agenda of the occupation. These suspicions gelled with some of Kennan's own concerns about the supposedly excessive reforms of the occupation and the two men struck up something of an association. Willoughby later showered Kennan with gifts to take back to Mrs. Kennan and for himself—including a samurai sword! Subsequently he corresponded with Kennan—whom he described as "a kindred spirit"—after the planner's return to the United States.[64]

The news of Kennan's memorable briefing presumably joined with Willoughby's assurances regarding Kennan changed MacArthur's attitude toward him. On March 5 the general met the diplomat alone for a long and comprehensive discussion. Prior to their meeting Kennan sent MacArthur a note conveying the message that many Washington policymakers thought the keynote of future occupation policy "should lie in the achievement of maximum stability of Japanese society" and raising U.S. security policy, economic recovery, and a relaxation in occupation controls as matters for discussion. MacArthur at their interview addressed each in turn. He spoke freely of his concept for an island defense strategy in the Western Pacific. He agreed that economic recovery should be made a primary objective of occupation policy but denied that there were additional moves he could take to achieve it. He defended the level of occupation control and particularly the reform measures, while explaining that some, such as the economic purge, were not as extreme as at times portrayed.[65]

MacArthur introduced his remarks by brazenly arguing that the Far Eastern Commission constituted an impediment to revision of occupation policy. Given the almost total control that SCAP exercised over the occupation Kennan demonstrated remarkable self-control to keep a straight face at this manufactured excuse to avoid any direct interference from Washington in the occupation. He went even further and offered MacArthur a way around his "difficulty" by cavalierly absolving him of any responsibility to the FEC. The

[63] See Cohen, *Remaking Japan*, p. 89.

[64] Kennan thanked Willoughby for "the lovely things you sent me at the hotel," and indicated his pleasure to "have such beautiful souvenirs of this brief visit," in Kennan to Willoughby, March 10, 1948, Papers of Major General Charles A. Willoughby, MacArthur Archives, Norfolk, Va. (facsimiles from Gettysburg College), R.G. 23B, Box 1. For examples of their subsequent correspondence see Willoughby to Kennan, April 8, 1948 (in which he pushed for a rapprochement with Franco); Kennan to Willoughby, May 20, 1948; Willoughby to Kennan, October 18, 1948; Kennan to Willoughby, October 27, 1948, in Willoughby Papers, R.G. 23B, Box 1.

[65] Kennan's memorandum of conversation, March 5, 1948, *FRUS* 1948, VI, pp. 699–706.

Planning Staff director pointed out that the terms of reference of the FEC called upon it only to outline policies for the implementation of the terms of surrender as based on the provisions of the Potsdam Declaration. He declared that these terms substantially had been carried out thus effectively terminating the FEC's policy-making functions—a view, incidentally, that would have shocked the other Allied members on the FEC.[66] In the resultant void Kennan suggested that the United States Government and MacArthur as its commander in Japan had to exercise independent judgment. Here Kennan tried to facilitate changes in occupation policy by removing MacArthur's disingenuous and self-imposed barrier to such changes. While Kennan recalled that MacArthur "slapped his thigh in approval" of his suggestion and that their meeting ended on friendly terms, he failed to convert the general to his view of the need for a shift in emphasis in the occupation. Soon after MacArthur indicated as much to Sir Alvary Gasgoigne, the head of the British Liaison Office, and complained about being treated by Kennan as a "purely American official."[67]

Kennan's astuteness allowed him to recognize that MacArthur had experienced no road to Damascus conversion and his report and recommendations eventually reflected this. But he took advantage of the elevated status which his long meeting with MacArthur accorded him and took up every opportunity to learn more of the occupation. He held further and more detailed discussions with SCAP staff in Tokyo. Then he moved from the capital and traveled with Green in a specially provided railway car to Kyoto and Osaka to observe more of the occupation firsthand.[68] As with the American occupation of Germany he didn't like what he saw. He deemed the occupation establishment "parasitical."[69] Its very maintenance preempted Japanese economic recovery. As for MacArthur's immediate headquarters, Kennan "recoiled at the 'stuffiness' and 'degree of internal intrigue' around MacArthur, which reminded him of 'nothing more than the latter days of the court of the Empress Catherine II, or possibly the final stages of the regime of Belisarius in Italy.' "[70] Indeed, Kennan raised pointed comparisons between MacArthur's court and the Kremlin under Stalin.[71] Nothing he saw or heard in Japan altered the critical views of the occupation which he had brought with him. Now, however, he could adopt an even more authoritative position in arguing for their adoption.

[66] On the position of the British see Roger Buckley, *Occupation Diplomacy: Britain, the United States and Japan, 1945–1952* (Cambridge, 1982).

[67] Gasgoigne to Foreign Office, 6 April 1948, FO 371/69886, PRO, quoted in Michael Schaller, "MacArthur's Japan: The View from Washington," *Diplomatic History* 10 (Winter 1986): 19.

[68] Interview with Amb. Marshall Green, July 6, 1978.

[69] Kennan, *Memoirs*, I, p. 387.

[70] Schaller, *The American Occupation of Japan*, p. 125. Schaller is here quoting from Kennan to Butterworth, March 9, 1948, PPS Records, Box 19, which he obtained through an FOIA request.

[71] Kennan to Butterworth, March 14, 1948, PPS Records, Box 19, cited in Schaller, *The American Occupation of Japan*, pp. 125–26.

POLICY RECOMMENDATIONS

Before departing Japan Kennan decided to wait for the arrival of William Draper's complementary mission focusing on the economic situation. Draper's party included prominent American business and industrial figures, among them Percy H. Johnston, chairman of the Chemical Bank (who served as nominal head of the mission); Robert F. Loree, former vice-president of Morgan Guaranty Trust, and chairman of the National Foreign Trade Council; and the former president of Studebaker, Paul Hoffman, whose appointment as head of ECA was announced during this mission. Just like Kennan, the Draper-Johnston mission began its investigation in Japan with predetermined conclusions. A scholarly critic of the mission remarked with some validity that "inasmuch as the mission, with no background on the Far East, drew up its recommendations, including a new set of reparation proposals on the basis of two weeks in Japan, it is clear that it did not come in search of information but rather a rostrum from which to enunciate the new policy."[72] The Draper-Johnston Committee made it obvious to SCAP that the problem in Japan was one of economic recovery.[73] Its report would combine with Kennan's report in formally altering policy in and towards Japan.

Kennan, after discussions with General Schuyler and with Green's assistance, wrote his report before he left Japan.[74] He already suffered from the painful illness that hospitalized him immediately upon his return to Washington. In shades of the Long Telegram, he dictated much of this report while he lay suffering in bed.[75] As with the earlier document his horizontal dictating position in no way inhibited his capacity to articulate his analysis and policy recommendations. He addressed first the question of a peace treaty. He advocated a nonpunitive treaty but explained that it should not be pressed for at that time. Instead the United States needed to concentrate on preparing the Japanese for the eventual removal of the occupation regime. After discussing security matters and the regime of control, Kennan moved on to occupation policy. Here he pointedly called for changes in existing policy and procedure. He advised that SCAP's functions be reduced to those of general supervision and counseled that it not press any further reform legislation on the Japanese government. As for existing reform measures he urged strongly that they be relaxed and provided specific details to this end with regard to the purge. After

[72] Hadley, *Antitrust in Japan*, p. 144.

[73] For detailed analysis of the Draper mission see Schonberger, *Aftermath of War*, pp. 180–90.

[74] Schuyler refers to his discussions with Kennan in his own "Notes on Far East Trip," April 10, 1948, in Records of U.S. War Department, Plans and Operations Division, R.G. 319, Decimal File, 091. Japan. (Obtained from facsimile in Marshall Library, Xerox 2328.) Schuyler's report was very supportive of Kennan's.

[75] Interview with Amb. Marshall Green, July 6, 1978. Green recalled that Kennan suffered from "ulcers."

these essentially corrective measures, he looked to the future and recommended that economic recovery be made "the prime objective of United States policy in Japan for the coming period." He outlined no detailed economic prescriptions because he knew this lay within the province of the Johnston Committee but he mentioned in general terms a U.S. aid program to stoke the Japanese economy, the revival of Japanese foreign trade, and a revised reparations program which would not handicap economic recovery.[76] He submitted this report (PPS/28) immediately upon his return to Washington on March 25. It was as Michael Schaller has noted "a comprehensive attack on MacArthur's program."[77] It served as a worthy successor to PPS/10 emphasizing, as had the earlier Staff paper, the strategic necessity of political and economic stability in Japan.

A month after Kennan submitted his report to the secretary of state the Johnston Committee submitted its report, for which Draper was largely responsible, to the Secretary of the Army. This report supplemented Kennan's. It provided more detailed recommendations on matters such as reparations, overcoming the economic uncertainty brought on by MacArthur's reform measures, and improving the climate for foreign investment in Japan. In addition to industrial recovery the report emphasized the importance of increasing Japan's merchant navy and warmly sponsored the American program for allocating funds to aid Japan's recovery.[78] When on May 20, 1948, the United States appropriated $150 million for the economic rehabilitation of Japan, it was attributed to the influence of the Johnston report and taken as an indication that a change of American policy towards Japan was underway.[79] This certainly was the case.

REVERSING COURSE

A change in formal policy, which would provide official sanction for redirecting Occupation policy, was indeed underway. Kennan's report served as the instrument for this change. At the end of April, Secretary Marshall described Kennan's paper on Japan policy to his fellow Cabinet members as "a very closely reasoned and persuasive document."[80] He indicated his intention to submit it to the National Security Council and then to the president. Prior to its submission to the NSC the interested divisions of the State Department con-

---

[76] PPS/28, "Recommendations with Respect to U.S. Policy Toward Japan," March 25, 1948, *FRUS* 1948, VI, pp. 691–96.

[77] Schaller, *Douglas MacArthur: Far Eastern General*, p. 151.

[78] The so-called Johnston report was submitted on April 26, 1948. It is discussed in Hadley, *Antitrust in Japan*, pp. 144–46.

[79] An example of Johnston's report being taken as a "turning point" in American policy are the comments of W. L. Holland, the Secretary General of the Institute of Pacific Relations, in his foreword to Edwin Martin's *The Allied Occupation of Japan*, pp. v–vii.

[80] Diary entry, April 30, 1948, Forrestal Diaries, Forrestal Papers, Box 4.

sidered Kennan's recommendations.[81] They did not quarrel with the main thrust of the proposals which began to gather an unstoppable momentum. When the Planning Staff director resumed his duties in the Department in late April he faced a veritable avalanche of issues dominated by the question of Western Union but he negotiated his way clear to hold discussions with Draper and General Schuyler and thereafter to make some comparatively minor revisions to his report. On May 26 George Butler, the Staff's deputy director, forwarded the revised version to Lovett for submission to the NSC.[82] The new paper (PPS/28/2) came with the joint recommendation of Kennan and Butterworth, who continued to cooperate well on this issue, advising approval by the NSC. Lovett forwarded the paper to the NSC on June 2, where Rear Admiral Souers, the Executive Secretary, referred the document—thereupon designated NSC 13/1—to the NSC Staff for its consideration and preparation of a report to the full Council.[83] The formal process to challenge MacArthur's control of the occupation and to alter the direction of it was well launched.

Running parallel to Kennan's efforts to change occupation policy through the NSC were his endeavors to impress on both the British and the Canadians the necessity of this new approach. The British, through Sir Alvary Gasgoigne, had complained at the time of the Kennan and Draper missions about the American failure to discuss what they correctly took to be "impending fundamental changes in American policy toward Japan."[84] Early in May Kennan, cognizant of these complaints, advised Marshall and Lovett that "a real job of diplomatic persuasion" would be required if the United States were to obtain the agreement of the majority of countries represented on the FEC to "any sensible occupation policy."[85] Conscious of the need to get the British on-side so that they might help in persuading other countries, particularly other members of the British Commonwealth, Kennan and Butterworth arranged for conversations with M. E. Dening, the assistant under secretary in the Foreign Office and the senior British official responsible for Far Eastern policy. In their discussions with him they argued against an early peace treaty for Japan and emphasized the need for "a program of recovery as opposed to

[81] For the generally supportive comments of the Economic Affairs and Occupied Areas divisions on Kennan's report see Memorandum by Assistant Secretary of State for Economic Affairs (Thorp) to Butterworth, April 6, 1948; and Memorandum by Assistant Secretary of State for Occupied Areas (Saltzman) to Butterworth, April 9, 1948, *FRUS* 1948, VI, pp. 964–66, 727–36.

[82] Memorandum from Butler to Marshall and Lovett, May 26, 1948, enclosing PPS/28/2, "Recommendations with Respect to U.S. Policy Toward Japan," *FRUS* 1948, VI, pp. 775–81.

[83] See NSC 13, June 2, 1948, and the attached note by the Executive Secretary to the NSC, National Security Council Documents, Modern Military Records, NA, Box 2.

[84] William Sebald (MacArthur's Political Adviser) passed on Sir Alvary's complaints in a cable to Marshall, March 29, 1948, a copy of which may be found in Leahy Files, Joint Chiefs of Staff Records, Modern Military Records, NA, Box 7.

[85] Kennan to Marshall and Lovett, May 5, 1948, Department of State Records, Decimal File, 740.0011 P.W. (peace)/4-2748.

reform, for stability as opposed to uncertainty.''[86] On a visit to Ottawa in early June Kennan placed similar views before the Canadians. He revealed the American apprehension—which he personally had done so much to foster—that a Japan turned free by a peace treaty would lack the economic and military resources to resist Soviet interference. He explained that the United States now favored a prolongation of the pretreaty occupation period during which controls over the Japanese government would be progressively relaxed and Japan would be assisted to again become an industrial power.[87] Kennan's encounters with the British and the Canadians were preliminary but important efforts to lay the groundwork among the close allies for the changes in occupation policy the United States was moving to implement. They again revealed Kennan as not simply a detached "planner" limited to offering counsel which others then implemented. He acted not merely as a navigator plotting a course but also proved capable of venturing into the engine-room of actual diplomacy to make progress along it. But in sharp contrast to the discussions with allies on the North Atlantic Treaty, where there was genuine exchange, on the Japanese matter the American mind was firmly made up. British reservations and requests for greater consultation proved no obstacle to the American determination to reverse course.[88]

NSC 13/1 arrived on the table of the National Security Council on September 30, 1948, after some detailed consideration especially concerning reparations payments. The Council, reflecting the consensus that Kennan and Draper had forged in Washington, adopted the draft report in slightly revised form (NSC 13/2) on October 7, and on October 9 Truman approved the NSC decision.[89] NSC 13/2 was the most important United States policy statement regarding Japan issued since 1945. Among policymakers in Washington it formalized the fundamental decision to alter the thrust of the occupation from reform to recovery. For Kennan it culminated over a year's effort to redirect Japanese occupation policy so that it would advance political, social, and economic stability which he deemed essential to make this strategically crucial nation less susceptible to internal upheaval that the Soviet Union might exploit. His effort was such that the historian of modern Japan, John W. Dower, has described him as "the father of reverse-course policy" and there is substantial

---

[86] For the discussions with Dening see memorandum of conversation by Lovett, May 27, 1948; and memorandum of conversation by Marshall Green, May 28, 1948, *FRUS* 1948, VI, pp. 782–85, 788–95.

[87] For Kennan's talks with the Canadians see the Memorandum prepared in the Canadian Department of External Affairs, June 3, 1948, *FRUS* 1948, VI, pp. 800–807; and Kennan to Marshall and Lovett, June 10, 1948, PPS Records, Box 13.

[88] For discussion of the British position on this question see Buckley, *Occupation Diplomacy*, pp. 159–70.

[89] See Souers to President Truman, October 7, 1948, which encloses NSC 13/2 on "Recommendations with Respect to United States Policy Toward Japan," *FRUS* 1948, VI, pp. 857–62.

truth to this assignation.[90] But Kennan worked in tandem with Draper and it was their partnership which ultimately prevailed. Both men deserve to share the credit—or blame—for the reversal in policy.

In his *Memoirs* Kennan claimed that his efforts on Japan "represented in their entirety a major contribution to the change in occupational policy that was carried out in late 1948 and in 1949." He even described his endeavors as, after the Marshall Plan, the most significant constructive contribution which he made in government.[91] Certainly Kennan played the central role in identifying and then articulating the need for a change in policy. After prompting from Davies Kennan's initial investigations shifted the State Department's attention from the nature of a peace treaty to the consequences of current occupation policy. He brought the department to focus on this matter. While his criticisms of SCAP's reform oriented occupation policies were shared both inside and outside the administration, Kennan's presentation of them was especially effective in convincing the senior State Department policymakers. Both Marshall and Lovett—neither of whom devoted major attention to Japan during 1947–1948 nor showed any personal inclination to challenge MacArthur—relied heavily on Kennan's analysis and recommendations. Precisely because of this Kennan's recommendations provided the basis for NSC 13/2 which became the official policy of the United States.

IMPLEMENTING THE NEW POLICY

While Kennan had played the principal role in devising the new occupation policy he passed the baton to Draper when it came time for its implementation.[92] Draper's key position in the Army Department and his commitment to enforce the new policy ensured that he became the point man in transforming the occupation.[93] In fact Draper had begun this process even before the new approach was accepted formally by the NSC. In May, 1948, he dispatched a carefully selected Deconcentration Review Board to Japan. This proved effective in blocking the MacArthur program to break up the Zaibatsu. It "whittled down the number of Japanese corporations facing deconcentration from the original 325 to thirty."[94] The congressional appropriation of funds for the economic rehabilitation of Japan also bore his mark. And when NSC 13/2 was accepted he wasted no time in enforcing its provisions. After discussions between the State and Army Departments, MacArthur was directed to implement the policy decisions of NSC 13/2—to eliminate restrictions on industry, to

---

[90] John W. Dower, "Rejoinder," *Pacific Historical Review* 57 (May 1988): 207.

[91] Kennan, *Memoirs*, I, p. 393.

[92] See Schonberger, *Aftermath of War*, pp. 195–97.

[93] Cohen refers to Draper as "the point man" in a different but related context. See *Remaking Japan*, p. 367.

[94] Schonberger discusses the matter in *Aftermath of War*, p. 81.

boost production, and to modify the purge.[95] But Draper determined that he couldn't rely on the existing SCAP authorities to oversee the new policy. Instead he arranged the appointment of a number of key officials who came to Japan to implement the program. First among these was the Detroit banker Joseph Dodge who arrived in early 1949 and orchestrated the economic stabilization plan.[96]

MacArthur at times disputed the Army Department's right to convey instructions to him as SCAP. He objected that the U.S. Government alone did not have the power to order him as Supreme Commander for the Allied Powers to change directives which had come through the FEC.[97] But with some of the wind knocked out of his sails by his humiliation in the 1948 Republican presidential primaries, MacArthur seemed less willing to battle Washington. As Michael Schaller has noted, while "he often criticized orders or delayed their implementation . . . [he] ultimately submitted."[98] By 1949 MacArthur and his SCAP officials had yielded substantial control of the occupation to officials like Dodge. And, in fact, MacArthur adopted increasingly conservative positions himself removing the chains from Willoughby who gleefully "began a search for conspiracies among Japanese leftists, suspected Comintern agents, and American liberals."[99]

In considering the implementation and the significance of the reverse course it is important to appreciate that it did not apply to the whole range of the reform agenda which SCAP had implemented. The surface democratic structures, the legal reforms, the changes in the status of women, and the variety of other important social reforms remained. The alterations in policy focused primarily in the economic domain but these had an inevitable major spillover into political life.[100] And such was the significance of the changes in these areas that they preserved and cemented in power the conservative economic

---

[95] For details see memorandum by Butterworth, October 27, 1948; and memorandum by Butterworth to Lovett, December 20, 1948, *FRUS* 1948, VI, pp. 878, 932–33.

[96] For a detailed discussion of Dogde's mission see Schonberger, *Aftermath of War*, pp. 198–235.

[97] MacArthur's position as outlined to his political adviser William Sebald is discussed in Sebald to John M. Allison, December 3, 1948, State Department Records, Decimal File, 740.0011 P.W. (Peace)/12-348.

[98] Schaller, *Douglas MacArthur: Far Eastern General*, p. 155. Schonberger argues persuasively that "MacArthur resisted NSC 13/2 in [only] two areas, the expansion of the national police organization and the return of purged individuals to public life." See his *Aftermath of War*, p. 83.

[99] Schaller, *Douglas MacArthur: Far Eastern General*, pp. 155–56. See also his *The American Occupation of Japan*, pp. 134–37.

[100] I find unpersuasive the conclusion of Justin Williams that "the Washington decisions, including the one on economic recovery, made no major impact on the occupation." For his argument see Williams, *Japan's Political Revolution Under MacArthur: A Participant's Account* (Athens, Ga., 1979), pp. 208–30. See also his "Completing Japan's Political Reorientation, 1947–1952: Crucial Phase of the Allied Occupation," *American Historical Review* 73 (June 1968): 1454–69.

and political elites which have governed Japan ever since. The leader of the conservative Democratic Liberal Party, Yoshida Shigeru, tellingly formed a new government in October 1948, and his political heirs subsequently have enjoyed virtually uninterrupted power.[101] The reprieved Japanese corporations reharnessed their energies and, with the close cooperation of the government, fostered the miracle of postwar economic development which now challenges the supremacy of the United States in the world economy. The Japanese political left found itself out in the cold. Critics of the reverse course have lamented these developments and expressed regret that the occupation failed in destroying entrenched conservative political and economic forces and proved unable to bring forth a more legitimately democratic and equitable society.[102] It is difficult to avoid some sympathy for this position—one's heartstrings normally are not tugged by concern for the Zaibatsu!—and yet it reflects a curious but characteristic American ethnocentrism. Perhaps also it underestimates the value of the political stability Japan has experienced over the past four decades. And, no doubt, it ignores Japan's reliability as a military ally of the United States for, although Kennan had not thought in these terms when challenging MacArthur's occupation policies, this became the next concern for American policymakers. Here Kennan drew the line.

A Neutral Japan?

Strategic concerns had been at the root of Kennan's apprehensions about Japan's occupation policy. Ironically, the acceptance of his critique of the occupation did not mean the endorsement of his view regarding Japan's place in America's global strategy. Kennan made this painful discovery during 1949 when his recommendations on American security policy in relation to Japan and on the timing of a peace treaty were rejected. For Kennan internal subversion and domestic upheaval comprised the real dangers. Consequently, he had recommended measures which aimed to ensure Japanese domestic cohesion and stability. He dismissed both the possibility of Russian military attack and the need for a long-term military relationship between the United States and Japan. The Defense Department disagreed. Perturbed by the deterioration of the Nationalist's position in China, uncertain about Russian intentions, and concerned to prevent any weakening of America's security position, the military began to consider the question of defending Japan and utilizing it in any conflict with the Soviets. The Defense Department strategists introduced the

---

[101] Once in power the political conservatives contributed to the change in occupation policy. This point is discussed in Ray A. Moore, "The Occupation of Japan as History: Some Recent Research," *Monumenta Nipponica* 36 (Fall 1981): 320.

[102] Howard Schonberger is a worthy representative of this position. See his "Conclusion" in *Aftermath of War*, pp. 279–85. For contemporary criticism see the observations by the Australian diplomat W. MacMahon Ball, *Japan: Enemy or Ally* (London, 1948), pp. 193–201.

necessity of maintaining American military bases and forces in Japan and raised the possibility of some Japanese rearmament.[103] On June 15, 1949, Secretary of Defense Louis Johnson submitted a Joint Chiefs of Staff paper on "Current Strategic Evaluation of the United States Security Needs in Japan," thereupon designated NSC 49.[104]

Kennan's comments on NSC 49 revealed his views. He discussed the JCS paper with his Staff colleagues on June 28 and then put pen to paper. He opposed the Joint Chiefs' proposal that American forces be retained in Japan after a peace treaty because he believed that this "would run counter to the objective of assuring Japan's political stability," which he consistently emphasized was of fundamental importance. He accepted that Allied forces should not withdraw from Japan until political stability and adequate defensive strength had been achieved there—until, in short, Japan was capable of standing on its own feet. From these two premises Kennan concluded that negotiations for a Japanese peace treaty should be postponed until Japan reached the stage when Allied forces could be withdrawn. He pungently observed that this lent renewed emphasis and urgency to the development of political and economic stability in Japan and he took the opportunity to promote the implementation on NSC 13/2.[105] Despite the Communist successes in China and America's disagreements with the Soviet Union, he possessed no desire either to use Japan as a base in American strategy against the Soviet Union or to lock Japan into a Western alliance. In his view American interests would be served adequately by the military-industrial potential of Japan simply being denied to the powers in the Kremlin. This could be guaranteed by the development of an independent and stable Japan which, as he explained to Rusk and Jessup, would restore the "natural balance of power." Kennan aligned himself with the earlier strategic outlook of Theodore Roosevelt and quoted favorably his remark to Senator Henry Cabot Lodge in 1905 that "It is best [that Russia] should be left face to face with Japan so that each may have a moderative action on the other."[106] But it was not to be.

As with his proposal for a reunified and neutralized Germany, Kennan found his proposals for an essentially neutral Japan rejected. During the fall of 1949 Secretary Acheson bowed to international pressure, applied by the British in particular, and agreed that the United States would turn its attention

[103] See Roger Dingman, "Strategic Planning and the Policy Process: American Plans for War in East Asia, 1945–1950," *Naval War College Review* 32 (November–December 1979): 4–21.

[104] NSC 49, "Current Strategic Evaluation of the U.S. Security Needs in Japan," June 15, 1949, National Security Council Documents, Modern Military Records, NA, Box 3.

[105] See Kennan's draft paper, June 28, 1949, PPS Records, Box 33.

[106] Memorandum from Kennan to Rusk and Jessup, September 8, 1949, under cover letter from Kennan to Rusk, October 6, 1949, PPS Records, Box 13, quoted in Schaller, *The American Occupation of Japan*, p. 182.

to a peace settlement with Japan.[107] Immediately the Pentagon objected that a peace treaty was "premature" unless it included provisions assuring the continuation of U.S. bases in Japan. Prolonged discussions on this question ensued between the State and Defense Departments. These soon focused more on the technicalities of arranging a continuation of the bases because the State Department acquiesced in the maintenance of American military presence in Japan.[108] As on the European security issue, with his defeats on the North Atlantic Treaty and the German question, Kennan's strategic vision for Japan found few takers. The Pentagon appeared to offer a more cautious and militarily sound course. Kennan's position had long been rejected when the Korean War broke out, but the North Korean aggression seemingly confirmed the necessity for American forces in Japan to maintain security in Northeast Asia. It served as an unnecessary but final nail in the coffin of notions about a neutral Japan.

With John Foster Dulles acting as principal negotiator the United States obtained the agreement of Japan to arrangements which ended the occupation while providing for the continued presence of American forces. On September 8, 1951, in San Francisco, the United States and its allies in the Pacific war —except the Soviet Union and China—signed a peace treaty with Japan. On the same day the United States and Japan signed a separate Security Treaty giving the U.S. the right to station its land, sea, and air forces in and about Japan.[109] Rather than risk the uncertainty of seeing Japan develop as an independent power the United States chose a strategy based on its alliance with a militarily weak and dependent Japan. The ultimate wisdom of this course is now being questioned in a climate of debates over burden-sharing and amidst recognition that America's direct commitment to Japan's defense allowed the Japanese to divert more of their own resources to their economic development while the United States committed more of its national treasure into less productive defense spending.[110] Kennan might be seen as providing early warn-

[107] In a discussion of Far Eastern Affairs in preparation for conversations with Bevin in September 1949, Butterworth informed Acheson "that the British were now desirous of pressing vigorously forward with the Japanese Peace Treaty." Report by Charles W. Yost, September 16, 1949, *FRUS* 1949, VII, pp. 1204–8. Bevin did put this view to Acheson who agreed to look at the "procedure for going forward with the Japanese peace treaty." See Acheson's record of his conversation with Truman informing him of this, September 16, 1949, State Department Records, Office of Executive Secretariat, Box 3.

[108] For details of the objections of the Pentagon and the subsequent discussions see Acheson, *Present at the Creation*, pp. 428–35. On this question see also Schonberger, *Aftermath of Peace*, pp. 240–43.

[109] See Dunn, *Peacemaking and the Settlement with Japan*; Bernard C. Cohen, *The Political Process and Foreign Policy: The Making of the Japanese Peace Treaty* (Princeton, N.J., 1957); and Ronald W. Pruessen, *John Foster Dulles: The Road to Power* (New York, 1982), pp. 432–98.

[110] Paul Kennedy's *The Rise and Fall of the Great Powers: Economic Change and Military Conflict from 1500 to 2000* (New York, 1987), pp. 459, 532–33, is instructive here.

ings against America's imperial overreach. He wanted Japan to resume the normal characteristics of a significant national actor able to play its part in balance of power calculations. Four decades later Japan hesitatingly moves to translate its economic strength into political and diplomatic influence and thus to play the role Kennan assigned to her, with what results we shall have to see.

SOUTHEAST ASIA AND THE NATIONALIST GROUNDSWELL

In his October 1947 paper (PPS/10) calling for emphasis on Japanese economic and political stability Kennan had raised the issue of the impact on Japan of its loss of markets and raw materials sources in Asia. Without this Asian trade, he explained, "Japan faces, even in the best of circumstances, an economic problem of extremely serious dimensions." As political stability seemed impossible without Japan's having "a fair chance of a satisfactory economic future" Kennan had confronted issues of economic policy.[111] This not only led to his concern about the reform measures within Japan but also led him to look at Japan's overseas economic needs. This in turn brought him to focus attention on an area which—the Philippines aside—had never been an American priority: Southeast Asia.[112] In his consideration of this area and its relationship to Japan, Kennan, as always on Asian matters, benefitted from the counsel of John Paton Davies.

Davies' attendance at a conference of American diplomatic representatives in Southeast Asia in June, 1948, stimulated his consideration of the region's importance. Serving as the State Department's representative at the meeting in Bangkok which brought together officials assigned to Burma, Indochina, Malaya, the Netherlands East Indies, the Philippines, Siam, India, and China, Davies bluntly stated—in a manner that presaged John Foster Dulles—that the United States was "tying Southeast Asia in as a regional block against Communism, just as we are trying to build up in Europe a regional organization against Communism and would like to do in the Middle and Near East." But Davies was attuned to the nationalist fervor running rampant in the region as independence movements strove to throw off colonial masters. He recognized the validity of these movements and worried that only the Communists exploited them. In Asia, he noted, "the Russians have captured the native movement and we are in opposition to them." The problem was that "on the Asiatic

---

[111] PPS/10, "Results of Planning Staff Study of Questions Involved in the Japanese Peace Settlement," October 14, 1947, *FRUS 1947*, VI, p. 541. Kennan was not the only one to make the connection. See the discussion in William S. Borden, *The Pacific Alliance: United States Foreign Economic Policy and Japanese Trade Recovery, 1947–1955* (Madison, 1984), pp. 108–9.

[112] For overviews of United States policy in Southeast Asia see Gary R. Hess, *The United States' Emergence as a Southeast Asian Power, 1940–1950* (New York, 1987); Russell H. Fifield, *Americans in Southeast Asia: The Roots of Commitment* (New York, 1973); and Andrew J. Rotter, *The Path to Vietnam: Origins of the American Commitment to Southeast Asia* (Ithaca, 1987).

groundswell the Russians are riding [while] we are bucking." The solution lay in the United States trying "to get on a groundswell ourselves."[113] This willingness to place the U.S. on the side of non-Communist nationalist movements battling against colonial powers, who also happened to be America's European allies like the Dutch, showed Davies at his insightful best. He saw the writing on the wall for the colonialists and wanted to establish Southeast Asia as an independent region. He appreciated well that over the long haul this would best serve America's national interest and began to develop a paper within the Planning Staff to this end.[114] He succeeded in persuading Kennan, who possessed no natural sympathies for Asian peoples struggling for independence, of the wisdom of this course.

Kennan adopted Davies' advice with a vengeance and applied it especially to Indonesia where the nationalist leader Sukarno led the movement to shed the rule of the Dutch and to establish a republic. At the end of 1948 Kennan wrote to Marshall and Lovett that Indonesia was "the most crucial issue of the moment in our struggle with the Kremlin." As he described the situation the Dutch had lost their authority so the choice confronting the Americans did not lay "between Republican and Dutch sovereignty of these islands but between Republican sovereignty and chaos." In a resort to almost histrionic hyperbole he then intoned to his superiors that "we know that chaos is an open door to communism." The fall of Indonesia to communism would mean the quick collapse of Siam and Malaya and lead to "a bisecting of the world from Siberia to Sumatra." Such a development, he warned, could "lead to communist denial of our east-west global communications" and would leave Australia critically vulnerable. And, in an early explication of a version of the domino theory, Kennan asserted that "it would only be a matter of time before the infection would sweep westward through the continent to Burma, India, and Pakistan." Turning to the other side of the coin, Kennan expounded on Indonesia's positive value to the United States. It was the "anchor in that chain of islands stretching from Hokkaido to Sumatra which we should develop as a politico-economic counter-force to communism on the Asiatic land mass."[115] With all this said Kennan proceeded to recommend pressuring the Dutch to concede, a course which incidentally the United States adopted during 1949.[116]

[113] See record of the Southeast Asia Regional Conference, June 21–June 26, 1948, in John F. Melby Papers, HSTL, Box 9.
[114] Davies already had a draft of this paper by late July. See Minutes of meeting, July 30, 1948, PPS Records, Box 32. Discussions on it involving various members of the regional offices continued off and on until early 1949. See minutes of meetings, November 24, 1948; December 8 and 14, 1948; March 3 and 23, 1949; PPS Records, Boxes 32 and 33.
[115] Kennan to Marshall and Lovett, December 17, 1948, PPS Records, Box 33.
[116] On American policy see Robert J. McMahon, *Colonialism and Cold War: The United States and the Struggle for Indonesian Independence, 1945–49* (Ithaca, N.Y., 1981), pp. 251–316.

Under Davies' influence Kennan not only developed a firm appreciation for the importance of Southeast Asia but also propagated this within the State Department in 1949. At the same time that they diminished China's importance to Western security Kennan and Davies emphasized the crucial role of the region to its south. Southeast Asia's strategic importance and its related indispensable part as both supplier of raw materials to Western Europe and Japan and potential market for manufactured goods assured it significance in American calculations.[117] When Acheson took over as secretary in January of 1949 and asked the Planning Staff for its advice in developing Southeast Asia policy, the two men were already well primed. The result of their endeavors, in which Davies played the key role, came in a study entitled "United States Policy Toward Southeast Asia" (PPS/51). Michael Schaller has argued that this document "formed the basis of Asian containment doctrine for the next two decades."[118] One might wish that its recommendations had been adopted in their entirety but tragically for the United States and for certain of the peoples of Southeast Asia this was not to be.

The planners sought to ring the death knell for European colonialism. They declared "19th century imperialism" to be "no longer a practicable system in SEA [Southeast Asia] excepting in the short run in Malaya."[119] The attempt to preserve it created only destructive political problems and left the region in an unsettled state where it could make but "limited contributions to ERP countries' self-support, to the solution of India's food problem or to the orientation of Japan's trade southward in search of survival." The Planning Staff reemphasized, as Kennan and Davies had done in 1948, the strategic importance of the region. Southeast Asia represented "a vital segment on the line of containment, stretching from Japan southward around to the Indian Peninsula. The security of the three major non-communist base areas in this quarter of the world—Japan, India and Australia—depend[ed] in a large measure on the denial of SEA to the Kremlin." This region needed to be viewed "as an integral part of that great crescent formed by the Indian Peninsula, Australia and Japan." What then could be done? For the Planning Staff, guided by Davies, "the first essential requirement for resistance to Stalinism" in this region lay in "the satisfaction of [its] militant nationalism." The Staff launched a powerful salvo against Dutch and French colonialism in Indonesia and Indochina

[117] For discussion on this see Schaller, *The American Occupation of Japan*, pp. 157–58. Schaller has led the way in showing the connection between Japan and Southeast Asia in American strategic planning. See his "Securing the Great Crescent: Occupied Japan and the Origins of Containment in Southeast Asia," *Journal of American History* 69 (September 1982): 392–414.

[118] Schaller, *The American Occupation of Japan*, p. 159.

[119] PPS/51, "United States Policy Toward Southeast Asia," March 29, 1949, in Nelson, ed., *The State Department Policy Planning Staff Papers*, III, pp. 32–58. All the quotations in this paragraph are drawn from this document.

respectively, describing it as "the greatest single immediate factor contributing to the expansion of communism in SEA." In light of this analysis it recommended that the United States persuade the Dutch and French to alter their policies. They suggested as a first step to this end cooperation with the British to outline the gravity and the reality of the overall situation to these rigid colonial powers. The Planning Staff wanted to eliminate the complications of colonial domination so that non-Communist Asian nationalists might more effectively oppose communism and allow for the economic development of their region in integral cooperation with Japan and Western Europe.[120]

Acheson received PPS/51 sympathetically and even engaged in conversations with Bevin on Southeast Asia coincident with the British Foreign Secretary's visit to Washington in April 1949 for the signing of the North Atlantic Treaty. But in terms of actual policy and actions the United States moved cautiously, somewhat to the dismay of the British who wanted to involve the Americans more deeply in this region in the battle against communism.[121] While the Truman administration applied some pressure to the Dutch it proved unwilling to do the same to the French, contrary to the recommendations of PPS/51. Instead it acquiesced in the French subterfuge to maintain their control of Indochina whereby they installed the former Emperor Bao Dai as head of a nominally independent Vietnam within the French Union—which the Staff had described as a "puppet regime" in anticipation of just such a move. The administration, as Michael Schaller correctly has pointed out, "heard only part of Kennan's message. It accepted the argument that Southeast Asia formed a critical link in the Great Crescent, but it ignored [the suggestion] that the United States move with, as far as possible, a real nationalist tide."[122] Future administrations would pay a high price for this partial acceptance.

Kennan and Davies continued their efforts throughout 1949 to engender a more positive American approach in Southeast Asia. In July Kennan submitted to Webb, Jessup, Bohlen, and Rusk a paper drafted by Davies outlining a program of specific actions "to create a new and hopeful atmosphere in our East and South Asian policy."[123] In the major National Security Council paper (NSC 48/2), "The Position of the United States with Respect to Asia" accepted at the end of 1949, the influence of the Planning Staff was still obvious in its close linkage of Southeast Asia with Japan. But, under Pentagon pressure, the

[120] Schaller discusses this at further length in *The American Occupation of Japan*, pp. 158–60.

[121] For details on British policy and their attitude to the Americans see Ritchie Ovendale, *The English-Speaking Alliance: Britain, the United States, the Dominions and the Cold War, 1945–1951* (London, 1985), pp. 154–78.

[122] Schaller, *The American Occupation of Japan*, p. 163. I have relied heavily on Schaller's excellent analysis of these matters.

[123] Kennan to Under Secretary et al., July 8, 1949, enclosing "Suggested Course of Action in East and South Asia," July 7, 1949, PPS Records, Box 33. This paper and its impact is discussed by Philip C. Jessup in *The Birth of Nations* (New York, 1974), pp. 24–26.

NSC's support for Asian nationalism was more ambiguous and its attention given to the Soviet military threat and the need for a military response more extensive than that of Kennan and his colleagues.[124] The American decisions in early 1950 to recognize the Bao Dai government in Vietnam and then to extend it military and economic assistance symbolized the new American position.[125] These decisions, which started the United States down the dangerous slope to its tragic and costly involvement in Vietnam, also indicated the rejection of Kennan's views. The outbreak of the Korean War, much to Kennan's dismay, cemented the United States in the more military oriented course it was pursuing in Asia.

In late August 1950, just before he left the State Department, Kennan made a final attempt to persuade Acheson of the dangers of what he termed "the Pentagon's present approach" to Far Eastern Policy matters. In his cover letter to Acheson he succumbed to the temptation of annoying self-pity and expressed the fear that "like many of my thoughts, [these] will be too remote from general thinking in the Government to be of much practical use to you."[126] In his paper Kennan then included some of the most prescient views on the American approach to Southeast Asia which would be offered for the next twenty years. Much of his paper focused on Japan and here he repeated his objections to continued United States military presence there and outlined the necessity to allow Japan to develop its own capability to resist Soviet pressure. When he turned to Southeast Asia Kennan addressed the Indochina situation with a chilling clarity, as can be seen in retrospect. "In Indochina," he told Acheson, "we are getting ourselves into the position of guaranteeing the French in an undertaking which neither they nor we, nor both of us together, can win." He advised that the French be told that their position was "basically hopeless." And the "founding father of containment" suggested that the preferable course involved permitting "the turbulent political currents of that country to find their own level," even if this meant "the spreading over the whole country of Viet-Minh authority."[127] Vietnam could be separated from the larger questions of the global contest with the Soviet Union.[128] Such sage

[124] NSC 48/2, December 30, 1949, NSC Documents, Modern Military Branch, NA, Box 2. For discussion of NSC 48/2 and the debate between State and Defense over it see Schaller, *The American Occupation of Japan*, pp. 195–211.

[125] On the American decisions see Gary R. Hess, "The First American Commitment in Indochina: The Acceptance of the 'Bao Dai Solution,' 1950," *Diplomatic History* 2 (Fall 1978): 331–50.

[126] Kennan to Acheson, August 23, 1950, Acheson Papers, HSTL, Box 65.

[127] Ibid., August 21, 1950.

[128] Kennan's views presaged the criticism of American involvement in Vietnam by scholars like George Herring who argues that "by wrongly attributing the Vietnamese conflict to external sources, the United States drastically misjudged its internal dynamics. By intervening in what was essentially a local struggle, it placed itself at the mercy of local forces, a weak client, and a determined adversary. It elevated into a major international conflict what might have remained a

views received no favorable response within the Truman administration. Kennan's influence over his nation's policy toward Asia had ended completely. His "ideas would surface again, some sixteen years later, when the Senate Foreign Relations Committee belatedly held hearings trying to trace the course which had brought us [the U.S.] that far."[129] Regrettably, by then it was too late.

---

localized struggle." See his *America's Longest War: The United States and Vietnam, 1950–1975*, 2d ed. (New York, 1986), p. 324.

[129] David Halberstam, *The Best and the Brightest* (New York, 1972), p. 340.

Fig. 5. Kennan's Staff circa 1948–1949. *From left to right*: Robert P. Joyce, Ware Adams, George H. Butler, George F. Kennan, John Paton Davies, Carlton Savage, unidentified, Dorothy Fosdick. Reprinted with permission of George F. Kennan and the Seeley G. Mudd Manuscript Library, Princeton University.

CHAPTER NINE

The Hydrogen Bomb and the Soviet Threat

BRITAIN AND EUROPEAN INTEGRATION

Early in 1949, the Commission on Organization of the Executive Branch of Government—known as the Hoover Commission after its chair, former president Herbert Hoover—submitted its hefty report to the Congress. In its section on the State Department the Commission favorably acknowledged the contribution of the Policy Planning Staff and described it as "a valuable aid to the top command of the State Department, especially as an 'anticipator' of problems." The Commission report, however, suggested that the Staff's effectiveness had been lessened particularly "by the tendency of the top command to utilize it on day-to-day problems."[1] In a written response to Under Secretary Webb, to which Kennan gave his approval, Deputy-Director George Butler accepted the validity of the Commission's observation and indicated the Staff's resolution to rectify the situation. Butler told Webb of the feeling of the Staff members that "we should not be drawn into operations and we shall make renewed effort to confine our activities to planning."[2] To enable the Staff to focus more on "planning," a State Department reorganization moved the liaison responsibilities with the National Security Council from Kennan to Dean Rusk as deputy under secretary for substantive affairs.[3] Appropriately unburdened, Kennan devoted a special effort throughout 1949 to the task of long-range planning. He confronted such complex questions as European integration and Britain's international role, international control of atomic weapons, and the development of the hydrogen bomb. In the end his attempts to look beyond the immediate horizon brought him little but defeat and frustration. The latter grew so intense that by the year's end he tendered his resignation as director of the Policy Planning Staff.

Kennan's concern with the long view drew him to the issue of European integration and union. American policymakers had pushed the value of eco-

---

[1] The Commission on Organization of the Executive Branch of the Government, *Report* (Washington, D.C., 1949), p. 55. The Commission report also mentioned as other factors inhibiting the effectiveness of the Planning Staff, its exclusive reliance for its staff on individuals with Foreign Service background and its reluctance to draw sufficiently upon the resources of other departments and agencies.

[2] Butler to Webb, March 14, 1949, PPS Records, Box 33.

[3] Nelson, "President Truman and the Evolution of the National Security Council," pp. 371–72.

nomic and political cooperation upon the Europeans from the time of the initiation of the Marshall Plan and by 1949 some limited progress had been made in this direction, especially through the Organization for European Economic Co-operation (OEEC). But the American views lacked specificity and clarity, especially regarding the role the United States expected Great Britain to play in a united Europe.[4] The need for greater coherence in the American approach stood out. This question of Britain's relationship with continental Europe also bore more than a little interest for policymakers in London. Early in the spring of 1949 Kennan took the initiative to connect with the British. He mentioned to Gladwyn Jebb, under secretary in the Foreign Office whose bailiwick included planning and who happened to be visiting Washington with Bevin for the signing of the North Atlantic Treaty, that he would like to talk over these matters to get a clearer sense of the British perspective.[5] Jebb proved quite amenable and soon after wrote Kennan inviting him to come to London for informal discussions with members of the Foreign Office on such matters of long-range policy as the integration of Europe and collaboration between the U.S., U.K., and Canada. Kennan advised the Staff of Jebb's invitation on April 11 and by the month's end he gained Acheson's approval of his acceptance. The secretary certainly had no objection to the talks and expressed the view that "they might be quite helpful."[6] Kennan set about to make sure this would be so.

At the very time when he witnessed the final interment of his Program A at the Paris CFM Kennan launched off on another major investigation of broad European issues. He used as his device in structuring the policy discussions in preparation for his meetings with the British one of the questions raised by Gladwyn Jebb, namely whether "the emergence of a United Western Europe (with or without the United Kingdom) postulates the formation of a third world power of approximately equal strength to the United States and the Soviet Union." Kennan put it more succinctly as "whether there are to be two worlds or three."[7] To assist in the consideration of this matter, plainly gargantuan in its implications, the Planning Staff director indicated his desire not only to have extensive consultations with officials within the administration but also to bring in distinguished outside consultants to benefit from their perspectives.[8] In doing so he carefully conformed to another recommendation of the Hoover Commission with regard to the Policy Planning Staff. He appears to have self-consciously sought to make the consideration of this matter a model exercise in long-term planning. On this issue the U.S. didn't confront an im-

---

[4] For Kennan's own discussion of these issues see *Memoirs*, I, pp. 449–50.

[5] Kennan mentions his taking the initiative in ibid., p. 451.

[6] Minutes of meeting, April 11, 1949, PPS Records, Box 32; Memorandum of conversation, April 28, 1949, Executive Secretariat Records, Box 1.

[7] Minutes of meeting, May 18, 1949, PPS Records, Box 32.

[8] Ibid., May 17, 1949.

mediate crisis situation. The demands of day-to-day policy did not dictate hasty action. In this rather unusual circumstance Kennan aimed to seize the opportunity to map out what kind of structure the United States should seek to foster in Europe.

In preparation for his meetings with the outside consultants Kennan and his colleagues began a series of discussions with key departmental officials, among them Dean Rusk, Theodore Achilles, Willard Thorp, and Henry F. Labouisse. Major General Truman H. Landon from the JCS staff and Harlan Cleveland from the Economic Cooperation Administration also joined in. A willingness to confront the large questions and to engage in sweeping judgments characterized these wide-ranging sessions. The meetings possessed a strongly nonbureaucratic flavor. With Kennan in the chair they took on the brainstorming character of a think-tank discussion. From the many words and ideas put forward some key thoughts began to emerge in Kennan's mind. The need to create some form of union in Europe strong enough and vast enough to incorporate Germany held pride of place. He joined to this a developing appreciation of Britain's unwillingness to yield any of its sovereignty to such a European union.[9]

Kennan staged two three-day conferences with his outside consultants during the first and third weeks of June.[10] He brought together a diverse but extraordinary group of individuals including physicist J. Robert Oppenheimer, then the director of the Institute for Advanced Study in Princeton, N.J., but whose stature derived from his directorship of the Los Alamos laboratory of the Manhattan Project; businessman Robert W. Woodruff, the chairman of Coca Cola Company; theologian Reinhold Niebuhr of Union Theological Seminary; Lieutenant General Walter Bedell Smith, then commanding the First Army but Kennan's former chief in Moscow and soon to be named Director of Central Intelligence; the political scientists Arnold Wolfers of Yale and Hans Morgenthau of the University of Chicago; and banker Frank Altschul, a trusted Kennan friend who would play such a crucial role in establishing Radio Free Europe. Along with these influential figures Kennan included most of the government officials he had met with previously and some others including John J. McCloy, the recently named U.S. High Commissioner for Germany. Together, as Michael Hogan has noted, "these men helped to launch the State Department's first full-blown effort to hammer out a policy on European unification."[11]

In his discussions with the consultants Kennan subtly but constantly supported the formation of a third force in Europe. In a clear demonstration that his specific defeat on Program A had not altered his general view of the neces-

[9] Ibid., May 20, 25, and 27, 1949; and June 3, 1949.

[10] For these deliberations and the participants see ibid., June 6–8 and 13–15, 1949.

[11] Hogan, *The Marshall Plan*, p. 258.

sities of the European situation, he observed that the United States should "be much more modest about [its] role in the world" and raised the possibility that the U.S. permit "something in the nature of a neutral force to grow up in Europe today between east and west," as a way of arranging the retirement of both the Americans and Soviets from Europe.[12] This European entity would need to be large enough to safely incorporate Germany and one which would simultaneously attract German loyalties and attention. While the consultants all backed measures to increase European economic and political cooperation they balked at Kennan's vision of an unaligned European union. As in the past the Soviet threat proved to be the rock upon which Kennan's arguments foundered. In an exchange with Kennan on how to avoid war with the Soviet Union, Bedell Smith commented that "our only hope of avoiding it is to retain such a preponderance of strength on our side that they won't dare."[13] Cutting Europe loose seemed risky in light of this analysis. Furthermore, most of the consultants questioned if the European entity envisaged by Kennan could contain German power especially, as they all conceded, as Great Britain would be unlikely to participate.

Kennan remained unperturbed by the failure of the consultants to endorse his ideas and held to them. Having benefitted from the consultants' advice he began to formulate his ideas in a formal manner so that he might broach them to Acheson before heading off for his conversations with Jebb and company in London. Here Kennan's confidence in his own thinking came to the fore. He made no great effort to present a consensus position of the consultants' views. The lowest common denominator didn't appeal to him. While he mentioned the consultants on occasion he largely set down *his* views in a paper (PPS/55) entitled "Study of U.S. Stance Toward Question of European Union."[14] He outlined that the prospects for greater international association in the future lay in two directions—on the one hand, between the United States, the United Kingdom, and Canada, and on the other, between the states of continental Europe. The latter association would depend on closer Franco-German understanding which Kennan argued both the Americans and the British must promote. Such a continental union notably would hold open a place for the East European states which he expected would gain their freedom eventually. Kennan emphasized that his suggestions aimed not "at achieving anything final and specific at [an] early date." Rather he sought to establish a "direction in which we would like to see events move."[15]

Acheson accepted PPS/55 as a planner's blueprint resulting from working

[12] Minutes of meeting, June 13, 1949, PPS Records, Box 32.

[13] Ibid.

[14] PPS/55, "Study of U.S. Stance Toward Question of European Union," July 7, 1949, in Nelson, ed., *SDPPSP, 1949*, III, pp. 82–100. Kennan emphasizes that these were his "personal" views in his *Memoirs*, I, p. 452.

[15] PPS/55, "Study of U.S. Stance Toward Question of European Union," July 7, 1949, p. 87.

level exploration. It implied no commitment on his part and with this understanding, following a discussion with Kennan on July 8, he voiced no objection to his Planning Staff director's using it as a basis for his discussions with the British.[16] With this approval Kennan crossed the Atlantic visiting first Paris and then London. The French officials of 1949 exhibited a deep and perhaps understandable fear, given their unfortunate past, of being left alone on the continent with the Germans. Their anxiety and suspicions quickened at suggestions from a key American official that they should take the lead in forging a European union while the British participated in an association with the United States from which they would be excluded. In a virtual paranoid manner they assumed that this meant the abandonment of France and would have no part of it.[17] Bruised but unbroken from this encounter Kennan traveled on to London. Here he found officials amenable to strengthening ties with the United States and the Canadians but much less enthusiastic for a third force on the continent. Rather the British, consistent with their positions on the North Atlantic Treaty and the division of Germany, saw themselves as playing an important role in a Western security structure which did not involve any surrender of national sovereignty but which linked them closely to the West Europeans.[18] As Kennan later disconsolately remarked, he returned to Washington "with empty hands."[19]

Kennan had won no converts to his views in either London or Paris, but the experience of this trip deepened his sense that the United States must enlarge and strengthen its relationship with Britain and Canada. A conversation over lunch with the capable Canadian ambassador in Washington, Hume Wrong, confirmed for him that the Canadians would support the further development of this triangular relationship.[20] Kennan, while usually noted for his expertise and interest in Russia and Germany, possessed his own strong appreciation for the "special relationship" between the United States and Great Britain. He was less of a public Anglophile than Acheson but he held a sympathy for Britain's peculiar international position—its far-flung strategic commitments, its leadership of the Commonwealth, and its crucial place in the international trading and monetary systems through its coordination of the sterling bloc. He enjoyed a friendly intimacy with British officials and possessed none of the animus toward John Bull that Americans of a more populist bent sometimes

---

[16] Kennan reviewed the conclusions of his paper at Acheson's daily meeting, July 8, 1949, and later discussed it with him. Memorandum of conversation, July 8, 1949, Executive Secretariat Records, Box 1; and Kennan's handwritten notation on Kennan to Acheson, July 7, 1949, PPS Records, Box 27.

[17] Kennan records the French reaction in his *Memoirs*, I, pp. 456–57.

[18] Kennan, *Memoirs*, p. 457. On Kennan's discussions with the British see also Kennan to Acheson and Webb, August 22, 1949, PPS Records, Box 27.

[19] Kennan, *Memoirs*, p. 457.

[20] See Kennan's report to Acheson on this meeting, August 2, 1949, PPS Records, Box 27.

affected. Kennan's favorable sentiments towards the British undoubtedly weighed into his calculations favoring the extension of associations between his nation and theirs.

Kennan's appreciation for the British position came into play more immediately as a result of the British financial crisis of 1949. The sterling bloc maintained an unfavorable trade balance with the United States—due in part to the American recession of 1949 and a decline in American demand—leading to the so-called dollar-gap and, by mid-1949, a dangerous running down of British financial reserves.[21] The situation demanded drastic action. Prior to taking it the British sought talks with Americans to discuss their position and to garner possible American support. Preparations for these talks quickly subsumed Kennan's attention and drew him away from his larger focus on European integration. However, the views he had developed regarding Britain's role in his larger consideration informed his attitudes on the matter of the dollar-sterling crisis.

To assist him and the Planning Staff in its consideration of issues arising from the British financial crisis Kennan requested that Paul Nitze, the deputy to the Assistant Secretary of State for Economic Affairs join the Staff. Nitze, whom Kennan had tried to recruit to the Policy Planning Staff at its outset only to be blocked by Acheson, agreed to assume responsibilities as deputy director.[22] He brought with him substantial economic expertise. An investment banker who worked through the 1930s with Dillon, Read and Company, he came to Washington in June 1940 as an assistant to James Forrestal. Thereafter he stayed in government service serving variously as financial director for the Coordinator of Inter-American Affairs, as chief of the metals and materials branch of the Board of Economic Warfare, as director of the foreign procurement and development branch of the Foreign Economic Administration, and as Vice-Chairman of the U.S. Strategic Bombing Survey. When he moved across to the State Department in 1946 Nitze had earned a reputation for "keen analytical abilities . . . but he was also known to be an aggressive, energetic executive with a knack for 'getting things done in a hurry.' "[23] At State he served as deputy-director of the Office of International Trade Policy in 1946 before moving to the Office of Economic Affairs from 1947 to 1949 where he

[21] On this subject see Scott Newton, "The 1949 Sterling Crisis and British Policy Towards European Integration," *Review of International Studies* 11 (July 1985): 169–82. For more general background see Susan Strange, *Sterling and British Policy: A Political Study of an International Currency in Decline* (London, 1971), pp. 55–63.

[22] Kennan announced Nitze's appointment to the Staff on August 1, 1949. See minutes of meeting, August 1, 1949, PPS Records, Box 32. Under Secretary Webb had earlier approached Nitze about coming to the Planning Staff. See memorandums of conversation, July 5 and 6, 1949, Executive Secretariat Records, Box 1.

[23] For the direct quotation on Nitze's executive capacity see David MacIssac, *Strategic Bombing in World War II: The Story of the United States Strategic Bombing Survey* (New York, 1976), p. 55. Consult this work for further details of Nitze's work on the Strategic Bombing Survey.

played an important role in implementing the Marshall Plan. When he arrived on the Staff he focused on the more technical economic aspects of the preparatory work for the talks with the British.[24] Kennan devoted himself to their political implications.

To Kennan's dismay Truman assigned the leadership of the American delegation to the forthcoming talks to his fellow Missourian, Secretary of the Treasury John W. Snyder. Snyder, a fiscal conservative, disliked the Attlee government's experiment in democratic socialism and exuded no sympathy for the British position. He intended to meet the British officials, led by Bevin and the Chancellor of the Exchequer Sir Stafford Cripps, with a coldly unforthcoming position and to make little effort to disguise his hostility to Britain's economic and social policies.[25] In the late stages of preparation for the talks Kennan intervened and introduced the political aspects of the problem to the cauldron of discussion. At a meeting with Acheson and Snyder on August 23 he pointed to the political damage that would be caused by treating the British with disdain, damage that would hurt the solidarity of the Western world. He acknowledged that the British needed to take drastic and painful measures but precisely because of this the United States needed to meet them with both a disposition of understanding and encouragement and a willingness to consider long-term solutions to the dollar-gap problem.[26] In the search for such long-term solutions Kennan hoped to push his idea for a closer economic association between the U.S, the U.K., and Canada.

Snyder remained unmoved by Kennan's reasoning but Acheson found him very persuasive.[27] The planner's concern for the British supported the secretary of state's own desire to sustain the Western alliance and tapped into his well-honed Anglo-American sentiments.[28] When the negotiations actually began Snyder led the U.S. delegation but as Hogan has noted "Acheson's view seemed to govern the outcome of the . . . talks."[29] After the British indicated their willingness to take major corrective measures, including a substantial

---

[24] On Nitze's work with the Staff see minutes of meetings, August 8, 9, 11, and 15, 1949, PPS Records, Box 32.

[25] Snyder was receiving advice which questioned the seriousness of the British problems and which led him to be suspicious that the British were simply after more assistance. See Martin to Snyder, August 30, 1949, on "Doubts re Urgency of the Immediate British Problem," Papers of John W. Snyder, HSTL, Box 34.

[26] See Kennan's diary entry of August 23, 1949, recorded in his *Memoirs*, I, pp. 459–60. For further discussion see Hogan, *The Marshall Plan*.

[27] Kennan and Nitze briefed Acheson further on the political implications of the problem. See memorandum of conversation, August 25,1949, Executive Secretariat Records, Box 1; and Acheson's Appointment Book, entry for September 2, 1949, Acheson Papers, HSTL, Box 45.

[28] Acheson also received advice to "show real sympathy for the British difficulties" from the American ambassador in London, Lewis Douglas. See Douglas to Acheson, August 15, 1949, Acheson Papers, HSTL, Box 64.

[29] Hogan, *The Marshall Plan*, p. 262.

devaluation of the pound, the Americans met them with a series of reciprocal and helpful measures.[30] Among these was a Kennan suggestion to establish a tripartite organization to investigate longer term solutions to the dollar-sterling issues. Kennan influenced these discussions through Acheson even though he chose not to participate in them.

In a fit of pique Kennan had asked Under Secretary Webb to excuse him from the talks. He preferred not to participate formally in a delegation led by Snyder.[31] His decision, however, reflected deeper concerns. The enormity of the obstacles to his turning into reality his vision for both an American association with Britain and Canada and a separate force in continental Europe now dawned upon him. The task of fashioning an understanding among Washington policymakers like Snyder seemed too daunting. The fierce reaction of the French to the Washington negotiations, which they feared foreshadowed the formation of an Anglo-Saxon bloc separate from Western Europe, only confirmed for Kennan the difficulties attendant to the pursuit of his approach. But he refused to give up.

After completion of the talks with the British Kennan again turned the attention of the Planning Staff back to the question of European union.[32] He wanted to produce a new draft of PPS/55 as he informed Acheson when the secretary of state joined a Staff discussion on October 11.[33] Kennan's general ideas about a separate U.S.-U.K.-Canada association distinct from a European union had now been exposed in the public domain through the courtesy of stories by Walter Lippmann and Joseph and Stewart Alsop.[34] Kennan aimed to shore up his defenses on this issue but the fire his position attracted proved overwhelming. A number of senior departmental officials, among them Willard Thorp, Llewellyn Thompson, and the redoubtable Hickerson attacked his basic idea.[35] Among Kennan's most cogent critics was his old friend Bohlen, now esconsced as David Bruce's deputy in the American embassy in Paris. On October 6 he wrote Kennan and informed him "of the considerable con-

[30] Hogan provides more detail in *The Marshall Plan*, pp. 262–63. See also Newton, "The 1949 Sterling Crisis and British Policy Towards European Integration," pp. 177–78.

[31] One should note, however, that he was not uninvolved during the talks. As he revealed in a later letter to Charles Bohlen he assisted Nitze in drafting part of the final communique and he engaged in talks on the problem of European unification with Gladwyn Jebb and Roger Makins of the Foreign Office at the time of the sterling-dollar talks. See Kennan to Bohlen, October 12, 1949, PPS Records, Box 27.

[32] Minutes of meeting, October 7, 1949, PPS Records, Box 32.

[33] Ibid., October 11, 1949.

[34] See *The Washington Post*, September 2 and 26, 1949, and October 11, 1949. On these stories see also Stewart Alsop to Kennan, October 13, 1949, Papers of Joseph and Stewart Alsop, Box 20.

[35] See Willard Thorp memorandum to PPS, October 14, 1949; Llewellyn E. Thompson memorandum to PPS, October 12, 1949; and John Hickerson memorandum to PPS, October 15, 1949, PPS Records, Box 27.

cern in French Governmental circles over the impression they have received (in no small measure from the Alsop and Lippmann articles on the subject) that the United States is moving towards a closer association with Great Britain at the expense of Western Europe.''[36] But Bohlen went beyond mere reportage of French concerns. He endorsed them in the strongest terms and argued that the United States must avoid giving the impression of maintaining a special relationship with Great Britain and Canada to the exclusion of the continental Europeans.

Kennan immediately penned a response in which he gave background to both the newspaper stories and the talks with the British and sought to demonstrate that French fears of a ''British desolidarization from the continent'' were baseless. In a mood of frustration he addressed head-on the persistent French fears that the United States might be weakening its commitment to the defense of the continent. ''If anyone can entertain the proposition that the efforts made in this Government to put through and implement the Marshall Plan, the Atlantic Pact and the Military Arms Program were some sort of a cynical joke,'' he observed, ''and that all these things were done only with a view to the sudden abandonment of the continent in precisely September 1949, I am afraid, then, there is no place here for rational argument.'' For Kennan the root of the problem lay with the French themselves—with their ''neuroses'' which led them to avoid facing up to their leadership responsibilities on the continent. He pointedly asked Bohlen if American policymakers had ''no choice but to cater to what is in reality the lack of confidence of the French in themselves.''[37]

Bohlen refused to let Kennan have the last word. He asked Kennan to face the fact that his concept implied not only a major departure from previous policy but also an inevitable weakening of the British commitment to the continent. And from this arose the ''fundamental fallacy'' of Kennan's position which in Bohlen's words was ''that there can be a feasible European integration without British participation to the maximum degree possible.'' As Bohlen explained it, without Britain the non-German parts of a European union would be insufficient to prevent German domination of such an entity. The non-German countries simply lacked the countervailing economic and military strength. In a forceful defense of the French he described it as ''unrealistic'' to expect them to take leadership in forming a union where German domination was more than likely. ''This is one case,'' he explained, ''where French 'hysteria' or neurosis is rooted in a very cold-blooded, realistic appraisal of the probable result.'' For Bohlen the problem lay less with France than with Britain, which he noted bluntly had been ''backsliding'' on European integration since 1948 and refusing to face the painful reality that it was no longer a

[36] Bohlen to Kennan, October 6, 1949, pps Records, Box 27.
[37] Kennan to Bohlen, October 12, 1949, pps Records, Box 27.

world power but only a European power. Far from French neuroses being the issue Bohlen laid the blame on the British attempt to maintain the "fiction" of world power status. As he noted, "she shrinks psychologically from becoming what the disagreeable facts may indicate, just another European power."[38] For him the time had come to stop pampering the British and accommodating their inflated sense of international importance and to confront them with the hard realities.

Unfortunately for Kennan and his position, he found himself opposed not only by Bohlen but the full complement of U.S. ambassadors in Europe. They came together in Paris on October 21–22 to discuss the whole question of European integration and the role of Britain. Kennan had established the agenda but he could not control the outcome of the meeting. The new Assistant Secretary of State for European Affairs, George W. Perkins, crossed the Atlantic to garner the views of the most senior American diplomats—among them David Bruce (Paris), Lewis Douglas (London), James C. Dunn (Rome), Alexander Kirk (Moscow), as well as Averell Harriman from ECA and John J. McCloy, the U.S. High Commissioner to Germany. He reported back to the secretary of state on October 22 that he had "found complete unanimity of opinion of all confreres here . . . that without the active participation of the UK, western European integration will have little if any value." Perkins conveyed directly to Acheson the same concerns that Bohlen put to Kennan. Without the British the western continental powers feared German domination. French leadership would be insufficient to bring about European integration without the participation of the United Kingdom.[39] For the American diplomats the time had come for Washington to pressure London to take up a leading role in the process of European integration.

With the weight of advice balanced so heavily against Kennan's position it is no wonder that Acheson decided against him and thus to encourage the British to lead Europe to unity. The problem with this approach, however, was that it left European integration hostage to British efforts, as Kennan had foreseen. And, Britain stubbornly refused to assume the European leadership role which the United States wanted to assign her. In late October Bevin wrote Acheson that Britain "cannot accept obligations in relation to Western Europe which would prevent or restrict the implementation of our responsibilities elsewhere," namely in the Commonwealth and the sterling area.[40] The British

---

[38] Bohlen to Kennan, October 29, 1949, PPS Records, Box 27. On this exchange between Kennan and Bohlen see also Ruddy, *The Cautious Diplomat*, pp. 94–95.

[39] Perkins to Acheson (No. 4422), October 22, 1949, copy in PPS Records, Box 27. On the deliberations of the diplomats see *FRUS* 1949, IV, pp. 342–44; and pp. 472–96.

[40] Bevin to Acheson October 26, 1949, quoted in Armin Rappaport, "The United States and European Integration: The First Phase," *Diplomatic History* 5 (Spring 1981): 139. On the British position see also Newton, "The 1949 Sterling Crisis and British Policy Towards European Integration," pp. 178–81.

feared the uncertainties involved. They felt content with the western security arrangements that had been forged and didn't want to risk them in any quixotic endeavors to create a European federation or union. Acheson chose not to pressure them to do so.[41]

In the end progress in European integration took place in spite of the uncompromising British refusal to participate in cooperative European endeavors. Ironically in light of Kennan's advice, it took place under *French* leadership in 1950 as Robert Schuman and Jean Monnet led the way in the creation of the European Coal and Steel Community which in turn led on to the Common Market.[42] Kennan welcomed these initiatives and the emergence of a limited European political identity under the leadership of Charles de Gaulle but these never matched the kind of third force he envisaged on the continent. Perhaps the Europe of 1992 and beyond will meet his expectations. This later Europe enjoys the participation of Britain, although one which, under the recent leadership of Margaret Thatcher, was still testy about the surrender of sovereignty and occasionally ambivalent about its status as simply a European power. Britain eventually recognized that its future lay primarily with Europe. This did not mean the end of its "special relationship" with the United States but it reflected the fact that this relationship never took on the breadth and depth which George Kennan had hoped to give it.[43] Kennan later referred to his proposed association of the United States, Great Britain, and Canada as his "fondest dream."[44] The recognition that the United States would not seek to bring this dream and its corollary of a continental European union into reality pained Kennan severely and provided part of the context for his resignation as director of the Policy Planning Staff.

RESIGNATION

The startling discovery by American intelligence in late August of 1949 and its confirmation in early September that the Russians had exploded an atomic device—three or four years ahead of most American estimates—shattered the implicit sense of security which their atomic monopoly had engendered among American policymakers. The shock caused by the Soviet explosion penetrated deeply within the administration and was compounded within two months by the final Communist conquest of all of mainland China. Not only had Soviet military capabilities increased tremendously with their possession of the atomic bomb but the balance of forces in Asia appeared to be moving in their

[41] Rappaport, "The United States and European Integration," p. 139.

[42] Ibid., pp. 139–49.

[43] For background see Wm. Roger Louis and Hedley Bull, eds. *The 'Special Relationship': Anglo-American Relations Since 1945* (Oxford, 1986).

[44] Kennan to Adam Watson, December 7, 1967, quoted in Mayers, *George Kennan and the Dilemmas of Foreign Policy*, p. 152.

direction. A strong response seemed called for to confront what most perceived as a heightened Soviet threat. During the latter months of 1949 and into 1950 the Truman administration debated the value of various measures—particularly the development of the hydrogen bomb—as suitable counters to the Soviet Union. The Policy Planning Staff participated centrally in the debate but during its course Kennan resigned as director. Paul Nitze replaced him. An understanding of the circumstances of this resignation serves here as a prelude to comprehending the discussions involved in framing the American response to the Soviet's successful atomic experiment and Kennan's part in them.

One view that needs to be banished quickly is that Kennan's resignation resulted from Acheson's desire to "gradually exclude" him from the policy-making elite in the department.[45] The secretary of state did nothing of the sort. Even though their substantive differences over policy continued to congeal in the latter part of 1949, Acheson included Kennan in the core group—along with Webb, Rusk, and Carlisle Humelsine from the Executive Secretariat—who attended his daily meeting right up until his departure from the directorship at the end of 1949. He consulted extensively with Kennan in the latter half of 1949 on issues like European integration even to the point of sitting in on Planning Staff meetings.[46] Kennan continued to bring issues to Acheson's attention for his discussion with the Staff, including a long discourse on the workings of the General Assembly of the United Nations, and Acheson remained interested in his work.[47] The bottom line, as the saying goes, is that Kennan chose to resign. Acheson in no way forced him out.[48]

A number of factors influenced his decision. In his own account Kennan highlights an organizational factor, namely a procedural change in the handling of Staff papers which Under Secretary Webb instituted in mid-Septem-

---

[45] For an example of this see John C. Donovan, *The Cold Warriors: A Policy Making Elite* (Lexington, Mass., 1974), pp. 73–74.

[46] At his daily meeting on October 10, Acheson indicated a desire to work more closely with the Policy Planning Staff and to place more of "the burden of the every-day operation of the Department," on Webb and Rusk. See memorandum of conversation, October 10, 1949, Executive Secretariat Records, Box 1.

[47] See Kennan's rather critical comments on the UN General Assembly in his memorandum to Acheson, November 14, 1949, PPS Records, Box 31. Also included here were comments on his work by Dorothy Fosdick which he described "as probably as useful corrective to my views." In his cover letter to Acheson Kennan noted that he was sending observations for his "private information." As he explained: "They aroused considerable pain even in my own Staff, and would have a positively fissionable effect on the Department at large." Kennan to Acheson, November 17, 1949, PPS Records, Box 31.

[48] Kennan recalled that "Mr. Acheson did not at all drive me from the Planning Staff. We had . . . high respect and even affection for each other." Kennan to author, September 6, 1979. Kennan, however, thought it "not unlikely that he was somewhat relieved that I myself decided to go and that he would be able to work with Mr. Nitze on the question of our military policy in the coming period."

ber 1949. Webb interfered with the direct submission of a Staff paper on Yugoslavia to the secretary. Instead he considered it at his regular under secretary's meeting with senior officers of the department and then returned it to the Staff to take account of some of the criticisms aired at this meeting. According to Kennan he saw this change as a threat to the integrity and purpose of the Staff and it prompted him to ask Webb on September 29 to relieve him as soon as possible of the director's responsibilities. He went further and actually expressed a desire to leave government service.[49] But his personal and professional reasons for resigning went far beyond his response to Webb's action. The under secretary's procedural change simply provided the spark to ignite them.

By early September Kennan had attracted to the Planning Staff the strongest complement of personnel since its formation. With Nitze as his deputy charged with general supervision and Savage's steady presence still on hand, Kennan then had an extremely able group of regional specialists to assist him. George Butler attended primarily to Latin America, John Paton Davies to Far Eastern Affairs, Ware Adams to European issues, while Robert Joyce handled intelligence matters and liaison with OPC. To these Staff stalwarts Kennan had added Lampton Berry, from the Division of Middle East Affairs, who handled the Near East and Africa; Dorothy Fosdick, who possessed a Columbia University Ph.D. and covered United Nations Affairs; and the able Robert Tufts who bore responsibility for economic affairs. It was a capable group without any weak link and Kennan had confidence in each member and worked well with them. His decision in early September to execute a major internal reorganization of the Staff and to create a special long-term planning section (consisting of himself, Nitze, and Savage, and others as needed) and a general departmental section suggests he intended to continue his work with the Staff.[50] But the very act of reorganizing the Staff reflected in a way his unease and underlying tension with his circumstances. This bubbled to the surface at the end of 1949.

The last months of 1949 brought Kennan a similar experience to the one he had suffered in Moscow under Averell Harriman in 1945–1946. Again this sensitive and emotional man felt frustrated, tired, and pessimistic as to his own future. He did not relish the role which his defeats on the German and Euro-

[49] Kennan, *Memoirs*, I, pp. 465–66. The Planning Staff's minutes do not provide full substantiation of Kennan's account but his recollection of the Staff paper being returned for further work is supported by the fact that on September 26 a Staff member was assigned to draft a "clarification" of PPS/60 (on Yugoslavia) which took into consideration the views of the European and Near Eastern and African Affairs divisions. See minutes of meetings, September 16, 19, and 26, 1949, PPS Records, Box 32.

[50] On the reorganization of the Staff into two sections and on the area responsibilities of its members see memorandum by Harry H. Schwartz, September 8, 1949, PPS Records, Box 33. Kennan outlined the changes verbally at the Under Secretary's meeting on September 9, 1949. See minutes of meeting, September 9, 1949, Executive Secretariat Records, Box 9.

pean integration issues cast him—that of a stimulator of debates which he was destined to lose. He did not possess the temperament to assume permanently the part of in-house dissenter. He wanted to influence policy and his growing inability to do so troubled him both professionally, because he believed the wrong course was being charted, and personally, because he was denied the rich satisfaction of having *his* advice accepted and implemented. He had, after all, once explained to Joseph Alsop that "the policy recommendations of an official like himself, with long expert training, should be treated like the diagnosis and prescriptions of a doctor."[51] And Kennan preferred patients, so to speak, who did not seek second opinions. He simply found it difficult to accept that his Planning Staff would not function "as the ideological inspirer and coordinator of policy."[52] His disillusionment mounted as he realized that Acheson considered him as just another policy adviser, albeit an important one.[53] Denied the special influence with the secretary of state which he had enjoyed with Marshall, Kennan's frustration with the crude and cumbersome processes of making foreign policy in a democracy showed through. His anger at the need to placate officials like Snyder or to persuade congressional committees fueled his discontent. David Lilienthal, the Chairman of the Atomic Energy Commission who worked closely with Kennan at precisely this time, remembered the planner's "gigantic intellectual impatience" which he thought then "was merely the result of a weary and highly motivated man's having to make a verbal attack on the roadblock to a particular result."[54] But later Lilienthal concluded that it reflected Kennan's more deep-seated difficulties with the processes of a democratic system, with "the give-and-take of a democratic society."[55] One need not engage in "psycho-babble" to suggest that these considerations, perhaps operative at a subconscious level, led to his frustration and thus to his resignation.

While the push factors carried most weight, the pull factors also operated. By late 1949 Kennan deservedly had developed a high reputation as a foreign policy analyst and lecturer. He started to receive offers for academic appointments which flattered him and played up to the scholarly bent he always had manifested. President Dwight Eisenhower of Columbia University tried to re-

[51] Alsop repeated this in a letter to Paul Nitze, December 10, 1949, Papers of Joseph and Stewart Alsop, Box 5.

[52] Kennan, *Memoirs*, I, p. 427. Also note here the observation of James Reston who noted that Kennan's pride was at stake and that he was a "proud man." Author's interview with James B. Reston, August 8, 1989.

[53] Loy Henderson is one who noted that Kennan "needed a boss who would appreciate him" and grew frustrated without it. Author's interview with Loy W. Henderson, Washington, D.C., June 28, 1978.

[54] David E. Lilienthal, *The Journals of David E. Lilienthal*, vol. 4: *Creativity and Conflict, 1964–1967* (New York, 1976), pp. 128–29.

[55] Ibid. On this point see also Joseph Alsop's comments in Alsop to Nitze, December 10, 1949, Papers of Joseph and Stewart Alsop, Box 5.

cruit Kennan to head the Institute for War and Peace Studies which he established during his short tenure there.[56] Kennan declined this offer but it lodged the possibility of an academic appointment firmly in his mind. He had long harbored the idea of getting away to think and to write.[57] And it's likely that he entertained the notion, from which most scholars are forced quickly to disabuse themselves, that he would be able to exercise considerable influence on public opinion and indirectly on policy from an academic position. Certainly Kennan knew that his resignation would not involve him stepping into a void and sure enough the offers flooded in when news of his impending departure from the State Department filtered out. Frank Altschul, an alumnus, and Arnold Wolfers, a regular Staff consultant, tried to attract him to Yale.[58] In "a sort of *tournee*," to use his own description, Kennan talked about possibilities at Dartmouth, Harvard, and M.I.T. and also considered opportunities with the Carnegie and Rockefeller foundations.[59] He finally decided to take up the offer of Robert Oppenheimer to join the Institute for Advanced Study at Princeton.

Whatever the relative weight of these reasons it is important to recognize that Kennan's resignation resulted from his own decision. Kennan admitted as much to Averell Harriman when he explained his decision as "the result of many considerations, most of which are personal. It reflects no bitterness; least of all any differences of opinion with the Secretary, who has always treated me, if anything, with much greater consideration than I deserve."[60] Acheson's reaction to it confirms the point. The secretary of state persuaded Kennan out of leaving government service entirely and offered him the alternative of a "leave of absence without pay" after which he would return to the department. Kennan accepted this offer and it was arranged that he would resign as Planning Staff director on December 31, 1949, and stay on as Counselor until June of 1950, whereupon he would take a one-year leave. Acheson appreciated that Kennan needed a break of sorts from the rigors to which he had long been subjected, a view incidentally endorsed by Charles Bohlen.[61] Kennan's

---

[56] Stephen E. Ambrose, *Eisenhower*, vol. 1: *Soldier, General of the Army, President-Elect, 1890–1952* (New York, 1983), p. 484.

[57] Averell Harriman noted this in his letter to Kennan after hearing of his resignation. Harriman also commented: "I don't know how the State Department is going to function any longer. Personally I will have no one to turn to with whom to think things through." Harriman to Kennan, December 19, 1949, Harriman Papers, Box 267.

[58] Altschul to Kennan, December 13, 1949, Altschul Papers, File 113a.

[59] See Kennan to Oppenheimer, February 13, 1950, Papers of J. Robert Oppenheimer, Library of Congress, Washington, D.C., Box 43.

[60] Kennan to Harriman, December 29, 1949, Harriman Papers, Box 267.

[61] In a talk at the National War College Acheson publicly observed that "the pressure every day of affairs which are borne in on men like Mr. Kennan is too much to stand year after year, and he has stood them since he entered the service of the United States at the age of twenty-two." Acheson's remarks, December 21, 1949, Papers of James E. Webb, HSTL, Box 20. When Kennan's resignation was finally announced Bohlen wrote Robert Lovett that he had "for some time

decision to resign didn't damage the genuine regard Acheson held for him. In December, when publicly referring to Kennan's departure, he admitted that "at first that filled me with despair. He is one of the most distinguished, if not the most distinguished Foreign Service Officer. I have rarely met a man the depth of whose thought, the sweetness of whose nature combined to bring about a real understanding of the underlying problems of modern life. But after I thought about the questions of his taking a sabbatical leave, it seemed to me it was the right and good thing to do." Acheson went on to assure his audience at the National War College that it would not be "an easy thing to have him go, even for a year," and that "we will eagerly welcome him back."[62] After allowing for the usual superfluities of farewell address, one must ask if Acheson's essential comments were sincerely meant. Given that he had no reason to dissemble and that such behavior was not in character for him, and also given his future use of Kennan in the department (as we shall see) and his continuing friendly relations with him and favorable references to him up to the time of Kennan's Reith lectures, one must conclude that they were.[63] Kennan certainly believed so. On the same day that he heard Acheson's remarks Kennan wrote to him that "I find no words to say how deeply moved I was by what you did and said this morning. Based on the past you did me too much honor. Perhaps the future can correct some of the disparity."[64]

Both Acheson and Kennan accepted that his leave would be temporary. Both began to refer to it as a sabbatical year and by the year's end Kennan went so far as to write Averell Harriman that "I do not feel that I am really leaving. I expect to be fairly near Washington next year and available for consultation; and in some ways I have a feeling that I may be able to contribute much more from that position than from the one I am now in."[65] In fact, in the summer of 1950, soon after he moved to Princeton Kennan returned to Washington and lunched with Acheson and Nitze who discussed some policy matter in front of him. "When I left the department," Kennan told them in

a feeling that a breathing spell for a year or so would not be at all a bad thing in his [Kennan's] case." Bohlen to Lovett, December 19, 1949, Records of Charles E. Bohlen, Box 3.

[62] Acheson's remarks, December 21, 1949, Webb Papers, HSTL, Box 20. I have found no contemporary private remarks which contradict these public utterances.

[63] As is discussed in more detail in the following chapter, Acheson's strong desire to have Kennan in the department is revealed by his future use of him during the early days of the Korean War; in the crisis situation following the intervention of the Chinese in Korea; in private discussions in mid-1951 with the Soviet U.N. delegate Jacob Malik to obtain a Korean War Armistice; and in his appointment of Kennan as ambassador to the Soviet Union. Also note Acheson's description of Kennan (along with Paul H. Nitze and C. B. Marshall) as a man of "deep insight and knowledge" in his "Introduction" to Louis J. Halle, *Civilization and Foreign Policy: An Inquiry for America* (New York, 1955), pp. xvi–xvii.

[64] Kennan to Acheson, December 21, 1949, Acheson Papers, HSTL, Box 64.

[65] Kennan to Harriman, December 29, 1949, Harriman Papers, Box 267.

response, "it never occurred to me that you two would make foreign policy without having first consulted me."[66] But that is precisely what they had proceeded to do. In fact they had begun their partnership well before Kennan formally left the department in June of 1950.

The close cooperation that quickly developed between Acheson and Nitze misled some historians to conclude that Nitze was handpicked by Acheson and assigned to the Planning Staff to establish better liaison with the strategic planners in the Defense Department. They present his appointment as the seed which grew to produce the seminal national security policy statement, NSC 68.[67] But, as we have seen, and as Nitze readily admits, he came to the Policy Planning Staff not as Acheson's choice but as Kennan's and he primarily came not to work on strategic planning but to tackle the problems associated with the British financial crisis and the trade imbalance between Europe and the United States.[68] Nitze had known Acheson slightly for quite some time owing to a close friendship between his father and the senior partner of Acheson's law firm, Mr. Edward Burling. During the war, however, some hostility developed between them as a result of clashes between Acheson's State Department and Nitze's Foreign Economic Administration. Nitze had no really close dealings with Acheson until 1949 when he supervised the department's preparatory work for the discussions with Cripps and Bevin.[69] During the actual negotiations, which occurred well after Nitze joined the Planning Staff, he served as departmental coordinator responsible for carrying out Acheson's assignments and for coordinating actions with the Treasury Department. It was here that Acheson recognized Nitze's abilities and their capacity to work well together. The temptation to read Nitze's appointment to the Planning Staff as illustrative of Acheson's desire to ease Kennan out and to effect a change in American military and strategic policy should be resisted. Such an analysis while blessed with fine symmetrical and dramatic qualities carries the burden of being wrong.

When the debate over how to react to the Soviet atomic explosion began Acheson had neither decided to exclude Kennan from policy-making nor assigned to Nitze any prominent or specific role in the strategic area. The Soviet atomic explosion was not used as a device by Acheson to seek the implementation of a new military and strategic policy. He entered the debate on how to respond to the Soviet atom bomb without a predetermined position or rigid views. Further, he entered it still prepared to consider the policy advice of George Kennan. With this understanding one can now turn to the debate itself.

[66] Nitze, *From Hiroshima to Glasnost*, p. 86.

[67] Among the first to do this was Paul Y. Hammond, "NSC 68: Prologue to Rearmament," in Warner R. Schilling, Paul Y. Hammond, and Glenn H. Snyder, *Strategy, Politics and Defense Budgets* (New York, 1962), pp. 287–88.

[68] Author's interview with Paul H. Nitze, June 30, 1978.

[69] Ibid.

THE HYDROGEN BOMB

In the years up to 1949 the Truman administration had not met the perceived Soviet challenge by initiating a major rearmament effort aimed at giving the United States a conventional force capability to counter possible Soviet aggression in Europe or elsewhere. Far from implementing such a measure Truman successfully sought, for reasons of political popularity and fiscal restraint, to sharply limit defense spending.[70] This in turn forced the American armed forces to rely increasingly on the atomic bomb in their plans to respond to any Soviet aggression. Indeed, by August 1949 American conventional forces were deemed capable of defending only the western hemisphere and the main Japanese Islands and perhaps of retaining communication lines to some bridgeheads in Great Britain, the Iberian Peninsula, and North Africa.[71] The Americans depended on the deterrent quality of their atomic monopoly to ensure that the Russians would not utilize their larger conventional forces.[72] The disquiet in different parts of the Truman administration which greeted the news of the Soviet possession of the atomic bomb was then quite understandable. It was soon channeled in a number of directions.

Within the State Department news of the Soviet A-bomb precipitated a renewed consideration of international control of atomic energy. The Policy Planning Staff guided by Kennan led this reconsideration. Kennan first had confronted issues related to atomic weapons while serving at the National War College in 1946–1947. Bernard Brodie served among his civilian colleagues there. Brodie had just edited *The Absolute Weapon: Atomic Power and World Order*, a pioneering work examining the strategic utility and importance of the new weapon. In discussions with Brodie and in his own lectures, Kennan developed his views on the subject. He reacted firmly against the new weapon. He later recalled having "an overpowering and instinctive distrust of this or any other of the weapons of mass destruction as possible useful factors in our political and military policy."[73] He viewed the use of the weapon against Ja-

---

[70] On the issue of limits on defense expenditures see Warner R. Schilling, "The Politics of National Defense: Fiscal 1950," in Schilling, Hammond, and Snyder, *Strategy, Politics and Defense Budgets*, pp. 1–266. For Truman's justification for his defense spending ceilings see his statement before the National Security Council in which he explained that "we must carefully balance the military requirements for national security against the economic and fiscal burdens of large military expenditures." Truman Papers, PSF, Box 150.

[71] On military capabilities note Defense Secretary James Forrestal's warning to Truman that on the given budget ceiling "we would probably have the capability only of reprisal against any possible enemy, in the the form of air warfare, using England as a base." Diary entry October 8, 1948, in Millis, ed., *The Forrestal Diaries*, p. 498.

[72] On the place of the atomic bomb in the Truman administration's concept of strategic deterrence see Gregg Herken, *The Winning Weapon: The Atomic Bomb in the Cold War, 1945–1950* (New York, 1980), p. 280.

[73] Kennan to author, September 9, 1979.

pan "as a regrettable extremism, born of the bad precedent of the conventional strategic bombings of the war just then ended and of the military fixations to which that war had conduced."[74] For him "the very development of weapons of this nature represented a philosophic mistake" and any attempt to "try to find a logical place for them in our policy could only lead us increasingly into the realm of total confusion."[75] The United States should not plan to use this weapon as part of its military strategy and policy. These views—"more instinctively than rationally arrived at" as he later put it—were deeply felt and held.[76]

Kennan's ideas about nuclear weapons did not prevent him gaining a good deal of experience in atomic energy areas during his tenure as director of the Staff. From 1947 onwards he dealt with such questions as international controls, the expansion of the atomic energy program, and Anglo-American-Canadian atomic cooperation particularly in the allocation of raw materials and the sharing of technical information.[77] The matter of Anglo-American cooperation on atomic energy matters brought Kennan into his first sustained association with J. Robert Oppenheimer when, in July 1948, the latter chaired a two-day meeting at Princeton of representatives from the State and Defense departments and the Atomic Energy Commission.[78] This association continued in a limited way in 1949 as Kennan called on Oppenheimer as a consultant to the Staff on the European integration question. It took on greater import once the news came in that the Soviets had the bomb.

At the very time that American intelligence discovered the Soviet atomic test Kennan was participating in discussions of the Anglo-American-Canadian Combined Policy Committee on atomic energy.[79] He quickly gained release from these time-consuming negotiations and, along with certain Staff members, began to devote attention to a major reevaluation of the U.S. position on international control and to the implications for American foreign policy of the

[74] George F. Kennan, *The Nuclear Delusion: Soviet-American Relations in the Atomic Age* (New York, 1982), p. xiv.

[75] Kennan to author, September 9, 1979.

[76] Kennan, *The Nuclear Delusion*, p. xv.

[77] For details see Richard G. Hewlett and Francis Duncan, *Atomic Shield, 1947–1952*, vol. 2 of *A History of the United States Atomic Energy Commission* (University Park, Pa., 1969), pp. 270–97, 304–5. See also McGeorge Bundy, *Danger and Survival: Choices About the Atomic Bomb in the First Fifty Years* (New York, 1988), p. 201.

[78] James W. Kunetka, *Oppenheimer: The Years of Risk* (Englewood Cliffs, N.J., 1982), p. 135.

[79] One should note that atomic matters were on Kennan's mind. In August 1949, he had considered the political implications of the Soviet Union's possessing an atomic bomb and had recommended a renewed attempt for international control of the weapon. See "Political Implications of Detonation of Atomic Bomb by the USSR," August 16, 1949, *FRUS* 1949, I, pp. 514–16. This paper, which concentrated on questions of detection and verification, is discussed in Herken, *The Winning Weapon*, pp. 299–301.

Soviet possession of the bomb.[80] On October 4 Under Secretary Webb formally charged the Planning Staff "to carry out a dress review of the U.S. Government position on atomic energy . . . in the nature of a complete re-evaluation of the situation."[81]

The Policy Planning Staff, however, held no monopoly on formulating a possible response to the Soviet's new atomic capacity. Some policymakers believed that the correct rejoinder lay in developing even more powerful weapons of mass destruction. With plans already in motion to expand the existing atomic energy program, a powerful group immediately questioned the sufficiency of this expansion and called for the development of a fusion nuclear weapon, the hydrogen bomb, known more simply as "the super."[82] It promised to be vastly more destructive than the fission atomic weapons used against Japan, a limited number of which now lay in the American stockpile. The strong-minded and relentless Lewis L. Strauss, one of the five members of the Atomic Energy Commission (AEC) chaired by Lilienthal, assumed the leadership and initiative among this group.[83] He had key support among the scientific community from Ernest Lawrence at Berkeley and most enthusiastically from Edward Teller, who had worked with Oppenheimer at Los Alamos during the war and who during 1949 returned there and campaigned vigorously for all-out research on the H-bomb. Senator Brien McMahon of Connecticut, the activist chairman of the Joint Committee on Atomic Energy, formed the third element of the powerful triad of support for the super.[84] As McGeorge Bundy has noted with measured understatement, "it was not a trivial group."[85] Strauss's knowledge that the FBI suspected Klaus Fuchs, a British physicist who had worked at Los Alamos during the war, of spying for the Soviet Union only strengthened his commitment to the super. In light of Fuchs' betrayal, Strauss feared that the super "was necessary not . . . to reestablish a lead over the Soviets but to keep up with them."[86]

The agitation of Strauss and his supporters persuaded AEC Chairman Lilien-

[80] For Kennan's relief from duties in the Combined Policy Committee on atomic energy see memorandum of conversation, September 27, 1949, Executive Secretariat Records, Box 1.

[81] Memorandum of conversation, October 4, 1949, Executive Secretariat Records, Box 1.

[82] On the expansion plans see Sidney Souers to Truman, October 10, 1949, attached to "Report to the President by the Special Committee of the National Security Council on the Proposed Acceleration of the Atomic Energy Program," October 10, 1949, Truman Papers, PSF, Box 200; and Lilienthal, *Journals*, 2, p. 577.

[83] See Richard Pfau, *No Sacrifice Too Great: The Life of Lewis L. Strauss* (Charlottesville, 1984), pp. 113–19; and Lewis L. Strauss, *Men and Decisions* (New York, 1962), pp. 216–23.

[84] For McMahon's considered views in support of the super's development see his memorandum to Truman, November 21, 1949, *FRUS* 1949, I, pp. 588–95.

[85] Bundy, *Danger and Survival*, p. 205.

[86] Pfau, *No Sacrifice Too Great*, p. 115. The FBI's suspicions turned out to be quite well founded. Fuchs confessed to passing information to the Soviet Union from 1942 to 1949 on January 23, 1950. On Fuchs see Robert Chadwell Williams, *Klaus Fuchs, Atom Spy* (Cambridge, Mass., 1987).

thal to agree to consider the matter.[87] As a first step he referred it to the AEC's General Advisory Committee (GAC)—a body of nine brilliant scientists and scientist-administrators chaired by Oppenheimer—for its recommendation. The GAC members met in Washington in late October. After intense deliberations, which included their being briefed by Kennan on the nature of the Soviet threat, they recommended against any all-out development of the super. The GAC offered both reasons of practicality (because it would interfere with the planned expansion of the atomic program), and morality (the super bomb would be "a weapon of genocide," and "a danger to humanity as a whole"), in support of its negative counsel.[88] But the virtually unanimous GAC recommendation against developing the hydrogen bomb failed to persuade its proponents. When the AEC met to formulate a recommendation to the president they split. Lilienthal and two colleagues sided with the Advisory Committee. But Strauss and the other AEC member, Gordon Dean, argued for the H-bomb's development.[89]

The division among the AEC members left Truman distinctly uncomfortable about making a decision. He needed and wanted further counsel. The admission in both the GAC report and the AEC recommendations that the decision on the super was not simply of a technical nature but also involved military and diplomatic considerations gave him a way to proceed. Advised by his naval aide, Robert L. Dennison, the president referred the whole question to a special subcommittee of the NSC comprising the secretaries of state and defense and the chairman of the AEC.[90] On November 19 he charged this subcommittee to "analyse all phases of the question including particularly the technical, military and political factors, and [to] make recommendations as to whether and in what manner the United States should undertake the development and possible production of 'super' atomic weapons."[91] He wanted the issues laid before him in an organized way to facilitate his making a considered and orderly decision. His assignment of the secretary of state to this subcommittee formally injected the State Department into the decision-making process regard-

[87] For further details on the complex matters described all too briefly in the following paragraph see the excellent study by Hewlett and Duncan, *Atomic Shield, 1947–1952*, pp. 369–91; Warner R. Schilling, "The H-Bomb Decision: How to Decide Without Actually Choosing," *Political Science Quarterly* 76 (March 1961): 24–46; and Bundy, *Danger and Survival*, pp. 206–9.

[88] On the recommendations of the GAC see Oppenheimer to Lilienthal, October 30, 1949, and the two enclosures of the same date in *FRUS* 1949, I, pp. 569–73.

[89] For the AEC recommendation and the reports of the individual commissioners see *FRUS* 1949, I, pp. 576–85, 596–99.

[90] See Dennison's memorandum for the president commenting on the Report of the Chairman of the Atomic Energy Commission, November 18, 1949, Truman Papers, PSF, Box 201.

[91] Truman to Executive Secretary of NSC (Souers), November 19, 1949, *FRUS* 1949, I, pp. 587–88. Truman's remarks to Acheson as to what he wanted from the committee are in memorandum of conversation with the president, November 21, 1949, Acheson Papers, HSTL, Box 64.

ing the hydrogen bomb, which had the effect of shifting the ground from underneath Kennan's study of international control measures.

Throughout October Kennan, Nitze, and other Staff members joined by R. Gordon Arneson, Webb's assistant on atomic energy policy, had held extensive discussions on international control and the implications of the Russian atomic explosion.[92] They called in a range of consultants from the Pentagon, the AEC, and the scientific community—among them Henry Smyth, a Commissioner; Carroll Wilson, the General Manager; and Dr. Kenneth S. Pitzer, the Director of the Division of Research, from the AEC. Also included were General Frederick H. Osborn, Deputy Representative on the U.N. Atomic Energy Commission; Dr. Karl T. Compton, Director of the Research and Development Board of the Defense Department; Cols. Don Z. Zimmerman, George W. Beeler, and F. W. Gibb from the Plans and Operations branch of the Army Department; Brig. Gen. James McCormack, Director of Military Application, AEC; Maj. Gen. T. H. Landon, of the Joint Strategic Survey Committee, Joint Chiefs of Staff; and Dr. Vannevar Bush, president of the Carnegie Institution and wartime Director of the Office of Scientific Research and Development. As this listing of consultants testifies these were serious discussions. The talks notably drew Nitze away from the economic policy arena into the realm of strategic policy. He brought to the discussions the same clinical capacity for analysis which he had demonstrated on the U.S. Strategic Bombing Survey. Nitze, as one close observer noted, "relied on numbers and facts, not on hunches."[93] He prized his capacity for rational calculation and preferred not to trust weighty matters to instinct. Here he differed from his Staff director and the consequences of their differing perspectives eventually emerged.

Acheson viewed the Staff study as very important. On November 3 he met with his planners for an "interim discussion on the general subject of international control of atomic energy." Well aware of the debate within the AEC over testing the H-bomb's feasibility Kennan questioned what would be accomplished if the United States developed the super "without showing the Russians any ray of light as far as their own policy is concerned."[94] He clearly wanted to investigate the possibility of international control before moving into any testing, let alone production of a fusion bomb. Interestingly, in view of his later decisions, Acheson tentatively suggested during the discussion "an 18–24 month moratorium on the super-bomb—bilateral if possible, unilateral if necessary—during which time you do your best to ease the international situation, come to an agreement with the Russians, put your own economic house in order, get your people's minds set to whatever is necessary to do, and

[92] For the minutes of meetings held on October 12, 14, 19, 21, and 24, 1949 see *FRUS* 1949, I, pp. 191–97, 204–5.

[93] Brandon, *Special Relationships*, p. 78. On Nitze see also Strobe Talbott, *The Master of the Game*, pp. 34–53.

[94] Minutes of meeting, November 3, 1949, PPS Records, Box 32.

if no agreement is in sight at the end of that time . . . then go ahead with overall production of both the super-bomb and the atomic bomb."[95] Now Acheson had not decided to recommend this course to the president. Here he engaged only in the exploration of ideas and the probing of possibilities. But his remarks suggest that at this point he still considered the subject of international control—to which he had made his own notable attempt through the 1946 Acheson-Lilienthal report—worthy of investigation, that he saw a linkage between international control and the development of the hydrogen bomb and gauged that some possibility existed for diplomacy to gain nuclear arms limitation.[96] Acheson's sentiments encouraged Kennan to pursue his investigation vigorously. The secretary of state indicated his further support of it when he advised the president that the State Department was making a complete review of international control and requested that no decisions be taken on atomic energy matters until the results of this review were submitted to him.[97] Truman, who at this time still awaited the AEC's report on the super, agreed to this. Kennan's efforts appeared to be directly related to American decision-making on the issue.

Throughout November and December Kennan formulated a paper on international control. He worked as a driven man, almost a man possessed. The heavy burden of emotional stress which he carried can be gauged from his surprising admission to Acheson soon after submitting his first draft that he "was tempted, day before yesterday, to go into the baby's room and say: 'Go on, get up. You're going to work today. I'll get in the crib.' "[98] He devoted himself fully to this subject, isolating himself even from his Staff colleagues. He later described the eventual product of his labors as being "in its implications one of the most important, if not the most important, of all the documents I ever wrote in government."[99] Even as he wrote it he invested heavy significance to the piece aiming to define through it the appropriate place in the world for these weapons which he abhorred. Kennan stayed with his larger focus even when Truman's request to the special subcommittee of the NSC transformed the immediate question for decision facing the State Department. Truman's instructions required Acheson to decide on the more narrow question of whether to develop the hydrogen bomb but Kennan continued to confront the admittedly related but larger questions of the role of nuclear weapons and the possibilities for international control of them. In so doing he distanced himself from the kernel of atomic energy policy formulation in the department. With

[95] Ibid.

[96] On the Acheson-Lilienthal Report see Acheson, *Present at the Creation*, pp. 151–56.

[97] Memorandum of conversation by Acheson, November 7, 1949, Executive Secretariat Records, Box 3.

[98] Kennan to Acheson, December 21, 1949, Acheson Papers, HSTL, Box 64. Kennan continued that he had "since existed only on the reflection that 'This, too, will pass.' "

[99] Kennan, *Memoirs*, I, p. 472.

Kennan preoccupied, Acheson placed Nitze, Arneson, and Adrian Fisher, the department's legal adviser, on the working group chaired by Souers of the NSC which he, Lilienthal, and Defense Secretary Johnson established to assist them.[100]

In retrospect, Kennan's not serving on this group—where assuredly his opposition to the hydrogen bomb would have been expressed eloquently and energetically—eased the task of the H-bomb's proponents. In the working group the State Department representatives lent no support to the opposition raised by those from the AEC. In fact Nitze, now working separately from Kennan, began to favor the testing of the super. Out of loyalty to his chief on the Staff—to whom, he recalled, "all of us who worked with him were absolutely devoted"—Nitze moved cautiously.[101] He did not aggressively press in the working group for a major acceleration of the program to test the feasibility of a thermonuclear reaction. He simply allowed the Defense Department members to push this position forcefully.[102] By December 19, however, he recommended to Acheson that Truman order the AEC to proceed with an accelerated program for testing the feasibility of the H-bomb while delaying any decision on a full production schedule.[103]

Kennan's advice differed sharply from Nitze's and their disagreement here launched a debate over these and related matters which the two men sustained for over four decades.[104] In his paper Kennan questioned both American concepts of and reliance upon atomic warfare, expressed deep anxiety over the dangers inherent in both American and Soviet possession of atomic weapons, and called fervently for a renewed attempt to reach a settlement with the USSR on international control. Naturally he opposed any development of the super before such attempts were made.[105] Kennan's paper manifested his passionate concern for humanity and the dire threat he perceived nuclear weapons to be. He attempted to confront the "political compulsions" that drove the arms race and strenuously argued, as he has ever since, that no American government should rely upon the first-use of nuclear weapons as a defense against

[100] For membership of the working group see *FRUS* 1949, I, p. 587 n. 2.

[101] Author's interview with Paul Nitze, June 30, 1978. Nitze further commented on Kennan: "He was and is a marvellous human being."

[102] The position of the Defense Department members of the working group held in part: "a. Possession of a thermonuclear weapon by the USSR without such possession by the United States would be intolerable. b. There is an imperative necessity of determining the feasibility of a thermonuclear explosion and its characteristics." See memorandum circulated by Defense members of working group, undated, *FRUS* 1949, I, pp. 604–10.

[103] Memorandum by Nitze, December 19, 1949, *FRUS* 1949, pp. 610–11. See also Nitze, *From Hiroshima to Glasnost*, pp. 87–92.

[104] On the Kennan-Nitze debate in its various incarnations see Gregg Herken, "The Great Foreign Policy Fight," *American Heritage* 37 (April/May 1986): 65–80.

[105] The final draft of Kennan's paper submitted after some revisions on January 20, 1950, is found in *FRUS* 1950, I, pp. 22–44. The early draft was discussed at the Secretary's Daily Meeting on December 15, 1949, and Acheson took a copy of it to read. Memorandum of conversation, December 15, 1949, Executive Secretariat Records, Box 1.

non-nuclear attack.[106] Kennan had reached these conclusions for the most part independently but drew sustenance from the fact that he found himself in essential agreement with Robert Oppenheimer.[107] Oppenheimer's enormous intelligence and true culture captivated Kennan as did the ready affection and comradeship which the physicist offered to him as another "scholar by nature."[108] Kennan would soon describe Oppenheimer as his "intellectual conscience."[109] Their deep, almost brotherly, bond—which led Kennan to defend Oppenheimer eloquently but unsuccessfully before his Personnel Security Board hearing in 1954 and which continued until Oppenheimer's death after which Kennan gave one of the eulogies at his memorial service—dated from this time.[110] The persuasive powers of the Kennan-Oppenheimer duo, however, proved inadequate in its first and most serious test over the hydrogen bomb.

Dean Acheson had the decisive responsibility for determining the recommendation to Truman. He not only faced a division within his own department between Nitze and Kennan but also found himself involved in a similar split within the special NSC subcommittee. At its first formal meeting on December 22 Louis Johnson argued for the super's development while Lilienthal opposed it. Acheson took no position here and arranged only for further study.[111] His friendship and respect for Lilienthal and also for Oppenheimer inhibited him from siding immediately with Johnson, although he leaned toward proceeding with a program to develop the new weapon. Earlier, after listening sympathetically to Oppenheimer argue against the H-bomb and in favor of attempts—including unilateral ones—at disarmament, Acheson told Arneson: "You know, I listened as carefully as I know how, but I don't understand what 'Oppie' was trying to say. How can you persuade a paranoid adversary to disarm 'by example.' "[112] Oppenheimer remembered that Acheson "was very depressed" by the whole issue and "wished that he could go along with their idea, but didn't think he would be able to." The secretary of state simply

[106] This point is made by Freeman Dyson in *Weapons and Hope* (New York, 1984), p. 178.

[107] Kennan met with Oppenheimer on November 16. The next day Oppenheimer wrote to him: "You will hardly need to be told how much I appreciated the opportunity that we had yesterday to talk of the present state of the atomic problem. To me, your visit was in all ways inspiriting, not only for the important new points of which you told me, but also for the spirit in which you are approaching the problem and for the sympathetic and non-doctrinaire framework of your own views." Oppenheimer to Kennan, November 17, 1949, Oppenheimer Papers, Box 43. Oppenheimer gave Kennan some further comments on international control issues.

[108] Author's interview with Kennan, March 6, 1989.

[109] Kennan to Oppenheimer, June 5, 1950, Oppenheimer Papers, Box 43.

[110] On Kennan at the Oppenheimer hearing see United States Atomic Energy Commission, *In the Matter of J. Robert Oppenheimer: Transcript of Hearing Before Personnel Security Board* (Cambridge, Mass., 1971), pp. 351–70. On the eulogy see Kunetka, *Oppenheimer*, p. 271.

[111] On the meeting of the subcommittee see Lilienthal, *Journals*, 2, pp. 613–14.

[112] R. Gordon Arneson, "The H-Bomb Decision," *Foreign Service Journal* 46 (May 1969): 29.

couldn't see "how any President could survive a policy of not making the H-bomb."[113]

As Acheson's remarks suggested his decision on control of atomic weapons and on the hydrogen bomb would be determined in relation to his analysis of the Soviet threat and his sense of Truman's responsibilities in dealing with it. Consistent with his decision-making on the German question he ultimately took what seemed the safer course, despite his earlier musings about a moratorium. Not surprisingly then, Kennan's long memorandum on international control of atomic energy failed to persuade him. In fact he later claimed that he told Kennan that "if that was his view he ought to resign from the Foreign Service and go out and preach his Quaker gospel but not push it within the Department," although, as with much Acheson later claimed to have said to and about Kennan, there is not the slightest evidence to support his recollection.[114] Whatever his private comments Acheson found the critiques of Kennan's paper much more persuasive. Arneson dismissed Kennan's view and argued that his memorandum was "based primarily on a fundamentally incorrect assumption; namely, that it is possible to achieve prohibition of atomic weapons and international control of atomic energy that has any meaning, without a basic change in Soviet attitudes and intentions, and, in fact, in the Soviet system itself."[115] Nitze, of course, also weighed in. While professing to agree with much in Kennan's paper he zeroed in on the real issue when he explained that it must be assumed that the Soviets were proceeding ahead with a program in the thermonuclear area and attested that "the military and political advantages which would accrue to the USSR if it possessed even a temporary monopoly of this weapon are so great as to make time of the essence."[116] This argument won the day. Convinced that a Soviet lead in nuclear weaponry represented a severe danger to American security and probably sensing the tide of Truman's own feelings on the matter, Acheson's course was set.

Acheson went beyond a mere recommendation in favor of the hydrogen bomb when he offered his counsel to Truman. On January 19 he informed Souers that he had "about reached the position that we should advise the President to go ahead and find out about the feasibility of the matter."[117] Johnson,

[113] These Oppenheimer reflections are drawn from notes of an interview which he gave to Warner Schilling, June 11, 1957. See the transcript in Warner Schilling folder, Oppenheimer Papers, Box 65.

[114] Acheson quoted in McLellan, *Dean Acheson: The State Department Years*, p. 176. McLellan quotes Acheson from an Oral History Interview which he conducted with him in April 1963.

[115] Arneson's memorandum on PPS Draft Paper on International Control of Atomic Energy, December 29, 1949, *FRUS* 1950, I, pp. 2–8. For a further Arneson critique of what he termed "the Kennan position" see the memorandum of January 24, 1950, included in his "The H-Bomb Decision, Part II," *Foreign Service Journal* 46 (June 1969): 25–26.

[116] Nitze's memorandum to Acheson, January 17, 1950, *FRUS* 1950, I, pp. 13–17.

[117] Memorandum of telephone conversation between Souers and Acheson, January 19, 1950, Acheson Papers, HSTL, Box 65.

who constantly pressured Acheson, already had unilaterally forwarded to the president a memorandum from General Omar Bradley supporting the H-bomb's development as a matter of top priority.[118] Acheson gained some slight revenge on the Defense Secretary when he reached a complementary decision to that on the H-bomb, namely that the administration required a major reexamination of America's military strategy in relation to its foreign policy. Lilienthal had prevailed on Acheson to seek an examination of this sort. He wanted it because he believed it would substantiate his argument that larger weapons of mass destruction would not strengthen national security.[119] Acheson thought of a reexamination in a somewhat different way. Kennan's incisive criticism had alerted him that American military policy lacked any clear nuclear strategy yet relied almost exclusively on atomic bombs as both defensive and offensive weapons. With this awareness and with Nitze's encouragement he perceived that a full review of foreign and defense policies would reveal this troubling reliance and, by implication, point to the need for a buildup of conventional forces.[120]

With considerable bureaucratic skill Acheson used his decision favoring investigation of the super's feasibility to facilitate the reexamination of foreign and defense policies which he knew the budget-conscious and perennially suspicious Johnson would be reluctant to accept. When he met Johnson and Lilienthal on January 31, 1950, the secretary of state held the casting vote. He and Johnson agreed to recommend the development of the H-bomb and then he combined with Lilienthal to ensure that the subcommittee's recommendation to the president included the call for a defense and foreign policy reexamination.[121] That same day the committee delivered these portentous yet straightforward recommendations to the president:

(a) That the President direct the Atomic Energy Commission to proceed to determine the technical feasibility of a thermonuclear weapon.

(b) That the President direct the Secretary of State and the Secretary of Defense to undertake a reexamination of our objectives in peace and war and of the effect of these objectives on our strategic plans, in light of the probable fission bomb capability and possible thermonuclear bomb capability of the Soviet Union.[122]

Truman immediately approved them.[123]

[118] Memorandum by Gen. Omar N. Bradley, Chairman, Joint Chiefs of Staff, January 13, 1950, Truman Papers, PSF, Box 114.

[119] Lilienthal, *Journals*, 2, pp. 620–21.

[120] Acheson, *Present at the Creation*, pp. 348–49.

[121] See Lilienthal, *Journals*, 2, pp. 623–32; and Arneson, "The H-Bomb Decision, II," pp. 26–27.

[122] For the subcommittee's report and recommendations see "Development of Thermonuclear Weapons," January 31, 1950, *FRUS* 1950, I, pp. 513–17.

[123] Truman made his decision public the same day. See his statement in *Public Papers of the Presidents of the United States: Harry S. Truman, 1950* (Washington, D.C., 1965), p. 138. For a comprehensive study of the military's role in Truman's H-bomb decision see David Alan Ro-

McGeorge Bundy noted recently that this Truman decision ranks "second in importance only to Franklin Roosevelt's commitment of October 1941 [to build the Atomic Bomb]; it led straight on, with no second thought by the president, to the world's first full-scale thermonuclear explosion, on November 1, 1952. For the human race there was no turning back. The first Soviet device was tested less than a year later."[124] Despite its hefty ramifications, Truman found it not a difficult decision at all. A few days after making it, Truman, the plain-speaking Missourian, told a White House Staff session "that we had got to do it—make the bomb—though no one wants to use it. But . . . we have got to have it if only for bargaining purposes with the Russians."[125] This dynamic of fear of the actual and potential capabilities of the opposing superpower constantly fueled the subsequent arms race.

The horrendous costs of the arms race over the following four decades and the widespread present-day support for arms control measures lends the quality of pathos to the courageous endeavors of men like Kennan and Oppenheimer to limit the development of nuclear weapons. Their efforts to foster international control arrangements certainly seems to place them on the side of the angels while leaving the H-bomb's proponents like Strauss and Teller among the seeming villains of the story. Yet the recent testimony of Andrei Sakharov reveals that caution is warranted in brandishing such designations. Soviet work on a thermonuclear bomb already had begun in 1948 when a theoretical group (which included Sakharov) was established under the leadership of Igor Tamm.[126] And as Sakharov clarified Stalin fully understood the potential of the new weapon and planned to develop and deploy it. Any American offer of either a moratorium on research or proposals for verifiable arrangements for nuclear arms control were destined to fail.[127] In such circumstances Truman's decision, albeit tragically, takes on a certain wisdom.

NSC 68 AND THE SOVIET THREAT

The State Department's direct interest in the H-bomb diminished once Truman accepted the recommendations of the special NSC subcommittee. The policymakers at Foggy Bottom left the mechanics of the weapon's development in the hands of the Defense Department and the Atomic Energy Commission.[128] They now centered their attention on the reexamination of objectives which

---

senberg, "American Atomic Strategy and the Hydrogen Bomb Decision," *Journal of American History* 66 (June 1979): 62–87. Also see Herken, *The Winning Weapon*, pp. 316–21.

[124] Bundy, *Danger and Survival*, p. 197.

[125] Diary entry, February 4, 1950, Eben Ayers diary, Eben A. Ayers Papers, HSTL, Box 17.

[126] David Holloway, *The Soviet Union and the Arms Race* (New Haven, 1983), pp. 23–25.

[127] Andrei Sakharov, *Memoirs*, trans. by Richard Lourie (New York, 1990), pp. 98–100.

[128] For details see Herbert F. York, *The Advisors: Oppenheimer, Teller and the Superbomb* (San Francisco, 1976), pp. 75–86.

Truman also had requested when approving the program to test the feasibility of thermonuclear weapons. A special interdepartmental committee of State Department and Pentagon representatives was formed to undertake this assignment. Under Paul Nitze's leadership this committee produced NSC 68, a paradigmatic document which has been described as "the first comprehensive statement of a national strategy" for the postwar period.[129]

Without contesting the ultimate importance of NSC 68, it can be seen as a postscript to the resolution of the debate within the State Department over the potential Soviet danger and over the possibility of negotiations with the USSR. Acheson's rejection of Kennan's advice on international control and his support for the H-bomb's development effectively culminated the debate. From then on Acheson targeted his efforts on moving the Truman administration to combat the Soviet threat most efficaciously. NSC 68 represented the working-out of plans to that end. The document offered no fresh position but rather fleshed out the stance which Acheson had reached during the course of the H-bomb discussions and then took it a stage further by prescribing actions. The secretary of state publicly revealed his position on February 8, 1950, when he argued that agreements with the Soviet Union were worthless, unless based on strength and backed by force. America's basic policy should be to create "situations of strength."[130] NSC 68 provided a full development of this thesis and, in very general terms, outlined the budgetary and military means to implement it. It was, as John Lewis Gaddis has noted, "as much a work of advocacy as of analysis."[131] Acheson himself later remarked that the purpose of NSC 68 was to "bludgeon the mass mind of 'top government.' "[132] Undoubtedly he had in mind the Defense Department, the Bureau of the Budget, and, while he would never have admitted it, the president himself.

Nitze oversaw the fundamental staff work on NSC 68, while working in close collaboration with Acheson and keeping him fully informed.[133] The new

[129] Senator Henry Jackson quoted in George and Smoke, *Deterrence in American Foreign Policy*, p. 26. For detailed analysis on the development, contents, and significance of NSC-68 see Paul Hammond's "NSC 68: Prologue to Rearmament"; Samuel F. Wells, Jr., "Sounding the Tocsin: NSC 68 and the Soviet Threat," *International Security* 4 (Fall 1979): 116–58; Joseph M. Siracusa, "NSC 68: A Reappraisal," *Naval War College Review* 33 (November–December 1980): 4–14; Sam Postbrief, "Departure from Incrementalism in U.S. Strategic Planning: The Origins of NSC-68," *Naval War College Review* 33 (March–April 1980): 34–57; John Lewis Gaddis, *Strategies of Containment*, pp. 89–126; and Marc Trachtenberg, "A 'Wasting Asset': American Strategy and the Shifting Nuclear Balance, 1949–1954," *International Security* 13 (Winter 1988/89): 5–18.

[130] "Peace Goal Demands Firm Resolve," extemporaneous remarks by Secretary Acheson at press conference, February 8, 1950, *Department of State Bulletin* 22 (February 20, 1950): 272–74.

[131] John Lewis Gaddis, "NSC 68 and the Problem of Ends and Means," *International Security* 4 (Spring 1980): 168.

[132] Acheson, *Present at the Creation*, p. 374.

[133] Interview with Paul Nitze, Arlington, Va., July 5, 1978.

Planning Staff director quickly enlisted the full support of his Staff colleagues, demonstrating once again that Kennan had been unable to inculcate his ideas and vision even among his closest collaborators. Indeed Kennan's friend, John Paton Davies, provided a key phrase for NSC 68—"to frustrate the Kremlin's design"—and yet again demonstrated the strength of his anti-communism, which nonetheless failed to save him from the ravages of McCarthyism.[134] George Kennan, however, played no direct role in the formulation of NSC 68. His influence emerged indirectly, of course. At the most basic level Kennan's revelation of the near exclusive American reliance on nuclear weapons for deterrence and as a response to possible Soviet aggression provided the departure point for Acheson and Nitze in their efforts to redress this situation.[135] He did most to alert them to the situation. More specifically, Nitze utilized in NSC 68 an analysis of the Soviet threat from a previously authorized NSC document (NSC 20/4), based on a draft authored by Kennan. Nitze presented the description of the threat as portrayed by Kennan as still valid but much more immediate in the early months of 1950.[136]

In NSC 68 Nitze portrayed the Soviet Union as inherently militant and expansionist "because it possesses and is possessed by a worldwide revolutionary movement, because it is the inheritor of Russian imperialism and because it is a totalitarian dictatorship." Having notched these three strikes against the Soviets, Nitze turned to the primary task at hand, the prescribing of American actions. He outlined four broad possibilities—a continuation of current policies and programs; a return to isolation; a preventive war; and a more rapid buildup of the political, economic, and military strength of the free world. He discussed then dismissed the first three options which served simply as straw men. He deemed only the last course as "consistent with progress toward achieving our fundamental purpose." NSC 68 held that "the frustration of the Kremlin design requires the free world to develop a successfully functioning political and economic system and a vigorous political offensive against the Soviet Union." These, in turn, required "an adequate military shield under

[134] Paul Nitze, *From Hiroshima to Glasnost*, p. 94.

[135] On this point see Sam Postbrief, "Departure from Incrementalism in U.S. Strategic Planning," p. 51. One can see an early indication of this in a Staff discussion, which Acheson attended, on October 11, 1949, the minutes of which read: "Mr. Kennan also mentioned the concept of retaliation by atomic bombing in the light of the knowledge that the Russians now have the atomic bomb and suggested that it may now be impossible for us to retaliate with the atomic bomb against a Russian attack with orthodox weapons. Mr. Nitze pointed out that this fact might make conventional armaments and their possession by the Western European nations, as well as by ourselves, all the more important; that it might be necessary, therefore, to lower rather than to raise civilian standards of living in order to produce arms as against consumer goods; and that this in turn might call for a different propaganda approach than the one we were presently using." Minutes of meeting, October 11, 1949, PPS Records, Box 32.

[136] On the connections between NSC 68 and NSC 20 see Joseph M. Siracusa, "NSC 68: A Reappraisal," pp. 4–14.

which they can develop." Getting to the proverbial bottom line, the document judged it necessary "to have the military power to deter, if possible, Soviet expansion, and to defeat, if necessary, aggressive Soviet or Soviet-directed actions of a limited or total character."[137] The required military power was interpreted generously and emphasis placed on the expansion of both conventional and nuclear forces.

This is not the place to describe how the outlook enshrined in NSC 68 came to dominate the thinking of policymakers in all sections of the Truman administration. We must acknowledge, however, that it eventually did, although the North Korean invasion of South Korea in June 1950 provided the crucial impetus to ensure its adoption. The Korean War "changed the whole frame of reference for policy" and allowed Acheson and Nitze to triumph by apparently confirming the analysis of NSC 68.[138] This national security document comprised the credo that Acheson had worked towards since assuming control of the State Department in January 1949. He had not brought it with him into office but had developed it through his consideration of issues like the German future and the division of Europe and the development of the hydrogen bomb. Acheson's adoption of the over-simplified, military-oriented approach of NSC 68 marked his final rejection of the views of George Kennan.

Kennan served as Department Counselor during the evolution of NSC 68 but his counsel regarding the proper methods to react to the Soviets found no audience. Acheson would seek his advice on specific matters, as during the early days of the Korean War, but it would always be within the context of the worldview framed in NSC 68. In the first half of 1950 the "author" of the containment doctrine watched as his State Department associates led the way in giving this doctrine an increasingly military character. As Kennan correctly recalled, his views conflicted with the dominant tendency to base American "plans and calculations solely on the *capabilities* of a potential adversary, assuming him to be desirous of doing anything he could do to bring injury to us, and to exclude from consideration as something unsusceptible to exact determination, the whole question of that adversary's real *intentions*."[139]

This dichotomy between intentions and capabilities proved utterly frustrating for Kennan. Late in 1949 in a meeting in Acheson's office he railed against reports of the British General Bernard Montgomery's calls for a conventional

---

[137] NSC 68, "A Report to the President Pursuant to the President's Directive of January 31, 1950," April 7, 1950, *FRUS* 1950, 1, pp. 246, 272–85. It is difficult to disagree with Herbert Feis's assessment made in 1953 that NSC 68 was "the most ponderous expression of elementary ideas not very coherently expressed." See transcript (p. 796) of Princeton Seminars, October 10–11, 1953, Acheson Papers, HSTL, Box 75.

[138] Hammond, "NSC 68: Prologue to Rearmament," p. 370. Hammond went so far as to argue that until the Korean War, NSC 68 was "threatened with irrelevancy."

[139] Kennan, *Memoirs*, I, p. 475. See also Kennan's comments of July 12, 1950, on this subject in *Memoirs*, I, p. 499.

force buildup. Kennan made the point "that what is necessary to win a war is not the same as what is necessary to deter an aggressor from waging a war."[140] Montgomery looked at Soviet military capabilities, pointed to the worst-case scenario in light of them and drew the obvious conclusion with regard to Western defense forces. Kennan didn't discount military capabilities but concentrated more on the likelihood of their use. He recommended that foreign policy and defense strategy be rooted more in an analysis of the adversary's intentions. But, as John Gaddis has explained, such an approach "would have required frequent reconsiderations, since intentions can change more rapidly than capabilities."[141] Such an approach failed to provide the clear-cut direction enamored by policymakers who must build a domestic consensus in support of foreign policy. In the end Acheson simply judged it too risky and tenuous and he adopted the alternative fleshed out in NSC 68.

Interestingly, Acheson allowed Kennan to go public with an expression of his views at the very time that NSC 68 received its final drafting. In the March 1950 issue of the *Reader's Digest*, Kennan published a short article entitled "Is War With Russia Inevitable?"[142] Stewart Alsop aptly referred to this essay in a column devoted to criticizing it as "the Kennan Swan Song."[143] Kennan argued, as he had from the time he assumed the directorship of the Policy Planning Staff, that the principal danger presented by the Soviet Union lay in its political expansion. He downplayed the Soviet military threat arguing that in Eastern Europe Soviet imperialism "bit off more than it could comfortably chew" and that its "resulting discomfort should make the Kremlin more wary, rather than less, about taking on much bigger bites just at this time." Kennan's benign, almost dismissive, attitude regarding the Soviet military threat also showed through in his assessment that the Russian possession of the atomic bomb "does not affect [the situation] very much."[144] Just as the principal danger from the Soviet Union lay in its political expansion so the requisite American response in Kennan's view lay primarily in the political rather than the military domain. Kennan explicitly warned, in an undisguised shot across the bow of the ideas of NSC 68, against being diverted "by a morbid preoccupation with what *could possibly happen if*."[145] He made a telling point and

[140] Summary of meeting, November 30, 1949, Executive Secretariat Records, Box 1.
[141] John Lewis Gaddis, "Was the Truman Doctrine a Real Turning Point?" *Foreign Affairs* 52 (January 1974): 401.
[142] George F. Kennan, "Is War with Russia Inevitable? Five Solid Arguments for Peace," *The Reader's Digest* (March 1950), pp. 1–9.
[143] Stewart Alsop, "The Kennan Swan Song," *Washington Post*, February 24, 1950, copy in Elsey Papers, HSTL, Box 62.
[144] Kennan, "Is War with Russia Inevitable?" p. 2.
[145] Ibid., p. 8. Also note Kennan's earlier warning to a National War College audience of the danger "that in our pre-occupation with a military contest . . . we will forget to do those things which might still keep such a contest from becoming a living reality." Kennan, "Where Do We Stand?" December 21, 1949, Kennan Papers, Box 17.

one that if acknowledged might have placed a brake on the military influence on American foreign policy after 1950. But Kennan had no real audience for this swan song. While retaining a deep sense of the validity of his own views, Kennan now stewed in a lonely dissent from the dominant foreign policy paradigm within the Truman administration. The period during which he made his major direct contribution to the formulation of American foreign policy had ended. He carried on in the Counselor's office, waiting to begin his sojourn at the Institute for Advanced Study, where he hoped to educate and raise the intellectual tone of the wider foreign policy debate. Just before his departure, however, the outbreak of war on the Korean Peninsula pulled him briefly back into the key decision-making councils.

CHAPTER TEN

Korean Dilemmas and Beyond

LATIN AMERICAN TRAVELS

For the majority of the first half of 1950 George Kennan operated at some distance from the center of policy-making in the State Department. He marked time while waiting for his leave to begin on June 30 and looked forward to his stay at the Institute for Advanced Study. But the outbreak of the Korean War delayed his departure for Princeton. The North Korean attack across the 38th parallel during Kennan's last scheduled week in the Counselor's office caused Acheson to request him to stay on temporarily and brought him back into the main action of policy determination. He played some role in formulating the initial American response to the North Korean aggression. Towards the end of August, however, he made his escape from Washington and took up his appointment with Oppenheimer and the other scholars at the prestigious Institute. The Korean War, however, provided subsequent occasions over the ensuing year to draw Kennan back into the policy-making process and kept him in contact with his colleagues in the department.

During the first months of 1950 when the politics of the Korean peninsula drifted far from the center of American concerns, Kennan uncharacteristically devoted some attention to Latin America. He undertook his first (and only) official visit to that continent which had resided at the outer periphery of the areas that claimed his attention as Director of the Policy Planning Staff. He first raised the possibility of such a trip with his Staff colleagues in November 1949. As he envisaged it then, he would visit not only Latin America but also Africa and perhaps the Near East "with a view to selecting material for a study of dependent areas."[1] He asked his associates for suggestions for his itinerary. By February he had lowered his sights somewhat and settled on a month-long visit to Latin America alone. The principal official obligation planned for his visit involved his participation in a regional conference of U.S. ambassadors to Latin American countries scheduled for early March in Rio de Janeiro.

Kennan left Washington by train on February 18 enroute to Mexico City, his first major port of call. His departure at this time took him away from the department during the main gestation period of NSC 68. Acheson later suggested that he dispatched Kennan on the Latin American tour precisely to remove him temporarily from the department in order to ease Nitze's preparation

---

[1] Minutes of meeting, November 25, 1949, PPS Records, Box 32.

of the national security statement. In his memoirs he wittily recalled that "when the argument reached the point which President George Vincent of the University of Minnesota has described as the 'you hold the sieve while I milk the barren heifer' stage, the way to peace and action required separating the chief contestants for a cooling-off period. Accordingly one [Nitze] stayed in Washington, one [Kennan] went to South America, and the third [Bohlen] to Europe."[2] Acheson's recollection plays a little fast and loose with the facts given that Kennan himself set about planning his trip long before Acheson secured Truman's approval to formulate the document which became NSC 68. Acheson might more accurately have said simply that he gave his benediction to Kennan's existing plans to visit south of the Rio Grande and appreciated the beneficial side-effects of his absence from the department at the time of NSC 68's formulation.

After a contemplative train ride that took him through St. Louis and San Antonio, Kennan reached Mexico City on February 21.[3] The Mexican capital made "a violent, explosive impression" upon him.[4] The negative experience there set the tone for his whole visit. He described Caracas in his diary as a "grotesque crevice of urbanization" while Rio repulsed him with its noise, traffic, and "unbelievable contrasts between luxury and poverty."[5] São Paulo was "still worse." Montevideo and Buenos Aires were more "relaxed" but not sufficiently so to lift his melancholy. On his return trip home, Lima "depressed" him while he sensed only a palpable "undercurrent of violence" during his brief stops in Central America. Additionally, he found his official meetings with Latin American leaders uniformly artificial and "meaningless."[6]

The decision of the Brazilian Communists to protest Kennan's visit further soured his experience in Latin America. On March 3 CIA Director Roscoe Hillenkoetter warned that the Communists were making extensive plans for demonstrations against Kennan's visit but advised that the Brazilian security forces would be able to control any public disorder.[7] In a perverse but nonetheless real illustration of the stature he had obtained by 1950, the local Communists, acting presumably with the approval of the Soviet propaganda machine, targeted Kennan as their "arch enemy," and as a "representative of the worst form of . . . 'Yankee Imperialism.' " Wall signs proclaimed him a "Fascist at heart" and advertised starkly: "*Fora Kennan*"—Kennan Go

[2] Acheson, *Present at the Creation*, p. 753.
[3] For Kennan's meditations and observations on this trip see his *Sketches from a Life*, pp. 129–34.
[4] Kennan, *Memoirs*, I, p. 476.
[5] Ibid., pp. 477–78.
[6] Ibid., p. 479.
[7] Hillenkoetter memorandum, "Appraisal of Communist-instigated anti-U.S. Demonstrations in Brazil," March 3, 1950, Truman Papers, Records of NSC, Box 3.

Home![8] In the end the promised demonstrations did not amount to much but the threat of violent protest forced Kennan to endure tight security arrangements both in Rio and São Paulo. There is surely some irony in the most senior American official committed to restraint in dealing with the Soviet Union being subjected to visceral Communist propaganda attack but Kennan failed to find the mood to appreciate it. This attack only added to his unfavorable impressions of Latin America, impressions which were not buoyed by the gloomy reports he heard at the Rio meeting from the various ambassadors on conditions in the respective countries to which they were assigned.[9] By the time he returned to Washington, Kennan had formed some strong views of the Latin American situation and these he determined to place before Acheson.

In his long report to the secretary of state, Kennan made no effort to avoid the danger of generalization about the vast and varied area south of the United States' border with Mexico.[10] He displayed neither hesitancy nor humility in commenting about an area whose initial acquaintance he had made barely a month before. Submitted on March 29, Kennan's report gave full vent to the critical views he had formed during his visit.[11] He deemed it unlikely "that there could be any other region of the earth in which nature and human behavior could have combined to produce a more unhappy and hopeless background for the conduct of human life than in Latin America." The problems of geography and the painful consequences of Spanish conquest and the adoption of the Spanish cultural and political traditions weighed on the Latin Americans and blocked their path to progress. "The shadow of a tremendous helplessness and impotence" lay over most of the Latin American world. The inability of the Latin Americans to face the "bitter realities" compounded the problem. In a blunt attack on the Latin American character Kennan argued that "in the realm of individual personality [the] subconscious recognition of the failure of group effort finds its expression in an exaggerated self-centeredness and egotism—in a pathetic urge to create the illusion of desperate courage, supreme cleverness, and limitless virility where the more constructive virtues are so conspicuously lacking."[12]

Despite this dismal portrayal, Kennan accorded Latin America some im-

[8] "Brazilian Reds Fail in Kennan Protests," *New York Times*, March 5, 1950, p. 27; and Kennan, *Memoirs*, I, p. 478.

[9] On the "gloomy" reports see the comment in "Kennan to Take Leave," *New York Times*, March 8, 1950, p. 6. On the conference see also "U.S. Envoys Close Parley in Brazil," *New York Times*, March 10, 1950, p. 16.

[10] Kennan pointed to this danger sometime later. See George F. Kennan, *The Cloud of Danger: Current Realities of American Foreign Policy* (Boston, 1977), p. 52.

[11] Memorandum by the Counselor of the Department to the Secretary of State, March 29, 1950, *FRUS* 1950, II, pp. 598–624. For a comment on this controversial report see Roger R. Trask, "George F. Kennan's Report on Latin America (1950)," *Diplomatic History* 2 (Summer 1978): 307–11.

[12] Kennan memorandum, March 29, 1950, pp. 600–602.

portance to U.S. strategic interests. The political support of the Latin American nations proved useful in world councils. Furthermore, Latin America possessed some raw materials essential to the United States prosecution of a war.
The Latin American Communists were a threat to these resources and constituted "our most serious problems in the area." He judged it important that the
United States move to counter the Communist advances in the region. This
could be done indirectly and would vary depending on the local situation. But,
in a harbinger of the tragic and constant support of the United States for the
Latin American national security states, Kennan allowed for "harsh governmental measures of repression," which might "proceed from regimes whose
origins and methods would not stand the test of American concepts of democratic procedure." As would be the case when later administrations justified
American support for despicable regimes like those of Augusto Pinochet in
Chile and the Argentine junta, Kennan justified support for such regimes and
methods on the grounds that they represented "the only alternatives, to further
Communist successes."[13] Beyond encouraging repressive anti-Communist
measures, Kennan argued that the United States exercise a firm hand in its
dealings with the Latin American nations. He concluded by emphasizing the
importance of keeping "before ourselves and the Latin American peoples at
all times the reality . . . that we are a great power; that we are by and large
much less in need of them that they are in need of us."[14] For Kennan, obtaining either the affection or the understanding of the Latin Americans mattered
much less than gaining their respect.

Kennan's paper caused a stir within the department. He aptly recalled that
it "came as a great shock to people in the operational echelons of the department."[15] The Assistant Secretary of State for Latin American Affairs, Edward
G. Miller, immediately reacted against it. Miller apparently feared the consequences of the report's harshly critical comments regarding Latin America and
its people being leaked to the press.[16] He prevailed upon Acheson to "forbid
its distribution within the department and to have all copies locked away and
hidden from innocent eyes."[17] Acheson's decision is understandable in light
of his interest in preventing unnecessary flare-ups in U.S. relations with Latin
American countries. His decision, however, meant that Kennan's report had
absolutely no impact on the policy of the United States towards the continent
to its south. Accepting this, one might also note that Kennan's report, while
undoubtedly "condescending and patronizing in parts," possessed a bizarre

[13] Ibid., pp. 603–7.
[14] Ibid., pp. 620–2. As Roger Trask noted Kennan was somewhat confusing in his recommendations for American policy. See Trask, "George F. Kennan's Report on Latin America (1950),"
p. 310.
[15] Kennan, *Memoirs*, I, p. 480.
[16] See Kennan's handwritten note on the copy of his Report found in Kennan Papers, Box 18.
[17] Kennan, *Memoirs*, I, p. 480.

kind of integrity.[18] Kennan articulated views which have been reflected in much of American foreign policy towards Latin America both before and after. He, at least, had the courage to articulate his views directly rather than weaving webs of pious rhetoric to disguise and mask policies which in reality differed little from what he outlined. Given the bleak history of United States relations with Latin America in the postwar period, one might speculate if the leaking of Kennan's report really could have done much further damage.

The embarrassment of having one of his reports denied distribution in the department turned out to be a tempest in a teapot. Few individuals were even aware of the matter and it did not affect the high reputation which Kennan now bore outside the department. Confirmation of the esteem in which he was held came with the conferral upon him of honorary degrees by Dartmouth and Yale.[19] Yale's citation paid tribute to Kennan's "long and varied service in which he showed not only competence in many special fields, but a great gift for the making of plans which require a largeness of mind transcending special fields."[20] Kennan welcomed but did not bask long in the glory of Ivy League commencement day honors and tributes. In any case North Korean actions interrupted any such basking.

RESPONDING TO NORTH KOREAN AGGRESSION

In the early morning of June 25, 1950 (evening, June 24, Washington, D.C. time), the North Korean Democratic People's Army launched a massive offensive across the 38th parallel into South Korea. A detailed analysis of the origins of the military conflict instigated by this attack need not detain us here, nor will any attempt be made to provide a comprehensive account of American decision-making with regard to the war which ensued.[21] Our more modest goal is to identify the nature and significance of Kennan's involvement in this decision-making, which took place in circumstances of real pressure. The North Korean attack caught all senior American officials by surprise and found them quite unprepared to respond to the North Korean aggression. No real contin-

---

[18] Trask, "George F. Kennan's Report on Latin America (1950)," p. 307.

[19] "Taste, Conscience Urged in Life Work," New York Times, June 12, 1950, p. 40.

[20] "Yale in Graduation Honors Its Leaders," New York Times, June 13, 1950, p. 32.

[21] The literature on the Korean War is large and impressive. Among the important works are Burton I. Kaufman, The Korean War: Challenges in Crisis, Credibility and Command (New York, 1986), which provides an excellent overview. On background to the War see James I. Matray, The Reluctant Crusade: American Foreign Policy in Korea, 1941–1950 (Honolulu, 1985); Charles M. Dobbs, The Unwanted Symbol: American Foreign Policy, The Cold War and Korea, 1945–1950 (Kent, 1981); and Bruce Cummings, The Origins of the Korean War: Liberation and the Emergence of Separate Regimes, 1945–1947 (Princeton, N.J., 1981). Cummings has argued that the Korean War was essentially civil in its origins. On the significance of the Korean War see Robert Jervis, "The Impact of the Korean War on the Cold War," The Journal of Conflict Resolution 24 (December 1980): 563–92.

gency plans existed. A North Korean attack had not entered seriously into American strategic and military planning.[22] The Truman administration needed to formulate an American response from scratch and time was of the essence.

Before June 1950, Kennan maintained a minimal involvement in Korean matters. He claimed in his *Memoirs* that prior to the outbreak of war on the Korean peninsula he had not been involved with any of the decisions relating to Korea.[23] As Director of the Planning Staff, however, he had offered views on American involvement in Korea in late 1947. Kennan took his lead from the Joint Chiefs of Staff who held "from the standpoint of military security, the United States has little strategic interest in maintaining the present troops and bases in Korea."[24] Kennan subsequently advised Marshall in early November 1947, in his review of the world situation, that "since the territory [South Korea] is not of decisive strategic importance to us, our main task is to extricate ourselves without too great a loss of prestige."[25] The military in fact pushed this process of extrication over the next two years while seeking to build up the South Korean defense forces. Furthermore, as is well known, Acheson excluded South Korea from the American "defense perimeter" in the Far East in his address of January 12, 1950.[26] Certainly the American commitment to South Korea did not appear a primary one, a position which Kennan supported. The North Korean attack altered all that.

Kennan spent the weekend of June 24–25 at his farm in southern Pennsylvania and only discovered news of the North Korean attack when he returned to Washington on Sunday afternoon—a full day after the first reports of the attack. He went immediately to the department and, indicative of his continuing stature there, joined Acheson, Jessup, Rusk, and H. Freeman Matthews in discussions designed to formulate recommendations for President Truman who was flying back to Washington from his home in Independence, Missouri. Acheson and Rusk already had shepherded through the United Nations Security Council—aided by the Soviet boycott of its meetings—a resolution calling for a ceasefire and the withdrawal of forces.[27] The question now on the table focused on the American response.

From the outset Kennan favored a strong response to the North Koreans.

[22] This point is made by Alexander George and Richard Smoke in their *Deterrence in American Foreign Policy*, p. 145.

[23] Kennan, *Memoirs*, I, p. 484.

[24] See Forrestal's memorandum to Secretary of State, September 26, 1947, Records of State Department, Decimal File, 740.00119 Control (Korea)/9-2647, in which he outlined the JCS views.

[25] PPS/13, "Resume of World Situation," November 6, 1947, *FRUS* 1947, I, p. 776.

[26] Acheson, "Crisis in Asia—An Examination of U.S. Policy," *Department of State Bulletin* 22 (January 23, 1950), pp. 111–18.

[27] On Rusk's key role with the UN resolution see Schoenbaum, *Waging War and Peace*, pp. 210–21.

He assumed that Kim Il-Sung would not have acted without at least obtaining Stalin's approval.[28] In the early days he perceived that the attack in Korea might be part of "an aggressive new worldwide push for extending Communist influence."[29] He did not view the conflict as essentially civil in nature with deeply indigenous roots.[30] Rather he concentrated on its global implications. A Communist victory in Korea would prove highly damaging to U.S. prestige and would serve to encourage further aggression. The United States needed to take actions to counter the North Koreans and this included the use of armed forces to repel them back across the 38th parallel. Furthermore, the U.S. would need to "assure that Formosa . . . did not fall into Communist hands." Such an eventuality on top of the North Korean attack would "disastrously" damage American prestige.[31] Kennan's colleagues shared such views and a consensus readily emerged. Kennan's views here were neither foundational nor decisive for Acheson, who from the outset had recognized that a strong response would be necessary, but they confirmed him in his position, coming from the senior Soviet expert in the department.[32]

Acheson took these strong views to a meeting at Blair House—(then serving as the presidential residence during White House renovations)—of the senior diplomatic and military advisers with President Truman later in the evening of June 25. According to Kennan, Acheson, on leaving to meet Truman at the airport, specifically left word for him to attend this meeting. But in the confusion of lists being sent to the White House staff his name was omitted and he could not attend this meeting which largely defined those who would join the president to determine policy in the ensuing days. The pain of this exclusion—understandable to any policymaker not included within the key decision-making group—penetrated through his recollection of it. "I found myself thus automatically relegated to the sidelines," Kennan noted, "attending the respective meetings in the Secretary's office, but not those that took place at the White House level."[33] At the first Blair House meeting Acheson rec-

[28] For Kim's obtaining Stalin's approval see Strobe Talbott, ed., *Khrushchev Remembers* (Boston, 1970), pp. 367–69.

[29] This was the consensus American position. See Robert J. McMahon, "The Cold War in Asia: Toward a New Synthesis?" *Diplomatic History* 12 (Summer 1988): 317.

[30] Interestingly, two years later he would refer to it in these terms in his dispatch from Moscow of September 8, 1952, entitled "The Soviet Union and the Atlantic Pact." Here he wrote that "it was our decision to treat a civil war as an act of international aggression and to involve the authority of the United Nations." See his *Memoirs*, II, p. 339.

[31] Kennan provides a good summary of his own position in *Memoirs*, I, p. 486.

[32] On Acheson see McLellan, *Dean Acheson*, p. 275.

[33] Kennan, *Memoirs*, I, p. 486. Regular State Department participants included Acheson, Webb, Matthews, Rusk, Hickerson, and Jessup. On the Defense side the participants included Secretaries Johnson, Pace, and Finletter; Generals Bradley, Vandenberg, and Collins; and Admiral Sherman. Kennan did get to attend one meeting with Truman on June 28, 1950. See Minutes of 58th meeting of NSC, June 28, 1950, Truman Papers, PSF, Box 208.

ommended that Truman order General MacArthur's Far Eastern Command to provide supplies and air cover to South Korea and to instruct the Seventh Fleet to prevent any attack on Formosa. Discussion on American policy resumed on June 26 with Acheson again leading the charge for a military commitment. At this meeting Rusk relayed "Mr. Kennan's estimate that Formosa would be the next likely spot for a Communist move."[34] By June 27 Truman briefed congressional leaders and informed them that American sea and air forces would assist the South Koreans and that the Seventh Fleet would prevent any movement across the Taiwan Strait. Also on June 27 the United States obtained Security Council approval for a second resolution which called on member states to "furnish such assistance to the Republic of Korea as may be necessary to repel the armed attack and to restore international peace and security."[35] By this time it was starkly apparent that the South Koreans were no match for the Northerners. The ROK army collapsed and retreated down the peninsula. The government of Syngman Rhee fled its capital of Seoul. Acheson now considered ground troops essential as did MacArthur. Truman quickly agreed. The president viewed the "Russian feeler in Korea" as "an exact imitation of Japan in Manchuria, Hitler in the Rhineland and Mussolini in Ethiopia," and he did not plan to engage in appeasement.[36] He authorized the use of ground forces without seeking any formal congressional approval by resorting to the UN Security Council resolution as a justification. By June 30, less than a week after the North Korean attack, the United States was, in Acheson's words, "fully committed in Korea."[37]

Kennan found the Truman decisions much to his liking, despite reservations about undertaking them under UN auspices. Stewart Alsop recalled seeing the State Department Counselor at a party "doing a little jig" as an "expression of [his] delight" at the decision to commit American forces to the defense of South Korea.[38] Kennan also appreciated the decision to deploy the Seventh Fleet to the Taiwan Strait, a decision which derived in part from the special call he had made to prevent what he considered the most likely next step in Communist aggression. Kennan worried little about the implications of the direct interference in the Chinese civil war which the deployment involved. He riveted his attention on developing a forceful American response. In doing so he briefly resumed a familiar role, that of acting director of the Policy Planning Staff. The outbreak of the Korean War found Paul Nitze salmon fishing in a remote region of New Brunswick, Canada, and it took him a number of

[34] Memorandum of conversation on "Korean Situation," June 26, 1950, Acheson Papers, HSTL, Box 65.

[35] UN resolution, June 27, 1950, *FRUS 1950*, VII, p. 211.

[36] Truman to Arthur H. Vandenberg, July 6, 1950, Truman Papers, PSF, Box 140.

[37] Acheson, *Present at the Creation*, p. 413.

[38] Stewart Alsop, *The Center: People and Power in Political Washington* (New York, 1968), p. 8.

days to return to Washington.[39] Kennan resumed leadership of the Staff in his absence and it proved a bastion of support for a strong response including the use of ground forces.[40] In these early days of warfare, Acheson who came under great pressure from the press, demonstrated his confidence in Kennan by suggesting to Truman that his Counselor might hold a press conference to address the situation. The White House press secretary, Charlie Ross, reported back to Acheson that Truman preferred Acheson to hold a press conference and Acheson abided by the president's wish.[41] Kennan's opportunity to play a more public role as a direct spokesman for American policy did not come to fruition. But Acheson employed his talents in a variety of other ways, including using him to brief the ambassadors from the NATO countries. With Nitze's return, Kennan's role changed somewhat to that of a " 'floating kidney' (i.e., outside the chain of command and one step removed from the real decisions).''[42] Nonetheless, he agreed to Acheson's request to postpone his departure and thereupon focused on specific issues relating to the war. The most important of these concerned the extent of the American commitment in Korea.

To Cross or Not to Cross the 38th Parallel

From the outset Kennan sought only the most limited of "limited wars" in Korea. He argued from the earliest days of the conflict that the American goal should be the restoration of the *status quo ante bellum*. He kept his passions under control and argued that the North Koreans need only be repelled to the 38th parallel but not punished further or destroyed.[43] Initially he simply assumed this to be the American position and briefed a group of NATO ambassadors to this effect.[44] But the military necessities, as interpreted by MacArthur and the Pentagon, began quickly to attack this position at the edges. On June 30 when Truman and the JCS formally authorized American ground forces they also gave MacArthur permission to extend his air operations over the north in order to establish air superiority and to aid his effort to deny the whole peninsula to the North Koreans.[45] Kennan accepted this decision as a necessary means to secure his end of repulsing the aggressors back beyond the 38th

[39] Nitze, *From Hiroshima to Glasnost*, pp. 101–3.

[40] Among the Staff members, Charles Burton Marshall pressed most vigorously for ground forces. See Charles Burton Marshall, *The Limits of Foreign Policy* (Baltimore, 1968), pp. 148–50.

[41] See Lucius Battle record of phone conversation with Charlie Ross, June 27, 1950, Acheson Papers, HSTL, Box 65.

[42] Kennan, *Memoirs*, I, p. 487.

[43] This relies on Roger Dingman, "1950: The Fate of a Grand Design," *Pacific Historical Review* 47 (August 1978): 469.

[44] Kennan, *Memoirs*, I, p. 487.

[45] Kaufman, *The Korean War*, p. 31.

parallel. It proved, however, to be the thin end of the wedge as Kennan later discovered.

Throughout July Kennan worked to establish as formal American policy the goal of simply repelling the North Koreans from the South. He exercised his influence most effectively through his former colleagues in the Policy Planning Staff. There, Kennan again found an ally in John Davies who exhibited a strong concern to prevent the United States being bogged down in a possible "Chinese quagmire." Davies recommended caution in dealing with the Chinese in order to prevent any military conflict with them and consequently advised that the United States should "endeavor through our propaganda and other means to let Peking know that we will not go beyond restoring the *status quo ante* [of] June 25."[46] The Staff, influenced by Kennan, began to consider the desirability of issuing a public statement clearly indicating the American intention of not proceeding beyond the 38th parallel. This developing stance evoked the opposition of John Allison, the Director of the Office of Northeast Asian Affairs. Allison believed that perpetuating the division of the country at the 38th parallel would "make it impossible 'to restore international peace and security in the area,' " as called for in the June 27 UN Security Council resolution. Furthermore, he deemed it appropriate to punish the aggressors in this instance, which he thought would have "a salutary effect upon other areas of tension in the world."[47] Another bureaucratic battle loomed.

The Planning Staff offered its considered view on July 22. It reflected advice which Kennan had conveyed directly to Acheson the previous day when he warned of the military dangers of proceeding too far up the neck of the peninsula and the risks of provoking direct Russian intervention.[48] The Staff developed this position and also warned of the danger of conflict with Chinese Communist forces. It concluded that "from the point of view of U.S. military commitments and strength, we should make every effort to restrict military ground action to the area south of the 38th parallel, to bring about a cessation of hostilities on acceptable terms as rapidly as possible, and to work for a situation that will minimize the requirements for U.S. forces in the Republic of Korea."[49] No less an authority than General Omar Bradley remarked later that "read in retrospect . . . this paper is full of good sense."[50] But the Planning Staff did not have the benefit of hindsight to support its case and the bureaucratic piranhas circled quickly to rip into its position.

[46] "Strength at the Center," July 4, 1950, PPS Records, Box 20. Davies' initials are on this paper, indicating his authorship.

[47] Allison to Rusk, July 15, 1950, *FRUS* 1950, VII, pp. 393–95.

[48] Kennan quoted directly from his diary notes of this meeting at Acheson's Princeton seminars, February 13–14, 1954, Acheson Papers, HSTL, Box 76, transcript p. 1306.

[49] Draft memorandum by the Policy Planning Staff, July 22, 1950, *FRUS* 1950, VII, pp. 449–54.

[50] Omar N. Bradley and Clay Blair, *A General's Life* (New York, 1983), p. 558.

John Allison led the attack on the PPS position. In the emotionally charged atmosphere of the time when talk of the "Munich analogy" was bandied about, Allison went for the jugular. He branded the Staff recommendation as "a policy of appeasement . . . a timid, half-hearted policy designed not to provoke the Soviets to war." Allison found no need for any compromise with North Korea, which, for him, possessed no legal status and owed its existence only to the Soviet Union. He presented any failure to reunify the Korean nation as "a shirking of our duty to make clear once and for all that aggression does not pay."[51] Under this Allison barrage and quite aware that Dean Rusk, John Foster Dulles, and the whole military establishment leaned towards Allison's position, Paul Nitze wilted somewhat. He agreed to revise the Staff memorandum.

On July 25 the Planning Staff offered a compromise position. It continued to warn of the dangers of crossing the 38th parallel but deferred any decision on the matter "until military and political developments provide . . . additional information."[52] In effect the Staff's modification of its position irreparably weakened the position of the opponents of crossing the 38th parallel. "From that point on," Robert Donovan accurately commented, "talk about stopping at the parallel dwindled."[53] The one institutional bastion of opposition declared itself neutral on the subject. Meanwhile the proponents of crossing the parallel, led by the Joint Chiefs of Staff, marshaled their forces further.[54] Only Kennan and Bohlen continued to make their opposition known.[55] The Truman administration made no decision at this point but the writing was on the wall.

Kennan refused to be captured by the seductive allure of teaching the Communist aggressors a lesson by rolling back their domination of the northern half of the peninsula. Such was his reserve and objectivity at the time that he even indicated in late July that the United States should not block the entry of the People's Republic of China into the United Nations. He proffered no regard for the PRC but simply suggested that the United States face the reality of its existence. But he swam here against an extremely strong current and his advocacy came to naught, except in that it earned him the suspicion of John Foster Dulles who reportedly concluded that Kennan "was a very dangerous man."[56] Such assignations as Dulles's of Kennan suggest why individuality

[51] Memorandum from Allison to Nitze, July 24, 1950, *FRUS* 1950, VII, pp. 458–61.

[52] Draft memorandum by PPS, July 25, 1950, *FRUS* 1950, VII, pp. 469–73. George Butler had played the principal role in drafting this memorandum.

[53] Robert J. Donovan, *Tumultuous Years: The Presidency of Harry S. Truman, 1949–1953* (New York, 1982), p. 270.

[54] Ibid., pp. 270–71; and Bradley, *A General's Life*, p. 559.

[55] Bohlen, *Witness to History*, pp. 292–93.

[56] Kennan, *Memoirs*, I, p. 259.

and courage to argue a dissenting opinion with conviction are usually in short supply in bureaucracies.

Kennan possessed both individuality and intellectual courage in good measure and these allowed him to make a final effort to influence Acheson. On August 23 he forwarded to the secretary of state a memorandum (dated August 21) giving his thoughts on Far Eastern Policy. Here he advised permitting Chinese membership of the UN, ending support for the French in Indochina, and the development of a neutral Japan. As for Korea, Kennan warned not only that the United States had ''not achieved a clear and realistic and generally accepted view of our objectives in Korea'' but also that ''sectors of our public opinion and of our official establishment are indulging themselves in emotional, moralistic attitudes toward Korea which, unless corrected, can easily carry us toward real conflict with the Russians and inhibit us from making a realistic agreement about that area.'' Turning to the requirements of American foreign policy, Kennan argued to Acheson that American security hardly required ''an anti-Soviet Korean regime extended to *all* of Korea for all time.'' He went even further and suggested that the U.S. could ''eventually tolerate for a certain period of time a Korea nominally independent but actually amenable to Soviet influence.'' Keeping Korea permanently out of the Soviet orbit simply lay beyond American capabilities.[57] Kennan knew full well that his views were not composed in tune with the tenor of the time but he hoped that they might signal some dangers for Acheson.[58]

Acheson rejected Kennan's warning signals. He remembered Kennan's memo as ''typical of its gifted author, beautifully expressed, sometimes contradictory, in which were mingled flashes of prophetic insight and suggestions, as the document conceded, of total impracticability.''[59] More powerful forces operated on Acheson. He recognized the difficulties from a military standpoint of simply stopping at the 38th parallel. MacArthur's troops, he wrote Nitze, could not be ''expected to march up to a surveyor's line and just stop.''[60] Beyond the pressures of military realities, Acheson faced mounting domestic political pressures. He knew well that charges of cowardice and appeasement would be flung at him if he persuaded Truman to halt at the 38th parallel. Politically, in order to silence his congressional critics, he ''needed a clear-cut victory, not a protracted stalemate.''[61] He decided to seek it, despite some lingering reservations. Truman accepted his recommendation which coincided with all the military advice he received. It would have been difficult for him to do otherwise. ''It would have taken a superhuman effort to say no,''

[57] Kennan memorandum to Acheson, August 21, 1950, Acheson Papers, HSTL, Box 65.
[58] Kennan to Acheson, August 23, 1950, Acheson Papers, HSTL, Box 65.
[59] Acheson, *Present at the Creation*, p. 446.
[60] Acheson to Nitze, quoted in Isaacson and Thomas, *The Wise Men*, p. 530.
[61] Isaacson and Thomas, *The Wise Men*, pp. 530–31.

Averell Harriman recalled of the time. "Psychologically, it was almost impossible not to go ahead and complete the job."[62] Truman was no superman.

While Washington debated crossing the 38th parallel, General MacArthur fashioned a military situation which added only further fuel to stoke the fires of those who sought to reunify Korea. After the tremendous early successes of the North Korean forces, MacArthur stemmed the tide and maintained a bridgehead on the Korean peninsula around the port of Pusan. There his ground forces held out while his air force began to inflict damage on the North Korean extended supply lines. On September 15 MacArthur launched a spectacular counterattack. The Eighth Army initiated its offensive from Pusan while the Navy and the marines conducted a dramatically successful amphibious assault against the port of Inchon, on Korea's west coast and almost two hundred miles behind the North Korean lines, just twenty miles from Seoul. This powerful combination soon had the North Koreans reeling in full retreat towards the 38th parallel. American units recaptured Seoul on September 28.[63]

MacArthur's exhilarating military victories had a steamroller effect and obliterated any further thoughts of stopping at the 38th parallel. The administration made no effort to explore Soviet feelers regarding a diplomatic solution to the conflict.[64] Instead, Truman formally authorized MacArthur to cross the parallel and to unify Korea. Despite warnings, from the Chinese in particular, the general's forces began to fight their way towards Pyongyang and beyond. George Kennan's effort to limit American objectives to the repulsion of the North Korean aggressors beyond the 38th parallel ended in failure. As events quickly would prove, however, much wisdom and prescience resided in the advice he offered.

KENNAN TO THE RESCUE

By the time MacArthur's forces crossed into North Korea, Kennan had made his way to Princeton's Institute for Advanced Study. A *New York Times* editorial wished him well and lauded him as one of the "most valued servants" of the State Department, the "outstanding expert on Russia," and as an "exceptional student of contemporary affairs." The *Times'* editorialist looked forward to Kennan's returning to the department "refreshed and ready for many more years of fruitful service."[65] Kennan certainly needed refreshment. He left Washington in late August thoroughly disillusioned with the state of American foreign policy. "Never before has there been such utter confusion in the public mind with respect to US foreign policy," he hyperbolically confided to his diary. "The President doesn't understand it; Congress doesn't un-

---

[62] Harriman quoted in Donovan, *Tumultuous Years*, p. 271.
[63] For further details see Kaufman, *The Korean War*, pp. 78–85.
[64] Ibid., p. 86.
[65] *New York Times*, August 26, 1950, p. 12.

derstand it; nor does the public, nor does the press. They all wander around in a labyrinth of ignorance and error and conjecture, in which truth is intermingled with fiction at a hundred points, in which unjustified assumptions have attained the validity of premises, and in which there is no recognized and authoritative theory to hold on to.'' Only the diplomatic historian, he thought, ''could unravel this incredible tangle.'' Perhaps the diplomatic historian could carry ''the public up to a clear and comprehensive view of the occurrences of these recent years.''[66] Thus, Kennan set about to study the past so as to dispel some of the confusions of the present.

At Princeton Kennan found himself inundated with requests to address various groups and associations. He fended most of these invitations off, even one conveyed on by Acheson who took the opportunity to assure Kennan that he was ''greatly missed in the daily councils on the fifth floor.''[67] Kennan rightly understood that his success in doing any ''serious academic work'' depended on his ''courage in ruling out distractions of all sorts.'' In replying to Acheson he informed him that he thought of him and his other colleagues often and found it ''hard to get used to the fact that I cannot even try to help any of you in the present travail.''[68] It seems he found the adjustment to life away from Washington difficult. He later admitted that ''after a few months I began to miss the operational side of life that I had become accustomed to in the Foreign Service. The stimulation of having things to do that I had to do.''[69] By late November he had clarified for himself that he wished to return to his ''regular profession, which is the service of the Government abroad.'' He wrote of his intentions to Acheson and explained that ''I have been long enough around Washington for a single spell and that for a whole series of reasons, including personal financial ones, I ought to go abroad again at this stage, rather than return to any policy-advisory function in Washington.''[70] Events in Korea, however, intervened to bring him back to Washington within the week.

After a series of warnings, which MacArthur chose to dismiss, the Chinese intervened in force in the last days of November 1950. The ferocious Chinese attack after November 28 caught MacArthur, who had just begun his ''home by Christmas'' offensive, by surprise. Within the week the general's forces were in full retreat. The military debacle seemed all the greater because the UN forces had appeared on the verge of final victory. Now questions were raised as to whether they could maintain a foothold on the peninsula.[71] Truman

---

[66] Kennan diary entry quoted in Kennan, *Memoirs*, I, p. 500.

[67] Acheson to Kennan, September 6, 1950, Acheson Papers, Box 32.

[68] Kennan to Acheson, September 12, 1950, Acheson Papers, Box 32.

[69] Entry February 1, 1970, Helen M. Lilienthal, ed., *The Journals of David E. Lilienthal*, vol. 7: *Unfinished Business, 1968–1981* (New York, 1983), p. 167.

[70] Kennan to Acheson, November 24, 1950, Acheson Papers, HSTL, Box 32.

[71] For further details see Kaufman, *The Korean War*, pp. 107–9.

gathered his advisers around him on November 28 to assess the disastrous situation. No one mentioned the goal of reunifying Korea. The military evoked no enthusiasm for the present battle. Acheson suggested only that the United States find some line and hold on to it.[72] But after a week of fighting this seemed beyond the capabilities of the American forces. On December 3 Acheson met with General Marshall, whom Truman had called on earlier to replace Louis Johnson as Defense Secretary, and the Joint Chiefs of Staff. The smell of defeat wafted in the air. Discussions focused on the benefits of a ceasefire and on the orderly evacuation of troops.[73] Kennan injected himself into the midst of this unhappy and depressed scene.

On December 1 Bohlen called Kennan from Paris and suggested he go to Washington to help out.[74] Kennan confirmed that his assistance could be utilized and reached the department on Sunday morning, December 3. He found Washington in "disarray."[75] Under Secretary Webb briefed him and based on military reports raised the specter of a complete withdrawal from Korea. He charged Kennan with analyzing the prospects for negotiations with the Russians on the Korean problem at the time.[76] In the afternoon Kennan sat in to hear Acheson's report to his senior advisers of his meeting with Truman and Marshall and had his assignment confirmed by the secretary.[77] He quickly set about his task aided by John Paton Davies and Frederick Reinhardt, a Soviet specialist in the department. Kennan concluded that "the present moment is probably the poorest one we have known at any time in the history of our relations with the Soviet Union for negotiations with its leaders." He persuasively argued that a prerequisite to satisfactory negotiations was "the demonstration that we have the capability to stabilize the front somewhere in the peninsula and to engage a large number of Communist forces for a long time."[78] He offered no easy escape for the United States. Before approaching a negotiating table the United States needed to demonstrate that it possessed some solid cards in its hand.

Kennan took his recommendations to Acheson's office at seven o'clock on that Sunday evening. He found Acheson still there and looking very tired. Kennan decided to hold off presenting his cautionary recommendations on negotiations and instead accepted Acheson's invitation to join him at his home for supper. There, they talked in general terms about the war but Acheson's indomitable spirit in the midst of his travails struck Kennan most deeply. He recalled feeling a "sympathy and solicitude" for Acheson which would sur-

---

[72] Notes on NSC Meeting, November 28, 1950, *FRUS* 1950, VII, pp. 1242–49.

[73] Memorandum by Jessup, December 3, 1950, *FRUS* 1950, VII, pp. 1323–34.

[74] Bohlen, *Witness to History*, pp. 294–95.

[75] Author's interview with Kennan, Princeton, N.J., March 6, 1989.

[76] Kennan, *Memoirs*, II, pp. 26–29.

[77] Report by Sheppard, December 3, 1950, *FRUS* 1950, VII, pp. 1336–39.

[78] Kennan quotes from his report in *Memoirs*, II, p. 29.

vive all their later disagreements. Knowing full well the frightful challenges that lay ahead of the secretary of state, Kennan rose early the next morning and wrote a personal letter to him which both men deemed of such significance that they included it in full in their respective memoirs. It awaited Acheson when he arrived in his office on December 4 and so moved was he by it that he read it to his staff meeting. Kennan wrote:

Dear Mr. Secretary:

On the official level I have been asked to give advice only on the particular problem of Soviet reaction to various possible approaches.

But there is one thing I should like to say in continuation of our discussion of yesterday evening.

In international, as in private, life, what counts most is not really what happens to some one but how he bears what happens to him. For this reason almost everything depends from here on out on the manner in which we Americans bear what is unquestionably a major failure and disaster to our national fortunes. If we accept it with candor, with dignity, with resolve to absorb its lessons and to make it good by re-doubled and determined effort—starting all over again, if necessary, along the pattern of Pearl Harbor—we need lose neither our self-confidence nor our allies nor our power for bargaining, eventually, with the Russians. But if we try to conceal from our own people or from our allies the full measure of our misfortune, or permit ourselves to seek relief in any reactions of bluster or petulance or hysteria, we can easily find this crisis resolving itself into an irreparable deterioration of our world position—and of our confidence in ourselves.[79]

This letter reflected the best of Kennan. He wasted no time reflecting on responsibilities for past mistakes nor in alluding to the perspicacity of his earlier warnings. He sought only to aid Acheson and through him his country. He addressed the situation as it existed and encouraged Acheson (and through him the whole administration) to face realities and then to muster the determination to confront the problems which existed.

Kennan's letter immediately benefitted Acheson. It appeared to boost his spirits and he followed up his reading of the letter by observing to his colleagues that they were being "infected by a spirit of defeatism emanating from headquarters in Tokyo."[80] To counter this he called for suggestions on how to bring about a redoubled and determined effort. The unlikely combination of Dean Rusk and Kennan came to the fore here. Kennan argued convincingly against negotiating with the Russians from a position of weakness and found agreement for his stance. Rusk and Kennan both evoked the memory of the British fighting on against overwhelming odds and called for the United States to muster its forces and hold on to some position in Korea. But did the Amer-

---

[79] Kennan to Acheson, December 4, 1950, Acheson Papers (Yale), Box 17.
[80] Acheson, *Present at the Creation*, p. 476.

ican military have the capacity to achieve this without resorting to extreme measures such as bombing Manchuria and thus widening the war? Acheson thought "the Military's will to resist" would need to be strengthened.[81] Acheson began the process by immediately calling General Marshall and encouraging him to think of holding on to a bridgehead rather than withdrawing. Marshall proved receptive to Acheson's suggestion and agreed with his use of "dogged determination." The only limitation he stipulated was that "we should not get ourselves into an irretrievable hole." Marshall also welcomed Acheson's further suggestion that Kennan and Rusk come across to the Pentagon to speak with him.[82]

Kennan and Rusk traveled over the Potomac to meet Marshall that very afternoon. Both felt a deep respect and admiration for their former chief under whom their respective careers had blossomed. But they were intent on stiffening the resolve of the military. Rusk outlined the importance of fighting on. Kennan supported him by explaining that a complete withdrawal would be mercilessly exploited by the Russians in any negotiations. Marshall accepted their points in principle but indicated his reluctance "to determine at the present moment whether any line or beachhead could be held." Rusk and Kennan refused to let the matter die at this point and pressed the general further. They denied trying to determine military policy and accepted that withdrawal might be necessary if it really was true that an attempt to hold a beachhead would mean the loss of the entire UN force or any other exorbitant consequence. But, they emphasized the costly political implications of any such decision and asked that these be kept in mind by the military authorities.[83] It is unclear what the "organizer of victory" in the Second World War thought of his two former subordinates pressuring him to adopt a particular military stance in Korea. Certainly, however, he possessed a clearer appreciation of the political importance of holding on in Korea after their visit.[84]

Kennan left Washington within days of his arrival but the fighting spirit he helped engender stayed on. Truman expressed it in his discussions with Clement Attlee on December 5. He told the British Prime Minister of the need to "hold the line in Korea," and made "it perfectly plain . . . that we do not desert our friends when the going is rough."[85] Truman, Acheson, and Marshall succeeded in encouraging the Joint Chiefs to stick with the battle in Korea, despite the loss of Seoul and Inchon in December of 1950. Early in 1951 the Eighth Army, now under the tough and capable General Matthew B. Ridg-

[81] Memorandum by Lucius Battle, December 4, 1950, *FRUS* 1950, VII, pp. 1345–46.
[82] Memorandum of Marshall-Acheson Telephone Conversation, December 4, 1950, Acheson Papers, HSTL, Box 65.
[83] Kennan's notes of this meeting, December 6, 1950, Acheson Papers, HSTL, Box 65.
[84] Pogue, *George C. Marshall: Statesman, 1945–1959*, pp. 467–68.
[85] Minutes of Second Meeting of President Truman and Prime Minister Attlee, December 5, 1950, *FRUS* 1950, VII, p. 1395.

way, stemmed the Chinese advance and launched a counteroffensive of its own that took the fighting back to the vicinity of the 38th parallel. From this position the United States revealed a willingness to consider a cease-fire and negotiations to reestablish the *status quo ante* June 25, 1950.[86]

Kennan judged his own role in the determination of American policy after the major Chinese intervention in Korea to be "relatively minor." As he portrayed it, he played "a small but not negligible part in steadying down the military." His assessment stands up well. Truman, Acheson, and Marshall bore the ultimate responsibility for providing leadership in these troubled times. Yet, Kennan aided them—especially Acheson and Marshall—in fulfilling their difficult leadership obligations at this time. One cannot measure the exact impact of Kennan's letter to Acheson but it appears to have served as an ignition device for the efforts to counter the pervasive defeatism within the administration. It should not be underestimated. Kennan's distinctive contribution lay in his clarifying that the United States should not rush into any negotiations. It needed to develop a hand to play with before meeting anyone over a negotiating table. This advice bolstered the arguments of Dean Rusk and Kennan on the necessity of garnering the fighting spirit and in ensuring that the United States fought on and avoided any precipitous and embarrassing withdrawal. Perhaps the American policy would have been the same had Kennan not journeyed down to Washington. Yet one must not dismiss the importance of key interventions by individuals at crucial moments and Kennan's may well have been one. He helped keep Washington together during one of its darkest moments of the postwar era.

BEHIND-THE-SCENES NEGOTIATOR

Kennan returned to Princeton and resumed his work. The products of his labors began to make their public appearance. The April 1951 issue of *Foreign Affairs* carried his essay, "America and the Russian Future," which explored the possibilities for political change in the Soviet Union.[87] That same month he traveled to the University of Chicago to deliver the Walgreen lectures. He arrived with but two of his six lectures completed and in a state of mind that can only be described as troubled. His surroundings depressed him and, as he recorded with seeming relish in his diary, he heard a "small inward voice . . . gleefully and melodramatically [say], 'You have despaired of yourself; now despair of your country.' "[88] Despite the pressures of composition and his inner turmoil, Kennan delivered incisive lectures that established him quickly as a major spokesman for the realist school in American foreign relations. Pub-

---

[86] Kaufman, *The Korean War*, pp. 144–49.

[87] George F. Kennan, "America and the Russian Future," *Foreign Affairs* 29 (April 1951): 351–70.

[88] Kennan, *Sketches from a Life*, p. 143.

lished as *American Diplomacy, 1900–1950*, they tellingly critiqued "the legalistic-moralistic approach to international problems," which, he sought to prove, ran "like a red skein through [the] foreign policy of the last fifty years."[89] Kennan's book made his name familiar to a generation of students of international relations but there remained only one audience that he really desired to influence—the makers of American foreign policy. Even while he worked on his Walgreen lectures, Kennan also attempted to influence the decisionmakers in Washington.

The matter of cease-fire arrangements for Korea prompted Kennan to offer his views to Acheson. Ridgway's success in stabilizing the front around the midsection of Korea provided a basis for negotiations which Kennan had realized did not exist during December 1950. Kennan explained that in order to obtain a cease-fire or an improvement in the situation in Korea it would be necessary "to deal with the Russians." The United States could not deal "only with their puppets." The time was ripe, he thought, to make contact through informal and secret channels. He suggested that this job be undertaken by "some intermediary who could be denied in case of necessity." In emphasizing the opportunity for negotiations Kennan warned again that any renewed attempt to push north of the 38th parallel would "invoke trouble." It would invite this time "the possibility of Soviet intervention."[90] Acheson read Kennan's advice and registered it without making any immediate decision.

Early in May 1951, the Soviet delegate to the United Nations Jacob Malik and his deputy Semem Tsarapkin gave a ride from the temporary UN headquarters in Lake Success into New York City to Frank Corrigan and Thomas Cory of the U.S. Mission to the UN. During the ride Malik spoke loquaciously about a range of matters in Soviet-American relations. He even inquired about George Kennan, whom he suggested had had "a great and unfortunate influence on United States' policy toward Russia."[91] Back in Washington, John Davies vested this conversation with significance and argued that the United States should follow up on Malik's evident willingness to talk about American-Soviet relations. Not to do so would only continue "relations with the U.S.S.R. on the basis of blind man's bluff without even attempting to discover whether the blindfold can be lifted a bit." He suggested that the person to engage in talks with Malik should not be "a high American official" but rather should be "in a position to speak with authority and in confidence for the Government."[92] He nominated Kennan for the role. Acheson decided to take up his suggestion.

Acheson determined to use Kennan to explore with the Soviet Union the

[89] George F. Kennan, *American Diplomacy, 1900–1950* (Chicago, 1951), p. 95.

[90] Reinhardt to Acheson (conveying Kennan's thoughts), March 17, 1951, *FRUS* 1950, VII, pp. 241–43.

[91] Memorandum of conversation, May 3, 1951, *FRUS* 1951, VII, pp. 401–7.

[92] Davies to Nitze, May 8, 1951, *FRUS* 1951, VII, pp. 421–42.

possibility of a cease-fire in Korea. On May 18 he saw Kennan in Washington and asked him to take on this assignment. Kennan readily agreed to do so and thereupon began the maneuverings to bring about a meeting with Malik.[93] He communicated with Malik through Tsarapkin and suggested a quiet talk. He temptingly added that "my diplomatic experience and long acquaintance with problems of American-Soviet relations should suffice to assure you that I would not make such a proposal unless I had serious reasons to do so."[94] Malik took the bait and agreed to meet Kennan at his summerhouse near Glen Cove, Long Island.

Kennan saw Malik twice. They first met alone on May 31 and spoke in Russian. Kennan introduced the matter of a cease-fire in Korea and delicately and skillfully sought to elicit Soviet attitudes on this subject. Malik, of course, evaded any direct response but agreed to meet again, thereby giving him a chance to consult with his superiors in Moscow.[95] The two men resumed their conversation on June 5. Malik now felt able to inform Kennan that the Soviets "wanted peace and wanted a peaceful solution of the Korean question—and at the earliest possible moment." Not being a participant in the Korean hostilities, Malik thought the Soviets could not appropriately take part in discussions over a cease-fire but he suggested that the United States approach the North Koreans and the Chinese directly.[96] In his analysis of Malik's comments Kennan focused especially on the words "at the earliest possible moment" and discerned that they should be interpreted as "a hopeful sign from the stand-point of arriving at an early cease-fire." He concluded by advising Acheson "to grasp at once the nettle of action directed toward achieving a cease-fire."[97] Kennan then continued to emphasize the need to pursue a cease-fire, writing to Acheson on June 20 that "my antennae tell me that if the Korean fighting does not stop soon, we should watch out for trouble."[98]

Acheson certainly wanted to avoid further trouble in Korea and favored a cease-fire but wondered "what we should do next" to bring it about.[99] Malik came to his rescue when he announced in the course of a UN radio program on June 23 that the Soviet people believed the Korean conflict could be settled. And, as a first step, he suggested, that "discussions should be started between the belligerents for a cease-fire and an armistice providing for the mutual withdrawal of forces from the 38th parallel."[100] The Truman administration acted on this suggestion and, after preliminary deliberations, the military authorities

[93] Kennan memorandum [undated], 1951, *FRUS* 1951, VII, pp. 460–61.

[94] Kennan to Tsarapkin, May 26, 1951, *FRUS* 1951, VII, p. 462.

[95] Kennan's report to Matthews, May 31, 1951, *FRUS* 1951, VII, pp. 483–86.

[96] Kennan to Matthews, June 5, 1951, *FRUS* 1951, VII, pp. 507–8.

[97] Ibid., pp. 509–11.

[98] Kennan to Acheson, June 20, 1951, *FRUS* 1951, VII, pp. 536–38.

[99] Acheson, *Present at the Creation*, p. 533.

[100] Kaufman, *The Korean War*, p. 191.

of each side began armistice discussions at Kaesong on July 10, 1951.[101] The negotiations to bring an end tò the Korean conflict proved long and wearisome in the extreme and the fighting dragged on at various levels of intensity for two more years.[102] The United States eventually negotiated an honorable settlement which, despite the tensions that prevail to this day on the Korean peninsula, permitted the secure development of South Korea. Kennan again had played "a small but not negligible part" in facilitating the cease-fire arrangements. Given the poor state of communications between the Soviet Union and the United States at the time, his quiet diplomacy proved extremely valuable in conveying to the Soviets the American interest in a cease-fire and in prompting a reciprocal Soviet concern. His work here effectively started the long negotiating process and should be so acknowledged. Furthermore, it revealed to Acheson Kennan's capabilities in dealing with the Soviets.

OH, TO MAKE POLICY AGAIN

Kennan's direct and influential involvement in the making of American foreign policy largely ended with his contributions to American policy in Korea. Afterwards his efforts to help direct the course of his nation's foreign policy brought him little but frustration. This frustration took on a deep character because Kennan proved quite incapable of ridding his system of the desire to participate in the formulation of foreign policy. His experience with the Policy Planning Staff had cast a permanent spell upon him. Even as he pursued a distinguished career as a historian during the 1950s the call to return to policy-making continued to resound within him. The life of a pure academic simply failed to satisfy him fully.

During his initial sabbatical from the Foreign Service, Kennan maintained a reasonably close connection to the policy-making process in Washington. His interventions on Korean matters reflect this. Also he continued his involvement with the intelligence community serving on the CIA's outside board of consultants—the "Princeton Consultants"—during 1950 and 1951. He still found himself in disagreement with many of the tenets of the foreign policy which Acheson pursued, especially regarding Germany, but personal bonds and shared experiences still linked him to the administration. These came into play when Acheson faced the task of selecting a new ambassador to the Soviet Union.

Kennan's background made him an obvious candidate for the ambassadorial post in Moscow. In 1949 the Foreign Service Board had mentioned him along with Bohlen as possible successors to General Bedell Smith in the event of his

[101] Ibid., pp. 192–201.

[102] Ibid., pp. 219–50. On the difficult negotiations see U. Alexis Johnson, *The Right Hand of Power* (Englewood Cliffs, N.J., 1984), pp. 120–22.

resignation.[103] Acheson instead had chosen his friend Alan Kirk to replace Smith but by the autumn of 1951 Kirk wanted to leave Moscow. Acheson decided to appoint Kennan and obtained Truman's approval to approach him.[104] He enlisted Bohlen to help persuade Kennan but this must not have been a difficult task.[105] When Acheson contacted him directly, Kennan declared himself anxious to take on the task, which was, he later remarked, one "for which my whole career had prepared me."[106] After the formal procedures had been carried out and Soviet agreement to the appointment obtained, Truman announced in December his intention to nominate Kennan as Kirk's successor.[107] The United States Senate confirmed the nomination unanimously on March 13 and Kennan took his oath of office as ambassador on April 2 at the State Department.[108] On May 5 he returned to Moscow but his concern and foreboding at the prospects of his mission already had emerged even before he touched Russian soil once again.

Kennan, not surprisingly, vested his mission to Moscow with significance. In fact, Harrison Salisbury, who observed him in Moscow in 1952, suggests that he brought to it "a mystical sense of purpose."[109] But it appears that Kennan stood alone in according this mission much importance. Truman gave him "no instructions of any kind," while Acheson gave him no "clue to the basic line of policy I was to follow in my new capacity."[110] The reality was that Truman and Acheson did not expect Kennan to undertake any initiatives in relations with the Soviet Union. They continued to focus their primary concerns on building the Western military capability and political alliance. Kennan sensed that he "was being sent on a mission to play a game at which I could not possibly win" but, more accurately, there existed no serious expectation that Kennan should engage the Soviets in any game at all.[111] U.S.-Soviet relations had reached their nadir.

Kennan harbored hopes that the Soviets might change their stance of near total antagonism and give some indication of a willingness to engage in discussion of the difficult issues which characterized their relations with the United States. Needless to say he desired to play some role in facilitating this. When he presented his credentials to Nikolay M. Shvernik, Chairman of the Presidium of the Supreme Soviet, on May 14, he outlined "the principal purpose of the Government of the United States in its relations with the Soviet

[103] Raundal to Peurifoy [undated, 1949], Truman Papers, Confidential File, Box 35.

[104] Acheson memoranda of conversation, October 6, 1951, *FRUS 1951*, IV, p. 1663 n. 3.

[105] Bohlen, *Witness to History*, p. 312.

[106] Memorandum of phone conversation, October 16, 1951, *FRUS 1951*, IV, p. 1663; and Kennan, *Memoirs*, II, p. 106.

[107] On the formal procedures and Truman's announcement see *FRUS 1951*, IV, pp. 1673–74.

[108] Editorial Note, *FRUS 1952–1954*, VIII, p. 967.

[109] Salisbury, *A Journey for Our Times*, p. 404.

[110] Kennan, *Memoirs*, II, p. 107.

[111] Ibid., p. 111.

Government [as] the peaceful adjustment of all those specific questions [the] solution of which requires agreement between the two governments.''[112] Here he engaged partly in the obligatory statement of hortatory formalities but these remarks also bore a personal investiture from him. Precisely because of his hopefulness that somehow or other he might effect a break-through to the Soviets by picking up on signals for improved relations, his actual experience proved all the more painful.

The Soviets showed no lessening in the intensity of their attitudes toward the United States and no openness of any sort towards the new American representative.[113] After a couple of months in Moscow Kennan wrote to Walter Lippmann that the metaphorical body of American-Soviet diplomacy had ''worn very thin.'' Indicative of his increasing doubts about the possibility of any achievement in his assignment, he lamented that it ''was unlikely that anything a single individual could do would help materially to restore flesh to its emaciated bones.''[114] By September his sense of professional isolation led him to suggest that the Soviet leaders effectively had ''broken diplomatic relations with the Western world.'' He complained in a long dispatch that ''the Western missions in Moscow have been isolated as completely and effectively as though they were on enemy soil in wartime.''[115] He confronted an even worse situation in the personal sphere than in his professional arena. He described his personal life to a friend at Princeton as ''bizarre and on occasion extremely unpleasant.'' The KGB controlled all his movements beyond the embassy and denied him contact with the Soviet citizenry. He lived as if afflicted with ''some sort of plague.''[116]

The combination of the frustration of his professional hopes and the savage personal isolation amounted ultimately to more than Kennan could stand. A small instance of cruelty by the Soviet police in denying to his young son the pleasure of the companionship of some Russian children finally caused Kennan to lose the patience and the collected disposition that ''professional'' diplomats supposedly should maintain.[117] While in transit through Berlin on his way to London for a meeting of American ambassadors in Europe, a journalist asked Kennan to describe how diplomats lived in Moscow. He compared the experience of living in Moscow to his experience as an internee in Nazi Germany. It was, he commented later and accurately, ''an extremely foolish thing

---

[112] Editorial Note, *FRUS* 1952–1954, VIII, p. 970.

[113] For a good overview of Kennan's ambassadorship in the Soviet Union see Mayers, *George Kennan and the Dilemmas of US Foreign Policy*, pp. 190–202. See also Kennan, *Memoirs*, II, pp. 112–57.

[114] Kennan to Lippmann, July 18, 1952, Lippmann Papers, Box 81.

[115] ''The Soviet Union and the Atlantic Pact,'' September 8, 1952, in Kennan, *Memoirs*, II, p. 344.

[116] Kennan to Berklie Henry, September 9, 1952, Oppenheimer Papers, Box 43.

[117] Kennan describes the episode and his reaction in *Memoirs*, II, pp. 157–58.

for me to have said."[118] It led to his being criticized by colleagues in the Foreign Service as "an indifferent diplomat."[119] Others had shared Kennan's thoughts but they managed not to voice them. Kennan's comment had come in an off-the-cuff remark but it nonetheless constituted a severe blunder and one for which the Soviets forced him to pay a high price. *Pravda* attacked him, the Soviet Government protested his comments, then declared him persona non grata and demanded his recall.[120] Soviet officials denied permission for Kennan to reenter their country. A plane was dispatched to Moscow to bring Mrs. Kennan and the children to join her shaken and shamed husband.

Kennan's defensive efforts to suggest that his expulsion owed to deeper Soviet motives against him rang rather feebly. His suggestions that his presence in Moscow was unwelcome to certain factions precisely because he was known "to be relatively moderate and conciliatory" and that certain officials within the Soviet hierarchy feared the possibility of his meeting with Stalin and clarifying the misinformation with regard to the outside world which the Soviet leader suffered under appear rather self-serving and designed to "salve [his] wounded ego."[121] Perhaps one day the internal processes of Soviet decision-making on this matter might become accessible to historians and Kennan's observations could be evaluated further. In the meantime it is safe to conclude that Kennan's ambassadorship had little impact on American policy toward the Soviet Union and, if anything, negatively affected (if that were possible) relations between the two antagonistic superpowers.

Despite the disastrous end to his brief and unhappy assignment in Moscow, Kennan made no plans to retire from the Foreign Service. He wanted to stay on at least until he could retire on a pension and indicated his willingness to serve "wherever the Government wishes me to serve."[122] Acheson made no decision on the matter before the year's end and consigned Kennan's future into the hands of John Foster Dulles who succeeded him as secretary of state when the Eisenhower administration took office in January of 1953. Kennan finally got through in March to see Dulles to talk about his position. The new secretary explained that "he knew of no 'niche' " in the department for Kennan at that time. Furthermore, the proponent of "liberation" noted, Kennan would have difficulty gaining Senate confirmation for any position because of

[118] Kennan, *Memoirs*, II, p. 159.

[119] U. Alexis Johnson, *The Right Hand of Power*, p. 316. Also see Jacob D. Beam, *Multiple Exposure* (New York, 1978), pp. 27–28; and the comments of John J. McCloy in Isaacson and Thomas, *The Wise Men*, p. 555.

[120] Note the comments of Andrei Gromyko on the incident in his *Memoirs*, trans. by Harold Shukman (London, 1989), pp. 302–3.

[121] See "Summary of Telegrams," September 29, 1952, Naval Aide Files, HSTL, Box 24; and Kennan, *Memoirs*, II, p. 165.

[122] Kennan revealed his plans to Oppenheimer in a letter, October 14, 1952, Oppenheimer Papers, Box 43.

his being tainted with "containment."[123] Kennan would need to serve out the required three months and retire from the Foreign Service. For all intents and purposes Dulles fired him. The Soviet specialist thought of himself as having been expelled by the State Department following upon his expulsion from Moscow.[124] Allen Dulles tried to recruit the man his brother had dismissed for the CIA which he now directed, but Kennan turned him down. Instead he served out his three months and on a pleasant June day in 1953 he quietly left the State department and drove off to his farm in Pennsylvania.[125]

Kennan did not drive off, however, into some sunset of anonymity. Even before he departed the corridors of Foggy Bottom, Kennan had been requested by President Eisenhower to participate in a top-secret review of national security policy which came to be known as "Operation Solarium"—after the White House solarium where some of the initial meetings took place. One could have expected that Kennan might have rejected this request in light of the Eisenhower administration's obvious reservations about appointing him to a position within the State department. But Kennan relished the opportunity to join this exercise and vigorously contributed to it working for six weeks in late June and July in basement rooms in the National War College. He headed one of the three teams assembled to argue for a particular line of strategy. Kennan's Task Force A supported the "continuation of the Truman strategy of 'containment' " while the other Task Forces defended respectively a strategy of nuclear "deterrence" and one of "liberation" or "roll-back."[126] When the exercise was completed, Kennan later commented, "it was the concept propounded by my team that received the presidential approval."[127] The comment of Eisenhower's assistant, General Andrew J. Goodpaster, that after the president's closing remarks at the final session of the exercise, "rollback was dead and that something in the area of containment or areas of interest would be pursued" lends credence to Kennan's observation.[128] But, as John Lewis Gaddis has demonstrated convincingly, "in practice the administration's strategic concept, which came to be known as the 'New Look,' managed to incorporate in one form or another all of the alternatives considered in [the] exercise." Furthermore, as he also noted, the containment option discussed in the Solarium exercise drew more upon NSC 68 than it did Kennan's more tex-

[123] Kennan recounted details of the meeting in Kennan to Oppenheimer, March 15, 1953, Oppenheimer Papers, Box 43.
[124] See Kennan's comments in C. L. Sulzberger, *Seven Continents and Forty Years*, p. 235.
[125] Kennan, *Memoirs*, II, pp. 170–89.
[126] For further details on Operation Solarium see Gaddis, *Strategies of Containment*, pp. 145–47; and William B. Pickett, "The Eisenhower Solarium Notes," *SHAFR Newsletter* 16 (June 1985): 1–10.
[127] Kennan, *Memoirs*, II, p. 182.
[128] Interview with Andrew J. Goodpaster by William B. Pickett cited in "Eisenhower Solarium Notes," p. 4.

tured notions of this strategy.[129] In short, Gaddis's work makes rather clear that Kennan's claim that while Dulles, in March, "had triumphed by disembarrassing himself of my person," he, in August, "had revenge by saddling him, inescapably, with my policy" is vastly overstated.[130] Kennan lent some assistance to the process of the Eisenhower administration's facing realities in U.S.-Soviet relations and helped skewer some of the more unrealistic promises of "liberation" generated by the 1952 election campaign. But he neither charted nor dictated the foreign policy of the Eisenhower administration—a policy for which Eisenhower, Dulles, and company rightly should take the credit or the blame.

His work on the Solarium Exercise completed, Kennan once again returned to his farm. In that rustic setting which he loved deeply he took the opportunity to contemplate his future. The immediate prospect was to return to the Institute for Advanced Study where he had a grant for one year. Longer term, he wrote to his friend Charlie Thayer, he had a "decision to make." His choice lay between "becoming a 'public figure' here at home"—which incredulously included the possibility of his running for public office—and being "a scholar and recluse and free-thinker" in which case he could say "the various unconventional things I actually believe." He leaned to the latter path—that of "intellectual eccentric"—and thought it might most profitably be pursued in Europe. The trends of the times, especially the rampaging McCarthyism, and the fact that most Americans "still find nothing wrong with the state of the country," led him to consider a sort of exile on the other side of the Atlantic.[131] In the end Kennan chose to stay in the United States and to pursue a scholarly career but he did not or could not adopt a reclusive posture, much to his occasional regret as the demands of contemporary occurrences pulled him away from his engagement with the past.

Kennan's various involvements and commitments prevented him simply withdrawing completely into some mythical ivory tower. He behaved more honorably and courageously than most of his contemporaries as he attempted to blunt the ravages of the McCarthyite scourge, although his forthright efforts in support of John Paton Davies and J. Robert Oppenheimer failed to produce their desired results.[132] The Republican exploitation of McCarthy's actions helped develop in Kennan a partisan edge. Furthermore, he found Adlai Stevenson an attractive figure. In light of this he took time away from the major study he had begun on Soviet-American relations from 1917 to 1920 to join a group of Democratic foreign policy experts in framing advice for Stevenson

---

[129] Gaddis, *Strategies of Containment*, p. 146.
[130] Kennan, *Memoirs*, II, p. 182.
[131] Kennan to Thayer, Charles W. Thayer Papers, HSTL, Box 3.
[132] Kennan treats this matter well in *Memoirs*, II, pp. 190–228.

with regard to foreign policy issues for the 1954 congressional campaign.[133] While he refused to become a regular member of this group, he gave other advice and support to Stevenson over the ensuing years.[134] Eisenhower's second victory in 1956, however, dashed hopes that Kennan might have entertained of returning to a responsible policy-making position in a Stevenson administration. He "was extremely disappointed, disgusted even, by the election" result and could "hardly bring himself to believe that Nixon could have been elected Vice-President," fearing that this meant he would eventually become president.[135]

By the time Kennan made his comments about the 1956 election it already had been clarified for him that his services would not be required by the Eisenhower administration. In June 1955, he wrote to his former colleague, Loy Henderson, who now served as Deputy Under Secretary for Administration in the department and requested a clarification of his status. As he outlined the issue to Henderson he remained subject to recall as a retired Foreign Service Officer until he turned 65. He explained that he had been offered the Eastman Professorship at Balliol College, Oxford, and asked if there was likely to be any claim made on him by the government which would prevent him from taking this appointment. Henderson checked with Under Secretary of State Herbert Hoover, Jr., who referred him on to Dulles. Henderson replied soon after and with "regret" told his onetime junior officer in Riga, Latvia, that "there is apparently no intention at the present time to recall you from your retirement."[136] No place existed in the policy-making establishment for Kennan, although officials of the administration still sought out his advice occasionally. Most notable among these was Allen Dulles who asked him in 1956 both to judge the veracity of the speech Nikita Khrushchev supposedly had given before the Twentieth Congress of the Soviet Communist Party condemning Stalin's despotism and to advise as to the use the United States should make of the speech.[137]

With no impediment placed in his way by the demands of government service, Kennan took up the appointment at Oxford in 1957–1958. He had won the Pulitzer Prize for his 1956 work *Russia Leaves the War* and clearly had a distinguished career ahead of him as a scholar. But he could not content himself with the satisfactions of his scholarly research and writing. He continued

[133] Others in the group included Chester Bowles, Thomas Finletter, Averell Harriman, Arthur Schlesinger, Jr., and Kennan's old colleagues from the PPS–Paul Nitze, Charles Burton Marshall, and Robert Tufts. See Bowles to Kennan, October 5, 1954, and attached memorandum, Chester Bowles Papers, Yale University, New Haven, Conn., Box 141.

[134] Mayers, *George Kennan and the Dilemmas of US Foreign Policy*, pp. 226–30.

[135] John Goldsmith, ed., *Stephen Spender: Journals, 1939–1983*, pp. 181–82.

[136] Kennan to Henderson, June 1, 1955; Hoover to Henderson, June 10, 1955; and Henderson to Kennan, June 18, 1955, in Loy W. Henderson Papers, Box 2.

[137] Khrushchev's speech is reprinted in Strobe Talbott, ed., *Khrushchev Remembers*, pp. 559–618. For Allen Dulles consulting Kennan see Winks, *Cloak and Gown*, p. 413.

to desire to influence the direction of his nation's foreign policy or, at the least, to contribute to the debate over it. To this end he accepted the invitation of the British Broadcasting Commission to deliver its Reith Lectures for 1957. Here, among other subjects, he addressed the German issue. He refused to surrender his earlier views and called again for the unification and neutralization of Germany and the disengagement of American, Russian, and British troops from the heart of Europe.[138] Prior to delivering his lectures Kennan wrote to Robert Oppenheimer that he looked forward to them "with unmitigated foreboding."[139] He was right to do so.

Kennan's remarks on Germany caused a stir. Acheson reacted apoplectically, dismissing his former subordinate as one who had never "grasped the realities of power relationships but takes a rather mystical attitude toward them."[140] The vituperative character of Acheson's attack shocked Kennan, who wrote Frank Altschul that "I am still utterly at a loss to understand it. We had always been friends; and mere disagreements about policy have never been occasions for public personal attacks in the world of human relationships to which I thought we both belonged."[141] Indeed, Acheson's berating of Kennan troubled many of their mutual friends, including those who tended to agree with the former secretary of state on the substance of the issue.[142] Acheson, as Foreign Policy Advisor to the Democratic Advisory Committee, wanted to make clear that Kennan's views did not represent those of the Democratic party and, also, to prevent their gaining any foothold within the Party and to limit their impact in Germany itself. "I can quite understand that the Kennan-Acheson brawl causes pain to our mutual friends," he wrote to Philip Jessup who had written to express concern about the vehemence of his attack on Kennan. But an aroused Acheson refused to back down. He explained to Jessup that "George always engenders more solicitude in others than he shows for others. But the self-deprecating garnishment of his lectures did not minimize their damaging, indeed reckless, content. I was not writing for our friends nor to put forward a gentle caveat. I was writing for the Germans to destroy as effectively as I could the corroding effect of what he had said and

[138] Kennan's Reith Lectures were published as *Russia, the Atom and the West* (New York, 1957).
[139] Kennan to Oppenheimer, October 24, 1957, Oppenheimer Papers, Box 43.
[140] Acheson's statement released on January 11, 1958, by the American Council on Germany, Acheson Papers, HSTL, Box 139.
[141] Kennan to Altschul, January 26, 1958, Altschul Papers, File 113b. On Kennan's reaction see also his letter to Dorothy Hessman, January 16, 1958, in Oppenheimer Papers, Box 43.
[142] On the reaction of friends see for example, Frank Altschul to Kennan, January 14, 1958, Altschul Papers, File 113b; Arthur Schlesinger, Jr., to Herbert Feis, January 29, 1958, Herbert Feis Papers, Library of Congress, Box 26; Chester Bowles to Kennan, January 28, 1958, Bowles Papers, Box 141; Philip Jessup to Dean Acheson, March 19, 1958, Jessup Papers, Container B-3.

the belief that he was a seer in these matters."[143] Acheson largely met success in his objectives. Despite the attention and the notoriety which his lectures received, Kennan effected no mass conversions to his views on Germany among Democrats or elsewhere. Certainly, the Republican administration made no adjustments in its policies because of them. In terms of actual policy the Reith Lectures were inconsequential.

Even before Kennan had absorbed the full barrage of Acheson's attack, Kennan, "cringing with horror and remorse" over the uproar caused by the lectures, expressed the hope to Oppenheimer that "it will be years before I again make a public statement about contemporary affairs."[144] But, of course, he couldn't fulfill his own hopes. Demonstrating inner strength, full confidence in his own intellectual convictions, and an inability to vacate the public stage, Kennan refused to be blasted off the field by Acheson. In the January 1959 issue of *Foreign Affairs* he published an article entitled "Disengagement Revisited" in which he replied to Acheson and other critics of the Reith Lectures.[145] Both this article and the Reith Lectures before it attracted favorable comment, although not full endorsement, from Senator John F. Kennedy of Massachusetts. Kennan appreciated Kennedy's favorable regard for his positions on negotiating with the Russians and he especially enjoyed reading of himself that "you have disposed of the extreme rigidity of Mr. Acheson's position with great effectiveness and without the kind of *ad hominem* irrelevancies in which Mr. Acheson unfortunately indulged last year."[146] Kennan began to extend some limited advice to the young senator.

During 1960 the young Senator Kennedy captured the Democratic nomination for president. During the campaign Kennan forwarded to him a lengthy review of the international situation along with suggestions as to how a new administration should regain the international initiative.[147] One careful observer has suggested that this letter resulted in part from Kennan's hope "to enjoy a high position in government" were Kennedy to emerge victorious.[148] This seems likely. After Kennedy narrowly defeated Richard Nixon and began the task of assembling his administration, Kennan waited in vain to be contacted and offered a position. As the year came to an end and in a state of obvious exasperation, he wrote to Walter Lippmann that "to date, [he] had not a single word since the election from anyone in Washington of or near the new administration—not even so much, in fact, as a personal word from a

[143] Acheson to Jessup, March 25, 1958, Jessup Papers, Container B-3.

[144] Kennan to Oppenheimer, December 17, 1957, Oppenheimer Papers, Box 43.

[145] "Disengagement Revisited," *Foreign Affairs* 37 (January 1959): 187–211.

[146] Kennedy to Kennan, January 21, 1959, quoted in Oral History Interview with George F. Kennan by Louie Fischer, March 23, 1965, John F. Kennedy Library, Boston, Mass.

[147] David Mayers discusses this in his *Kennan and the Dilemmas of US Foreign Policy*, pp. 207–8.

[148] Ibid., p. 207.

friend." Kennan then got to the real source of his irritation. "Meanwhile," he continued, "the senior assignments in the State department have all been made; and even the one embassy—namely, to India—for which I should have thought myself particularly suited, has, as I understand it, already been offered elsewhere."[149]

Kennan clearly had hoped that Kennedy might install him into a policy-making position in the State Department but it was not to be. He felt the rejection deeply. "Had I taken a less prominent part, in recent years, in the public debates on questions of national policy, I could let this pass without drawing any drastic conclusions from it; but in the circumstances I can regard it only as a sign of deliberate repudiation, and one that comes to me with particular force inasmuch as it proceeds from people who were, in large part, my friends and colleagues, who stand on the same side of our political life, and who professed at the time to have been shocked at the enigmatic and cavalier manner in which, eight years ago, Mr. Dulles dismissed me from the public service."[150] Kennan, thereupon, announced to Lippmann his intention to retire from the field of public debate and affairs. His remarks here clarify just how desperately he wanted to return to a position in which he might contribute to the formulation of American foreign policy. He had endured a virtual eight-year exile as a result of Dulles's decision to force him out of the department. Now it seemed like that exile would continue.

Eventually—January 23, 1961, to be precise—Kennedy offered him a choice between the ambassadorships to Poland and Yugoslavia and he took the latter.[151] The ambassador-designate recognized that he resided on the periphery of policy-making and it must have galled him a little to see his former colleague Dean Rusk occupying the secretary of state's office, but such was Kennan's desire to return to government service that he gladly accepted the Yugoslav post, conveniently ignoring his own earlier plans to retire from public affairs.[152] He apparently even got caught up in the mood of Camelot, which Charles Bohlen's wife Avis described well as similar "to the days—almost of the war—conferences—meetings at all times—dinner parties and receptions again filled with people eager to talk and exchange ideas and information.

[149] Kennan to Lippmann, December 28, 1960, Lippmann Papers, Box 81.

[150] Ibid.

[151] Kennan, *Memoirs*, II, pp. 267–68.

[152] Kennan's respect for Rusk diminished as the decade wore on. By the end of 1965 he wrote Walter Lippmann that "I would not wish to exaggerate the relative deficiencies of our present leadership in foreign affairs—we have had plenty of incompetence, God knows, at times in the past. But I am daily depressed, particularly as concerns the leadership of the Dept. of State itself, by evidence of lack of any adequate understanding for world realities and their true relationship to one another; of smugness and total absence of humility; of a dreadful inability to relate military effort to political purpose; and of an obsession with the danger of appearing weak—an obsession which is itself the surest sign of real inner weakness." Kennan to Lippmann, December 19, 1965, Lippmann Papers, Box 81.

Most exciting." She wrote her brother Charlie Thayer in February that "George Kennan was here for two days—looks 20 years younger and is so full of smiles and cheer and dying to get started."[153] But the smiles soon faded.

Kennan's ambassadorship to Yugoslavia provided him satisfaction in a personal sense but little professional fulfillment. Within seven months of his arriving in Belgrade he wrote home to Robert Oppenheimer that he felt "no very stirring sense of usefulness at this point." He expressed a sympathy for Kennedy and a desire to "help him more" but, with this not a real possibility, he raised the prospect of his returning to the Institute where since 1956 he had held a permanent appointment.[154] Kennan's disgust with Congress's revocation in 1962 of Yugoslavia's Most Favored Nation trading status and his disappointment at Kennedy's lukewarm support for his efforts to overturn this eventually prompted his resignation in 1963.[155] At a deeper level, however, Kennan's inability merely to represent policy formulated by others caused his resignation. Although he possessed long training in the Foreign Service he could not content himself with a diplomat's role. His experience from 1947 to 1950 had cast an indelible stamp upon him. He had reveled in the formulation of foreign policy then and had hoped to do so again. As he returned to Princeton after his service in Yugoslavia he sensed that his chance to participate directly in the making of his nation's foreign policy had ended. And he was right.

Kennan continued to engage in commentary on foreign policy matters from that time through to the present. Indeed, his public prominence remained high as a stream of additional books and articles flowed from his eloquent pen. His role, however, was limited to that of a sage trying to influence elite and public opinion and thereby to exercise some indirect impact upon policy. In this role he dissented thoughtfully on the painfully divisive question of American participation in the Vietnam conflict; he offered constructively critical support to the Nixon-Kissinger policy of detente with its prospects for improved U.S.-Soviet relations; and he passionately opposed the nuclear arms race that characterized the late Carter and early Reagan presidencies.[156] Such were his efforts that he has been described as "the conscience of American foreign policy."[157] Additionally, Kennan turned his attention to a wide array of other issues—the student movement of the sixties, civil rights, the environment,

[153] Avis Bohlen to Thayer, February 22, 1961, Thayer Papers, Box 1.

[154] Kennan to Oppenheimer, December 8, 1961, Oppenheimer Papers, Box 43.

[155] Kennan, *Memoirs*, II, pp. 292–311.

[156] For discussion of Kennan's views on these great issues see Mayers, *George Kennan and the Dilemmas of US Foreign Policy*, pp. 275–332; Hixson, *George F. Kennan: Cold War Iconoclast*, pp. 221–96.

[157] Gregg Herken, "The Great Foreign Policy Fight," *American Heritage* 37 (April/May 1986): 80.

immigration to the United States, the social fabric of America.[158] His views were occasionally outrageous, usually insightful, invariably interesting, and they have attracted the attention of a surprising number of analysts who have struggled to categorize Kennan's philosophic outlook.[159] No further such analysis is needed here in this study of Kennan's contribution to the making of American foreign policy. Instead, an overall evaluation of Kennan's importance and contribution as a maker of American foreign policy is required.

[158] For an intriguing discussion of Kennan's views on such matters see Stephanson, *Kennan and the Art of Foreign Policy*, pp. 211–55.

[159] Consult the previously cited works by David Mayers, Anders Stephanson, and Walter Hixson.

America's Global Planner?

GEORGE F. KENNAN'S time in the mainstream of American foreign policy formulation was relatively brief. Essentially it was limited to his tenure as director of the Policy Planning Staff and a short stint as Counselor in the State
Department immediately afterwards. Much to his dismay his further service
as a diplomat in Moscow and in Belgrade afforded him little involvement in
the making of foreign policy. As we have seen, Kennan was forced to transfer
his energies from the making of foreign policy to writing of its making in
works of historical scholarship and in articles and lectures aimed at influencing
contemporary policymakers and opinion. Yet, while his service at the center
of foreign policy-making was brief, it coincided with and contributed to an
enormously formative period in American diplomacy. Who would dispute
Dean Acheson's finely understated observation that "the postwar years were
a period of creation"?[1] During this period the fundamental postwar world
structure was shaped and America's basic role was established for a generation
until Vietnam and in fact beyond. The American commitment to restore and
to secure Western Europe and to pursue stability in the Far East laid the foundations for four decades of American foreign policy.

Indeed, only in the late 1980s did American officials come to speak regularly of being in "an era of transition" in which "the postwar system is being
transformed and a new environment is emerging," and in which the United
States and the West could move "beyond containment."[2] Such views emerged
in response to the collapse of communism, to the end of Soviet political domination in Eastern Europe, and to plans for the retraction of Soviet military
power from the heart of Europe. Commentators proclaimed that the Cold War
had ended and argued that "the familiar guideposts of American foreign policy have disappeared."[3] There may be some exaggeration here but it is clear
that in response to new world circumstances the United States is engaged already upon a process of redefining its international role. The full extent and
direction of this redefinition is not apparent as yet and the successful exercise
of American power against Iraq in early 1991 by no means made the way

[1] Acheson, *Present at the Creation*, p. xviii.
[2] Statement by Secretary of State James Baker to Senate Foreign Relations Committee, Washington, D.C., June 20, 1989, *Current Policy Document*, no. 1186 (Washington, D.C., 1989).
President Carter, of course, offered such thoughts early in his presidency but was singing a rather
different tune by the end of it.
[3] Michael Mandelbaum, "The Bush Foreign Policy," *Foreign Affairs* 70, no. 1 (1991): 6.

clear. Suggestions aplenty are bandied about but there is no consensus at this stage. Should the United States seize the "unipolar moment" and lay down and enforce rules for world order?[4] Or should the U.S. acknowledge it is no longer a superpower capable of dominating the international system and turn primarily to confront its pressing domestic problems?[5] Such questions as these will need to be faced as America fashions its place in the post–Cold War world. They need not be addressed here. What the historian might note, with all due modesty of course, is that as the United States continues—during the 1990s and beyond—to redefine its own role in the world in response to changing international realities it might be helpful that it have some intelligent grasp of the past, and especially a grasp of how the essential foundations for the foreign policy which served the nation for forty years came to be. Might one suggest in the familiar refrain of historians that while such a knowledge of the past will not provide specific answers to the questions and challenges of the present it will allow for more wisdom and perspective in addressing them.

This study of American foreign policy from 1947 to 1950 reveals clearly that this policy was not simply a "working-out" of a clearly delineated doctrine or strategy of containment. Nor can it be presented as conforming to any other deliberately fashioned schema. Although President Truman and his advisers determined as early as 1946 that Soviet actions endangered American security and resolved to meet this danger, no explicit course of action was charted for them.[6] Only in a piecemeal and staggered manner did the Truman administration decide upon the major elements of the American response to the Soviet Union. Each element resulted from a complex of both particular and constant factors—political, strategic, economic, personal—as this investigation, hopefully, has made clear. Indeed, the containment doctrine, it must be said, did not dictate the policies determined from 1947 to 1950 but rather the policies gave form and meaning to the doctrine. This is not to suggest, as has the political scientist Robert Jervis, that "incoherence . . . characterized U.S. foreign and defense efforts" during this period.[7] Instead, it establishes that foreign policy neither was built in accord with the design of a single architect—whether Kennan or another—nor conformed to any overarching strategy. The latter came about only with the implementation of NSC 68 under the impetus of the Korean War.[8] Thus, Henry Kissinger's suggestion that

[4] This is the suggestion of Charles Krauthammer in "The Unipolar Moment," *Foreign Affairs* 70, no. 1 (1991): 24–33.

[5] See William Pfaff, "Redefining World Power," *Foreign Affairs* 70, no. 1 (1991): 34–48.

[6] See John Lewis Gaddis, *The United States and the Origins of the Cold War, 1941–1947* (New York, 1972), pp. 282–315.

[7] Robert Jervis, "The Impact of the Korean War on the Cold War," *The Journal of Conflict Resolution* 24 (December 1980): 563.

[8] See John Lewis Gaddis, "Was the Truman Doctrine a Real Turning Point?" *Foreign Affairs* 52 (January 1974): 386–402.

"George Kennan came as close to authoring the diplomatic doctrine of his era as any diplomat in our history" stands in need of some revision.[9]

The foreign policy framed from 1947 to 1950 is not susceptible to a simple mono-causal explanation. In this period, however, political and strategic factors clearly were the most significant in the development of the major constituent parts of U.S. foreign policy. All the principal policymakers perceived the Soviet Union as a threat to the basic American interest of maintaining an external environment conducive to its survival and prosperity. This recognition, spurred along by the Soviet domination of half of Europe, dictated the need for a response. To accept this concern for national security as the principal motive for American action, however, does not explain much about the content and shape of policy because the central question here must be not why the United States acted but why it acted in the *way* that it did. This is the principal question addressed in this study of George Kennan.

The structure of American foreign policy was built stone by stone, as it were, in reaction to pressing needs and challenges. American policymakers simply struggled to respond to a succession of international crises—Western Europe's political weakness, economic dislocation, and military insecurity; the diverse Communist challenges in China, Italy, and Greece; the conundrum of Palestine; the power vacuums in Germany and Japan; the opportunity presented by Titoism; and the perceived threat posed by Soviet military power and atomic capability. Through addressing these various situations a foreign policy emerged. It developed functionally and through being called forth by circumstances more so than by being imposed upon them. As Kennan admitted late in 1949, American policy since World War II was not "based on any global plan" but owed much to "a great deal of improvisation."[10] This point deserves emphasis and might well be appreciated by those who campaign for more long-term planning by romanticizing the Truman period as some kind of golden age for such.

As the foregoing infers Kennan did not write any blueprint for American foreign policy which other officials merely accepted and implemented. Neither the Long Telegram nor the "X" article should be interpreted as a prescriptive tract which provided detailed instructions. Kennan did not play the role of a powerful architect whose planning provided the instructions for building the structure of foreign policy. Rather, he served as one of the on-site builders who contributed in important ways to the eventual structure which emerged. These builders—the policy-making core of the State Department—op-

---

[9] Henry Kissinger, *White House Years* (Boston, 1979), p. 135.

[10] Kennan's views given at a briefing for Indian Prime Minister Nehru, October 13, 1949, Acheson Papers, HSTL, Box 64. A classic case to confirm this point is the evolution of policy toward Greece over the period 1947 to 1949. See Howard Jones, *"A New Kind of War": America's Global Strategy and the Truman Doctrine in Greece* (New York, 1989).

erated in essence without agreed architectural plans. They debated and then determined the nature and shape of the structure as they went along.

Kennan, of course, possessed a coherent strategy designed to restore the balance of power in both Europe and Asia. He deemed the Soviet threat to be essentially political rather than military and aimed to ensure political and economic stability in the key industrial areas of Western Europe and Japan so that they, in large part independently of the United States, might be capable of resisting this Soviet threat. He brought this strategic vision to all the issues which he confronted as is readily apparent in his support for the Marshall Plan, for German unification, and for the reverse course in Japan.[11] But he never succeeded in effectively securing the full adoption of his strategy within the Truman administration. His strategy or global plan informed *his* contributions to policy formulation but he needed to win the internal debate over specific policies in order for it to influence the approach pursued by the United States. Kennan's realist worldview rightly is an object for intellectual curiosity but those who would seek to understand his importance and contribution must know just which of his specific ideas and plans he managed to translate into reality. One should note, however, before passing to this question that Kennan's ideas on policy rested upon two important understandings—a sure appreciation of the danger and horrors of totalitarianism (in Kennan's case, the Stalinist variation) and a recognition that there were limits to American action in the world—which have an enduring relevance.[12]

Kennan's accomplishments in the actual making of foreign policy are striking. There seems no second-level State Department official in this century who could match the breadth of his contribution. Along with his few Planning Staff colleagues Kennan fashioned, through his actions both before and after Marshall's Harvard address, the American strategy to provide for the development of an economic aid program for Europe. He proved influential in determining the nature and extent of the support which the United States rendered to the non-Communist governments of Italy and Greece—in the case of the former, favoring vigorous support, while in the latter objecting successfully to the use of combat forces. He had a most salient impact on the formulation of American policy toward Northeast Asia. He helped establish the quite basic premise of Japan's greater importance relative to China in the region and ensured that the United States government operated from that premise. Additionally, he influenced specific policy toward both Japan and China. On China, Kennan, aided by John Paton Davies, took a leading part in developing the policy of

[11] The most coherent presentation of Kennan's strategy is provided by John Lewis Gaddis in *Strategies of Containment*, pp. 27–51.

[12] Kennan wrote to Acheson in 1949 that "whoever, peering from the comfortable distance of the bourgeois-liberal world, views Stalin as just another successful political leader pushing his people firmly but roughly along the path of history, has failed to grasp the cataclysmic horror of modern totalitarianism." Kennan to Acheson, July 8, 1949, Acheson Papers, HSTL, Box 64.

limited assistance without deep involvement which led to the China Aid Act. He constantly and successfully opposed efforts to involve the United States more deeply on the side of the Nationalists. In terms of policy toward Japan, both as implemented and as formally enunciated, Kennan's contribution was decisive. Initially, he shifted the focus of attention away from the nature of a peace treaty to the consequences of the occupation policies then being implemented by MacArthur. Then, in tandem with William Draper, he stood at the center of the successful effort to redirect these occupation policies toward economic recovery. The extent of Kennan's influence upon American policies in Asia, an area of little familiarity to him, ironically necessitates the judgment that his impact there far exceeded his influence on American policy in Europe.

Of course, there was a debit side to the Kennan balance sheet on policy formulation. The negotiation of the North Atlantic Treaty represented a clear rejection of his strategic vision, even though he participated in some of the discussions which shaped the historic treaty. The lack of interest in his proposal for a long-term US-UK-Canada association distinct from the European Union marked a similar rejection. More fundamentally, Acheson's decision to eschew the Kennan-sponsored efforts for German reunification and to press ahead with the formal partition of Germany revealed the planning chief's failure to secure the application of his strategic vision in Europe. Kennan's endeavors in Europe foundered ultimately because he could not persuade his superiors and colleagues that the Soviet threat was limited and essentially political. Kennan based his analysis on an assessment of Soviet intentions rather than capabilities. His fellow policymakers found it unpersuasive, especially after the Soviets exploded an atomic weapon. Even those uncertain about Soviet intentions, such as Acheson in his initial days as secretary of state, were not prepared to run any risk of being wrong. They could not ignore the Soviet threat. This guaranteed Kennan's defeat not only on the North Atlantic Treaty and Germany but also on Japanese security policy and the hydrogen bomb issues. NSC 68 served to formalize the rejection of Kennan's strategic vision.

These defeats on specific policies, substantial though they were, do not warrant any questioning of Kennan's central place in American foreign policy formulation during the period of his directorship of the Policy Planning Staff. Aside from the president and the respective secretaries and under secretaries of state, he was the one official who addressed the whole range of foreign policy concerns. Through his concurrent responsibilities as Director of Policy Planning and as the State Department Consultant to the National Security Council Kennan found himself at the vortex of the policy-making process. Many of the Planning Staff papers, after approval in the State Department, became the bases for NSC papers. In short, Kennan played a crucial role in making the newly established NSC system work. Sidney Souers' work as executive secretary of the NSC concentrated more on the administrative domain.

Kennan provided the substance, the basic staff work, which constituted the departure point for much of the NSC's actions.

He also played a significant role in devising new and controversial weapons for the American diplomatic arsenal. He helped in developing the covert capabilities of OPC under Frank Wisner. Along with his close aide and friend Robert Joyce, Kennan contributed to the planning of certain of the operations undertaken by OPC. Also notable was his role in developing instruments of propaganda, among which Radio Liberty and Radio Free Europe were the most significant. Kennan showed no reluctance to enter the fray of implementing policy. His involvements reveal him to be much more than the departmental gadfly of his own later description. Certainly he was not inept in the game of bureaucratic politics but he played it in a straightforward and honorable manner. He had few of the talents for scheming or secrecy or manipulation which characterize supposed masters in the art of bureaucratic infighting such as Henry Kissinger or Richard Perle. His dearth in this area should not disguise the fact that his influence effectively was felt throughout the State Department, the NSC, and the intelligence community. Few of the operators among the veterans of the "guerrilla warfare" of more contemporary policy-making during the Carter and Reagan administrations have matched his achievement.[13]

Kennan's impact rested on the depth and force of his analyses and recommendations, on the reputation he and his Staff earned by its initial success on the Marshall Plan, and on the access afforded him by the secretaries of state. Both George Marshall and Dean Acheson valued him and his Policy Planning Staff. According to Acheson, Marshall had seen the function of the Planning Staff as "being to look ahead not into the distant future but beyond the vision of the operating officers caught in the smoke and crises of current battles."[14] Kennan's Staff never fully met this expectation because from the outset the group was not concerned with planning divorced from operations but was involved integrally in policy-making. Nonetheless, neither Marshall nor Acheson ever appeared perturbed by this development because both appreciated that the Planning Staff under Kennan, even though engaged in the battles of the moment, brought to policy formulation what Thomas Etzold has called "a long perspective on American interests in foreign affairs."[15] Under Kennan's directorship the Planning Staff never really anticipated events but in reacting to them, even in virtual crisis situations, it had a capability to frame policies which had validity over the longer term. The response to the economic disar-

[13] Dean Rusk describes contemporary policy-making as "guerrilla warfare" in *As I Saw It*, p. 135.

[14] Acheson, *Present at the Creation*, p. 214.

[15] Thomas H. Etzold, "Organization for National Security, 1945–50," in Etzold and John Lewis Gaddis, eds., *Containment: Documents on American Policy and Strategy, 1945–1950* (New York, 1978), p. 22.

ray in Europe in mid-1947 and to Tito's break with Stalin exemplify the point. Perhaps such a long view is the best one might expect from such an agency which hopes to retain its contact with and relevance to those who ultimately endorse policy.

The Policy Planning Staff revolved around Kennan. As its pivotal figure he provided much of its intellectual power and capably exploited the access afforded him. On most issues his was the dominant voice. On certain major policy elements, however, he received substantial assistance from particular Staff members. Joseph Johnson, Jacques Reinstein, and Col. Charles Bonesteel ably supported him on the Marshall Plan. Ware Adams gave him special assistance on German policy as did Robert Joyce on intelligence matters. Most important, John Paton Davies contributed as a virtual equal partner in helping frame Kennan's policy advice on China, Japan, and Southeast Asia. In addition to these individual efforts all Staff members acted in support of Kennan by criticizing, demanding clarification, and refining his ideas and proposals in order to strengthen his analysis.[16]

Kennan's Planning Staff worked cohesively. Although vigorous discussion took place within it, no real subgroups or intragroup conflict developed. All Staff members were loyal to Kennan but their loyalty seems to have been extended to him personally and to have required him to stake out a basic position which they then could support. In the case of the North Atlantic Treaty, where the Planning Staff acted on a major issue in Kennan's absence, it lent support to a proposal which he opposed. The ease with which Nitze assumed control of the Planning Staff and used its members in the drafting of NSC 68 suggests that, while Kennan enjoyed his colleagues' personal loyalty, he had not managed to convert them fully to his basic ideas on how the United States should deal with the Soviet Union.

Under Kennan's directorship the Planning Staff had no formalized modes of procedures. What characterized it principally was a willingness to discuss the difficult policy problems it confronted not only among its own members but also with outsiders. The Staff constantly sought and remained receptive to information and advice from sources beyond the group itself. It displayed a readiness to build upon and organize existing ideas and proposals. It sought advice and obtained proposals from other members and sections of the State Department, as in the case of the Marshall Plan, and from outside consultants,

---

[16] Ware Adams recalled that "we'd all gather around the table and George would start talking. And . . . very often none of us would say a word, but we'd just be looking at him. And he, by watching us, seemed to know what we were thinking . . . he could tell a person's slant . . . toward a particular subject by bouncing ideas off him and noticing the angle at which they bounced. Rather often he wouldn't have to ask; he'd say, oh yes, you mean so-and-so, don't you? And there'd be a nod, and on he'd go, changing his course to take account of this other factor he may have, for the moment, overlooked." Ware Adams interview, September 30, 1970, C. Ben Wright Collection, Marshall Library.

as in the development of proposals on German policy and on Japanese occupation policy. The Staff's skill and capacity to utilize the ideas of others contributed to the successes it enjoyed from 1947 to 1950.

The key to the Planning Staff's success during this period, however, was its director. Kennan established it as a vital contributor to the process of foreign policy formulation. In light of this, we must ask if it is apposite to describe him as "America's Global Planner" as Brooks Atkinson first did well over four decades ago. The answer rendered here is a much qualified yes. Obviously Kennan did not frame a grand design which others implemented. Only certain elements of his strategy were accepted and implemented. But even if his contribution to designing American postwar foreign policy were to be limited only to the Marshall Plan, or Japan, or China, or even Yugoslavia, he would still warrant recognition for his decisive role.

When Kennan left the directorship of the Policy Planning Staff at the end of 1949, his friend Joseph Alsop described him aptly as a "brilliant, disinterested and courageous public servant in action." Alsop typically had to go further and hyperbolically compare the experience of watching Kennan to that of a collector of Chinese porcelain encountering "a flawless piece of Soong eggshell ware."[17] Be that as it may, Alsop's initial assessment stands the test of time. Kennan was a determined and principled official and a man of estimable character. In his Walgreen lectures he spoke favorably of the characteristics embodied in men such as Elihu Root, Charles Evans Hughes, and Henry L. Stimson—"that pattern of integrity of mind and spirit, moderation and delicacy of character, irreproachable loyalty in personal relations, modesty of person combined with dignity of office, and kindliness and generosity in the approach to all who were weaker and more dependent."[18] Despite his being burdened with inner turmoil, anxieties, and insecurities, Kennan possessed such qualities in good measure. One hopes that they might still be appreciated in those who are called on to determine the nation's foreign policy.

To appreciate Kennan's contribution and endeavors allows for a more full comprehension of the role of others in the making of American foreign policy. Kennan's defeats on the North Atlantic Treaty and on the German issue make clear the significant influence of the West European powers, especially Britain and France, in influencing American foreign policy during this period. They took up the challenge of Marshall's economic assistance offer, provoked discussions for American involvement in a regional security pact, and prevented a further attempt to unify Germany. Much of the American response to the Soviets in Europe resulted from genuine consultation among the Western powers. Among the Europeans, the British Foreign Secretary Ernest Bevin stands head and shoulders above any contemporary in his capacity to influence Amer-

---

[17] Alsop to Kennan, December 31, 1949, Alsop Papers, Box 5.
[18] Kennan, *American Diplomacy*, p. 92.

ican foreign policy. Bevin's biographer, Alan Bullock, rightly has assigned his subject "to that small group of men who can be said to have had a decisive impact on the history of their time."[19] Much of this impact derives from his success in swaying American diplomacy in certain key directions.

This examination of Kennan as policymaker also serves to highlight the significance of the Office of European Affairs under the directorship of John D. Hickerson. The external pressure applied by the Western European nations was usually complemented and reinforced by the activities of this office. Both were able to exploit—most notably on the German issue—Acheson's desire to maintain Western unity. Both sought far stronger security links between the United States and Western Europe than Kennan favored. Among the second level policymakers beneath the president and the respective secretaries of state, the wily and ebullient Hickerson emerges as the most influential in formulating the American response to the Soviet Union in Europe—certainly he was more influential than Kennan. Hickerson has never received either the scholarly or popular renown extended to Kennan but in this study devoted to the latter the capability of the former must be acknowledged. Hickerson worked with Theodore Achilles, Robert Murphy, and others to effectively design the extraordinary American commitment to Western Europe that endured for forty years and provided the umbrella under which the Europeans enjoyed unprecedented prosperity and experienced real security not only from the Soviet Union but from the fratricide which characterized so much of their past.

Ultimately Truman, Marshall, and Acheson bore responsibility for the foreign policy which such figures as Kennan and Hickerson helped to forge. In the case of the president and Secretary of State Marshall, however, they relied heavily on the recommendations that came up to them. Truman prided himself on "his ability to delegate responsibility and to back up those he trusted" and his involvement in foreign policy-making illustrates well his capacity in this regard.[20] Except in crisis situations such as the Berlin Blockade and the Korean War, the White House was simply not the source of the major policy proposals. Determination of American policy on Palestine/Israel stands as the great exception and serves only to confirm the larger point. On this issue Truman later railed against "second or third echelon [officials] in the State Department" for trying to sabotage his policy and to make their own. He recalled, in his usual feisty manner, that he "wanted to make it plain that the President of the United States . . . is responsible for making foreign policy."[21] But the record reveals clearly that essentially Truman approved policy but did not formulate it. "Unlike Roosevelt," as Alonzo Hamby has noted, Truman never suffered from "the illusion that he could function without the distraction

---

[19] Bullock, *Ernest Bevin: Foreign Secretary*, p. 857.

[20] Alexander L. George, *Presidential Decisionmaking in Foreign Policy: The Effective Use of Information and Advice* (Boulder, Colo., 1980), p. 151.

[21] Truman, *Memoirs*, II, pp. 164–65.

of a State Department."[22] In Marshall and Acheson he appointed strong secretaries of state and accepted guidance from them. A large part of his success
as president resides in his wisdom in choosing not to be his own secretary of
state—a wisdom not demonstrated by all his successors. George Kennan had
little direct contact with Truman beyond a few scattered meetings to which he
accompanied Marshall or Lovett. But his influence was exerted efficaciously
precisely because of Truman's ready acceptance of State Department counsel.

George Marshall shared with Truman a capacity to delegate. Dean Rusk,
one of his subordinates, recalled that he "delegated massively, and if he found
that he couldn't delegate effectively to a particular person, he would replace
him."[23] Marshall delegated much of the work of departmental supervision and
the "selling" of foreign policy to the public and the Congress to his loyal
deputy Robert Lovett. His delegation for the actual development of policy
went to the officers one rung down from Lovett such as Kennan and Hickerson. Marshall never entered the Policy Planning Staff conference room to
brainstorm with his planners. He waited for the policy paper or recommendation to come to him and then he acted upon it. If adopted, he then bore responsibility for it and carried it to Truman for approval.[24] Under Marshall's
leadership the State Department reached the height of its influence in the postwar period. But, as we have seen, the general never articulated a coherent
foreign policy strategy which his department implemented. He resembles Truman in that he approved rather than formulated policy. In this he differed
substantially from his successor.

Acheson did not become secretary of state convinced that negotiation with
the Soviet Union was useless and that building up Western political and military strength to contain communism was the only viable course. Contrary to
conventional interpretations Acheson exhibited an initial caution about policy,
perhaps even indecision, which clarifies further how this period must be understood as a working toward a coherent strategy rather than the implementation of a predetermined one. But Acheson explored the options and then
played the decisive role in framing the strategy which came to be known as
containment. Events during 1949, including dealing with the Russians at the
Paris CFM and the Soviet atomic explosion, shaped him and led him to adopt
the concept that possession of strength, especially military strength, was the
way to meet the Soviet Union in world affairs. This view provided the basis
for NSC 68. The Korean War seemingly confirmed it. In taking this view, for
which he adeptly obtained Truman's approval, Acheson rejected the advice of
Kennan, which contributed to the Planning Staff director's decision to resign.
During the course of Kennan's directorship the United States virtually had

[22] Alonzo Hamby, "Harry S. Truman: Insecurity and Responsibility," in Fred I. Greenstein,
ed., *Leadership in the Modern Presidency* (Cambridge, 1988), p. 65.
[23] Rusk, *As I Saw It*, p. 132.
[24] Author's interview with Kennan, March 6, 1989.

worked its way to a coherent foreign policy, but Kennan disagreed with the end result. As he rightly has maintained ever since, he objected to the military character of the measures which Acheson eventually sponsored and which made containment a reality.

Finally, we might ask what the Policy Planning Staff's involvement in making foreign policy in the late 1940s has to teach those charged with this responsibility in the present and future. What made Kennan's Planning Staff an effective instrument of government and is this relevant in our own time and beyond? Certainly some rather elementary points can be made regarding the Policy Planning Staff. Its import and influence over U.S. foreign policy from Kennan's tenure as director down to the present depends heavily on the secretary of state serving as the senior presidential adviser on foreign policy. If the secretary of state is not a significant force in making foreign policy—as with William P. Rogers in Richard Nixon's first presidential term—then the Planning Staff is automatically hobbled. If the secretary of state is engaged upon a constant struggle within the administration for control of foreign policy—as with Cyrus Vance during the Carter presidency—then the Staff's impact is more limited. In short, its influence is derived from and dependent upon that of the secretary of state. It has proved most effective with a strong Secretary at the helm—such as Kennan's Staff with Marshall, Nitze's with Acheson, Robert Bowie's with John Foster Dulles, and Winston Lord's with Henry Kissinger (during the second Nixon/Ford presidential term).

After acknowledging this dependency, however, the question of what makes for an effective Staff needs some answer. Here the attributes which allowed for Kennan's initial success must be present and these are far easier to recite than to implement. Firstly, the capacity to provide superior analysis and advice and to do it quickly is fundamental. Secondly, unquestioned access to and a close working relationship with the secretary of state is almost as important as the first. Lastly, and largely as a synergy of the first two, a reputation is necessary which ensures both that its work is accorded high respect within the government and that it obtains cooperation from bureaucratic units which are larger and determined to protect certain interests. In all of this the role of the Planning Staff director is crucial. There must be a personal chemistry between this person and the secretary to allow for an extremely close working relationship, although this does not necessarily require personal friendship as the case of Marshall and Kennan amply demonstrates. Simply put, the planning chief must be part of the inner core of departmental advisers and must be perceived as such. But, more than this, the chief planner must bring a strong knowledge and experience of international affairs along with a capacity for independent thought, powerful analysis, and tough judgment. If the chief planner is to serve effectively he must be more than an echo of his superior and must bring his own ideas and thinking to the secretary to guide policy formation. It is here that Kennan's example in the office has been telling. He established this office as a key location in the State Department from which to influence policy and won for the position a certain prestige. Surely his success is partly responsible for the array of talented individuals—among them Paul Nitze, Robert Bowie, Walt W. Rostow, George McGhee, Henry Owen, Gerard Smith, Winston Lord, Anthony Lake, and Richard Solomon— who willingly have taken on the job intent in their own ways on replicating Kennan's feat.

Kennan's determination to keep his group small and cohesive has stood the test of time and seems an essential condition for a successful planning team. A small group wastes less time on its own administration and allows for greater flexibility in confronting an array of issues. As Kennan's Staff displayed well the Planning Staff must be able and willing to garner and utilize the ideas of others. It can be a testing ground of sorts for policy ideas. Indeed, a key part of its function must lie in transforming a variety of suggestions and proposals into coherent policy recommendations. In this process the Planning Staff can serve as a vehicle to link the secretary of state to other divisions of that large department. The geographic divisions can channel ideas through the Planning Staff and argue for them there. In a somewhat similar manner, as Kennan's Staff revealed through the use of outside consultants, the Planning Staff can be the point of contact where advice is drawn from figures outside the government and where some effort is made during the embryonic and preliminary stages of policy development to begin to build public support for it. This may be an increasingly important undertaking for any administration intent on building a broad consensus for an altered American world role.

With the unraveling of the Cold War the United States now must navigate within a more uncertain even if more malleable international environment than that which prevailed since the late 1940s. The rapidly changing international scene presents a challenge to contemporary policymakers equal in complexity if less threatening than the one which Kennan and his colleagues faced over forty years ago. Calls are uttered from a variety of sources for a new American grand strategy to guide the ship of state through the rocks and shoals of the next decade and into the next century. But this study suggests that notions of a *new* grand design are somewhat misplaced and facile. It would be more mature and appropriate for the United States to develop its foreign policy pragmatically in a more deliberate case-by-case manner and in light of a clear assessment of international developments. This means that the United States should not delude itself that it can or should quickly reformulate the role it must play in the world. With an eye on the late 1940s Americans might appreciate that this is something that develops from the endeavors of policymakers across a range of issues rather than being concocted magically into being. One can only hope that the present and future makers of foreign policy might grasp realities as effectively as did their forebears after World War II and share something of the integrity and intelligence of men such as George F. Kennan.

Appendix A

Policy Planning Staff Papers, 1947–1949

Appendix B

Consultants Who Appeared Before the Policy Planning Staff, 1947–1949 (Partial List)

Dean Acheson, formerly Under Secretary of State

Frank Altschul, National Planning Association

James Angel, Professor, Columbia University

Hamilton Fish Armstrong, Editor, *Foreign Affairs*

Ray Atherton

Capt. B. L. Austin, USN

Joseph Ballantine, Brookings Institution

Lt. Col. George W. Beeler, USA

Sarah Gibson Blanding, President, Vassar College

Bernard Brodie, Professor, Yale University

Col. H. A. Byroade, USA

William R. Castle, formerly Under Secretary of State

Selden Chapin, Minister to Hungary

John L. Collyer, President, B. F. Goodrich Company

Lt. Col. J. W. Coutts, USA

Monnett B. Davis, Ambassador to Panama

Walter J. Donnelly, Ambassador to Venezuela

William J. Donovan

Eugene H. Dooman, FSO, Ret.

Lewis Douglas, Ambassador to Great Britain

Allen Dulles

Frederick Dunn, Professor, Yale University

Brooks Emeny, President, Foreign Policy Association

John K. Fairbank, Professor, Harvard University

Marion B. Folsom, Treasurer, Eastman Kodak Company

Col. A. Gerhart, USA

Joseph C. Grew, formerly Under Secretary of State

Maj. Gen. Alfred M. Gruenther, USA

Col. Richard A. Gruffendorf, USAAF

Col. P. M. Hamilton, USA

John M. Hancock, Lehman Brothers

Col. E. S. Hartshorne, USA

Donald R. Heath, Minister to Bulgaria

Calvin B. Hoover, Professor, Duke University

Philip Jessup, Ambassador-at-Large

Nelson Johnson, formerly Minister to Australia

Lt. Col. George M. Jones, USA

John Lockwood, formerly Deputy Director, ARA

Capt. R. N. McFarlane, USN

Donald McKay, Professor, Harvard University

Edward S. Mason, Professor, Harvard University

John Miller, National Planning Association

Ludwell L. Montague, CIA

Hans J. Morgenthau, Professor, University of Chicago

Robert D. Murphy, Political Adviser, Berlin

Reinhold Niebuhr, Union Theological Seminary

Maj. Gen. Lauris Norstad, USA

J. Robert Oppenheimer, Director, Institute for Advanced Study, Princeton

Leo Pasvolsky, Brookings Institution

Wallace B. Phillips, President of U.S. Chamber of Commerce in London

Joseph M. Proskauer

John D. Rockefeller III

Comdr. Finn Ronne, USMR

David N. Rowe, Professor, Yale University

Arthur Schoenfeld, Minister to Rumania

General Cortlandt Van R. Schuyler, USA

Adm. F. P. Sherman, USN

Lt. Col. W. M. Skidmore, USA

Capt. H. P. Smith, USN

Walter Bedell Smith, Ambassador to U.S.S.R.

Robert Strauss-Hupe

Charles P. Taft, President, Federal Council of Churches of Christ in America

Jacob Viner, Professor, Princeton University

William Vogt, Pan American Union

Father Edmund Walsh, S.J., Regent, School of Foreign Service, Georgetown University

James P. Warburg

Col. C. B. Westover, USA

Brayton Wilbur, formerly President of U.S. Chamber of Commerce

Edward P. Williams, NSRB

Karl A. Wittfogel, Professor, Columbia University

Arnold Wolfers, Professor, Yale University

Robert W. Woodruff, Chairman, Coca Cola Company

Adm. Edmund T. Woolridge, USN

Mary C. Wright, Professor, Stanford University

P. Latimer Yates, Food and Agriculture Organization

Col. Don Zimmerman, USA

Contents to Bibliography

Bibliography

Primary Sources

Manuscript Collections

BENTLEY HISTORICAL LIBRARY, THE UNIVERSITY OF MICHIGAN, ANN ARBOR, MICH.
Arthur H. Vandenberg Papers

COUNCIL ON FOREIGN RELATIONS ARCHIVES, NEW YORK, N.Y.
Records of Groups
Records of Meetings

DOUGLAS MACARTHUR MEMORIAL ARCHIVES AND LIBRARY, NORFOLK, VA.
Douglas MacArthur Papers
Courtney Whitney Papers
Charles A. Willoughby Papers

FIRESTONE LIBRARY, PRINCETON UNIVERSITY, PRINCETON, N.J.
John Foster Dulles Papers

GEORGE C. MARSHALL LIBRARY, LEXINGTON, VA.
Larry I. Bland Collection
W. Walton Butterworth Papers
George C. Marshall Papers
Forrest C. Pogue Materials
James W. Riddleberger Papers
U.S. Department of the Army, Plans and Operations Division, Miscellaneous Papers on Greece, Japan and Germany (RG 319)
C. Ben Wright Papers (Kennan Biography Project)

HARRY S. TRUMAN LIBRARY, INDEPENDENCE, MO.
Dean G. Acheson Papers
George V. Allen Papers
Eben A. Ayers Papers
Ralph Block Papers
William L. Clayton Papers
Clark M. Clifford Papers
Matthew J. Connelly Papers
Jonathan Daniels Papers
George M. Elsey Papers
Thomas K. Finletter Papers
A. Robert Ginsburgh Papers
S. Everett Gleason Papers

Stanton Griffis Papers
Paul G. Hoffman Papers
Joseph M. Jones Papers
Dan A. Kimball Papers
Charles P. Kindleberger Papers
David D. Lloyd Papers
John F. Melby Papers
Edward G. Miller Papers
Charles S. Murphy Papers
Frank Pace, Jr., Papers
J. Anthony Panuch Papers
Sumner T. Pike Papers
Harry B. Price Papers
William M. Rigdon Papers
Frank N. Roberts Papers
Samuel I. Rosenman Papers
Charles G. Ross Papers
John W. Snyder Papers
Sidney W. Souers Papers
Stephen F. Spingarn Papers
Charles W. Thayer Papers
Harry S. Truman Papers: Central Files
Harry S. Truman Papers: Post-Presidential Files
Harry S. Truman Papers: President's Official File
Harry S. Truman Papers: President's Secretary's File
Harry S. Truman Papers: Records of the National Security Council
James E. Webb Papers
Chaim Weizmann Archives, Rehovoth, Israel (copies)

HERBERT H. LEHMAN SUITE, COLUMBIA UNIVERSITY, NEW YORK, N.Y.
Frank Altschul Papers

HOUGHTON LIBRARY, HARVARD UNIVERSITY, CAMBRIDGE, MASS.
Ruth Fischer Papers
Joseph Grew Papers

JOHN F. KENNEDY LIBRARY, BOSTON, MASS.
John F. Kennedy Papers: President's Official File
Arthur M. Schlesinger Papers
James P. Warburg Papers

LIBRARY OF CONGRESS, WASHINGTON, D.C.
Joseph and Stewart Alsop Papers
Tom Connally Papers
Joseph E. Davies Papers
Herbert Feis Papers
W. Averell Harriman Papers

Loy W. Henderson Papers
Philip C. Jessup Papers
William D. Leahy Papers
J. Robert Oppenheimer Papers
Robert P. Patterson Papers
Laurence A. Steinhardt Papers

NATIONAL ARCHIVES, WASHINGTON, D.C.
Diplomatic Branch:
Department of State Records: Central Decimal Files, 1945–1949
Department of State Records: Executive Secretariat Files
Department of State Records: Personnel File 123, George F. Kennan
Department of State Records: Records of Charles E. Bohlen, 1941–1952
Department of State Records: Records of the Inter and Intra Departmental Committees (RG 353)
Department of State Records: Records of the Office of European Affairs, 1942–1947 (H. Freeman Matthews and John D. Hickerson Files)
Department of State Records: Records of the Policy Planning Staff
Modern Military Branch:
Central Intelligence Agency Records: Arthur B. Darling and Ludwell Lee Montague Histories
National Security Council Documents
U.S. Joint Chief of Staff Records: (RG 218) Central Decimal File, 1948–1950
U.S. Joint Chiefs of Staff Records: William D. Leahy Records

SEELEY G. MUDD MANUSCRIPT LIBRARY, PRINCETON UNIVERSITY, PRINCETON, N.J.
Bernard M. Baruch Papers
James V. Forrestal Papers
George F. Kennan Papers
Arthur Krock Papers
David E. Lilienthal Papers

STERLING MEMORIAL LIBRARY, YALE UNIVERSITY, NEW HAVEN, CONN.
Dean G. Acheson Papers
Robert O. Anthony Collection of Walter Lippmann
Hanson Baldwin Papers
Samuel Flagg Bemis Papers
Chester Bowles Papers
Arthur Bliss Lane Papers
Max Lerner Papers
Walter Lippmann Papers
Arnold Wolfers Papers

Documents

Bundy, Harvey H., and James Grafton Rogers. *The Organization of the Government for the Conduct of Foreign Affairs: A Report With Recommendations Prepared for the Commission on Organization of Executive Branch of the Government*. Washington: U.S. Government Printing Office, 1949.

Division of the Federal Register, National Archives. *United States Government Manual*. Washington: U.S. Government Printing Office, 1947–1950.

Etzold, Thomas H., and John Lewis Gaddis, eds. *Containment: Documents on American Foreign Policy and Strategy, 1945–1950*. New York: Oxford University Press, 1978.

Great Britain, Parliament. *Parliamentary Debates*. 1947–1950. London: His Majesty's Stationary Office, 1947–1950.

Nelson, Anna Kasten, ed. *The State Department Policy Planning Staff Papers*. 1947–1949. New York: Garland, 1983.

Truman, Harry S. *Public Papers of the Presidents of the United States: Harry S. Truman*. 1947–1950. Washington: U.S. Government Printing Office, 1963–1965.

U.S. Atomic Energy Commission. *In the Matter of J. Robert Oppenheimer: Transcript of Hearings Before Personnel Security Board*. Washington: U.S. Government Printing Office, 1954.

U.S. Civil Service Commission. *Official Register of the United States*. 1947–1950. Washington: U.S. Government Printing Office, 1947–1950.

U.S. Congress. *Congressional Record*. 80th and 81st Congresses. Washington: U.S. Government Printing Office, 1947–1950.

U.S. Congress. House. Committee on Foreign Affairs. *Emergency Foreign Aid: Hearings*. 80th Congress, 1st Session. Washington: U.S. Government Printing Office, 1947.

U.S. Congress. Senate. Committee on Foreign Relations. *European Recovery Program: Hearings*. 80th Congress, 2d Session. Washington: U.S. Government Printing Office, 1948.

U.S. Congress. Senate. Committee on Foreign Relations. *Interim Aid for Europe: Hearings*. 80th Congress, 1st Session. Washington: U.S. Government Printing Office, 1947.

U.S. Congress. Senate. Committee on Foreign Relations. *Mutual Defense Assistance Program, 1950: Hearings*. 81st Congress, 2d Session. Washington: U.S. Government Printing Office, 1950.

U.S. Congress. Senate. Committee on Foreign Relations. *North Atlantic Treaty: Hearings*. 81st Congress, 1st Session. Washington: U.S. Government Printing Office, 1949.

U.S. Congress. Senate. Committee on Government Operations. *Administration of National Security: Hearings and Staff Reports*. 88th Congress. Washington: U.S. Government Printing Office, 1965.

U.S. Congress. Senate. Committee on Government Operations. *Organizing for National Security: Hearings, Studies, Staff Reports and Recommendations*. 3 vols. 86th and 87th Congresses. Washington: U.S. Government Printing Office, 1961.

U.S. Congress. Senate. Select Committee to Study Government Operations with Respect to Intelligence Activities. *Final Report: Supplementary Detailed Staff Reports on Foreign and Military Intelligence: Book IV*. 94th Congress. Washington: U.S. Government Printing Office, 1976.

U.S. Department of State. *The Biographical Register of the Department of State*. Washington: U.S. Government Printing Office, 1947–1950.

U.S. Department of State. *The Department of State Bulletin*. 1947–1950. Washington: U.S. Government Printing Office, 1947–1950.

U.S. Department of State. *Foreign Relations of the United States*. 1945–1952. Washington: U.S. Government Printing Office, 1967–1988.

Personal Correspondence

John Paton Davies, Jr., January 14, 1987.

John D. Hickerson, September 20, 1978.

George F. Kennan, September 14, 1978; December 14, 1978; February 22, 1979; April 23, 1979; August 10, 1979; August 16, 1979; September 6, 1979.

James McCargar, March 15, 1990.

Interviews

John Paton Davies, Asheville, North Carolina, August 12, 1986.

Marshall Green, Department of State, Washington, D.C., July 6, 1978.

Loy W. Henderson, Washington, D.C., June 26, 1978.

John D. Hickerson, Atlantic Council of the United States, Washington, D.C., July 6, 1978.

George F. Kennan, Princeton, New Jersey, March 6, 1989.

Franklin Lindsay, Washington, D.C., February 27, 1990.

Charles Burton Marshall, Arlington, Virginia, June 22, 1978.

James McCargar, Washington, D.C., February 28, 1990.

Paul H. Nitze, Arlington, Virginia, June 30, 1978; July 5, 1978.

James Reston, *The New York Times* Offices, Washington, D.C., August 8, 1989.

Carlton Savage, School of International Service, American University, Washington, D.C., June 22, 1978.

Oral Histories

COLUMBIA UNIVERSITY ORAL HISTORY PROJECT

Charles E. Bohlen; Harvey H. Bundy; W. Averell Harriman; Robert Lovett; John J. McCloy; Marshall Plan Project; Walter Lippmann

DULLES ORAL HISTORY COLLECTION (PRINCETON UNIVERSITY)

Theodore Achilles; Stewart Alsop; Charles Bohlen; James F. Byrnes; Lucius Clay; W. Averell Harriman; John D. Hickerson; George F. Kennan; John J. McCloy; H. Freeman Matthews; Robert D. Murphy; Lauris Norstad

FOREIGN AFFAIRS ORAL HISTORY PROGRAM, GEORGETOWN UNIVERSITY LIBRARY

William Attwood; Robert R. Bowie; Marshall Green

GEORGE C. MARSHALL LIBRARY, LEXINGTON, VA.

GEORGE C. MARSHALL INTERVIEWS AND REMINISCENCES FOR FORREST C. POGUE, 1956–1957

ORAL HISTORY INTERVIEWS IN C. BEN WRIGHT'S KENNAN BIOGRAPHY COLLECTION

Ware Adams, September 30, 1970

Charles E. Bohlen, September 29, 1970

Benjamin V. Cohen, September 29, 1970
William Crawford, September 29, 1970
Dorothy Hessman, October 1, 1970
Carlton Savage, September 30, 1970
Llewellyn E. Thompson, September 30, 1970

HARRY S. TRUMAN LIBRARY ORAL HISTORY COLLECTION
Theodore Achilles; George E. Allen; Eben A. Ayers; Robert W. Barnett; David E. Bell; Ralph Block; Winthrop G. Brown; David K. E. Bruce; John C. Campbell; Matthew J. Connelly; Jonathan Daniels; William H. Draper, Jr.; Robert L. Dennison; George M. Elsey; Thomas K. Finletter; Gordon Gray; Loy W. Henderson; John D. Hickerson; Paul G. Hoffman; Benjamin M. Hulley; Marx Leva; Edwin A. Locke, Jr.; John Maktos; Edward S. Mason; Clifford C. Matlock; Charles S. Murphy; Charles S. Murphy, Richard Neustadt, David Stowe, James E. Webb (joint interview); Frank Pace, Jr.; James W. Riddleberger; Samuel I. Rosenman; Francis Russell; Charles E. Saltzman; Durward V. Sandifer; Joseph C. Satterthwaite; Philip D. Sprouse; Isaac N. P. Stokes; John L. Sullivan; Harry H. Vaughan; Edwin M. Wright

HARRY S. TRUMAN LIBRARY: HARRY B. PRICE INTERVIEWS ON THE MARSHALL PLAN
Charles Bohlen; Hugh Gaitskell; W. Averell Harriman; George F. Kennan; George C. Marshall; James Reston; Francis Wilcox

JOHN F. KENNEDY LIBRARY
Dean G. Acheson; Charles E. Bohlen; Roger Hilsman; George F. Kennan; Llewellyn E. Thompson

Newspapers and Periodicals

New Republic, 1947–1950
New York Times, 1947–1950
Saturday Evening Post, 1947–1950
Time, 1947–1950
U.S. News, 1947–1950

Published Memoirs, Diaries, and Papers

Acheson, Dean G. *Present at the Creation: My Years in the State Department*. New York: W. W. Norton, 1969.
———. *Sketches From Life of Men I Have Known*. New York: Harper, 1961.
Achilles, Theodore C. "US Role in Negotiations that Led to Atlantic Alliance, Parts 1 & 2," *NATO Review* vol. 27, nos. 4 & 5 (1979), pp. 11–4, 16–19.
Adenauer, Konrad. *Memoirs, 1945–1953*. Chicago: Henry Regnery, 1966.
Allison, John M. *Ambassador from the Prairie or Allison Wonderland*. Boston: Houghton Mifflin, 1973.
Anders, Roger M., ed. *Forging the Atomic Shield: Excerpts from the Office Diary of Gordon E. Dean*. Chapel Hill: The University of North Carolina Press, 1987.
Anderson, Clinton P. *Outsider in the Senate*. New York: World, 1970.

Arneson, R. Gordon. "The H-Bomb Decision," *Foreign Service Journal* 46 (May 1969): 27–29; (June 1969): 24–27, 43.

Aron, Raymond. *Memoires*. Paris: Julliard, 1983.

Attlee, Clement. *Twilight of Empire: Memoirs of Prime Minister Clement Attlee*. New York: A. S. Barnes, 1962.

Attwood, William. *The Twilight Struggle: Tales of the Cold War*. New York: Harper and Row, 1987.

Bailey, Thomas A. *The Marshall Plan Summer: An Eyewitness Report on Europe and the Russians in 1947*. Stanford: Hoover Institution Press, 1977.

Balfour, John. *Not Too Correct an Aureole: The Recollections of a Diplomat*. Wilton, Salisbury, Wiltshire: Michael Russell, 1983.

Ball, George W. *The Past Has Another Pattern: Memoirs*. New York: W. W. Norton, 1982.

Barkley, Alben W. *That Reminds Me*. Garden City, N.J.: Doubleday, 1954.

Baruch, Bernard. *The Public Years*. New York: Holt, 1960.

Beam, Jacob D. *Multiple Exposure: An American Ambassador's Unique Perspective on East-West Issues*. New York: W.W. Norton, 1978.

Beaulac, Willard L. *Career Ambassador*. New York: Macmillan, 1951.

Berle, Beatrice Bishop, and Travis Beal Jacobs, eds. *Navigating the Rapids, 1918–1971: From the Papers of Adolf A. Berle*. New York: Harcourt Brace Jovanovich, 1973.

Bidault, Georges. *Resistance: The Political Autobiography of Georges Bidault*. London: Weidenfeld and Nicholson, 1965.

Bingham, Jonathan B. *Shirt-Sleeve Diplomacy: Point 4 in Action*. New York: John Day, 1953.

Blum, John Morton, ed. *Public Philosopher: Selected Letters of Walter Lippmann*. New York: Tickner and Fields, 1985.

Bohlen, Charles E. *Witness to History, 1929–1969*. New York: W. W. Norton, 1973.

Bowles, Chester. *Promises to Keep: My Years in Public Life, 1941–1969*. New York: Harper and Row, 1971.

Braden, Spruille. *Diplomats and Demagogues: The Memoirs of Spruille Braden*. New Rochelle: Arlington House, 1971.

Bradley, Omar N., and Clay Blair. *General's Life: An Autobiography of General of the Army Omar N. Bradley*. New York: Simon & Schuster, 1983.

Brandon, Henry. *Special Relationships: A Foreign Correspondent's Memoirs from Roosevelt to Reagan*. New York: Atheneum, 1988.

Briggs, Ellis. *Farewell to Foggy Bottom: The Recollections of a Career Diplomat*. New York: David McKay, 1964.

Bullitt, Orville H., ed. *For the President: Personal and Secret, Correspondence Between Franklin D. Roosevelt and William C. Bullitt*. Boston: Houghton Mifflin, 1972.

Bush, Vannevar. *Pieces of the Action*. New York: William Morrow, 1970.

Byrnes, James F. *All in One Lifetime*. New York: Harper and Bros., 1958.

Cabot, John M. *First Line of Defense: Forty Years' Experiences of a Career Diplomat*. Washington: School of Foreign Service, Georgetown University, 1979.

Childs, J. Rives. *Foreign Service Farewell: My Years in the Near East*. Charlottesville: University Press of Virginia, 1969.

Clark, Mark W. *From the Danube to the Yalu*. New York: Harper and Bros., 1954.

Clay, Lucius, D. *Decision in Germany*. New York: Doubleday, 1950.

———. *Germany and the Fight for Freedom*. Cambridge, Mass.: Harvard University Press, 1950.

Clifford, Clark, and Richard Holbrooke. *Counsel to the President: A Memoir*. New York: Random House, 1991.

Clubb, O. Edmund. *The Witness and I*. New York: Columbia University Press, 1974.

Conant, James B. *My Several Lives: Memoirs of a Social Inventor*. New York: Harper and Row, 1970.

Connally, Tom. *My Name is Tom Connally*. New York: T. Y. Crowell, 1954.

Dalton, Hugh. *Memoirs*. Vol. 2: *High Tide and After, 1945–1960*. London: Frederick Muller, 1962.

Davies, Jr., John Paton. *Dragon by the Tail: American, British, Japanese and Russian Encounters with China and One Another*. New York: W. W. Norton, 1972.

Dixon, Piers. *Double Diploma: The Life of Sir Pierson Dixon, Don and Diplomat*. London: Hutchinson, 1968.

Dobney, Frederick J., ed. *Selected Papers of Will Clayton*. Baltimore: Johns Hopkins University Press, 1971.

Dulles, John Foster. *War or Peace*. Rev. ed. New York: Macmillan, 1957.

Eden, Anthony. *Full Circle: The Memoirs of Anthony Eden*. Boston: Houghton Mifflin, 1960.

Eichelberger, Clark M. *Organizing for Peace: A Personal History of the Founding of the United Nations*. New York: Harper and Row, 1977.

Emmerson, John K. *The Japanese Thread: A Life in the Foreign Service*. New York: Holt, Rinehart & Winston, 1978.

Galbraith, John Kenneth. *A Life in Our Times: Memoirs*. Boston: Houghton Mifflin, 1981.

Gromyko, Andrei. *Memoirs*. Trans. by Harold Shukman. London: Hutchinson, 1989.

Harriman, W. Averell. *America and Russia in a Changing World*. New York: Doubleday, 1971.

Harriman, W. Averell, and Elie Abel. *Special Envoy to Churchill and Stalin, 1941–1946*. New York: Random House, 1975.

Henderson, Sir Nicholas. *The Birth of NATO*. London: Weidenfeld and Nicolson, 1982.

Hoover, Calvin B. *Memoirs of Capitalism, Communism and Nazism*. Durham: Duke University Press, 1965.

Howley, Frank. *Berlin Command*. New York: G. P. Putnam's, 1950.

Hughes, H. Stuart. "The Second Year of the Cold War: A Memoir and an Anticipation," *Commentary* 48 (August 1969), pp. 27–32.

Jebb, Gladwyn. *The Memoirs of Lord Gladwyn*. London: Weidenfeld and Nicholson, 1972.

Jessup, Philip C. *The Birth of Nations*. New York: Columbia University Press, 1974.

Jones, Joseph M. *The Fifteen Weeks*. New York: Viking, 1955.

Johnson, U. Alexis. *The Right Hand of Power*. Englewood Cliffs, N.J.: Prentice Hall, 1984.

Kennan, George F. *Memoirs, 1925–1950*. Boston: Little, Brown, 1967.

———. *Memoirs, 1950–1963*. Boston: Little, Brown, 1972.

———. *Sketches From a Life*. New York: Pantheon Books, 1989.

Khrushchev, Nikita S. *Khrushchev Remembers*. Boston: Little, Brown, 1970.

Kindleberger, Charles P. *Marshall Plan Days*. Boston: Allen & Unwin, 1987.

Kirkpatrick, Ivone. *The Inner Circle*. London: Macmillan, 1959.

Kissinger, Henry. *White House Years*. Boston; Little, Brown, 1979.

Krock, Arthur. *Memoirs: Sixty Years on the Firing Line*. New York: Funk and Wagnall, 1968.

Langer, William L. *In and Out of the Ivory Tower: The Autobiography of William L. Langer*. New York: N. Watson Academic Publications, 1977.

Lash, Joseph P., ed. *From the Diaries of Felix Frankfurter*. New York: W. W. Norton, 1975.

Lie, Trygve. *In the Cause of Peace: Seven Years With the United Nations*. New York: Macmillan, 1954.

Lilienthal, David E. *The Journals of David E. Lilienthal*. Vol. 2: *The Atomic Energy Years, 1945–1950*. New York: Harper and Row, 1964.

———. *The Journals of David E. Lilienthal*. Vol. 6: *Creativity and Conflict, 1964–1967*. New York: Harper and Row, 1976.

———. *The Journals of David E. Lilienthal*. Vol. 7: *Unfinished Business, 1968–1981*. New York: Harper and Row, 1983.

Lodge, Henry Cabot. *The Storm Has Many Eyes: A Personal Narrative*. New York: W. W. Norton, 1973.

MacArthur, Douglas. *Reminiscences*. New York: McGraw-Hill, 1964.

McGhee, George. *Envoy to the Middle World: Adventures in Diplomacy*. New York: Harper and Row, 1983.

McLellan, David C., and David C. Acheson, eds. *Among Friends: Personal Letters of Dean Acheson*. New York: Dodd & Mead, 1980.

Meyer, Cord. *Facing Reality: From World Federalism to the CIA*. New York: Harper and Row, 1980.

Millis, Walter, ed. *The Forrestal Diaries*. New York: Viking, 1951.

Murphy, Robert D. *Diplomat Among Warriors*. New York: Doubleday, 1964.

Nitze, Paul H. *From Hiroshima to Glasnost: At the Center of Decision*. New York: George Weidenfeld, 1989.

Pearson, Lester B. *Mike: The Memoirs of the Right Honourable Lester B. Pearson*. Vol. 1: *1897–1948*. Vol. 2: *1948–1957*. New York: Quadrangle, 1972, 1973.

Philby, Kim. *My Silent War*. London: Granada, 1968.

Pickersgill, J. W., and D. F. Forster. *The MacKenzie King Record*. Vol. 4: *1947–1948*. Toronto: University of Toronto Press, 1970.

Poppe, Nicholas. *Reminiscences*. Ed. Henry G. Schwartz. Bellingham, Wash.: Western Washington University Press, 1983.

Reid, Escott. *Time of Fear and Hope: The Making of the North Atlantic Treaty, 1947–1949*. Toronto: McClelland and Stewart, 1977.

Ridgeway, Matthew B. *Soldier: The Memoirs of Matthew B. Ridgeway*. New York: Harper and Bros., 1956.

Rusk, Dean, with Richard Rusk. *As I Saw It*. New York: Norton, 1990.

Sakharov, Andrei. *Memoirs*. Trans. by Richard Lourie. New York: Knopf, 1990.

Salisbury, Harrison E. *A Journey for Our Times: A Memoir*. New York: Harper and Row, 1983.

———. *A Time of Change: A Reporter's Tale of our Time*. New York: Harper and Row, 1988.

Smith, Jean Edward, ed. *The Papers of General Lucius D. Clay: Germany, 1945–1949*. 2 vols. Bloomington: Indiana University Press, 1974.

Smith, Walter Bedell. *My Three Years in Moscow*. Philadelphia: J. B. Lippincott, 1949.

Spender, Stephen. *Journals: 1939–1983*. Ed. by John Goldsmith. London: Faber and Faber, 1985.

Stikker, Dirk U. *Men of Responsibility: A Memoir*. New York: Harper and Row, 1966.

Strang, Lord. *Home and Abroad*. London: Andre Deutsch, 1956.

Strauss, Lewis L. *Men and Decisions*. New York: Doubleday, 1962.

Sulzberger, Cyrus L. *A Long Row of Candles: Memoirs and Diaries, 1934–1954*. New York: Macmillan, 1969.

———. *Seven Continents and Forty Years: A Concentration of Memoirs*. New York: Quadrangle, 1977.

Talbott, Strobe, ed. *Khrushchev Remembers*. Boston: Little, Brown, 1970.

Teller, Edward. *The Legacy of Hiroshima*. Garden City, N.Y.: Doubleday, 1962.

Truman, Harry S. *Memoirs*. Vol. 1: *Year of Decisions*. New York: Doubleday, 1955.

———. *Memoirs*. Vol. 2: *Years of Trial and Hope*. New York: Doubleday, 1956.

Vandenberg, Jr., Arthur, ed. *The Private Papers of Senator Vandenberg*. Boston: Houghton Mifflin, 1952.

Villard, Henry Serrano. *Affairs at State*. New York: T. Y. Crowell, 1965.

Warburg, James P. *The Long Road Home: The Autobiography of a Maverick*. New York: Doubleday, 1964.

Wedemeyer, Albert C. *Wedemeyer Reports*. New York: Holt, 1958.

White, Theodore H. *In Search of History: A Personal Adventure*. New York: Warner Books, 1978.

Whitney, Courtney. *MacArthur: His Rendezvous With History*. New York: Knopf, 1956.

Williams, Justin. *Japan's Political Revolution Under MacArthur: A Participant's Account*. Athens, Ga.: University of Georgia Press, 1979.

Willoughby, Charles A., and John Chamberlain. *MacArthur, 1941–1951*. New York: McGraw-Hill, 1954.

Wilson, Evan M. *Decision on Palestine: How the U.S. Came to Recognize Israel*. Stanford: Hoover Institution Press, 1979.

Yoshida, Shigeru. *The Yoshida Memoirs: The Story of Japan in Crisis*. London: Heinemann, 1961.

Yost, Charles W. *The Conduct and Misconduct of Foreign Affairs: Reflections of U.S. Foreign Policy Since World War II*. New York: Random House, 1972.

SECONDARY SOURCES

Books

Adams, Larry L. *Walter Lippmann*. Boston: Twayne, 1977.

Allison, Graham T. *Essence of Decision*. Boston: Little, Brown, 1971.

Alsop, Joseph, and Stewart Alsop. *We Accuse! The Story of the Miscarriage of American Justice in the Case of J. Robert Oppenheimer*. New York: Simon & Schuster, 1954.

Alsop, Stewart. *The Center: People And Power In Political Washington*. New York: Harper and Row, 1968.

Ambrose, Stephen E. *Eisenhower: Soldier, General of the Army, President Elect, 1890–1952*. New York: Simon & Schuster, 1983.

———. *Rise to Globalism: American Foreign Policy, 1938–1980*. 2d rev. ed. New York: Penguin Books, 1980.

Anderson, David L. *Imperialism and Idealism: American Diplomats in China, 1861–1898*. Bloomington: Indiana University Press, 1985.

Anderson, Terry H. *The United States, Great Britain and the Cold War, 1944–1947*. Columbia: University of Missouri Press, 1981.

Arkes, Hadley. *Bureaucracy, The Marshall Plan and The National Interest*. Princeton, N.J.: Princeton University Press, 1972.

Backer, John H. *The Decision to Divide Germany: American Foreign Policy in Transition*. Durham: Duke University Press, 1978.

———. *Priming the German Economy: American Occupation Policies, 1945–1948*. Durham: Duke University Press, 1971.

———. *Winds of History: The German Years of Lucius DuBignon Clay*. New York: Van Nostrand Reinhold Co., 1983.

Bain, Kenneth Ray. *The March to Zion: United States Policy and the Founding of Israel*. College Station, Texas: Texas A&M University Press, 1979.

Baldwin, Hanson W. *The Price of Power*. New York: Harper & Bros., 1947.

Barnes, William, and John Heath Morgan. *The Foreign Service of the United States: Origins, Development and Functions*. Washington: Historical Office, Department of State, 1961.

Barnet, Richard. *The Alliance: America-Europe-Japan, Makers of the Postwar World*. New York: Simon & Schuster, 1983.

Barnett, O. Doak. *China on the Eve of Communist Takeover*. New York: Frederick A. Praeger, 1963.

Beal, John Robinson. *Marshall in China*. New York: Doubleday, 1970.

Beichman, Arnold. *The "Other" State Department: The United States Mission to the United Nations*. New York: Basic Books, 1968.

Bell, Coral. *Negotiation From Strength: A Study of the Politics of Power*. London: Chatto and Windus, 1962.

Bellush, Bernard. *He Walked Alone: A Biography of John Gilbert Winant*. The Hague: Mouton, 1968.

Bernstein, Barton J., ed. *Politics and Policies of the Truman Administration*. Chicago: Quadrangle, 1970.

Best, Richard A., Jr. *"Co-operation With Like-Minded Peoples": British Influences on American Security Policy, 1945–1949*. Westport, Conn.: Greenwood Press, 1986.

Bethell, Nicholas. *The Great Betrayal: The Untold Story of Kim Philby's Biggest Coup*. London: Hodder and Stoughton, 1984.

———. *The Last Secret: Forcible Repatriation to Russia, 1944–1947*. London: Andre Deutsch, 1974.

Betts, Richard E. *Soldiers, Statesmen and Cold War Crises*. Cambridge: Harvard University Press, 1977.

Bingham, June. *Courage to Change: An Introduction to the Life and Thought of Reinhold Niebuhr*. New York: Charles Scribner's Sons, 1972.

Blum, Robert M. *Drawing the Line: The Origin of the American Containment Policy in East Asia*. New York: W. W. Norton, 1982.

Bohlen, Charles E. *The Transformation of American Foreign Policy*. New York: W. W. Norton, 1969.

Borden, William S. *The Pacific Alliance: United States Foreign Economic Policy and Japanese Trade Recovery, 1947–1955*. Madison: University of Wisconsin Press, 1984.

Borg, Dorothy, and Waldo Heinrichs, eds. *Uncertain Years: Chinese-American Relations, 1947–1950*. New York: Columbia University Press, 1980.

Borklund, Carl W. *Men of the Pentagon: From Forrestal to McNamara*. New York: Praeger, 1966.

Borosage, Robert L., and John Marks, eds. *The CIA File*. New York: Grossman Publishers, 1976.

Bowie, Robert R. *Shaping the Future: Foreign Policy in an Age of Transition*. New York: Columbia University Press, 1964.

Browder, Robert Paul. *The Origins of Soviet-American Diplomacy*. Princeton, N.J.: Princeton University Press, 1953.

Brown, Seyom. *The Faces of Power: Constancy and Change in United States Foreign Policy from Truman to Johnson*. New York: Columbia University Press, 1968.

Buckley, Roger. *Occupation Diplomacy: Britain, the United States and Japan, 1945–1952*. Cambridge: Cambridge University Press, 1982.

Buhite, Russell D. *Patrick J. Hurley and American Foreign Policy*. Ithaca, N.Y.: Cornell University Press, 1973.

———. *Soviet-American Relations in Asia, 1945–1954*. Norman: University of Oklahoma Press, 1982.

Bullock, Alan. *Ernest Bevin: Foreign Secretary, 1945–1951*. New York: W. W. Norton, 1983.

Bundy, McGeorge. *Danger and Survival: Choices About the Atomic Bomb in the First Fifty Years*. New York: Random House, 1988.

Burdick, Charles Burton. *An American Island in Hitler's Reich: The Bad Nauheim Internment*. Menlo Park, Calif.: Markgraf Publishing Group, 1987.

Campbell, John C. *Tito's Separate Road: America and Yugoslavia in World Politics*. New York: Harper and Row, 1967.

Campbell, John Franklin. *The Foreign Affairs Fudge Factory*. New York: Basic Books, 1971.

Caraley, Demetrios. *The Politics of Military Unification: A Study of Conflict and the Policy Process*. New York: Columbia University Press, 1966.

Carr, Albert Z. *Truman, Stalin and Peace*. Garden City, N.Y.: Doubleday, 1950.

Cheever, Daniel S., and H. Field Haviland, Jr. *American Foreign Policy and the Separation of Powers*. Cambridge: Harvard University Press, 1952.

Childs, Marquis W., and James B. Reston, eds. *Walter Lippmann and His Times*. New York: Harcourt, Brace, 1959.

Clifford, Clark M., Eugene V. Rostow, and Barbara W. Tuchman. *The Palestine Question in American History*. New York: Arno Press, 1978.

Cline, Ray S. *Secrets, Spies and Scholars: Blueprint of the Essential CIA*. Washington, D.C.: Acropolis Books, 1976.

———. *Washington Command Post: The Operations Division*. United States Army in World War II: The War Department. Washington: U.S. Government Printing Office, 1951.

Cohen, Bernard C. *The Political Process and Foreign Policy: The Making of the Japanese Peace Treaty*. Princeton, N.J.: Princeton University Press, 1957.

Cohen, Michael J. *Palestine and the Great Powers, 1945–1948*. Princeton, N.J.: Princeton University Press, 1982.

Cohen, Theodore. *Remaking Japan: The American Occupation As New Deal*. New York: The Free Press, 1987.

Cohen, Warren I. *New Frontiers in American–East Asian Relations*. New York: Columbia University Press, 1983.

Colby, William, and Peter Forbath. *Honorable Men: My Life in the CIA*. New York: Simon & Schuster, 1978.

Coleman, Peter. *The Liberal Conspiracy: The Congress for Cultural Freedom and the Struggle for the Mind of Postwar Europe*. New York: The Free Press, 1989.

Corson, William R. *The Armies of Ignorance: The Rise of the American Intelligence Empire*. New York: The Dial Press/James Wade, 1977.

Crozier, Brian. *Strategy for Survival*. London: Temple Smith, 1978.

Cummings, Bruce. *The Origins of the Korean War: Liberation and the Emergence of Separate Regimes, 1945–1947*. Princeton, N.J.: Princeton University Press, 1981.

Davids, Jules, ed. *Perspectives in American Diplomacy: Essays on Europe, Latin America, China and the Cold War*. New York: Arno, 1976.

Davidson, Eugene. *The Death and Life of Germany: An Account of American Occupation*. New York: Knopf, 1961.

Davies, John Paton. *Foreign and Other Affairs*. New York: W. W. Norton, 1964.

Davis, Lynn Etheridge. *The Cold War Begins: Soviet-American Conflict Over East Europe*. Princeton: Princeton University Press, 1974.

Davison, W. Phillips. *The Berlin Blockade: A Study in Cold War Politics*. Princeton, N.J.: Princeton University Press, 1958.

DeConde, Alexander. *The American Secretary of State: An Interpretation*. New York: Praeger, 1962.

Dennett, Raymond, and Joseph E. Johnson, eds. *Negotiating With the Russians*. Boston: World Peace Foundation, 1951.

Destler, I. M. *Presidents, Bureaucrats and Foreign Policy*. Princeton, N.J.: Princeton University Press, 1972.

Destler, I. M., Leslie H. Gelb, and Anthony Lake. *Our Own Worst Enemy: The Unmaking of American Foreign Policy*. New York: Simon & Schuster, 1984.

Dobbs, Charles M. *The Unwanted Symbol: American Foreign Policy, The Cold War and Korea, 1945–1950*. Kent, Ohio: Kent State University Press, 1981.

Donovan, John C. *The Cold Warriors: A Policy-Making Elite*. Lexington: D. C. Heath, 1974.

Donovan, Robert J. *Conflict and Crisis: The Presidency of Harry S. Truman, 1945–1948*. New York: W. W. Norton, 1977.

———. *Tumultuous Years: The Presidency of Harry S. Truman, 1949–1953*. New York: W. W. Norton, 1982.

Dower, John W. *Empire and Aftermath: Yoshida Shigeru and the Japanese Experience, 1878–1954*. Cambridge, Mass.: Council on East Asian Studies, Harvard University, 1979.

———. *War Without Mercy: Race and Power in the Pacific War*. New York: Pantheon Books, 1986.

Druks, Herbert M. *Harry S. Truman and the Russians, 1945–1953*. New York: Robert Speller and Sons, 1966.

Dunn, Frederick S. *Peacemaking and the Settlement with Japan*. Princeton, N.J.: Princeton University Press, 1963.

Dyson, Freeman. *Weapons and Hope*. New York: Harper and Row, 1984.

Eckes, Alfred E. *A Search for Solvency: Bretton Woods and the International Monetary System, 1941–1971*. Austin: University of Texas Press, 1975.

Elder, Robert E. *The Policy Machine: The Department of State and American Foreign Policy*. Syracuse: Syracuse University Press, 1960.

Estes, Thomas S., and E. Allan Lichtner, Jr. *The Department of State*. New York: Praeger, 1976.

Etzold, Thomas H. *Aspects of Sino-American Relations Since 1784*. New York: New Viewpoints, 1978.

———. *The Conduct of American Foreign Relations: The Other Side of Diplomacy*. New York: New Viewpoints, 1977.

Farnsworth, Beatrice. *William C. Bullitt and the Soviet Union*. Bloomington: Indiana University Press, 1967.

Feis, Herbert. *The Birth of Israel: The Tousled Diplomatic Bed*. New York: W. W. Norton, 1969.

———. *From Trust to Terror: The Onset of the Cold War*. New York: W. W. Norton, 1970.

Ferrell, Robert H. *George C. Marshall*. Vol. 15 of *The American Secretaries of State and Their Diplomacy*. Ed. Robert H. Ferrell. New York: Cooper Square Publishers, 1966.

Fifield, Russell. *Americans in Southeast Asia: The Roots of Commitment*. New York: Thomas Y. Crowell, 1973.

Finletter, Thomas K. *Power and Policy: U.S. Foreign Policy and Military Power in the Hydrogen Age*. New York: Harcourt, Brace, 1954.

Fitzsimons, M. A. *Foreign Policy of the British Labour Government, 1945–1951*. Notre Dame: University of Notre Dame Press, 1953.

Fulbright, J. William. *The Price of Empire*. New York: Pantheon Books, 1989.

Gaddis, John Lewis. *The Long Peace: Inquiries into the History of the Cold War*. New York: Oxford University Press, 1987.

————. *Strategies of Containment: A Critical Appraisal of Postwar American National Security Policy*. New York: Oxford University Press, 1982.

————. *The United States and the Origins of the Cold War, 1941–1947*. New York: Columbia University Press, 1972.

Ganin, Zvi. *Truman, American Jewry, and Israel, 1945–1948*. New York: Holmes & Meier, 1979.

Gardner, Lloyd C. *Architects of Illusion: Men and Ideas in American Foreign Policy, 1941–1949*. Chicago: Quadrangle Books, 1970.

Gardner, Richard N. *Sterling-Dollar Diplomacy: The Origins and the Prospects of Our International Economic Order*. Rev. ed. New York: McGraw-Hill, 1969.

Garwood, Ellen Clayton. *Will Clayton: A Short Biography*. Austin: University of Texas Press, 1958.

Gellman, Barton. *Contending with Kennan: Toward a Philosophy of American Power*. New York: Praeger, 1984.

George, Alexander L., and Richard Smoke. *Deterrence in American Foreign Policy: Theory and Practice*. New York: Columbia University Press, 1974.

George, Alexander L. *Presidential Decisionmaking in Foreign Policy: The Effective Use of Information and Advice*. Boulder: Westview, 1980.

Gerson, Louis L. *John Foster Dulles*. Vol. 17 of *The American Secretaries of State and Their Diplomacy*. Ed. Robert H. Ferrell. New York: Cooper Square Publishers, 1958.

Gilpin, Robert. *American Scientists and Nuclear Weapons Policy*. Princeton, N.J.: Princeton University Press, 1962.

Gimbel, John. *The American Occupation of Germany: Politics and the Military, 1945–1949*. Stanford: Stanford University Press, 1968.

————. *The Origins of the Marshall Plan*. Stanford: Stanford University Press, 1976.

Gleason, Philip. *Keeping the Faith: American Catholicism, Past and Present*. Notre Dame, Ind.: University of Notre Dame Press, 1987.

Golay, John Ford. *The Founding of the Federal Republic of Germany*. Chicago: University of Chicago Press, 1958.

Goldman, Eric F. *The Crucial Decade and After: America, 1945–1960*. New York: Knopf, 1966.

Gormley, James L. *The Collapse of the Grand Alliance, 1945–1948*. Baton Rouge: Louisiana State University Press, 1987.

Graebner, Norman A., ed. *An Uncertain Tradition: American Secretaries of State in the Twentieth Century*. New York: McGraw-Hill, 1961.

Grose, Peter. *Israel in the Mind of America*. New York: Knopf, 1983.

Guhin, Michael A. *John Foster Dulles: A Statesman and His Times*. New York: Columbia University Press, 1972.

Hadley, Eleanor M. *Antitrust in Japan*. Princeton, N.J.: Princeton University Press, 1970.

Halberstam, David. *The Best and the Brightest*. New York: Random House, 1972.

Halle, Louis J. *Civilization and Foreign Policy: An Inquiry for Americans*. New York: Harper and Bros., 1955.

Halle, Louis J. *The Cold War as History*. New York: Harper and Row, 1967.

Halperin, Morton H. *Bureaucratic Politics and Foreign Policy*. Washington: Brookings Institution, 1974.

Hamby, Alonzo. *Beyond the New Deal: Harry S. Truman and American Liberalism*. New York: Columbia University Press, 1973.

Hammond, Paul Y. *Organizing for Defense: The American Military Establishment in the Twentieth Century*. Princeton, N.J.: Princeton University Press, 1961.

Hammond, Thomas T., ed. *Witnesses to the Origins of the Cold War*. Seattle: University of Washington Press, 1982.

Harbutt, Fraser J. *The Iron Curtain: Churchill, America and the Origins of the Cold War*. New York: Oxford University Press, 1986.

Harper, John Lamberton. *America and the Reconstruction of Italy, 1945–1948*. Cambridge: Cambridge University Press, 1986.

Harr, John Ensor. *The Professional Diplomat*. Princeton, N.J.: Princeton University Press, 1969.

Harries, Meirion and Susie. *Sheathing the Sword: The Demilitarization of Japan*. New York: Macmillan, 1987.

Hartmann, Susan M. *Truman and the 80th Congress*. Columbia: University of Missouri Press, 1971.

Hathaway, Robert M. *Ambiguous Partnership: Britain and America, 1944–1947*. New York: Columbia University Press, 1981.

Haviland, Henry Field et al. *The Formulation and Administration of U.S. Foreign Policy*. Washington: Brookings Institution, 1960.

Haynes, Richard F. *The Awesome Power: Harry Truman as Commander in Chief*. Baton Rouge: Louisiana State University Press, 1973.

Healey, Denis, ed. *The Curtain Falls: The Story of the Socialists in Eastern Europe*. London: Lincolns-Prager, 1951.

Herken, Gregg. *Counsels of War*. New York: Oxford University Press, 1987.

———. *The Winning Weapon: The Atomic Bomb in the Cold War, 1945–1950*. New York: Knopf, 1980.

Herring, Jr., George C. *Aid to Russia, 1941–1946: Strategy, Diplomacy and the Origins of the Cold War*. New York: Columbia University Press, 1973.

———. *America's Longest War: The United States and Vietnam, 1950–1975*. 2d ed. New York: Knopf, 1986.

Hess, Gary R. *The United States' Emergence as a Southeast Asian Power, 1940–1950*. New York: Columbia University Press, 1987.

Heuser, Beatrice. *Western 'Containment' Policies in the Cold War: The Yugoslav Case, 1948–53*. London: Routledge, 1989.

Hewlett, Richard G., and Francis Duncan. *Atomic Shield: 1947–1952*. Vol. 2 of *A History of the United States Atomic Energy Commission*. University Park: Pennsylvania State University Press, 1969.

Hogan, Michael J. *The Marshall Plan: America, Britain and the Reconstruction of Western Europe, 1947–1952*. New York: Cambridge University Press, 1987.

Holloway, David. *The Soviet Union and the Arms Race*. New Haven: Yale University Press, 1983.

Holt, Robert T. *Radio Free Europe*. Minneapolis: University of Minnesota Press, 1958.

Hoopes, Townsend. *The Devil and John Foster Dulles*. Boston: Little, Brown, 1973.

———. *The Limits of Intervention*. New York: David McKay, 1969.

Hoxie, R. Gordon. *Command Decision and the Presidency: A Study of National Security Policy and Organization*. New York: Reader's Digest Press, 1977.

Huntington, Samuel P. *Common Defense: Strategic Programs in National Politics*. New York: Columbia University Press, 1961.

Hyman, Sidney. *The Lives of William Benton*. Chicago: University of Chicago Press, 1969.

Iatrides, John O., ed. *Greece in the 1940s: A Nation in Crisis*. Hanover: University Press of New England, 1981.

Ireland, Timothy P. *Creating the Entangling Alliance: The Origins of the North Atlantic Treaty Organization*. Westport, Conn.: Greenwood Press, 1981.

Isaacson, Walter, and Evan Thomas. *The Wise Men: Six Friends and the World They Made*. New York: Simon & Schuster, 1986.

Jackson, Henry M., ed. *The Atlantic Alliance*. New York: Praeger, 1967.

———. *The National Security Council*. New York: Praeger, 1965.

———. *The Secretary of State and the Ambassador*. New York: Praeger, 1964.

James, D. Clayton. *The Years of MacArthur*. Vol. 3: *Triumph and Disaster, 1945–1964*. Boston: Houghton Mifflin, 1985.

Janis, Irving, L. *Victims of Groupthink: A Psychological Study of Foreign Policy Decisions and Fiascoes*. Boston: Houghton, Mifflin, 1972.

Jeffreys-Jones, Rhodri. *The CIA and American Democracy*. New Haven: Yale University Press, 1989.

Johnson, Richard A. *The Administration of United States Foreign Policy*. Austin: University of Texas Press, 1971.

Jones, Howard. *"A New Kind of War": America's Global Strategy and the Truman Doctrine in Greece*. New York: Oxford University Press, 1989.

Kahn, Jr., E. J. *The China Hands: America's Foreign Service Officers and What Befell Them*. New York: Viking, 1975.

Kaplan, Lawrence S. *The United States and NATO: The Formative Years*. Lexington: University of Kentucky Press, 1984.

Karnow, Stanley. *Vietnam: A History*. New York: Viking Press, 1983.

Kaufman, Burton I. *The Korean War: Challenges in Crisis, Credibility and Command*. New York: Knopf, 1986.

Kennan, George. *Siberia and the Exile System*. 2 vols. New York: Century, 1891.

———. *Tent Life in Siberia*. Rev. ed. New York: G. P. Putnams, 1910.

Kennan, George F. *American Diplomacy, 1900–1950*. Chicago: University of Chicago Press, 1951.

———. *The Cloud of Danger: Current Realities of American Foreign Policy*. Boston: Little, Brown, 1977.

———. *The Nuclear Delusion: Soviet-American Relations in the Atomic Age*. New York: Pantheon Books, 1982.

———. *On Dealing With the Communist World*. New York: Harper & Row, 1964.

Kennan, George F. *Realities of American Foreign Policy*. Princeton, N.J.: Princeton University Press, 1954.

————. *Russia, the Atom and the West*. New York: Harper, 1958.

————. *Russia and the West Under Lenin and Stalin*. Boston: Little, Brown, 1961.

Kennedy, Paul M. *The Rise and Fall of the Great Powers: Economic Change and Military Conflict from 1500 to 2000*. New York: Random House, 1987.

Kepley, David R. *The Collapse of the Middle Way: Senate Republicans and the Bipartisan Foreign Policy, 1948–1952*. New York: Greenwood Press, 1988.

Keyserlingk, Robert W. *Fathers of Europe: Patriots of Peace*. Montreal: Palm Publishers, 1972.

Kindleberger, Charles P. *American Business Abroad*. New Haven: Yale University Press, 1969.

————. *Marshall Plan Days*. Boston: Allen & Unwin, 1987.

Kirkendall, Richard S., ed. *The Truman Period as a Research Field: A Reappraisal, 1972*. Columbia: University of Missouri Press, 1974.

Kohler, Foy D. *Understanding the Russians: A Citizen's Primer*. New York: Harper and Row, 1970.

Kohler, Foy D., and Mose L. Harvey, eds. *The Soviet Union, Yesterday, Today, Tomorrow: A Colloquy of American Long Timers in Moscow*. Coral Gables: Center for Advanced International Studies, University of Miami, 1975.

Kolko, Joyce and Gabriel. *The Limits of Power: The World and United States Foreign Policy, 1945–1954*. New York: Harper and Row, 1972.

Kolodziej, Edward A. *Uncommon Defense and Congress, 1945–1963*. Columbus: Ohio State University Press, 1966.

Kovrig, Bennett. *The Myth of Liberation: East-Central Europe in U.S. Diplomacy and Politics Since 1941*. Baltimore: Johns Hopkins University Press, 1973.

Kuklick, Bruce. *American Policy and the Division of Germany: The Clash With Russia Over Reparations*. Ithaca: Cornell University Press, 1972.

Kunetka, James W. *Oppenheimer: The Years of Risk*. Englewood Cliffs, N.J.: Prentice-Hall, 1982.

Kuniholm, Bruce R. *The Origins of the Cold War in the Near East: Great Power Conflict and Diplomacy in Iran, Turkey, and Greece*. Princeton, N.J.: Princeton University Press, 1980.

LaFeber, Walter. *America, Russia and the Cold War, 1945–1971*. 2d ed. New York: John Wiley, 1972.

Larson, David L. *United States Foreign Policy Toward Yugoslavia, 1943–1963*. Washington: University Press of America, 1979.

Larson, Deborah Welch. *Origins of Containment: A Psychological Explanation*. Princeton, N.J.: Princeton University Press, 1985.

Lauren, Paul Gordon, ed. *The China Hands' Legacy: Ethics and Diplomacy*. Boulder: Westview, 1987.

Leary, William M. *Perilous Missions: Civil Air Transport and CIA Covert Operations in Asia*. Birmingham: University of Alabama Press, 1984.

Levering, Ralph B. *American Opinion and the Russian Alliance, 1939–1945*. Chapel Hill: University of North Carolina Press, 1976.

————. *The Public and American Foreign Policy, 1918–1978*. New York: William Morrow, 1978.

Lieberman, Joseph I. *The Scorpion and the Tarantula: The Struggle to Control Atomic Weapons, 1945–1949*. Boston: Houghton, Mifflin, 1970.

Lippmann, Walter. *The Cold War: A Study in U.S. Foreign Policy*. New York: Harper, 1947.

Litchfield, Edward H. et al. *Governing Postwar Germany*. Ithaca: Cornell University Press, 1953.

Loftus, John. *The Belarus Secret*. New York: Knopf, 1982.

Louis, Wm. Roger, and Hedley Bull, eds. *The 'Special Relationship': Anglo-American Relations Since 1945*. Oxford: Clarendon Press, 1986.

Louis, Wm. Roger, and Robert W. Stookey, eds. *The End of the Palestinian Mandate*. Austin: University of Texas Press, 1986.

Lundestad, Geir. *The American Non-Policy Towards Eastern Europe, 1943–47: Universalism in an Area not of Essential Interest to the United States*. New York: Humanities Press, 1975.

McCloy, John J. *The Atlantic Alliance: Its Origin and Its Future*. New York: Columbia University Press, 1969.

————. *The Challenge to American Foreign Policy*. Cambridge: Harvard University Press, 1953.

McGeehan, Robert. *The German Rearmament Question: American Diplomacy and European Defense After World War II*. Urbana: University of Illinois Press, 1971.

McInnis, Edgar W. et al. *The Shaping of Postwar Germany*. New York: Praeger, 1960.

MacIssac, David. *Strategic Bombing in World War Two: The Story of the United States Strategic Bombing Survey*. New York: Garland, 1976.

McLellan, David S. *Dean Acheson: The State Department Years*. New York: Dodd, Mead, 1976.

MacMahon, Arthur W. *Administration in Foreign Affairs*. Birmingham: University of Alabama Press, 1953.

McMahon, Robert J. *Colonialism and Cold War: The United States and the Struggle for Indonesian Independence, 1945–49*. Ithaca: Cornell University Press, 1981.

McNeill, William H. *Greece: American Aid in Action, 1947–1956*. New York: The Twentieth Century Fund, 1957.

————. *The Greek Dilemma: War and Aftermath*. Philadelphia: J. B. Lippincott, 1947.

Maddox, Robert James. *From War to Cold War: The Education of Harry S. Truman*. Boulder: Westview, 1988.

Manchester, William. *American Caesar: Douglas MacArthur, 1880–1964*. Boston: Little, Brown, 1978.

Marshall, Charles Burton. *Beyond the Cold War: Essays on American Foreign Policy in a Changing World Environment*. Chicago: Rand McNally, 1965.

————. *The Exercise of Sovereignty: Papers on Foreign Policy*. Baltimore: Johns Hopkins Press, 1965.

————. *The Limits of Foreign Policy*. Baltimore: Johns Hopkins Press, 1968.

Martin, Edwin W. *Divided Counsel: The Anglo-American Response to Communist Victory in China*. Lexington: The University Press of Kentucky, 1986.

388 · Secondary Sources

Matloff, Maurice. *Strategic Planning for Coalition Warfare, 1943–1944*. United States Army in World War II: The War Department. Washington: U.S. Government Printing Office, 1959.

Matray, James I. *The Reluctant Crusade: American Foreign Policy in Korea, 1941–1950*. Honolulu: University of Hawaii Press, 1985.

May, Ernest R. *"Lesson" of the Past: The Use and Misuse of History in American Foreign Policy*. New York: Oxford University Press, 1973.

———. *The Truman Administration and China, 1945–1949*. Philadelphia: Lippincott, 1975.

Mayers, David Allan. *Cracking the Monolith: U.S. Policy Against the Sino-Soviet Alliance, 1949–1955*. Baton Rouge: Louisiana State University Press, 1986.

———. *George Kennan and the Dilemmas of US Foreign Policy*. New York: Oxford University Press, 1988.

Mazuzan, George T. *Warren R. Austin at the United Nations, 1946–1953*. Kent: Kent State University Press, 1977.

Medvedev, Roy. *Let History Judge: The Origins and Consequences of Stalinism*. New York: Columbia University Press, 1989.

Mee, Charles L., Jr. *The Marshall Plan*. New York: Simon & Schuster, 1984.

Meilinger, Phillip S. *Hoyt S. Vandenberg: The Life of A General*. Bloomington: Indiana University Press, 1989.

Merkl, Peter. *The Origin of the Western German Republic*. New York: Oxford University Press, 1963.

Merli, Frank J., and Theodore A. Wilson, eds. *Makers of American Diplomacy*. New York: Charles Scribner's Sons, 1974.

Messer, Robert L. *The End of an Alliance: James F. Byrnes, Roosevelt, Truman, and the Origins of the Cold War*. Chapel Hill: University of North Carolina Press, 1982.

Mickelson, Sig. *America's Other Voice: The Story of Radio Free Europe and Radio Liberty*. New York: Praeger, 1983.

Miller, James Edward. *The United States and Italy, 1940–1950: The Politics and Diplomacy of Stabilization*. Chapel Hill: University of North Carolina Press, 1986.

Milward, Alan S. *The Reconstruction of Western Europe, 1945–1951*. London: Methuen, 1984.

Moore, Ben T. *NATO and the Future of Europe*. New York: Harper, 1958.

Morgan, Kenneth O. *Labour in Power, 1945–1951*. Oxford: Clarendon Press, 1984.

Morgan, Roger. *The United States and West Germany, 1945–1973: A Study in Alliance Politics*. London: Oxford University Press, 1974.

Mosely, Leonard. *Dulles: A Biography of Eleanor, Allen and John Foster Dulles and Their Family Network*. New York: Dial Press/James Wade, 1978.

Moss, Norman. *Men Who Play God: The Story of the H-Bomb and How the World Came to Live With It*. New York: Harper and Row, 1968.

Nagai, Yonosuke, and Akira Iriye, eds. *The Origins of the Cold War in Asia*. New York: Columbia University Press, 1977.

Nitze, Paul H. *The Recovery of Ethics*. New York: Council on Religion and International Affairs, 1960.

———. *United States Foreign Policy, 1945–1955*. New York: Foreign Policy Association, 1956.

Osgood, Robert E. *NATO: The Entangling Alliance*. Chicago: University of Chicago Press, 1962.

Ovendale, Ritchie. *The English-Speaking Alliance: Britain, the United States, the Dominions and the Cold War, 1945–1951*. London: George Allen & Unwin, 1985.

———, ed. *The Foreign Policy of the British Labour Governments, 1945–1951*. Leicester: Leicester University Press, 1984.

Paterson, Thomas G., ed. *Cold War Critics: Alternatives to American Foreign Policy in the Truman Years*. Chicago: Quadrangle Books, 1971.

———. *Containment and the Cold War: American Foreign Policy Since 1945*. Reading, Mass.: Addison-Wesley, 1973.

———. *Soviet-American Confrontation: Postwar Reconstruction and the Origins of the Cold War*. Baltimore: Johns Hopkins University Press, 1973.

Patterson, James T. *Mr. Republican: A Biography of Robert A. Taft*. Boston: Houghton Mifflin, 1972.

Payne, Robert. *The Marshall Story: A Biography of General George C. Marshall*. New York: Prentice Hall, 1951.

Pelling, Henry. *Britain and the Marshall Plan*. Houndmills, Basingstoke: Macmillan, 1988.

Peterson, Edward N. *The American Occupation of Germany: Retreat to Victory*. Detroit: Wayne State University Press, 1978.

Pfau, Richard. *No Sacrifice Too Great: The Life of Lewis L. Strauss*. Charlottesville, Va.: University Press of Virginia, 1984.

Phillips, Cabell B. *The Truman Presidency: History of a Triumphant Succession*. New York: Macmillan, 1966.

Podhoretz, Norman. *The Present Danger*. New York: Touchstone/Simon & Schuster, 1980.

Pogue, Forrest C. *George C. Marshall: Statesman, 1945–1959*. New York: Viking, 1987.

Powers, Thomas. *The Man Who Kept the Secrets: Richard Helms and the CIA*. New York: Knopf, 1979.

Prados, John. *Presidents' Secret Wars: CIA and Pentagon Covert Operations Since World War II*. New York: William Morrow, 1986.

Price, Don, ed. *The Secretary of State*. Englewood Cliffs, N.J.: Prentice Hall, 1960.

Price, Harry B. *The Marshall Plan and Its Meaning*. Ithaca: Cornell University Press, 1955.

Pringle, Robert. *Indonesia and the Philippines: American Interests in Island Southeast Asia*. New York: Columbia University Press, 1980.

Pruessen, Ronald W. *John Foster Dulles: The Road to Power*. New York: The Free Press, 1982.

Quester, George H. *Nuclear Diplomacy: The First Twenty-five Years*. New York: Dunellen, 1970.

Rabel, Roberto G. *Between East and West: Trieste, the United States, and the Cold War, 1941–1954*. Durham: Duke University Press, 1988.

Raucher, Alan R. *Paul G. Hoffman: Architect of Foreign Aid*. Lexington: The University Press of Kentucky, 1985.

Rearden, Steven L. *History of the Office of the Secretary of Defense: The Formative*

Years, 1947–1950. Washington, D.C.: Historical Office, Office of the Secretary of Defense, 1984.

Reed, Bruce, and Geoffrey Williams. *Denis Healey and the Politics of Power*. London: Sidgwick and Jackson, 1971.

Rogow, Arnold. *James Forrestal: A Study of Personality, Politics and Policy*. New York: Macmillan, 1963.

Rose, Lisle A. *After Yalta: America and the Origins of the Cold War*. New York: Charles Scribner's Sons, 1973.

———. *Dubious Victory*. Kent, Ohio: Kent State University Press, 1973.

———. *Roots of Tragedy: The United States and the Struggle for Asia, 1945–1953*. Westport, Conn.: Greenwood Press, 1976.

Rositzke, Harry. *The CIA's Secret Operations: Espionage, Counterespionage, and Covert Action*. New York: Reader's Digest Press, 1977.

Rostow, Walt. *The Division of Europe After World War II: 1946*. Austin: University of Texas Press, 1981.

———. *Europe After Stalin: Eisenhower's Three Decisions of March 11, 1953*. Austin: University of Texas Press, 1982.

Rotter, Andrew J. *The Path to Vietnam: Origins of the American Commitment to Southeast Asia*. Ithaca: Cornell University Press, 1987.

Rubin, Barry. *Secrets of State: The State Department and the Struggle Over U.S. Foreign Policy*. New York: Oxford University Press, 1985.

Ruddy, T. Michael. *The Cautious Diplomat: Charles E. Bohlen and the Soviet Union, 1929–1969*. Kent, Ohio: Kent State University Press, 1986.

Russell, Ruth B. *The United Nations and United States Security Policy*. Washington: The Brookings Institution, 1968.

Sapin, Burton M. *The Making of United States Foreign Policy*. Washington: Praeger, 1966.

Schaller, Michael. *The American Occupation of Japan: The Origins of the Cold War in Asia*. New York: Oxford University Press, 1985.

———. *Douglas MacArthur: The Far Eastern General*. New York: Oxford University Press, 1989.

———. *The United States and China in the Twentieth Century*. New York: Oxford University Press, 1979.

———. *The U.S. Crusade in China, 1938–1945*. New York: Columbia University Press, 1979.

Schilling, Warner R., Paul Y. Hammond, and Glenn H. Snyder. *Strategy, Politics and Defense Budgets*. New York: Columbia University Press, 1962.

Schlesinger, Jr., Arthur M. *The Vital Center: The Politics of Freedom*. Boston: Houghton Mifflin, 1949.

Schmitt, Hans A., ed. *U.S. Occupation in Europe After World War II*. Lawrence: Regents Press of Kansas, 1978.

Schoenbaum, Thomas J. *Waging Peace and War: Dean Rusk in the Truman, Kennedy and Johnson Years*. New York: Simon & Schuster, 1988.

Schonberger, Howard B. *Aftermath of War: Americans and the Remaking of Japan, 1945–1952*. Kent, Ohio: Kent State University Press, 1989.

Schulzinger, Robert D. *The Wise Men of Foreign Affairs: The History of the Council on Foreign Relations*. New York: Columbia University Press, 1984.

Schwartz, Thomas Alan. *America's Germany: John J. McCloy and the Federal Republic of Germany*. Cambridge, Mass.: Harvard University Press, 1991.

Sharp, Tony. *The Wartime Alliance and the Zonal Division of Germany*. Oxford: Clarendon Press, 1975.

Shepley, J. R., and C. Blair. *The Hydrogen Bomb: The Men, The Menace, The Mechanism*. New York: David McKay, 1954.

Shlaim, Avi. *The United States and the Berlin Blockade, 1948–1949: A Study in Crisis Decision-making*. Berkeley: University of California Press, 1983.

Shoup, Larry, and William Minter. *Imperial Brain Trust: The Council of Foreign Relations and United States Foreign Policy*. New York: Monthly Review Press, 1977.

Simpson, Christopher. *Blowback: America's Recruitment of Nazis and Its Effects on the Cold War*. New York: Weidenfeld & Nicholson, 1988.

Simpson, Smith. *Anatomy of the State Department*. Boston: Houghton Mifflin, 1967.

Siracusa, Joseph M., ed. *The American Diplomatic Revolution: A Documentary History of the Cold War, 1941–1947*. Port Washington, N.Y.: Kennikat Press, 1977.

———. *New Left Diplomatic Histories and Historians*. Port Washington, N.Y.: Kennikat Press, 1973.

Smith, Gaddis. *Dean Acheson*. Vol. 16 of *The American Secretaries of State and Their Diplomacy*. Ed. Robert H. Ferrell. New York: Cooper Square Publishers, 1972.

Smith, Jean Edward. *The Defense of Berlin*. Baltimore: Johns Hopkins University Press, 1963.

Smith, Michael Joseph. *Realist Thought From Weber to Kissinger*. Baton Rouge, La.: Louisiana State University Press, 1986.

Snell, John L., ed. *The Meaning of Yalta: Big Three Diplomacy and the New Balance of Power*. Baton Rouge, La.: Louisiana State University Press, 1956.

Snetsinger, John. *Truman, The Jewish Vote and the Creation of Israel*. Stanford, Calif.: Hoover Institution Press, 1974.

Spaulding, E. Wilder. *Ambassadors Ordinary and Extraordinary*. Washington: Public Affairs Press, 1961.

Spiegel, Steven L. *The Other Arab-Israeli Conflict: Making America's Middle East Policy From Truman to Reagan*. Chicago: University of Chicago Press, 1985.

Stavrianos, L. S. *The Balkans Since 1453*. New York: Holt, Rinehart & Winston, 1958.

Steel, Ronald. *Imperialists and Other Heroes: A Chronicle of the American Empire*. New York: Random House, 1971.

———. *Walter Lippmann and the American Century*. Boston: Little, Brown, 1980.

Stephanson, Anders. *Kennan and the Art of Foreign Policy*. Cambridge, Mass.: Harvard University Press, 1989.

Stern, Philip M. *The Oppenheimer Case: Security on Trial*. New York: Harper and Row, 1969.

Stiller, Jesse H. *George S. Messersmith: Diplomat of Democracy*. Chapel Hill: University of North Carolina Press, 1988.

Strange, Susan. *Sterling and British Policy: A Political Study of an International Currency in Decline*. London: Oxford University Press, 1971.

Stromberg, Roland N. *Collective Security and American Foreign Policy: From the League of Nations to NATO*. New York: Praeger, 1963.

Stuart, Graham H. *The Department of State: A History of Its Organization, Procedure and Personnel*. New York: Macmillan, 1949.

Stueck, William Whitney, Jr. *The Road to Confrontation: American Policy Toward China and Korea, 1947–1950*. Chapel Hill: The University of North Carolina Press, 1981.

————. *The Wedemeyer Mission: American Politics and Foreign Policy during the Cold War*. Athens, Ga.: The University of Georgia Press, 1984.

Stupak, Ronald J. *The Shaping of Foreign Policy: The Role of the Secretary of State as Seen by Dean Acheson*. Racine: Odyssey Press, 1969.

Stursberg, Peter. *Lester Pearson and the American Dilemma*. Toronto: Doubleday, Canada, 1980.

Talbott, Strobe. *The Master of the Game: Paul Nitze and the Nuclear Peace*. New York: Knopf, 1988.

Taubman, William. *Stalin's American Policy: From Entente to Detente to Cold War*. New York: W. W. Norton, 1982.

Thomas, Hugh. *Armed Truce: The Beginnings of the Cold War, 1945–46*. New York: Hamish Hamilton, 1987.

Thompson, Kenneth W. *Interpreters and Critics of the Cold War*. Washington: University Press of America, 1978.

————. *Political Realism and the Crisis of World Politics*. Princeton, N.J.: Princeton University Press, 1960.

Tint, Herbert. *French Foreign Policy Since the Second World War*. London: Weidenfeld and Nicholson, 1972.

Tompkins, C. David. *Senator Arthur Vandenberg: The Evolution of a Modern Republican, 1884–1945*. East Lansing: Michigan State University Press, 1970.

Treverton, Gregory F. *Covert Action: The Limits of Intervention in the Postwar World*. New York: Basic Books, 1987.

Truman, Margaret. *Harry S. Truman*. New York: William Morrow, 1973.

Tuchman, Barbara. *Practicing History*. New York: Ballantine Books, 1981.

Tucker, Nancy Bernkopf. *Patterns in the Dust: Chinese-American Relations and the Recognition Controversy, 1949–1950*. New York: Columbia University Press, 1983.

Ulam, Adam. *Expansion and Coexistence: The History of Soviet Foreign Policy, 1917–1967*. New York: Praeger, 1968.

————. *The Rivals: America and Russia Since World War II*. New York: Viking, 1971.

Vali, Ferenc A. *The Quest for a United Germany*. Baltimore: The Johns Hopkins University Press, 1967.

Walker, J. Samuel. *Henry A. Wallace and American Foreign Policy*. Westport: Greenwood, 1976.

Walker, Richard L., and George Curry. *E. R. Stettinius, Jr. and James F. Byrnes*. Vol. 14 of *The American Secretaries of State and Their Diplomacy*. Ed. Robert H. Ferrell. New York: Cooper Square Publishers, 1965.

Walton, Richard J. *Henry Wallace, Harry Truman and the Cold War*. New York: Viking, 1976.

Warburg, James P. *Germany—Bridge or Battleground*. New York: Harcourt, Brace, 1947.

——. *Germany: Key to Peace*. Cambridge: Harvard University Press, 1953.

Ward, Robert E., and Sakamoto Yoshikazu, eds. *Democratizing Japan: The Allied Occupation*. Honolulu: University of Hawaii Press, 1987.

Watt, D. Cameron. *Succeeding John Bull: America in Britain's Place, 1900–1975*. Cambridge: Cambridge University Press, 1984.

Weil, Martin. *A Pretty Good Club: The Founding Fathers of the U.S. Foreign Service*. New York: W. W. Norton, 1978.

Weiler, Peter. *British Labour and the Cold War*. Stanford: Stanford University Press, 1988.

West, Rebecca. *The New Meaning of Treason*. New York: Viking, 1964.

Westerfield, H. Bradford. *Foreign Policy and Party Politics: Pearl Harbor to Korea*. New Haven: Yale University Press, 1965.

Wexler, Imanuel. *The Marshall Plan Revisited: The European Recovery Program in Economic Perspective*. Westport, Conn.: Greenwood Press, 1983.

White, Theodore H. *Fire in the Ashes: Europe in Mid-Century*. New York: Sloane, 1953.

Williams, Francis. *Ernest Bevin: Portrait of a Great Englishman*. London: Hutchinson, 1952.

Williams, Justin. *Japan's Political Revolution Under MacArthur: A Participant's Account*. Athens, Ga.: University of Georgia Press, 1979.

Williams, Robert Chadwell. *Klaus Fuchs, Atomic Spy*. Cambridge, Mass.: Harvard University Press, 1987.

Willis, F. Roy. *The French in Germany, 1945–1949*. Stanford. Stanford University Press, 1962.

Wilson, Theodore A. *The Marshall Plan: An Atlantic Venture of 1947–1951*. New York: Foreign Policy Association, 1977.

Winks, Robin W. *Cloak and Gown: Scholars in the Secret War, 1939–1961*. New York: William Morrow, 1987.

Wittner, Lawrence S. *American Intervention in Greece, 1943–1949*. New York: Columbia University Press, 1982.

Wolfe, Robert., ed. *Americans as Proconsuls: United States Military Government in Germany and Japan, 1944–1952*. Carbondale, Ill.: Southern Illinois University Press, 1984.

Wolfe, Thomas W. *Soviet Power and Europe, 1945–1970*. Baltimore: Johns Hopkins University Press, 1970.

Wolff, Robert Lee. *The Balkans in our Time*. Rev. ed. Cambridge, Mass.: Harvard University Press, 1974.

Xydis, Stephen. *Greece and the Great Powers, 1944–1947: Prelude to the Truman Doctrine*. Thessaloniki: Institute for Balkan Studies, 1963.

Yergin, Daniel. *Shattered Peace: The Origins of the Cold War and the National Security State*. Boston: Houghton Mifflin, 1977.

York, Herbert F. *The Advisors: Oppenheimer, Teller and the Superbomb*. San Francisco: W. H. Freeman, 1976.

Articles

Acheson, Dean G. "The Eclipse of the State Department," *Foreign Affairs* 50 (July 1971): 593–606.

———. "The Illusion of Disengagement," *Foreign Affairs* 36 (April 1958): 371–82.

Adams, Ware. "The Policy Planning Staff," *American Foreign Service Journal* 24 (September 1947): 7–9.

Adler, Les K., and Thomas G. Paterson. "Red Fascism: The Merger of Nazi Germany and Soviet Russia in the American Image of Totalitarianism, 1930s–1950s," *American Historical Review* 75 (April 1970): 1046–64.

Altschul, Frank. "The Cold War," *New York Herald Tribune*, September 16, 1947.

Annan, Noel. "Dean Acheson," *The Yale Review* 77 (October 1988): 463–77.

Atkinson, Brooks. "America's Global Planner," *New York Times Magazine* (July 13, 1947), 9, 32–33.

Baldwin, Hanson W. "Big Boss of the Pentagon," *New York Times Magazine* (August 29, 1948), 9, 38–39

Barnes, Trevor. "The Secret Cold War: The c.i.a. and American Foreign Policy in Europe, 1946–1956. Part I," *The Historical Journal* 24 (June 1981): 399–415.

———. "The Secret Cold War: The c.i.a. and American Foreign Policy in Europe, 1946–1956. Part II," *The Historical Journal* 25 (September 1982): 649–71.

Beloff, Max. "The Conscience of George Kennan," *Encounter* 40 (April 1973): 15–19.

Berger, Henry W. "Bipartisanship, Senator Taft, and the Truman Administration," *Political Science Quarterly* 90 (Summer 1975): 221–37.

Bloomfield, Lincoln P. "Planning Foreign Policy: Can It Be Done?" *Political Science Quarterly* 93 (Fall 1978): 369–91.

Blum, Robert M. "Surprised by Tito: The Anatomy of an Intelligence Failure," *Diplomatic History* 12 (Winter 1988): 39–57.

Boyle, Peter G. "Britain, America and the Transition from Economic to Military Assistance, 1948–1951," *Journal of Contemporary History* 22 (July 1987): 521–38.

———. "The British Foreign Office and American Foreign Policy, 1947–1948," *Journal of American Studies* 16 (December 1982): 373–89.

Braden, Tom. "The Birth of the cia," *American Heritage* 28 (February 1977): 4–13.

Brands, Henry W. Jr. "Redefining the Cold War: American Policy toward Yugoslavia, 1948–60," *Diplomatic History* 11 (Winter 1987): 41–53.

Brzezinski, Zbigniew. "How the Cold War Was Played," *Foreign Affairs* 51 (October 1972): 181–209.

Buckley, Gary J. "American Public Opinion and the Origins of the Cold War: A Speculative Reassessment," *Mid-America* 60 (January 1978): 35–42.

Buhite, Russell D. " 'Major Interests': American Policy toward China, Taiwan, and Korea, 1945–1950," *Pacific Historical Review* 47 (August 1978): 425–51.

Caldwell, Dan. "Bureaucratic Foreign Policy-Making," *American Behavioral Scientist* 21 (September 1977): 87–110.

Campbell, John F. "An Interview with George F. Kennan," *Foreign Service Journal* 47 (August 1970): 18–23.

Carleton, William G. "Brain-Trusters of American Foreign Policy," *World Politics* 7 (July 1955): 627–39.

Carpenter, Ted Galen. "United States' NATO Policy at the Crossroads: The 'Great Debate' of 1950–1951," *The International History Review* 8 (August 1986): 389–415.

Cashman, Greg, and Arthur N. Gilbert. "Some Analytic Approaches to the Cold War Debate," *History Teacher* 10 (February 1977): 263–80.

Clayton, William L. "GATT, The Marshall Plan and OECD," *Political Science Quarterly* 78 (December 1963): 493–503.

Coffey, John W. "George Kennan and the Ambiguities of Realism," *South Atlantic Quarterly* 73 (Spring 1974): 184–98.

Cohen, Warren I. "Conversations with Chinese Friends: Zhou Enlai's Associates Reflect on Chinese-American Relations in the 1940s and the Korean War," *Diplomatic History* 11 (Summer 1987): 283–89.

Colbert, Richard G., and Robert N. Ginsburgh. "The Policy Planning Council," *United States Naval Institute Proceedings* 92 (April 1966): 73–81.

Diebold, William, Jr. "The Marshall Plan in Retrospect: A Review of Recent Scholarship," *Journal of International Affairs* 41 (Summer 1988): 421–35.

Dingman, Roger. "Strategic Planning and the Policy Process: American Plans for War in East Asia, 1945–1950," *Naval War College Review* 32 (November–December 1979): 4–21.

———. "1950: The Fate of the Grand Design," *Pacific Historical Review* 47 (August 1978): 465–71.

Dulles, John Foster. "A Policy of Boldness," *Life* 32 (May 1952): 146–60.

Duncan, Francis. "Atomic Energy and Anglo-American Relations, 1946–1954," *Orbis* 12 (Winter 1969): 1188–1203.

Dunn, Keith A. "A Conflict of World Views: The Origins of the Cold War," *Military Review* 57 (February 1977): 14–25.

Eckes, Alfred A. "Open Door Expansionism Reconsidered: The World War II Experience," *Journal of American History* 59 (March 1973): 902–24.

Eisenberg, Carolyn. "Reflections on a Toothless Revisionism," *Diplomatic History* 2 (Summer 1978): 295–305.

———. "Working-Class Politics and the Cold War: American Intervention in the German Labor Movement, 1945–1949," *Diplomatic History* 7 (Fall 1983): 283–306.

Etzold, Thomas H. "Organization for National Security, 1945–50," in Etzold and John Lewis Gaddis, eds. *Containment: Documents on American Policy and Strategy, 1945–1950* (New York, 1978).

Falk, Stanley L. "The National Security Council Under Truman, Eisenhower and Kennedy," *Political Science Quarterly* 79 (September 1964): 403–34.

Feaver, John H. "The China Aid Bill of 1948: Limited Assistance as a Cold War Strategy," *Diplomatic History* 5 (Spring 1981): 107–20.

Fischer, John. "Mr. Truman's Politburo," *Harper's Magazine* 202 (June 1951): 29–36.

Folly, Martin H. "Breaking the Vicious Circle: Britain, the United States, and the Genesis of the North Atlantic Treaty," *Diplomatic History* 12 (Winter 1988): 59–77.

Foschepoth, Josef. "British Interest in the Division of Germany after the Second World War," *Journal of Contemporary History* 21 (July 1986): 391–411.

Fox, William T. R. "Civilians, Soldiers and American Military Policy," *World Politics* 7 (April 1955): 402–18.

Franklin, William M. "Zonal Boundaries and Access to Berlin," *World Politics* 16 (October 1963): 1–31.

Frazier, Robert. "Did Britain Start the Cold War? Bevin and the Truman Doctrine," *The Historical Journal* 27 (September 1984): 715–27.

Friedman, Edward. "Was Chinese-American Hostility Inevitable?" *Reviews in American History* 15 (September 1987): 499–506.

Gaddis, John Lewis. "Containment: A Reassessment," *Foreign Affairs* 55 (July 1977): 874–87.

———. "The Corporatist Synthesis: A Skeptical View," *Diplomatic History* 10 (Fall 1986): 357–62.

———. "The Emerging Post-Revisionist Synthesis on the Origins of the Cold War," *Diplomatic History* 7 (Summer 1983): 171–90.

———. "Intelligence, Espionage, and Cold War Origins," *Diplomatic History* 13 (Spring 1989): 191–212.

———. "NSC 68 and the Problem of Ends and Means," *International Security* 4 (Spring 1980): 164–70.

———. "Was the Truman Doctrine a Real Turning Point?" *Foreign Affairs* 52 (January 1974): 386–402.

Garson, Robert. "American Foreign Policy and the Limits of Power: Eastern Europe, 1946–50," *Journal of Contemporary History* 21 (July 1986): 347–66.

———. "The Role of Eastern Europe in America's Containment Policy, 1945–1948," *The Journal of American Studies* 13 (April 1979): 73–92.

Gati, Charles. "What Containment Meant," *Foreign Policy* 7 (Summer 1972): 22–40.

Gimbel, John. "On the Implementation of the Potsdam Agreement: An Essay on U.S. Postwar Policy," *Political Science Quarterly* 87 (June 1972): 242–69.

Grant, Natalie. "The Russian Section, A Window on the Soviet Union," *Diplomatic History* 2 (Winter 1978): 107–15.

Hamby, Alonzo. "Harry S. Truman: Insecurity and Responsibility," in Fred I. Greenstein, ed., *Leadership in the Modern Presidency*. Cambridge: Harvard University Press, 1988, 41–75.

Hammond, Paul Y. "The National Security Council as a Device for Interdepartmental Co-ordination: An Interpretation and Appraisal," *American Political Science Review* 54 (December 1960): 899–910.

Harrington, Daniel. "Kennan, Bohlen and the Riga Axioms," *Diplomatic History* 2 (Fall 1978): 423–37.

Hathaway, Robert M. "Truman, Tito, and the Politics of Hunger," in William F. Levantrosser, ed. *Harry S. Truman: The Man from Independence*. New York: Greenwood Press, 1986.

Henrikson, Alan K. "The Creation of the North Atlantic Alliance, 1948–1952," *Naval War College Review* 32 (May–June 1980): 4–39.

Herken, Gregg. "The Great Foreign Policy Fight," *American Heritage* 37 (April/May 1986): 65–80.

Herring, George C. " 'Peoples Quite Apart': Americans, South Vietnamese, and the War in Vietnam," *Diplomatic History* 14 (Winter 1990): 1–23.

Hess, Gary R. "The First American Commitment in Indochina: The Acceptance of the 'Bao Dai Solution,' 1950," *Diplomatic History* 2 (Fall 1978): 331–50.

———. "The Iranian Crisis of 1945–46 and the Cold War," *Political Science Quarterly* 89 (March 1974): 117–46.

Hitchens, Harold L. "Influences on the Congressional Decision to Pass the Marshall Plan," *Western Political Quarterly* 21 (March 1968): 51–68.

Ho, Zhigong. " 'Lost Chance' or 'Inevitable Hostility?' Two Contending Interpretations of the Late 1940s Chinese-American Relations," *The SHAFR Newsletter* 20 (September 1989): 67–78.

Hodgson, Godfrey. "The Establishment," *Foreign Policy* 10 (Spring 1973): 3–40.

Hoffman, Stanley. "After the Creation, or the Watch and the Arrow," *International Journal* 28 (Spring 1973): 175–84.

Hogan, Michael J. "Paths to Plenty: Marshall Planners and the Debate over European Integration, 1947–1948," *Pacific Historical Review* 53 (August 1984): 337–66.

Hudson, Daryl J. "Vandenberg Reconsidered: Senate Resolution 239 and American Foreign Policy," *Diplomatic History* 1 (Winter 1977): 46–63.

Jackson, Scott. "Prologue to the Marshall Plan: The Origins of the American Commitment for a European Recovery Program," *Journal of American History* 65 (March 1979): 1043–68.

Jervis, Robert. "The Impact of the Korean War on the Cold War," *Journal of Conflict Resolution* 24 (December 1980): 563–92.

Jessup, Philip C. "The Berlin Blockade and the Use of the United Nations," *Foreign Affairs* 50 (October 1971): 163–73.

———. "Park Avenue Diplomacy—Ending the Berlin Blockade," *Political Science Quarterly* 87 (September 1972): 377–400.

Kaplan, Lawrence S. "The Cold War and European Revisionism," *Diplomatic History* 11 (Spring 1987).

———. "The Korean War and U.S. Foreign Relations: The Case of NATO," in Francis H. Heller, ed., *The Korean War: A 25 Year Perspective*. Lawrence: The Regents Press of Kansas, 1977.

———. "Toward the Brussels Pact," *Prologue* 12 (Summer 1980): 73–86.

———. "The United States and the Origins of NATO, 1946–1949," *Review of Politics* 31 (April 1969): 210–22.

Kazin, Alfred. "Solitary Expert: The Case of George F. Kennan," *Atlantic Monthly* (January 1968): 59–67.

Kedourie, Elie. "From Clerk to Clerk: Writing Diplomatic History," *American Scholar* 48 (Autumn 1979).

Kennan, George F. "After the Cold War: American Foreign Policy in the 1970s," *Foreign Affairs* 51 (October 1972): 210–27.

———. "America and the Russian Future," *Foreign Affairs* 29 (April 1951): 351–70.

———. "America's Administrative Response to Its World Problems," *Daedalus* 87 (Spring 1958): 5–24.

———. "Disengagement Revisited," *Foreign Affairs* 37 (January 1959): 187–210.

———. "Flashbacks," *The New Yorker* 61 (February 25, 1985): 52–69.

Kennan, George F. "The Future of Our Professional Diplomacy," *Foreign Affairs* 33 (July 1955): 566–86.

———. "An Historian of Potsdam and His Readers," *American Slavic and East European Review* 20 (April 1961): 289–94.

———. "History and Diplomacy as Viewed by a Diplomatist," *Review of Politics* 18 (April 1956): 170–77.

———. "Is War with Russia Inevitable? Five Solid Arguments for Peace," *The Reader's Digest* (March 1950), 1–9.

Kennan, George F., Paul H. Nitze, Robert R. Bowie, Gerard C. Smith, and Christian A. Herter (Symposium). "Planning in the Department," *Foreign Service Journal* 38 (March 1961): 20–24.

"X" [George F. Kennan]. "The Sources of Soviet Conduct," *Foreign Affairs* 25 (July 1947): 169–82.

———. "Tribute to General Marshall," *New York Times*, October 18, 1959, p. 8E.

———. " 'X' Plus 25: Interview with George F. Kennan," *Foreign Policy* 7 (Summer 1972): 5–21.

Kindleberger, Charles. "The Marshall Plan and the Cold War," *International Journal* 23 (Summer 1968): 369–82.

Kirkendall, Richard S. "Election of 1948," in Arthur M. Schlesinger, Jr., ed. *History of American Presidential Elections, 1789–1968*, vol. 8. New York: Chelsea House Publishers, 1985, pp. 3099–3145.

Kissinger, Henry A. "Conditions of World Order," *Daedalus* 95 (Spring 1966): 503–29.

Knight, Jonathan. "George Frost Kennan and the Study of American Foreign Policy: Some Critical Comments," *Western Political Quarterly* 20 (March, 1967): 149–60.

Knight, Wayne. "Labourite Britain: America's 'Sure Friend'? The Anglo-Soviet Treaty Issue, 1947," *Diplomatic History* 7 (Fall 1983): 267–82.

Kousoulas, D. George. "The Truman Doctrine and the Stalin-Tito Rift: A Reappraisal," *South Atlantic Quarterly* 72 (Summer 1973): 427–39.

Kreiger, Wolfgang. "Was General Clay a Revisionist? Strategic Aspects of the United States Occupation of Germany," *Journal of Contemporary History*, 18 (April 1983): 165–84.

Kuklick, Bruce. "A Historian's Perspective: American Appeasement of Germany, 1941–1951," *Prologue* 7 (Winter 1976): 237–40.

———. "The Origins of the Marshall Plan" [Review Essay], *Reviews in American History* 5 (June 1977): 292–98.

LaFeber, Walter. "Kissinger and Acheson: The Secretary of State and the Cold War," *Political Science Quarterly* 92 (Summer 1977): 189–97.

———. "NATO and the Korean War: A Context," *Diplomatic History* 13 (Fall 1989): 461–77.

Leary, William M., and William Stueck. "The Chennault Plan to Save China: U.S. Containment in Asia and the Origins of the CIA's Aerial Empire, 1949–1950," *Diplomatic History* 8 (Fall 1984): 349–66.

Lees, Lorraine M. "The American Decision to Assist Tito, 1948–1949," *Diplomatic History* 2 (Fall 1978): 407–22.

Leffler, Melvyn P. "The American Conception of National Security and the Beginnings of the Cold War, 1945–48,'' *The American Historical Review* 89 (April 1984): 346–81.

———. "From the Truman Doctrine to the Carter Doctrine: Lessons and Dilemmas of the Cold War," *Diplomatic History* 7 (Fall 1983): 245–66.

———. "The United States and the Strategic Dimensions of the Marshall Plan," *Diplomatic History* 12 (Summer 1988): 277–306.

Levine, Steven I. "A New Look at American Mediation in the Chinese Civil War: The Marshall Mission and Manchuria," *Diplomatic History* 3 (Fall 1979): 349–75.

Lowenthal, Richard. "The Shattered Balance: Estimating the Dangers of War & Peace," *Encounter* 55 (November 1980): 9–14.

Lundestad, Geir. "Empire By Invitation? The United States and Western Europe, 1945–1952," *The SHAFR Newsletter* 15 (September 1984): 1–21.

McLean, David. "American Nationalism, the China Myth, and the Truman Doctrine: The Question of Accommodation with Peking, 1949–1950," *Diplomatic History* 10 (Winter 1986): 25–42.

McLellan, David S. "Who Fathered Containment?" *International Studies Quarterly* 17 (June 1973): 205–26.

McMahon, Robert J. "The New Cold War in Asia: Toward a New Synthesis?" *Diplomatic History* 12 (Summer 1988): 307–27.

Magstadt, Thomas M. "Understanding George Kennan," *Worldview* 27 (September 1984): 7–10.

Maier, Charles S. "The Two Postwar Eras and the Conditions for Stability in Twentieth-Century Western Europe," *The American Historical Review* 86 (April 1981): 327–52.

Mallalieu, William C. "The Origin of the Marshall Plan: A Study in Policy Formation and National Leadership," *Political Science Quarterly* 73 (December 1958): 481–504.

Mark, Eduard M. "Allied Relations in Iran, 1941–1947: The Origins of a Cold War Crisis," *Wisconsin Magazine of History* 59 (Autumn 1975): 51–63.

———. "American Policy Toward Eastern Europe and the Origins of the Cold War, 1941–1946: An Alternative Interpretation," *Journal of American History* 68 (September 1981): 313–36.

———. "Charles E. Bohlen and the Acceptable Limits of Soviet Hegemony in Eastern Europe: A Memorandum of 18 October 1945," *Diplomatic History* 3 (Spring 1979): 201–13.

———. "The Question of Containment: A Reply to John Lewis Gaddis," *Foreign Affairs* 56 (January 1978): 430–40.

May, Ernest R. "The American Commitment to Germany, 1949–55," *Diplomatic History* 13 (Fall 1989): 431–60.

———. "The Development of Political-Military Consultation in the United States," *Political Science Quarterly* 70 (June 1955): 161–80.

———. "The Nature of Foreign Policy: The Calculated Versus the Axiomatic," *Daedalus* 91 (Fall 1962): 653–67.

Mayers, David. "Nazi Germany and the Future of Europe: George Kennan's Views, 1939–1945," *International History Review* 3 (November 1986): 550–72.

Merrick, Ray. "The Russia Committee of the British Foreign Office and the Cold War, 1946–47," *Journal of Contemporary History* 20 (July 1985): 453–68.

Messer, Robert L. "Paths Not Taken: The United States Department of State and Alternatives to Containment, 1945–1946," *Diplomatic History* 1 (Fall 1977): 297–319.

Miller, James E. "Taking Off the Gloves: The United States and the Italian Elections of 1948," *Diplomatic History* 7 (Winter 1983): 35–55.

Milward, Alan S. "Was the Marshall Plan Necessary?" *Diplomatic History* 13, (Spring 1989): 231–253.

Miscamble, Wilson D. "Anthony Eden and the Truman-Molotov Conversations, April, 1945," *Diplomatic History* 2 (Spring 1978): 167–80.

———. "The Evolution of an Internationalist: Harry S. Truman and American Foreign Policy," *Australian Journal of Politics and History* 23 (August 1977): 268–83.

———. "George F. Kennan, The Policy Planning Staff and the Origins of the Marshall Plan," *Mid-America: An Historical Review* 62 (April–July 1980): 75–89.

———. "Harry S. Truman, The Berlin Blockade and the 1948 Election," *Presidential Studies Quarterly* 8 (Summer 1980): 306–16.

———. "The Origins of the North Atlantic Treaty: Policy Formulation in the Department of State," in Roger J. Bell and Ian J. Bickerton, eds., *American Studies: New Essays from Australia and New Zealand*. Sydney: ANZASA, 1981, 236–56.

Moore, Ray A. "The Occupation of Japan as History: Some Recent Research," *Monumenta Nipponica* 36 (Fall 1981): 317–28.

Morgan, George. "Planning in Foreign Affairs: The State of the Art," *Foreign Affairs* 39 (January 1961): 271–78.

Mosely, Philip E. "Soviet-American Relations Since the War," *Annals of the American Academy of Political and Social Science* 263 (May 1949): 202–11.

Nelson, Anna Kasten. "President Truman and the Evolution of the National Security Council," *Journal of American History* 72 (September 1985): 360–78.

Newman, Robert P. "The Self-Inflicted Wound: The China White Papers of 1949," *Prologue* 14 (Fall 1982): 141–56.

Newton, Scott. "The 1949 Sterling Crisis and British Policy Towards European Integration," *Review of International Studies* 11 (July 1985): 169–82.

Nitze, Paul H. "Assuring Strategic Stability in an Era of Detente," *Foreign Affairs* 54 (January 1976): 207–32.

———. "Atoms, Strategy and Policy," *Foreign Affairs* 34 (January 1956): 187–98.

———. "Foreword," in William Schneider, Jr., and Francis P. Hoebner, eds., *Arms, Men and Military Budgets*. New York: Crane Russak, 1976, xi–xv.

———. "The Role of the Learned Man in Government," *Review of Politics* 20 (July 1958): 275–88.

———. "The Strategic Balance Between Hope and Skepticism," *Foreign Policy* 17 (Winter 1974–1975): 136–56.

Ovendale, R. "Britain, The United States, and the Recognition of Communist China," *The Historical Journal* 26 (March 1983): 139–58.

Pachter, Henry. "The Intellectual as Diplomat: A Critical Discussion of George F. Kennan," *Dissent* 15 (March/April 1968): 161–70.

Pfau, Richard. "Containment in Iran, 1946: The Shift to an Active Policy," *Diplomatic History* 1 (Fall 1977): 359–72.

Pickett, William B. "The Eisenhower Solarium Notes," *The SHAFR Newsletter* 16 (June 1985): 1–10.

Pollard, Robert A. "Economic Security and the Origins of the Cold War: Bretton Woods, the Marshall Plan, and American Rearmament, 1944–50," *Diplomatic History* 9 (Summer 1985): 271–89.

Poole, Walter S. "From Conciliation to Containment: The Joint Chiefs of Staff and the Coming of the Cold War, 1945–1946," *Military Affairs* 42 (February 1978): 12–16.

Postbrief, Sam. "Departure from Incrementalism in U.S. Strategic Planning: The Origins of NSC–68," *Naval War College Review* 33 (March–April 1980): 34–57.

Powers, Richard. "Who Fathered Containment?" *International Studies Quarterly* 15 (December 1971): 526–43.

Propas, Frederic L. "Creating a Hard Line Toward Russia: The Training of State Department Soviet Experts, 1927–1937," *Diplomatic History* 8 (Summer 1984): 206–26.

Quade, Quentin L. "The Truman Administration and the Separation of Power: The Case of the Marshall Plan," *Review of Politics* 27 (January 1965): 58–77.

Rappaport, Armin. "The United States and European Integration: The First Phase," *Diplomatic History* 5 (Spring 1981): 121–49.

Raucher, Alan. "The First Foreign Affairs Think Tanks," *American Quarterly* 30 (Fall 1978): 493–513.

Reynolds, David. "The Origins of the Cold War: The European Dimension, 1944–1951," *The Historical Journal* 28 (June 1985): 497–515.

Roberts, Chalmers M. "How Containment Worked," *Foreign Policy* 7 (Summer 1972): 41–53.

Roberts, Frank K. "Soviet Policies Under Stalin and Khrushchev: A Comparison Based on Personal Experiences between 1939 and 1962," *South Atlantic Quarterly* 72 (Summer 1973): 440–50.

Rose, Lisle A. "The Trenches and the Towers: Differing Perspectives on the Writing and Making of American Diplomatic History," *Pacific Historical Review* 55 (February 1986): 97–101.

Rosenberg, David Alan. "American Atomic Strategy and the Hydrogen Bomb Decision," *Journal of American History* 66 (June 1979): 62–87.

Roskin, Michael. "From Pearl Harbor to Vietnam: Shifting Generational Paradigms and Foreign Policy," *Political Science Quarterly* 89 (Fall 1974): 563–88.

Rostow, Eugene. "Searching for Kennan's Grand Design," *Yale Law Journal* 87 (June 1978): 1527–48.

Ruddy, T. Michael. "Realist Versus Realist: Bohlen, Kennan and the Inception of the Cold War," *Midwest Quarterly* 17 (January 1976): 122–41.

Sander, Alfred D. "Truman and the National Security Council: 1945–1947," *Journal of American History* 59 (September 1972): 369–88.

Schaller, Michael. "Consul General O. Edmund Clubb, John P. Davies, and the 'Inevitability' of Conflict Between the United States and China, 1949–50: A Comment and New Documentation," *Diplomatic History* 9 (Spring 1985): 149–60.

Schaller, Michael. "MacArthur's Japan: The View from Washington," *Diplomatic History* 10 (Winter 1986): 1–23.

———. "Securing the Great Crescent: Occupied Japan and the Origins of Containment in Southeast Asia," *Journal of American History* 69 (September 1982): 392–414.

Schilling, Warner R. "The H-Bomb Decision: How to Decide Without Actually Choosing," *Political Science Quarterly* 76 (March 1961): 24–46.

Schlesinger, Jr., Arthur M. "The Cold War Revisited," *New York Review of Books* 26 (October 25, 1979): 46–52.

———. "Origins of the Cold War," *Foreign Affairs* 46 (October 1967): 22–52.

Schonberger, Howard. "The Japan Lobby in American Diplomacy, 1947–1952," *Pacific Historical Review* 46 (August 1977): 327–59.

Scott, Andrew M. "The Department of State: Formal Organization and Informal Culture," *International Studies Quarterly* 13 (Spring 1969): 1–18.

Shaw, Yu-ming. "John Leighton Stuart and U.S.-Chinese Communist Rapprochement in 1949: Was There Another 'Lost Chance in China'?" *The China Quarterly* 89 (March 1982): 74–96.

Siracusa, Joseph M. "NSC 68: A Reappraisal," *Naval War College Review* 33 (November–December 1980): 4–14.

Smith, E. Timothy. "The Fear of Subversion: The United States and the Inclusion of Italy in the North Atlantic Treaty," *Diplomatic History* 7 (Spring 1983): 139–55.

Smith, Jean Edward. "General Clay and the Russians: A Continuation of the Wartime Alliance in Germany, 1945–1948," *Virginia Quarterly Review* 64 (Winter 1988): 20–36.

Stefan, Charles G. "The Emergence of the Soviet-Yugoslav Break: A Personal View from the Belgrade Embassy," *Diplomatic History* 6 (Fall 1982): 387–404.

Trachtenberg, Marc. "A 'Wasting Asset': American Strategy and the Shifting Nuclear Balance, 1949–1954," *International Security* 13 (Winter 1988/89): 5–49.

Trask, Roger R. "George F. Kennan's Report on Latin America (1950)," *Diplomatic History* 2 (Summer 1978): 307–11.

Turpin, William N. "Foreign Relations, Yes; Foreign Policy, No," *Foreign Policy* 8 (Fall 1972): 50–61.

Ulam, Adam B. "The Cold War According to Kennan," *Commentary* 55 (January 1973): 66–69.

Ullman, Richard H. "The 'Realities' of George F. Kennan," *Foreign Policy* 28 (Fall 1977): 139–55.

Wagner, R. Harrison, "The Decision to Divide Germany and the Origins of the Cold War," *International Studies Quarterly* 24 (June 1980): 155–90.

Walker, J. Samuel. "The Confessions of a Cold Warrior: Clinton P. Anderson and American Foreign Policy, 1945–1972," *New Mexico Historical Review* 52 (April 1977): 117–34.

Warner, Geoffrey. "The Truman Doctrine and the Marshall Plan," *International Affairs* 50 (January 1974): 82–92.

Wells, Samuel F., Jr. "Sounding the Tocsin: NSC 68 and the Soviet Threat," *International Security* 4 (Fall 1979): 116–58.

Whelan, Joseph G. "George Kennan and His Influence on American Foreign Policy," *Virginia Quarterly Review* 35 (Spring 1959): 196–220.

Wiebes, Cees, and Bert Zeeman. "The Pentagon Negotiations March 1948: The Launching of the North Atlantic Treaty," *International Affairs* 59 (Summer 1983): 351–63.

Williams, Justin. "American Democratization Policy for Occupied Japan: Correcting the Revisionist Version," with "Rejoinders" by John W. Dower and Howard Schonberger, *Pacific Historical Review* 57 (May 1988): 179–218.

————. "Completing Japan's Political Reorientation, 1947–1952: Crucial Phase of the Allied Occupation," *American Historical Review* 73 (June 1968): 1454–69.

Wright, C. Ben. "Mr. 'X' and Containment," *Slavic Review* 35 (March 1976): 1–31.

Yarmolinsky, Adam. "Bureaucratic Structures and Political Outcomes," *Journal of International Affairs* 23 (1969): 225–35.

————. "The Military Establishment (or How Political Problems Become Military Problems)," *Foreign Policy* 1 (Winter 1970–71): 78–97.

Yost, Charles W. "The Instruments of American Foreign Policy," *Foreign Affairs* 50 (October 1971): 59–68.

Zeeman, Bert. "Britain and the Cold War: An Alternative Approach. The Treaty of Dunkirk Example," *European History Quarterly* 16 (July 1986): 343–67.

Unpublished Materials

Denman, Dorothy I. "The Riddle of Containment: As Reflected in the Advice and Dissent of George F. Kennan." Ph.D. diss., University of Miami, 1975.

Landa, Ronald Dean. "The Triumph and Tragedy of American Containment: When the Lines of the Cold War Were Drawn in Europe, 1947–1948." Ph.D. diss., Georgetown University, 1971.

McCullough, David. "Dean Acheson, A Remembrance." Address delivered April 6, 1989, Washington, D.C.

Newman, Jr., Parley W. "The Origins of the North Atlantic Treaty: A Study in Organization and Politics." Ph.D. diss., Columbia University, 1977.

Powers, Richard James. "Kennan Against Himself?: From Containment to Disengagement. A Decade of U.S. Foreign Policy Making as Focused on the Ideas and Concepts of George F. Kennan, 1947–1957." Ph.D. diss., Claremont Graduate School and University Center, 1967.

Schwartz, Thomas Alan. "From Occupation to Alliance: John J. McCloy and the Allied High Commission in the Federal Republic of Germany, 1949–1952." Ph.D. diss., Harvard University, 1985.

Siracusa, Joseph M. "Paul H. Nitze, NCS 68, and the Soviet Union: In Search of a Cold War Paradigm." Paper delivered at Western Social Science Association Meeting, Denver, April, 1978.

Wright, C. Ben. "George F. Kennan, Scholar-diplomat, 1926–1946." Ph.D. diss., University of Wisconsin, 1972.

Index

Italicized page numbers indicate photographs.

Acheson, Dean Gooderham: as consultant to PPS, 363; correspondence from Kennan to, 30, 40, 325; and development of hydrogen bomb, 302–4, 305–7, 309; and division of Germany, 148, 158–62, 163–77 passim, 229, 341–42, 350; and European integration, 282, 284–85, 287–88, 290–91; and European recovery, 46–47, 50, 51, 53–54, 55; Kennan's relationship with, 157–58, 162, 292, 294, 295–96, 327, 334, 341, 351, 355–56; and Korean War policy, 319, 320–22, 328–30, 331, 332–33; and North Atlantic Treaty, 123n.39, 135, 229; and NSC 68, 309–12, 314–15; as secretary of state, 5, 135, 154–58, 296–97; as under secretary of state, 4, 5, 6, 26, 30, 159; and selection of Kennan to head PPS, 6–7, 9, 10, 11, 37, 218; and selection of staff for Kennan, 37–39; and U.S. policy in China, 229–34, 236, 237, 239, 240, 241, 242, 243; and U.S. policy in Japan, 271; and U.S. policy in Latin America, 317; and U.S. policy in Southeast Asia, 275, 276, 277
Achilles, Theodore C., 117, 122, 124, 125, 126, 131, 137, 147n.19, 283, 354
Adams, Ware, 42, 48, 151, 166, 280, 293, 352
Adenauer, Konrad, 173–74, 201n.107
Advisory Steering Committee (State Department), 71
AEC. See Atomic Energy Commission
agricultural production, European, 61
Albania: covert operations in, 203, 207–9; Soviet control of, 81, 178, 205
Allied Control Council (Berlin), 141
Allison, John, 323, 324
Alsop, Joseph, 36, 109, 111, 157, 215, 223, 232n.78, 260, 288–89, 294, 353
Alsop, Stewart, 111, 288–89, 312, 321
Altschul, Frank, 204, 283, 295, 341, 363

"America and the Russian Future" (Kennan), 331
American Council on Japan, 256
American Diplomacy, 1900–1950 (Kennan), 332
AMTORG Trading Corporation, 240
Angel, James, 363
Anglo-American-Canadian Combined Policy Committee, 299
Annan, Noel, 155
anti-Semitism: Kennan accused of, 102; State Department accused of, 83
Arabs, 13–14. *See also* Palestine
Argentina, 315
Armour, Norman, 105, 122
arms race, 308, 344
Armstrong, Hamilton Fish, 67, 111n.158, 148, 363
Arneson, R. Gordon, 302, 304, 305, 306
Arnold, Maj. Gen. A. V., 89
Atherton, Ray, 363
Atkinson, Brooks, 353
Atlantic Council of the United States, 137
atomic bombs, 247, 298–308
Atomic Energy Commission (AEC), 294, 299, 300, 301, 304, 308
Attlee, Clement R., 126n.52, 141, 287, 330
Austin, Capt. B. L., 363
Austin, Warren, 99
Australia, 274, 275
Austria, 71
Azerbaijan region (Iran), 25
Azores, 19

Babcock, Stanton, 261
Bain, Kenneth R., 99
balance of power: in Asia, 291–92, 349; in Europe, 73–74, 117, 146, 349
Balfour, John, 53, 54, 56
Ballantine, Joseph, 252, 363
Bao Dai (emperor of Indochina), 276, 277
Barry, Gerald, 53

Iran, 32, 88
"Iron Curtain" speech (Churchill), 27, 114
Isaacson, Walter, 19
Israel, 100–101. *See also* Palestine
"Is War With Russia Inevitable?" (Kennan), 312
Italian Communist party (PCI), 80, 84, 86–87, 103–5, 114
Italy: in CEEC, 61; Communist and Soviet interest in, 44, 74, 75–76, 79–80, 84–87, 88, 102–6, 107, 111–12, 187, 349; covert operations in, 103, 106, 199; economic recovery in, 60, 71, 79–80, 85; and North Atlantic Treaty, 116, 132, 135

Jacobsen, Eddie, 99
Japan: assistance of Soviets in war against, 22; demilitarization of, 248, 250, 251, 254, 255, 256, 269–70; democratization of, 248, 250, 254, 255, 256; economic recovery of, 46, 250–52, 254, 256–58, 262, 263, 264–65, 273; importance of to U.S. foreign policy, 217, 220, 253, 254, 271, 275; and nationalism in Southeast Asia, 273–78; neutrality of, 270–73, 325; U.S. occupation of, 75, 247–50, 252–58, 262–63, 266, 272; U.S. postwar policy in, 13, 264–73
JCS. *See* Joint Chiefs of Staff
Jebb, Gladwyn, 114n.6, 124, 282, 284, 288n.31
Jellicoe, Earl, 209
Jervis, Robert, 347
Jessup, Philip C., 157, 163–71 passim, 176, 234, 236, 238n.102, 240, 242, 271, 276, 319, 341, 364
Johnson, Joseph E., 38, 39, *42*, 48, 70, 352
Johnson, Louis, 167, 169, 195, 232, 271, 304–7, 320n.33, 328
Johnson, Lyndon B., 243
Johnson, Nelson T., 224, 364
Johnston, Percy H., 264
Joint Chiefs of Staff (JCS), 76, 91, 94, 98, 125, 130, 167, 200n.102, 218–19, 224, 232, 234, 271, 319, 322, 324, 328, 330
Jones, Lt. Col. George M., 364
Jones, Howard, 89
Jones, Joseph, 32, 69n.113
Joyce, Robert P., 110, 184n.31, 186, 194, 199, 205, 208–10, *280*, 293, 351, 352

Kalinin, Mikhail, 16

Kaplan, Lawrence, 45
Karalekas, Anne, 210
Kauffman, James Lee, 256–57
"Keep Left" group, 114n.3
Kelley, Robert, 14
Kennan, Annelise Sorensen (wife), 15, 35, 110n.154, 337
Kennan, Florence James (mother), 11
Kennan, George (cousin of grandfather), 12, 16n.66, 258–60
Kennan, George Frost: as ambassador to the Soviet Union, 296n.63, 334–37, 346; as ambassador to Yugoslavia, 196, 197n.89, 343–44, 346; children of, 15, 35, 336, 337; as Consultant to NSC, 77–78; and development of hydrogen bomb, 298–308; and division of Germany, 143–54, 159–77 passim, 341–42, 350; early diplomatic career of, 13–28; early interest in Soviet Union, 12, 13–15; education of, 11–15; and European integration, 281–91; and European recovery, 43–74 passim, 349, 351; first appointment in Soviet Union (1933–37), 15–17; health of, 16, 17, 24, 25, 28, 35, 67, 128, 145, 147, 187, 189, 264; honorary degrees awarded to, 318; at Institute for Advanced Study, 295, 313, 314, 326, 327, 331, 339, 344; and interest in languages, 12, 13–14, 143; interned by Nazis, 19, 336; Long Telegram by, 25–28, 348; marriage of, 15; and Mediterranean (Italy, Greece, and Palestine) crises, 75–112 passim; at National War College, 6, 7, 28–33, 29, 47, 70, 217, 298; and Operation Solarium, 338–39; opposition to North Atlantic Treaty, 116–20, 127–32, 133–36, 350; at Oxford, 340; photographs of, *xx*, *29*, *42*, *259*, *280*; resignation of, 246, 291–97, 326; role in Korean War policy, 314, 318–31, 332–34; second appointment in Soviet Union (1944–46), 20–24, 215, 293; selected to establish PPS, 6–7, 8, 9–11, 13, 28, 33–40; and U.S. domestic politics, 36, 69, 344–45; and U.S. policy in China, 213–46 passim, 349–50; and U.S. policy in Eastern Europe, 179–211 passim; and U.S. policy in Japan, 247–73 passim, 350; and U.S. policy in Southeast Asia, 273–78 passim; and U.S. policy in Yugoslavia, 190–97; visit to Japan by, 253, 254, 258–65, *259*